*For John Cushman*

# CONTENTS

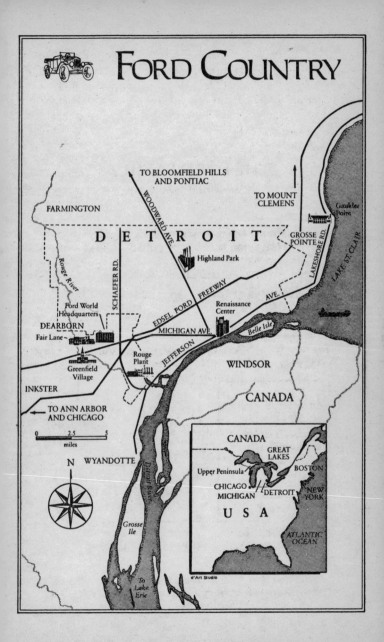

# THE FORD FAMILY

## A Simplified Family Tree

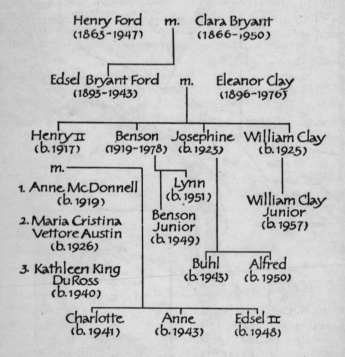

*This chart shows those Fords mentioned in the text. For a full genealogy of all the descendants of Henry Ford I, see the Appendix, The Ford Family, on page 791.*

# THE MEN AND
# THE MACHINE

One day in November 1975, a few weeks before Henry Ford II left his second wife, Cristina, he felt a sharp pain in the left side of his chest. He was out for a walk when it happened. Some neighbours saw him strolling, a tall, patrician figure with a paunch, and when he went down they ran out to help. They found Henry Ford II sitting on the kerb,[1] winded and scarcely able to speak.

It was not quite what it seemed. It was angina, said the doctors, not a heart attack. But it spelt out the same thing: a narrowing of the arteries, a shortage of blood to the heart, an urgent need for some serious medical attention—and most of all, that disquieting tap on the shoulder, a reminder of mortality.

Fords live long and Fords live short. Old Henry Ford I was eighty-three when he died. But his grandson was not yet sixty, and here it was already, that tightening of the chest with a final grip about it. Angina pectoris. It does not have a pleasant ring.

The bad heart ran in the family. Henry's brother Benson had frightened himself with a heart attack while he was still in his thirties. Their mother had lived with angina for years and years.

At Ann Arbor they recommended a bypass, and quickly too. They had Henry's clothes off and the suite ready even as they went through their investigations. The specialists at the Ford Hospital were more reassuring. They thought that pills would do the trick—and in the end, Henry Ford II listened to no less than six top-level medical opinions before deciding that he would, in fact, do without the bypass. He would keep going on the glyceryl trinitrate pills, and he would also do as the doctors ordered: aim at a change of lifestyle, get more exercise, try to avoid quite so much stress.

By the time he had got the diagnosis, the worst of the stress was behind him. Leaving Cristina had taken care of that. Until the policeman had stopped him in Santa Barbara, he had been living a double life, stealing away on "business trips," working late at the office, encouraging his wife to spend more time away. No wonder he had felt under pressure.

The publicity had been purgatory—an auto king caught driving drunk, and with his mistress too. But with the scandal had come a certain relief. It had brought it all out in the open. It had forced him to make a decision between his two women, and he had opted for the new one. He had packed his bags and moved out of the lakeshore.

But now this had happened—and the message that it carried was very clear. The doctors, the pain, the catheters, the drips—it could only mean one thing for the company. It was almost exactly thirty years since Henry II had taken over at Ford. He had run the company ever since, but now he would have to set about choosing somebody to succeed him, and that brought up the big question, the question that Henry had been trying to postpone—the question of Lee.

As you drive into Detroit from the airport, your eye is caught by a tall sign on your right. It looks like the mileage counter in the middle of a car's speedometer, and as you stare at it for a second or two, the figure on the right-hand end clicks down. It is not a poster. It is the real thing: a massive electronic counter which is keeping the tally, not of miles, but of the automobiles being produced by the car companies of the Motor City.[2]

The counter clicks down every second or so in a good year when the cars are coming off the lines 34,000 a day, 8 million a year—for this is the motor capital of the world. There are motor industries in Japan, Germany, Britain, in every industrialized country, but they are scattered. Nowhere else have the carmakers all congregated in one single, grey, smokey location to build their cars together—and of all Motown's carmakers, no name has quite the magic of Ford.

It is the four-letter word you cannot escape in Detroit. Ford Hospital, Ford Auditorium, Ford Road—you are even driving on the Edsel Ford Freeway as you come in from the airport. It runs right through Ford country, the flat, pale green Michigan landscape where Henry Ford I grew up. He was born here, the founding father, in Dearborn, the village that became a town and is now a suburb tacked on to the western side of Detroit, and just off the freeway, to your right as you hit the city, is the factory which produced most of his cars, and is still producing them: the Ford Rouge River plant.

It is an awesome sight, the Rouge, a vast looming mass of chimneys and towers and acres of zigzagged, notched roofs. The line started running there in 1918, when America wanted mass-produced warships and turned to Henry Ford, the genius of mass production, to see if his magic could be rubbed from cars onto boats. The line has been running ever since, with a few pauses for retooling, and the Fords have rolled off by the million: the Model T, the Model A, the Thunderbird, the Mustang.

When old Henry Ford built the Rouge, it was the largest industrial complex on earth, a modern wonder of the world, and it retains its power to this day: the blast furnaces, the coking ovens, the slab-sided lake tankers at anchor, unloading the coal and ore which feed the belly of the beast.

He had a vision, Henry Ford. He wanted it all. Other carmakers put the bits together, but he wanted to go right back to the earth, to quarry out the raw materials that made up his cars. So he bought coal mines and iron mines in northern Michigan. He bought a piece of Brazil where he could grow rubber: Fordlandia, a little Ford settlement in a clearing beside the Amazon. He bought whole hillsides of pine forests for his station wagons—and to transport it all back to Dearborn he built his very own Ford fleet.

The boats still sail into the Rouge—the *Henry II*, the *Benson*, the *William Clay*, their prows commemorating Fords dead and living, for this is a family firm. Even the blast furnaces have names, and they are Fords as well.

On the other side of Miller Road are the staff parking lots, where only the insensitive would park a Nissan or Chevrolet, and connecting them to the factory is a steel bridge, the overpass, across which the workers file night and day. One May afternoon in 1937, when the shifts were changing, Walter Reuther and three other union organizers were beaten up on the overpass in broad daylight by thugs of the Ford Service Department, and it was down below on Miller Road in those years that four hunger marchers who had come to the Rouge gates got Ford's answer. They were shot dead.

This is one of capitalism's altars, a vast, satanic cathedral of private enterprise. All night the Rouge growls, its fires and flares casting flickering shadows, its furnaces glowing dull red around the base of its huge brooding bulk.

Cars will not be fired in crucibles like this for much longer. There are robots in the wings with pincers, men in white coats. But here, for the time being, are the industrial guts of America. Europe has its palaces, but America celebrates her native genius with monuments of a rougher sort.

This is the story of the world's largest family-controlled business and of the family that built it and control it to this day. Run your finger down the Fortune 50, the roll call of the largest industrial corporations on earth, and at number four you come to Ford.* Only General Motors and some oil companies are larger, and they are controlled by the votes of their shareholders. Ford is also controlled by shareholder votes, but some 40 percent of them, the effective working

___

* In 1985, *Fortune* listed the world's largest industrial corporations as (1) Exxon, (2) Royal Dutch Shell, (3) General Motors, (4) Mobil, (5) Ford, (6) British Petroleum, (7) Texaco, (8) IBM, (9) Dupont, and (10) AT & T.[3] As this book goes to press, *Fortune*'s preliminary figures show Ford overtaking Mobil (and General Motors overtaking Royal Dutch Shell and Exxon).

majority, are all in the hands of the Ford family, the present-day descendants of Henry Ford I.

The story is largely a tale of two Henrys—of old Henry Ford, who created the business, and of young Henry Ford, his grandson, who saved it from his grandfather's caprice. In between them came Edsel Ford, young Henry's father, old Henry's son, the lost generation, cruelly smothered in his lifetime by his visionary, tyrannical father, overshadowed in death by his son's achievement—and by the ugly, ill-starred car named in his honour in the late 1950s.

It is a story in which the truth can prove elusive. In 1964 representatives of the Ford Motor Company removed large sections of Edsel Ford's private papers from the Ford Archives in Dearborn, and the whereabouts of those documents today is a mystery. Henry Ford II has personally destroyed the medical records of his father and grandfather. He put them through the paper shredder in his own office, together with most of the documents from his own private and business files,[4] an annihilation for which he remains defiantly unapologetic.

"Why the hell shouldn't I destroy them?" he asks.[5]

Henry Ford II does not like books being written about him, or about his family. "With any luck," he said on first meeting this author, "I'll be dead by the time your book comes out."[6]

He granted polite but cautious cooperation with the preparation of this book—one interview at the outset, and one interview when the book had been completed and was sitting ready to go on press. Lee Iacocca granted no interview at all. But many other people close to both men have been willing to speak, and the source notes following the text list more than 180 on-the-record interviews, including every significant member of the Ford family today.

In order to write this book, the author took his family from London to live for more than two years in Michigan. He drove the freeways, met the car men, and tried briefly working on the assembly line—Henry Ford's own creation—in pursuit of the flavour of the Motor City.

15

It is a curious place, this motor capital of the world. Dynamic and tedious, cultured and banal, Detroit and its paradoxes have been shaped by the Ford story, and they have given shape of their own to the plot. The climax to the tale, the battle between Henry Ford II and Lee Iacocca, derives much of its bitterness and poignancy from the claustrophobia of life in this very particular corner of southeast Michigan—and it is with a European visitor to Michigan more than 150 years ago that the story can begin.

**Part One** The Rise of Henry Ford

# 1

## FARMBOY

When Alexis de Tocqueville landed in America in May 1831, he was disappointed to find the place so civilized. He was expecting savagery. So, forsaking New York and the cities of the East, the Frenchman went in search of the raw, wild heart of the continent, and as he headed inland, he asked people where the real frontier was. Where were the Indians?

Ten years ago, he was told, they were here. There, five years. There, two. Tocqueville arrived in settlements where men told him, "I cut down the first tree of the forest."[1] But the traveller was in search of "the utmost limits of European civilization,"[2] and not until he caught a glimpse of America's great inland seas did he get an idea of where those limits might lie. Arriving in Buffalo on the shore of Lake Erie in July 1831, Tocqueville was told that there was a steamer leaving in twenty-four hours for Detroit and the Michigan territory. There he would find his savagery.

Michigan did not disappoint him. A mile out of Detroit the forest started, and for whole days, as Tocqueville travelled, he scarcely saw the sun through the trees. When he heard the sound of the cowbells which the pioneers placed around their animals' necks, he knew that he was approaching a settlement, and the next sign was trees that seemed to have been struck by sudden death. Tocqueville was travelling in July, but the branches of these trees looked petrified, leafless, as though it were the middle of winter. Lacking time to fell them properly, the frontiersmen had carved rings around their bark to cut off sap and stop the foliage that would shade their crops.

The pioneer would come forward to greet his visitor, but as he extended his hand, his features did not express goodwill

19

or pleasure. His hospitality was complete in all the formalities, but somehow, Tocqueville felt, it was quite devoid of warmth. The man would only speak to ask questions, and having gained the information he desired, he would fall silent again.

As Tocqueville travelled onwards, every settler was the same, consumed almost totally by the challenge of his own survival, and as the Frenchman filled his notebooks with the thoughts that were to form the basis of his classic *Democracy in America*, he pondered on this curious people to whom belonged the future of the New World: "a restless, calculating, adventurous race which sets coldly about deeds that can only be explained by the fire of passion, and which trades in everything."[3]

Beneath the frozen trees of the Michigan forests, the Frenchman had discovered what was to make America so successful—and what was to make for success in America: "a nation of conquerors . . . who only cherish those parts of civilization and enlightenment which are useful". The demands of frontier life had wrapped the American pioneer's psyche in an egotism so formidable that conventional standards were overwhelmed. Blame or disapproval seemed irrelevant.

"Can a man capable of such sacrifices be a cold, unfeeling being? Should one not rather recognize that he is consumed by some burning, tenacious, implacable passion of the mind?"[4]

It was in a clearing in the Michigan woods that Henry Ford was born on July 30, 1863.

The Ford family arrived in Michigan the year after Tocqueville's visit. They came from Ireland in 1832. Henry was born some thirty years after their arrival, and in that time Michigan had lost a little of its savagery. It had been promoted from territory status to become a state of the union, and its principal town, the port of Detroit, was a thriving commercial centre. But it was still a frontiersman's world—rail fences, rough roads, the air sharp with the smoke of burning stumps—and the best paths through the woods were still the trails made by the Indians. Dearbornville, later Dearborn, the settlement in which Henry Ford was born, was the first clearing along the forest route that the tribes had been padding for centuries between the Detroit River and what is now Chicago.

The first Fords had settled in Dearborn because it was virgin territory. The thing about Michigan, Tocqueville had discovered, was that the land was so cheap. "An acre in Michigan," he wrote, "never costs more than ten shillings when the land is still uncultivated. That is about the price of a day's labour. So a labourer can earn enough in a day to buy an acre."[5]

This was the reason why so many Irish were drawn to Michigan, along with even more Germans, Scandinavians, and Poles—peasants working hard to turn themselves into yeoman farmers. The Ford family bought their uncleared forest land from the government, cut their rings around the trees, and started hacking fields and paddocks out of the wilds. When Henry Ford was growing up in the 1860s, wolves were still shot in the surrounding forests for bounty, and men came home with deer and wild turkey for supper. In springtime the women went out in the woods to tap the maple trees, gather the sap, and boil it down into syrup, since there was no white sugar. Tea was a luxury, coffee even more so, and an orange at Christmastime could be a once-a-year treat.[6]

"The first thing that I remember in my life is my Father taking my brother John and myself to see a bird's nest under a large oak log twenty rods East of our home," Henry Ford was to write when he was fifty. "I remember the nest with 4 eggs and also the bird and hearing it sing. I have always remembered the song, and in later years found that it was a song sparrow. I remember the log layed in the field for a good many years."[7]

In the later stages of his adult life, Henry Ford jotted down memories like this in little blue padded notebooks small enough to slip into a shirt pocket. The pages are small and perforated, the size of a calling card, and on them he also scribbled phone numbers, grandchildren's birthdays— and some appalling jokes:

> *What is it the sign of when you sit down on a* bee?
> *Sign of an Early Spring.*[8]

Henry's memory of the bird's nest under the fallen log was one of his longer reminiscences, and he accompanied it with a drawing to show the exact location of the nest with the log in the field in front of the home that was his birthplace.

Today Henry Ford's birthplace is a tourist attraction, a plain, white, woodframe house, painstakingly restored by him in later life to recreate the setting of his childhood. Its ground floor is occupied by two parlours, one for everyday use, leading off the dining room and kitchen, and another, best, "Sunday" parlour, which occupies the front of the building. In the centre of this somewhat funereal chamber, well clear of the fireplace, stands an ornate oval stove with its pipe going straight up through the ceiling; this pipe emerges through the middle of the floor in the bedroom above, to turn a sharp right angle in midair and then exit through the wall. It was in this bedroom that Henry Ford was born a few hours after dawn on the morning of July 30, 1863.

With its bare boards, oil lamps, and sparse decoration of needlework mottoes on the walls, the Ford home strikes the modern eye as rather threadbare—even with the best crockery put carefully on display. But in 1863 it represented quite a solid home for a farmer. When an illustrated atlas of Detroit and its surrounding countryside was being prepared in 1876,[9] it was the Ford farm that was chosen to show off the best of Dearborn—a planked house surrounded by neat picket fences, well-tended orchards, and quite a collection of stables and outbuildings. It looks the sort of establishment owned by a man who counted for something in the community, and by that date William Ford, Henry's father, was indeed a man of substance.

It has suited the popular imagination to see Henry Ford as a poor boy who pulled himself up from nothing, but this is a truer picture of his father, William, who had crossed the Atlantic steerage in the 1840s, a refugee from the Irish potato famine. The Fords had been poor Protestant settlers in southern Ireland, tenant farmers scratching a bare sort of living from the countryside outside Cork.[10] William's uncles abandoned the struggle and emigrated to America in the 1830s, and in 1847 William's branch of the family followed them. The Fords who were already in Michigan lent the new arrivals the money they needed to buy land, and by the time of Henry's birth in 1863 they had come to be one of the more important families in the Dearborn area, owning several hundred acres and enjoying connections with the prosperous Irish community in Detroit, the marketplace where they sold their farm produce.

Henry Ford was to go through life a loner. He was to show great generosity to his wife's family and to his relatives on his mother's side, and he was to provide modest support for his sister Margaret, widowed at an early age. But he was never on close terms with his brothers, or with any other relative who bore the name of Ford. It was as if he resented sharing any of the glory of the name he made famous.

All the other Fords, however—his father, uncles, and cousins—worked well together. There was clearly a great deal of cooperative effort involved in the two-stage migration which got the clan started in America, first searching out Dearborn as a promising base and then helping the second wave of arrivals to get established there. Henry's father, William, worked as a carpenter for quite a time, travelling all over the Midwest to build the wagon sheds, stations, and other structures required by the expanding American railway system. With his savings he increased his landholdings—120 acres in 1864, the year after Henry was born, and the year in which William also completed the formalities of becoming a U.S. citizen.[11]

A photograph of William Ford in later life shows him as foreman of a Dearborn jury, seated heavily in formal three-piece suit, with a solid watch chain strung across his waistcoat. He is surrounded by the eleven other good men and true. William Ford had come a long way since he disembarked from steerage: he had become a local road commissioner, a member of school boards, a Justice of the Peace after 1877, and a church warden as well, though he was something of a freethinker. His small library included the works of Herbert Spencer, the controversial philosopher who preached evolution, and who also popularized the notion of sociology as a valid subject of serious study. In his second-best parlour William Ford hung a Masonic plaque— a disembodied, all-seeing eye captioned with the words *Faith, Hope and Charity*—and his son Henry was later to add Masonic membership to his own oddly radical ragbag of beliefs and allegiances.

William Ford had met his wife, Mary Litogot, when he went to do some carpentry work for a neighbour, a fellow settler from southern Ireland, Patrick O'Hern. O'Hern came from Fair Lane in the city of Cork,* some thirty miles from the village of Clonakilty where the Fords had been farmers, and he had married an older woman when he got to Michigan.[12] Unable to have children of their own, the O'Herns had adopted two little girls, and it was with the younger of these, Mary Litogot O'Hern, that William Ford fell in love. He married her on April 25, 1861, and their first child, a little boy, died at birth early in 1862. So when Henry Ford arrived in the summer of the following year, he was Mary and William's eldest child.

In later years Henry Ford was to commission elaborate investigations to find out more about the origins of his mother, Mary Litogot, but his agents could discover only a few vague details, most of which turned out to be tragic. Her natural mother had died, no one knew how, when Mary was a baby; her natural father, a carpenter, was said to have

---

* Following the independence of Southern Ireland, Fair Lane was renamed, and is today known as Wolfe Tone Street, after the leader of the Irish uprising of 1798.

been killed in a fall from a roof; one of her brothers had accepted $1,000 to serve in the place of a neighbour in the Civil War draft, and had been killed in the first few months.

The one surviving portrait of Mary Litogot shows her as plain and rather full-faced, with dark eyes and glossy brown hair, which she parted in the middle. Her children recalled her as busy, alert, and quick. Henry Ford remembered that he idolized her when he was a boy, and he unashamedly cherished her memory to his dying day. "She taught us what the modern family needs to learn," he recalled when he was sixty: "the art of being happy with each other." He felt his mother to have been the parent who set the tone of the household: "She made it a good place to be."[13]

When he was seven Henry Ford went to school, a single-room establishment in Dearborn, well over a mile's walk away from home. All the grades, from one to eight, crammed together into four double rows of desks in front of the single teacher—who was usually a man in winter. Every spring, however, the male teacher went out to the fields, to be replaced in the classroom by a woman; and for the same reason, children who were in the higher grades tended to leave school at that time of year, not to return until after the harvest.

The Dearborn schoolhouse was a tall, simple, redbrick structure, surmounted by a bell tower which summoned the children from fields miles away. In front of the teacher's dais stood a large stove. "When a boy got in trouble he was brought up front and placed . . . directly under the teacher's eye," remembered Henry later. "You could get a good view of the stove in that location."[14]

The spelling in Henry Ford's notebooks suggests that he may well have been placed in front of the classroom stove quite often, but otherwise he seems to have been a reasonable student. He read well enough to get by as an adult—though it sometimes suited him to pretend otherwise—and there was never anything wrong with his adding and subtracting. Henry was no delinquent: his best friend at school was the

brightest pupil in the class, a studious dark-haired boy called
Edsel Ruddiman.

"We started school off with a song or a prayer," remembered Henry's sister Margaret, who joined the school four
years later. "There wasn't any set schedule. It depended on
the mood of the teacher. . . . There were two classes in
spelling, one before noon and one before the close of school.
We had reading, writing and arithmetic. Our writing was
on old copybooks. We had spell-downs and spelling bees.
We had to read our lessons over several times to enunciate
and learn the pronunciation. They tried to teach moral
lessons, too, from things we read. The McGuffey Readers
were our first books."[15]

The *Eclectic Readers* of William Holmes McGuffey shaped
the minds of a whole generation of Americans. Filled with
dramatic illustrations and simple moral tales in which bad
boys came to bad ends and good boys ended up President,[16]
they were used by schools in practically all thirty-seven
states in the 1870s. They were a reminder that this was a
nation founded by Puritans. In the world of McGuffey, Right
and Wrong were like Black and White. You distinguished
between them with something called your Conscience. But
on occasions, the moralizing developed away from the Ten
Commandments in some original directions. William
McGuffey was a teacher at various small-town Ohio colleges
in the years that he produced his Readers, and his thought
contained a raw streak of Midwest radicalism. A section
called "Things by Their Right Name," for example, redefi-
ned *soldiers* as "murderers."

In later life, when Henry Ford had the means to do just
about anything that he cared to, he determined to reacquaint
young America with McGuffeyland, and he went to some
trouble to exhume the Readers and get them reprinted. The
single-room Dearborn schoolhouse with its dunce's cap,
willow cane, and American flag on the wall had provided
him, he felt, with an ideal start in life.

*

Tales of Henry Ford's infant mechanical prowess, his devising of gadgets and tinkering with tools, have clustered around the accounts of his youth like miracles around the boy Jesus. Shown the inside of a watch for the first time at the age of seven, we are told, he became a passionate watch repairer, swapping marbles with other boys for clock wheels. Inspired by a visit to the Nicholson File Company in Detroit, runs another story, he went back home to Dearborn to make his own file by hand, then used it to shape his mother's knitting needles into miniature screwdrivers. He fashioned tweezers from his mother's corset stays, he nearly lost the tip of one finger while investigating a threshing/harvesting machine, and he blew a hole through his lip when a steam boiler with which he was experimenting exploded. To judge from his own recollections in his notebooks, and in the numerous secondhand accounts based on interviews in which the anecdotes had obviously flowed free, the infant Henry Ford was forever dismantling, investigating, and generally displaying his mechanical genius in all directions.

But at least one member of his immediate family felt that Henry's memories of his childhood suffered from a certain poetic license. To her dying day, his sister Margaret protested at the way in which her brother restored the old Ford homestead, refurnishing his bedroom there with a little watchmaker's bench and tools. There was never any such bench up there, she insisted.

Henry told an oft-repeated tale that he would slip out of the house after dark to collect neighbours' watches, and then bring them home to repair them.

"I never knew of him going out at night to get watches," said Margaret.[17]

Her brother's most dramatic story involved a dam which he built near the schoolhouse with the help of other boys, constructing a waterwheel as a power source. This was connected by a rake handle to an old coffee-bean grinder with which the boys experimented under Henry's supervision, trying to grind up clay, potatoes, and even some small pieces of gravel, which threw off sparks. The youthful researchers failed to dismantle their dam after they had completed their experiments, so that it overflowed in the night, flooding the neighbouring potato field. According to Henry, the farmer was enraged by the devastation. He demolished the dam and complained vociferously to Henry's teacher.

But sister Margaret could remember no such flooding and drama. "It was just a small dam," she remarked.[18]

Margaret Ford Ruddiman was not noted for more than the normal human ration of envy and spite. Her husband, James, was the brother of Henry Ford's great school chum, Edsel Ruddiman, and through adult life, she stayed on rather better terms with Henry than did either of his brothers. She never denied Henry's penchant for tinkering: "When we had mechanical or 'wind up' toys given to us at Christmas," she remembered, "we always said, 'Don't let Henry see them! He just takes them apart!'"[19] But Margaret did feel quite strongly that, when it came to the record of the childhood they had shared, Henry had a tendency not exactly to lie, but, well, to exaggerate a little.

"It was neither as colorful and romantic as it has been painted," she declared, looking back in 1953, "neither was it as full of hardship."[20]

In 1876, however, when Henry Ford was not quite thirteen, his childhood was split in two—and, in one sense, ended—by a drama that it was scarcely possible to exaggerate. In the middle of March that year, Mary Litogot Ford went into labour for the birth of her eighth child. After her first, stillborn, child had come Henry (1863), John (1865), Margaret (1867), Jane (1869), William Junior (1871), and Robert (1873), so the new arrivals in the upstairs room where the stovepipe came up through the floor had become quite routine occurrences.

But this time something went wrong. The baby was lost, and twelve days later, on March 29, 1876, Mary Litogot Ford died. She was thirty-seven years old.

Henry Ford never forgot the grief and shock of his mother's death. He felt, he said later, as if "a great wrong had been done to me."[21] His home and family suddenly seemed "a watch without a mainspring."[22] It was as though he had lost a soulmate—"she read what was in my mind. . . . It was a way she had"[23]—and for the rest of his life he cherished the lessons that he ascribed to her:

She taught me that disagreeable jobs call for courage and patience and self-discipline, and she taught me also that "I don't want to" gets a fellow nowhere. . . .

My mother used to say, when I grumbled about it, "Life will give you many unpleasant tasks. . . . Your duty will be hard and disagreeable and painful to you at times, but you must do it. You may have pity on others, but you must not pity yourself."[24]

In all manner of ways the adult Henry Ford was to revere his mother's memory with a fervour that amounted to fixation. When visitors praised his notably clean and tidy factories, he would ascribe their neatness to his mother's influence. When the time came to restore his birthplace, it was the artefacts connected with her which were given most significance, so that it became as much a memorial to Mary Litogot Ford as it was to him. Henry had the original backyard sifted and excavated for pottery shards, and he then commissioned lovingly faithful reproductions of all the crockery she had used. When interviewed, the farmboy who became one of the richest men in the world had a simple explanation of his success: "I have tried to live my life as my mother would have wished"[25]—and no matter how hardened success made Henry Ford, the mention of the woman who had died when he was just twelve never failed to elicit from his chiseled features something that was close to tenderness.[26]

A few months after his mother's death, one day in July 1876, the young Henry Ford was riding with his father in a horse-drawn wagon towards Detroit, when he saw a steam engine coming towards him, propelled by its own power.

"I remember that engine," he declared forty-seven years later, "as though I had seen it only yesterday."

It was the first vehicle not drawn by horses that Henry Ford had ever seen.[27] As the engine stopped to let the Fords' horses go by, "I was off the wagon and talking to the engineer before my father, who was driving, knew what I was up to."[28]

The steam "engine" was nothing resembling the antique steamers and locomotives, with funnel and broad wheels, which are sometimes seen today at fairgrounds, gaudily painted and restored. It was a plain, homemade adaptation of the upright boilers used by American farmers at this time to power small machinery. Fat and round, it looked rather like an overgrown stove. Wood was shovelled in through a stove door at the bottom and burned to heat water in the boiler above. The resulting steam power drove a wheel at the side.

These engines were common sights on American farms by the end of the nineteenth century. Broad webbing belts ran around the drive wheel to carry power to threshing machines, corn huskers, or circular saws. But the owner of the machine Henry saw that day had fitted his engine with an ingenious adaptation that caught the boy's interest.

"I had seen plenty of these engines hauled around by horses," he later wrote, "but this one had a chain that made a connection between the engine and the rear wheels of the wagon-like frame on which the boiler was mounted."[29]

The chain enabled the steam engine to shift itself forward under its own power, and the engineer showed the boy how the chain could be disconnected on arrival at its destination, and then be replaced by a belt to drive stationary farm machines in a conventional fashion. Henry noted that the power unit had been made by Nichols, Shepard & Company of Battle Creek, Michigan—and years later, in a court case which revealed some sad gaps in other areas of his memory and knowledge, he showed that on this matter, at least, his recollection was vivid and accurate:

*Q.* How many turns a minute did these Nichols, Shepard & Co. engines run?

*A.* I suppose about 200.

*Q.* Why do you suppose; why don't you remember?

*A.* Because I never counted them.

*Q.* Why do you guess 200?

*A.* Because I asked the man that was running it how fast the engine ran and he told me 200 turns a minute; and I have never forgotten it.

*Q.* And you remember that ever since you were a boy of twelve?

*A.* Yes, sir, as distinctly as anything I can remember yesterday.[30]

Henry Ford always regarded his encounter with the moving engine as his meeting on the road to Damascus. He had come face to face with his destiny. Great men tend to rewrite their own histories, and Henry Ford rewrote his more than most. But in this case we can accept his own interpretation of events. With Henry still recoiling from the shock of his mother's death, groping through the pain of bereavement for some fresh basis for his life, it is easy to see how his surprise encounter with this novel, noisy, and powerful machine could take on a special drama for him.

Yet the purpose that was generated in young Henry Ford by this new enthusiasm—a machine which would not just turn watch hands or the workings of an old coffee grinder, but could actually create its own motion—had a sadder, tainted side. Henry remembered fondly that his mother had encouraged his natural abilities before her premature death. But the antithesis of Henry's love for his mother was a conviction that his father was opposed to his mechanical ambitions, and Henry's subsequent accounts of his adolescence paint a picture of increasing conflict between himself and his father.

The conflict is implied in the very tale of meeting the machine—"I was off the wagon and talking to the engineer before my father, who was driving, knew what I was up to"[31]—and a few lines later it is made explicit: "My father was not entirely in sympathy with my bent towards mech-

31

anics."[32] Henry Ford always explained the disputed work-bench in his bedroom in terms of his father's displeasure. He had to work secretly in his room, he claimed, with only a lantern between his feet to keep him warm—and the curious creeping out on night collections of watches to repair was also, he said, a consequence of his father's hostility.[33]

The thesis, as Henry Ford later developed it, was that his father wanted to tie his son down to the land. "He thought that I ought to be a farmer,"[34] he told Samuel Crowther, a journalist he commissioned to ghostwrite the authorized version of his life in 1922, and at about the same time Ford gave interviews to the writer Allan L. Benson, who repeated a similar story. "His heart was always in his mechanical pursuits, which his father detested, because he realized that they were leading the lad away from the country."[35] Benson repeated the tale of the secret bedroom workshop—"he worked with his tools always against the wishes of his father" —and the writer embellished the adventure of the night watch repairing with a stealthily saddled horse, miles of riding across the Michigan countryside, and weary home-comings at three o'clock in the morning.[36]

Not surprisingly, sister Margaret's memory differed from this picture of a punitive parent intent on stifling young Henry's natural impulses. "Father never forbade him to repair neighbors' watches," she said. Indeed, Margaret Ford Ruddiman could remember William Ford teaching his son how to repair things around the home. "Since father was handy with tools," she said, "he was very proud that Henry had inherited his ability to fix things."[37]

As Margaret Ford Ruddiman remembered it, her father, William, the onetime railway carpenter, maintained quite a sophisticated workshop on the Ford farm to which friends and neighbours would resort for help, and it was here, not up in his bedroom, that she saw her brother Henry serving his apprenticeship as a mechanic. She could recall him working there on a latch device which would open heavy gates without the need to get down off a wagon.

"Father was quick to recognize Henry's ability in making

new things," she wrote. "He was very understanding of Henry's demands for new tools for the shop and ours was one of the best equipped in the neighborhood."[38]

William Ford was certainly a man with mechanical experience and tastes. In 1876, the same year that his wife died, he travelled to Philadelphia to the great fair celebrating the centenary of America's independence. Displayed for visitors in Philadelphia's huge Machinery Hall were steam-powered locomotives, drills, lathes, and ploughs, a self-propelled "steam road-roller"—and also at least seven examples of an altogether newer, lighter, and more efficient power unit, the internal-combustion engine.

It seems inconceivable that William Ford did not return from Philadelphia in 1876 impressed by what he had seen and eager to communicate his enthusiasm to his eldest son. Margaret, then aged nine, later recalled her father talking about the big city and the wonders he had seen, particularly the machinery that was on display. When it came to mechanical progress, William Ford was no Luddite. Appointed to a local commission to investigate the desirability of streetcars coming out to Dearborn, he was one of those who voted in favour.

So why was it impossible for the great mechanic, Henry Ford, to admit that he had anything for which to thank his father, who clearly had mechanical aptitude and tastes? Ever eager to give credit to his mother, who died before he entered his teens, he could not bear the idea that his father, who survived until Henry was in his forties, had anything to do with his success.

Mary Litogot Ford died in childbirth, and, just entering the years of sexual consciousness, her eldest son would have been well aware of who was the cause of that condition. Henry Ford wanted someone to blame, and the pain and revulsion wrapped up in his trauma are indicated by the ultimate adolescent fantasy he fashioned: that his father's hostility drove him to run away from home.

Allan Benson told the story most succinctly, at the end of a chapter about the disagreements between father and son:

Thus for a time the struggle went on between the father's will and the son's determination. One day, when the boy was 16 the struggle ended. The mother had died three years before, the old home did not seem the same, and the call of the city silenced everything else in the boy's heart. Without saying a word to anyone, he walked 9 miles to Detroit, rented a room in which to sleep, and sought employment in a machine shop.[39]

"I was all but given up for lost," declared Henry Ford through the ghostwriter Samuel Crowther, describing how he left home to become "an apprentice in the machine shop of the Drydock Engine Works."[40] Both these accounts, published in the early 1920s, echo an earlier version by two other authors, Horace Arnold and Fay Faurote, who came to Detroit to make the first detailed study of Henry Ford's assembly line in 1914. Describing their hero's early years, Arnold and Faurote tell how "the boy Henry left the farm, against his father's commands"—but their version differs from the others in one interesting respect. They specify that Henry Ford started work in "Flower Brothers' machine shop,"[41] not the Dry Dock Company, as he informed Samuel Crowther.

Now it so happened that a mechanic called Frederick Strauss, who was to work closely with Henry Ford at different times between 1878 and 1902, later committed his memories to paper, and Strauss could recall precisely when he first met the man who put the world on wheels. It was in the Flower Brothers' machine shop, and in slightly unusual circumstances:

One morning I brought some valves into the office and while I was there I saw Henry Ford's father, and Henry was with him. I didn't know who they were, but the next day Henry came to work. . . . They put Henry in with me, and he and I got chummy right away.[42]

Strauss recalled these early days at Flower Brothers in a letter that he wrote several decades later to Henry Ford's private secretary, Frank Campsall, and Strauss discovered that he had unwittingly stumbled upon a subject of some embarrassment to his former friend:

When I wrote this letter to Mr. Campsall about Henry, Henry denied that he had ever worked at Flower Brothers at all. He told [Campsall] that I must be mistaken, that I must have taken someone else for him. He said he had never worked there. I got a letter from Mr. Campsall telling me this. . . .[43]

But Strauss was quite sure that he had not been mistaken. Next time he met Henry he brought the subject up again, and, face to face, he extracted the admission: "Fred, you were right. I remember very well when the both of us worked at Flower Brothers."[44]

Frederick Strauss came to the conclusion that, for his own reasons, Henry Ford "never wanted anybody to know that he had worked at Flower Brothers"—and Strauss wasted no further thought on the subject. But Margaret Ford Ruddiman tried to take things further, confronting her brother with the difference between the story that he was giving to the world and the truth as they both knew it: "Henry and I discussed this many times," she said, "but he put off doing anything about correcting the stories. . . ."[45]

It is clear, however, that the Flower brothers, James, George, and Thomas, were acquaintances, if they were not close friends, of the Ford family in Dearborn. All born in England, the brothers had worked for a period as mechanics on the Michigan Central Railroad, and William Ford may well have met them there when he was working for the railroad as a carpenter. He certainly knew them as customers of his farm, since Margaret can remember the Flower brothers visiting the Ford homestead.

"Quite often," she wrote, "when Mr. Flower needed an extra order of hay delivered, he and his wife would drive out on a Sunday to give the order and have a visit with old friends."[46]

So the pieces fall into place. Henry Ford's father was on good terms with the men who offered his son his first job. "Apparently Henry's father knew the Flowers," remembered Strauss, "and came in and talked to them about Henry working in the shop."[47] Far from playing the wicked

35

ogre, William Ford acted as a supportive, caring parent, yet in later years Henry Ford lied and tried to suppress the evidence that made this clear. It suited him to create for the world's benefit—and, more important, for his own—the fantasy of conflict between himself and his father, when the reality was, in fact, considerably less dramatic.

"There were family discussions and differences of opinion as there are in all normal families," declared Margaret Ford Ruddiman as she recalled her childhood, "and no doubt there were many times when Father questioned the wisdom of Henry's decision." But as the Ford children grew up on their Dearborn homestead in the 1870s, there was little disagreement or conflict over the likely destiny of the eldest son who had displayed such aptitude for matters mechanical.

"We knew," said Margaret, "that at some time Henry would go to Detroit. . . ."[48]

# 2

## MACHINE AGE

The city of Detroit into which Henry Ford walked on December 1, 1879, was the oldest major settlement on the shores of the Great Lakes, more than a century older than Chicago. The French were the first white men to conquer the lakes, and it was a Frenchman who had founded the city of Detroit: Antoine Laumet de La Mothe Cadillac, a Gascon soldier of fortune who sailed up the Detroit River in July 1701.

"The climate is temperate, and the air purified through the day and the night by a gentle breeze," enthused Cadillac soon after his arrival. "The skies are always serene, and spread sweet and fresh influence."[1]

The very first French explorers to come sailing up the Detroit River in the seventeenth century had thought they were on their way to the riches of the Indies. They soon discovered they had to make do with the fur trade, but this proved profitable enough. Cadillac was one of the *coureurs de bois*, the freebooting trappers who made their living from both the English colonists and the Indians, and it was he who first grasped the strategic importance of the narrow stretch of water that ran between the lakes Erie and St. Clair.[2]

If France could control these narrows, he argued in the proposal he submitted to King Louis XIV in December 1698, she would have a stranglehold on the trade passing through to the eastern two thirds of the Great Lakes system. A fort controlling the narrows would also represent a clever outflanking of the English in the struggle for North America. This argument evidently swayed Count Pontchartrain, the Sun King's Minister of the Marine. "The King has . . . ordered me to send you immediately to Canada," he wrote in 1700, "to take prompt possession of the straits."[3]

When Cadillac reached the straits in the summer of 1701 with a party of fifty soldiers, fifty *coureurs*, a hundred friendly Indians, and two Jesuits, he decided to dig in on that kink in the river's course where, by a freak of geography, the land that is now the United States lies briefly to the north of Canada. He named his settlement in honour of the Minister who had sent him there, *Fort Pontchartrain du Détroit*—Fort Pontchartrain of the Strait[4]—and for the next half century Detroit flourished, on the whole, as well as Cadillac had predicted. The trappers who used it as a base cornered a major share of the Great Lakes' fur trade. The French were able to establish friendly relations with the local Indians, and a growing number of settlers established successful farms along the narrows of the river and up into Lake St Clair.

The soft and easily worked soil of Michigan proved to be astonishingly fertile. Beans, peas, squash, and melon ballooned to vast proportions. Corn reached ten or twelve feet in height.[5] It was a "land without stones," and the French planted acres of orchards: plums, apples, cherries, and pears. Detroit became especially famous for its pear trees. The settlers organized their land as thin strip farms, long ribbons of cultivation that ran back inland for several miles from narrow waterfronts, and the names of these original settlers have survived today in the street names of Detroit. Rivard, Cadieux, Dubois, Gratiot—the geography of the Motor City still retains a curiously French flavour, although the inhabitants do their best to camouflage it, "Dubois" being pronounced "De Boys," and "Gratiot" being rendered to rhyme with "Crash It."

With the British takeover of French Canada in 1760, Detroit became more of a garrison town. The French farmers, some of them by now quite substantial landowners, got on reasonably well with the British commandant and his officers, but the Indians were less happy with their new overlords. In 1763 the chief of the Ottawas, Pontiac, led an assault which almost destroyed Detroit, and for five months the inhabitants were held besieged inside the stockade. Then the outbreak of the American Revolution made the city on the strait a crucial base against the rebellious seaboard colonists, and the British paid bounties to Indians who brought rebel scalps into the fort. Records show payments for several hundred of these grisly trophies every season—at $5 per scalp.[6]

Although the victory of the infant United States theoretically consigned Detroit and the Michigan Peninsula to the triumphant colonists, Britain held on to the settlement for more than a dozen years in a dispute over compensation to her loyalists. It was not until 1796 that General Anthony Wayne finally occupied the town in the name of the United States, and then the British recaptured it again in the war of 1812. So when Henry Ford came to live in Detroit in 1879, the town had been continuously American for less time than it had been a European colony. The principal sport of the male inhabitants was still cricket, and it was not until Frank Woodman Eddy, founder of the Detroit Athletic Club, arrived in 1876 that the cricket pitch was surrendered to a more proper pastime: baseball.[7]*

By the middle of the nineteenth century, you could tell you were near Detroit several hours before you reached the city from the pall of smoke that hung over it. There were not many of the old pear trees left. A census of 1870 showed that the city contained rather fewer than 80,000 inhabitants, a third the size of conurbations on the eastern seaboard, while in terms of manufactured products, Detroit barely scraped into the American top twenty. But the city was already embarked upon the extraordinary expansion which was to make it the powerhouse of the American economy in its most glorious years. In 1899 it was Number 10 among the cities; by the mid-1920s it had become Number 3 in productive wealth, outranked only by Chicago and New York.

* Cricket, however, is still a summer sport in Detroit. It is played on Belle Isle by blacks of Caribbean origin.

The key to this spectacular growth had been the commencement in 1817 of the Erie Canal, which, by opening a waterway from Buffalo to New York, was to give all the settlers of the Great Lakes safe and direct access to the Atlantic and the world beyond. In the summer of 1818, a little steamboat called *Walk-in-the-Water* had puffed, sailed, and paddled her way into Detroit, making the trip from Buffalo, over 200 miles away, in little more than a day and a half—a journey which sailing ships could sometimes take over a week to cover.

It was the beginning of a major shift in the economic orientation of America. Boston, Philadelphia, and Baltimore, the principal ports along the eastern seaboard, had always laid claim to being the principal American cities. Now they had to yield ground to New York and the centres of population that started to mushroom along the new Great Lakes hinterland—Buffalo, Cleveland, Toledo, Detroit, even Milwaukee and Chicago. The world was turned upside down. By 1850 Detroit was closer in time to Liverpool than she had been to Cincinnati in 1800.[8] Goods and money circulated that much quicker, and so did people. The Fords were just a few among tens of thousands of immigrants to the Michigan area in the years between 1830 and 1860, when the city's population doubled every decade.[9]

The wealth of Detroit was based, in part, simply upon the natural resources of the 50,000 square miles of Michigan to which it was the gateway. The rich fishing grounds of the Great Lakes—25 percent of all the fresh water on earth —had never been commercially exploited: now sturgeon, pickerel, pike, and bass were fished in bulk, and by 1830, seven vessels were busy shipping salted fish to the East. Lumber made the fortune of many a Michigan tycoon as the virgin forests of the territory were brought crashing down; and soon after the territory became fully incorporated as a state in 1837, natural riches were discovered below the earth which far exceeded anything that anyone had had a right to expect.

Surveying the Upper Peninsula one day in 1844, Dr.

Douglas Houghton, elected mayor of Detroit in 1842, was perplexed to see his compass spinning. It indicated magnetic north to lie first to the east, then to the north, then to the south and west of him, and it took a little time for the mayor to work out, with his companions, that he was in the middle of one of the largest deposits of iron ore on earth. Drawn to the area by this discovery, other prospectors hit upon the largest single mass of copper ever discovered. From 1847 until the late 1880s, Michigan led the world in copper production. She also became a primary source of lead and salt, and her fertile soil provided the basis for vast agricultural enterprises. The D. M. Ferry Company, which shipped seeds to pioneers, became the largest seed company in the world, and in Battle Creek, Michigan, Mr. Post and the Kellogg brothers created a new industry based on the humble cornflake.

Detroit became the staging post and port through which the riches of Michigan reached the wider world—just as Cadillac had predicted—and by the time Henry Ford came to town in 1879, the wealth was starting to show. Most of the streets were paved with cedar blocks bound together with gravel and tar, a mixture which could become treacly in the hot Michigan summers, but which served the needs of horse-drawn traffic well enough. The road down which Henry walked from Dearborn was made of cedar planks, and that supported quite heavy wagon trains, as well as the occasional steam engine. Since 1830, no less than ten different railroad companies had run their lines into Detroit, and several of them came by the world's first rail-ferry. Heavy barges floated passenger coaches and freight cars across the river from Canada, where the settlement previously known as "The Ferry," or South Detroit, was renamed Windsor in 1836 in a defiant assertion of un-Detroitness.

Inside Detroit itself, there were over twenty miles of street railway, the streetcars all drawn by teams of horses, and an impressive network of heavy cast-iron gas and naphtha lamp standards—though this street lighting was only switched on for three weeks out of four. For the fourth week of every month the city fathers relied on the light of the full moon, having to husband their resources to cater to all the needs of their exploding population.

Detroit was a literate city. It boasted one of the finest municipal libraries in the Midwest, and when Thomas Alva Edison was a boy selling newspapers and snacks on the morning express from Port Huron, he had killed his days in Detroit before the train went back in the evening inside the reading room of the Young Men's Christian Association. Edison moved off east later, but Detroit felt she could claim a share of the credit when he publicly exhibited his incandescent electric light bulb in 1879.

Mechanical innovation was already the hallmark of Michigan and of her principal city. In 1848 the first iron furnace to the west of Pittsburgh had started smelting in Detroit. The first 100-percent-iron vessel built in America came from the yards of the Detroit Dry Dock Company, and this same firm was later to fire the first steel plant in North America using the Bessemer process. The local deposits of lead and salt laid the basis for a flourishing chemical industry, founding the fortunes of Dow and Parke Davis. A new soda ash and alkali plant on the Detroit riverfront made the city the chief soap-manufacturing centre in the Western Hemisphere—and when the Detroit Capital Copper and Brass Rolling Works were completed in 1881, *they* were the largest in the world.

As the nineteenth century reached its climax, Detroit was becoming the cutting edge of the American economy. Some magic wand seemed to have blessed the place. A fish merchant called William Davis dreamed up the idea of refrigerating a railroad car, and in May 1869, George Hammond, a Detroit butcher, agreed to risk a consignment of beef in one of Davis's new contraptions. The beef reached Boston unspoiled.

In the event, the beef business went to Chicago, but the manufacture of metal cookers and stoves was an industry which did not get away. Jeremiah Dwyer, whose father had

42

bought a farm close to Dearborn at about the same time that the first Fords settled there, saw how eager people were to improve on the open hearth as a means of cooking and heating their homes. The open, red iron mines scarring the Upper Peninsula provided the raw material, and in 1864 the Detroit Stove Company went into business. Within a matter of years the city's ironworks were producing 150,000 stoves annually, in 700 different models, and such were the economies of mass production and steam transportation that these undercut even their European competitors.[10]

This was the flurry of inventiveness and profit which Henry Ford entered when he started his apprenticeship at the James Flower & Brothers Machine Shop in December 1879. It was one of the smaller factories in the city, but it had a reputation for thorough workmanship and for training its apprentices well. Among the other graduates of Flower Brothers was David Dunbar Buick, who made his money in plumbing and bathroom fittings before turning his attention to cars.

"It was a great old shop," remembered Henry Ford's workshop companion Fred Strauss. "They manufactured everything in the line of brass and iron—globe and gate valves, gongs, steam-whistles, fire hydrants, and valves for water pipes. . . . They made so many different articles that they had to have all kinds of machines, large and small lathes and drill presses. . . . They had more machines than workmen in that shop." [11]

This was one of the lessons which Detroit was teaching America. Nothing could beat the right machine. The city's entrepreneurs were moving towards that specialization of function to which the adult Henry Ford was to give such triumphant expression in the moving assembly line, and at his own lowly level, Henry the apprentice was a part of it in the early 1880s. After the months at Flower Brothers, which he forgot about, he moved on to the Detroit Dry Dock Company—the pioneers of iron ships and Bessemer steel— and this became the official beginning of his working life.

Henry Ford had a very precise memory indeed, when he

cared to. The engineering inspiration behind the Detroit Dry Dock Company was a construction engineer, Frank Kirby, and Henry remembered all his life how, one day, this rich and famous man noticed the young apprentice struggling to push a heavy wheelbarrow up a steep gangway into a ship.

"Stick in your toe-nails, boy," called out Kirby, "and you will make it!"

"Well," recalled Ford when he told this story later, "I have been sticking in my toe-nails ever since."[12] When in the 1920s Henry Ford constructed his long, colonnaded Engineering Laboratory in Dearborn, and decided to emblazon the names of the world's great scientists and inventors along the frieze, there alongside Galileo, Copernicus, Edison, Newton, and Faraday is carved in characters of equal majesty the name of K I R B Y.

While Henry Ford worked at the Detroit Dry Dock Company he lived in rented lodgings close by. His landlady charged him $3.50 a week for room and board, and to make up the gap between that and his $2.00 wage, Henry put his Dearborn watch-repairing experience to remunerative use. He took evening work, for another fifty cents a night, with a jeweller, Robert Magill, cleaning and repairing watches. He would slip down the road to Magill's every evening when he got home from work, and at week-ends too—though the jeweller would not let him into the front shop, since he feared his customers might doubt the workmanship of one so beardless.[13]

Henry Ford looks very boylike in the first photograph we have of him since he was a baby, a group pose by several dozen soiled and rumpled workers outside the Dry Dock works. He stands at the very back, among the apprentices with his mechanic's cap, showing no signs of fatigue from holding down two jobs at once. "No work with interest is ever hard," he said later.[14] Indeed, Henry Ford felt that a man intent on success ought to keep his mind occupied day and night. "If he intends to remain always a manual laborer, then he should forget about his work when the whistle blows, but if he intends to go forward and do anything, the whistle is only a signal to start thinking. . . ."[15]

One subject on which Henry Ford started thinking was the possibility of going into some sort of business—the watch business, perhaps. He worked out that he could build a good, serviceable timepiece for around thirty cents if he produced 2,000 a day, he said later. But he could not see himself disposing of over half a million watches a year, and he gave up the idea. He left the Detroit Dry Dock engine works sometime in 1882, and having completed his mechanical apprenticeship to his own satisfaction before the age of twenty, Henry decided to go back to the farm.

When Henry Ford had worked in Detroit as a young apprentice, he had left his workshop every autumn to go home and help his father bring in the harvest. Now, at the age of nineteen, he gave up life in the city to work on the land. He was to remain on the land until he was nearly thirty.

For his own reasons, Henry Ford, the famous industrialist, liked to impress interviewers with his dislike of life on the farm. But a shrewd reporter sent to interview the great man on his tractor development in the 1930s was not deceived. "When you first meet him," he wrote, "you think that he is a mechanic with a bent for farming: later you decide that he is a farmer with a bent for mechanics"[16]

There was, in truth, less contradiction than this paradox proposed. The steam engine which had inspired the boy Henry in the months following the death of his mother had been an agricultural machine. When as an adult he started work on an internal-combustion engine, he seems to have been thinking about how this power source could be applied to some form of tractor—and it was an agricultural machine that persuaded him to forsake the Dry Dock works in 1882, and to come back to live in Dearborn.

A neighbour of the Fords, John Gleason, had bought a

little portable steam engine from the Westinghouse Company, and it had gone wrong. Gleason had planned to use it for his own threshing and sawing, and to rent it out around the neighbourhood, but the mechanic he had hired was not up to the job.

"I have an idea he was afraid of his machine," said Henry, who was called in to lend a hand. "To tell the truth, I was frightened myself."[17] But the months at Flower Brothers and the Dry Dock Company had not been in vain. "I went to work around that little engine . . . and getting a grip on the engine, so to speak, I got a grip on myself."[18]

At the end of a day's work, Henry felt he knew all he needed about the Westinghouse portable steam engine, and that was the beginning of a long, happy summer shepherding it around the Dearborn area on behalf of Farmer Gleason.

I was paid three dollars a day and had eighty-three days of steady work. I travelled from farm to farm, and I threshed our own and the neighbors' clover, hauled loads, cut cornstalks, ground feed, sawed wood. It was hard work. I had to fire [it] myself and the fuel most generally was old fence-rails, though it would burn coal the few times coal was to be had. I became immensely fond of that machine. . . . I have never been better satisfied with myself than I was when I guided it over the rough country roads of the time.[19]

Many years later, Henry Ford started a search for the little steam engine he had steered around the Michigan countryside in the summer of '82.[20] He could remember its serial number, 345, and with the help of the Westinghouse Company, he eventually tracked it down to a farm in Pennsylvania, where it was languishing, decrepit and rusting. Henry had the machine repaired, oiled, and polished, brought it back to Dearborn, put water in the boiler, stoked up the fire—and then threshed with it again on his sixtieth birthday. You can take the boy out of the country, but you can't take the country out of the boy.

This was the happiest period of Henry Ford's life, and he would hark back to these years increasingly as he got older.

His search for old 345, sending out his agents to scour the countryside regardless of expense, was, in some ways, a search for his own youth, a quest for the fresh and innocent Henry Ford that the successful, hard-nosed industrialist had lost sight of. That old steam engine was his Rosebud.

Through working on Westinghouse No. 345, Henry had got to know the local representative of the company, and this opened the way to more work for him when his season with Farmer Gleason came to an end. Henry became area demonstrator and repairman for the Westinghouse Company in southern Michigan, travelling around the countryside with a bag of tools to operate and service the company's machines.

It was the ideal job for an independent young man just entering his twenties. Henry was his own master, caring for the puffing, chattering engines that he loved so well. He was comfortably paid. He was quite important. He was a figure of magic when he strolled into a village, children crowding around to ask him questions—as he had asked questions of that engineer on the road to Detroit. For a day or so the wandering mechanic was the focus of interest in that community, welcomed into its homes, and sharing in its rituals, especially at harvest time.

Henry Ford loved it, and in later life, every year in September, the limousines would go out to round up friends and relatives from the Dearborn area.[21] A field would be found. Scythes would be sharpened, old wooden reapers and threshers put through their paces. Cooks from the auto baron's kitchen would bring out the hampers, and the wooden trestle tables would be set up under the trees. The steam engine was the idol at the feast. Henry would tend it lovingly, feeding the boiler, shooing children away from the long webbing belt that ran to a corn husker or cider press. Then, all around the old machine, the man who put the twentieth century on wheels would lead his guests through the fond, bucolic rituals of a nineteenth-century harvest home.

Henry remembered those years as idyllic, but they were not. The Midwest countryside through which he travelled in the middle of the 1880s was going through some painful adjustments to the modern world, and the anger and tension which those generated were stimulating some oddly complicated new ideas. In 1882, the year in which Henry Ford left Detroit to return to the farm, Michigan elected itself a Greenback governor.[22]

Michigan had been safely Republican for nearly thirty years, but the steadily falling price of farm produce had created hardship and discontent across the state. People were leaving the land. When Henry Ford had gone to start work in Detroit in 1879, he was just one of thousands of farmboys heading into town—and the farming families who were left behind were no better off for having one less mouth to feed.

It was part of a general problem afflicting America's central farm belt. At the root of the trouble were machines like the ones that Henry Ford was tending. Mechanization was vastly increasing the volume of produce pouring from the prairies and meadows of the Midwest, and this was sending agricultural prices on a downward curve that was accentuated by improvements in transportation: railways and steamships meant that American farmers had to compete with producers across the globe.

The farmer did not understand this. If he was more productive by making use of machines, he should be earning more money, not less, and from his puzzlement and anger sprang a variety of political action groups with remedies to suggest. The National Greenback Party took its name from the paper money—"greenbacks"—issued during the Civil War without gold backing, thus producing inflation, which had suited the rural community very well indeed. Most farmers held their land on mortgages, and as the value of money fell, so it eased the burden of their debt. The coming of peace, however, had brought a return to strict monetary policies. The greenbacks were redeemed. The dollar was linked to gold again. Inflation slowed, and suddenly a farmer's obligations became a real burden to him, especially as his income shrank from the falling price of his produce. The Greenbackers called for a return to easy money, for paper currency that was unhampered by—or only loosely linked with—gold or silver, and the technicalities of these matters became the hot topic of political debate.

As young Henry Ford walked or rode from farm to farm with his bag of tools in the 1880s, an early version of the home-appliance serviceman, he found himself listening to farmers who rolled words like *bimetalism* around their tongues as easily as they discussed backsetting, silage, or the price of feed. The mysteries of the currency were held to be the secret of happiness by the 154,451 Michiganders who voted for Josiah W. Begole, the Greenbacker who took the governorship with Democratic backing in 1882;[23] and if Begole himself had a hard time explaining precisely what his various metallurgical nostrums stood for, he and his supporters had no difficulty at all knowing what they stood against.

Railroad tycoons, eastern bankers, city slickers in general, middlemen, moneylenders, Jews—this was the demonology of rural Michigan at the end of the nineteenth century, and though the Greenbackers did not last, the grass-roots movements that took their place shared the same assumptions. There was the Grange (the National Grange of the Patrons of Husbandry), a Mason-like secret society which had been at work since 1867, campaigning against railroad freight charges and organizing cooperative buying schemes to cut out middlemen's profits on everything from reapers to calico.[24] The Grange championed temperance, staging teetotal square dances and hoedowns to prove that farming —and virtue—could be fun. Most notable of all, the Populist Party, a coalition of ex-Greenbackers and other activists, gathered strength through the 1880s and 1890s to launch its own presidential candidates: James B. Weaver in 1892 and, in 1896, "The Great Commoner," William Jennings Bryan.

Populism was a great rural shout of rage. It was Tocqueville's pioneers hitting back. They had cleared their forests, but now they were getting cheated of their just desserts. Embracing a multitude of rallying points—the Greenback call for easy money, regulation of the railroads, government loans to farmers, and a graduated income tax that would hit the rich as well as the poor—populism was a radical programme, progressive for its day.

But the roots of the movement were also deeply traditional, based on a strong-grounded belief in conspiracy— a conspiracy hatched somewhere out there in the East— and a warm nostalgia for the golden age which the men of the city had somehow stolen from the men of the soil. Populists looked back to an age of pastoral content and plenty, redolent with the scent of crushed grass, when upstanding men with calluses on their hands would tell you the truth, look you straight in the eye, and pick at their teeth with a straw.

This was the vanished world which Henry Ford, later in life, was to seek to recapture—although he more than anyone was instrumental in its destruction. As wealth gave the great carmaker the means to give shape to his beliefs, those beliefs turned out to be very much those of a late-nineteenth-century Michigan farmer: temperance, an odd familiarity with currency theories, mistrust of the eastern establishment, and a particular mistrust of Wall Street, moneylenders, and the Jews.

Henry Ford made no apology for this. He was not the sort of self-made man who was embarrassed by his background. On the contrary, he was proud of it. The real America, the seventy-one-year-old Henry told an interviewer in July 1935, was not to be found in cities like New York or Chicago. "America," he said, "is out there among the old village sites, the small towns, and the farms."[25]

In January 1884, Henry Ford received a letter. "Dear Friend," it began, "I suppose you think I was never going to write to you." The letter is unsigned, but it sounds as if it came from some fellow apprentice who, like Henry, had gone back to the farm:

I have been rasseling the cross cut Saw most of the time since I been hom. . . . I suppose you and your mash tripped the lite fantastic toe newyears night. I was down to the rink newyears and skated a rooler clean off my skates . . . this is all at present Old chum Write soon.[26]

*Mash* was the 1880s vogue word for sweetheart. Lithe, active, full of ideas, and bubbling over with himself, Henry Ford was a handsome man. All his life he was a good dancer. Women found him attractive, and though we do not know the name of the "mash" with whom he tripped the light fantastic on New Year's night of 1884, there is no doubt about the identity of his dancing partner the following year.

On January 1, 1885, the inhabitants of Greenfield, the township next to Dearborn, gathered to welcome the New Year at the Martindale House, a white clapboard inn generally considered a cut above the normal rural hostelry. It was close enough to Detroit for people to ride out to, with quite a respectable restaurant—the sort of place you could take a young lady to dinner—and a ballroom which the Greenfield Dancing Club had hired for their New Year's celebration.

Quite a few Fords went over to Greenfield in a party that evening. Henry later remembered dancing a foursome with his second cousin Annie, but the person who really impressed him was Annie's friend, a small, vivacious girl with bright, dark eyes and chestnut-coloured hair, Clara Jane Bryant.

"I knew in half an hour she was the one for me," Henry informed an interviewer in 1923.

"He shouldn't have told you that," said his wife when she heard what he had said—and, though it was nearly forty years later, a definite blush rose to the cheeks of the former Miss Clara Jane Bryant.[27]

In the Ford Archives at Dearborn today is a dance programme that preserves the memory of that romantic occasion: "New Year's Ball, January 1st 1885," it announces in ornate gothic script beneath a fine steel engraving of the Martindale House. Printed on thick, white folded card, with a long, dark tassel hanging down from one corner, it is an impressive tribute to the Greenfield Dancing Club, whose name is printed at the foot of the programme.

But the club's name is printed in a typeface which did not exist in 1885, and the fine steel engraving is based, down to the last tree and bush, on a photograph of the Martindale House taken in the 1920s. The programme is, well, not exactly a forgery, since there is no evidence of Henry Ford ever claiming this to be the very dance programme he held on the night he met Clara, but it is, at the least, another example of his congenital reshaping of history.

There was no especially sinister reason for him to make the country square dance where he met his wife appear a grander occasion than it really was. Perhaps at some later date he just felt a sentimental urge to relive the occasion. But clearly the man who said "history is more or less bunk"* had a more than normal preoccupation with his own history, and, when he had the chance, he could not resist the temptation to give it a little polish.

The truth seems to have been that the couple's first meeting on January 1, 1885, meant rather less to Clara Bryant than it did to the young man who snatched one quick dance with her.

"She had quite a few beaux," remembered Margaret Ford Ruddiman, who was already a friend of hers. "She was a popular girl, very sociable."[28] And the lady herself was, later, quite emphatic: "He made absolutely no impression upon me. And I didn't see him again until a year later. . . ."[29]

Clara Bryant was more impressed the second time around. "He was so different from all the other young men I had known," she remembered. Other boys talked to her about "how good the music was and all that sort of thing." But Henry had sharp, vivid, oddly practical notions, and he got Clara involved in them:

---

* See chapter 14, pages 293–4.

I remember he showed me a watch that he'd fixed himself to tell sun time and standard time—standard time was just coming in then, and he explained how he'd done it. I remember going home and telling how sensible he was, how serious-minded. That was the beginning. . . .[30]

The courtship picked up speed. Henry and Clara started attending dances together. "At those parties they had a man who played the dulcimer," remembered Margaret Ford Ruddiman, who sometimes escorted the couple as a friendly chaperone. "He was a cripple. This instrument would be on a table, and he played it with little mallets, and called off the dances as he played. He played really beautiful music."[31]

As a romantic touch, Henry invested in a high, curve-fronted light sleigh—a "cutter"—painted a shiny dark Brewster green, and he would take Clara out on excursions through the forest, the bells on the harness of the Ford farm horse a-jingling.

On Valentine's Day 1886, he wrote to her in the fine, firm hand he had temporarily acquired from the Goldsmith, Bryant & Stratton Business University, a Detroit commercial college. Henry had enrolled there for classes in mechanical drawing, bookkeeping, and business practice, the only formal business training he ever had—and perhaps Clara Bryant had something to do with it. Goldsmith, Bryant & Stratton do not, however, seem to have had much impact upon Henry Ford's punctuation:

DEAR CLARA

*I again take the pleasure of writing you a few lines. it seems like a year since i seen you. it don't seem mutch like cutter rideing to night, does it but i guess we will have some more sleighing . . .*

*Clara Dear you did not expect me Friday night and i think as the weather is so bad, you will not expect me tonight. but if the weather and roads are good you look for me Friday or Saterday night for the Opera or Sunday night or Monday night at the party . . . Clara Dear you can not imagine what*

*pleasure it gives me to think that i have at last found one so loveing kind and*
*true as you are and i hope we will always have good success.*
  *Well i shall have to Close*
*wishing you all the joys of the year and a kind Good Night.*

  *May Flowerettes of love around you bee twined*
  *And the Sunshine of peace shed its joy's o'er your Minde*
                              *FROM ONE THAT DEARLY LOVES YOU*
                                                    H.[32]

The couple were married on Wednesday, April 11, 1888
—Clara's twenty-second birthday—standing side by side in
the front parlour of the Bryants' house at Greenfield, not far
from Dearborn. William Ford and Martha Bryant, Clara's
mother, signed the marriage certificate as witnesses. Clara
wore a gown she had made herself—Margaret Ford Ruddiman helped dress her in it—and Henry wore a blue suit.
After the ceremony, Clara's brothers brought out supper
and served it at two tables set out across the end of the
dining room. The presents were placed on display on one of
the beds upstairs.[33]

The honeymoon was on the little farm where Henry Ford
had been living for the past two years. When he first came
back from Detroit he had moved into the family homestead
with his father, but in 1886 old William had offered his son,
now twenty-three, eighty acres of forest land which William
had bought back in the 1860s and had never got around to
clearing. The lumber promised a chance to make some
money—Henry could cut it and trim it with his beloved
steam machines—and there was a small, rough wooden
house on the place which, with a bit of work, could provide
a pleasant home for a young married couple.

Margaret Ford and her brothers John and William Junior
had helped Henry get his little dwelling decorated and
cleaned up in time for his wedding. But Clara wanted a
proper home of her own, and almost as soon as they got
married, Henry started setting aside some of his lumber to
construct a new house to his wife's specifications. He sawed
quite a lot of it himself, and in little more than a year he

had the new place completed: a low, geometric structure with fancy, turned balustrade work around the roof and verandah that gave it the air of a gingerbread cottage. It was quite the prettiest home that Henry and Clara Ford were ever to live in, and they christened it "The Square House."

Clara Bryant had been raised to be a farmer's wife—her father farmed some forty acres—and from the start of her marriage she took charge of the household finances. Before long she had saved enough to open a bank account. The Bryants were always careful with money—too careful, some said—and in later years Clara would take exception to the stories of Henry Ford's penniless youth. The youth she had married was not penniless.

Henry had turned his lumber clearing into a rudimentary business. Receipts survive from a Detroit furniture company to which he supplied elm strips. A receipt for tolls totalling $11.45 shows he made numerous shipments down the plank road to Detroit, and he suffered from the scourge of every small businessman, the late payer. One ledger shows a James Ford, a Sam Ford, and a George Ford owing him several hundred dollars—though perhaps the family were so casual with Henry because he was himself a late payer. His father, William, got annoyed at one point, and gave notice to the local bank that he would not be held answerable to his son's creditors.[34]

Henry Ford was not a conventional farmer. He cultivated a small area he had cleared as a vegetable garden, and he raised enough livestock for his and Clara's own domestic needs. But it was his machines that he loved, and his bachelor days as a wandering mechanic had spread his name around as someone who could tackle problems that defeated other men. For two summers he took on assignments for the Buckeye Harvester Company, setting up and repairing their "Eclipse" portable farm engines.[35] He was called into Detroit on several occasions to carry out repairs, and at least once, he travelled on quite a distant assignment —to the town of Alpena, Michigan, on Lake Huron, over

200 miles north of Detroit. Henry sailed there on one of the Great Lakes steamer lines.

"I wish you were here," he wrote home to Clara. "I bet i will never go so far from you again . . . i am very busisy they want me to stay but i will bee home for it don't seam as though I can stay another day without YOU."[36]

A few months later Henry was called in to Detroit again, this time to look at the engine that was all the rage of the mechanical world: "the silent Otto." Not a steam device but one of the new internal-combustion engines, this power unit had been developed by the German Nikolaus August Otto, one of whose collaborators had been Gottlieb Daimler. It was remarkably light, compact, and regular by comparison to anything Henry had seen before. It was fired by gasoline on a novel four-stroke system: on its first stroke the piston would draw an explosive charge into the cylinder; the second stroke would compress this charge; ignition would then explode the charge, the resulting expansion driving the piston for its third stroke; and the final stroke would exhaust the burnt gases, clearing the cylinder to start the cycle again.

When he got home, Henry tried to explain this to Clara on the back of a sheet of music from the household organ, which she had been playing when he walked in. He sketched out how he felt that this sort of engine, which was being used in Detroit in a soda-bottling plant, could be mounted on wheels and adapted to propel itself—rather as the upright boiler he had seen when he was thirteen had been adapted to move the wagon that carried it.

Henry felt sure he could make such a self-propelled vehicle himself. But internal-combustion engines relied on electricity for their firing cycle, and in working with steam engines he had not learned enough about this. So, scouting around Detroit, Henry had secured the offer of employment at a substation of the Edison Illuminating Company as a mechanic-engineer. At a wage of $45 per month, it was a good job, and Henry told Clara that he wanted to take it. If Clara was willing, they could move straight away, and he could start work.

In all the versions of this story later related by Henry himself, and by Clara, it is clear that Henry Ford sprang this idea on his wife almost totally unprepared—and, not surprisingly, Clara was horrified, since it meant uprooting and moving into Detroit. It "almost broke her heart," she confided later to her sister-in-law Margaret Ford Ruddiman.[37] She loved the wooden Square House which she had designed. She was near her family and friends there, and she had, apparently, been given no reason to see her future other than in terms of the eighty acres that Henry had cleared.

Henry, however, saw no reason to stay out in the country. Having shuttled back and forth to Detroit quite often, he did not find the idea of the move very complicated. It did not mean giving up his plot of land in Dearborn. He had got interested in a new, more sophisticated type of machine which he could only really learn about by moving into town. And besides, as he said later, "The timber had all been cut."[38]

# 3

## FIRST FORD

Bell and the telephone, Edison and the light bulb, the Wright brothers and the aeroplane. Henry Ford and his motorcar fit neatly into this familiar pantheon of American hero-inventors—except that Henry Ford was not an inventor. Bell, Edison, and the Wright brothers all personally devised the machines that made them famous but Henry Ford's achievement was built upon the work of others.

When Henry moved to Detroit in September 1891 to start work at the Edison Illuminating Company,[1] there were already factories producing cars on a regular commercial basis in France. Words like *automobile*, *chauffeur*, and *garage* are reminders of the early lead that the French established in the automotive field, building on a basis of German technology. The honours for the very first car of all are usually shared between Gottlieb Daimler and Karl Benz, sometime in 1885 or 1886. In America it was the Duryea brothers, Charles and Frank, who could claim the first publicly verified demonstration of a gasoline-powered vehicle, at Springfield, Massachusetts, in September 1893—twelve months after Henry Ford had moved with his wife to Detroit. The following summer Elwood Haynes exhibited the car he had designed for the Apperson brothers of Kokomo, Indiana,[2] and a year after that there were enough rudimentary machines in existence for the *Chicago Times-Herald* to organize America's first-ever car race. Held on Thanksgiving Day 1895, the race followed a fifty-two-mile course up and down the Chicago lakeshore in a raging snowstorm, and of the six cars that started, only two managed to complete the course. The winner, a Duryea, came in at an average speed of 6.66 miles per hour.[3]

While the Chicago race attracted nationwide attention, it

58

was not until this time—the autumn and early winter of 1895—that Henry Ford was anywhere close to constructing a machine that could fairly be described as an automobile. He had spent the previous four years supervising the generators of the Edison Illuminating Company.

Operating a power station is largely a matter of making sure that the machines are properly set up. After that, they will take care of themselves with routine maintenance, and Henry Ford appears to have had the knack of running a trouble-free shop. He managed to simplify things that could have been complicated—he devised a boring bar which greatly eased the chore of boring out clogged cylinders[4]— and his superiors at the Edison Company rewarded him with wage rises, promotions, and a certain freedom.

Henry took over some spare space at the power station as a private workshop for his own mechanical experiments, and when the generators gave him leisure—which they did, most of the time—he would retreat to his own little room to fiddle with scraps of metal and electric coils. It was here that his friend from Flower Brothers, Frederick Strauss, caught up with him:

Other fellows would come sit in there. Henry had a little lathe. He had this idea of making a little gasoline engine out of scrap. We didn't work every night. We would just joke away. Sometimes we would work and sometimes not. It took us about six weeks to get this little engine built.

Saturday nights we had quite a crowd. Henry had some sort of a magnet. He could draw people to him; that was a funny thing about him.

When you are building a little engine, one thing goes after another. You bore out the cylinder, and you know you've got to make a piston, and you know you've got to have a cylinder head.

We had an awful time with the ignition. . . .[5]

Henry Ford liked to tell the tale of how he took the ignition home with him late one Christmas Eve, to the lodgings that he and Clara had taken at 58 Bagley Avenue in Detroit. The Bryants were due in from Greenfield next day, and Clara was busy getting the meal prepared when Henry walked in with the little engine he had been working on. It had a crude spark plug which he connected to the household electrical supply, but he needed Clara's help to start the engine. She would have to drip gasoline into the fuel intake, he explained, and turn a valve, while he spun the flywheel. This would suck gas and air into the cylinder and, hopefully, start internal combustion.

History records not even the slightest remonstrance from Clara Bryant Ford on that Christmas Eve in the 1890s as she set aside her cooking to drip gasoline into the oily device that her husband was clamping to the sink. She dripped the first time, adjusting the intake valve as Henry spun the flywheel, and the kitchen light flickered. This time the engine only coughed, but with a slight adjustment, another spin, and another drip, it suddenly belched into life, shooting flames and smoke from its exhaust and nearly shaking the kitchen sink from its moorings.

When Henry Ford was less obsessed than he customarily was with his latest project or invention, he reflected on his good fortune in having a wife so docile and uncomplaining, and he decided that she qualified for the title "The Believer." Clara had given up life in her beloved Square House in the country to come to the dirt and noise of Detroit. She had moved through several sets of dingy lodgings before settling in half of a two-family home on Bagley Avenue—and on the Christmas Eve when her husband requested that she drop everything to minister to his noisy and highly dangerous gasoline engine, she not only had to worry about her parents coming for dinner next day, she had a six-week-old baby sleeping in the room next door.

Henry and Clara Ford's only child was born on November 6, 1893. Dr. David O'Donnell, who assisted, was just setting up in practice after medical school. He did not have enough money for a horse and carriage, so he rode out to attend Mrs. Ford on a bicycle, with his doctor's bag tied on front. The birth was quite an easy one, but a few years later Clara Ford went into hospital for a major operation which is said to have been a hysterectomy.[6] The details can never be known—Henry Ford II has had his grandparents' medical records destroyed—but it is certain that Henry Ford took against doctors from this date onwards, and also that he had no more children by Clara.

The Fords decided to christen their son Edsel, though it is doubtful if they knew its meaning, "Rich Unto Himself,"[7] nor the Germanic root from which this curious name derived: Attila.[8] They chose the name because of Henry's best friend at school, Edsel Ruddiman, who was soon to become a member of the family through the marriage of his brother James to Henry's sister Margaret. Edsel had been one of the cleverest boys in the one-room schoolhouse at Dearborn, and Henry, a much less brilliant student, seems to have hero-worshipped him just a little. Edsel had gone on to university and became a well-paid chemist-pharmacist. Certainly by 1893 Dr. Edsel Ruddiman had made more of himself than the rather shiftless farmboy-turned-mechanic who, at the age of thirty, was spending most of his nights tinkering in a back room or laughing and joking with the boys.

The birth of his son in November 1893, however, appears to have injected new resolution into Henry. He was called out in that month from the substation where he worked to repair some steam engines at the main powerhouse of the Edison Illuminating Company, and he performed so well that he was transferred permanently there, with an increased salary of $75 a month. Soon afterwards he was promoted to chief engineer, at a salary of $100, and around this time he was also hired to teach evening classes for machinists at the Detroit YMCA.[9]

The contacts which Henry Ford made in these new positions seem to have crystallized his mechanical thinking. At the YMCA one of his pupils was a gifted young mechanic who had lived for a time in Germany, Oliver Barthel. Either through Barthel or, possibly, through his new status as chief Edison engineer, Henry got to know Barthel's employer, Charles B. King, an unusual and stimulating talent. Neither Barthel nor King admitted a limit to human speculation.

They were attracted to psychic experimentation, and they debated with each other theories of eternalism and reincarnation. King believed that human inventiveness was a special, undying essence which was preserved in the "immortal mind"—a theory which, later, was to shape some of Henry Ford's own thinking.

More practically, in the mid-1890s, Barthel and King were engaged in research into the horseless carriage. King had acted as an umpire in the momentous Chicago motor race of 1895, riding in one of the Benz cars because his own horseless carriage was not sufficiently developed to enter. When the driver he was umpiring collapsed through the strain and exposure of more than ten hours in driving snow, King took over the wheel to pilot the Benz home a gallant second.

King was an enthusiast. Recalling his pioneer days at the age of seventy-eight for the benefit of the *New Yorker*, he leapt from his chair and paced up and down with excitement at the memory of all the possibilities the world had offered him in the mid-1890s. "I was bursting with ideas," he exclaimed, "—bursting!" [10] His inventions included a pneumatic hammer and a steel brake beam, both of which went into successful production. But when he met Henry Ford, it was the horseless carriage that had him on the boil, and his enthusiasm was infectious.

In mechanical terms, Henry Ford appears to have consecrated most of his twenties and thirties to the joy of tinkering. His expertise with machinery was considerable, but it was undirected: watches, farm machines, electrical generators —almost anything that whirred and got his fingers oily. Henry Ford has conventionally been depicted as forsaking his farm in September 1891, in the Horatio Alger tradition, intent on devising a horseless carriage in Detroit, but this squares neither with his four years of dabbling once he got there, nor with his own testimony.

He told Samuel Crowther in 1926, "The idea of a [horseless] carriage at first did not seem so practical to me as the idea of an engine to do the harder farm work. . . . a tractor to attend to the excessively hard labour of ploughing." The farmboy was still thinking, evidently, in rural terms. "I felt perfectly certain," he said, "that horses, considering all the bother of attending them and the expense of feeding, did not earn their keep. . . . To lift farm drudgery off flesh and blood and lay it on steel and motors has been my most constant ambition."[11]

In later years, Henry Ford was to claim that he had experimented from the moment of his arrival in Detroit—and even while still living on the farm—with tractorlike devices powered by a rudimentary internal-combustion engine. But there is no proof of this. From 1903 onwards, soon after he became a serious car-maker, Henry was embroiled in the Selden Patent Suit, a momentous and long-drawn struggle with George Selden, an inventor who attempted to patent and monopolize the motorcar. In this battle it was important for Henry Ford to claim that he had been seriously working on the internal-combustion engine rather earlier than he had, and after the suit was over, the dates to which he had laid claim became fixed as the official chronology of his early car experiments. For many years Ford publicists gave out 1893 as the date of Henry Ford's first motorcar.

January 1896, however, is a much more plausible starting point. This was the month when Henry Ford visited his friend Charles Brady King in his office and happened to catch sight of two copies of *The American Machinist* on King's desk. These magazines, dated November 7, 1895, and January 9, 1896, contained a two-part article on how to build a simple gasoline engine from odds and ends, and Oliver Barthel, who was in the office at the time, recalled Henry saying, "I want to build one of these."[12]

Sometime after this, George Cato, an electrician who worked for Henry at the Edison plant, remembers his boss showing him one of the magazines with the do-it-yourself instructions, and making the comment that "a barrel of money was to be made in it."[13]

George Cato was one of a group of mechanical enthusiasts at the power station who had been working with Henry

Ford on the little engines and ignition systems he had been playing with in his private workroom. Two others were James W. Bishop and Edward S. "Spider" Huff. With Henry they made up a quartet of gas-engine fanatics at the electricity plant, escaping whenever they could from the antiseptic turbines, to the noise, dirt, and explosions of primitive cylinders and firing plugs.

Ford, Bishop, Cato, and Huff came to form a fine mechanical team, and they laid the basis of their teamwork in the moments that they stole together from the Edison company. When the time arrived for the serious building of a motorcar, however, the centre of their activities shifted from the power plant to a shed at the back of Henry's lodgings at 58 Bagley Avenue. It was a small, plain brick shed, later preserved and restored by Henry Ford, like so many of the shrines of his early career. It had small windows, a narrow door, and just enough room in the middle for Henry's do-it-yourself machine. There cannot have been much space to spare in the shed when four grown men were working inside it together.

Today car enthusiasts can build or modify engines from ready-made component parts, but in 1896 Henry Ford and his collaborators had to build everything themselves. For the heart of their motor, they took a length of scrap pipe from an old steam engine, reamed out the inside to a bore that was later measured as 2.565 inches, cut the pipe into two eleven-inch lengths—and there they had their cylinders.[14] Fuel was fed to the engine by the simple device of placing the gas tank above it, so that gasoline would flow into the manifold by gravity. Power was transferred to the wheels by a ten-foot length of chain from the Indianapolis Chain Company, and Charles King obtained this chain for Henry, according to King's diary, on May 27, 1896.[15]

Charles King, who was already working on a horseless carriage of his own, was a month or so ahead of Henry. With Barthel's help, he had fitted a four-cylinder engine onto a wooden wagon, and on March 6, 1896, he had trundled it out on a public demonstration at a speed of just five miles per hour. Cycling beside him as he went was Henry Ford.

"The first horseless carriage seen in this city was out on the streets last night," reported the *Detroit Free Press* on March 7, 1896.[16] The *Detroit Journal* carried an interview with the proud inventor in which, predicting great things, King stated that the Prince of Wales had recently ordered a similar vehicle. "They are much in vogue," he said, "among the English aristocracy."[17]

King's boast carried an important clue to the difference between his own machine and the vehicle that Henry Ford was working on. King was thinking in traditional terms. His vehicle was, literally, a horse-less carriage—designed for the elite who traditionally bought carriages drawn by horses. It was a wooden cart with a motor inside, and, at 1,300 pounds, the vehicle was doing well if it exceeded five miles per hour.

Henry Ford's machine, on the other hand, had a top speed of over twenty miles per hour.[18] This was remarkably fast by the standards of the time, and the secret of the car's speed was its weight—little more than 500 pounds. With its engine removed, a man could lift it quite easily.[19]

"Fat men cannot run as fast as thin men," declared Henry Ford some years later, "but we build most of our vehicles as though dead-weight fat increased speed. . . . I cannot imagine where the delusion that weight means strength came from."[20] It seemed obvious to Henry. The early internal-combustion engines were precarious, fragile things. Saving even a few pounds of a vehicle's weight could considerably reduce the strain on them—and that meant that they would break down less frequently. They would also go faster and consume less fuel. Reducing weight usually involved reducing materials, which, in turn, meant reducing cost as well.

Lightness, speed, reliability—and a low price. Henry Ford's ideas were already starting to crystallize around the principles that were to create the car for the masses. There is no evidence that Henry was consciously thinking or talking in these terms in 1896. He cannot be credited, at this stage, with anything like a long-term master plan. But, by accident or instinct, Henry Ford had settled, in his very first car, upon the ingredients that were to make for his subsequent success.

He called his car the Quadricycle, which was exactly what it looked like, two bicycles side by side. It had thin, spindly, bicycle-like wheels, a bicycle seat, and a frame that was scarcely visible. Henry covered up the workings with a wooden cabinet that he could sit on, and he ran a cosmetic sheet of wood across the front, but even then the machine had a remarkable resemblance to a baby carriage.

By the beginning of June 1896, it was nearly ready. Clara later remembered that, at the end, Henry worked almost twice around the clock to get it finished.[21] "We often wondered when Henry Ford slept," remarked Charles T. Bush, of the Strelinger Company, which had sold Henry his bolts, screws, and nuts.[22]

Finally, in the small hours of June 4, 1896, it was complete. Clara was there—she often stayed up to keep her husband company—and so was Jim Bishop, one of the comrades from work. Jim was to be the outrider on the first expedition, escorting Henry on his bicycle, as Henry had escorted Charles King. But as the two men readied themselves to push the Quadricycle out into the street, Henry Ford realized the most ridiculous mistake. He and his helpers had been so intent on building up the Quadricycle over the past weeks, testing its two cylinders and fitting all the parts together, that they had forgotten they were doing this with the aim of one day taking the machine out through the door—and the door was only a standard one.

At this point, doubtless, Henry Ford would have brought the entire shed and the rest of Bagley Avenue crashing down if he had to. He got an axe, demolished the door frame, knocked out several courses of bricks, and finally the machine was free. Clara came out to wish the car Godspeed, with a shawl over her head and an umbrella, since there was a light rain falling. Henry turned on the current from the battery, adjusted the gasoline, and placed his thumb and finger over the device that he used as a choke. He turned over the flywheel, the engine sputtered, and the Quadricycle came to life.

To steer his little ship, Henry had fashioned a tiller, long and curved, with a button on the end connected to what passed for his car horn—a domestic doorbell screwed to the front. But at two in the morning, there were few enough people to signal on the historic first ride of Henry Ford. When the Quadricycle, humiliatingly, broke down in front. of the Cadillac Hotel on Washington Boulevard, a group of revellers came out to witness Henry and the faithful Jim Bishop derisively while the two men carried out running repairs. But with a new valve-stem nut and spring, the engine came to life again, and then it was back to Bagley Avenue for a few snatched hours of sleep.

Next morning Clara made the two men some breakfast, after which, as usual, they went off to work.

The Quadricycle was not up to long trips to start with. It needed some steering improvements, and also some metal-work strengthening to its frame. But Henry Ford learned from each excursion, modifying as he went along—it was both a fault and virtue of his that he could not let well enough alone—and before too long he was ready to venture the eight miles out to Dearborn.

His sister Margaret later remembered the little car's arrival, driving along somewhat atilt:

The wheels on one side were high in the center of the road. Henry had built the car in such a way that the distance between the wheels was less than that of wagons and carriages, so drove in this way on a road which had a rut. Clara and Edsel were on the front seat with him and all of them were sitting on the slanted seat. I remember Edsel was a very small boy in dresses at this time and he was held tightly by his mother on her lap.[23]

Edsel was only two or three years old at the time. "Of course," he said as an adult, slightly muddling up his dates, "I don't remember the first automobile that my father made, for he got it running to his satisfaction the year after I was born and sold it two years later. But I do well remember that the Mayor of Detroit came to see . . . because I was standing at the window, watching for him to come in. It must have been around election time. We had a picture of him in the window."[24]

The Fords had the mayor's picture in their window because he was a friend of theirs. William C. Maybury came from an Irish family who had grown prosperous on real estate and who had helped out the Fords when they first arrived in Michigan. William Ford and Mary Litogot had had their wedding party in the grand front parlour of the Maybury mansion, and now in 1897, William Maybury was extending a helping hand to their son. Starting in January of that year and continuing on into 1898, William Maybury provided Henry Ford with the financial backing to build a successor to the Quadricycle.

The new Ford looked much more like a proper motorcar —high wheels, a luxurious, padded double bench seat, brass lamps, and two rakishly combined running boards and mudguards which gave the vehicle a racy air. In terms of looks, the vehicle stood comparison with any horseless carriage of its day, and its engineering could stand equal scrutiny. In 1898, R. W. Hanington, an engineer who had worked in the East for a period with Charles Duryea himself, came through Detroit on an expedition investigating the latest automobile developments in America, and he subjected Henry Ford's new car to a stringent inspection:

No compensating gear is shown on the rear axle. This device has been found absolutely essential. . . .

The design of the motor is excellent . . . similar to that of the Springfield Duryea's wagon. The sparker is better however. . . .

The cooling tanks show ingenuity and thought. The idea is not original . . . but has not been carried out in such detail. The Duryea wagons have no device for cooling. . . . The carburetor is good. The measuring device is complete and ingenious. . . .

The whole design strikes me as being very complete, and worked out in every detail . . . the carriage should equal any that has been built in this country.

The success of a motor-wagon seems to rest on its ability to keep in order and run over all kinds of roads without breakdowns or hitches, and the first wagon to do this will be the successful one.[25]

This final thought was precisely that of William H. Murphy, another of Detroit's Irish. The Murphys, like the Mayburys, had their fingers in many pies, from downtown real estate to a share in the Edison Illuminating Company, and William Murphy had long been a horseless-carriage enthusiast. Back in 1883, reading a newspaper report that Philadelphia had just acquired a horseless fire engine propelled by steam, he had made a quick journey and bought the same wagon for the Detroit Fire Department.[26]

Sometime in the first half of 1899, Henry Ford gained an audience with this promising potential backer, and William Murphy's response showed that he understood the fledgling automobile business. If Ford could drive him in his car out to Farmington to the northwest of Detroit and then back to the city via Pontiac, a triangular odyssey of over sixty miles, without a breakdown, then Murphy would take the whole thing seriously.

A few months later, probably sometime in July, Henry turned up again at the Murphy residence, ready for some driving. Murphy got in the car. He kept a careful log of the trip, noting the amount of fuel consumed, and the condition of the roads covered, together with the overall performance of the car, and on arriving back in Detroit in good time and without accident, he announced himself fully satisfied.

"Well," he declared, "now we will organize a company."[27]

When the Detroit Automobile Company—mechanical superintendent, Henry Ford—announced its formation on August 5, 1899, it was the first automobile manufacturing company ever to be established in the city of Detroit.[28]

"We have several new devices in connection with the construction of our automobiles, on which patents are now pending," announced the company secretary, Frank R.

Alderman, who addressed himself immediately to one of the early consumer complaints about gasoline vehicles. "We have solved the problem of overcoming bad odor by securing perfect combustion," he said, "and with our improved method of applying the power to the rear axle, and of keeping all the machinery hidden from sight, we will have a fine motor carriage."[29]

Capitalized at $150,000, the Detroit Automobile Company was quite the most solid amalgamation of assets placed behind any American horseless carriage to date. Most of the gifted tinkerers who were creating cars in these final months of the nineteenth century were struggling along on income from their sales, or on the patronage of one rich man. But three years after completing his Quadricycle, Henry Ford had managed to marshall behind himself the main pillars of the establishment of Detroit.

William Maybury, the first backer of all, was nothing less than the mayor of the city. William Murphy, whose excursion to Farmington and Pontiac had proved the crucial spark, was a multi-millionaire. Significant shareholdings were held by the brothers James and Hugh McMillan, who controlled a complex network of shipping lines, railroads, banks, insurance companies, and other enterprises ranging from the Michigan Telephone Company to the Detroit Dry Dock Company, where Henry Ford had once worked. Dexter M. Ferry, the seed king, bought shares. So did U.S. Senator Thomas W. Palmer of Michigan. Other shareholdings were held by the Peck family, who owned the Edison Illuminating Company; Frederick Osborne, head of one of Detroit's leading brokerage firms; and Frank Woodman Eddy, the successful businessman best known for founding the Detroit Athletic Club and converting the cricket pitch over to baseball.[30]

This was a cast-iron crowd to run with, the sort of men who decide who stands for what at election time and have their names over buildings downtown, and Henry was taking few risks when he handed in his notice at the Edison plant on August 15, 1899.[31] He tried to persuade his little team of helpers there to join him, but only Edward "Spider" Huff would take the risk. Frederick Strauss, Henry's friend from Flower Brothers, decided to sign on, and one day in 1899, Henry took Strauss along to 1343 Cass Avenue, which was to be the factory and workshop of the new company:

When we got in there it opened our eyes. It was just perfect for our shop. The place was empty. There wasn't a thing in there except an engine and a boiler and a main line of shaft. . . . The first thing I did was start to get the boiler and engine ready.[32]

The Detroit Automobile Company already had an automobile that it could put into production: the car in which Henry had driven William Murphy to Farmington and Pontiac. But this was not, in fact, the vehicle that they decided to manufacture. Instead, on January 12, 1900, they unveiled a completely new sort of vehicle, a horseless delivery wagon, high, black, polished, and slab-sided, with a little covered balcony projecting from the front to hold a driver and a mate.

The company's mechanical superintendent introduced this novel offering to the press. SWIFTER THAN A RACE-HORSE IT FLEW OVER THE ICY STREETS, ran the headline in the *Detroit News-Tribune* for February 4, 1900. THRILLING TRIP ON THE FIRST DETROIT-MADE AUTOMOBILE WHEN MERCURY HOVERED ABOUT ZERO.

Henry took a reporter from the *News-Tribune* on a test run which inspired the newspaperman to poetic lengths:

There has always been at each decisive period in this world's history some voice, some note, that represented for the time being the prevailing power. There was a time when the supreme cry of authority was the lion's roar. Then, came the voice of man. After that it was the crackle of fire. . . . And now, finally, there was heard in the streets of Detroit the murmur of this newest and most perfect of forces, the automobile, rushing along at the rate of 25 miles an hour . . .

It was not like any other sound ever heard in this world. It is not like the puff! puff! of the exhaust of gasoline in a river launch; neither is it like the cry! cry! of a working steam engine; but a long, quick, mellow gurgling sound, not harsh, not unmusical, not distressing; a note that falls with pleasure on the ear. It must be heard to be appreciated. And the sooner you hear its newest chuck! chuck! the sooner you will be in touch with civilization's latest lisp, its newest voice. . . .[33]

Would it take a long time to learn to drive, the reporter wanted to know?

"In a few days, maybe a few hours," replied Ford, "there's little to learn. Ride a bicycle? It's the same thing."

"But that puffing! Isn't she liable to blow up?"

"Nothing to blow up."

"But we are sitting on top of three gallons of gasoline!"

"That's nothing. It's perfectly safe. There is no fire about here. And then, we are in the open air."

The wagon drove past the shop of a saddler and harness maker. "His trade is doomed," declared Henry with some satisfaction.[34]

The story of this test drive was splashed, with a dramatic picture, across the front of the *News-Tribune*'s feature section, and it revealed a previously unguessed-at side of Henry Ford. Normally rather shy, and by no means a public speaker, Henry was wondrously at ease with the press. Set a reporter in front of Henry Ford with a notepad, and the carmaker became a fountain of quips and quotes—at least so long as he was talking about one of his motorcars.

With an intuitive gift for making slightly provocative remarks, Henry Ford gave newspapermen exactly what they wanted, and this appeared to help the Detroit Automobile Company off to a good start in February 1900. The company had plans for several other cars as well as the delivery van, and in the next few months it manufactured around a dozen vehicles. By November 1900, however, little more than a year after its foundation, the Detroit Automobile Company had ceased trading, and two months later, official notice of its dissolution was filed in the State Capitol at Lansing.

Henry blamed the failure on his backers—"a group of men of speculative turn of mind," he complained later, whose aim was "to exploit." They had no sympathy, he said, with his own objective, which was to make a better car for the public, "and being without authority other than my engineering position gave me, I found that the new company was not a vehicle for realizing my ideas but merely a money-making concern."[35]

Ford's biographers have tended to take their cue from this, explaining the failure of the Detroit Automobile Company in terms of Henry's "perfectionism." He wanted a better car, while his backers were only interested in the quick buck. But the investors in the Detroit Automobile Company were scarcely fly-by-night characters. Between August 1899 and November 1900, they stood a loss of some $86,000 before they threw in the towel, and to judge from the recollections of Frederick Strauss, it was not so much they as Henry Ford who showed a lack of commitment. Henry's successor to the Quadricycle, the vehicle demonstrated on his excursion with William Murphy, had been the trigger for forming the company, yet for some reason, Henry held back his designs for this car. The workshop at 1343 Cass Avenue was kitted out, the machine tools were purchased, and the mechanics had been hired, but, remembered Fred Strauss:

Henry wasn't ready. He didn't have an automobile design. To get the shop going, Henry gave me some sketches to turn up some axle shaftings. I started machining these axle shaftings to show them we were doing something. It was just to get it going but they didn't belong to anything. We never used them for the automobile. It was just a stall until Henry got a little longer into it.[36]

Henry never got into it. The Cass Avenue factory was on the outskirts of Detroit, and he would go off into the nearby woods, saying that he was going to do some designing. Strauss and the other mechanics in the shop saw less and less of him—"he might come in every day for about an hour or two"—and when eventually his directors got tired of this and forced a showdown, Henry continued to play truant. "If they ask for me," he told Strauss, "you tell them that I had to go out of town."[37]

It was extraordinary behaviour for a man of nearly forty who had had a company tailor-made around his own special expertise and ambitions. Fred Strauss explained Henry's dog-in-the-manger attitude in terms of his backers' refusal to give him "a better settlement," and this is in line with Henry's complaints about "exploitation" and his own lack of authority. He evidently decided, within a matter of months, that he wanted a better deal. Throughout his career, Henry Ford was to drop out at crucial moments like this, withdrawing from a difficult situation like a hermit, because he could not get his way.

Henry's backers, however, do not seem to have been that awkward or unreasonable to deal with. William Maybury, the family friend, personally stood most of the $86,000 loss, and William Murphy retained enough confidence in Henry to back him in another project within a year of the Detroit Automobile Company's collapse. It is difficult to see why Henry Ford found it so painful to discuss his problems with these men that he had to run away to the woods.

Over the debris of the Detroit Automobile Company lingers the unmistakable impression that Henry Ford got out of his depth, for producing cars to sell in quantity required very different skills from designing and producing a single prototype. One particular design had to be "frozen," and then a long process of thought and experimentation was needed to sort out the practical problems of producing multiple copies of each part. "You would be surprised," said an evidently chagrined Frank Alderman, company secretary in February 1900, "at the amount of detail about an automobile."[38]

It was the mastery of manufacturing detail that was to separate the tinkerers from the carmakers in the early years of automobile development. An efficient and economic manufacturing process was the key to whether money was made, or lost—and Henry Ford's record at the Detroit Automobile Company suggests that he had not as yet realized this. Abandoning his tested prototype for a completely different sort of vehicle, the delivery van, and talking to Fred Strauss about "designing" in the woods, Henry had not yet come to terms with the new dimension he was working in. He was no longer a power-station supervisor, fiddling with engines in a back room as a hobby.

Compared to America's other automotive pioneers like Duryea, Haynes, or even Charles B. King, Henry Ford had come quite late to the business of carmaking. The Detroit Automobile Company had offered him a chance to catch up, or even to get ahead of the game—and Henry had muffed it.

# 4

# RACING

In January 1901, Clara Ford decided to mark the dawning of a new century by keeping a diary of her own activities in it. She did not manage to maintain this New Year's resolution much longer than most other people do, and she never attempted such a chronicle again. But starting with the month in which the Detroit Automobile Company filed its dissolution papers—an event which goes unrecorded in Clara's journal—we have a vividly detailed picture of life as lived by Henry, thirty-seven, Clara, thirty-four, and the growing Edsel Ford, now just seven years old.

*January 11, 1901.*
Snowed all day. Edsel got soaking wet. He and Grandpa [Ford] played checkers. Edsel cheated awful and beat every game. Went to bed so full of laughs he could not say his prayers.
*Sat. January 12.*
Went downtown, got Edsel shoes and leggings. Went into Sheaffer's store to hear the music. After supper we tried to learn Grandpa to play cards. . . .
*Sun. January 13.*
Edsel and I went to S[unday] School. . . . Came home, had dinner, then Henry fixed Edsel's old sleigh to take him coasting, but Edsel would not go, said sleigh was no good. He was sent up stairs for punishment for his pride. He was sorry.[1]

In adult life Henry Ford's attempts to impose his own values upon his son were to make for tragedy, but so long as Edsel was a little boy, Henry was the indulgent father.

*January 19.*
Henry bought Edsel new coaster.[2]

Henry Ford was an active, enjoyable parent for a seven-year-old boy to have. Henry loved gadgets, and he loved showing Edsel how to use them. He had bought a camera quite early in the 1890s, and his snapshots are full of clowning and goonery. There is Henry in 1907, when he was forty-four, turning a cartwheel for Edsel's benefit. There is the pair of them, half a dozen years earlier, turning hay together. There are several pictures of Edsel playing with his father's cars—Henry taught the boy to drive, and let him drive unaccompanied, when he was eight—and there is a fancy-dress picture in which Clara pretends to be a cowboy, while Edsel, horsing about in the foreground, makes a silly face at the camera.[3]

With the failure of the Detroit Automobile Company, Henry Ford had more time to spend with his family. April 11, 1901, was Clara's thirty-fifth birthday—as well as the Fords' thirteenth wedding anniversary—and Henry took his wife down to Hudson's, Detroit's up-and-coming department store.

*April 11.*
Henry bought me a pair of patent-leather shoes and a pair of black silk hose. . . .
*April 20.*
Went downtown met Henry at Hudson's. Tried to change my shoes but could not. Got my money back. . . .[4]

Clara's diary petered out shortly after this, but before it did, she made one entry which offers a clue as to why her husband was more carefree than might be expected of a man who has just had a $150,000 company fold under him.

*April 5.*
Henry and Mr. Murphy went out with automobile to Farmington around to Orchard Lake on to Pontiac back home. Started half after two back at 6.[5]

William Murphy had not been discouraged by the failure of the Detroit Automobile Company. He had lost money in the venture, but that counted for little in the scale of his lumber fortune. He had the motoring bug. He evidently enjoyed the long test runs to Farmington and Pontiac with

Henry, and he was still more excited by the project that Henry was hatching for that summer: a racing car.

Every early carmaker raced. How else to prove the product in an age before *Consumer Reports*? Newspapers did not yet have motoring correspondents, and, until the winter of 1900, motor shows were still subsections of bicycle shows and fairs. Auto races were to the early 1900s what space shots are today. They combined drama—real human courage and danger—with the visible demonstration of technical progress, a chance for ordinary mortals to witness man expanding the limits of his day.

At the turn of the century, almost every car race was faster than the previous one. In September 1900, the cream of East Coast society had gathered at Newport, Rhode Island, to watch William K. Vanderbilt win a five-mile-race in under nine minutes—better than thirty-three miles an hour—and later that month Alexander Winton, a Cleveland manufacturer whose reputation had been made largely by his racing activities, defeated a field of strong competitors over a fifty-mile course in Chicago. Winton had kept up an average speed of over thirty-eight miles an hour, and his victory gave him a double preeminence. It made him both racing champion and dominant U.S. car manufacturer, and his products were advertised nationwide: "Always ready for use!" "Never gets 'winded'!" "Away with the whip!"[6] When it became known that Winton would be bringing one of his machines to Detroit late in 1901 to compete against all comers, the challenge was inescapable.

The race was to be held on October 10, 1901, at a track just constructed beside the lakeside resort of Grosse Pointe, to the east of Detroit. Henry had been working on his own racing machine since the spring, if not earlier—the vehicle in which he took William Murphy out on April 5 was probably a prototype—and in May, with Murphy's backing, he started serious work on the racer, recruiting a team that included Charles B. King's former helper, Oliver Barthel, and the electrician from the Edison plant, Edward "Spider" Huff. Huff was credited officially with the car's induction coil, and he also worked with Barthel on the device that turned out to be the Ford racer's most lasting contribution to automotive history: a special spark coil which they took to Barthel's dentist, Dr. W. E. Sandborn, who made a porcelain insulating case for it—the forerunner of the modern spark plug.[7]

The machine itself was built on the same principles that had made the Quadricycle such a success. Henry had sold his first machine to finance his work on its successors, and in April 1899, he had received a note from its latest owner, A. W. Hall of 255 Woodward Avenue.

You will be surprised when I tell you that the little carriage is still doing its usual duty. I disposed of it this spring and the little rig was still in fair shape after all the banging around that it has had, and I guess you know that was considerable. . . .

I was out in Chicago all last fall, and looked over the few horseless rigs there, and among them all I did not see one I would of rather had than that little rig, for when it comes right down to simplicity, they were not in it.[8]

Simplicity was the keynote of Henry's racer. It had just two cylinders, developing twenty-six horsepower, and on paper, this did not match up to the other machines entered for the Grosse Pointe race. Henri Fournier, French holder of the world mile record, drove a sixty-horsepower car, Alexander Winton's machine packed forty, and William K. Vanderbilt, Jr. commanded equal power in his "Red Devil," a fearsome, imported beast which was said to have cost $7,000 in customs' duties alone. Ford's entry, which he did not officially register until the day before the race, scarcely matched up to these, and when both Fournier and Vanderbilt scratched, it seemed that there was only one man in it. Alexander Winton's sales manager, Charles Shanks, had a word with the race organizers about the aesthetics of the victory trophy. The bay window of his Cleveland dining room was rather bare, so the trophy was chosen accordingly—a fine cut-glass punchbowl which would look just right in the Winton bay window.[9]

At the turn of the century, it was scarcely possible to see Grosse Pointe as you approached it across the waters of Lake St. Clair. A few gingerbread villas and the eaves of the odd Swiss boathouse broke the profile of the prevailing greenery, but most of the place was just trees.[10] It was the summer refuge of Detroit's elite.

Grosse Pointe was too far from town for people to live there on a regular basis. One enterprising group of residents had clubbed together to purchase their own little commuter yacht which steamed them to work and back in the summer, and a couple of the truly affluent had yachts of their own. Their boats lay at anchor off their estates, the crews up at dawn each day, holystoning the decks and rubbing the brasswork till it glistened. But these were summer indulgences. Grosse Pointe was a resort, not a suburb, and with winter everyone went back to their mansions on Woodward Avenue.

As the contestants arrived in Grosse Pointe for the great automobile race, the autumn exodus was just beginning. Yachts were being beached and verandahs shut down. At the racetrack itself, a mile-round circuit constructed on open ground, workmen were dumping earth to bank up the corners, for Alexander Winton was planning an attempt on the world mile speed record. Fournier, the Frenchman, was due to make an attempt in New York on the same day, and the promoters of the Grosse Pointe race wanted the honour for Detroit.

They offered a full card of events, to test vehicles of every variety. The first race was for steamers over five laps, their fastest mile being covered in just under two minutes. Then it was the turn of the electric cars. None of them could manage a mile in less than four minutes, and it was left to Alexander Winton to demonstrate the superiority of gasoline-powered engines by driving an exhibition mile in 1 minute 12.4 seconds, a whole second faster than the latest mark set by Henri Fournier. A world record had come to Detroit—for an hour or so at least. In New York later that same afternoon, Henri Fournier was to lower his fastest mile to 1 minute 6.8 seconds.

Now came the event that had been the talk of Detroit for weeks. Judge Phelan had adjourned the Recorder's Court at one o'clock that day so that the city's lawyers and their clients could attend, and they swelled a crowd of more than 8,000 spectators. The race itself, however, threatened to be something of an anticlimax, for only three competitors made it to the starting line—and one of them had a leaking cylinder and could not start. So that left just two combatants: the new world-record holder and ace motor manufacturer, Alexander Winton, and the Dearborn country boy and failed manufacturer, Henry Ford. The organizers said they were cutting the originally scheduled length of the race from twenty-five miles to ten because the previous races had gone on longer than expected. But they were probably being polite. This was clearly going to be a one-way contest, and there would be little suspense or fun to be had from watching Alexander Winton circle the track for fourteen extra laps.

Winton made his mastery apparent from the start. He went straight into the lead, and though there was a suspicion that Ford's car might have the speed to overtake him, Henry did not appear to have the expertise. He had concentrated on the mechanics of his machine, not the driving, so he lost ground on every turn, having to shut off power and coast out wide.

Crouched down beside him on the running board, gripping special handles, the faithful Spider Huff was riding postillion, and he leant out gallantly, extending his body wide and low into each corner, trying to pull the car tighter into the curve. But in vain. After three laps covered, Winton was at least a fifth of a mile up, and the race seemed over.

But then Henry Ford started to catch up. He gained perceptibly on Winton in every straight. He and Huff got a rhythm going on the curves, and by the sixth lap they had cut back Winton's lead significantly. The champion was losing power.

"A thin wreath of blue smoke appeared at the rear of the machine," reported the *Detroit Tribune*, "and it gradually increased to a cloud."[11] Winton's postillion was his sales manager, Charles Shanks, chooser of the cut-glass punchbowl, and Shanks tried desperately to execute running repairs, leaning over to pour oil into the engine.

But it was no good. In the seventh lap, right in front of the grandstand, Henry Ford shot ahead, and he stayed there to the end, Winton losing ground all the way.

Clara Ford was one of the delirious spectators. "I wish you could have seen him," she wrote in a letter to her brother Milton Bryant.

The people went wild. One man threw his hat up and when it came down he stamped on it, he was so excited. Another man had to hit his wife on the head to keep her from going off the handle. She stood up in her seat & screamed "I'd bet Fifty dollars on Ford if I had it."[12]

It was a great and famous victory, thoroughly earned. A driver who wins a modern motor race through the mechanical failure of his rivals might well feel less than satisfied. But on October 10, 1901, at Grosse Pointe, the blue smoke from Alexander Winton's engine, and the ability of Henry Ford's racer to keep on going, reflected directly on each man's ability to address the problem that mattered more to early motorists than manoeuvrability and speed. Mechanical reliability was the real challenge facing Henry Ford and his more famous rival, and Henry Ford had won that battle hands down.

Watching the race on that autumn day in 1901 by the banks of Lake St. Clair were a number of men who decided to think again about Henry Ford—and Clara Ford got a fine cut-glass punch-bowl to put in her front window.

On September 6, 1901, a little over a month before the Grosse Pointe race, William McKinley, just reelected President of the United States, was shot down, to die eight days later. The entire nation was plunged into mourning.

On the day of the funeral, two minutes' silence was proclaimed in memory of the slain President, and in the Detroit workshop where Henry Ford and his friends were tuning up their racer for its encounter with Winton next month, work ceased and the men laid down their tools. Their thoughts turned to sombre things, and as they talked, Oliver Barthel handed Henry a thin volume which had, he said, shaped his own thinking greatly: *A Short View of Great Questions*, by Orlando Jay Smith.[13]

Henry took the book and read it. The essays outlined three theories of man's origin and destiny: "the theory of Materialism," that life begins with birth and ends with death; "the theory of Theology," that man is born with an immortal soul; and "the theory of Reincarnation," the belief that every human spirit is eternal and moves after the death of one body to inhabit another.

Henry Ford was impressed. He does not seem to have possessed any deep spiritual or philosophical convictions prior to this. Back in Dearborn, Edsel Ruddiman and he used to walk four miles to church and back every Sunday but, according to Ruddiman, "Neither of us was very religious. . . . It was more to be together and to be doing something than to go to church."[14]

After he had first come to Detroit, Henry had gone through a phase of church sampling. He later described himself trying out different forms of worship on succeeding Sundays, always emerging with the feeling that he knew no more than when he had gone in. But in 1901 Henry Ford was approaching the age of forty, and in Oliver Barthel's thin volume, he finally found a set of spiritual clothes in which he could feel comfortable.

The belief that the human soul lives on after death, carrying the things which it has learned in one existence on with it into the next, is very appealing—and once you have accepted the basic assumption, it makes perfect sense of the eternal questions that trouble man. Where do we come from? Where are we going? Why are some born to a happy lot, while others have to cope with distress?

Reincarnation is a simple, logical answer to all these doubts and fears. We have always existed, and our spirits are part of the eternal reality. As we strive and learn in one existence, so we carry the progress we have made to the next. This is the point of struggling hard through life, because if we can manage to ascend two or three rungs on the human ladder in this existence, we shall start off next time from the more elevated position that we have earned.

"Every experience is worth having," explained Henry Ford later. "Work is futile if we cannot utilize the experience we collect in one life in the next."[15] This is how believers in reincarnation explain child prodigies. Mozart brought his creativity with him from his previous existences. The same went for Henry Ford: he was an "old soul."

One attraction of reincarnation, if you are as compulsive and egocentric as Henry Ford later became, is that you have no one to thank for your own achievements but yourself. Your drive and ideas derive from your own previous lives as you yourself have chosen to live them, not from "blood" or heredity—and certainly not from how your father brought you up.

Henry Ford felt that reincarnation pulled together so many of the contradictory strands in his character. The outbreak of the First World War in Europe was to find him a convinced pacifist, and when people asked him the roots of this, he would explain it in terms of his immediately previous life. His birthday in Dearborn on July 30, 1863, fell at the end of the month that had started with the Battle of Gettysburg, so he decided that he must have been a soldier, killed in the Civil War. It was this experience that had inspired his hatred of fighting and bloodshed, he would say.[16]

It might seem a simplistic explanation, but that was precisely why Henry Ford embraced it. He was a simple man. His great gift, the secret that was to make him successful, was his ability to make complex things simple. In 1901, at the age of thirty-eight, he still gave only intermittent indications of the great achievements ahead, but he always looked back to the moment when Oliver Barthel handed him *A Short View of Great Questions* as one of the turning points in his life.[17]

"It was as if I had found a universal plan . . . ," he said later. "Time was no longer limited. I was no longer a slave to the hands of the clock. There was time enough to plan and to create."[18]

On November 30, 1901, just seven weeks after Henry's famous victory over Alexander Winton at the Grosse Pointe track, articles of incorporation were filed in Detroit for the Henry Ford Company, a manufacturing enterprise capitalized at 6,000 ten-dollar shares, 1,000 of which were awarded to Henry Ford by his backers in return for his designs and expertise, and for the use of his name. The racing car had paid off.

The five investors who, led by William Murphy, each staked $10,000 to back Henry Ford at the end of 1901 had all lost money in the Detroit Automobile Company, but they had witnessed Henry's convincing victory over the premier motorcar maker in America. Wisened by their previous experience, the syndicate laid private plans to avoid a second debacle. It proved just as well that they did.

Only four days after the Henry Ford Company was formed, Clara Ford wrote to her brother Milton Bryant, then working as a drug salesman in Kentucky.

Henry has worked very hard to get where he is. That race has advertised him far and wide. And the next thing will be to make some money out of it. I am afraid that will be a hard struggle. You know rich men want it all . . . [19]

Clara must have been taking her cue from Henry, for he was already up to the same sort of tricks that had brought down the Detroit Automobile Company.

After his victory over Winton, Henry had travelled to the New York Auto Show, where he was lionized as a home-grown automotive hero. There he met Henri Fournier to discuss a joint attempt on the Frenchman's latest world record, and, down in Kentucky, brother-in-law Milton Bryant, something of a wheeler-dealer, fancied he could stage such a challenge near Louisville. Milton proposed himself as Henry's racing manager, and, less than two months after William Murphy and his partners had put their money into the Henry Ford Company, Henry expressed himself as keen on the idea of the challenge.

DEAR BROTHER,

*If I can bring Mr. Fournier in line there is a barrel of money in this business. It was his proposition and I don't see why he won't fall in line. If he don't, I will challenge him untill I am black in the face. As for managing my end of the racing business, I would rather have you than anyone else that I know of. My Company will kick about me following racing, but they will get the Advertising, and I expect to make $ where I can't make c[ents] at Manufacturing* ... [20]*

Henry wrote this letter on the impressive notepaper of the Henry Ford Company—"Builders of High-Grade Automobiles and Tourist Cars. Makers of Automobile Specialities and Spark Coils." The letterhead featured a striking picture of the machine that had defeated Winton, and the company's plan seems to have been to manufacture and sell a line of cars derived from this successful and famous prototype. Oliver Barthel was hired to work full-time on the project.

But Henry Ford had enjoyed the taste of glory on the Grosse Pointe track. "He did not seem inclined to settle down to a small car production plan," remembered Barthel. "He talked mostly about wanting to build a larger and faster racing car."[21] Instead of pushing ahead with a conventional production vehicle for the general market, Henry secretly began work on another, faster racing machine, and he enlisted Barthel to help him with it.

Moonlighting had become a habit with Henry Ford. He had worked on the Quadricycle in time filched from his employers at the electrical plant, and once he found himself in similar circumstances—at the Detroit Automobile Company, and now in the company bearing his own name —he reverted to the same pattern of behaviour. He knew how to win commitment, but he did not know how to give it.

"Mr. Ford seemed to have a dual nature," Oliver Barthel said later. "One side of his nature I liked very much and I felt that I wanted to be a friend of his. The other side of his nature I just couldn't stand. It bothered me greatly."[22]

William Murphy and his partners were on the watch. One day Murphy came into the plant unexpectedly, and he caught Barthel working on the new racer. "He told me not to do it, and that he would fire me," said Barthel. "If I valued my job, I'd better not do any work on it."[23]

Murphy could see that Henry Ford was playing the old game—and the businessman had already worked out a contingency plan. Murphy worshipped at the same church as Henry M. Leland, a director and partner in Leland & Faulconer, which was one of the finest machine shops in Detroit. Leland had worked on the strong and delicate gears of the Columbia chainless bicycle, and he was also producing components for Ransom E. Olds, the Lansing carmaker who had come to Detroit and who was, in 1902, on his way to producing 2,500 units of his little curved-dash Oldsmobile, the world's first low-priced car to be produced in any quantity.[24] Solid, reputable, and established, Henry Leland served first as an adviser to William Murphy, and then, as things got out of hand at the Henry Ford Company, Murphy brought him in to sort out the problems on the shop floor itself.

Matters came very swiftly to a head. Leland, the older man, receiving his brief as a troubleshooter directly from William Murphy, felt he could tell Henry Ford what to do. "Mr. Ford," remembered W. W. Pring, an employee in the workshop, "wasn't the type of man to take it, because Mr. Ford still understood that he was still in the designing end."[25]

When the clash came, Ford's partners took Leland's side, and early in March 1902, only four months after the formation of the Henry Ford Company, Henry Ford was shown the door. He took with him a $900 cash settlement, the designs for his new racing car—but not the designs for the car he was supposed to have put into production—and the company's undertaking to remove his name from their masthead, which they lost no time in doing.

In an historical flight, Murphy and his partners rechristened themselves the Cadillac Automobile Company. Taking Henry's car, they removed his power unit and replaced it with a precision single-cylinder engine produced by Henry Leland. The Cadillac went on to establish an unparalleled reputation for quality and reliability, and in 1909 it became the flagship of the fledgling General Motors Corporation. But originally it was a Ford.

Managing to close down two manufacturing companies in less than two years was, in its way, quite an achievement. Henry Ford's double failure reflected his personal insecurity and his lack of direction. He seemed to be scared of success.

Yet Henry appears to have survived his two debacles with remarkable equanimity. The world may have assumed he was rudderless, but Henry himself never admitted to the slightest personal doubt. He sailed through a couple of episodes that would have bruised the psyche of most normal mortals—and he later explained this in terms of the inner knowledge to which he had been led by Oliver Barthel.

"I feel that I have never done anything by my own volition," he declared in 1928. "I was always pushed by invisible forces within and without me. . . . I was forty when I went into business, forty when I began to evolve the Ford plant. But all the time I was getting ready."[26]

By the time Henry Ford delivered these words, he had made himself the richest and most famous man in America. He was entitled to his sense of destiny. In a sense, his was the very best explanation for his success of all, since, when he was a young man, there had indeed been invisible forces pushing around him in every direction.

When Henry Ford came to Detroit, went back to the country, and then came back to Detroit again, he had been one of hundreds and thousands of farmboys doing the same across the country. He was part of America's great nineteenth-century migration to the cities. In tearing up his rural roots, it was not surprising that he should feel the aimlessness and insecurity later manifested in his nostalgia for a pastoral idyll that had never been.

On the other hand, the economic wave that Henry Ford was riding was a very real one. There *were* jobs in town. In America at the turn of the century there were opportunities for a poor boy to make himself rich with a completeness that has seldom existed before or since. In his chosen field, Henry Ford could afford to let two companies die under him—and probably a good few more until he found what really suited him.

Between 1900 and 1908 no less than 502 American companies were formed to manufacture automobiles. Three hundred and two of these dropped out or entered another line of business,[27] but that still left 200 survivors. By 1910, when the American automotive industry was really hitting its stride, there were nearly 300 different makes of automobile being manufactured in various parts of the country,[28] and as late as 1917, after many shakedowns and mergers, there were 23 carmaking companies in Detroit alone, with 132 parts firms supplying them with components.[29]

The jobs and backing were there for the right person. When Henry had left the Detroit Automobile Company, he had immediately found financial backing for his racer, and now, in the spring of 1902, even before he had parted company with Murphy and his backers for the second time, he had found himself another patron: Tom Cooper, a cycling champion who, through exhibitions and endorsements, had made himself rich on the bicycle mania of the 1890s, and who wanted to make the switch to the latest speed craze.

"Tom Cooper . . . has got the racing fever bad," Clara wrote to her brother Milt in March 1902, a week before Henry's final severance from the Henry Ford Company. "He is very anxious to get a good racing car."[30]

By early May, Henry Ford and Tom Cooper were in partnership constructing two machines with Cooper's money, both of them named after famous express trains of the time: "The Arrow" and "999." Henry Ford's 999 was then the largest and most powerful American car ever built, nearly ten foot long, rated at seventy horsepower, with four massive cylinders, each of them the size of a small powder keg.

"The roar of those cylinders alone was enough to half kill a man," remembered Henry later. "There was only one seat. . . . We let them out at full speed. I cannot quite describe the sensation. Going over Niagara Falls would have been but a pastime after a ride in one of them."[31]

These leviathans were the work of a new mechanical partner in Ford's life, C. Harold Wills, a young draughtsman who may possibly have done some work with Henry earlier, but who was fully in harness by the summer of 1902. The C. before Harold stood for Childe. Wills's Welsh parents were evidently poetry lovers, and though he was always embarrassed by his first name, there was something Byronic about him. Tall, handsome, and proud, C. Harold Wills was a swashbuckler, and the practical application of his artistic side was consummate ability as a draughtsman. He filled a crucial gap in Henry Ford's own repertoire of skills, for he could execute precise mechanical drawings, and through the summer of 1902 he worked on the engines of the Arrow and 999. Alexander Winton was due for another challenge race at the Grosse Pointe track in October, and 999 was selected as the machine to do battle with him.

But 999 was a difficult car to drive. Tom Cooper tried a test drive in it and promptly thought better of his motor-racing ambitions. He brought in a friend, another cyclist, Barney Oldfield, who was something of a daredevil, and though Oldfield had never actually driven a motorcar before, he accepted the challenge. "I might as well be dead," he said, "as dead broke."[32]

When race day came, Oldfield charged 999 into battle with the happy ignorance of a neophyte. He slammed his foot down on the accelerator at the start and didn't raise it until he had crossed the finish line, not slackening in the slightest on the corners. Winton, who had christened his car

"The Bullet," held the pace for a lap or so, then gave up. The only other driver with a chance was Charles Shanks, Winton's sales manager, and 999 lapped him before the end, completing the five-mile course in 5 minutes 28 seconds, a new American record—less than 1 minute 6 seconds per mile.

This second Ford victory in less than a year started Barney Oldfield on a successful career as a motorcar racer. Six weeks later he got 999 down to 1 minute 1.2 seconds for the mile, and in later years he liked to say that he and Henry Ford had "made" each other, Ford by building the car and Oldfield by driving it. "But," Oldfield used to add, "I did much the best job of it."[33]

Henry Ford, however, had reached another dead end. On October 25, 1902, when it won its victory, 999 had not even been his, for he had had a falling out with Cooper and had sold the car to him. Henry had caught Cooper "in a number of sneaky tricks," reported Clara to her brother Milt on October 27, 1902. Cooper, she explained, "was looking out for Cooper and Cooper only." This, of course, was precisely what all Henry's previous partners would have said about Henry.

There had been talk of Milton Bryant and Henry forming some sort of racing circus and travelling around the country with Cooper, and Clara was very pleased that this would not now happen. "I am glad we are rid of him," she wrote to her brother. "I would not like you or Henry to travel with him. He thinks too much of low down women. . . ."[34]

# 5

## DR. PFENNIG BUYS A CAR

When Diego Rivera, the Mexican painter, came to Detroit in the 1930s to start work on his epic tribute to the American industrial spirit, the Detroit Industry frescoes, the artist was taken on a tour through the great grey mass of plants and smokestacks that made up the landscape of the Motor City, and his guide, Dr. William Valentiner, director of the city's art museum, tried to explain to the Mexican how it all came about.

Valentiner thought that the climate had a lot to do with it—"certainly almost the worst in the United States. Only the very strong could survive." Valentiner, an aesthetic German who did not find life in southeast Michigan much to his taste, compared Detroit to two of Europe's more austere cities, Berlin and Madrid, both of them founded comparatively recently in places naturally hostile to human habitation. "To defeat the conditions imposed by earth and sky at Detroit," he said, "required intensive labor by energetic men who were not tempted by pleasure and play." [1]

Hard work did have a lot to do with it, and perhaps the climate was a reason for that. Staying indoors and building motorcars is just about the most exciting thing you can do in the depths of a long, harsh Detroit winter, with not a single hill to shield you against the cold air coming south from Hudson Bay.

But there were other, more kindly gifts of nature—like Michigan's great beds of copper and iron ore, which provided the raw material for Detroit's flourishing metalworkers and machine shops. There was the local coal which was so plentiful, but which, when it came to burning, did not really heat too well. This inclined Detroit's shipyards to favour gasoline as a power source for their launches and lake vessels, so that Detroit engineers came to know about internal-combustion engines when others were still working with steam.

The lumber counted for much, those miles and miles of dense Michigan forest which had made Detroit a centre of railcar and horse-drawn-carriage making. These two industries generated the army of expert leather workers, upholsterers, and carpenters whose skills transferred so well to working on the developing motorcar. Until the 1920s, large parts of most automobiles were constructed out of good, old-fashioned wood.

And Detroit did a few things to help itself. After a spate of labour trouble in the 1880s, its employers got together to fight unionization, and the EAD, the Employers' Association of Detroit, became known throughout America for the thoroughness with which its spies and thugs infiltrated labour organizations, broke up strikes, and provided the city's hiring offices with blacklists of potential troublemakers. Attracted by Detroit's fierce protection of employer interests, the Burroughs Adding Machine Company decamped there in 1904 from St. Louis, where it was having labour trouble,[2] and the open shop was one of the reasons why the Packard Motor Company uprooted from Ohio in 1903 and shifted its works to Detroit.[3]

Packard also shifted, however, because its new backers, Henry B. Joy and Truman H. Newberry, were both Detroit men—part of the same well-heeled network as William Murphy, the McMillan brothers, and the other early backers of Henry Ford. They were the princes of Griswold Street, Detroit's own little Wall Street, and their investment instincts were telling them to make a switch, as the traditional iron, copper, and lumber sources of the city's private fortunes were on the wane.

It was the men they backed, however, who were the most important factor of all, the men with gasoline in their veins, the enthusiasts, the fanatics who seemed happier going broke on the right machines than making money with the wrong ones. Sometimes friends, sometimes rivals, they fed off each other, copying, competing, striking sparks to create in one small locality a compound reaction whose explosive energy far exceeded their powers as individuals or as a group: Henry Ford cycling beside the buggy of Charles B. King, Henry Leland shouldering Ford aside, Ransom E. Olds buying components from Leland, Olds himself throwing off apprentices like Roy D. Chapin who went on to create companies of their own.

It took some time. U.S. carmaking did not start in Detroit, but in the East, in New England. Later, Alexander Winton made his cars at Cleveland, Elwood Haynes in Indiana. Until 1905 Indianapolis contained more auto plants than did any city in Michigan.[4] But by the beginning of the twentieth century, Detroit's vortex was spinning—the population had more than doubled between 1880 and 1900[5]—and as the vortex turned, it sucked in more and more suppliers and outside capital.

Motor manufacturing has since developed elsewhere in the world, but in no other major country has it concentrated in one exclusive geographic locality as it has done in America. The complex interaction of economic and human chemistry which occurred in south-east Michigan in the early years of this century occurred only once, and the consequence was Detroit, the Motor City—a creation unique then and ever since.

When Henry Ford was superintending the coal-fired boilers of the Edison Illuminating Company in the early 1890s, he had purchased his fuel from an enterprising and energetic young coal merchant, Alex Y. Malcomson.

"This is to certify," runs a testimonial dated from Henry's time with Edison,

that before awarding the contract for coal for the season of 1894 —1895, we made tests of the different grades of coal from several of Detroit [*sic*] largest coal merchants, and found that the Acme Pea and Acme Nut and Slack coal furnished by Elex Y. Malconson [*sic*] in point of quality and price, was unexcelled, in fact we consider it the finest coal ever burned at our plant.[6]

Malcomson, born in Scotland in 1865, had started work as a grocery clerk when he came to Detroit, but when he saw the booming city's need for coal, he had switched to that business. Most Detroit coal suppliers used large wagons hauled by four or six horses. Malcomson used smaller wagons, hauled by just two, which enabled him to make more deliveries faster, and to supply domestic as well as commercial users.

"Hotter than sunshine" was the slogan of Malcomson's coal, and his business grew rapidly. From a single horse and cart, operating on credit, he expanded to 10 coalyards, 110 wagons, and 120 horses by the early years of the twentieth century.[7] He also owned a Winton automobile and wanted to invest in motorcar production, for having successfully sniffed out one commercial growth area, he felt certain that motorcars were another.

Henry Ford and Malcomson were talking business by the summer of 1902. On August 16, the two men met in the office of Malcomson's lawyer, John W. Anderson, and four days later they signed an agreement to go into partnership under the name of Ford & Malcomson Ltd., with the object of producing a passenger car.[8] Henry surrendered a half interest in all his patents, tools, models, and drawings, promised to hand over one of his two racing cars on completion, and also undertook to devote his time to building a model of the proposed passenger car.

This was all promised at the time when Henry was supposed to be completing his racers for competition that autumn in collaboration with Tom Cooper. Rather than Cooper's "sneaky tricks," it appears more likely that it was Henry's new agreement with Malcomson that ended Henry's racing partnership with the cycling champion.

As a child of rural populism, Henry Ford always professed contempt for the ethics of "big business," but when it came to the pursuit of his own interests, he demonstrated an opportunism to rival that of any robber baron. In splitting with Cooper, Henry was scuttling his third commercial partnership in as many years, and the prospects of his relationship with Malcomson lasting very much longer seemed slight in 1902, since the coal merchant was a character of the same water. Opportunistic, restless, and compulsive, Alex Y. Malcomson specialized in spreading himself thin.

But this very tendency to bite off more than he could chew proved the saving of the enterprise, for spread so thin and mortgaged so deep that he did not dare tell his own bankers he had taken on yet another venture, Alex Malcomson opened his motor-business account in another bank, and he put this account in the name of his chief clerk and cashier at his coalyard, James Couzens.

If one man were to be singled out for his contribution to the achievement of Henry Ford, it would have to be the coalyard clerk James Couzens. Pudgy, dyspeptic, and indefatigable, Couzens had all the ambition and self-importance of a municipal mayor or U.S. senator, both of which he later became. He was a humourless man. When James Couzens smiled his annual smile, it was said, the ice on the Great Lakes started to break.[9] Almost ten years younger than Henry Ford, he was one of the large number of English-speaking Detroiters who had been born across the river in Canada.* Couzens got his first job in Detroit checking freight-car cargoes, which included coal, and he had given Alex Malcomson such a hard time over his late shipments and payments that the coal merchant had hired him to do the same job for him.[11]

Henry Ford could not have had a harder taskmaster. Behind his wire-framed pince-nez, Couzens's sharp little eyes were focused directly on business, and he was, at the outset, less than enthralled by the motorcar venture in which

* In 1900 about 96,000 of Detroit's residents—a third of the total—were foreign born. One third of these were of German extraction, and a quarter were English-speaking Canadians. Other major groups of newcomers included some 14,000 Poles and 6,400 Irish.[10]

his employer's impetuousness had embroiled him. There was something rather raffish, not quite respectable, in the fly-by-night beginnings of the car business, companies opening and closing almost daily, hick mechanics walking off with their investors' money—and Henry Ford's own record in this respect was not encouraging.

Still, the basic mechanical prototype which Henry brought to Ford & Malcomson Ltd. was a good one. In terms of external appearance, it looked almost identical to the car he had been developing for Murphy at the Henry Ford Company. It was difficult, indeed, to distinguish Henry's car at a glance from the vehicle that now contained Leland's single-cylinder engine, the One Lung Cadillac.

But Henry Ford had been working on a new engine, and it proved to be a sturdy one. If James Couzens was to prove the partner that Henry needed for business discipline, then C. Harold Wills, the engineer who had worked with him on 999, was his mechanical catalyst. For more than a dozen years Ford and Wills were to provide the mechanical core for all the extraordinary developments that carried the name of Ford, and in 1902 they came up with a bright, new idea for their engine: as a result of their racing experience, the two men decided to try setting the two cylinders of their passenger car vertically instead of horizontally. This greatly reduced engine wear and vibration, thus increasing power, and it proved to be a milestone in automotive technology. Cylinders have been vertical, or just about vertical, ever since.

The new car was to be known as the Model A—a robust, practical, modern name signifying no nonsense, while also hinting at the possibility of progression through succeeding letters of the alphabet. Somewhere in the psyche of Henry Ford was a homing device that could latch unerringly upon the contemporary imagination, and his draughtsman Harold Wills displayed a similar intuition.

Soon after the second Ford victory at the Grosse Pointe track, it was decided that the Ford and Malcomson partnership, when properly capitalized, would be known as the

Ford Motor Company, and Wills turned his mind to a trademark. Wills had earned pocket money as a boy by printing up calling cards, for which he had used a home printing set with a graphic and flowing script. The "F" had a particular swash to it, bearing a strong resemblance to the signature of Henry himself, so when the question of a Ford logo arose, Wills rummaged in his attic for his old printing set. Thus was born the trademark whose appearance, in its oval blue lozenge, was to announce in every corner of the world that the twentieth century had arrived.

The Model A was not to be manufactured by the Ford Motor Company, for early automobile makers were essentially designers, assemblers, and marketers of cars. Having perfected their prototype, they would farm out the manufacture of its parts. To this day, 5,000 or 6,000 of the 13,000 or so parts that go into every modern car produced by Detroit's Big Three carmakers, Ford, Chrysler, and General Motors, are produced by independent outside parts manufacturers. Carburetors, dashboard instruments, hood ornaments, whole bodies on occasions—the companies which manufacture these parts may well be producing very similar components for rival manufacturers, and when Detroit is referred to as the Motor City, it is as much because of these several thousand parts suppliers and their agents as because of the better-known firms which buy from them.

In 1903 the Ford Motor Company subcontracted the wooden body shells and leather upholstery of the Model A out to the C. R. Wilson Carriage Company—a horse-drawn-carriage company nimble enough to move with the times. For the car's mechanical components, Ford turned to the machine shop run by a couple of red-haired and rumbustious brothers, John F. and Horace E. Dodge, two young mechanics who had built up a thriving business supplying mechanical components to order all over the Midwest. Dodge Brothers was one of the first Detroit machine shops to move on from making miscellaneous parts—for steam engines, bicycles, firearms, or whatever—and to concentrate on manufacturing parts for motorcars. The brothers had already produced transmissions for Ransom E. Olds, and when Henry Ford brought his Model A designs to them in the spring of 1903, they were considering another supply contract for the Oldsmobile.

It has sometimes been said that the Dodge brothers were so impressed by the design for the Model A that they decided to concentrate on that, dropping Oldsmobile, but Henry's engineering was not that much better than that of Ransom E. Olds. The attraction of the Ford car, thanks to Alex Malcomson's lack of cash, was that undertaking to produce it offered the Dodges a better business deal. Carmakers usually expected forty to sixty days' credit from their suppliers, but Malcomson's credit rating was so low that he had to offer the Dodge brothers payment for the first 100 chassis C.O.D., with payment due within fifteen days on every subsequent consignment. If Ford and Malcomson faltered on this stringent schedule, then all unsold machinery would become the property of the Dodge brothers.

The Model A would have to be assembled quickly and well—and it would have to sell fast—to meet these terms and still stand a chance of survival. Compared to his previous ventures, Henry Ford's partnership with Malcomson was a precarious, undercapitalized affair, and any hint of his previous behaviour—going off on other projects, or tinkering and refusing to "freeze" his design—would almost certainly result in yet another humiliating failure. In February 1903, Ford and Malcomson signed their contract with the Dodge brothers for the supply of 650 Model A engines, transmissions, and axles at $250 each—a commitment to pay $162,500 within a matter of months. Now all they had to do was raise the money.

The investors in Henry Ford's previous automobiles appear to have grouped themselves together with very little difficulty, as Detroit's old-boy network usually did, and the amounts they staked were only very small portions of their personal fortunes. But some of the men who assembled to back the Model A in the spring and summer of 1903 had far more difficulty finding funds—and it took Alex Malcomson more than six months to find them.

The first was the easiest. John S. Gray, a banker who wore a velvet collar on his coat, was Malcomson's uncle, and the coal merchant was already quite heavily in debt to him. So when the Dodge brothers' first deliveries brought $5,000 due in the middle of March 1903, with the prospect of another $5,000 being needed within a month, Gray had the choice of paying up or saying goodbye to a still larger sum. Gray found the $10,000 himself, with another $500—but his contribution carried a price.

Ford and Malcomson seem to have hoped, at the outset of their venture, to float their partnership fifty–fifty, without outside help; but costs rose higher than Ford had predicted, and Malcomson could produce less ready cash than he had promised. So John Gray became the first and principal member of a wider partnership, of which he insisted on being president. His $10,500 was held to represent 105 shares in the new company.

The Dodge brothers agreed to come in for 50 shares each, in lieu of $7,000 in materials, with a promise to pay $3,000 cash. A cousin of Malcomson's, Vernon C. Fry, decided to risk $5,000, as did Albert Strelow, a painting and woodworking contractor who had built Malcomson's coalyards. John W. Anderson and Horace H. Rackham, a pair of lawyers who derived much of their business from collecting Malcomson's debts and formalizing his expanding business empire, took on 50 shares each, and two of Malcomson's staff, James Couzens and a bookkeeper, Charles J. Woodall, scraped together their savings for 25 and 10 shares respectively. Couzens could not actually raise all the $2,500 which his shareholding represented, so he persuaded his sister, Rosetta, a schoolteacher, to hand over half of her $200 life savings to make up the balance.

The only investor in the Ford Motor Company whose personal fortunes were not already linked in some way to Alex Malcomson was Charles H. Bennett, a mechanically minded businessman who ran an airgun-making company.

Planning to buy an Oldsmobile, he had tested the Model A prototype and been impressed.

This ragbag of investors—most of whom were drawn into the venture because they had so much already staked on Malcomson that they could scarcely afford to see him fail—held their first stockholders' meeting on the night of Saturday, June 13, 1903, and voted John S. Gray their president. Henry Ford and Alex Malcomson were credited with $25,500 each for the machinery, patents, and designs which they jointly put into the company, and this entitled them to 255 shares each. If the two men were in agreement, they controlled the company with 51 percent of the 1,000 votes. On June 16, 1903, papers of incorporation were filed at the State Capitol in Lansing, and the Ford Motor Company was officially in business.

Less than four weeks later it was virtually bankrupt.

By June 1903, Henry Ford, Harold Wills, and their team of mechanics had already been operating for some time in a workshop to the east of Detroit in Mack Street, today known as Mack Avenue. The building belonged to the contractor-stockholder Albert Strelow, who converted it for a rent of $75 a month. The plan was that the engines, transmissions, and chassis from the Dodge brothers would be brought here—by horse and cart—to be married with the C. R. Wilson bodies (bodies $52, upholstered seats $16 each) and with wheels from the Prudden Company of Lansing ($26 per set). A good stock of parts had accumulated by the beginning of June, and a dozen workmen were hired at $1.50 a day to start assembling.

James Couzens had worked out the sums precisely. The basic machinery from the Dodge brothers would cost $250. Body, wheels, and other parts came to an additional $134. Labour costs totalled $20, and he set aside $150 for selling costs, to include advertising, salaries, and commissions. This added up to a total expenditure of $554, and the car would be offered for sale at $750, leaving a margin of $196 per unit.

Deduct $46 for contingencies, and that left a clear profit of $150 per car.[12]

Couzens's calculations also covered the first, but by no means the last, optional extra to be offered with the motorcar. For an additional $100, purchasers could order a tonneau, a purpose-built, upholstered seating compartment which could be attached behind the front bench seat, thus transforming a two-seater into transport for four. The profit to Ford on this attractive feature was an additional $50.

The figures made sense, the parts came in, and the workmen in the Mack Street shop started to assemble. But while money continued to flow out, none was coming back. While Henry Leland over at the Cadillac Company was producing vehicles against firm orders, Ford and Malcomson had committed themselves to production long before they had any definite customers lined up, and the stubs from James Couzens's accounts ledger show the effect this had on the cash flow.

The first cheque book of the Ford Motor Company shows an opening balance of $19,500 on June 27, 1903, but already Couzens had had to start issuing cheques:

| No. 1 June 26, 1903 | to pay the Dodge Brothers for parts delivered | $10,000.00 |
| No. 2 June 26, 1903 | to the Hartford Rubber Co. 64 tires @ $10 | $ 640.00 |
| No. 3 June 26, 1903 | to C. Harold Wills Sundry shop expenses | $ 22.02 |

The expenses continued: $1.15 to Western Union, $1.79 for blueprints, $31.40 for some new furniture for Couzens's office, and some really big payments as well, another $5,000 to the Dodge brothers. By cheque stub No. 61—July 10, 1903, to the Moreton Truck Company for cartage, $18.91— things were really serious. The balance had sunk to $223.65. Albert Strelow, the builder and landlord of the company's plant, paid in his $5,000 stake money next day, so the balance looked healthier, and there were other stockholders who had still to produce the cash they had pledged.

But would they pay up if the business cash flow remained oneway? It was not until July 15, 1903, that there was a first solid entry in the credit column:

| (Chicago Ill Trust & Sav) | Dr. E. Phenning | $850.00 |
|---|---|---|

James Couzens unfortunately misspelt the name of the historic first purchaser of a car from the Ford Motor Company. Dr. E. Pfennig, a Chicago dentist, bought himself a Model A—and he ordered a tonneau as well.* Dr. Pfennig's payment of the full cash price through the Illinois Trust and Savings Bank represented a turning point in the fortunes of the Ford Motor Company, and from $223.65 onwards, its cash flow went one way only.

In January 1904, Henry Ford bought his first dress suit. It cost him $65,[13] and he could well afford it, for Dr. Pfennig's purchase of a Model A the previous summer had proved to be the first in a very avalanche of sales. By the end of March 1904, the Ford Motor Company had sold 658 automobiles with a margin over expenses of $98,851[14]—a profit per car of $150, as James Couzens had calculated.

The shareholders who had been corralled with such difficulty the previous spring lost no time reaping the dividends of their happy investment. In November 1903, the directors voted $10,000, in January 1904 came a further $20,000, and in June of that year a final share-out brought the returns on the first twelve months of operation to the grand total of $98,000—which meant that the investors in the Ford Motor Company had effectively got their money back inside a year.

* For seventy-five years it was believed that Dr. Pfennig was a doctor, and his historic purchase was often cited as an example of how physicians were one of the first groups to make professional use of the horseless carriage. But in preparing for their seventy-fifth anniversary celebrations in 1978, Ford researchers located Dr. Pfennig's granddaughter, who informed them he had been a dentist.

Henry Ford's own share of the payout was the best part of $25,000, and he had not put up a penny.

In October 1903, Albert Strelow had added an extra storey to the Mack Street plant, but sales were growing so fast it was clear that new premises would be needed. In April 1904, a special meeting of stockholders approved the acquisition of a fresh factory site at the junction of Piquette and Beaubien Avenues, near Grand Boulevard on the northern edge of Detroit, and by the beginning of 1905 the company had settled in its spacious new headquarters.

"We are now turning out 25 machines a day on an average," James Couzens told the *Detroit Journal*, "and giving employment to 300 men."[15]

"Home of the Celebrated Ford Automobile," proclaimed a huge white-lettered sign that ran along the side of the new Piquette Avenue factory—which stands to this day in Detroit, near the junction of the Chrysler and the Edsel Ford freeways. The entire plant covered 1.4 acres. In addition to the main building, there were a separate power plant, paint shop, and testing laboratory. A large open yard served as a testing ground for the cars as they came out of assembly.

It was a flourishing, busy business, with twenty-five vehicles leaving each day, and the parts for twenty-five more arriving. James Couzens's office was on the ground floor, but since he believed in working his staff hard and hiring no more than were absolutely necessary, his empire was squeezed into a corner surrounded by the machine shop, electrical department, and despatch area. Even with sales flowing at over 600 cars a month, the administrative staff of the Ford Motor Company was barely enough to occupy three automobiles.[16]

Henry Ford himself thoroughly approved of this, for he had little time for paperwork. Searching vainly for a lost invoice one day, Frank L. Klingensmith, one of Couzens's clerks, eventually tracked Henry down to the assembly floor and asked him if he had seen it.

"It might be upstairs," replied Ford vaguely, and going up to Ford's office, Klingensmith discovered enough pending correspondence to fill two wastepaper baskets. There were important letters, bills, and even cheques for quite substantial sums, all set aside by Henry without even being opened.

"From now on," Couzens told Klingensmith, "it will be part of your job to open Mr. Ford's mail."[17] But Klingensmith found that getting Henry Ford to apply his attention to more than one short letter at a time was an uphill task, for Henry was much happier out in the design laboratories with Harold Wills and Spider Huff.

Ford, Wills, and Huff were forever making changes. The carburettors installed by the Dodge brothers in the original Model A proved unsatisfactory, and so did a replacement set of devices. They telegraphed George Holley, a young mechanic from Pennsylvania who had been dabbling with small cars and motorcycles fitted with his own simple air-and-gasoline mixer, and together Ford, Wills, and Holley worked out a sturdy, reliable, and cheap carburettor significantly ahead of any other on the market.

James Couzens made it his job to stop such modifications interrupting the flow of cars to cash-paying customers. When Henry had tried to hold back the very first consignment of Model As for improvement in the summer of 1903, Couzens had brushed his objections aside, had escorted the vehicles to the railhead, and had personally nailed shut the doors of the freight cars.

"Stop shipping," he said, "and we go bankrupt."[18]

Couzens was the sales manager of the new enterprise, and the work he did establishing a network of agents to sell Henry Ford's cars may well have been his single greatest contribution to the fortunes of the Ford Motor Company. In 1903 there was no such thing as a car dealer. Blacksmiths, bicycle dealers, farm-machine salesmen—all sold automobiles on the side, and often they doubled as driving schools, creating new customers in a nearby field liberally sprinkled with straw barriers.

It was Couzens's task to sort through the available hucksters to come up with an aggressive and enterprising salesforce whose credit was good enough to pay for vehicles as they received them, cash on the nail. By 1905 he had built up a cadre of 450 such agencies, from the Duerr-Ward Company in New York, right across the country to San Francisco, where William L. Hughson, a bicycle-parts salesman, purchased $5,000 worth of Model As in the summer of 1903 for West Coast distribution, and thus became the world's first Ford dealer.[19]

In 1904 Henry Ford had his photograph taken, his first official company portrait, and it is instructive to compare it with photographs taken two, three, or even ten years earlier. In one sense there is no change. Henry Ford looks no older. With his moustache shaved off, in fact, he looks rather younger and fresher. He obviously has a good many miles left in him.

But in another sense, Henry Ford looks completely different, and the difference lies in small things: in the eyes, in the crisp clothes, in the set of the jaw. It is a professional portrait, of course, cleverly lit, designed to make him look good. But there is something more, a sense of power and assurance that comes from Henry himself. Suddenly, and for the first time, Henry Ford looks as he was to look for the rest of his life, no longer Henry the shiftless, Henry the tinkerer, Henry the moonlighter, but Henry Ford the successful businessman, Henry Ford the carmaker, Henry Ford the captain of industry. In fact he finally looks like Henry Ford.

In 1904, for their second year of operations, the Ford Motor Company announced three completely new models —the Model B, the Model C, and the Model F—but, in what was to become the best Detroit tradition, two of these cars were not new at all. The models C and F were updated versions of the Model A, with slightly different engines and trimmings to justify increased prices of $800 and $1,000 respectively. The really new model was the Model B, a larger, more powerful car, claimed to be "the first four-cylinder car for general road use."[20] The Model B was considerably bigger and heavier than the Model A—and, at $2,000, considerably more expensive. With differentiated products at $800, $1,000, and $2,000, the Ford Motor Company was moving after less than a year into the modern pattern of marketing cars for every pocket.

The company was still some way, however, from producing a really budget-price car. Ford's cheapest offering was $150 more than the "Merry Oldsmobile," America's best-selling car popularized by a song of the period—and the figures for Ford's second year reflected this. Sales continued to expand, but not quite at their original phenomenal rate, and the Model B moved especially slowly. For the company's third sales season, starting in the spring of 1905, the Model B was dropped.

Yet this was not without heated debate between the directors of the Ford Motor Company. After two years of doing business together, differences were starting to develop between Ford and Malcomson, and new model policy became the battleground. With the move to the expanded premises at Piquette Avenue at the beginning of 1905, Ford and Wills had gone back to the drawing board to make a fresh beginning on a moderately priced automobile that would incorporate all they had learned from the inexpensive Model A, and from its derivatives, the C and F. (There was never a Model D or E, for reasons unspecified.)

But Malcomson wanted to move the product range upmarket, and he got Ford and Wills to design a grand-luxury touring car with a six-cylinder engine: the Model K. The coal merchant was convinced that the future of the automobile lay in this direction, and market trends apparently favoured his arguments. From 1903 to 1907, the proportion of cars costing more than $1,375 showed significant annual increases, for as the car habit caught on, it was the rich who came in faster—and expensive cars meant higher profits per unit.

If Henry Ford had truly been as opposed to the expensive Model K as he later claimed, then he would never have designed it in the first place. But he did genuinely differ with Malcomson on the commercial path that their company should pursue: in May 1905, he gave an interview prophesying "Ten Thousand Autos at $400 Apiece" to the *Detroit Journal*.[21] This difference of opinion was paralleled in at least one other automobile company at this time.

Fred L. Smith, who owed his position in the Olds Motor Works to his father's mining and lumber fortune, wanted, like Malcomson, to move the Olds company away from cheap cars—and, perhaps also like Malcomson, he was attracted by the prestige of dealing in the aristocratic end of the market. Finding Ransom E. Olds opposed to him, Smith pushed the inventor out of the company—together, later, with the company's enterprising sales manager, Roy D. Chapin, who promptly set up on his own in the Hudson Motor Company, aiming at the cheap-to-moderate sectors of the market. The Hudson Motor Company flourished. The Oldsmobile company, as run by Fred Smith, did not.

Business partners all over America were having similar disagreements at this time. Throughout the nineteenth century, the great challenge to entrepreneurs had been technical questions of how to produce, and the principal challenges had been matters of manufacturing practice. But by the early years of the twentieth century, many of these practical problems had been solved, and the new challenge was how and where to sell all the things that were now being produced in such volume. Marketing—the ability to identify the right group of customers and sell to them—was the new key to business success.

The traditional high-profit consumer market was the rich and the affluent middle classes. But Henry Ford was one of those who was sensing that a much larger, and potentially richer, market lay elsewhere. Forty-two years old, suddenly wealthy after years of failure, he could easily have pursued the path favoured by Smith and Malcomson, both younger men. That was the safe and obvious way. But, as at every other juncture in his life, Henry Ford opted for the radical solution, the unconventional. It was partly his instinct—his own original "genius," which, he believed, had lived before him and was learning so much for yet another existence. It was partly, to be sure, plain prejudice, the country-boy suspicion of the upper crust—and it was also, given the context in which Henry now found himself, facing down the last partner with whom he had to share, a matter of sheer ambition. Confronted by one final obstacle to securing control over his own destiny, Henry Ford had the appetite to fight over just about anything.

Alex Malcomson also seems to have been ready for a showdown. Contemplating the dramatic expansion of the car company, he had come to regret his decision to leave his own interests in Couzens's hands, and he tried to regain his foothold. He proposed that his former clerk should return to the coal business where he had started, while Malcomson moved in to play a more active role in the car company.

Couzens, not unnaturally, refused, and Henry Ford backed him up. "I told Malcomson that I did not want him but that I wanted his man Couzens," he said later.[22]

It was an unlikely friendship that James Couzens and Henry Ford had struck up together. Ford could never work closely with other strong men. He had to beat them into submission, or else wriggle away in the strange fashion in which he had evaded his earlier business partnerships. But with Couzens, from the start, he had established a relationship that extended beyond mutual self-interest, and which seems somehow to have thrived for a season upon the odd moods and fits to which both men were subject.

"What do you think we ought to ask from those fellows?" Ford had demanded of Couzens as they had gone home together, discussing their salaries after the very first meeting of stockholders on June 13, 1903; and as the history of the Ford Motor Company developed, it became very much the story of Ford and Couzens, the most active constituents, on one side, and "those fellows"—including Malcomson—on the other.

When the showdown came, however, it was not a question of Ford and Couzens versus the rest. Malcomson was supported by his cousin Vernon Fry and by Charles H. Bennett.

But his uncle, John Gray, backed the two men whose day-to-day energies had generated a 100 percent return on his investment in less than a year, and so did all the other stockholders—including even the brothers John and Horace Dodge, who stood to suffer, in the short term, from the manoeuvre that Ford and Couzens had devised to rid themselves of Malcomson.

Setting aside the issue of personalities, and even the large-versus small-car debate, the time had come for the Ford Motor Company to do some hard thinking. After two years' successful trading, turning out a respectable twenty-five vehicles a day from the spacious new Piquette Avenue premises, the company still had not developed beyond being an assembly plant. Ford engines, chassis, brakes, gears, and axles—the bulk of the car was all put together by the Dodge brothers at their own works, before being shipped over to Piquette Avenue. This meant that the Dodge brothers were profiting twice, through their supply contract with Ford, as well as through their investment. There had already been some arguments over the quality of the Dodges' workmanship and finish, but more important to Ford and Couzens, intent on increasing production speed and quantity, the two-stage process was costing valuable time and money.

As Ford and Harold Wills had worked on their new cheap car, the intended successor to the bottom-of-the-range models A, C, and F, they had wrestled with the problem of price and had come to see that the secret of getting this down lay in improving production techniques: increasing volume and flow, and thus saving on man-hours. But they could only do this effectively if they themselves controlled the entire production process, which meant taking the engine and chassis assembly away from the Dodge brothers and setting up a manufacturing facility of their own. This dovetailed with Ford and Couzens's desire to shift the company in the direction of high-volume, low-price production—and it also provided a satisfyingly neat device for edging out Malcomson.

On November 22, 1905, the Ford Manufacturing

Company was incorporated with a capital of $100,000 and the stated object of producing engines, running gears, and other types of automobile parts and appliances—the very manufacturing which the Dodge brothers had hitherto executed for the Ford Motor Company. Ford Motor and Ford Manufacturing now stood side by side, but with a significantly different pattern of shareholding. Alex Malcomson had no interest whatever in the new manufacturing company, and John Gray explained to Vernon Fry how this bicorporate juggling was essentially a device to squeeze out the coal merchant.

"I have Mr. Ford's promise," said Gray, "that when they get things straightened out with Mr. Malcomson, the Ford Manufacturing Company is to be taken into the Ford Motor Company, just as if it had never existed."[23]

The threat to Malcomson was obvious. Not only was he being excluded from a new development that was as large as the original enterprise, if not larger, it would also be possible for the manufacturing company to set the prices it charged Ford Motor. So if Henry, James Couzens, and the majority of shareholders who supported them really wanted to, they could drain all the profits out of the original company simply by raising the price that Ford Motor had to pay Ford Manufacturing for its parts.

Malcomson prepared to do battle, and his case was a strong one, since the new manufacturing company was, in essence, a conspiracy by one group of shareholders at the expense of another. But moving, as usual, with too much speed and insufficient thought, the coal merchant announced the creation of an automobile enterprise of his own, the Aerocar Company, and he plunged straight into the building of a three-storey factory intended to turn out 500 touring cars a year.

It was a fatal mistake, for now it was not Malcomson but his rival stockholders who had legitimate cause for complaint. It would scarcely be proper for Malcomson to go on receiving Ford dividends which he could use to build up a rival concern, and on December 6, 1905, a resolution moved by the lawyer Horace Rackham and seconded by Henry Ford called for Malcomson's resignation.

At first the coal merchant refused. He blustered and talked of a lawsuit. But after several months' reflection, Malcomson sued for terms, entering into negotiations for the sale of his stock in May 1906. Shortly afterwards, the three stockholders who had taken his side, Charles Bennett, Vernon Fry, and Charles Woodall, also sold out their shares. Albert Strelow, the building contractor, had originally backed Couzens and Henry, but in a cavalier fit which must go down as one of the greatest miscalculations of business history, he now decided that his money would be better off in a Canadian gold-rush project, so he sold out as well.

The Ford Motor Company's Articles of Association laid down that all such sales had to be to existing shareholders, and so, in the wake of Malcomson's departure, the company's stockholding now took on a simplified pattern. The lawyers, Anderson and Rackham, continued to hold 50 shares each, as did the Dodge brothers, John and Horace. The banker John Gray's holding remained at 105, this being passed on to his family after his death in July 1906, while James Couzens had profited from the reshuffling to build up his holding to 110––or rather, to 109, with one more share representing the original stake of his sister Rosetta.

But all these holdings only totalled 415, and the remaining 585 shares in the Ford Motor Company, which rapidly reabsorbed the Ford Manufacturing Company as Henry had promised, were now held by Henry Ford himself. He had a private arrangement with Harold Wills to pay a small proportion of his dividends to him, and it would suit Henry in the immediate future to stay on good terms with James Couzens. But in the final analysis, Henry Ford had no need of either of these men, and henceforward, his control over the Ford Motor Company would be absolute.

In the spring of 1906, Henry and Clara Ford played host to an English couple, Mr. and Mrs. Percival Perry. Perry was a car enthusiast who had helped sell the first automobiles to be used as taxis in the streets of London: three imported Model B Fords, which the authorities had insisted should be painted white as a warning to pedestrians. In Detroit, the Ford Motor Company had been internationally minded from the start, selling its sixth Model A to Canada in August 1903, and Percival Perry came to Michigan in 1906 in hopes of securing the exclusive rights to market Ford cars in Great Britain.

He arrived in the middle of the turmoil attending Henry Ford's split with Malcomson, and the journal of his trip provides a vivid glimpse of the Ford Motor Company in its earliest years.[24] Since business was the object of his visit, he started off with John Gray, the president of the company —"a dear old man," thought Perry.

"Well," said Gray, when the Englishman had explained his mission, "I guess you'll have to see Henry," and he put Perry on a streetcar to the Piquette Avenue plant. There the Englishman met Harold Wills, dressed in greasy overalls, as well as Henry Ford, who genially invited Perry and his wife to come and stay in his own home while they were in Detroit.

The Fords still occupied modest quarters. They had plans to build in one of the prestigious new developments out along Woodward Avenue, but for the time being, they were in a rented home on Harper Avenue, not far from the Piquette plant, and the accommodation was cramped when there were guests in the house. Perry had to race the twelve-year-old Edsel to the bathroom every morning.

It was a teetotal household. "Won't you have some fruit-juice?" Henry Ford would ask. The beverage was a fortified tonic called "Malto Grape," which he ordered in bulk from a company in Paw Paw, Michigan.[25]

Percival Perry took to Henry Ford. The carmaker had an unmistakable streak of genius, he decided—though he could also sense the complications which were later to cause him to revise his initially favourable estimate. Perry thought he could trust Henry, that he was "a man to whom you would give your last penny." He describes Ford as having an

113

impish sense of fun—"a proper Puck"[26]—and other eyewitnesses in these years paint a picture of Henry laughing and joking at work with Wills and Huff, handing out trick cigars, wiring up doorknobs, and stripping off to engage in impromptu boxing matches in the middle of research debates over some knotty problem.[27]

Springtime does not come to most men in their mid-forties, but in Henry's case it had. He was still living in rented lodgings, but he knew it was not for long. He was still locked in battle with Malcomson, but he could see the way clear beyond that. He was just entering that phase in his life when everything went right for him, when he was to strike every ball sweet and true, and when he was to have that exhilarating feeling of watching it soar out of sight. In the summer of 1907 he took Edsel and Clara to Atlantic City for a holiday, and there, at the age of forty-three, in the middle of the beach, Henry Ford took a run in the sand and turned a cartwheel, right in front of everyone.

We know about the cartwheel because Henry turned it in front of his camera.

"That guy has a bird in his head," said one ex-Ford worker, explaining why he still liked Henry, even though the worker reckoned himself to have been wrongfully dismissed.[28]

The bird in Henry's brain in 1907 was the cheap car, the car that everyone could afford, and the notion had been flittering around his head for some time. "The way to make automobiles," he had told the lawyer Anderson in 1903, "is to make one automobile like another automobile, to make them all alike . . . just as one pin is like another pin when it comes from a pin factory"—and now Henry Ford had the wherewithal to make that vision come true.

On the July day in 1906 that Henry had bought out Malcomson's stock, he asked one of his mechanics, Fred Rockelman, to drive him home, as he quite often did. As they motored along towards Harper Avenue in the sticky Detroit gloaming, the new majority stakeholder in the Ford Motor Company grew positively expansive.

"Fred," he declared, "this is a great day. We're going to expand this company, and you will see that it will grow by leaps and bounds. The proper system, as I have it in mind, is to get the car to the multitude."[29]

**Part Two** Glory Days

# 6

## MODEL T

*I will build a motor car for the great multitude. It will be large enough for the family, but small enough for the individual to run and care for. It will be constructed of the best materials, by the best men to be hired, after the simplest designs that modern engineering can devise. But it will be so low in price that no man making a good salary will be unable to own one—and enjoy with his family the blessing of hours of pleasure in God's great open spaces.*

HENRY FORD, 1907[1]

Henry Ford's car for the people, the car that was to make him famous, and which was to transform the face of America, was an unusual notion in 1907. It sprang from Henry's populist instincts, his chip on the shoulder which resented the rich and fat's monopoly on the good life, and from his generous, almost didactic impulse to share the joy of machines with the world.

Yet the idea was not unique to Henry Ford. Other carmakers had tried to manufacture an inexpensive, mass-produced car. Henry's ambition was distinguished by generating the technology, the solid engineering innovations, to make it happen.

In 1905 Henry was at a race meeting, watching Malcomson's beloved Model K, the company's top-of-the-range six-cylinder heavyweight, when there was a smashup involving a French racer. Henry had been noticing for some time how certain components of European cars seemed to be much lighter and stronger than their American equivalents, and now, examining the wreckage of the French car, he picked up a little valve strip stem which was exceptionally light and tough.

"That is the kind of material we ought to have in our cars," he said, and he initiated an inquiry into precisely what sort of steel the valve strip stem was made of.[2] It turned out to be an alloy of vanadium, which no American foundry then knew how to incorporate into steel. Making vanadium alloy required a furnace heat of 3,000 degrees Fahrenheit, and ordinary furnaces could not get above 2,700.

Henry found a small steel company in Canton, Ohio, to experiment with the process:

I offered to guarantee them against loss if they would run a heat for us. They agreed. The first heat was a failure. Very little vanadium remained in the steel. I had them try again, and the second time the steel came through. Until then we had been forced to be satisfied with steel running between 60,000 and 70,000 pounds tensile strength. With vanadium, the strength went up to 170,000 pounds.[3]

In March 1907, Ford took delivery of what the company claimed to be the first shipment of vanadium steel made in America. Produced in Canton exclusively for Ford cars, it had ten times the tensile strength of metal that the Carnegie Steel Company was currently turning out for armour-plate experiments.

"Vanadium steel resists shock," reported the *Detroit Journal*, "—either one blow or a series of lighter ones, or minute vibrations . . . to a greater extent than any other metal."[4]

The first Ford to benefit from the use of vanadium steel was the Model N, a robust open car developed from the models A, C, and F, and unveiled in January 1906. On New Year's Day, James Couzens announced that the new car would cost only $450, and that the Ford Motor Company would be producing 10,000 Model Ns every year:

We are making 40,000 cylinders, 10,000 engines, 40,000 wheels, 20,000 axles, 10,000 bodies, 10,000 of every part that goes into the car—think of it! Such quantities were never heard of before. . . .[5]

In January 1906, the Ford Motor Company was still entangled with Alex Malcomson. The coal merchant was fighting to hang on to the company he had started, and he did not, in fact, relinquish his shares until May of that year.

But Henry Ford and James Couzens already felt confident of their eventual victory, and the proclamation of the Model N was their defiant assertion of the new direction they were now going to take.

Mass production was a long-established tradition in American industry: Singer sewing machines, McCormick reapers, the small-arms manufacturing of Samuel Colt. Now Ford and Couzens were proposing to apply mass production to the car industry for the first time in a thoroughgoing way. Ransom E. Olds had managed to turn out 5,000 of his "Merry Oldsmobiles" in 1903 before his backers took his company upmarket. In 1906, Ford and Couzens were aiming at double that.

They soon discovered that mass production was easier said than done. In the absence of the moving assembly line which was, eventually, to prove the secret to the smooth production of cars in bulk, they had to go for sheer weight of numbers: more workstations, more men, more machines. They had more than doubled their own capacity, thanks to the workshops of the Ford Manufacturing Company, but when Model N production started in the spring of 1906, it was still a two-legged operation, as it had been from the start with the Dodge brothers. The engines and chassis were produced in the manufacturing workshops, then moved over to be assembled at the Piquette Avenue plant.

It was autumn before all the logistics of men and machinery had been worked out properly, and Ford and Couzens found it was impossible to hold to the price of $450 which had been their objective. They tried to stick below $500, and then $550, but in the end the Model N came out at $600.

Still, even at this price, the first of Henry Ford's cars for the people represented better value than anything else on the market. The Model N had a compact and rugged four-cylinder engine, the first time an inexpensive car had ever had such a strong power unit. Its ignition, developed by Spider Huff along with Ford and Wills, still was not perfect, but it was the basis of an electrical system superior to

121

any of the competition. Above all, the Model N was a comparatively light car, and it got lighter over the months as Henry Ford and Harold Wills worked vanadium steel into its components.

It seemed obvious that Ford should set up its own metallurgical laboratory to further its expertise with vanadium and other alloys, and Harold Wills, who had taken a special interest in the vanadium breakthrough, proposed that this be headed by a qualified scientist. Henry Ford disagreed. "Make an expert of Wandersee!" he said, John Wandersee being a mechanic who had started his career with Ford sweeping the factory floor.

Throughout his career, the Dearborn boy who had left the one-room schoolhouse before he was fifteen was touchy on the subject of higher education. It was much overrated, in his opinion—job seekers who touted their university qualifications to Henry Ford invariably received short shrift —and John Wandersee proved the point. Cars for the people, by the people. The former factory-floor sweeper went away for three months' training, and on his return, he set up and ran a set of metallurgical laboratories for Ford which remained, for many years, the foremost in America.

After its initial production delays, the Model N eventually vindicated all that had been hoped for by Ford and Couzens —as well as proving the wisdom of their split with Malcomson. In the twelve months up to September 1906, when the company had been offering quite a range of models, they had sold only 1,599 cars—96 less than they had sold in the previous year. But dropping almost everything to concentrate on the mass-produced Model N, they achieved spectacular results. By September 30, 1907, they had sold a total of 8,243 cars, almost five times more than in their best year ever. This brought them a gross return of $4,701,298, and for the first time, an annual profit of over $1 million.[6] Henry redesigned the Model N to produce an upmarket version, the Model R; and further tinkerings were incorporated into a vehicle with a single-seat tonneau to the rear: the Model

S. By the sales season of 1908, the Ford Motor Company had just seven letters to go before they would reach the end of the alphabet.

Soon after the 1905 move to Piquette Avenue, Henry Ford had offered a job to an ambitious young woodworker of Danish birth, Charles E. Sorensen. Ford had got to know Sorensen in 1902 while he was working on his racer 999, for the young Dane, muscular and athletic, was a bicycling friend of Tom Cooper, and Cooper had brought Sorensen in on the project to make models—or "patterns"—of various components out of wood.

Henry Ford liked this. Never very happy with blueprints, he found it so much easier to work three-dimensionally, and he hired Sorensen—at $3 a day—to bring his pattern-making skills to the Ford Motor Company. As Henry worked on refinements to the Model N, he came to rely quite heavily on Sorensen's ability to convert his ideas and rough sketches into solid form, and early one morning in the winter of 1906–07, he turned up as usual in the pattern-making department.

"Come with me, Charlie," he said, "I want to show you something."[7]

Ford led Sorensen to the top floor of the building, one end of which had not been occupied by assembly work.

"I'd like to have a room finished off right here in this space," he said. "Put up a wall with a door in big enough to run a car in and out. Get a good lock for the door. . . . We're going to start a completely new job."[8]

Charles E. Sorensen always dated the inspiration for the Model T Ford from Henry's experiments with vanadium and heat-treated steels. These had demonstrated how it was possible to build a car that was stronger, lighter, and faster than any that had been built before, and while these new steel alloys were first tried out in parts of the Model N, they were now to be deployed much more ambitiously in the "completely new job" that was taking shape behind the locked door at the top northern end of Piquette Avenue.

Joseph Galamb, a gifted young Hungarian engineer who had worked in German automobile plants before coming to Detroit, was in charge of the think tank.

"Mr. Ford first sketched out on the blackboard his idea of the design he wanted," remembered Galamb later. "He would come in at seven or eight o'clock at night to see how they were getting along."[9]

By the end of the year the team was working till ten or eleven every night.

"Mr. Ford followed out the design very closely," said Galamb, "and was there practically all the time. There was a rocking chair in the room in which he used to sit for hours and hours at a time, discussing and following out the development of the design."[10]

The rocking chair had belonged to Henry's mother.

The Model N's four-cylinder engine had been an innovation in the low-priced field, but the engine itself had not been that simple. Each enclosed cylinder had been cast separately, then bolted together.[11] Henry Ford's idea for the Model T was that the core of the power unit should be one single casting that contained all four cylinders. After Sorensen had struggled for some time with the practical difficulties of this, Henry came up with a further suggestion: why not slice the block off across the top?[12]

Thus was born the basic configuration of the modern internal-combustion engine: the single cylinder block with a separate, bolt-down cylinder head on top. Open at top and bottom, the block could be machined and manufactured to close tolerances, and it made for an arrangement that was easy to service.

Henry wanted something strong and flexible in the way of gears. The teeth on the soft steel transmission cogs used in many cars of the day were easily stripped, so Joseph Galamb refined quite an old, preautomotive gearing system which involved continuously circulating fabric bands—the system which Ford had already been using on its previous models. Henry never believed in novelty for its own sake. The moving-band system was less obviously strong than an all-steel transmission, but it was much lighter, and since it did not rely on resistance, it was also immensely more durable. Sorensen made wooden models of the gearing wheels involved, and he showed them to Henry Ford.

"First designs were way oversize on what Mr. Ford thought they should be," remembered Sorensen. "It was astonishing to see how closely he sensed the sizes required for the different gears."[13]

From these experiments came the Model T's memorable "planetary" transmission, a primitive sort of automatic gear, worked by three footpedals: a brake, a pedal for forward, and a pedal for reverse. Orchestrating them was an acquired art, rather like playing the organ. The whole body was engaged. But once mastered, all sorts of tricks became available—notably the capacity to shoot straight from forward into reverse, thus making it possible to "rock" the car out of a pothole.

Spider Huff worked, as usual, on the electrics, coming up with a heavy flywheel studded with sixteen copper coils and magnets—a magneto—which would, for the first time in a low-priced car, produce sparks for the cylinders. Until this date, dry batteries had usually supplied the sparks for auto engines,[14] and Huff's magneto meant that the Model T, when well tuned, could actually start and operate without a battery of any sort. When tested on the road, however, Huff's ingenious device kept failing—until Henry Ford came into the workroom one day with several large maple syrup boiling kettles that he had brought in from Dearborn.

"Charlie," he said, "the trouble with that plate [the magneto] is that we have not insulated it properly."[15]

Sorensen and Ford worked on the syrup kettles to turn them into pressure cookers, put the magnetos inside, and then pressure-packed the kettles with heavy impregnating varnish of the type used at this time for electrical insulation. They then removed the varnished-soaked magneto, placed it in a paint-baking oven, waited six hours, and observed the result. The varnish had totally hardened in and around the magneto coils, rather like a modern plastic coating, and there were no insulation problems with the device again.

"Mr. Ford and I worked about forty-two hours without letup," remembered Charles E. Sorensen, "from the time we started until the job was complete."[16]

For more than a year Henry Ford laboured, night and day, with his helpers in the room at the top of the Piquette Avenue plant. As Galamb and Sorensen both remembered it, he was involved in everything: the electrics, the transmission, the four-cylinder block, and the extensive use of vanadium steel. When the team looked at the crankshaft made of the new alloy, they could not believe it would work. It seemed so frail and small compared to any other crankshaft they had seen. But when they gave it a shock test, it easily withstood double the load that it would get in the actual operation of the engine.[17]

Now approaching his mid-forties—he celebrated his forty-fifth birthday three months before the Model T was unveiled—Henry Ford was at the height of his powers. He had consolidated control of his company, and he had also consolidated control of himself. He was tinkering, playing, and testing as he had a dozen years earlier in his spare room at the Edison plant, but now he had the money to try just about anything—special forgings, wooden models, impact tests. He had built up a team which, though largely self-taught like himself, ranked among the finest automotive engineers in Detroit—and Henry himself was seeing so sharp and so true. He threw himself into every detail, insisting on getting small things absolutely right, going for innovation when it tested properly, but sticking to the tried-and-true when it did not. He never lost sight of the ultimate, overall objective. He had a vision of what his new car should look like. From all the improvisation, hard thought, and hard work came a machine that was at once the simplest and the most sophisticated automobile built to date anywhere in the world. When advance circulars for the Model T were sent out to Ford dealers in the spring of 1908, the reception of the claims made on behalf of the car verged on incredulity.

"We must say it is almost too good to be true," wrote a Detroit dealer to the company, while an Illinois agent seems to have treated the thing as a huge joke. "We have carefully hidden the sheets away and locked the drawer, throwing the key down the cold-air shaft."[18] The dealer's anxiety appears to have been that if the Model T was really as good as Henry Ford said it was, and if his customers found out, then he would not be able to off-load his existing stocks of the Model N.

When the car finally went on the market at the beginning of October 1908, the wildest predictions were fulfilled. The first public advertisements for the Model T appeared on a Friday, and "Saturday's mail," reported the *Ford Times*, "brought nearly one thousand enquiries. Monday's response swamped our mail clerks, and by Tuesday night, the office was well nigh inundated."[19]

Orders flooded in, with hard cash, and by the end of the winter Ford had to announce that the company could not take any more. They had sufficient advance orders to consume the entire factory output until the following August— and by the end of September 1909, more than 10,000 cars had been sold, bringing in over $9 million, a 60 percent increase on the turnover of the previous year.[20]

The immediate appeal of the Model T was based, as Henry Ford had intended, on its sturdiness, power, and value for money. It was not really that inexpensive as yet —reductions in price were to come in later years, with increases in production. In 1908 the car cost $825, which was quite a substantial price when compared to the average teacher's annual salary of $850. When adjusted to modern values, the sticker on a Model T Ford would work out today at around $9,400. (Ford's closest modern equivalent in terms of size and capacity, the Ford Tempo, retails at just under $7,000.)[21]

There were cheaper cars on the market in 1908, but not one could offer such a combination of innovation and reliability, making the Model T genuinely state-of-the-art. The formidable four-cylinder power unit, the semiautomatic planetary transmission, the magneto which did away with the need for heavy, dry-storage batteries—all these were new, as was the fact that the transmission, axles, and general workings of the car were completely enclosed and protected against rain, dust, and knocks by lightweight steel casings.

These pressed-steel stampings were engineering breakthroughs in themselves. They came from a Buffalo machine shop, the John R. Keim Mills, which had illustrated the creative possibilities of the relationship between car manufacturer and supplier. Keim's engineers had wondered whether they could apply their steel-stamping techniques to automotive parts, had approached Ford with the idea, and had then worked with Harold Wills and Charles Sorensen to perfect the stampings for the Model T. At this stage in his career, Henry Ford was not too proud to accept ideas from elsewhere. ·

There was scarcely a component of the Model T which did not contain some fresh development to excite automotive enthusiasts, but the guiding theme of all of them was simplicity—and this was Henry Ford's supreme contribution to his supreme creation.

Ford's gift was to cut through to the essence of things, to disentangle complexities, to plough through detail to arrive at the unvarnished idea at the back of his head. Ordinary motorists did not need to know about the tensile strength of vanadium steel, nor the mysteries of the planetary transmission. They just knew that their Ford stood up to bumps, and that it did not strip its gears.

"No car under $2000 offers more," proclaimed the Model T's advertising, and for once, in the long and dishonourable history of automobile advertising, the claim was absolutely correct. Hard thinking, imaginative innovation, and thorough testing had produced a vehicle that was to prove more than just a means of transportation: it was to provide America, and the world, with a whole new way of life.

One of the attributes of the Model T was its ability to inspire affection in its drivers. People gave it a name, usually female—though not invariably so. When E. B. White was a young writer just out of Cornell in the early 1920s, he decided to drive across America in search of work and raw material, and for the expedition he purchased a Model T, which he christened Hotspur.[22]

Starting the Model T's engine, White later remembered, was a ritual all its own. You had to be careful not to put your thumb around the starting handle. If you did, you risked breaking an arm or wrist:

The trick was to leave the ignition switch off, proceed to the animal's head, pull the choke (which was a little wire protruding through the radiator) and give the crank two or three nonchalant upward lifts. Then, whistling as though thinking about something else, you would saunter back to the driver's cabin, turn the ignition on, return to the crank, and this time, catching it on the down stroke, give it a quick spin with plenty of That. If this procedure was followed, the engine almost always responded—first with a few scattered explosions, then with a tumultuous gunfire, which you checked by racing around to the driver's seat and retarding the throttle. Often, if the emergency brake hadn't been pulled all the way back, the car advanced on you the instant the first explosion occurred, and you would hold it back by leaning your weight against it. I can still feel my old Ford nuzzling me at the curb, as though looking for an apple in my pocket.[23]

The nuzzling came from the planetary transmission, which gave the Model T a constant, trembling impulse to move forward, even when the car was in neutral. This may have been why people felt that their Model T had a personality which they wished to enhance. White remembered how, the moment he acquired Hotspur, he drove straight to the blacksmith to have his army trunk fixed to the running board with two iron brackets. Supplying accessories for the car became an industry in its own right: a Ruby Safety Reflector for a glowing red rear, radiator "Motor Wings" for a Pegasus touch in the front, a set of anti-rattlers (98 cents), and a rearview mirror. The list was endless. At the height of the Model T's popularity in the early 1920s, the Sears, Roebuck catalogue featured no less than 5,000 different items that could be bolted, screwed, or strapped to the vehicle.

It was partly that the car emerged almost naked from the showroom: the original models came without speedometer, windshield wipers, or even doors, and the gas gauge was a long thin stick that you had to find for yourself and insert in the tank. But perhaps it was also because, when confronted with the first truly standardized machine for individual conveyance, human nature felt an irresistible need to personalize it.

The Model T turned out to be exactly what was needed by a restless population trying to fill up a continent. Farmers took to it in large numbers. The car had quite extraordinary suspension, two huge, crude, transverse springs, one in the front, one in the back. These springs were little more sophisticated, from the engineering point of view, than the suspension on the average hay wagon, but this suited them ideally to the rutted mud and gravel roads of the time. When E. B. White travelled across the continent as late as 1922, he encountered not a single inch of made-up roadway all the way from Minnesota to Spokane, Washington, a distance of more than 1,000 miles; and when Edsel Ford travelled from Detroit to San Francisco in 1915 on a similar expedition, he encountered conditions that were still worse: potholes, fissures, clouds of dust, and ceaseless bumping.[24]

These were the conditions for which the Model T was designed, and which it so triumphantly overcame with its transverse springs and wobbly, almost double-jointed wheels. Many carmakers of the time aimed at rigidity, but the Model T was so flexible that if you drove it diagonally across railroad tracks, you could actually feel it bend. It was the car of rural America, the twentieth-century equivalent of the covered wagon—and until the 1920s America was still very much a rural society. Almost as soon as the Ford Motor Company started making money, Henry Ford had started trying to develop a tractor, transferring the mechanics of the Model A and its successors to primitive machines which he tried out on land he bought at Dearborn. As his motorcar components succeeded or failed in these tough, demanding testbeds, so the Model T took shape. A machine that could not work on the land was not a real machine, to Henry Ford's mind—hence the resilient steel, the one-piece cylinder block which could not shake to pieces, and those springs.

Henry Ford took great delight in demonstrating how his beloved Model T was the farmer's friend. He would cock it up on one side and remove a wheel in order to run a power belt from the exposed hub to a circular saw or corn husker, as if the car was old 345 reincarnated. But the American farmer had no need of such a lesson. He knew that he had found a friend the day that his Model T got him into town in half an hour—and the same went for the farmer's wife.

"You know, Henry," wrote a farmer's wife to him from Rome, Georgia, in 1918, "your car lifted us out of the mud. It brought joy into our lives. We loved every rattle in its bones. . . ."[25]

A woman need no longer be imprisoned in the farmhouse, or in any other house. The Model T could take her to the shops, to a job, to study. Gertrude Stein loved her Model T, demonstrating her liberation by driving it through the snow and the mud of Flanders, where she served as a volunteer nurse during the First World War, and she delighted in mechanical discussions. According to Ernest Hemingway, Stein's famous phrase about a lost generation, *une génération perdue*, originally came from a French garage owner's diatribe against a young mechanic who had failed to look after Miss Stein's Ford properly.[26]

By the end of the First World War, Ford had achieved such dominance of the automobile market in North America —and virtually everywhere else in the world—that almost half the cars on earth were Model Ts. More than 15 million of them were produced before Henry finally shut down the line in 1927. They swarmed everywhere, transforming the way people lived and thought and had fun—family outings, picnics, lovers' trysts. The freedom which the car offered loosened existing ties and created new ones. Together with radio, it was the people's car which transformed America from a continent of separate settlements into one vast neighbourhood.

Lean, rangy, and occasionally fairly cussed, the Model T was rather like Henry Ford himself, and through knowing the car, people felt that they had got to know its maker. It endeared itself to all manner of folks. When Prohibition came, the first bootleggers found it the fastest and most efficient conveyance for transporting their contraband. With room for ninety gallon-size jars of alcohol, it could carry a cargo worth $3,600. The Model T converted a plaything of the European rich into the birthright of the American masses, and it started off that strangest of love affairs, the enduring emotional relationship between the American and his car.

Sinclair Lewis, the novelist, was a Model T owner, and though his writing won him the Nobel Prize, that award did not give him half the pleasure, according to his wife, as that moment on a California evening when "he stopped the Ford neatly in front of the stone carriage step and called out to Father and Mother and me as we sat on the porch after supper, 'How about a little ride?'"

The Lewises owned and loved their car for many years, cherishing it as if it were a child, until 1916, when they sold it to a couple of female university students who came to drive it away one evening. Grace Hegger Lewis stood with her husband watching the shiny fenders and the single glowing red kerosene taillight of their car bounce off into the distance, and when their first Model T had finally vanished out of sight, she sat down on the front porch and unashamedly cried.[27]

On September 15, 1909, as the Model T was just approaching its first birthday, breaking ever more sales records and setting the Ford Motor Company on its way to becoming the largest car manufacturer in the world, a judgement in the Circuit Court of the Southern District of New York appeared to call everything into question. The Association of Licensed Automobile Manufacturers, twenty-six of America's most prominent carmakers, had brought suit against Ford claiming patent infringement, and Judge Charles Merrill Hough upheld their claim. The Ford Motor Company would have to pay millions of dollars in back royalties to the ALAM. Far worse, it would have to admit defeat in a fierce and bitter battle which it had been waging from the very moment of its creation.

The case stemmed from the patent of George Baldwin Selden, a lawyer-inventor from Rochester, New York, whose most original creation had been a machine for making barrel hoops until, late in the 1870s, he latched onto the work being done in Europe on the internal-combustion engine. As a lawyer, Selden specialized in patents, and he set his mind to working out the precise legal definition and wording of a patent that would give him the sole right to license and charge royalties on future automobile development in America.

In 1899 Selden had gone into partnership with a group of Wall Street investors who saw the chance to cut themselves in on the profits of the growing American car industry, and when this syndicate tried to enforce Selden's patent against the five largest U.S. carmakers of the day, they met with surprising success. Rather than fight Selden, the carmakers—who included Alexander Winton—decided to join him, since an alliance would save them a costly legal case and also offer them the chance to license or control their commercial rivals in the future. Thus was born, in March 1903, a few weeks before the formal incorporation of the Ford Motor Company, the Association of Licensed Automobile Manufacturers.

In the throes of trying to launch his own company with Malcomson, Henry Ford's first reaction to the formation of the ALAM was to try to join it.

"Henry Ford called on me one morning," remembered Fred L. Smith, treasurer of the Olds Motor Company and acting president of the ALAM, ". . . and wanted to know if, in case application was made, membership in the association would be granted them."[28]

Ford made this approach in June or July of 1903, and it sounds as if he was, at this stage, willing to join up with the ALAM, along with Winton and all the others. Certainly Alex Malcomson and his fellow investors, led by the prudent John Gray, would have welcomed additional security at this perilous initial stage of their enterprise.

But Fred Smith was dismissive. "I told him I did not think an application from the Ford Motor Co. at that particular moment would be considered favorably.... I remember solemnly telling Henry Ford that his outfit was really nothing but an 'assemblage plant.'"[29] When Smith met later with Henry's fellow directors, he followed a similar line.

James Couzens was incensed. "Selden can take his patent and go to hell with it!" he roared, according to one account of the meeting.[30]

"You men are foolish," counselled Smith. "The Selden crowd can put you out of business—and will."

"Let them try it," responded Henry Ford,[31] and when a few days later the ALAM formally declared war, Ford and Couzens were ready with an announcement in the *Detroit Free Press*.

"To Dealers, Importers, Agents and Users of our Gasoline Automobiles...," promised the Ford Motor Company: "We will protect you against any prosecution for alleged infringements of patents."

The Ford advertisement dismissed Selden's claim, defiantly stating what every automotive engineer—and even the members of the ALAM itself—knew very well. "The Selden Patent ... does not cover any practicable machine, no practicable machine can be made from it and never was."

The announcement concluded in fighting terms.

We are the pioneers of the GASOLINE AUTOMOBILE. Our Mr. Ford also built the famous "999" Gasoline Automobile, which was driven by Barney Oldfield.... Mr. Ford, driving his own machine, beat Mr. Winton at Grosse Pointe track in 1901. We have always been winners.[32]

For nearly six years the Ford Motor Company fought the ALAM in a series of closed hearings and at one memorable encounter on a racetrack near Guttenberg, New Jersey, where, on June 14, 1907, George Selden solemnly produced a full-scale working version of the horseless carriage which he claimed to have been working on all those years ago. Started by an air compressor inside a shed, with all the lawyers and court officials standing around, Selden's machine coughed into life, ran five yards, and then stopped dead.

Judge Charles Merrill Hough, however, felt that the mechanical failure of the Selden buggy had little relevance to the case. By the judge's reading of the patent, Selden was not claiming to be the inventor of specific mechanical devices. His claim was to have combined a number of preexisting elements into a new "harmonious whole capable of results never before achieved,"[33] and on this criterion, Judge Hough upheld the Selden patent in 1909.

"Nothing now remains," exulted Alexander Winton on behalf of the ALAM, "but to exact from all trespassers a share of that income they have enjoyed for years without letters patent."[34]

It was a heavy blow for Henry Ford and his colleagues. Through all the trouble and expense of the suit, Ford and Couzens had remained confident of victory, and Judge Hough's decision caught them off balance. "We thought we were in great jeopardy," remembered the lawyer, John Anderson, later. "We were feeling very blue indeed." [35]

Suddenly the Ford Motor Company stood alone. Other carmakers who had been cheering Ford on in expectation of victory—and royalty exemption—fell silent, and within a matter of weeks of the judgement, no less than thirty independent carmakers had caved in and agreed to pay tribute to the ALAM. Chief amongst these was the new conglomerate being formed by the entrepreneur William

Durant, the General Motors Corporation, which comprised Cadillac, Buick, Oldsmobile, and a number of other companies, and which, it was announced on October 19, 1909, had paid the ALAM $1 million in back royalties.[36]

But Henry Ford held firm. "We will fight to a finish," he telegraphed his dealers on the day after the decision.[37] Henry had already put up bonds totalling $12 million to indemnify any Ford dealer or customer who might be prosecuted by the ALAM, and he reasserted his pledge.

"There will be no let up in the legal fight," he declared, promising to take his fight all the way to the Supreme Court if need be.[38] The Ford Motor Company had done more to advance the industry than "any dozen other manufacturers," he said, and the patent was a "freak among alleged inventions . . . worthless as a patent and worthless as a device."[39]

"There's a man for you, a man of backbone," declared the *Detroit Free Press* admiringly on March 1, 1910, in an editorial entitled "Ford, the Fighter." "As a human figure he presents a spectacle to win the applause of all men with red blood; for this world dearly loves the fighting man."[40]

On January 9, 1911, Henry Ford's stand was finally vindicated. The appeals court found for him, and in terms so absolute that there was clearly little point in the Selden forces fighting on. Judge Hough's decision was dismissed, the ALAM was disbanded, and, thanks almost entirely to Henry Ford, the American car industry was liberated from what soon came to be seen as an audacious and shameless conspiracy to limit its freedom.

It was a famous victory, bravely fought and deservedly won. After his defeat in September 1909, Henry Ford could easily have settled for a quiet life and joined the ALAM, since the association had been keen to settle with him for the sake of peace. The Selden royalty payments would have been no problem for Ford with the Model T selling so well. But partly through principle and partly through sheer obstinacy, Henry had hired new lawyers and battled on. He refused to compromise. He applied the same ruthless simplicity to fighting the Selden case as he had to the creation of the people's car—and his victory in 1911 was the beginning of the emergence of Henry Ford as a public figure.

If the name of Ford meant anything at all to Americans at the end of the first decade of the twentieth century, it was associated with a cheapish brand of motorcar. No one could put a face or personality to it. But with his fight against the Selden patent, Henry Ford, the man, started to take on an identity of his own. The report of his 1911 victory in the appeals court was the first occasion that his name had ever featured in a Detroit newspaper front page lead[41]—and, given the nature of his lone crusade against the "Motor Trust," it was a brave and iconoclastic debut. Innovator, giant-killer, and tribune of the people, a new American folk hero was beginning to stand revealed.

The Ford factory at Highland Park lies just past Manchester Street as you drive north on Woodward Avenue. You go past the Pretzel Bowl Saloon and the Tender Trap ("Topless Entertainment, Businessmen's Lunches") and there, on the right, it stands, flat-roofed, long and low, an endless white rectangular framework trimmed with strips of red brickwork and windows—acres and acres of windows. Highland Park today hovers on the edge of dereliction, one among the scores of other deserted factories that dot the drab wasteland stretching between downtown Detroit and the affluent suburbs, and its office section stands completely empty. Flakes of distemper have formed snowdrifts across the stairs where James Couzens's clerks scurried seventy-five years ago.

But a million square feet of the factory area is still used by the Ford Motor Company—for storage. When a Thunderbird line shuts down in St. Louis or an Escort line in Mexico, the machines that might one day be useful somewhere else are brought to Highland Park, and here they sit, fuzzing gently with dust: paint ovens, seat moulders, body presses, and, at the end, some robot welders with shiny rod arms, their pincers ready to jerk back into life if ever the call to duty comes.

It is an eerie, silent, waiting world, and in one corner are the cars, wrecks all and twisted horribly. Some are the objects of corrosion experiments, sitting here waiting to see how long a pound of salt will take to eat into their carcase. Others are just wrecks, the remnants of crashes whose details are wired onto them with tags, each its own mangled memorial to some life lost or item of human beauty blighted —and thus the subject of a court case which will keep them from the wrecker's yard for a season, perversely cherished.

Inside you realize that the lowness of the building is an optical trick, a visual function of its sheer width, for in fact the Highland Park plant stands a full four storeys tall. You see it most clearly if you walk to where the floors come to a stop in the middle of the factory, and you suddenly find yourself staring up into a high, soaring cathedral nave that extends from floor to skylight. There are two of these surprises that run from one end of the building to the other, long skinny canyons lit by grey filtered sunlight—and projecting out into them, irregularly, from every section of every floor, are dozens of angular little balconies.

These were the dumping areas into which moving cranes would deposit parts. Screws, springs, nuts, and bolts— almost everything a worker needed was brought to him by a crane, a conveyor belt, or a gravity slide, for the rule at Highland Park was that men never moved from their work, the work came to them. It is because of this rule that Highland Park today remains more than just any other redundant Detroit workshop that time has passed by. Highland Park was the logical development of Henry Ford's people's car, the source of a manufacturing innovation which was to transform the texture of twentieth-century life as much as the car itself did, for in this now-mouldering old factory was created the moving assembly line.

Henry Ford's first cars, like the other automobiles produced back in the early years of this century, were put together in logical, cost-saving stages from the start. It was the way Henry had seen machine shops operating in Detroit in the 1880s and 1890s, an efficient, disciplined sequence which saved money and time—the same system of mass production that was fuelling economic takeoff all over America at the end of the nineteenth century.

But innovators like Singer, McCormick, and Samuel Colt mass-produced their consumer goods on a system best described as the process line. The sewing machine—or reaper or firearm—was built up as it passed through the factory in a series of jerks. In the case of automobiles, teams of mechanics would build up engines on stationary cradles in one particular workshop. These would then be shifted to the next shop, where men gathered around to fit axles and wheels, and when this process had been completed, the chassis would be moved off again to the upholstery shop.

The process line embodied calculated, progressive movement, but there was no continuous flow. The closest to a continuously moving line was the dressing rail from which carcases hung in the Chicago slaughter yards. Butchers cut off legs and haunches as the carcases travelled past—a sort of dis-assembly line.

When Henry Ford moved to Highland Park, it gave him the chance to get down to first principles. In April 1907, the same month in which the Manufacturing Company was amalgamated back into the Motor Company after Malcomson's departure, the Ford directors agreed to purchase the fifty-seven-acre site on the outskirts of Detroit, hitherto a racecourse, and planning started in tandem with the work that Henry, Galamb, Wills, and Sorensen were doing on the Model T. For his people's car, Henry Ford wanted a factory that was not just the world's biggest. It had to be the world's best.

He was fortunate in finding an architect whose appetite for innovation matched his own. Albert Kahn, the son of a rabbi, born and educated in Germany, had developed an interest in the new method of construction just coming into use at the beginning of the century—reinforced concrete, a method by which concrete beams, brittle on their own, were given added strength by being poured around a basketwork of steel rodding. It was cheaper and more flexible than building with brick or with a solid steel skeleton. Using reinforced concrete an architect could, for the first time, create really wide, open factory areas which had the added advantage of being virtually fireproof, since concrete, unlike steel, is a poor conductor of heat.

Albert Kahn's first reinforced-concrete factory in Detroit had been built for the Packard Car Company in 1905, and it demonstrated the virtues of his system: less vibration, less fire risk, more open floor spaces in which machinery could be shifted and rearranged—and amazing expanses of windowpanes which, at a stroke, turned every other factory into a prison workshop by comparison. This was clearly the way to build Highland·Park, and Ford and Kahn turned out to be kindred spirits. They had a mutual delight in setting up technical problems and then vaulting over them—and the consequence on the site of the former racecourse was an inspired, airy creation with huge areas of floor space lit by 50,000 square feet of Kahn's windows from the sides and from above, a building that was hailed at its opening in December 1909 as Detroit's own "Crystal Palace."

When Model T production started at Highland Park in the early months of 1910, the process was initially organized very much as it had been at Piquette Avenue. Movement was still only rudimentary. The cars sat on their cradles while the work teams swarmed around them, making them up in batches of fifty, and the assembly process did not start moving until the cars had been fitted with their wheels, from which point they could be pushed from station to station.

But the Model T was impatient. It imparted an urgency of its own to the manufacturing process—18,664 cars sold in 1909–10, and 34,528 in 1910–11.[42] Demand was so compelling. Even with the extra workstations that could now be deployed within the light and airy acres of Highland Park, the Ford Motor Company just could not keep up with its order book. The cars were packed into railcars and whisked away as they were completed. In 1911–12 production doubled yet again, to an incredible 78,440—and still the orders kept on coming. Somehow the company had to speed up even more. It had to find ways to improve, to get ever more efficient. The people's car had to get out to the people, and from this mechanical imperative came the machinery to accomplish it.

There was no one begetter of the continuously moving assembly line. Kahn's flexible new plant provided the context. Ford himself, with Galamb and Wills, provided a product engineered for mass production—the three men designed components like the single-piece four-cylinder block which, in other cars, might be made up of eight or more separate pieces. Charles Sorensen, his pattern-making days behind him for good, was playing an increasing role in choreographing production, along with P. E. Martin, a French Canadian who had been with the company since its days at Mack Avenue. They were assisted by Clarence W. Avery, a young teacher at Edsel Ford's school, until he caught Henry's eye. Along with what seems to have been a remarkably creative team of foremen and supervisors, this group worked through 1910 and 1911 to smooth and speed production of the Model T.

In 1912 they received a fresh injection of personnel. The lightweight steel axle housings stamped out on the presses of the Keim Mills in Buffalo had proved so integral to the success of the Model T that Henry Ford had bought up the company in 1911, lock, stock, and barrel. When, in the following year, a strike threatened production in Buffalo, he promptly closed down the plant and had the crucial presses shipped to Highland Park, where they were stamping out axle housings again within three days. Henry had not taken long to master the gentle arts of tycoonery.

With the Keim Mills presses came the Keim Mills personnel: William H. Smith, who had first proposed the steel axle housing to Ford; John R. Lee, a manager whose personnel techniques were soon to develop another new field at Highland Park; and a Danish-born engineer, William S.

Knudsen, whose contribution to the Ford Motor Company's expansion was to match that of his compatriot Charles Sorensen. These men enriched still further the engineering expertise at Henry Ford's disposal, and ever-more-accurate engineering was the prerequisite of faster production.

In 1908 Henry M. Leland had astonished the members of the Royal Automobile Club by having three of his Cadillac cars dismantled at Brooklands, and by having the component parts thoroughly mixed up. His engineers then set to work, taking any available part, and built the cars up again in front of the RAC members' eyes, driving them off in triumph around the track.

Today we take it for granted that the most intricate pieces of a car's machinery can be replaced with an off-the-shelf duplicate. But in 1908, a car engine was still seen as an individually crafted organism, a handmade job. That was how most engines had to be made, since the engineering of their parts was seldom consistent. There were few components that did not arrive from the machine shop without the need for some extra filing or adjustment before they could be incorporated into an engine, and the secret of the phenomenal quantity and speed with which Henry Ford had produced first the Model N and then the Model T had lain in the quality of Ford machining.

"One of Mr. Ford's strong points was interchangeability of parts," remembered Max Wollering, who had supervised the manufacture of parts for the Model N. "He realized as well as any other manufacturer realized that in order to create great quantity of production, your interchangeability must be fine and unique in order to accomplish the rapid assembly of units. There can't be much hand work or fitting if you are going to accomplish great things."[43]

Interchangeability had been the Ford watchword in the Piquette days, together with the logical arrangement of machines to create a sequential production flow, and the same principles were extended at Highland Park.

"Each piece is machined in a jig, so that every one is absolutely interchangeable," marvelled one observer in the autumn of 1910, who could discover "no filing, grinding, sawing, or hammering of parts to make them fit."[44] No other plant in Detroit could match the vast Keim presses which stamped crankcases from flat sheets of steel and could produce the ninety-five tubes and sheet-metal pins needed to make up a radiator at one single stroke.[45]

Henry Ford, Wills, Galamb, and Sorensen were like children as they sniffed out new machine tools that could cut out a manufacturing stage, or increase the accuracy of milling or grinding by 1/10,000 of an inch. If they found a new device, they scrapped all the old ones, and though Couzens sometimes protested at the cost, his figures nearly always reflected the dividends of the reinvestment.

One craze that Couzens certainly did subscribe to was the science of Taylorism which hit Detroit around this time. Frederick "Speedy" Taylor, father of the stopwatch-and-clipboard approach to factory life, had begun making time-and-motion studies of machine shops in the early 1880s, and in 1911 he published *The Principles of Scientific Management*, a work which made his creed an instant management vogue —the early equivalent of *Parkinson's Law* or *The Peter Principle*, if somewhat more humourless.

A thoroughgoing fanatic like Henry Ford, Taylor lived out Taylorism in his personal life, perfecting a device that woke him up if ever he was so unscientific as to doze off in a chair. He lectured on several occasions in Detroit, and in 1909 he had made a memorable speech to the Packard management which lasted no less than four hours. Some of his audience may well have had their stopwatches on him by the end of his presentation, but he impressed the people who mattered, and Packard was promptly "Taylorized." Time-and-motion techniques became the norm all over Detroit. It was the genius of the Ford system, however, to go beyond Taylor, whose "science" was focused on the time that one man took to do a job. Why use a man at all, was the Ford question, if a machine could do the job instead?

The world's first moving assembly line came in the spring of 1913, in the magneto department at Highland Park.[46]

Workers lined up side by side, facing the flywheels designed by Spider Huff. These flywheels rested on waist-high metal shelving along which the components could be slid, and below the shelf each man had a bin containing just one or two simple components.

Until this date the magneto assemblers had worked at benches with a complete range of magnets, bolts, and clamps, each of them fitting together some thirty-five to forty complete flywheel magneto assemblies in the course of a nine-hour day. Now they were each assigned just one or two of the twenty-nine different operations that went into the assembly—a magnet to place, a couple of nuts to start or tighten before they pushed the assembly down to their neighbour—and immediately their production time fell quite noticeably. With the old system it had taken at least fifteen minutes to produce one magneto. Now the assembly time was thirteen minutes ten seconds.

When the waist-level shelving was replaced by a rather more elevated, motorized conveyor belt which set the pace for the line, production time fell still more; and when further analysis refined the division of tasks along the belt, the average assembly time per magneto fell to seven minutes, and then to five. Through the introduction of continuous movement, it had become possible for one man to do the work which had previously occupied three or four—nor was there any longer the need for the worker to be especially skilled. Any manual labourer could do the job.

Soon another conveyor belt was carrying engines along, and their crankshafts and pistons were fitted as they moved. The making of transmissions was similarly analysed and its component stages strung out along a moving belt. Suddenly, in the summer of 1913, the production managers at Highland Park had a problem. These new continuously moving assembly systems were producing so much that they were threatening to flood the final chassis assembly—the conclusion of the whole production process generally thought of when people refer to "the" assembly line.

Stopwatches went into action. An analysis of production

at Highland Park that August showed 250 assemblers and 80 parts carriers working nine hours each per day for twenty-six days to complete 6,182 chassis and motors—an average of twelve and a half man-hours per chassis. As an experiment, a crude moving line was set up, with a rope running 250 feet down the factory from one chassis to a winch which hauled the rope in slowly across the floor. As the chassis moved, a team of six assemblers kept pace with it, picking up parts as they needed them from strategic dumps along the way—and lo and behold, the average number of man-hours needed to complete a chassis using this method fell to five hours and fifty minutes.

Eliminating the trotting escort, and repositioning the assembly workers in stationary positions along a moving line that had been raised to just above waist height cut production times even more dramatically. Work was analysed still more thoroughly and subdivided accordingly.

"The man who places a part does not fasten it," said Henry Ford. "The man who puts in a bolt does not put on the nut; the man who puts on the nut does not tighten it."[47] Average chassis assembly time fell to ninety-three minutes.

The lesson was obvious. Within months Highland Park was a buzzing network of belts, assembly lines, and subassemblies: a dashboard assembly line, a front-axle assembly line, a body-and-top assembly line. The entire place was whirled up into a vast, intricate, and never-ending mechanical ballet.

"Every piece of work in the shops moves," exulted Henry Ford; "it may move on hooks, on overhead chains . . . it may travel on a moving platform, or it may go by gravity, but the point is that there is no lifting or trucking. . . . No workman has anything to do with moving or lifting anything."[48] Let the conveyor do the walking. "Save ten steps a day for each of 12,000 employees, and you will have saved fifty miles of wasted motion and mis-spent energy."[49]

Ford output figures rose dramatically. Highland Park's

1911–12 production of 78,440 Model T's had been achieved with a work force of 6,867. The following year production more than doubled, and the work force more than doubled as well. But when, in 1913–14, production nearly doubled yet again, the number of workers needed to manufacture this dramatically increased number of cars did not increase. This was the year in which the moving assembly line was introduced, and thanks to its efficiencies, the size of the work force at Highland Park actually fell, from 14,336 workers to 12,880.[50] In his drive to produce the people's car, Henry Ford had turned a giant key that admitted him to a magical new world.

# 7

# BIRDS AND THE SPIRIT

In July 1913, Henry Ford celebrated his fiftieth birthday, and the milestone evidently prompted some stock-taking. It was on October 28 of this year that he scribbled down his very first childhood memory: his recollection of going out with his father to gaze at the four little sparrows' eggs in their nest beneath the fallen oak tree.[1]

But Henry did not waste too much time looking back. Nineteen thirteen was the year the moving assembly line came to Highland Park, and Henry Ford's fifties were to prove the most expansive and adventurous decade of his entire life. At a stage when most people are slowing down, Henry Ford was scaling extraordinary new peaks of power, wealth, and creativity. Far from losing momentum, he was intensifying his capacity to do several things at once. Through the summer months of 1913, he was working on the details of the belts, chutes, and slides which were to revolutionize the twentieth-century workplace. In the middle of all this, he found time for a holiday which was to have still greater implications for his own spirit.

The break came as a result of an unusual friendship he had just developed. On December 6, 1912, the bird-lover John Burroughs—author, poet, disciple of Thoreau and Emerson, and, at seventy-five, the Methuselah of American naturalists—received an unexpected item of mail: "I had a surprising letter. Mr. Ford, of automobile fame, is a great admirer of my books—says there are few persons in the world who have given him the pleasure I have. . . . He wants to present me with a Ford automobile all complete. . . . There shall be no publicity in connection with it."[2]

Henry Ford had been stung by some criticisms Burroughs

had been making of the industrial desecration of America, and of the impact of the motorcar in particular. The naturalist had complained that the automobile was going to kill the appreciation of nature, and Henry Ford evidently hoped that the present of a Model T might change the old man's mind.

It did. Burroughs was alarmed when the machine first arrived at his farm in the Catskills, and it took him some time to tame it: he had to have a young relative drive him around. But once the naturalist had mastered the mysteries of the planetary transmission, he took over the wheel himself, and he was soon to be seen, white-bearded and behatted, bobbing across the New York countryside from hide to hide, touring his bird-watching sites. The resilient, lightweight Model T actually brought the old man into closer contact with the countryside in some respects—as Henry Ford intended. Burroughs wrote to thank his unexpected benefactor, and when the two men met in Detroit in June 1913, Burroughs discovered that Henry Ford had a surprising and impressive knowledge of birds.[3]

Henry Ford dated his interest in wildlife and nature back to his earliest childhood, to that first glimpse of the little sparrows' eggs. The McGuffey Readers had fortified his interest. "Don't Kill the Birds!" was the theme of one lesson in Reader Three, one of McGuffey's many earnest attempts to teach little country boys not to take wildlife for granted.

Almost as soon as Henry started making money, he had started buying up farmland and forest around Dearborn, partly for his primitive tractor experiments, but partly also in order to create bird sanctuaries. His interest was evident even in the midst of all the machinery at Highland Park. It was always very difficult to lay hands on Henry there, for he liked to spend his time roaming the engineering laboratories or the assembly floor, and his grand, rather bare, wood-panelled presidential office was the last place to expect him. If by chance you should happen to corner him there, however, it was quite probable that you would find the president of the Ford Motor Company on the opposite side of the room from his desk, peering down the bird-watching telescope that he kept by the window.

Since ornithology was one minor relief from Henry Ford's compulsive inability to think about anything much except his car, his wife encouraged his unexpectedly nonmechanical preoccupation. When he first expressed an interest in one of Burroughs's books, Clara had bought him the complete set, and she found that they had "quite a marked effect on his attitude of mind." Burroughs's writing about nature "started new currents" in Henry, she found, and these "stuck by him."[4] In December 1912, the same month in which he wrote out of the blue to Burroughs, and just as Highland Park's manufacturing revolution was gathering momentum, Henry Ford decided to lend his support to the Weekes-McLean Bill, a proposal to protect migratory birds, which had been put before Congress in 1909 but had been marking time ever since.

This was Henry Ford's first venture into the political arena. At the same time as he was working with Wills, Avery, and his other lieutenants on the revolution of the moving assembly line, he was mobilizing Ford dealers across the country to lobby their congressmen and to get local schoolchildren and wildlife societies to do the same. Capitalizing on the public eminence that had started to grow with his victory in the Selden Patent Suit, he sent personal requests to Thomas Edison and John D. Rockefeller to use their influence—though it was probably the grass-roots pressure stirred up through the Ford dealer network which proved more important. The Weekes-McLean Bill became law in 1913.

John Burroughs had come to visit the Fords in Detroit just before Henry's fiftieth birthday, and he invited the couple back three months later to sip at the wellsprings of contemporary American mysticism in Massachusetts. In the first week of September 1913, the old naturalist took Henry Ford to Walden Pond and into Concord, where Ralph Waldo Emerson's house stood very much as he had left it, and also to the Sleepy Hollow cemetery nearby, last resting place of the philosopher, as well as of Nathaniel Hawthorne, Louisa May Alcott, and that archetypal thinker-in-the-woods, Henry David Thoreau.

Burroughs recruited Frank Sanborn, a biographer of Emerson, to show Henry Ford around these shrines of American transcendentalism, but it was Burroughs himself whom Henry always credited with opening his eyes to the confused yet uplifting message preached by the Sage of Concord.

"Not only did he know Emerson by heart as an author, but he knew him by heart as a spirit," Ford later told Samuel Crowther. "He taught me to know Emerson. He had so saturated himself with Emerson that at one time he thought as he did and even fell into his own mode of expression."[5]

A slender, worn blue volume found among Henry Ford's possessions after his death gives some clue to the chord that was startlingly struck in the carmaker by his exposure to the thought of Ralph Waldo Emerson in the summer of 1913. It is a pocket-size collection of Emerson's essays—"The World's Classics," published by the Oxford University Press—and down the inside of the frayed dust jacket, scrawled in Henry's spidery handwriting, are a series of page numbers with his comments beside them: "Good," "Beauty," "our spontenious action the Best."[6]

The flyleaf of the book shows that it was published in 1936. But Henry Ford was quoting Emerson in interviews from January 1915 onwards,[7] and we know that by 1921 or 1922 at the latest, there were in his library several copies of Emerson's essays. According to one visitor, these books were visibly "soiled by use."[8] So the annotations on Henry's 1936 edition suggest either that he lost or gave away his original editions, or else that he wore them all out, and then laboriously reread and reannotated this one.[9]

Henry Ford was not a great reader. When he read aloud it was slowly and haltingly. But for this very reason, the things that Henry did manage to read made that much more of an impression on him—and this proved the case with the essays of Ralph Waldo Emerson.

It was Emerson's concept that God resides in the soul of

every man—"a man contains all that is needful to his government within himself"—which appears to have offered Henry Ford a new vision of how he might come to terms with his own restless spirit.

"As there is no screen or ceiling between our heads and the infinite heavens," runs a passage on one of the marked pages, "so there is no bar or wall in the soul where man, the effect, ceases, and God, the cause begins."[10]

Emerson's recipe for releasing the divinity that resides within each of us was that we should escape from the stultifying limitations of reason and surrender to the more erratic, but also more creative, impulses of our own particular genius.

"Only in our easy, simple, spontaneous action are we strong," runs a passage in Ford's book beside which there is a pencilled check mark. "We love characters in proportion as they are impulsive and spontaneous," explains another marked page. The logical corollary of this was that too much rationalization could be a dangerous thing.[11]

"Our painful labors are unnecessary and fruitless," runs a passage on page 97, which was endorsed in Ford's handwriting as "Good."

These arguments made such sense of Henry Ford's erratic, whimsical life to date, crowned so late and unexpectedly with success. He had followed his own hunches, defying the attempts of three groups of rich and rational men to harness him systematically to their own designs, and in the end, his own hunches had paid off. Individuals must learn, argued Emerson on another marked page, that they are not "leaning willows" and that they should not be afraid to detach themselves from their fellows. "With the exercise of self trust," promised the philosopher, "new powers shall appear."[12]

Emerson had special words for those rare spirits who were brave enough to strike out in life on their own: "a class of men . . . so eminently endowed with insight and virtue, that they have been unanimously saluted as divine. . . . They are usually received with ill-will, because they are new."

This was a consoling thought for a naive and thin-skinned character who was just beginning to encounter that envy with which the world blights success, and it was marked second on the list of key pages in Henry's little blue book, obviously representing a heartfelt theme.

"To be great is to be misunderstood," stated the essay on "Self Reliance." "Beware when the great God lets loose a thinker on this planet. Then all things are at risk."[13]

Emerson spun off thoughts which harmonized with Henry Ford's existing belief in reincarnation—"the spirit sports with time, can crowd eternity into an hour, or stretch an hour to eternity"—and, most satisfying of all, none of this transcendental mysticism contradicted the main passion and purpose of Henry's life. On the contrary, stated Emerson, "machinery and transcendentalism agree well."[14]

Opening his mind to the "technological sublime," the philosopher had come to believe, more than twenty years before Henry's birth, that machines were "new and necessary facts" which, when designed and employed with integrity, were essentially in harmony with nature. The sharply engineered lines of the frontiersman's axe, the technology of the steam locomotive opening up the prairies, the aero-efficient billowing of the clipper ship—all these were examples of mechanization which brought Americans into closer contact with the natural mysteries of their own continent. To that list it was already proper to add by 1913 the mechanical ingenuity and ruggedness of Henry Ford's own creation, the Model T motorcar.

Henry Ford returned to Detroit in the autumn of 1913 buzzing with his newly discovered divinity. Emerson had articulated the magic in him, the aptitude that Henry had conjured from somewhere in his psyche to wrestle with the secrets of nature and to fashion artefacts that were prized and coveted by his fellow men. His was the magic of the smith in a primitive society, the wizard who wrought life out of hammer and fire. As Henry Ford struggled with the final triumphant details of his moving assembly line—an

alchemy which was to transform industrial life for millions
—he might well mark the page in Emerson's essay "Circles"
—"when these waves of God flow into me, I no longer
reckon lost time. . . . These moments confer a sort of omni-
presence and omnipotence."

Almost every day in these intoxicating months, Henry
Ford, with the help of his Highland Park lieutenants, was
making some new discovery which saved production time,
increased production efficiency, confirmed how clever he
was, and made him richer than ever. It was a heady period
in his life, rich in fulfillment that is given to few men or
women to enjoy, and it is not surprising that it might drive
Henry Ford to look for, and be receptive to, some exterior
psychic validation. There are many mystical creeds which
contradict or nullify material achievement, but in the teach-
ings of Ralph Waldo Emerson, Henry Ford had found a
philosophical framework which gave a deeper meaning, and
added a more than material value, to the technological
revolution he was accomplishing at Highland Park.

As 1913 drew to a close, the Ford ego stood at an all-time
high. But Henry's newfound spiritual mentor preached more
than self-love and the glory of the Great God Me. If God
moved in you, said Emerson, then you were a rare and lucky
human being, and you should be aware of that.

"It is as easy for the strong man to be strong," he wrote
on one page which Henry Ford marked with uncharacteristic
humility, "as it is for the weak to be weak."[15]

Narcissism alone was not enough. It was the duty of those
heroes who were fortunate enough to be "victory organized"
to help those lesser mortals who still had not discovered how
to realize their own potential. "Emerson said that the chief
want in life is somebody to make us do what we can do,"
declared Henry Ford, and as 1913 turned into 1914, he set
out to be precisely that somebody.

Detroit's car factories, like industries throughout America
—and, indeed, the rest of the early twentieth-century world
—operated on the crude basis of "lay on, lay off." When

there was work to do, workers were hired and paid for it. When there was no work, they were sent home without pay. If there was an inventory to be taken, or a new production line to be set up, the ordinary assembly workers waited at home, without pay, while the specialized job was done, and they just hoped that when production started up again, they would get their jobs back. The same went for Christmas and other holidays. Men filed out of the factory gate on Christmas Eve not knowing when they would get paid next, and they then waited in limbo for two or three weeks until the factory siren sounded again.

It was on the occasion of one such lay-off—at Christmas 1913—that James Couzens stood by his office window in Highland Park, looking down on the thousands of employees trudging out with their lunch pails into the cold of Woodward Avenue.

"We had been driving our men at top speed for a year," he later recalled, "and here we were turning them out to spend the Christmas holidays with no pay. The company had piled up a huge profit from the labor of these men; the stockholders were rolling in wealth, but all that the workers themselves got was a bare living wage."[16]

Couzens subsequently claimed that the "gross injustice of all this" prompted him to bring about what happened next, but his is only one version of events.[17] Henry Ford later remembered how just before this Christmas he was walking through the factory with his son, Edsel, now just twenty and starting work in the business, when they came across two men, dirty, bruised, and sweating, attempting to beat each other's brains out. Henry was appalled that his son should be the witness to such depravity, and as he pondered on what turned potentially sensitive human beings into insensate brutes, his mind moved in the same novel direction which appears to have inspired Couzens and a group of other senior executives when they gathered with Henry in the empty Highland Park plant early in January 1914 to discuss production and costs for the coming year. It was resolved, and a meeting of the directors held on January

5 confirmed the resolution, that the Ford Motor Company would, at a stroke, more than double its basic rate of take-home pay to the unheard-of figure of $5.00 a day.

Henry Ford had never had a reputation for being especially generous to his workers. He was no Scrooge, but he had never paid any more than the going rate: $1.90 or so to Model T production workers for a ten-hour day in 1908, rising gradually to an average of around $2.50 (with a minimum of $2.34) by 1913.[18] He had paid out annual production bonuses on a modest scale—very modest when compared to the huge dividends that the shareholders had regularly voted themselves—and during the autumn of 1913, John R. Lee, the recruit from the Keim Mills, had been carrying out a thoroughgoing reform of the company's wage structure.

Aimed at reducing labour turnover and creating a more stable and committed work force at Highland Park, Lee's 1913 reforms had produced an October wage increase of around 13 percent, with an ingenious job-ladder system which could raise the pay of some elite workers from the $2.34 minimum to over $4.00 a day.[19]

But this paled beside the massive across-the-board pay rise proposed less than three months later, which was coupled to a reduction in working hours. The new $5.00 minimum was to apply to an eight-hour day—this additional flourish being achieved by replacing the two existing nine-hour shifts with a nonstop rotation of eight-hour shifts around the clock. So the Ford Motor Company got more production, and the workers put in fewer hours. It was almost too clever to be true.

Henry Ford, whose nose for publicity had developed with his victory over Selden and the ALAM, knew he had a good story for the local papers, and by lunchtime on January 5, 1914, reporters were out at Highland Park being briefed by James Couzens on the pay scheme approved by the directors only a few hours earlier.

It was, in fact, quite complicated, for the basic rate of pay to Ford workers would remain around the $2.34 level set by John R. Lee a couple of months earlier. The magic $5.00 figure was reached by adding a "profit-sharing" bonus which was even larger than the basic wage, but which had to be earned. Workers would be required to put in six months' service to qualify for the bonus, they had to be at least twenty-two years old—unless they were married or were supporting a widowed mother or next of kin—and there was a string of other conditions revolving around Ford's hope that each of his employees should lead "a clean, sober and industrious life."[20]

But all these complexities were, for the moment, by the way. Five Dollars a Day was the story. It was a pay rise so massive as to appear impossible, a defiance of the laws of gravity, and it was emblazoned in headlines across the country. "A blinding rocket through the dark clouds of the present industrial depression," declared the *Cleveland Plain Dealer*. "A magnificent act of generosity," declared the *New York Evening Post*. Some editorialists grew positively reverential. GOD BLESS HENRY FORD, proclaimed a headline in the *Algonac Courier* over a story which described the carmaker as "one of God's noblemen."[21]

The *Detroit News*, one of America's first afternoon papers, had carried the story on the same Monday of the announcement, and by two o'clock the following morning, men were already gathering in the cold and dark outside the Highland Park employment office. By the time dawn was clear enough to reveal the huge F O R D block letters that were suspended between the factory's towering smokestacks, there were some 10,000 men milling together against the railings. The temperature was well below freezing—under ten degrees Fahrenheit[22]—and raw gusts of snow were swirling around the silent multitude, many of whom were without proper shoes and were dressed only in rags. The Detroit Poor Commission was distributing relief to more than 19,000 people that winter, the highest figure the city had known for nearly twenty years.[23]

Highland Park needed 4,000 or 5,000 fresh hands to man

its additional eight-hour shift, but this gathering of recruits was overwhelming. "No Hiring" signs were put out, and the crowds dispersed slightly. But by next day they were swelled by more job seekers from out of town, and the numbers grew in succeeding days as men arrived from as far away as Milwaukee and Chicago.

By the middle of January 1914, there were 15,000 desperate men gathering every morning to jam Woodward Avenue and Manchester Street, which led to the Highland Park employment office. Attempts by Ford agents to mingle with the crowd, surreptitiously handing out hiring slips to likely looking prospects, only intensified the problem, since rumours that hiring had finally started increased numbers still more.

Fights broke out. There were attempts to bribe or intimidate Ford personnel, and the general atmosphere of beseeching panic drove the supplicants to pathetic lengths. Greying men shoved newspapers into their shoulders and applied boot polish to their hair in attempts to make themselves more eligible. Some men were starving, others were getting drunk—and all of them were getting angry. It was an impossible situation. On Saturday, January 10, 1914, large signs were posted in several languages announcing that hiring had ceased. Newspaper announcements attempted to discourage any more of the unemployed who were by now hurrying to Detroit from all over the Midwest.

But many men had travelled, in hope and desperation, without the money to get home. There were still 10,000 massed in Manchester Street when work started at the factory again the following Monday morning, and the sight of Ford workers, well fed and clothed, pushing their way through the crowds, brandishing their coveted metal work badges—their passports to privilege—was too much. The supplicants turned on them, and the pathetic crowd became a threatening mob. Bricks were hurled. There was jeering, chanting. Men linked arms to throw themselves against the factory gates, trying to break them down, and the Highland Park Police were summoned. A fire hose was unrolled, and when this was greeted with derision, the water was turned on, icing its victims' clothes into hard, chilly boards almost as it struck home in the nine-degree weather.

The demonstration ended as the crowd broke for cover, drenched and shivering. But as they retreated, a few had the satisfaction of upturning and looting the lunch and cigar stands of the vendors who made their business at the Ford factory gates.[24]

Cartoonists had greeted the original announcement of the Five Dollar Day with fantasies of fur-coated Ford workers reclining in chauffeur-driven limousines—"Hawkins, will you step over to the pay window and get my wages? I quite overlooked the matter last week."[25] But the Manchester Street riot displayed a different picture, and it gave the American business establishment the chance for a heartfelt "told you so." The *New York Times* had actually prophesied "serious disturbances" as a result of the Ford initiative, which it condemned as "distinctly Utopian and dead against all experience," while the *Wall Street Journal* accused Henry Ford of "economic blunders if not crimes," which would soon "return to plague him and the industry he represents, as well as organized society." In a naive wish for social improvement, declared the newspaper, Ford had injected "spiritual principles into a field where they do not belong" —a heinous crime—and captains of industry lined up to condemn "the most foolish thing ever attempted in the industrial world." If other employers followed Ford's example, complained the president of the Pittsburgh Plate Glass Company, "it would mean the ruin of all business in this country. . . . Ford himself will surely find that he cannot afford to pay $5 a day."[26]

Henry Ford himself, of course, could quite easily afford his pay increase, for what he was aware of, and what his critics were not, was the massive saving in labour costs that had been created by the continuously moving assembly line. Two new lines, one of them driven by an endless chain, were being rigged in Highland Park during that very 1913–14

Christmas lay-off, and when raised to waist level, these were to cut assembly time down to 93 man-minutes per car, from 728 a year earlier.

On these figures Henry Ford could afford a wage increase to nearly $20 a day. He was living and thinking in a different world from the one his critics still inhabited—and it turned out that he was not being particularly generous, in any case. James Couzens had estimated that the Five Dollar Day would cost the company $10 million in the course of the first year, but he discovered, in fact, that it amounted to rather less than that. For the same twelve-month period, the shareholders voted themselves dividends totalling $11.2 million. "Profit-sharing" was profit-making.

Still, Henry Ford and his colleagues had not been sure of this when they took their momentous decision at the beginning of 1914. They did have huge back orders for cars, and a few months' experimentation had given them an inkling of the economies that their new production process would bring, but there was true generosity, and not a little rashness, in their initiative.

Emerson definitely had something to do with it. In later years his essay on "Compensation" was said to be Henry Ford's favourite, and in "Compensation" the philosopher addressed himself specifically to labour and the proper wage. "In labor as in life," wrote Emerson, "there can be no cheating. The thief steals from himself. The swindler swindles himself."[28] When we buy a broom, a wagon, a knife, or some other everyday object, he argued, we are buying the application of "good sense" on the part of a manufacturer or labourer to a perceived common need, and that "good sense" has a price.

Trying to chisel down the price of labour is self-defeating. You get what you pay for. A wise employer should educate his workers, argued Emerson, and should generally seek to raise the level of their "good sense," vision, and quality of life. The employer who took the time to do this would be rewarded in more than monetary terms.

"Human labor," he wrote, "through all its forms, from

the sharpening of a stake to the construction of a city or an epic, is one immense illustration of the perfect compensation of the universe. The absolute balance of Give and Take, the doctrine that everything has its price—and if that price is not paid, not that thing, but something else is obtained."[29]

Until the winter of 1913–14, Henry Ford had not been paying his workers "the price." He had not passed on to them the immense economies created by the moving assembly line, and instead of getting "that thing" which he wanted, Henry Ford had been getting "something else"— an extraordinary increase in labour turnover which threatened all the advantages promised by his new production techniques. His workers simply did not like the moving assembly line and the pressure it put on their customary work practices, and they declined to cooperate in the most basic fashion. They looked for jobs elsewhere. By December 1913, turnover had reached 380 percent at Highland Park—which meant that Ford had to hire 963 men to keep 100[30]—and when the directors decided to issue a Christmas bonus that month to men who had worked with the company for three years or more, they found that only 640 qualified, out of some 15,000 employees.[31]

This presented Henry Ford with a real problem. What was the use of his new system if it drove his workers to work in other people's factories? The moving line was saving time and money on the assembly floor, but it was generating forbidding new expenses in terms of hiring and training, and at the very moment Henry was grappling with this problem—which was as new and mystifying, in its own way, as the moving assembly line itself—he had come into contact with Emerson, who suggested both a diagnosis and a cure:

Always pay; for first or last you must pay your entire debt. . . . He is great who confers the most benefits. He is base—and that is the one base thing in the universe—to receive favors and render none. . . . Beware of too much good staying in your hand. It will fast corrupt, and worm worms.[32]

This was precisely what had been happening at Highland Park—and money alone was not enough. John R. Lee's wage reforms of October 1913 had offered money, quite a lot of it. Yet less than three months later Henry Ford scrapped them—to Lee's considerable anger. The company personnel expert "became pretty nasty,"[33] according to Charles Sorensen, when his carefully constructed wage scale was set aside.

But Henry Ford was now looking beyond mere wages for something better than money—compensation in the full Emersonian sense.

Henry Ford always liked to present the Five Dollar Day as a hardheaded matter of "efficiency engineering"[34] with "no charity in any way involved,"[35] and he took pleasure in subsequently reporting it to be "one of the finest cost-cutting moves we ever made."[36] But he also believed that the natural mechanisms of free enterprise have moral consequences, as he explained to the minister of his local church, the Reverend Doctor Samuel S. Marquis:

There are thousands of men out there in the shop who are not living as they should. Their homes are crowded and unsanitary. Wives are going out to work because their husbands are unable to earn enough to support the family. They fill up their homes with roomers and boarders in order to help swell the income. It's all wrong—all wrong. It's especially bad for the children. . . .

Now, these people are not living in this manner as a matter of choice. Give them a decent income and they will live decently— will be glad to do so. What they need is the opportunity to do better, and someone to take a little personal interest in them— someone who will show that he has faith in them.[37]

Henry Ford was casting himself as this "someone," the Emersonian hero "to make us do what we can do." "We want to make men in this factory as well as automobiles," he told Samuel Marquis,[38] and the key to his exercise in human restructuring was the careful distinction between the basic wage and shared profits, which newspapers had tended to overlook in their fixation with the miraculous $5.00 figure.

"By share of profits," explained a volume of *Helpful Hints and Advice to Employees*, "is meant that sum which is put into the pay envelopes each pay day over and above the sum earned and paid as wages."[39] The Ford employee could count on his basic wage as he could at any other factory, but he could only expect his share of the profits if he could demonstrate that he was saving it or investing it in a fashion that would be "of permanent benefit" to himself and his family. As Samuel M. Levin put it in the 1920s, the Ford worker was paid $2.34 (the basic wage) for his day's work, and $2.66 (the profit-sharing bonus) to live in the style that Henry Ford considered appropriate.[40]

Company inspectors from a new, specially created "Sociological Department" would visit his home to check on this, and they would investigate, if necessary, questioning wife and neighbours, to make sure he was not frittering his share of Ford profits away on extravagances and wild living.

Today, of course, the politest reaction to such an exercise in paternalism would be to inquire whether the shareholders of the company were also being investigated to make sure that they were spending their share of the profits wisely. Viewed from the perspective of the 1980s—and from 1984 in particular—it is difficult not to see the Ford Sociological Department, with its inspectors busybodying their way into workers' homes, in Orwellian terms, arrogant and sinister.

But in 1914 Big Brother had his uses for the average Detroit workingman, who could probably speak little English. As the first beneficiaries of the new wage system left Highland Park with their pay in January 1914, reported the *New York Times*, they were met by a small army of cast-off wives, loose women, bill collectors, writ servers, and salesmen of every imaginable item from sewing machines to insurance.[41]

With the sudden, spectacular development of the car industry, Detroit had become a boomtown, America's latest end of the rainbow—one of those "roaring, impromptu cities" described by Robert Louis Stevenson, "full of gold and lust and death"[42]—and the pressures on Ford workers

162

were legion. There were 1,600 licensed bars in the city, and at least 1,000 that were unlicensed; they were known as "blind pigs." There were opium dens and gambling houses, and, most numerous of all, there were brothels—more brothels than churches, in fact. Detroit in these years could boast over 500 whorehouses, a figure that can be arrived at with some certainty, since they were licensed and supervised, after a fashion, by the police.

Most of the single men who came to Detroit to work in the car factories found themselves lodgings in rooming houses, whose beds were quite often rotated in eight-hour shifts to match the time-tables of the machine shops, and for these men the city's houses of ill repute offered more than just sex. They provided just a little of the warmth and comfort of home, and, like the bars, they were usually organized on an ethnic basis. Miss Hattie Miller ran the city's most exclusive establishment, while the Bucket of Blood Saloon catered to a less fastidious clientele. The city fathers tried to camouflage the problem by changing the names of streets as they became too notorious—Croghan became Monroe, Champlain's new identity was Lafayette East—but the results were cosmetic. A check of twenty-two licensed employment agencies revealed that seventeen of them were supplying girls for immoral purposes. Talent scouts ranged as far as Europe, reporting back in code that "the cigars . . . are fine, young and good looking." Even some of the city's immigrant hostels and mission shelters, ostensibly dedicated to the protection of newly arrived families, worked to channel single girls into prostitution. Crime flourished.[43]

"Unscrupulous agents, schemers and fakers are abroad in the land," the Ford Motor Company warned its employees. "The Company will not approve, as profit-sharers, men who herd themselves in overcrowded boarding houses which menace their health. Select a home where there are few boarders or roomers, the surroundings clean and wholesome, paying particular attention to the sanitary conditions." Graphic photographs illustrated the difference between "an unhealthy bedroom, a breeder of tuberculosis" and "a good, clean room with plenty of light and air."

The Sociological Department was equally rigorous with workers who had acquired houses of their own. "Employees should not sacrifice their family rights, pleasures and comforts, by filling the house with roomers and boarders, nor endanger their children's morals or welfare by allowing them to associate with people about whom they know little." Photographs showed how to cultivate "a neat clean yard in which the owner may take pride," as opposed to "a filthy back yard; a breeder of disease." There were even illustrations to demonstrate the difference between "a profit-sharing" and "a non-profit-sharing dining room."

Cleanliness was next to Fordliness:

Employes should use plenty of soap and water in the home, and upon their children, bathing frequently. Nothing makes for right living and health so much as cleanliness. Notice that the most advanced people are the cleanest.[44]

The inspectors of the Sociological Department drove off into the slums of Detroit to check that these rigorous standards were being adhered to. There were about fifty of them to start with, each responsible for 700 or so employees, and they were expected to make at least a dozen house calls every day, checking off information about marital status, religion, citizenship, savings, health, hobbies, life insurance, and countless other questions listed on a long blue-and-white form. It was a formidable agenda to get through, and to speed the task each inspector was provided with a brand new Model T, a driver, and an interpreter appropriate to the neighbourhood to which they were assigned. Working as a team, the trio could compile impressive dossiers on everything from the character of the district to the adequacy of the family diet, but they were urged to inject "deep, personal interest" into their inquiries.[45] The success of their visits would depend greatly on the rapport they could establish with wives, children, and other relatives, who often spoke even less English than the head of the family.

Language was a real problem in the Ford work force. A

survey carried out in November 1914 showed that only 29 percent of Ford workers were American-born—and that the 71 percent of foreigners came from no less than twenty-two different national groups.[46] Highland Park was a veritable Tower of Babel. To survive as a cohesive production unit the immigrants clearly had to be taught English, and from May 1914, English-language classes based on the direct, Berlitz method became compulsory for all foreign-born Ford workers who wanted to earn their profit-sharing bonus. The classes were conducted, after work hours, under the supervision of 150 or so English-speaking workers—who taught without pay—and at the end of the course the successful students went through a ritual that was part church service, part rite of initiation.

"Across the back of the stage was shown the hull and deck of an ocean steamship at Ellis Island," described one eyewitness to the graduation ceremony. A gangway led down from this ship and, in the dim light, a "picturesque figure" appeared at the top of the gangway, dressed in a foreign costume and carrying his possessions wrapped, Dick Whittington-like, in a bundle tied to a stick over his shoulder. It was the first graduate of the after-hours language classes, and one by one the other graduates followed him down the gangway into "an immense caldron across which was painted the sign *Ford English School Melting Pot.*" Each successful graduate entered the Melting Pot in his foreign costume, carrying a sign indicating the country he had come from. But minutes later they all emerged from the great cauldron "dressed in American clothes, faces eager with the stimulus of new opportunities. . . . Each man carried a small American flag in his hand."[47]

This was Emerson *pace* the U.S. Immigration Department. To be reborn was to become an American citizen.

Female workers were not originally included in the profit-sharing system of the Five Dollar Day, for Henry Ford was an unashamed male chauvinist, in an age when few men were not.

"We expect the young ladies to get married," he explained blithely to a reporter who asked him why his plan made no provision for female workers; and though this omission was soon rectified, it scarcely altered the basic philosophy of Henry Ford.

"I consider women only a temporary factor in industry," he informed the readers of *Ladies' Home Journal* in 1923. "Their real job in life is to get married, have a home and raise a family. I pay our women well so they can dress attractively and get married."[48]

Still, Henry Ford employed more women than did most other employers in Detroit, and at better wages. By the standards of contemporary enlightenment he operated at quite a high wattage.

He was even more progressive when it came to the employment of the handicapped. As hiring started under the Five Dollar Day, the Ford employment office was instructed that only contagious disease was a reason for turning men away. Work should be found for cripples to do, and John Lee had his data on the 7,882 different jobs in the plant analysed so that they could be matched to the needs of specific physical disabilities.

By 1919 Ford was employing 9,563 men and women with some kind of handicap—out of a total work force of 44,569. One had no hands, 4 had lost both legs or feet, 4 were totally blind, 37 were deaf and dumb, 60 were epileptics, 1,560 had hernias. There was a special, segregated building for workers who had contracted tuberculosis. All these cripples and invalids were paid the full rate of pay, with profit-sharing bonus.[49] Few of these employees could have got work anywhere else but Highland Park, and Henry Ford liked to boast that their gratitude inspired them to repay him with added productivity.

Wearing his hard-boiled boss's bowler hat, he liked to claim the same for the 400 to 600 ex-convicts that he also employed, many of them paroled early from prison by a private arrangement with the courts. These redeemed criminals gave him a better day's effort, he would say, than his

law-abiding workers. He was not doing anybody any favours
—though when not playing Mr. Gradgrind, Henry Ford
would confess to attempting a little human reprogramming:

Blindfold me and lead me down there into the street and let me
lay my hands by chance on the most shiftless and worthless fellow
in the crowd and I'll bring him in here, give him a job with a wage
that offers him some hope for the future, some prospect of living a
decent, comfortable and self-respecting life, and I'll guarantee that
I'll make a man out of him.[50]

Adam Smith had preached capitalism as the handmaiden
of the common good, and in the happy and heady years in
which Henry Ford now found himself leading capitalism up
onto a new plateau, he had no doubt that the wealth generated by his moving assembly line was having a genuine
moral impact on mankind. The people's car had led to the
moving assembly line, and now the moving line was in turn
revealing itself to be an engine of enormous potency for
Henry Ford, the social engineer.

"Books, mechanics, commerce, and science, the motor
car," declared Henry, all were creating a fresh dimension
in the workplace that was bringing about new ways of
thinking and doing—"a new world, a new heaven, and a
new earth."[51]

One week after the announcement of the Five Dollar Day,
the *Detroit Times* sent a reporter to investigate the impact of
the new scheme upon Ford workers, and it seemed to him
that heaven had come down to relocate itself in Highland
Park.

"Enemies are friends, universal brotherhood has come
with industrial freedom," he declared. As he walked around
the factory, he was sure that, above the roar of machinery,
he could detect "a faint happy sound that is the singing of
happy men." Ford workers, he reported, could now be
recognized by a new set of distinguishing marks: "a lightness
of step, a smile that glows through the mask of oil and dirt,
a lifting of tired shoulders, a gleam of manhood to eyes that

167

were weary."[52] Utopia, it appeared, had been achieved at a stroke.

The men who actually got their faces covered with oil and dirt, eight hours a day, six days a week, have recorded less glowing memories—like the recruitment parade inside Highland Park where, stripped naked "like a bunch of cattle at a stock show," new workers underwent a minute and humiliating physical examination. "I could not help but think," wrote one of them, "that once a year the Ford Motor Company's high executives from Mr. Ford on down should make a similar display."[53]

Charles A. Madison was a worker who left the Dodge Brothers' plant in pursuit of high wages at the beginning of 1914 when the Five Dollar Day was announced. But after only a week at Highland Park, he returned to Dodge. He had not realized he would have to work six months before qualifying for his profit-sharing bonus, and even at $5.00 a day he decided he could never work at Ford. He had intellectual tastes and had felt "too fatigued after leaving the Ford factory to do any serious reading or attend a play or concert."

Madison settled for $3.00 a day, the more relaxed and friendly atmosphere of the Dodge plant, and the energy and appetite for some life of his own after he had clocked out from work. His brief week at Ford remained in his mind

a rancorous memory—a form of hell on earth that turned human beings into driven robots. I resented the thought that Ford publicists had made the company seem beneficent and imaginative when in fact the firm exploited its employees more ruthlessly than any of the other automobile firms, dominating their lives in ways that deprived them of privacy and individuality.[54]

Madison had found himself shadowed by stopwatch wielders and harassed by his foreman, who seemed harassed in turn by his own superiors. The only way Madison could keep up with his production schedule, he discovered, was to work right through his eight-hour shift without a break,

munching on a sandwich while endeavouring to keep pace
with his machine—"no allowance was made for lunch, toilet
time, or tool sharpening"—and once he had proved capable
of maintaining that rate for a day, working flat out and
pushing himself to the limit, he was ordered to work still
faster.[55]

Madison was a victim of "speed-up," the new word that
had entered the workingman's language with the introduction of the continuously moving assembly line. Sales decided
to cut prices, Production decided to increase volume, and,
down on the line, the ordinary worker found that the belt
was moving past him just a little faster, and that the foreman
was asking for just one extra component or so every hour—
a dozen or so extra per day.

"The chain system you have is a *slave driver*!" wrote the
wife of one worker to Henry Ford on January 23, 1914. "*My
God!* Mr. Ford. My husband has come home & thrown
himself down & won't eat his supper—so done out! Can't
it be remedied? . . . . That $5 a day is a blessing—a bigger
one than you know but *oh* they earn it."[56]

Five dollars' worth of work meant five dollars' worth of
pressure—and of discipline. In the same month that the
new, enlightened system of profit-sharing was announced,
900 Ford employees were dismissed because, as Greeks and
Russians of the Orthodox faith, they had taken time off work
to celebrate Christmas as it fell by their Orthodox calendar
—in January.[57] God and "efficiency engineering" did not
always go together.

Late in 1915 the Reverend Samuel Marquis left his Detroit
Parish to work full-time for the Ford Sociological Department, and he found that the criticism most frequently made
of the Five Dollar Day was that it had paid off. It put
more dollars into Henry Ford's pocket than he paid out,
complained other employers that the minister talked to, so
it amounted to no more than "a crafty scheme for getting
more work out of his men"[58]—and the Reverend Marquis
would agree with this: "Mr. Ford . . . never maintained that

his profit and bonus schemes were a means for distributing charity."[59] Working in his own self-interest, Henry Ford had appealed to the self-interest of his workers—to their mutual profit.[60]

The statistics were impressive. Valued at $3.25 million at the beginning of 1914, the homes of Ford workers were valued at over $20 million two years later, and though this 900 percent increase was partly a function of inflation and the growing size of the Highland Park work force, it principally reflected an improvement in living conditions. The proportion of "poor" homes in the local housing stock fell from 20 percent to 2 percent, while average savings in bank accounts and real-estate equities rose in the same period from $196 to $750 per worker.[61]

"It would almost have required the use of a rifle in order to separate the average Ford employee from the payroll," observed Leslie McDonnell, a Ford worker who noted how Highland Park employees had come to display their plant badges with all the ostentation of Masonic lodge members in their regalia.[62] With his pay in his pocket, the Ford employee found himself the most desired object of Detroit shops and business houses. The cartoonists' fantasies of fur-coated workers had turned out to be not that far from reality.

This was the enduring significance of the Five Dollar Day. Within a few years, inflation was to erode its stunning, seemingly impossible magnitude as a recompense for eight hours' labour. Other Detroit factories were soon to pay as much, once they had caught up with Henry Ford's production methods, while the benevolence of the Sociological Department was to wilt with time.

But the principle that workers in high-profit, high-volume industry should be paid high wages endured in America, because, as the labour leader Walter Reuther put it, "mass consumption makes mass production possible."[63] Wage earners were also wage spenders, and, twenty years before Keynes, Henry Ford demonstrated the importance of consumption in fuelling economic growth.

The Five Dollar Day was the answer to capitalism's dilemma at the beginning of the twentieth century: who was going to buy all the artefacts that entrepreneurs had developed the capacity to produce? The answer was right in front of them, working at the machines inside their factories, and the ramifications of paying out a higher proportion of profits in wages—and, later, in other benefits—extended far beyond the simple economic mechanisms of production, consumption, and exchange.

In 1917 the Russian Revolution was to generate a new moving force in twentieth-century history, but three years prior to that Henry Ford had demonstrated at Highland Park how workers need not become the enemies of big business. High wages could turn them into partners and accomplices—shareholders in capitalism to a genuine, integrated degree that extended far beyond the pious terminology of profit-sharing schemes. Whether the employer liked it or not—and the day was to come when Henry Ford did *not* like it—the payment of a decent, living, spending wage was to become the prerequisite for the survival of modern, Western free enterprise.

The Five Dollar Day raised the pain threshold of capitalism, and the history of the last seventy years suggests it is possible to say rather more for it than that. Through birds, Burroughs, Emerson, an appetite for profits—and just plain luck—Henry Ford had unwittingly stumbled on a new set of economic laws. Hailed and cursed for his role in enslaving the modern world to the automobile and to mass production, he must also stand at the bar of history for afflicting modern mass society with yet a further mixed blessing: affluence.

# 8

## THE PEACE SHIP

*Some people must dream broadly and guilelessly, if only to balance those who never dream at all.*

—ARTHUR M. SCHLESINGER. JR.[1]

*Our spontaneous acteoin* [sic] *is always best. . . . You have got to keep doing and going.*

—JOTTING FROM HENRY FORD'S NOTEBOOKS[2]

On the summer's evening in 1906 when Henry Ford had been driving home in triumph, exultant finally to have bought out Alex Malcomson and thus win control of the company that bore his own name, he had sketched an ambitious picture of the blessings that his people's car could bestow upon mankind. "If you get people together so that they get acquainted with one another . . . ," he had promised Fred Rockelman sitting beside him, "the car will have a universal effect. We won't have any more strikes or wars."[3]

Americans greeted the outbreak of the Great War in Europe in August 1914 less with horror than with disbelief, for the dozen or so preceding years, which had been a twilight for Europe's empires, had been a time of exuberance and vital growth on the other side of the Atlantic—the bright and hopeful dawning of a new century. So when Americans heard about the grim slaughter in the trenches, and the obscure Balkan disputes that had provoked it, it seemed to them incredible "that such an archaic institution should be revived in modern Europe."[4]

In the United States this was the progressive era. Woodrow Wilson had just been elected President, and he had chosen "The Great Commoner," William Jennings Bryan, the Populist presidential candidate of the 1890s, to be his

Secretary of State. Finally given the opportunity to put his pacifist principles into practice, Bryan had devoted much of his energy to the negotiation of "cooling-off" treaties in which America used her good offices around the world to persuade quarrelsome countries to refrain from fighting for twelve months while their complaints were investigated. Bryan supervised nearly thirty such treaties, which he prized as his greatest achievement. To the American ambassador involved in each successful negotiation, he would send a congratulatory paperweight beaten from an old War Department sword into the shape of a ploughshare.[5]

With optimism, naivety, and a fair amount of arrogance, America assumed that her own national experience was the pattern for constructive integration which the whole world would eventually follow. "The United States," declared "Old Gray" in *The New Nobility*, the best-selling novel which articulated so many American assumptions at the end of the nineteenth century, "is merely a model in small for the United States of the world."[6]

This Americanization of human progress conveniently ignored the fact that the greatest bloodletting anywhere on earth in the fifty years prior to 1914 had been the American Civil War. Its trauma lay at the root of a broad consensus of pacifism that married well with the country's traditional isolationism, especially in the farm belt, whose assumptions Henry Ford shared.

"To my mind," he told the *New York Times* early in 1915, echoing his childhood readings of McGuffey, "the word 'murderer' should be embroidered in red letters across the breast of every soldier."[7] Wars were the consequence, he declared, of secret manipulation by moneylenders and munitions makers. Wall Street, he suspected darkly, had a great deal to do with it.[8]

Henry developed this populist theme in June 1915, when he called a press conference to announce a successful outcome to his ongoing quest to apply the internal-combustion engine to the land. After half a dozen years of experiments, he thought he had finally worked out a practicable tractor he could offer to the farmers of America, and he felt that the productivity this would stimulate had a wider dimension. Thanks to his tractor, small farmers could keep working their land. "If we can keep our people working," he said, "America will never be dragged into war. . . . The parasite known as the absentee owner fosters war. New York wants war. New York wants war, but the United States doesn't. The people west of New York are too sensible for war."[9]

It occurred to the editor of the *Detroit Free Press* that there might be a good article in the local carmaker's thoughts on the European war, and he despatched Theodore Delavigne, one of his brighter young reporters, to get the story. Delavigne had quite recently distinguished himself by identifying a clock in the Highland Park offices as of English manufacture, and this mechanical connoisseurship had won him Henry's special attention. So the eager young writer was soon taking notes on the Ford view of war as he wandered at the great man's side through the wild acres of Dearborn forest which Henry had brought together as his own private bird sanctuary.

The Ford Motor Company had become quite international since it sold its sixth car to Canada in 1903. Ford factories and agencies were springing up in England, France, and other corners of the world. In 1912 Henry had visited his English and French operations in an extended summer expedition with Clara and Edsel, and this seems to have made him specially conscious of his international influence. He would rather burn a factory down, he said, than let it produce cars that might be used for military purposes, and he declared himself ready to finance a "world-wide campaign for universal peace" to the tune of $1 million. In fact, he would do better than this. He was willing to "give everything I possess" if he could stop war and the stockpiling of arms in America.

"You mean that, Mr. Ford?" asked the red-headed Delavigne, scenting the main line of his story.

"Yes sir, in heaven's name, I do," replied Henry, blithely

authorizing Delavigne to take everything he had said and put it all down, as he saw fit, in his own words.[10]

The story was headlines in the *Free Press* next morning—HENRY FORD TO PUSH WORLD-WIDE CAMPAIGN FOR UNIVERSAL PEACE: Will Devote Life and Fortune to Combat Spirit of Militarism Now Rampant—and, like the story of the Five Dollar Day a year earlier, it was picked up by newspapers all over the country. Early in September 1915, a follow-up from Delavigne's flowing pen gave more details: there would be money to endow a prize for the writing of an antiwar history, and a programme of investments all over the world to encourage the production of farm tractors and other "implements of peaceful labor." Henry thought that there was money to be made from peace, and he argued pacifism as embodying the same paradox as his famous wage increase of the previous year. To do the moral thing might appear utopian, but it was, in reality, the hardheaded route to increased prosperity and profits.

The Five Dollar Day, however, had not been the idea of Henry Ford alone. It had evolved from his discussions with the very shrewd engineers and businessmen who ran Ford with him on a day-to-day basis, in contrast to his pacifist notions which were steaming directly out of his own head. These were untempered by anyone else's reflection or debate —James Couzens, indeed, was fiercely opposed to his colleague's views—and the lure of money for peace projects provoked approaches from all manner of eccentrics and charlatans. Every one of these was screened and firmly rejected by Ernest Liebold, the stiff, Germanic private secretary who had taken over the running of Henry's private office from Frank Klingensmith, and who had found much of his time taken up with protecting his master from the consequences of his own generosity.

Liebold was out of town, however, inspecting Ford branches in the Denver area when Madame Rosika Schwimmer presented herself at Highland Park on November 17, 1915.

A dark-haired, square-jawed Jewish Hungarian, Rosika

Schwimmer was not exactly in the charlatan class. She had campaigned sincerely and energetically for peace and for women's rights in Europe, and she was in Detroit completing a lecture tour of America propagating these causes. But the aggressiveness and paranoia which surrounded Madame Schwimmer's good intentions had alienated steadier pillars of the American peace movement like Jane Addams, the pioneer social worker who was later to become a Nobel Peace Laureate. Every project espoused by Madame Schwimmer came, somehow, to revolve around the flamboyant and erratic personality of Madame Schwimmer herself. Her ability to inspire those exposed to her impassioned eloquence tended to generate heat rather than light, and this proved the case when Rosika Schwimmer was ushered into the presence of Henry Ford in November 1915 to explain her recipe for ending the war in Europe. She carried with her, in a voluminous black handbag, notes of conversations she had held with various European leaders, and these provided proof, she maintained, that a genuine wish for peace existed on both sides of the conflict. She felt sure that an independent, neutral peace initiative from the outside would receive a warm welcome from the combatant governments, and she invited Henry Ford to become the sponsor of this initiative.

Henry Ford proved, over the years, to have something of a weakness for strong women who knew what they wanted from him. Clara Ford might be "The Believer," but she always seems to have kept her husband healthily in awe of her, and the same proved the case with Rosika Schwimmer. Henry invited her to join him for lunch after their first meeting on Wednesday, November 17, 1915. Next day she was granted another interview, and on the following day, Friday, November 19, she was invited to his home, together with the journalist Theodore Delavigne and Louis Lochner, a young peace worker from Chicago who had been a student activist and now supported a peace plan which was similar to Madame Schwimmer's, but which also called for official U.S. government involvement. Delavigne and Lochner were evidently intended as counterweights to the overwhelming

Madame Schwimmer. Henry also enlisted his firmest buttress of all.

"I think I'd like my wife's judgement on this," he said, and left Rosika "to talk things over" with Clara, while he nimbly skipped out for a drive around Dearborn to show off his tractor experiments to the two men.

But on his return, Henry discovered that Clara had been as captivated by Rosika Schwimmer as he was. It was agreed that he would travel to New York that very weekend to work out the details of his own contribution to the initiative with the leaders of the American peace movement, and a fruitful and extraordinary day was rounded off by the twenty-two-year-old Edsel Ford, who entertained the assorted peace crusaders with a virtuoso performance on his set of drums.[11]

It was on the long train journey from Detroit to New York that Louis Lochner first began to wonder whether Henry Ford's sponsorship represented a totally unmixed blessing for the American peace movement. As Henry explained his ideas, he used the young man as a sounding board, watching him closely while he tried out various epigrams and slogans —"Men sitting around a table, not men dying in a trench will finally settle the differences"—and when he sensed an encouraging response he would say, "Make a note of that; we'll give that to the boys when we get to New York."[12] By "the boys" Henry Ford meant the press.

Since the Selden Patent Suit, Henry Ford had developed a voracious appetite for reading stories in the papers about himself. In 1913 his name still had not made it to the American *Who's Who*, but the publicity attending the Five Dollar Day had transformed him into a national celebrity whose views were sought by journalists on every subject— and Henry loved it. He had proved, in fact, to have rather a flair for publicity. After fifty years of obscurity, he had stepped out onto the public stage with a ready-rounded instinct for the telling phrase or gesture that newsmen could turn into a story. The previous summer he had promised

Ford customers their own form of "profit-sharing"—a re-
bate on any new car they purchased if Ford sales exceeded
300,000 units in the year—and he had made good his
promise: a refund to every purchaser of some $50.[13] Now he
was searching for a similar grand gesture in his two-day-old
commitment to the peace campaign.

The opportunity came before the end of his first meeting
over lunch with Jane Addams, Lochner, Schwimmer, and
other peace activists on Monday, November 22, 1915. The
main topic of discussion was the nature and agenda of the
delegation that America should send to conciliate in Europe,
and someone mentioned, half in jest, the idea of chartering
a special ship for the purpose. Until this point Henry Ford
had been conspicuous for his silence—the complicated discussions as to who should do precisely what and when had
been serious and detailed—but with the mention of a special
"peace ship" he came to life. It was a grand yet simple
gesture that everyone would understand. It cut through all
the complexities in appealing and dramatic terms. Henry
could see the front pages already.

His lunch companions were not enthusiastic. Jane
Addams disliked the idea as flamboyant. Henry was due to
go to Washington the next day, in any case, to meet President
Wilson and encourage him to put some official weight behind
a peace initiative from America. That would represent really
solid progress, and it would be foolish to compromise anything that might come out of the meeting with the President.

Henry Ford listened to the objections, went back to his
hotel, and ignored them completely. He summoned steamship agents to his suite, and by that evening he had taken
over most of the first-and second-class accommodation on
the *Oscar II*, a vessel of the Scandinavian-American line that
was due to leave New York in just eleven days' time.

President Wilson had not been very keen to see Henry
Ford, and his eventual consent to a meeting on Tuesday,
November 23, 1915, was principally for public-relations
purposes. Granting the car-maker an audience was an easy

way to demonstrate his concern for peace without having to do anything concrete about it, and when he met Henry, he was flabbergasted not only to be invited aboard the Peace Ship—about which he knew nothing—but to have the invitation extended to his son-in-law, Secretary of the Treasury William McAdoo, Mrs. McAdoo, and another daughter, Margaret Wilson. The President should bring them all along for the ride, suggested Henry Ford, next Saturday week.

"The President is a small man," muttered Henry Ford to Louis Lochner as he left the White House, evidently surprised that Wilson should not wish to entrust his personal prestige and that of the American government to the vague and unpredictable fate of Henry's Peace Ship. The carmaker felt he had done his best to put the President at ease, lolling with one leg over the arm of his chair and telling the latest Ford joke about the man who asked to be buried in his Model T because it had pulled him out of every other hole he had been in. This had elicited a limerick from the President in response, and Henry could not understand how such convivial beginnings had led to a blank refusal.

There was more disappointment in store. Henry had promised reporters that he would have a peace story for them by the following day, Wednesday, November 24, and he had one of his slogans ready: "We'll get the boys in the trenches home by Christmas." He felt sure that this promise, coupled with the drama of his Peace Ship, would guarantee generous coverage, with or without the co-operation of the President.

Louis Lochner, however, was apprehensive. He had already noted Henry's preference for sensation over solid thought, and how this was often coupled to a surprising shyness when dealing with people en masse. Fluent and persuasive in the presence of two or three respectful listeners, Henry Ford could become tongue-tied and awkward in front of a crowd. He fidgeted and stammered, and his self-confidence evaporated. Public speaking was not included in his repertory of talents.

Lochner's solution was to bring in a sympathetic expert,

Oswald Garrison Villard, editor of the *Evening Post*, to offer some professional advice, and Villard tried to modify Henry's impossible "home by Christmas" pledge. The *Oscar II* was not scheduled to dock in Europe until December 16 at the earliest.

But the Ford performance was unimpressive:

"Well, boys, I've got the ship . . ."

"What ship, Mr. Ford?"

"Why, the *Oscar II*."

"Well, what are you going to do with her?"

"We're going to stop the war."

"Going to stop the war?"

"Yes, we're going to get the boys out of the trenches by Christmas."

"But how are you going to do it?"

"Oh, you'll see."

"Where are you going?"

"I don't know."

"What country will you head for?"

"I don't know."

"But what makes you think you can put it over?"

"Oh, we have had assurances."[14]

It was a dismal, embarrassing display—"so extraordinary," wrote Villard later, "that I have no parallel to it in all my experience."[15] Cornered in the first minute, Henry had tried to deflect questioning to Villard and Lochner beside him, but his evasion only made his interrogators the more insistent, and their doubts were reflected in the coverage next day. GREAT WAR ENDS CHRISTMAS DAY: FORD TO STOP IT, sneered the *New York Tribune*.[16] Henry had got his front-page attention, but hardly in the fashion he had predicted. "Repeated questions," reported the *Detroit Free Press*, "disclosed not the slightest evidence that Mr. Ford has a definite plan as to what he is going to do when he gets to Europe."[17]

This was no more nor less than the truth. Henry Ford's biographers have customarily placed the blame for the failure of the Peace Ship upon the eccentricities of Rosika

Schwimmer, and certainly her melodramatic style made things worse. When Henry had talked of "assurances" at his press conference, he had been referring to the documents that she carried in her handbag, and which she refused to allow anybody to see.

But it was Henry's own decision to attach his name to such flimsy stuff, and the indecent rush with which the Peace Ship was chartered was his responsibility alone. His developing addiction to personal publicity had led him to confuse genuine action with the more glamorous but empty facsimile of action enshrined in the newspaper headline. And this was one occasion when Emerson did not serve him well: spontaneity and impulse were better suited to other problems.

Peace sounded a simple idea, but it was not. Henry Ford had set himself to tackle a vexed and complex conundrum that was peculiarly resistant to the bold and wilful approach that had served him so well in other situations. His peace crusade was doomed from the start as a viable initiative— though, as a media event, of course, it made wonderful news, since failure often makes a better story than success. It is certainly more amusing.

The Ford Peace Ship had a propitious name, for Oscar II was the mild-mannered Swedish king who presided over the bloodless separation of Norway from Sweden, and made something of a profession for himself as an arbitrator in international disputes. But the brief deadline before the liner's departure from New York on Saturday, December 4, 1915, provided busy and substantial American peace sympathizers with little more than a week to rearrange their schedules.

Henry had originally hoped to invite a crowd of friends and celebrities to join him on his peace expedition—he had developed quite an appetite for the company of the rich and famous—but his haste provided the perfect excuse for refusal. Thomas Edison and John Wanamaker, the Philadelphia store magnate, had made encouraging noises, but

181

suddenly they had previous engagements. William Jennings Bryan, recently departed from the Wilson administration in protest at "preparedness"—Wilson's willingness to extend solid help to the Allies—was a perfect candidate, but, as the expedition's total absence of guaranteed strategy became obvious, he too made his excuses.

At least the refusal of John Burroughs, the bird-lover, had the virtue of honesty. "Mr. Ford's heart is bigger than his head . . . ," said Burroughs. "He might as well try to hasten Spring as to hasten peace now. I told him as much."[18]

As the date for sailing drew near, others close to Henry Ford echoed the advice of Burroughs, and none more vehemently than Clara Ford, who had had a decided change of heart on the subject of Rosika Schwimmer. The Amazonian activist had turned out to have a sweet tooth for luxury, masterminding the preparations for the voyage from a plush suite in the Biltmore Hotel, firing off cables at the rate of $1,000 a day, and even ordering herself a "peace wardrobe" of evening dresses and fur coats at Henry Ford's expense.

"All I have to do is wave my wand," she told Louis Lochner with delight, ". . . and lo! it appears."[19]

Clara Ford was furious. Rosika Schwimmer had the temerity to send her a necklace as a thank-you for her help in the early stages, and Clara later let her know precisely what she thought of it. "The way Mr. Ford's name and money was used was shameful," she wrote to her, "and you were the leader."[20]

Clara flatly refused to accompany her husband on the *Oscar II*, and she tried to prevent him from sailing as well. It was only six months since the *Lusitania* had gone down. There were mines strung across the sea approaches to Europe, and she had ghastly visions of their only son being left fatherless.[21] In later years Clara was to recall her distress at the Peace Ship as the most miserable period of her marriage. "There were times when I couldn't understand all that he was doing. . . . I wouldn't go . . . but let's not talk about it."[22]

She enlisted the help of her minister from Detroit, the

Reverend Samuel Marquis, and also a young chauffeur-
bodyguard from the Ford factory, Ray Dahlinger, and on
the night before the *Oscar II* was due to leave, Marquis sat
up until dawn with the Fords, trying to dissuade Henry
from sailing.[23]

Marquis failed, but to placate his wife, Henry agreed to
take the minister and Dahlinger on the voyage with him,
one to watch over him spiritually and the other to provide
physical protection. Marquis could see that Henry was
playing a "hunch," and since so many previous Ford
hunches, equally foolhardy, had succeeded, it was difficult
to convince him why this one should fail.

The scene at Hoboken pier on the raw, cold morning of
Saturday, December 4, 1915, fully justified Clara Ford's
fears. "Nobody knew where to go, nobody was in charge of
anything, nobody knew anything," reported the *Detroit Free
Press*.[24]

Rosika Schwimmer had hired a "Social Director" to provide entertainment on the voyage, and, dressed in beret,
smock, and yellow spats, he was stirring up the enthusiasm
of the substantial crowd. There were 15,000 people, by one
account, who came to see the *Oscar II* set sail. Each time the
Social Director spotted anyone of interest walking up the
gangplank, he would raise his megaphone, shout, "Hip,
Hip, Hooray!" and try and coax him to make an impromptu
speech—but he had a thin time of it. The fifty or so crusaders
who had jumped at the chance of a trip to Europe at Henry
Ford's expense were obscure folk on the whole—ministers,
academics, students—and as they milled around on the
quay, among a consignment of office desks ordered too late
by Madame Schwimmer and left behind, there was little to
distinguish them from the ordinary steerage travellers and
eight bewildered first-class passengers who had purchased
tickets on the *Oscar II*, in all innocence, for a routine transatlantic voyage.

Thomas Edison, whom Henry had recently enlisted as a

friend in rather the same way that he had got involved with John Burroughs, did turn up to wish the expedition Godspeed, and Henry tried to persuade him to stay. "I'll give you a million dollars if you'll come," he bellowed into the deaf man's ear. But Edison did not appear to hear him, smiled benignly, and returned to dry land.

Rival bands, on ship and shore, played "I Didn't Raise My Boy to Be a Soldier," Henry Ford threw roses, Clara Ford cried, and two of the delegates chose this moment to get married in the main saloon, so that they could travel together respectably. As one well-wisher, who gave his name as "Mr. Zero," leapt into the icy waters of the Hudson on a demonstration swim for peace, the general atmosphere seemed well symbolized by the mascots sent on board the liner by someone with a sense of fun: two squirrels in a cage. The joke referred to the animals' diet, and to make it clearer, they were accompanied by a large box of raisins "To Go with the Nuts."[25]

The chaos became less amiable once the *Oscar II* lost sight of shore. The overall plan of the expedition was to sail to Norway, and then travel on by land through Sweden, Denmark, and Holland, all neutral countries, where it was hoped that a programme of lectures and meetings would generate a popular demand for peace which the combatant countries could not ignore. But with little to do on the liner except argue out the details of this programme, together with a manifesto that would lend some shape to their nebulous goals, the fifty-five peace delegates were soon at each other's throats. Madame Schwimmer had hired no less than thirty-one administrative staff to service the clerical needs of the venture (along with 20,000 large envelopes, 565 reams of paper, 1,778 pencils, and 5 gross of rubber erasers),[26] and the production and duplication of rival memos and agendas grew fast and furious. All this was watched with great amusement by the vast party of newspapermen on board—there were forty-four journalists travelling at Henry Ford's expense—and their sardonic despatches home set the tone of derision with which the outside world followed the progress of the *Oscar II* across the Atlantic.

Rosika Schwimmer became a particular focus of controversy, making much of the documents in her mysterious black handbag, but obstinately refusing to let anyone see them. She might have fared better with a sense of humour —"Don't be hypocritical!" she snapped when the journalists applauded her appearance at one press conference—and, overflowing with her own importance, she ostentatiously avoided all meals and social gatherings, spending most of her time withdrawn and darkly secluded in her stateroom "like a great spider, weaving the web of her plans"[27]

Henry Ford, by contrast, quite won over his companions. Naive and eccentric though he might be, he was demonstrably sincere, and, unlike Madame Schwimmer, he did not give himself airs.

"I came to make fun of the whole thing," said one reporter, "but my editor is going to have the surprise of his life. . . . I believe in Henry Ford and I'm going to say so."[28]

Less accustomed than they might pretend to daily contact with multimillionaires, the journalists were impressed by Henry's willingness to spend time talking with them, and they were disarmed by his innocence—"a mechanical genius with the heart of a child."[29] One went so far as to compare him to Lincoln, and even to "a sort of inarticulate Christ."[30] On the seventh day out of New York, the press corps held a meeting to discuss how to extricate their newfound hero from the disaster to which the Peace Ship was clearly heading.

"The men are going to see Henry Ford through on this deal," cabled the representative of the *New York Tribune*, "no matter what happens to the party. . . . Ford is a white man —and most emphatically sincere. We ought to know, we lived with him. And we are not hypnotized."[31]

It was twelve degrees below zero when the *Oscar II* finally reached Norway, docking at Oslo on December 18, 1915, in the small hours of the morning. Henry Ford insisted on walking through the dark and snowy streets to his hotel, where he promptly collapsed. He had started a cold during the voyage when a rogue wave had washed over him, and his protectors, Marquis and Dahlinger, were rightly concerned about his health. They tucked him up in bed in a suite that could only be reached through their rooms, and when the Norwegian press were finally summoned to his presence on December 22—the day when, coincidentally, the expedition's bespatted Social Director actually died of pneumonia that he had contracted during the voyage—they discovered a disoriented, weakened man, dressed in his nightshirt and quite disinclined to talk about his Peace Ship.

Henry was back on the subject of his tractor again, and of how he hoped that this would lift drudgery from mankind. It would revitalize postwar Europe, he explained, and, since he had not patented the invention, it also offered armament manufacturers an alternative source of profit. His hope was that they might give up making rifles and convert their factories to tractor production instead.

"He must be a very great man," pondered one of his hearers, "who permits himself to utter such foolishness."[32]

At four o'clock the following morning, Henry Ford's steamer trunks were sent down from his room. Samuel Marquis had learned that there was a liner returning from Bergen to New York later that day, and Henry, weakened and dispirited, did not argue with his pastor's feeling that he should be on it.

"Guess I had better go home," he said, "to Mother."[33]

Rosika Schwimmer, still up at that hour drafting yet another document, got wind of her patron's departure and organized an interception party down in the hotel lobby. But Ray Dahlinger and Samuel Marquis joined forces to form a "flying wedge" out through the doors to a waiting taxi, and with an undignified scuffle and shouts of "Kidnapping!" Henry Ford abruptly took his leave of the peace companions that he had first met in Detroit little more than one month previously.

*

Travelling back home across the Atlantic, Henry Ford did some serious talking to Samuel Marquis about the Peace Ship, and why he had risked so much upon it.

"I do not want the things money can buy," he said. "I want to live a life, to make the world a little better for having lived in it."[34]

Marquis reflected that Ford would stand a better chance of achieving his ambition if he avoided areas where he had no experience. He should "follow the example of a good shoemaker," thought the minister, "and stick to his last."[35]

Both men braced themselves for yet more ridicule when they got home, since Henry's desertion had effectively removed whatever slight chance of success his peace initiative had ever had. Yet the failure of the Peace Ship produced a surprising turn of sentiment in America. "No matter if he failed," declared the *New York American*, admitting that it had lampooned Henry Ford as much as anyone had in the recent weeks, "he at least TRIED."[36] Henry returned home wreathed with the pathos of a Don Quixote. It was better "a thousand times [to] be branded a fool in the service of humanity," declared the Rabbi Joseph Krauskopf of Philadelphia, "than be hailed a hero for having shed rivers of blood"[37]—and most Americans agreed with him.

Small-town newspapers editorialized particularly in favour of the carmaker. The *Springfield Republican* hailed him as "God's Fool," while the *Saginaw Herald* compared him to the farmer who stood on the railtracks to defy the train. People might not respect his judgement, "but they admire his nerve and extend him sympathy."[38] The Peace Ship joined the Selden Patent Suit and the Five Dollar Day as components in the legend of Henry Ford—the small man fighting for his principles against the world—and grass-roots America loved him the more.

Henry Ford, however, loved himself the less. He always liked to claim that ridicule did not bother him: "the more criticism that comes the better," he declared in conformity with Emerson's teaching, "by criticism I get my education."[39] But he was whistling in the dark. The failure of the Peace

187

Ship hurt Henry Ford very deeply, and unable to accept his own responsibility for it, he looked around for others to blame.

Rosika Schwimmer was an obvious target, and in the most unpleasant way. In later years Henry Ford's virulent anti-Semitic campaigns were to make up one of the darker chapters in his life, and he would hark back to his ill-starred adventure with the Hungarian Jewess as the beginning of it all. The Peace Ship incident, he would maintain, was the first time he had personal experience of the mischievous links between radicalism and the Jews; and though he continued to support his peace commission for some time after he had abandoned it to its own devices in Norway (Henry was to spend nearly half a million dollars supporting the project before the participants themselves threw in the towel in 1917), his relations were all conducted through Louis Lochner, not the woman whose inspiration first got him involved.

The Peace Ship was the first obvious failure that Henry Ford had experienced for many years, and his ego had got used to an unremitting diet of success. He had come to take adulation for granted, and ridicule caught him off guard, though he would never admit it. It soured his once-fresh and sprightly optimism—and the humiliation was to prove a turning point in his life. Increasingly suspicious and embittered, Henry Ford began to show that his idealism had a darker side.

# 9

# BLOOD MONEY

Soon after Henry Ford became a public figure, the *New York Herald* sent one of its writers, William Richards, to ask ten questions of the carmaker. The plan was to print the great man's replies just as he gave them, one to ten.

Henry came up with good, strong answers to four of the questions, but there were four more to which he firmly declined to respond. He did not know the answers to those, he said, and he dismissed the ninth question as a trick—which Richards had to admit it was. So that left the final question, query ten, as a last chance to salvage at least half the content of the quiz.

"Mr. Ford," inquired William Richards, "the *Herald* wishes to know how you feel to be the world's first billionaire."

Henry Ford had not, in fact, quite attained billionaire status at this time, but he had reached a high plateau of wealth where the distinction was fairly irrelevant, and he endeavoured for a moment to address his mind to the question, squirming in his chair and twisting a leg over one arm of it, before abandoning the effort.

"Oh, shit!" he replied,[1] and the *New York Herald* had to make do with just four answers to its quiz.

The people's car had made Henry Ford very rich indeed. By the beginning of January 1916, when Henry got home from his Peace Ship expedition, the Ford Motor Company had paid out some $52 million in dividends to its stockholders, and Henry's personal share of that was over $30 million[2]—received, until 1913, totally free of income tax.

Money itself never mattered that much to Henry Ford. He cared very much about power, and he obviously cared about his cars. But beyond having an apparently limitless

189

wardrobe of immaculately tailored grey suits, which he wore crisp and pressed every day, he enjoyed few indulgences. He was not obviously a greedy man. For someone who had had to watch every dollar for four fifths of his life, Henry Ford displayed a remarkable indifference to material things. Searching through the pockets of one of his suits one day, his wife, Clara, came across a cheque which he had not cashed—for $75,000.

The Fords had taken their time building and moving into a home of their own, 66 Edison Avenue, a self-important stone-trimmed mansion not far from Highland Park—and they did not stay there very long.[3] The problem was people, for the publicity generated by the Five Dollar Day transformed their lives. Newspapermen, job seekers, do-gooders, speculators—an endless succession of mendicants haunted their front porch, taking up station as early as six o'clock in the morning, and it was quite impossible to go out for a walk at any time of day.

As Samuel Marquis told it, taking the air with Henry Ford in the years after January 1914 was rather like promenading with the Sun King through the suppliants at Versailles.[4]

"People are always stopping Mr. Ford," complained Clara, "asking for a million dollars."[5]

Clara Ford never cared greatly for public attention, and after a while even her husband's appetite for it grew jaded. The problem was where to go to get away from it. As inner Detroit became more and more industrialized in the first two decades of the century, the men who had made their money from the grime and congestion started the exodus that was to become one of the main dynamics of the city's history. More and more of the grand mansions along Woodward Avenue were getting torn down to be replaced by offices and shops, and the merchant princes were moving out with their families, usually towards the east.

Detroit's original drift to the suburbs was in the direction of Grosse Pointe, which had been brought into commuting distance by the motorcar and the surfaced roadway:

America's first-ever concrete street had been laid in Detroit in 1909.[6] Grosse Pointe was leafy, peaceful, and exclusive, and Henry Ford decided to join the flock of prominent Detroiters who were building their homes there. He purchased 300 acres of lake frontage and commissioned plans for a grand house and estate.

But then Henry had second thoughts. He had never felt happy with the old families of Detroit—and the feeling was mutual. The Five Dollar Day had earned him pariah status in the eyes of the local business establishment, and it was difficult to see Henry receiving a very warm welcome in the Grosse Pointe Club, whose claims to social preeminence were indicated by its recent change of name to the Country Club of Detroit. The obvious place for the Dearborn boy was in Dearborn, and that was the conclusion to which Henry himself soon came. He had been buying up land there, in any case, since 1908 to provide peace and seclusion for his beloved birds. Why should he not share a little of it with them?

So in February 1914, work began on a new home for Henry Ford in the middle of the woods at Dearborn. He decided to name it Fair Lane, after the area in Cork which had been the home of his mother's adoptive father, Patrick O'Hern—the grandfather who first gave him his love of birds.[7] The new house promised to be a spectacular work of architecture, since Henry's nonconformist instincts led him to commission the design from the Chicago office of Frank Lloyd Wright. Wright's "Prairie school" specialized in unconventional, modern responses to a natural setting, and Fair Lane's forested situation on a rise overlooking the Rouge River offered the wild style of Midwest backdrop which inspired some of the architect's most dramatic work.

But in 1909 Frank Lloyd Wright had run off to Europe with the wife of one of his clients, leaving his office in the hands of a young German, Hermann von Holst, and Henry did not like von Holst's designs. He turned them over to be modified by a Pittsburgh interior decorator, William H. Van Tine, who had made his reputation as an efficient supervisor of building works rather than as a designer,[8] and the result was a catastrophe: a heavy, brooding hodgepodge of styles, part Victorian mausoleum, part Spanish hacienda. Built of dismal grey limestone blocks, Fair Lane would have looked depressing anywhere, but it was particularly lumpish when deposited upon the banks of the River Rouge.

Fair Lane cost the Fords over $1 million (some $30 to $40 million in today's values), and there was only one beautiful room in the entire building: the powerhouse. This was a spare, clean chamber which Henry had designed himself —he had been an electrical engineer, after all, until motorcars had sidetracked him—and he created a very Ritz of power stations, all marble and gleaming brass dials and pipes. Around the floor were set out little generators, raised on plinths like so many modern sculptures, and all of them were powered from a fourteen-foot waterfall that had been created by damming the Rouge outside.

The Fair Lane turbines, in fact, generated enough electricity to provide power for the whole of Dearborn for many years, and the first room that Henry showed visitors was always his powerhouse. The equipment even comprised a socket into which Clara could insert the plug of her electric car. Regularly redecorated, its metalwork rubbed and cherished every day, the high-vaulted room was like a place of worship for Henry Ford, a chapel to his own peculiar movings of the spirit, and at the top of the green-painted walls was set a row of brass grilles depicting robins who smiled down on it all—homage to the Emersonian reassurance which Henry needed, that the mechanical strivings of technology were ultimately in harmony with nature.[9]

Henry's private power station was connected to the main house by an underground tunnel lined with massed pipes and cables—three quarters of a mile of brass tubing went into Fair Lane and 135 miles of electric conduit[10]—and the mansion was amply provided with creature comforts. Every bathroom had four taps yielding well-water and rainwater, both hot and cold, as well as nozzles which shot out hot air for hair-drying on command. The marble benches around the indoor swimming pool were continually warmed to comfort the posteriors of those who sat upon them, and the same heating pipes extended outside to prevent the 500 birdbaths scattered around the estate from freezing up in winter. Henry's personal retreat inside the house was a "Field Room" lined with rough-hewn timbers to give the impression one had entered a log cabin somewhere out in the Michigan woods. "Chop your own wood," admonished a huge beam over the fireplace which Henry had carved with a saying of Thoreau's, "and it will warm you twice."

Fair Lane was large and comfortable, but it was scarcely lush or glamorous. For all its size, the house was rather homely. Its principal attraction for Henry was being a few steps from the Dearborn woods that surrounded it—and many of the mansion's more opulent features, like the heated swimming pool, were provided not for Henry and Clara themselves but for young Edsel Ford. The boy who in Edison Avenue had slept in a bedroom off his parents' room[11] was now given his own suite of rooms—complete with a sleeping porch looking out over the river—a full-size bowling alley beside the swimming pool, a billiard room whose table had a tasteful oyster-grey baize, and the lion's share of the gardens, which were landscaped for his benefit into a private golf course. Henry and Clara Ford dearly loved their only son, and when they moved into their new home in January 1916, they looked forward to many happy years of sharing it with him.


Edsel Bryant Ford got his own car when he was eight years old. In the absence of a legal minimum driving age, he drove himself to and from school in it, and he spent hours tinkering in the workshop that his father equipped for him; filling his schoolbooks with drawings of cars.

Edsel was quite a good student—his grades seldom dropped below the B+ level on his report cards—and his marks for Mechanical Drawing and Geometry were an unbroken string of As.[12] But when school was over, the boy liked to drive straight to the Ford factory. He would sling his satchel on a desk in the offices and go off to look at the latest developments in the experimental laboratories. Towards the end of the afternoon, the clerical staff would notice Henry Ford coming into their department to scan their desks. The moment he saw the satchel he would smile and make his way off busily to join his son.

Edsel Ford loved and admired his father hugely, and his affection was reciprocated. Henry Ford displayed unashamed sentimentality towards children throughout his life, and he included his own son in that. Clara and Henry were always most at ease in their own small family unit—they were homebodies—and they seem to have treated their only son as an equal and a companion from the beginning. When the couple took out the Quadricycle for test runs in the 1890s, little Edsel was always with them, muffled up and wedged between his parents on the driver's seat, and as they puttered around Detroit in one of the first horseless carriages ever seen, the three Fords became quite a familiar local sight. They were recognized as a unit.

There had never been any question that Edsel would go into his father's business. Henry always wanted it, and Edsel always wanted what his father wanted. He clearly had the grades to go to college, and there was no financial problem about him going to the most expensive Ivy League school. But Henry's mistrust of higher education applied even more to his son than it did to other people, so Edsel went straight into the business on leaving school. In 1915, aged twenty-one, he was made company secretary and he was given a place on the board of directors. It was taken for granted that he would be taking over the Ford Motor Company one day.

Around the factory people knew him as "Mr. Edsel." He was quiet and modest. He did not throw his weight around. He treated men like Charles Sorensen with the same respect he showed his father—whom he always addressed as "Father," not "Dad"—and, as he moved around Highland Park, discreetly watching and listening, he earned respect himself. Nobody disliked Mr. Edsel.

Physically he resembled his father, though his features were somewhat softer and darker. He was small and neat, and he had the same dapper style of dress. Like Henry, Edsel Ford invariably presented himself to the world in well-cut, fresh-pressed suits. His shoes were custom-built, slightly pointed, with sensible, thick soles, the footwear of an English country gentleman[13]—and there was, indeed, something of the aristocrat about Edsel. For all his modesty, he had self-assurance and a polished, second-generation sense of style.

Samuel Marquis noted the young man's sense of *noblesse oblige*. Marquis was working with Edsel on a Ford committee to organize a new system of profit-sharing—$10 million was due to be distributed throughout the work force—when news came of a threatened electrical cut-off caused by a shortage of coal. This would mean laying off the men and shutting down the factory for an indefinite period, and most of the committee saw little point in continuing to work out the details of how to give away $10 million of company money. But Edsel disagreed.

"If there is a prospect of closing down the plant," he said, "the men will only need the bonus all the more."[14]

Considerate and dutiful to a fault, Edsel Ford imitated his father's habit of keeping notebooks, but his private jottings reveal a freer, more fun-loving character. He had an endearing weakness for bad jokes—"the hen is the only creature that ever got rich by laying around"—and there is also some evidence of a valuable quality which his father did not possess: the ability to laugh at himself.

"Bad headache," runs one entry in a diary he kept on his journey to Europe with his parents in 1912. "Too much Paris."[15]

Edsel made up lists of the latest jazz songs that caught his fancy, and he evidently had romantic yearnings, for as well as "Alexander's Ragtime Band" and "I Want to Be in Dixie," his list included such ballads as "Let's Make Love Among the Roses." On the surface he appeared to be a young man who was quite content with his life, his work hours spent earnestly at the factory, and the pattern of his leisure time still revolving largely around his parents. But one of the snatches of lyric that Edsel Bryant Ford took the trouble to write down in his notebooks suggested he was looking for more in his life than an oyster-grey billiard table and a golf course of his own: "*for every boy whose lonely there's a girl whose lonely too.*"[16]

Miss Annie Ward-Foster taught the social graces to the young rich of Detroit. Her dancing classes were an adolescent rite of passage. Young ladies brought their pink dancing shoes in monogrammed, velvet, drawstring bags and were accompanied by a female chaperone. Young gentlemen wore white gloves, ties, and suits. Miss Ward-Foster, a lively lady of uncertain age, presided over the meeting of the sexes with a watchful eye and a pair of castanets which she would clack firmly at the slightest hint of improper behaviour.

"It is the gentlemen who lead on the dance floor. Ladies *follow*."[17]

Miss Ward-Foster held her dancing classes in a room over the Woman's Exchange, a high-class craft centre whose half-timbered facade squeezed incongruously between the high-rise offices in the middle of Detroit. It was here beside Grand Circus Park that Edsel Ford first met and paid court to an energetic little person whose young life was already crammed with basketball, ice-skating, and all manner of good works.

Miss Eleanor Clay came from one of Detroit's leading commercial families. Joseph L. Hudson, Eleanor's uncle, had arrived from Newcastle-on-Tyne in the middle of the nineteenth century and had taken up shopkeeping with some success, developing a department store which had become one of the premier trading posts of Detroit. A red carpet extended from the front doors of Hudson's imposing emporium on Woodward Avenue to the kerb, and uniformed doormen waited there all day long to help down the ladies who drove up in their carriages. The wealth of the Hudson clan was rather too recent for them to come out of the very top drawer of local society, but no one doubted that they ranked higher than the gasoline aristocracy.

Joseph Hudson looked after his family. When his sister Eliza lost her husband, William Clay, in 1908, he took her into his own home along with her daughters, Eleanor and Josephine, and after his own death in 1912, the girls and their mother went on living in the grand Hudson mansion on Boston Boulevard. One of the lesser benefits that Eleanor Clay was to bring with her marriage into the Ford family was unlimited credit at Hudson's, and a discount on all purchases as well.

The courtship was discreet. Edsel Ford's parents had no thought of their son settling down and marrying at the age of twenty-two. Eleanor Clay still had not graduated from Liggett School, where she was a star pupil, and Miss Liggett wanted her to go on to Vassar. But the two young people evidently knew their own minds, and by the spring of 1916, they had arrived at a private "understanding."

In the summer of 1916, Eleanor Clay helped organize a fete-cum-garden party for Tau Beta, a local philanthropic women's club, and her young friend Katie Shiell, who helped her put on a pageant by the cream of Miss Ward-Foster's dancing pupils, noticed for the first time how close were the attentions being paid to Eleanor by Edsel Bryant Ford. Ellie Clay was running a stall where the contestants had to throw coins into a tin basin on the grass. If the coin stayed in the basin, they won a dollar. If it bounced out, the money went to Tau Beta. For some reason Edsel Ford seemed to find this game quite the most riveting of all the diversions on offer in the garden. He spent the afternoon tossing dollar bills well wide of the basin.[18]

The couple's engagement was announced in June 1916, on the same day that Ellie Clay graduated from Liggett, and they married on November 1, 1916. The ceremony was held in the Hudson mansion on Boston Boulevard—a substantial redbrick edifice, but by no means the most impressive residence in the street. Somewhat to the disappointment of waiting reporters, it was conducted "as quietly, as simply as though they were the children of obscure families." There was "no pomp, no magnificent ceremony."[19]

Eleanor had gone to New York to arrange dresses for herself and her bridesmaids in an exotic, Russian style, but the reporter from the *Free Press* had been hoping for much more: "I don't think," he sniffed, "I saw $1000 of jewels"[20]

On January 14, 1917, Louis P. Lochner returned to America to report on the progress of Henry Ford's Peace Commission. The survivors of the Peace Ship had remained in Europe for the twelve months since Henry had deserted them, supported by Ford funds. They had kept on trying to interest European governments in their offers of independent mediation, and back in New York Henry was waiting on the quay to greet Lochner and receive a personal report on how things had gone.

Henry Ford might have abandoned the Peace Ship, but he had by no means abandoned peace. He had spent nearly half a million dollars on maintaining his Peace Commission in Europe. On his return from Norway, he had financed an expensive advertising campaign in the country's largest newspapers, savagely attacking "preparedness" and the "munitions interests" whose thirst for profit was pushing America to provide more support to Britain and the Allies.[21] He had spent a further $50,000 on advertisements supporting Woodrow Wilson's reelection on a peace platform in 1916,[22] and when he met with Lochner he remained enthusiastic about the chances of neutral mediation ending the war. Peace was his hope, he declared on January 30, 1917.

Two days later, on February 1, 1917, Germany announced its intention of resuming unrestricted submarine warfare on any shipping, neutral or otherwise, that was suspected of bringing succour to the Allies, and on February 3 Woodrow Wilson responded by severing U.S. diplomatic ties with Germany.

Suddenly war loomed as a real prospect for America, and when Henry Ford was questioned on February 5 about his own attitude towards this, he declared that the entire production facilities of Ford, consecrated until the previous week to the cause of peace, would now be harnessed for war. Henry Ford, who had promised to burn Highland Park down rather than produce munitions, now pledged himself ready to turn out tanks, aeroplanes—whatever instrument of human destruction the government might commission. He had his own personal proposal for a small, one-man submarine which would carry a "pill on a pole. . . . That is, a pole on the front end of a submarine with a pill—bomb —on the end of it." The submarine would run beneath the enemy battleship, explained Henry, attach its pill, and blow the enemy out of existence.[23]

This abrupt conversion from bleeding-heart pacifist to bloodthirsty Mars did not impress the U.S. Assistant Secretary of the Navy. Mr. Ford, suggested the young Franklin D. Roosevelt, had thought a submarine was "something to eat" until he saw the chance of some free publicity.[24]

But Henry's sudden about-face was not that untoward. President Wilson, who now led America into war, had been campaigning for conciliation and "peace without victory" until only a few days before breaking with Germany on the submarine issue, while even that great beater of plough-shares William Jennings Bryan was now proclaiming Americans' willingness "to die for their liberty."[25] Populists might be pacifists, but they were patriots first and foremost. "A declaration of war," said Bryan, "closes discussion."[26] America's right to make money anywhere and anyhow she chose was sacred, and German submarine attacks on American shipping had aroused deep anger in the U.S., even among those opposed to sending supplies to Britain.

Henry Ford promised that he would operate his factories for war "without one cent of profit."[27] Getting rich on the national war effort would, he said, be "like taking blood money,"[28] and he was willing to turn his hand to just about anything. Steel helmets, ammunition boxes, armour plating, aeroplane engines, tractors, gasmasks—Highland Park turned out all of these. The Model T went into Army service both as it was and adapted into an ambulance. Henry also proposed encasing it in metal for use as a minitank, and he was quite unperturbed when his experiments ended with numerous machines ignominiously upended in trenches. It was all part of the plan, he explained, since mass production had brought a new disposable dimension to war. The stranded tanks could serve as trench-crossings for the army that followed them.

The throwaway tank never reached the battlefield, but another exercise in mass-produced weaponry fared better. Focusing on the U-boat threat, the U.S. Navy had designed a fast, lightweight submarine chaser, and Ford got the job of mass-producing these specialized "Eagle" boats. Charles Sorensen was tied up putting Henry's beloved tractor into production, so the job of supervising Eagle boat production went to Ford's other Scandinavian lieutenant, William Knudsen, the recruit from Keim Mills.

The Eagle boat held special appeal for Henry Ford. It was a fresh mechanical challenge and a much-publicized novelty which placed Ford at the heart of the national war effort. But it also offered him the opportunity to advance a private plan which had become the next stage in his ambition: a spectacular follow-up to the moving assembly line.

Highland Park, the world's largest factory complex, had become too small for Henry Ford. By 1915 the plant was turning out a quarter of a million Model Ts a year, and it had the capacity to more than double that. But Henry wanted more. Having mastered the production of cars, he wanted to master the raw material that went into cars—the rubber and wood, and, in particular, the coal and iron that made up the steel. He had a vision of a total plant, the ultimate factory, where the raw materials poured in at one end and the finished cars came out at the other.

Henry had found a site for his superplant in the summer of 1915. He bought land down in the marshes where the

Rouge River flowed into the Detroit River. The company's other stockholders—the Dodge brothers, in particular—were unhappy at the massive capital investment it would take to develop the site, but the naval contract to manufacture Eagle boats now gave Henry the chance to put in some improvements—at somebody else's expense. The Rouge River needed deepening and the marshes needed draining, and as part of the Eagle boat contract, the U.S. government agreed to foot the bill for this.

There were some unhelpful members of Congress who could not understand why the U.S. taxpayer had to produce $3.5 million[29] to set Henry Ford up in yet another line of business and create a shipyard in the middle of some Dearborn meadows. But the Navy's own shipyards were overwhelmed with war work, and it was suggested, though not promised, that Ford would buy back the plant when the war was over.[30]

Early in 1918 work started on a huge Eagle boat assembly building stretched out beside the Rouge River by Albert Kahn. Never before had ships been built indoors, and the building was revolutionary in other respects: it was more than half a mile long, with steel-framed, hundred-foot-tall walls which were nothing but undisturbed expanses of glass. Building B, as it became known, made architectural history, and it stands on the Rouge site to this day, worn and grimy, but with the light still streaming magically through its walls onto the assembly line that now produces four-, six-, and eight-cylinder Mustangs.[31]

On May 7, 1918, the keel of the first Eagle boat was laid, and only eight weeks later, on July 10, it was launched from a massive 225-foot-long steel trestle which slid down into the Rouge, released its hull, and then returned back to land for the next one. "An Eagle a Day Keeps the Kaiser Away," proclaimed celebratory banners brandished by Ford workers. Building B contained three production lines each carrying seven boats, which made the Eagle the first ship ever produced on a mass-assembly basis, and patriotic fervour hailed the Eagle as further evidence of the genius of Henry Ford.

"Warships While You Wait," exclaimed the *New York Times*.[32]

But when Armistice came in November 1918, it turned out that Henry Ford's Eagle boat production had not been quite as spectacular as the carmaker had given the world to believe. In fact, of the 112 boats ordered from Ford at a cost of some $46 million, only seven had been completed and despatched, and only one was actually in commission—still undergoing preliminary sea trials.

Ford blamed the vessel's naval designers, who had changed specifications several times and had considerably hampered production. But the truth was that William Knudsen's engineers had found it harder to adapt their motorcar production techniques to shipbuilding than they had anticipated. They did not hit their stride until after the war was over, and the Ford Motor Company finally delivered sixty Eagle boats to the U.S. Navy. The Navy did not invite Henry Ford to build ships for it again.

With the declaration of war in April 1917, Edsel Bryant Ford, aged twenty-three, had appealed to his draft board for exemption from military service. He was already engaged in important war work supervising Ford munitions production, argued company lawyers on his behalf, and though the draft board rejected this argument in October 1917, a fortunate change in regulations placed Edsel in Class 2-A, as having dependents—his first son, Henry Ford II, had been born in September 1917—and in Class 3-L, as being indispensable to a war industry. Of the seven persons in the world certain to go through the war unscathed, remarked Congressman Nicholas Longworth sardonically, six were the sons of the Kaiser, and the seventh was Edsel Ford.[33]

Posterity has tended to take the side of Edsel Ford in his evasion of military service during the First World War. "It took more courage for Edsel Ford not to put on a uniform," declared Edwin Pipp, one of Henry Ford's severer critics in later years, "than it would have taken to put one on"[34]— Pipp's point being that Edsel's open refusal to serve was

202

more honest than the sly methods by which other rich young men bought themselves safe commissions in Washington. When questioned personally on the subject, Edsel stated, "I am perfectly willing to be drafted with the rest of the young men of this community."[35] It was only at his father's insistence that he had applied for draft exemption.

But this was the trouble with Edsel Ford, and it was to provide the tragic theme for his entire adult life. He was not his own man. Generous, civilized, and kind, Edsel Ford had that polish and sensitivity with which the second generation of a business dynasty can often smooth and amplify the raw achievement of its thrusting founder. Edsel was, in personal terms, immensely more humane than his father, and he possessed all the ingredients for true greatness, except the most important: independence of spirit. He was totally incapable of resisting his father's will, even on matters that related to his most cherished principles, and he paid a painful price for this. Newspapers pointed out how on the day that Quentin, the son of Teddy Roosevelt, had been killed in an air battle, Edsel Ford and his wife were entertaining friends at an expensive and fashionable club, while his father's sponsoring of the Peace Ship laid Edsel open to obvious jibes. Henry Ford was more successful, declared *Detroit Saturday Night*, in keeping his own boy out of the trenches than in getting the other boys out by Christmas.[36]

Edsel's draft refusal was made a public issue by his father's decision to stand for election to the U.S. Senate in the autumn of 1918. In 1916, local political activists had nominated Henry Ford in several of the Midwest presidential primaries, and it was a measure of the quixotic appeal which the Peace Ship had added to Henry's name that the Ford candidacy attracted an astonishing response. In Michigan, Henry's nomination secured 83,000 votes against the 78,000 won by Senator William Alden Smith, and in Nebraska, the very heartland of populism, he had come close to defeating Senator Albert Cummins. The farmers loved Henry: in Missouri, the southern headquarters of rural agitation, a poll in the *St. Louis Times* showed Henry Ford heading a list of presidential candidates.[37]

There is some evidence that, in best folk-hero tradition, the "Henry for President" movement received a little help along the way. Local Ford dealers were initially involved in the promotion of these theoretically spontaneous candidacies, and the trails from them all led back to Ernest Liebold in Henry Ford's private office. But Henry himself steadfastly maintained that he was not a candidate for President in 1916, and he proved it by endorsing Woodrow Wilson's reelection campaign and by giving Wilson heavy advertising support. Largely concentrated in California, Ford's advertising proved a crucial factor in Wilson's narrow victory in that state.

Wilson won California by just 4,000 votes, giving him the presidency in his close-fought struggle with Charles Evans Hughes, and two years later Wilson turned to Henry Ford for help again. The President could foresee trouble fighting his peace plans through Congress, particularly in the Senate, where the Republicans held a majority. If Henry Ford could win Michigan for the Democrats, it would sway the balance of power in Wilson's favour, and in June 1918 the carmaker was summoned to the White House to receive an invitation from the President.

Mr. Ford, we are living in very difficult times—times when men must sacrifice themselves for their country. . . . You are the only man in Michigan who can be elected and help to bring about the peace you so much desire. I wish you therefore to overcome your personal feelings and interests and make the race.[38]

The *New York Times* pointed out that Henry Ford's candidacy "would create a vacancy both in the Senate and in the automobile business," and Henry's friends were scarcely more encouraging.

"What do you want to do that for?" asked Thomas Edison, now quite a frequent guest at Fair Lane. "You can't speak. You wouldn't say a damned word. You'd be mum."[39]

Mum was the way Henry Ford chose to play his campaign

for the Senate in 1918. He had done well in the Farm Belt primaries of 1916 by staying at home and doing nothing, and he decided to adopt the same reclusive tactics again. He declined to make any public speeches; he issued no public statements, with the exception of a declaration of support for female suffrage; and although he had demon-strated the power of political advertising in his support of Woodrow Wilson two years earlier, he now perversely refused to spend a cent on advertising himself.

His Republican opponents had a field day at the expense of his pacifism and his son's draft refusal. "Why not," inquired one newspaper, "send the indispensable Edsel to the Senate?" So it was rather surprising, when the votes were finally counted, that Henry Ford only lost the election by 212,487 to 220,054, with a recount bringing the margin down to 212,751 against 217,088. If Henry Ford had bothered to sway just 2,200 of the voters who opposed him in November 1918, he could have become a U.S. senator.

The man who won the election, Truman H. Newberry, came from the Detroit–Grosse Pointe elite for whom Henry had come to feel such hostility. Partly in reality, but more particularly in the developing paranoia of Henry Ford, Newberry was part of the establishment which had cham-pioned George Selden and had ridiculed the Five Dollar Day, and Newberry's narrow victory in the 1918 senatorial election stung Henry Ford to an urgent and passionate commitment that he had never demonstrated during the campaign itself.

Suddenly Henry cared very much about winning. He filed for a recount and, with the help of Harvey Firestone (his principal tyre supplier, who had come up from Akron, Ohio, to lend his shoulder to the campaign), he set about proving that the election had been rigged. Private detectives were hired to dig out evidence that Newberry and his supporters had exceeded the legal limits on campaign spending. Vocal in a way he had never been when some direct speaking might have won him the battle cleanly, Henry Ford pushed his way back into the newspapers to denounce the hidden monied "interests" who were behind his defeat. He condemned the easy old targets—Wall Street and the bankers—and, for the first time publicly, he identified a sinister new scapegoat. Newberry, he told a onetime president of the Detroit Board of Commerce, was the tool of an "influential gang of Jews."[40]

The smear was quite unfounded. Newberry was, if anything, even more anti-Semitic than Ford—there were certainly fewer Jews in the clubs he belonged to than were working in the Ford factories. But truth played a small part in the vendetta that Henry Ford was to wage for more than four years to sour and spoil the victory that Newberry had won over him. More than forty private investigators combed Michigan under the direction of Bernard M. Robinson, a Firestone attorney, to gather evidence that Newberry's campaign spending amounted to at least $176,000,[41] comfortably exceeding the limits on campaign spending set by law. Henry Ford then brandished this figure as proof of the monied conspiracy that had defeated him.

"If they would spend $176,000 to win a single Senate seat," he complained, "we may be certain they would spend $176,000,000 to get control of the country."[42]

But the self-righteousness sat ill upon him, for Henry Ford had spent considerably more than $176,000 promoting causes that were dear to him, and he had never scrupled to try and buy America around to his own way of thinking. His campaign against Truman H. Newberry had little to do with patriotic concerns. Henry Ford was a poor loser. He was out to get yet another of his social superiors who had bested him.

He finally got satisfaction in 1922 when a Democratic majority was restored to the Senate. Two Democratic senators announced their intention of reopening the Newberry case—which had been fought through various courts with the decision going both ways—and, facing the inevitable, Newberry stepped down. In his letter of resignation he reluctantly conceded defeat to "political persecution," complaining that "hundreds of agents" had "hounded and terrified" men all over Michigan.[43] Once back in private life, he took consolation from waging a social vendetta of his own. If there had ever been any doubt as to the antipathy between the barons of Grosse Pointe and the multimillion-aire carmaker of Dearborn, it was now removed, and the feud extended to the womenfolk. Mrs. Truman H. Newberry made a point of absenting herself from any social gathering to which an invitation had been extended to "that man."[44]

In the early months of 1922, a volume entitled *The Truth About Henry Ford* extolled the many virtues of the carmaker, among them the generosity with which he had donated all the profits he had made from war production, some $29 million, to the U.S. Treasury.[45] The author, Mrs. Sarah T. Bushnell, thanked Mrs. Henry Ford in her preface for supplying her with most of the data in the book. "For months she gave me liberally of her time in order that I might compile this volume and verify my facts."[46]

Andrew W. Mellon, the U.S. Secretary of the Treasury, was mystified to read Mrs. Bushnell's claim, since he had no recollection of $29 million being paid to the Treasury, and he set a clerk to check his memory. "The records of the Treasury do not show any such sum received," he wrote to Henry Ford on March 16, 1922, "and in fact there appears to be no record whatever of such a donation." Could Ford, perhaps, shed some light on the matter?[47]

A week later, Ernest Liebold replied to Mellon on his master's behalf saying that Henry Ford had not authorized Mrs. Bushnell's book, and had not even seen it. "Consequently, he feels no responsibility for its circulation or statements it may contain."[48]

But neither Mellon nor the media were prepared to let the matter stand at that. Henry had made much, during the war, of his refusal to accept "blood money" from his munitions work. Now, in the spring of 1922, it turned out that Henry Ford had not paid a single cent to the Treasury. The War Department and Navy Department also consulted their ledgers and announced that Ford had invoiced the government, and had been paid, the full price for every Eagle boat, steel helmet, and ammunition box that his company had produced. Mrs. Bushnell's book, suggested *Detroit Saturday Night*, should be subtitled "What We Would Like The World To Think About Pa."[49]

Shamed into a show of action, and engaged once again in political campaigning which required some sort of public explanation, Henry Ford let it be known in the autumn of 1923 that the "huge job" of working out precisely what he owed the government was still being worked on, and that when the audit was completed, he would, of course, "do as he said."[50] The *New York Times*, however, reported that far from $29 million, the actual amount of the refund Ford was contemplating was in the area of $1,750,000.[51]

How much money Henry Ford made out of World War I has never been precisely established. Ford's official biographers, Professor Allan Nevins and Frank Ernest Hill, used company records to show a gross profit on war contracts of over $8 million—$4,357,000 after tax. Ford's own 58.5 percent share of this would have been just under $2.5 million, which came down, after personal income tax, to only $926,780.46—less than a million dollars.

But this figure is implausibly low. Total Ford profits for both war work and civilian production in the eighteen months of war had reached some $78 million by December 1918,[52] which means that Nevins and Hill set war work at no more than 6 percent of the activity of the Ford factories for this period. In November 1917, the Ford lawyers representing Edsel in his draft-evasion case claimed that the company was taking on war contracts at the rate of $40 million a month.[53] Calculating on this basis, one arrives at a sum much closer to Mrs. Bushnell's $29 million profit for Henry—and this figure, in any case, could only have come from the Fords themselves.

Whatever the precise sum, however, the U.S. Treasury never received a penny of it—and the most mysterious aspect of the entire episode was the way in which the legend refused to die.

In the summer of 1935, a dozen years after the subject had been thoroughly aired, *Detroit Saturday Night* published a history of the Ford Motor Company which stated that "Henry Ford turned back to the government every cent of profit he had made from war contracts,"[54] while three years later, a couple of local Lutheran ministers who decided to honour Henry Ford on his seventy-fifth birthday singled out for special praise the fact that he was the "only rich man of note who had an opportunity to coin money out of the blood of the nations during the World War, and refused to do so." The ministers hailed Henry Ford as "the outstanding citizen of America and of the world."[55]

It is not known where the Detroit newspaper and the reverend gentlemen gathered their misinformation, and in accepting the ministers' birthday compliments, Henry Ford was too polite to correct them. But in 1935, *The Triumph of an Idea*, a pocket biography of Ford by Ralph H. Graves, had solemnly repeated the story of how Henry paid back every penny of his war profits to the U.S. Government, and as late as 1940, anyone who contacted the Ford Public Relations Department in search of accurate information about the company's founder was sent a copy of Mr. Graves's book, free of charge.

# 10

## NO STOCKHOLDERS, NO PARASITES

*Money the* Root *of all* Eval. . . .
—JOTTING FROM HENRY FORD'S NOTEBOOKS[1]

John Reed, the radical journalist, was mesmerized by Henry Ford when he met the carmaker in the autumn of 1916:

A slight, boyish figure, with thin, long, sure hands, incessantly moving; unshaven—the fine skin of his thin face browned golden by the sun; the mouth and nose of a simple-minded saint; brilliant, candid, green eyes, and a lofty forehead rising to shining gray hair like the gray hair of youth; the lower part of his face extraordinarily serene and naive, the upper part immensely alive and keen.[2]

Reed, soon to eulogize the Russian Revolution and help found the Communist Labor Party in America, was no lover of rich businessmen. Touring the Detroit area, he was full of scorn for the local fat cats, an unscrupulous gang of "mushroom millionaires," in his opinion, living ostentatiously in their Grosse Pointe villas and carving up the city for the benefit of themselves, the private street-railway company, and "the liquor interests."

But Henry Ford, in Reed's judgement, was different.

He hasn't a villa at Grosse Pointe; he lives on a farm in the little village of Dearborn, ten miles from Detroit. He does not move in Detroit's select social circles; he prefers sitting on a neighbour's back porch of an evening and talking things over with the farmers. He belongs to none of the exclusive clubs frequented by his fellow-millionaires. And, frankly, they hate him.[3]

Reed was so bewitched by Henry Ford that he was even ready to stretch the truth for him—Fair Lane was hardly a farm, except, perhaps, in terms of acreage. The revolutionary had fallen under the spell to which so many people succumbed when they met Henry Ford face to face—his earnestness, his quirky ideas, his bluntness, his "mind of appalling simplicity."

John Reed had come to Detroit to meet a tycoon, but he felt he had come into contact with the real heart of America: energetic, rural, idealistic. "Only the people of the Middle States—farmers and farmer stock—conserve the distinctive flavor," he wrote. Reed entitled his profile of Henry "Industry's Miracle Worker," because he trusted the man. Henry Ford might be rich, but he was not a bloated plutocrat. Beneath his wealth, felt the revolutionary, Henry remained simple, self-made—"practical."

John Reed might have been advised to consult a few other self-made, "practical" men before he finally made his mind up about Henry Ford. James Couzens together with the Dodge brothers, John and Horace, had known Henry a great deal longer than Reed had—had known him, and had watched him change from the days when they were all simple, practical men together—and by October 1916, they had come to form rather a different estimate of his character and ambitions. James Couzens, indeed, was no longer working for the Ford Motor Company.

Since 1908, one of Couzens's responsibilities in his overall supervision of the sales and marketing of Ford cars had been the *Ford Times*, a house journal considerably more sprightly and readable than the general run of such organs. In September 1915, Henry Ford had had Theodore Delavigne's original and momentous article about his peace plans reprinted in the paper, and as his pacifist ardour increased, Henry had an even more outspoken piece prepared for the October issue. This was a scathing criticism of American willingness to extend war loans to Britain and France. Lord Balfour was about to bring an allied commission to the U.S. in search of financial aid, and the *Ford Times* proposed that the visitors should be "kicked off the dock."

"Henry," said Couzens, "that editorial in the *Ford Times* can't go."

"I own fifty-nine percent of the stock of this company," retorted Ford, "and I guess it can go if I say so."

"That is true," responded Couzens, "but I resign."[4]

James Couzens sat down, wrote out his resignation as business manager, put on his hat, and then drove into Detroit to get his version of the story into the newspapers before Henry could. His resignation as vice-president and treasurer was accepted on October 13, 1915, though as the largest Ford shareholder after Henry himself, he retained his 11 percent stake in the company and his seat on the board.

James Couzens had been entertaining political ambitions for some time. He had already got started on the career that was to make him, within a few years, mayor of Detroit and to take him eventually into the U.S. Senate—where, ironically, he succeeded to the seat vacated by Truman H. Newberry. As a public supporter of Woodrow Wilson's policy of "preparedness," Couzens could hardly allow his views to be pilloried by the company of which he was the day-to-day business manager.

But, like a good politician, James Couzens had chosen his resignation issue carefully. His relations with Henry Ford had been deteriorating for some time. He had grown less and less amused by his partner's willingness to take sole credit for every achievement of the Ford Motor Company. He could remember nailing up those railcars in the very earliest days, when it had been his prudence and ability to discipline Henry which had been the saving of the enterprise, and as he contemplated his future career, he felt the time had come for James Couzens to emerge from the shadow of Henry Ford.

Henry, for his part, was also ready for a parting of the ways. He had grown less and less tolerant of his partner's caustic tongue, and when the disagreement came up over the pacifist editorial, he later confided to Edwin Pipp, he rather welcomed the chance for a showdown.

"Fine," he said to himself. "That's a dandy way out of it," and he "stood pat."[5]

Breaking with the Dodge brothers proved a more long-drawn process. In August 1913, John Dodge had resigned from the Ford board of directors,[6] having given notice the previous month that the Dodge Brothers' machine shop would cease supplying Ford with parts in one year's time. John and Horace Dodge had made their fortunes both as suppliers to the Ford Motor Company and as stockholders, but now they had decided that they wished to produce a cheap car of their own.

The two brothers retained their Ford shareholdings, however. They were planning to find much of the capital for their car company from their share of the massive dividends that Ford was firing out almost monthly—the Dodges were to net $1.22 million in 1914 alone[7]—and this was the cause of the trouble, since Henry Ford, quite understandably, did not appreciate the spectacle of Ford profits going to finance a rival car—particularly when the Dodges' car turned out to be rather a good one.

Among its several criticisms of the Five Dollar Day, the *Wall Street Journal* suggested that Henry's apparent generosity in paying out $10 million to his workers was no more than a way of spiting the Dodge brothers; it was $10 million that he did not have to share with his old partners. This was scarcely an explanation of the Ford Sociological Department and the elaborate profit-sharing scheme, but it was an accurate enough interpretation of the tactics that Henry adopted next. His much-publicized repayment of some $50 to every purchaser of a Model T in 1914 removed $11 million from the profits of the company at a stroke, thus denying the Dodges a million dollars they had been counting on. In August 1916, Henry finally brought matters to a head. The company had by then accumulated some $58 million in profits, and he announced that rather than distribute this to the shareholders, he was planning to reinvest it in several new projects, notably his new superplant down by the Rouge River. No more special dividends would be declared.[8]

It was a challenge which the Dodges could not ignore. On November 2, 1916, they responded with a suit in the Michigan State Circuit Court requiring the Ford Motor Company to pay out at least 75 percent of its cash surplus to the shareholders immediately—some $39 million—and when Henry Ford refused, the war was on.

One of the Dodge brothers' complaints against Henry Ford was his policy of continually reducing the price of his cars. The Highland Park sales office was flooded with orders that it could not meet, but instead of raising his prices, as he could well have done, Henry kept on cutting them. This defied the conventional laws of profit-taking, and it was difficult for the Dodges not to see the price cuts as an attack upon their dividends.

Henry Ford, however, disagreed. His own shareholding in the company was nearly six times larger than the Dodge brothers', so if he hurt them 10 percent, he hurt himself 58.5. "I do not believe that we should make such an awful profit on our cars," he told the *Detroit News* on November 14, 1916. "A reasonable profit is right, but not too much."[9]

Henry expressed this noble sentiment within a few days of receiving the Dodge brothers' writs, and it was clearly an appeal on his part to public sympathy. It was a fair appeal for him to make, however, since his policy of cutting the price of his cars went back many years, and it certainly predated his dispute with the Dodge brothers.

I hold that it is better to sell a large number of cars at a reasonably small margin than to sell fewer cars at a large margin of profit. I hold this because it enables a larger number of people to buy and enjoy the use of a car and because it gives a larger number of men employment at good wages. Those are two aims I have in life.[10]

This was a classic exposition of what had become the Ford manufacturing philosophy. The price of the Model T had been raised at the end of the first year's production, but thereafter it had been reduced progressively and dramatically—from $825, the car's original price in 1908, down to $440 by October 1914, and still lower by August 1916, to only $345.[11] These extraordinary price cuts were one of the reasons why Henry Ford was liable to be called a miracle worker by magazine writers. Henry always took great pleasure in spelling out the magic paradox by which he managed to keep on cutting his prices—and make his company even more money in the process.

Every time you reduce the price of the car without reducing the quality, you increase the possible number of purchasers. There are many men who will pay $360 for a car who would not pay $440. We had in round numbers 500,000 buyers of cars on the $440 basis, and I figure that on the $360 basis we can increase the sales to possibly 800,000 cars for the year—less profit on each car, but more cars, more employment of labor, and in the end we get all the profit we ought to make.[12]

This explained precisely why Henry Ford had become the largest carmaker in the world—the 390,000 vehicles he produced in 1915 represented 44.6 percent of all the cars manufactured in America[13]—and it made the Dodge brothers look both greedy and shortsighted, since the basic intent of their lawsuit was to secure themselves fatter dividends and to prevent Henry from allocating so much of his profits to price-cutting and reinvestment.

But this was not quite the whole story, for Henry Ford was in business to make money like any other industrialist, and although he presented himself as the fearless framer of new economic laws, the evidence suggests that he stumbled on these new truths of the mass market by accident. He deserved full credit for his vision of the people's car, and its accomplishment was a triumph. But Henry's own personal drive, the inner motivation that made Henry Ford tick, was not all sweetness and light.

Success seldom satisfies the hunger that creates it, and in the case of Henry Ford, the public acclaim that success had brought had stimulated his reluctance to share, his paranoia and sensitivity, and the angry, go-it-alone spirit that had stalked the corridors of the Ford psyche in his disputes with his earliest backers. These psychoses were not unique to Henry Ford: no businessman can succeed without selling his soul, in some measure, to their dark demands. But in 1916, the Dodge brothers did have good reason for believing that their partner's growing appetite for control and for omnipotence was coming to threaten the safety of their own investment.

The issue that had driven them to law was Henry's dream of a vast new manufacturing complex, his factory to end all factories beside the Rouge River. The government was to help develop this in 1918 through the Eagle boat contract, but in 1916 the site was just open marshland. It represented a monstrous, scarcely believable capital investment, and it was to pay for this that Henry had announced his intention of withholding dividends from his stockholders.

Early one morning in July 1915—the summer before the Peace Ship expedition—Henry had taken Charles Sorensen and a group of his other executives to look at the Rouge site. Covering more than 2,000 acres, it was a flat, open expanse of soggy farmland close to two local railways, and this rail access would obviously be helpful to any new plant. But what had caught the imagination of Henry Ford was the sight of the Rouge River, a wide if shallow stream at this point, flowing down through the fields to the Detroit River and the Great Lakes beyond. Henry could visualize the ore boats sailing in with their coal and iron from the mines of northern Michigan to service his own blast furnaces, while huge cargo ships would go sailing out again taking finished Ford motorcars across the oceans of the world—"to England, France, Germany, South America, Australia, and the Orient." [14] Henry could own his own coal mines, his own iron mines, his own forests, his own rubber plantations even, and he could also create a Ford navy to bring all the raw materials to his doorstep. The name of Ford would come to stand for a veritable industrial empire.

The Rouge would be the start of it. Fred Gregory, the Dearborn realtor who handled Henry's land purchases, was instructed to assemble a team of agents who could descend on the local farmers all in one day. The land was purchased in Henry Ford's own name and with his own money, not by the Ford Motor Company, and Henry announced that the Rouge project was a personal one. His intention was to start producing his tractor there. A new company was incorporated, Henry Ford and Son (the Ford tractor was to be called a Fordson), and when Henry spoke to the local paper, the *Dearborn Independent*, he presented the enterprise as a purely family affair. The production of the tractor on this new Rouge River site, he said, would involve "no stockholders, no directors, no absentee owners, no parasites."[15]

The Dodges might resent this jibe, particularly since they had been anything but parasitical in the early days of Ford development, but they had no grounds for complaint so long as the Rouge development was kept separate from the motor company.

John Dodge soon started picking up worrying rumours that it was not. Henry Ford was carrying out many of the experiments for his tractor, it seemed, using men and materials from Highland Park. There was talk that he might use the existing Model T engine in the new machine, and Henry was also fond of talking in unguarded moments about his grandiose plans for steel production.[16] If he really intended to build his own blast furnaces on the Rouge site, this represented a massive capital outlay that could not possibly be for the benefit of the tractor alone. It would take an output of at least a million vehicles a year to justify the expense of blast furnaces—and that had major implications for the car company. John Dodge requested a meeting.

The Dodge brothers met with Henry Ford early in 1916 in their own offices in Detroit, and the discussions started amicably. Henry had brought along C. Harold Wills for reinforcement, and the two men were able to satisfy the Dodges that the tractor project would not be at the expense of the motor company. They were keeping careful records of all resources that had been diverted to tractor development, they said, and Henry promised to repay this to the company in full.

But then John Dodge happened to express regret at the recent departure of James Couzens, and this touched a sore spot with Henry.

"It was a very good thing," he stated with some fervour, that Couzens had left. "Now they would be able to do things that before Mr. Couzens had prevented. . . . They were going to double the size of the Highland Park plant and double the output of cars and sell them at half price."

Suddenly Henry Ford's true ambitions stood unveiled, and he was no longer sweet reasonableness.

"The stockholders had already received a great deal more than they had put into the company . . . ," he told John Dodge with feeling, and he did not propose to pay any more. He was going "to put the earnings of the company back into the business so as to expand it."[17]

John Dodge responded that if Henry really wanted to be able to do whatever he liked with the company's money, then he should pay for the privilege: he should buy out his fellow stockholders. That would give him 100 percent control—and the Dodges were willing to negotiate a price.

But Henry Ford dismissed this suggestion out of hand. "He had control," Dodge later remembered him saying, "and that was all he needed."[18]

On December 30, 1918, Henry Ford resigned from the presidency of the Ford Motor Company. Aged fifty-five, he now wished, he said, to devote his principal energies "to building up other organizations" with which he had a connection, and his place at Ford was taken by his son, Edsel, who was elected to the company presidency at a salary of $150,000 a year.[19]

To emphasize his resignation, Henry left Detroit, decamping with Clara to Altadena in southern California for a prolonged holiday in the sun, while the world wondered what his new projects might be.

On March 5, 1919, the *Los Angeles Examiner* provided an answer. HENRY FORD ORGANIZING HUGE NEW COMPANY TO BUILD A BETTER, CHEAPER CAR, ran the headline.

"His idea," reported the *Examiner*, "is to make a better car than he now turns out and to market it at a lower price, somewhere between $250.00 and $350.00."[20] Henry's "Huge New Company" would be set up in direct competition with the old Ford Motor Company, and the carmaker seemed quite indifferent to the effect this would have on the enterprise that he had spent more than fifteen years building up.

"Why," he told the *Examiner* vaguely, "I don't know exactly what will become of that."[21]

The prospect of America's most successful industrial enterprise being toppled by its own creator prompted headlines across the country, and Henry was happy to hold court for the reporters who came scurrying to Altadena.

The present Ford Motor Company employees number about 50,000 in the actual manufacture of its cars. Our new company will have four or five times that number. . . . The new car is well advanced, for I have been working on it while resting in California. . . . We shall have a plant on this coast and all over the country. In fact, we propose to dot the whole world with our factories.[22]

Enticed by the employment prospects, fifty-one Chambers of Commerce across America sent telegrams to Detroit urging the advantages of their own community as a site for one of the new Ford factories.[23] Gathering all the telegrams and newspaper cuttings together back at Highland Park, Ernest G. Liebold delighted in the furore that his master's announcement had created. "I do not believe," he confided to Gaston Plantiff, the Ford manager in New York, "[that] any of the stockholders are at all pleased over it."[24] This, of course, was the object of the exercise. Henry Ford's "Huge New Company" was a negotiating ploy, the same game he had played a dozen years earlier with Alex Malcomson. On February 7, 1919, just a month before Henry's sensational announcement, the Michigan State Superior Court had finally come to a verdict in the case of the Dodge brothers versus the Ford Motor Company, and had found against the company. After more than two years of litigation and appeals, Ford had been ordered to pay out $19,275,385 to its stockholders—with interest of around $1.5 million.

The money itself scarcely mattered. As holder of 58.5 percent of the shares, Henry himself would collect the bulk of the dividends. The issue was control. Justice Russell C. Ostrander of the Michigan State Superior Court had conceded several points of the Ford case, praising the "philanthropic and altruistic" motives behind certain aspects of company policy, and he had removed the obstruction which a lower court had placed upon the development of steel blast furnaces at the Rouge River site. "Judges are not business experts," he declared. Developing the Rouge project was a legitimate option within the commercial discretion of the company.

On the other hand, the judge did not approve the whimsical treatment of the men who had once risked their own money to help Henry Ford set up his business, men who still held a 41.5 percent stake in the enterprise between them.

"The record, and especially the testimony of Mr. Ford," said the judge, "convinces that he had to some extent the attitude towards shareholders . . . that they should be content to take what he chooses to give them."[25] This was both "arbitrary" and illegal. "A business corporation is organized and carried on primarily for the stockholders," declared the judge, and he enjoined that the future conduct of the Ford Motor Company should pay proper consideration to the stockholders' interests.[26]

Here was the rub, for Henry Ford had got fond of running his own company in his own way. Since the departure of John Dodge and James Couzens, the Ford board of directors had been rubber-stamping Henry's decisions without question. The only board members actively involved in the company were Edsel Ford and Frank Klingensmith.* Now Henry would have to take account of the views of the Dodges —and, worse, of James Couzens. Talking to the *Los Angeles Examiner* in March, he did not deny that his decision to strike out on his own was prompted by the judgement against him: "I must do business on the basis I think is right; I cannot do it on another."[28] In his populist mode, Henry spoke airily of devising "some system of common partnership wherein those who work as a result of investing their money and those who work otherwise will be partners."[29] But, more honestly, he told another reporter that "the new company will be owned entirely within our family, and thus can be directed without outside interference."[30]

The Dodge brothers, of course, had proposed precisely this during the confrontation that had driven them to litigation back in 1916. If Henry Ford wished to run the Ford Motor Company as an absolute monarch, he had only to buy out the minority stockholders. The Dodge brothers had professed themselves willing to sell out, and later, in court, their attorney, Elliott G. Stevenson, had indirectly ventured towards this same point—stirring an unexpected and revealing response.

"If you sit there until you are petrified," shot out Henry Ford with sudden venom, "I wouldn't buy the Dodge brothers' stock!"

"I didn't ask you to buy the Dodge brothers' stock," responded the startled Stevenson.

"Nor any other stockholders' stock," persisted Ford, ignoring the attorney. "I don't want any more stock."[31]

Stevenson did not pursue the point, but he had got Henry Ford to make a revealing admission. Henry was not just trying to exclude the Dodges and the other stockholders from having any future say in the company, he was trying to cut them all off without a penny, since the long-term

* From 1913 the members of the Ford board were Henry himself, Edsel, Klingensmith, David Gray (John Gray's heir), the lawyer Horace Rackham, and James Couzens. Couzens, however, had not been an active member after his resignation as business manager.[27]

consequence of his both withholding dividends and declining to buy back shares would be to make the shares themselves virtually worthless. No one was likely to pay much for shares that yielded meagre and whimsical dividends. Henry's "Huge New Company" was part of the same strategy: who would now put up the money for a 41.5 percent Ford stockholding, or any part of it, if Henry Ford himself was not involved in the company? In February 1919, before Henry's announcement of a new car and rival enterprise, S. K. Rothschild had offered the Dodges $18,000 for each of their 2,000 Ford shares. In March 1919, after the announcement, the going price for the Dodges' stock went down to $12,500, while the Gray shares were put out to option at only $9,000 each.[32]

Henry Ford had maintained in court that the Ford Motor Company was "organized to do as much good as we can, everywhere, for everybody concerned," and that he personally was only interested in making money "incidentally"[33] —thus prompting the judge to compliment him on his philanthropy and altruism. But ten years later, discussing the claims of his fellow shareholders, Henry was more direct.

"Personally," he told the *Detroit Times* in February 1927, "I never would have paid them a cent."[34]

In April 1919, Henry's Detroit representatives completed the play. Asked directly whether his project of a new company was not just a means of forcing the Dodge brothers and the other minority shareholders to sell out cheaply, Henry Ford had replied, "We . . . will not buy a share of anybody else's stock."[35]

But as the Dodge brothers and the other minority shareholders found themselves mysteriously approached in the following weeks by would-be Ford share purchasers, it became clear that the threads all led back to Henry, working through Edsel in Detroit. The bidding started at $7,500 per share. The Dodge brothers responded with their $12,500 price—and $12,500, in the end, became the price that the Fords had to pay. The lawyers John Anderson and Horace

Rackham both settled for this sum, and so did the heirs of the banker John Gray.

Only James Couzens held out for more, since it was little over a dozen years previously that he himself had devised the tactic of starting up a new company to frighten off Alex Malcomson. James Couzens was not an easy man to scare, and he finally settled for just over $13,000 per share on behalf of himself and his sister Rosetta, the schoolteacher whose original $100 stake was consequently priced at $262,036.67.

None of the minority shareholders had done that badly:[36]

| Shareholder | Investment in 1903 | Dividends 1903–1919 | Sold for in 1919 |
|---|---|---|---|
| Dodge brothers | $10,000 | $ 9,500,000 | $ 25,000,000 |
| John W. Anderson | $ 5,000 | $ 4,750,000 | $ 12,500,000 |
| Heirs of John Gray | $10,500 | $ 9,975,000 | $ 26,250,000 |
| Horace Rackham | $ 5,000 | $ 4,750,000 | $ 12,500,000 |
| James Couzens | $10,900 | $10,355,000 | $ 29,308,858 |
| Rosetta Couzens | $ 100 | $ 95,000 | $ 262,036 |
| Totals | $41,500 | $39,425,000 | $105,820,894 |

These were massive sums. This group of original investors in the Ford Motor Company had received the largest return on risk capital in recorded business history. But Henry Ford had not done that badly himself, for if he could buy 41.5 percent of his company for some $105 million, this set the company's total value at little more than $250 million, and in 1919 the Ford Motor Company was certainly worth a great deal more than that. A few years later, Henry was to receive an offer of $1,000 million from a financial syndicate for the 100 percent shareholding he held with Edsel,[37] which would suggest that the shareholdings of James Couzens, the Dodge brothers, and the rest were actually worth four times more than Henry paid for them. Small wonder that when, in July 1919, Henry was brought the news that the last of the minority stockholders had finally consented to his hard-driven terms, he "danced a jig all around the room."[38]

Henry Ford now held a degree of control over his own company unrivalled by the greatest pharaohs of American capitalism: John D. Rockefeller held no more than two-sevenths of Standard Oil at the height of his power.[39] Henry was free to realize his most voracious dreams of empire. In 1920, following contemporary business wisdom, the Ford Motor Company reorganized as a Delaware corporation to take advantage of that state's laissez-faire attitude to company regulation and disclosure. The Ford family share-holding was redistributed to give Henry 55 percent, Edsel 42, and Clara 3, and there was no more mention of the sensational new car that Henry had dreamed up in Altadena, California. In July 1919, an awkward reporter from the *New York Times* tried to resurrect the issue, inquiring about the new enterprise which had so excited Henry Ford only a few months earlier, but he was brushed aside.

"Of course," said Edsel Ford, "there will be no need of a new company now."[40]

Little more than a year later, one chilly May morning in 1920, the Ford family were on parade at their new manufacturing site on the banks of the Rouge River—three generations of them: old Henry himself, Edsel in the middle, and Edsel's two-and-a-half-year-old son, Henry Ford II. Freed from the constraints of the Dodge brothers and the other minority shareholders, Henry had built up the Rouge site sufficiently for steel making to begin, and Henry the Younger had been assigned the task of firing the first blast furnace.

"The fun of playing with matches," reported the *Detroit News*, "was almost too much for Henry II."[41] Edsel and Eleanor's elder son displayed an unfamiliarity with the craft of fire starting that was a credit to his governess. But his grandfather helped him, and soon the oil-soaked kindling and coke inside the furnace were blazing fiercely. The watching crowd cheered, and wrapped in his grandfather's boney embrace, the chubby-cheeked Henry, who was wearing a beaver fur hat for the occasion, got the idea. He joined in the general merriment, "clapping his hands and shouting gleefully."[42]

John Reed was not a witness to this cosy dynastic scene, a celebration in the best traditions of bloodstock capitalism. He was in Moscow in May 1920, where he died that same year and was buried, with great honours, in the Kremlin. Comparing Reed's 1916 assessment of Henry Ford, the Miracle Worker, with Henry's sly and greedy behaviour in his battle with the Dodge brothers, it would be easy to say that Henry Ford had hoodwinked the journalist completely. In ousting his minority shareholders, Henry Ford had displayed the rapacity of any run-of-the-mill moneybags. What price now the simpleminded saint?

The Reverend Samuel Marquis, a thoughtful, dispassionate man who got very close to the complex soul of Henry Ford, did not have an easy answer to that question. Working beside Henry in the Sociological Department, Marquis had come to feel that Henry's moral qualities and impulses were "some of the highest and noblest I have ever known grouped in any one man."[43] Henry was not the classic rich man of the Biblical parable, thought Marquis, coldly ignoring the beggar at his gate as part of the system, a necessary evil that he could do nothing about. "Lazarus," he wrote, "would not lie unnoticed very long at the gate of Henry Ford."[44]

But Marquis had also seen the other side: the angers, the jealousies, the scheming. He had been on the receiving end of it himself, and he had seen other men suffer from it cruelly. "There rages in him," he wrote, "an endless conflict between ideals, emotions and impulses as unlike as day and night— a conflict that at times makes one feel that two personalities are striving within him for mastery." It seemed to Samuel Marquis that this conflict could, on occasions, be seen on the outside, that it actually manifested itself physically on the features, in the very stance and posture, even, of Henry Ford.

On a good day, wrote Marquis, Henry stood "erect, lithe, agile, full of life, happy as a child, and filled with the child spirit of play." Out of the eyes of the carmaker there shone "the soul of a genius, a dreamer, an idealist . . . a soul that is affable, gentle, kindly, and generous to a fault." But the very next day Henry Ford could be exactly the opposite. His body became drooped and shrunken.

His face is deeply lined, and the lines are not such as go to make up a kindly, open countenance. The affable, gentle manner has disappeared. There is a light in the eye that reveals a fire burning within altogether unlike that which burned there yesterday.[45]

When the driving passions inside Henry Ford stood revealed, the change was sudden, dark, and terrible, and his pastor searched for some explanation of the astonishing transformation. It was as if, he said, the inventor of the assembly line had not yet assembled himself.

**Part Three** Grass-Roots Hero

# 11

## EVANGELINE

On Monday, April 9, 1923, just before noon, a baby boy was born at the Henry Ford Hospital in Detroit. He weighed seven pounds eleven ounces and his mother, Mrs. Evangeline C. Dahlinger, a twenty-nine-year-old shorthand-typist, was a healthy young woman whose delivery went without complications. It was a routine birth that would, normally, have excited no special attention.

But later that day the staff of the hospital were startled by the arrival at the maternity ward of Mr. Henry Ford himself, who wished to set eyes upon the newborn baby. Miss Lynch, the nurse in the maternity ward, was especially surprised, since Mr. Ford informed her that she would not be working at the hospital any longer and that she was to accompany Mrs. Dahlinger when she took her son home. Miss Lynch's new responsibility would be to act as nurse and to care exclusively for the little boy,[1] since, Mr. Ford made it clear, this was a child in whom he had a special interest.

Having made the Ford Motor Company 100 percent his own, Henry Ford seems to have felt that he should expand his interests somewhat. He had always had a twenty-two-track mind, spinning off ideas to let them fall where they might—wage rises that provided the excuse for social engineering, saving the birds, stopping the war. Nobody could accuse Henry Ford of limited horizons.

But the great central theme of his life had been his car—the Model T, how to perfect it, and how to produce it in ever-greater quantities—and, bound up with this, the company that had in some ways become the instrument of the car itself. The Model T kept on selling in ever greater and greater quantities: 472,350 in 1915–16; 730,041 in 1916–17; 933,720 in 1920–21.[2] Through the early 1920s it sold consistently above the million mark. It needed modification as it went along—mildly different body shapes, an electric self-starter, some dashboard instruments—but, in general terms, it took care of itself, and as the Model T continued to outsell the competition, Henry came to feel that he did not need another product. The maintenance of the car that had made him became an article of faith, indeed, and he felt free to turn his mind in other directions. He became a publisher; he bought a railway; he built aeroplanes; he developed his own, especially Henry Ford-style of hospital; he took on the Jews; he tried to save the blacks; he explored new routes towards his cherished aim of reconciling industrialization with the countryside; he laid a fair claim to inventing the supermarket; he gave American farmers a new cash crop; he took a more than casual run at the White House. It was not enough to have created a machine that became an American institution. Henry Ford wanted to become an institution himself—a foursquare, indispensable, larger-than-life American hero. And in the midst of accomplishing this, he also found time for Evangeline Dahlinger.

She was an attractive young woman, dark, short, and self-assured. She was just over five feet tall, with bright eyes and a provocative toothy grin. She came of French-Canadian stock, and her maiden name was Côté. Her father had fallen ill when she was in her teens, and to support the family Evangeline had taught herself shorthand and got a job in the stenographic department at Highland Park.

When Evangeline Côté joined Ford in 1909, she was just sixteen years old, and she rose rapidly on the wave of expansion that followed the introduction of the Model T. By 1912 she was head of the stenographic department, aged only nineteen, and C. Harold Wills, then at the peak of his influence in the company, picked her out to be his personal secretary.

Wills was something of a ladies' man. Dapper and well aware of his good looks, he made a hobby of collecting precious stones which he wore on stickpins and cufflinks. Some people thought that Wills was ostentatious. He would dive his hand into his pocket at the slightest excuse to show off the gemstones that he carried around with him. But he was no miser. He would make presents of his treasures to those who won his favour—Charles Sorensen was startled on one occasion to be presented with a diamond ring[3]— and Evangeline Côté certainly took his fancy.

Wills, however, was not the only admirer of Evangeline. Henry Ford also took a shine to the vivacious young stenographer whom he started to meet in his assistant's office, where he spent quite a lot of time in 1913 and 1914, collaborating through the heady months which produced first the moving assembly line and then the Five Dollar Day. Evangeline soon found herself working for both men, dividing her time between them. She was willing to work late at the office, and when she did, Henry Ford himself would take her home.[4]

Evangeline was a woman who had the ability to get things done. She was not afraid to make decisions on her own initiative, and this won her the especial favour of Ford, who liked to delegate problems to subordinates and then forget about them. When he developed an interest in restoring his birthplace, the old wooden homestead built by William Ford, Evangeline took over the project and handled all the details for him.

Henry Ford appears, sexually, to have been a vigorous man—and an ambitious one. Among his personal papers at the Ford Archives in Dearborn there survives a document dated October 1945, when Ford was eighty-two, written in the hand of his doctor, the osteopathic physician Lawson B. Coulter. It is a prescription for an ammoniated mercury salve with the instruction "Apply to skin & rub in well daily." Since ammoniated mercury has no conventional medical uses, the salve must, in some way, be connected with the paper that accompanies it, also in Dr. Coulter's hand: an explanation of aphrodisiacs and their uses.[5]

Harry Bennett, the ex-sailor who entered Ford employment at the end of the First World War, and who was, in time, to get closer to the carmaker than almost anyone outside the family, had a curious experience one day when his employer asked him to arrange the repatriation of a Finnish serving girl who had been working at Fair Lane. Her name was Wantatja, and it seemed she had been walking in the garden on one occasion when, quite by chance, she had come across Mr. Ford, standing behind a hedge and patting the hand of a second serving girl called Agnes, who was crying bitterly.

Mr. Ford hastened to explain to Harry Bennett that he had been doing nothing at all improper behind the hedge. He had only been "comforting" Agnes, he said, because of some, unspecified, grief. But he was worried lest Wantatja might have picked up the wrong impression of his behaviour, and might go carrying this to Mrs. Ford—who would naturally be distressed. So "it might be wise," Mr. Ford suggested, if Harry could arrange "to send Wantatja back from whence she came."[6]

Fixing things was Harry Bennett's speciality, and Wantatja found herself back in Finland with little delay. But her brother, who lived in Michigan, took exception to his sister's rapid and unexplained disappearance from the United States. He found it most mysterious, and failing to secure any satisfaction in his attempts to see Henry Ford, he lodged formal complaints with both the Michigan State Police and the FBI. It took quite some effort to silence him—but silencing was another of Harry Bennett's specialities.

Mr. Ford was still worried, however. Perhaps it would be a good idea, he suggested, if, for safety's sake, the other maid, Agnes, were to leave the Dearborn area as well. In this case there proved to be a brother on hand who was cooperative. Harry Bennett was able to arrange a good job for Agnes's brother 2,000 miles away on the West Coast, and Agnes was persuaded to go out and join him.

Harry was just leaning back congratulating himself on the efficiency with which he had taken care of his master's little problems, when his phone rang. It was Mr. Ford.

"Is Agnes happy out on the West Coast?" he inquired.

"Sure . . . ," replied Harry. "You'll never hear any more from her."

"Oh, won't I?" responded Henry Ford. "Well, she's right here in Dearborn."[7]

Somebody in the servants' hall had been tittle-tattling, it seemed. Mrs. Ford had got to hear of it, and she had hired a Pinkerton detective, who had managed to get Agnes traced and brought back to Dearborn for cross-examination.

What happened thereafter is uncertain. "This time I'll handle it," Henry Ford informed Harry Bennett, and he evidently did, since no more was heard on the subject of Agnes—nor of Wantatja, for that matter. Mr. Ford presumably managed to convince Mrs. Ford that his activities out in the garden were quite innocent, and that his elaborate attempts to get rid of the two girls—together with their own versions of these strange goings-on—did not spring from a guilty conscience.

The story of Henry Ford and the serving girls is a bizarre episode, and it is quite possible that Harry Bennett made the whole thing up. He was a mischievous man, and if Henry Ford is presumed to have been a saint and devoid of original sin, then Agnes, Wantatja, and their brothers could be written off as no more than figments of Bennett's frequently malicious imagination. But since the drift of Henry Ford's later life displayed a conspicuous tendency to gratify his own appetites and to exploit the power that his wealth gave him over other men, there is no reason to believe that he did not also seek, on occasions, to extend his power over women. Power, wealth, and appetite were certainly potent components of his long and complex relationship with Evangeline Dahlinger.

It was strange that Henry never made much secret about it. It was not unheard-of for rich and powerful men to have lady friends, but the tradition was to maintain them with discretion, behind closed doors. "That," Alex Dow, Henry's former employer at the Edison Illuminating Company, liked to say, "is what doors are for." Dow, who had risen to be quite a figure in Detroit, kept a succession of ladies in an apartment in Indian Village, and he liked to lecture his former protégé on the etiquette of such arrangements, discretion being of the essence.[8]

Discretion, however, was foreign to Henry Ford's nature. He did not mind if Evangeline appeared publicly by his side, and the photographs survive—Henry and Evangeline at a football game, Evangeline in fancy dress, Evangeline the only woman with Henry in a group of visiting celebrities that included Will Rogers. The pictures make up an extraordinary and flagrant display, and it seems unthinkable that Henry Ford did not appreciate the clear message which was carried by the presence at his side of this attractive young woman, thirty years his junior. There is no trace of Clara, nor of any other woman. It is as if Henry regarded himself as being blessed by some special dispensation that rendered him immune to the ordinary rules of public conduct. Or perhaps his self-absorption had become so overpowering that he really believed the world thought as he wanted it to think—that his relationship with Evangeline must be perfectly proper because she had, in 1917, got married to somebody else.

Ray Dahlinger had been the bag-man on Henry's ill-fated Peace Ship venture. He had physically transported the gold necessary to maintain the expedition in an age before traveller's cheques, and he had displayed his prowess as a bodyguard in the ill-tempered skirmish that had attended his master's predawn departure from Oslo. He owed everything to Henry Ford. Official versions of his career described him as having started at Highland Park with work as a "test driver," but the evidence suggests that Ray Dahlinger's early test-driving was limited to starting up vehicles as they came off the assembly line, parking them in the delivery yard, and then running back to collect the next one. It was a job where success depended on being quick on your feet.

With Harry Bennett, Ray Dahlinger made up one of the ill-assorted bunch of retainers who were coming to gain increasing importance in the world of Henry Ford. Part housecarls, part cronies, they had few qualifications that would obviously commend them for any conventional employment. They were not engineers, accountants, or production men. Their functions were ill-defined. They were henchmen whose powers and status derived exclusively from their loyalty to Henry Ford and from their ability to fix things for him—and Ray Dahlinger fixed a lot of things for his master when he married Evangeline Côté on February 20, 1917.

John Dahlinger, the baby born to Evangeline in April 1923, came later to believe that the man whom he was brought up to call "Dad" had, at one time, been deeply and genuinely in love with his mother. John discovered some beautiful love letters which Ray Dahlinger had written to Evangeline in the early stages of their relationship. But there is no evidence that Evangeline wrote any back. Her diary for the years 1917 to 1923 was centred upon her activities with Henry Ford, according to her son, who published short extracts from the diary in 1978; and with John's birth in April 1923, the love letters between Mum and "Dad" stopped. Ray and Evangeline Dahlinger had shared the same bedroom until that date, but the appearance of the baby boy who meant so much to Henry Ford caused Ray Dahlinger to move out. Henceforward he slept in a bedroom of his own, and it was on the other side of the house.[9]

The world will never know whether the baby born to Evangeline Dahlinger in April 1923 was fathered by her husband or by Henry Ford—and it is quite possible that Evangeline did not know either.

"I don't want to talk about it," she said on the one occasion that her son tried to raise the question that meant so much to him.[10]

John Dahlinger took his mother's evasiveness as confirmation of the legend generally regarded in Dearborn as an established truth, that he was the natural son of Henry Ford. If it had not been true, it would have been perfectly easy for his mother to tell him so, and "I don't want to talk about it" was the code he remembered from his childhood for subjects that were to be swept under the carpet.

Yet it is also quite possible that Evangeline was genuinely uncertain as to the paternity of her only child. Ray Dahlinger was sharing her bed and appears to have assumed that the child was his own, until it was born, when Henry Ford proceeded to lay claim to the boy in his own very positive style. Evangeline was caught in the middle, and if she had been sleeping with both men, then "I don't want to talk about it" was probably the most honest answer she could give.

It was certainly Henry Ford who created the ambiguity surrounding the parentage of John Dahlinger. Having visited the hospital within hours of the boy's birth and having commandeered a nurse to look after him, he then presented John with his own, Ford, christening gown to be baptized in. He insisted that the baby should sleep in the same turned-wood crib in which he had slept as an infant, and when John was a month old he gave him a present that was as lavish as it was inappropriate for a four-week-old child: a real, live Shetland pony.

Irving Bacon, an amateur artist whose paint-by-numbers style had earned him the position of court painter to Henry, was sent over to the Dahlingers' home. His commission was to decorate the nursery of Baby John, and Bacon was amazed to see looming above all the toys on the porch a large working model of a Fordson tractor in shiny aluminium.

"It must have cost plenty, I thought to myself, and I bet the Boss gave it to the baby. . . . The Dahlingers seemed to really have a pull."[11]

The pull extended to Ford dealerships for Evangeline's father and brother, and a 200-acre farm for Ray's mother beside a lake at Belleville, thirty miles southwest of Dearborn. This was part of a little empire of Ford farms that was being pushed out into Michigan west of Fair Lane and the Rouge, for Henry had ideas about how industry could be brought into harmony with the countryside. He also liked to eat the good, fresh, unprocessed food that he remembered

from his childhood. Ray Dahlinger was given the manager-
ship of the Ford farms, and one of his most important
duties was arranging the daily deliveries of new-laid eggs,
home-made butter, and unpasteurized milk to Fair Lane
and to the Edsel Ford home on the other side of town.

The Dahlingers themselves started off their married lives
in a large farmhouse beside the Ford dairy in Dearborn, but
Evangeline wanted something grander, and Henry Ford
gave it to her: 150 acres close to Fair Lane that he had
earmarked for Edsel. Henry conveyed the land to the Dahlingers for one dollar, and the mansion, designed to Evangeline's specifications, was built by Ford-employed workmen.

Ray Dahlinger, who professed himself happy living in
the old farmhouse, used to describe this new home as the
"goddamn castle," and there was no doubt it represented
the particular fulfillment of Evangeline's fantasies: it had a
gatehouse staffed by a twenty-four-hour guard, three barns,
a blacksmith's shop, a lake with skating house, a half-mile
track for exercising the horses that Evangeline liked to breed,
a quarter-mile cinder track, a six-car garage, a greenhouse
with servants' quarters, a boathouse, a farmhouse with
three more garages, a family-sized house known as "the
carpenters' shanty," and the main Tudor-style manor house
itself, elaborate with luxuries and refinements of all sorts,
including a Tudor-style secret staircase that led up to the
dressing room and to the bedroom suite of Evangeline.[12]

Just up the Rouge River from Fair Lane—Henry Ford
had an electric boat that would bring him gliding upstream
for impromptu visits—the Dahlinger home was Dearborn's
second-most-magnificent residence, and it represented only
one part of the Dahlingers' property holdings. Henry Ford
gave them a 300-acre farm near Romeo, Michigan, complete
with 300 cows; and up in Michigan's northern peninsula he
bought them a vacation estate beside the Huron Mountain
Club, the retreat where the elite of Chicago and Detroit
took refuge from the humidity of high summer. Evangeline
developed both properties in characteristic style, turning the
Romeo spread into a stud farm where she bred high-pedigree

bloodstock, and enlarging her Upper Peninsula home with a proliferation of guest cabins and other facilities that included a docking ramp for her own personal seaplane, a Curtiss flying boat with Hispano-Suiza engine.[13]

On no one did Henry Ford lavish money as he did on Evangeline Dahlinger. Friends of Clara Ford pursed their lips grimly when discussion turned to the lavish lifestyle of the former stenographer and her test-driver husband, but nobody could claim that Clara was ill-treated by Henry, nor that he did not love her in his fashion.

"If I were to die and come back to another life," he said on several occasions, "I would want the same wife."[14]

He has to be taken at his word. There are contradictions between what Henry said and what Henry did in many areas of his life, but those close to Henry and Clara Ford are unanimous that theirs was a strong and constant partnership, and that Evangeline came to be not so much a threat as, in some ways, a buttress to their alliance. Clara eventually worked out an accommodation of her own with Evangeline, and by the end of Henry's life there was a fair case for arguing that the very best friends the Fords had were the Dahlingers.

Henry and Clara had so much in common. They came from the same rural background; they had shared so much. When Henry got home of an evening to Fair Lane, he would let out a birdlike warble as he walked through the front door, and from wherever she was in the house, Clara would respond with a similar call.

She appears to have understood her husband and his roving eye, and her strategy towards it was a realistic policy of containment—from discouraging his association with the cyclist who favoured "low down women," to tracking down the errant Agnes on the West Coast. Clara was no prude. Her principal charitable interests were homes for fallen women which she sponsored in both Dearborn and Detroit, where she provided generous but brisk assistance to unmarried mothers who were attempting to start a new life.[15]

238

*William Ford,*
*Henry's father*

ogot Ford,
mother

n, Henry's
from the
Historical
ne County,
6

There was certainly a period when Clara's wifely dislike of Evangeline was quite tangible. Commissioned to commemorate on canvas the great banquet that Henry Ford threw in 1929 in honour of Thomas Edison and his invention of the electric light, Irving Bacon made the mistake of including Mrs. Dahlinger among those present.

"Take her out," ordered Henry sharply. "Mrs. Ford wouldn't like for her to be in it."[16]

But with the years, feelings mellowed. Whatever physical dimension there had been to the relationship of Henry and Evangeline seems to have cooled with the birth of John, and Clara made a point of being as welcoming to the little boy as her husband was. John was invited over to Fair Lane when the Ford grandchildren came to play, and the Dahlingers worked hard at making themselves useful to Clara. As manager of the Ford farms and estates, Ray was responsible for many of the practical aspects of her life, from getting furniture shifted to supervising the gardeners who cared for her beloved rose garden, and Evangeline was not too proud to lend a hand. She helped Mrs. Ford with her correspondence and ran errands for her. Henry was a teetotaller, but Clara did take comfort from the occasional glass of Red Rock beer, which she purchased in dainty, pony-sized bottles, and she also appreciated a restoring nip of cherry brandy. Cherry Heering was her favoured brand, and Evangeline knew where to obtain this beverage in bulk for her, at a cut-price rate.

There were few things Clara Ford appreciated more than a bargain. She was a frugal soul, and that, in Harry Bennett's opinion, was a delicate way of putting it. When Fair Lane was being constructed, she was responsible for the gardens, which she placed in the care of the great Midwest "naturalist" landscaper, Jens Jenssen, and Jenssen's plaintive requests in the account files for the payment of quite minor sums make vivid and painful reading.[17] Her niece, Grace Prunk, remembers Aunt Clara spending most of a morning driving around New York City in a chauffeured limousine looking for a drugstore that did not charge more for a hairnet than the price Clara considered proper: ten cents.[18]

She was most famous for her thrift when it came to socks. She had darned Henry's hose in their days of comparative poverty on the farm and during their pilgrimage through the lodging houses of Detroit, and she did not see why she should stop darning just because he had made a bit of money since then. New socks were an extravagance that offended her principles of sound housekeeping, and she kept a vigilant eye open lest her husband surrender to this prodigality. Henry had to conspire with her maid Rosa to keep any new pairs of socks that he purchased out of Clara's sight,[19] and to keep his wife happy he would make a point of putting on darned ones in the morning and leaving the house wearing them. Later in the day, however, his car was not infrequently to be seen idling outside one of the menswear shops in Dearborn while the owner of the world's greatest automobile company sent inside for a quick purchase. The experience of sharing a car with a man worth a billion dollars while he struggled to change his socks was, reported Harry Bennett, a unique one.[20]

Clara's frugality can also be presumed to have had its effect upon Henry's attitude towards Evangeline Dahlinger. Money is a potent element in the self-esteem of most rich men, and there are few more effective ways of frustrating their potency than denying them the opportunity to spend it. So Henry Ford must have found it quite refreshing that at least one of the women in his life could savour the pleasure of owning her own private flying boat with an Hispano-Suiza engine.

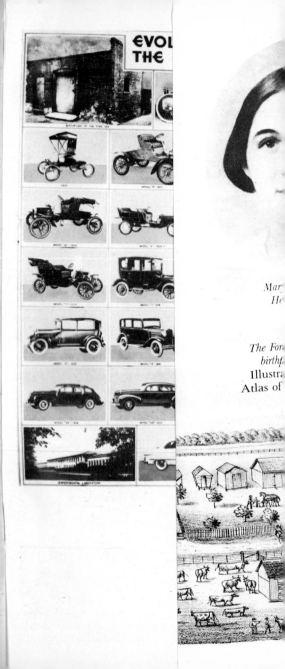

Mar
He

The For
birthf
Illustra
Atlas of

**Above** *Henry Ford in 1880, aged seventeen, an apprentice at the Detroit Dry Dock Company*

**Left** *Clara Bryant Ford in April 1888, the month of her wedding and her twenty-second birthday*

*Henry Ford, around thirty years of age (rear row, third from right) with his fellow workers at the Detroit Edison Illuminating Company, c. 1892*

*Home photography, 1896. Clara and Henry Ford with Edsel, aged three*

*Town and country. Edsel outside 58 Bagley Avenue with Clara, c. 1894, and at Dearborn with Henry, c. 1905*

*Father and son. Henry and Edsel in a Ford Model F, c. 1905*

*Henry Ford, 1893*

*Henry Ford with Barney Oldfield and 999 in 1902*

*Alex Malcolmson (centre) in the office of his coal company. Standing, right, James Couzens. The man seated, left, with cigar, is thought to be the banker John Gray*

*Ford's Piquette Avenue plant, 1906-7. In the foreground, Model K's*

*On duty. Henry Ford's first
official portrait, 1904*

*At ease. Henry, aged forty-three, turns a cartwheel for Edsel and Clara at
Atlantic City Beach, 1907*

*The first moving assembly. The magneto line, Highland Park, 1913*

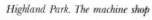

*Highland Park. The machine shop*

*Model T*
*A car for all the people*

John Burroughs
Aug 27 1913

**Above** *John Burroughs and his Model T, August 1913*

**Left** *Henry Ford beside the Rouge River during the building of Fair Lane*

*Highland Park, 1913. One day's output*

*English-language classes at Highland park, 1915*

*To save the world*　　　　*Rosika Schwimmer and handbag*

*The Peace Ship sets sail, December 1915*

*First crossing. Henry, Clara, and Edsel Ford en route to Europe, 1912*

*Fair Lane in 1920*

*Henry Ford at fifty,
summer 1913*

*Henry Ford II, aged two and a half, lights the first blast furnace
at the Rouge Plant, May 1920*

# 12

## CHRONICLE OF THE NEGLECTED TRUTH

*I am going to print the truth. I am going to tell the people what they need to know. I am going to tell them who makes war, and how the game of rotten politics is worked. I am going to tell them how to get the idle land into use. . . .*

— HENRY FORD TO UPTON SINCLAIR, MAY 1919[1]

In November 1918, Henry Ford bought himself a newspaper. It was the logical thing to do, given the problems he so often seemed to encounter with the media, forever making fun of his attempts to accomplish a little good in the world. If Henry Ford had a publication of his own, he would be able to take on the big, nationally known newspapers and magazines at their own game—except that, being Henry Ford, he did not choose to acquire a publication of national stature. He purchased his own, local newspaper, the *Dearborn Independent*.

The *Independent* was a typical small-town publication which had been in business since the turn of the century. It had built itself a modest list of about a thousand subscribers, and Henry liked its name. "Independent," he felt, was a good description of his own beliefs, and he was tickled by the notion that the small rural community in which he grew up should acquire a certain fame of its own, for his plans were ambitious. If Henry Ford could turn floor sweepers into metallurgical experts, he could make a national platform of his local newspaper. He visualized the *Dearborn Independent* being distributed to newsstands across the country—a homely, "plain-folks" publication that would sell so well it could get itself racked up alongside the *New York Times* and the *Wall Street Journal*.

In keeping with these plans, Henry purchased a large-capacity printing press, and he expanded the paper's editorial staff, shifting the entire enterprise from its existing offices to the tractor plant he had built across Michigan Avenue from Fair Lane. With the end of the war, tractor production had been moved down to the Rouge to take over Building B from the Eagle boats, and the *Dearborn Independent* moved into the area that the tractors had left. Henry had all sorts of ideas for his new publication, and, now it was situated in a factory, it struck him that its articles could well be prepared on assembly-line principles, one writer supplying the facts, another the humour, another the editorial comment, and so on.

This idea did not, in the end, prove practical. The writers he recruited rebelled at the notion. But they were good writers: Henry was offering the literary equivalent of the Five Dollar Day, and he raided the best talent in Detroit. Edwin G. Pipp, the first editor of the *Dearborn Independent* under Ford ownership, was previously editor-in-chief of the *Detroit News*, and Pipp brought half a dozen top writers with him.

The first issue of the *Dearborn Independent* appeared on January 11, 1919—five cents a copy, one dollar for a whole year of weekly issues—and it proclaimed a progressive, libertarian manifesto. "Into the new time with all its prophetic forces," promised its leading editorial, "the *Dearborn Independent* comes to put its shoulder to the car of social justice and human progress."[2] Finally Henry could present the world with the particular mixture of Emersonian optimism and Bible-belt populism that made up his personal credo: the evils of absentee ownership, support for Woodrow Wilson's League of Nations plan, the need for better housing, a call to turn the competing telegraph and telephone companies into a government-owned national service—and why not, at the same time, nationalize the railways as well? You could just see the farmers nodding in approval. There was much suspicion of big business, bankers, and Wall Street, and there was vehement endorsement of temperance, prohibition, and women's rights.

These last were causes particularly dear to the heart of the *Independent*'s owner, and the structure of the publication was built around a central feature entitled "Mr. Ford's Own Page," an unpredictable assortment of epigrams and anecdotes that represented the wit and wisdom of Henry Ford: "The man who sees is master," "Opportunity will not overlook you because you wear overalls." Careful to point out that it was in no way an organ of the Ford Motor Company, the *Dearborn Independent* proudly offered itself as a personal crusade on the part of Henry Ford himself. "I have definite ideas and ideals that I believe are practical for the good of all," he said, "and intend giving them to the public without having them garbled, distorted or misquoted."[3]

Henry Ford, however, did not write "Mr. Ford's Own Page," for while happily convinced, as he had been on the Peace Ship, that his personal talents would bring success in virtually any field in which he chose to apply them, he had no stomach for writing. Instead, he would dictate his views to the journalist specially charged with the production of "Mr. Ford's Own Page," an eloquent but alcoholic columnist brought from the *Detroit News* by Edwin Pipp, William J. Cameron.

William Cameron was to play a prominent role in the public persona which Henry Ford developed through the 1920s and 1930s. There was a sense, indeed, in which William Cameron *was* that persona, since he possessed the extraordinary ability to pick up the abrupt, enigmatic remarks that his employer loved to throw out and make sense of them. Henry Ford, it was once said, spoke in telegrams, and it was Cameron's gift to convert these into lucid, flowing sermons of considerable grace and persuasiveness which he set down on paper in the *Dearborn Independent* and, in later years, delivered on the radio. During the 1930s, one of America's most popular radio programmes was the *Ford Sunday Evening Hour*, a potpourri of light music and classical selections broadcast live from Dearborn and Detroit, and the centrepiece of the entertainment was a mellifluous homily—

a little nugget of Ford wisdom—polished and delivered by William Cameron.

Cameron always delivered his sermonettes as coming directly from Henry Ford himself. Over the years he built up a whole theology, a polished Ford canon of beliefs, which he referred to as such—*Ford Ideals* was the title of one collection of his pieces—and never once did the master find cause to rebuke his interpreter for misrepresentation, exaggeration, or embellishment.

The empathy between Ford and Cameron was the more remarkable for the dissimilarity in their personal habits. Resolutely overweight and overindulgent, Cameron had something about him of W. C. Fields. Yet Henry Ford, usually so unforgiving of personal frailty, chose to turn a blind eye to the lapses of his amanuensis—even though there were occasions when, it was said, William Cameron had to be propped up at the microphone in the Ford broadcasting auditorium on a Sunday night.

The two men did share similar roots in the populist ferment of the late nineteenth century—Cameron once named the idols of his youth as Robert Ingersoll and William Jennings Bryan[4]—and they had the same weakness for exotic codes of personal belief. Cameron, who had been a preacher at one stage in his career, was an adherent of the British Israelites, a sect who interpreted data derived from the Great Pyramid as proving that they were descended from the "Lost Tribes" of Israel.

Professionals were not overly impressed by "Mr. Ford's Own Page," nor by the *Dearborn Independent* as a whole when it appeared. *Detroit Saturday Night* described it as the "best weekly ever turned out by a tractor plant"[5]—but that was just the sort of comment you would expect from the professionals. Henry Ford was very pleased with his own, homegrown publication, and he liked to refer to it as the "Chronicler of the Neglected Truth."

In the summer of 1919, the staff and officers of the *Dearborn Independent* were shifted, for a season, to Mount Clemens, a spa town fifteen miles to the northeast of Detroit. The black and sulphurous waters of Mount Clemens had a wondrous effect upon eczema, arthritis, and all manner of other ailments, drawing invalids from every corner of the Midwest, but Henry Ford did not take his journalists to Mount Clemens for a health cure. He had got himself involved in yet another lawsuit, and the venue for it had been set in this town which smelled of rotten eggs.

In June 1916, President Wilson had called up reservists of the National Guard to police America's southern border following raids and incursions from Mexican guerrillas, and the *Chicago Tribune* had taken it upon itself to investigate the attitude of major employers to this call-up. Would they continue to pay those members of their work force who were mobilized? The *Tribune*'s Detroit correspondent could not contact Henry Ford personally, so he put the question to Frank Klingensmith, the faithful personal secretary who had risen, since James Couzens's departure, to the Ford board of directors and to the position of Treasurer. Klingensmith carried out many of Couzens's functions as business and administrative manager, and he informed the *Tribune* reporter that any Ford employees who left their jobs to serve in the National Guard would be neither paid nor reinstated.

This was, in fact, untrue. Klingensmith had spoken to the *Chicago Tribune* without consulting his employer, and Ford policy towards the eighty-nine employees who did go off to serve on the Mexican border proved to be both liberal and patriotic. All were given special, numbered badges which entitled them to their jobs on their return, and the Sociological Department set up a programme to visit and help the families left behind by the absent heroes.[6]

Still, without checking, the *Tribune* ran Klingensmith's statement on June 22, 1916, under the headline "Flivver Patriotism"—*flivver* being a popular slang expression for a cheap car, and for a Ford in particular. Next day the *Tribune* followed this with an editorial denouncing Henry Ford "not merely as an ignorant idealist, but as an anarchistic enemy of the nation which protects him in his wealth." Although

Henry seems to have shrugged off this attack, his lawyer, Alfred Lucking, was incensed by it. Lucking was at that time in charge of Henry's legal dispute with the Dodge brothers, and he urged Henry to hit back against the *Chicago Tribune* and sue them for libel.

"Well," responded Henry, dropping another of the throw-away remarks with which he regularly banana-skinned his own career, "you'd better start suit against them."[7]

Wary of hometown prejudice, Lucking sought to have the libel action heard in Detroit rather than in Chicago. But the *Tribune* lawyers opposed a Detroit venue for the same reason, and that was how the case of Henry Ford versus the *Chicago Tribune* came to be held on neutral ground, among the steam chambers and pumprooms of the town principally noted until that date for the large numbers of people to be seen walking its streets in bathrobes.

Mount Clemens was not all rheumatism and rubdown parlours. There was a flourishing amusement park which featured "Leap the Dips," a giant roller coaster claimed to be the "largest in the world," and the therapies on offer extended beyond bitter water purges at five cents for half a gallon. Miss Mae McKenna, proprietress of the spa's most successful bordello, was one of the sights of the town, promenading of an afternoon, impeccably coiffed and costumed, in her open late-model touring car—driven by a female chauffeur.[8]

The circus that descended on Mount Clemens in the summer of 1919 provided excitement to match anything the spa had known. Newspapers and wire services from all over America sent more than fifty correspondents to report the trial day by day. Each side had hired legal teams which multiplied as only high-paid lawyers can. They, in turn, had summoned a bizarre and colourful crowd of expert witnesses. In order to prove the patriotic necessity of defending the border with Mexico, the *Tribune* had shipped to Michigan twenty Texan cattle ranchers who paraded around Mount Clemens for a month in cowboy regalia, complete with six-shooters, while the Ford lawyers responded, for reasons which are now obscure, with more than a hundred Mexicans wearing their sombreros.[9]

It was to present his own point of view in this mêlée that Henry Ford shifted the staff of the *Dearborn Independent* to Mount Clemens in the summer of 1919. Edwin Pipp, Bill Cameron, and the other writers on the paper were going to put out their material on a more than weekly basis. Convinced that "powerful enemies" manipulated the established wire services, Henry had determined that his own views would be more faithfully reported by a news agency of his own, so Pipp and his staff were established in an office across the road from the courthouse, and the "Mount Clemens News Bureau" set about transmitting the testimony of Henry Ford to America.

It was an elaborate operation, for while producing weekly copy for the *Dearborn Independent*, the Mount Clemens News Bureau also provided a stream of pro-Ford stories which were wired to twelve strategic distribution points around the country. Here the material was set in type and then cast into printing plates that were sent off, free of charge, to any paper content to print this ready-made Ford version of the truth. Nearly 3,000 daily and weekly newspapers signed up to participate in this extraordinary—and expensive— exercise in mass-produced propaganda. Back in Mount Clemens on a huge wall map, some 12,500 blue pins indicated the location of publications that were considered favourable to Henry Ford. Hostile publications were indicated by yellow pins: 397 of them.[10]

Henry Ford needed all the propaganda he could get, for Alfred Lucking, whose indignation had first provoked the confrontation, had made a fatal error in his framing of the case. If Lucking had sued solely on the words *anarchist* and *anarchistic*, Ford's legal position would have been virtually impregnable, since previous cases had clearly established that these terms were libelous. But Lucking had chosen to make his complaint against the entire editorial, which included the phrase "ignorant idealist," and this widened the battleground immeasurably, for it offered the lawyers of the *Chicago Tribune* the chance to broach a much more open question: whether or not Henry Ford, the great carmaker, could be considered "ignorant."

Too late, Lucking realized his mistake and instituted a crash course in American history, current affairs, and virtually anything else that the *Tribune* lawyers might ask his client. But Henry was not a good student. Edwin Pipp sat in on the painful hours of coaching.

Lucking would begin with, "Now don't forget this; remember the evacuation of Florida . . ."

But Ford would be out of his seat, looking out of the window.

"Say, that airplane is flying pretty low, isn't it?" he would ask.

Again Lucking would steer him to the chair, but Ford would hop to the window with: "Look at that bird there; pretty little fellow, isn't it?"[11]

If Henry Ford had been cross-examined on his knowledge of birds, he would have been on strong ground, but the lawyers of the *Chicago Tribune* chose instead to probe his knowledge of American history:

*Q:* Have there been any revolutions in this country?
*A:* Yes.
*Q:* When?
*A:* In 1812.
*Q:* One in 1812, eh? Any other time?
*A:* I don't know of any others.
*Q:* Do you know that this country was born in a revolution?
*A:* Yes, in 1776.
*Q:* Did you forget that revolution?
*A:* I guess so. . . .
*Q:* Do you know what forced us into the Revolutionary War?
*A:* No, I do not. . . .
*Q:* Do you know of any great traitors?
*A:* No.
*Q:* Did you ever hear of Benedict Arnold?
*A:* I have heard the name.
*Q:* Who was he?
*A:* I have forgotten just who he is. He is a writer, I think.[12]

"Outrageous, cruel," hissed Alfred Lucking, watching his

client's performance with helpless fury. "A shame to subject that man to such an examination."

There was a plausible explanation of Henry's extraordinary answer to the question about America's most famous traitor: Horace L. Arnold was a writer who had spent several months at Highland Park researching *Ford Methods and the Ford Shops*, the book which first described the working of the moving assembly line. But Henry Ford was guilty of inattentiveness and sloppy thinking, at least, at a moment that called for applied thought and concentration on his part, and it was difficult for the most impartial witness to his testimony not to conclude that a charge of ignorance could be sustained against him. Asked to define "a large mobile army," he came up with "a large army mobilized," and as a meaning for "ballyhoo" he offered, "Oh, a blackguard or something of that nature."

Leaning back ostentatiously in his chair, clasping one knee to his chest and smiling benignly through his succession of gaffes, Henry Ford seemed determined to play the hayseed.

*Q:* Mr. Ford, I have some hesitation but in justice to yourself I shall ask this question: I think the impression has been created by your failure to read some of these things that have been presented to you, that you could not read. Do you want to leave it that way?

*A:* Yes, you can leave it that way. I am not a fast reader and I have the hayfever and I would make a botch of it.[13]

A sign outside the Mount Clemens courtroom declared: "If you spit on the floor in your own house, do it here. We want you to feel at home." But if Henry Ford hoped that this beer-and-sawdust attitude guaranteed sympathy for his low-brow performance on the witness stand, the verdict of the jury in the *Chicago Tribune* trial provided him with a grave disappointment. In July 1919, the eleven local farmers and one public roads' inspector who had sat through nearly fourteen weeks of testimony found against the *Tribune*, and ordered that the newspaper should pay costs. Henry Ford was clearly not an anarchist, in their opinion. But when invited to express their view on the newspaper libel, and to set a value on the difference between Henry Ford as depicted by the *Tribune* and Henry Ford as they had seen him, the jury awarded the carmaker damages in the sum of just six cents.

"The mystery is finally dispelled," declared the *Nation*, when it heard the verdict. "Henry Ford is a Yankee mechanic, pure and simple; quite uneducated, with a mind unable to 'bite' into any proposition outside of his automobile and tractor business. . . . He has achieved wealth but not greatness." There was something pitiful, if not tragic, about his unveiling. "We would rather have had the curtain drawn, the popular ideal unshattered."[14]

Henry Ford's summer in Mount Clemens provided educated America with yet another opportunity to indulge in ridicule at the carmaker's expense. Ford's intellectual qualities had been tested, declared the *New York Times*, and "he has not received a pass degree."

But, not for the first time, middle America came to a different conclusion. Arthur Brisbane, the Hearst columnist who was syndicated in rural publications across the country, urged his readers to show their feelings, and the response was overwhelming.

"If busy with your crops," suggested Brisbane, "cut this out and mail it with your name signed: 'Dear Ford: I am glad to have you for a fellow citizen and I wish we had more of your brand of anarchism, if that is what it is. Yours truly: Sign here———.'"[15]

Religious sentiment figured strongly in the thousands of responses to Brisbane's invitation. Ordained ministers sent prayers for Henry's deliverance from the hands of the Philistines, and more than one pointed out that Jesus Christ had been an anarchist.[16] It might have been the propaganda of the *Dearborn Independent*/Mount Clemens News Bureau, but more probably it was because Henry Ford had revealed himself, yet again, to be as flawed and fallible as any other of his fellow Americans. His very nakedness when subjected to the city-slicker cleverness of the *Tribune* attorneys struck a chord with thousands who were equally hazy on their knowledge of the American Revolution, and who would have been even more reluctant to read aloud in public. One of the questions to which Henry had not known the answer was the meaning of "chili con carne"—and many Americans saw no reason why he should. It spoke well for his mistrust of things foreign and unconventional.

"We sort of like old Henry Ford, anyway," declared the *Ohio State Journal*.[17]

Just before the Mount Clemens jury announced its verdict, Henry Ford took a holiday. It was another of his excursions with John Burroughs, the naturalist, and for their 1919 expedition the two bird-lovers were joined by Thomas Edison and Harvey Firestone, the tyremaker. This quartet had gone camping in the Adirondacks the previous summer, and the men had enjoyed the experience so much they decided to make it an annual ritual.

Their 1919 project was to blaze a trail eastwards through the forests of upstate New York to New England, but their paraphernalia meant that they were scarcely roughing it: half a dozen cars and trucks with chauffeurs and attendants, a Model T fitted out as a mobile kitchen, a kitchen tent with refrigerator, and a dining tent with an upright table that seated twenty. The "vagabonds," as they termed themselves, revelled in the adventure of sleeping under canvas, but each man had his own ten-by-ten tent complete with floor, electricity, folding cot, mattress, blankets, sheets, and pillow, and when they emerged every morning for breakfast, each was immaculate in collar, formal tie, and three-piece suit.

John Burroughs was the chronicler of the expeditions. "When we have settled on a camping site," he wrote about the 1918 trip, "Mr. Edison settles down in his car and reads or meditates; Mr. Ford seizes an axe and swings it vigorously till there is enough wood for the campfire."[18]

There was no doubt who was the most energetic member of the party.

Mr. Ford is a runner and a high kicker, and frequently challenges some member of the party to race with him. He is also a persistent walker, and from every camp, both morning and evening, he sallied forth for a brisk half-hour walk. His cheerfulness and adaptability on all occasions, and his optimism in regard to all the great questions, are remarkable.[19]

Henry Ford's relationships with both John Burroughs and Thomas Edison contained strong elements of hero worship, and Burroughs reciprocated the sentiment. The white-bearded old naturalist cherished Henry Ford for his imaginative, visionary side.

Notwithstanding his practical turn of mind, and his mastery of the mechanic arts ... he is through and through an idealist. This combination of powers and qualities makes him a very interesting and, I may say, loveable personality. He is as tender as a woman, and much more tolerant.[20]

After the ordeal of Mount Clemens, a little mutual admiration did not come amiss. The great men sat around the campfire at night coaxing Edison to reminisce about his inventions and marvelling as the chemical formulae rolled off his tongue. They debated literature, Edison proposing *Les Misérables* as the great novel of his lifetime, with Burroughs demurring. From an artistic point of view he considered it "a monstrosity," and he thought no more of Edison's nomination for the world's greatest poem, Longfellow's "Evangeline"—though Edison's suggestion may have been mischievously inspired.

Every stream that the campers encountered awakened Henry Ford's mania for waterpower. He would stride up and down the bank, pointing out all the energy going to waste, and dilating on the benefits that would accrue from harnessing it, as he had done at Fair Lane. John Burroughs, meanwhile, was concerned with a different sort of practicality, teaching his fellow campers how to prepare a Burroughs speciality, the Brigand Steak: cut a strong green branch that will not burn, spear it with one whole steak, a few slices of bacon, and a couple of whole onions, and then hold over the fire, turning frequently.[21]

Shinning up trees, exploring old watermills, and rolling up their trouser legs to paddle in forest pools, the four famous men were like so many little boys—and, Henry Ford being Henry Ford, their escapades were captured by newsreel cameramen and relayed to movie theatres across the country. News photographers were on hand wherever the white-haired Huckleberry Finns halted, to record the satisfying sight of great American inventor-heroes getting back to the authentic soil from which America's greatness sprang.

MILLIONS OF DOLLARS WORTH OF BRAINS OFF ON A VACATION, ran the headlines. GENIUS TO SLEEP UNDER THE STARS.[22]

The rural excursions of Henry Ford and his famous friends provided regular summer features for American newspapers between the years 1918 and 1924, and their emblematic character was made clear when others got in on the act: President Harding joined the Ford caravan for one trip. But America might have been surprised by some of the conversations that took place around the campfire when the great men settled down for the night.

"Mr. Ford," recorded John Burroughs in his diary of the 1919 trip, "attributes all evil to the Jews or the Jewish capitalists—the Jews caused the war, the Jews caused the outbreak of thieving and robbery all over the country, the Jews caused the inefficiency of the Navy of which Edison talked last night . . ."[23]

Henry Ford's anti-Semitism first came into the open on May 22, 1920, in the year following the *Chicago Tribune* trial, when the *Dearborn Independent* featured an unsigned article on its front cover: "The International Jew: The World's Problem." Its facts were spurious and its arguments predictable, but its message was very, very simple indeed.

There is a race, a part of humanity which has never yet been

253

received as a welcome part, and which has succeeded in raising itself to a power that the proudest Gentile race has never claimed —not even Rome in the days of her proudest power.

For the next ninety-one issues, from the spring of 1920 until the beginning of 1922, the *Dearborn Independent* hammered at the same theme every week: the corrupting influence of the Jews on American politics, public life, finance, living habits, and morality in general. Proudly and prominently proclaimed, with the name and prestige of Henry Ford behind them, the articles were a sustained outpouring of prejudice the like of which had never been seen in America, before or since.

The roots of Henry Ford's anti-Semitism went back to his farmboy, populist suspicion of financiers and middlemen. "He called all the moneylenders of the world 'Jews,'" remembered his sister Margaret.[24] Entire generations were introduced to the children of Israel by way of Shylock and Fagin, and in the years before the Holocaust, anti-Semitism was a common, lazy way of thought for whole classes of society. Henry Ford had some close associates who propagated entrenched, anti-Semitic views. Thomas Edison habitually groused about Jewish conspiracies—he was a poor businessman, and his inventions had never made him the money he thought he was entitled to—while Henry's German private secretary, Ernest Liebold, who was to create his own empire, in the style of Ray Dahlinger and Harry Bennett, from the patchiness of Ford's panoramic attention span, appears to have imported his notions undiluted from Prussia.[25]

Henry himself explained it in terms of the Peace Ship. He told several people that the voyage of the *Oscar II* had opened his eyes to the sinister influence wielded by the Jewish race, and this was taken as a reference to Madame Rosika Schwimmer and another of the peace delegates, Herman Bernstein, owner-editor of a liberal newspaper, *The Day*.[26] It was quite simple, said Henry. The world was controlled by gold, and the gold was controlled by the Jews.[27] Explaining life's woes in terms of precious metal made perfect sense to someone raised in the Greenback paranoia of the 1880s.

But the paranoia had a deeper cause, for whatever the Jewish involvement in the Peace Ship might have been, the episode stood first and foremost in Henry's life for failure—massive and surprising failure after the preceding, glorious years of success.

Emerson taught his followers to learn from such episodes. Failure was even more useful to a man, said the philosopher, than success. The wise man had the ability to learn from his critics and from the faults and weaknesses that his enemies might identify. "It is more his interest than it is theirs to find his weak point," runs one of the marked passages in Henry's little blue book of essays,[28] and Henry Ford would earnestly try to follow that advice. Edwin Pipp could remember Henry poring over column after column of bitter criticism and ridicule of him without wincing.

"They are right in this. They have got it on us there; let's correct that," he would say.[29]

But this strategy only seemed to work with the little things. When it came to truly serious shortcomings—the congenital gaps in the circuitry that led to débâcles like the Peace Ship or the Mount Clemens trial—Henry Ford simply did not have the mental equipment to accept his own responsibility for his failure, let alone to analyse it. His defence mechanisms were so strong that they blanked out the possibility of self-blame. He sought consolation in his own success in other fields, and in the conviction that some exterior force must be responsible for his failure in this particular, isolated instance. He looked outside himself for simplistic, mechanical explanations of what had gone wrong, and this made him bitter and mistrustful, easy prey for conspiracy theories. Failure was no corrective for Henry Ford. On the contrary, it fed his paranoia; and in the spring of 1920, when the failure of the Peace Ship had been so recently compounded by his own crushingly incompetent performance in the Mount Clemens trial, it was not surprising that he should be feeling a little persecuted.

"The capitalistic newspapers began a campaign against me," he complained in the summer following the Mount Clemens verdict. "They misquoted me, distorted what I said, made up lies. . . . The invisible government got at its work."[30]

Anti-Semitism is one of the ultimate communal and personal paranoias, and the "invisible government" was a favourite code word of prejudice in the early years of this century. It derived from the *Protocols of the Learned Elders of Zion*—the tsarist forgery purporting to be the transcripts of conversations between senior Jewish leaders, the "Learned Elders of Zion," and Freemasons, as they laid their plans to destroy Christian civilization and take over the world. Familiar with the concepts of the *Protocols*, Ford and Liebold were shown copies of the work itself soon after their anti-Semitic articles started, and from August 1920 onwards, the *Protocols* provided a cornerstone for their campaign, quoted as an authority, issue after issue, as if they were the gospel truth.

In retrospect, it seems such flimsy stuff. Jazz, revealed the *Dearborn Independent*, was part of the international conspiracy. Never mind that it was played by blacks. "The mush, the slush, the sly suggestion, the abandoned sensuousness of sliding notes are of Jewish origin."[31] Short skirts and rolled-down stockings were the work of the Jews who owned the garment industry. Rising rents stemmed from the Jewish landlord. "The present Jewish government of Russia was transported almost as a unit from the lower East Side of New York," thus proving that "the Bolshevik revolution was a carefully groomed investment on the part of international Jewish finance."[32] America as a whole was getting corroded by it, resulting in "a marked deterioration in our literature, amusements, and social conduct . . . a general letting down of standards."[33] It was not "the robust coarseness of the white man, the rude indelicacy, say, of Shakespeare's characters, but a nasty Orientalism which has insidiously affected every channel of expression." All of this was traceable "to one racial source."[34]

256

The articles thrived on the inversion of the truth. If people scoffed at the notion of a Zionist conspiracy, that only proved there really was one.

This concealed international control of the world flourishes because people do not believe that it exists. They don't see how it can exist. . . . Someday a world-wide exposure will be made and many things explained which have always puzzled the plain people. . . . We shall see that much which we have charged up to the "mystery of life" has really been the deliberate effect of a deep-wrought, unified international but private program.[35]

This was pure, undiluted Henry Ford. The practical, week-to-week impetus for his anti-Semitic propaganda of the 1920s and 1930s came from others. William Cameron wrote the columns, often with very little detailed reference to Henry personally, and Ernest Liebold supplied most of the data and development of the ideas. The private secretary was probably the central driving force of the entire campaign, courting the spies and riffraff which it was easy to recruit from Russian emigres in the years following 1917. Liebold hired private detectives to gather dirt on prominent Jews. He organized the reprinting of the *Dearborn Independent* articles as a series of books, *The International Jew*, and he also published an edition of the *Protocols* themselves.* These books were distributed all around the world in the early 1920s—they had a particular impact in pre-Hitler Germany—and they survive to this day, circulated and reprinted by racist groups, as enduringly potent and poisonous as nuclear waste.

---

* Always suspect, the *Protocols* were totally discredited in August 1921, when Philip Graves demonstrated how they had been copied, word for word in places, from an obscure French satire of the nineteenth century. The Russian historian Burtsev later produced evidence to show how the documents had been concocted as part of the tsarist authorities' campaign to discredit their Marxist critics, who were frequently, though by no means invariably, Jews. Ernest Liebold shrugged this off. "If you will carefully read our articles," he wrote in January 1921, "you will find we have at no time guaranteed their authenticity. We have merely stated what they contain and have paralleled this with what actually took place and are leaving it to the mind of the public to judge."[36]

But Cameron and Liebold were only delegates. They were as much the extensions of Henry Ford's complex genius as were Wills, Sorensen, or any of the other technicians who handled the mechanical details of his cars. The basic drive, the impetus for the campaign, came from Henry Ford himself—and from deep within him. He was the Great Simplifier. Seeing the obvious solution which lay at the heart of a complex problem was his particular talent, and since it worked so well with cars, he did not see why it should not work equally well with the "mystery of life": the complex, discouraging realities of existence "which have always puzzled the plain people."

The "invisible government" was the simple, obvious solution which required to be revealed, and he, Henry Ford, would be the revealer. For the great carmaker, anti-Semitism was the intellectual equivalent of vanadium steel or the moving assembly line.

The articles stopped, mysteriously, as abruptly as they had started. One morning in January 1922, William Cameron walked into his office, to find Henry Ford waiting for him.

"You're late, aren't you?" said Ford, and before Cameron could attempt an excuse, his boss continued, "I want you to cut out the Jewish articles."

Cameron had become editor of the *Dearborn Independent* within weeks of the "International Jew" series starting. Edwin Pipp had resigned in disgust at the articles and had set up his own newspaper, *Pipp's Weekly*, largely dedicated to publishing corrective truths about the newspaper that had been founded to publish corrective truths.

"Put all your thought and time to studying and writing about this money question," Ford continued. "The Jews are responsible for the present money standard, and we want them on our side to get rid of it."

Ernest Liebold arrived soon afterwards and suggested that the Jews and the money standard could both be dealt with at the same time, but Henry Ford was adamant.

"The Jewish articles must stop," he said, "and Cameron must go to work on the money question."[37]

Several reasons have been proposed for Henry Ford's sudden and, as it proved, temporary change of heart. There had been lawsuits, and threats of lawsuits. The Hollywood producer William Fox had pointed out that if Henry Ford could flood newsstands with anti-Jewish propaganda, then he, Fox, could flood movie theatres with footage of Ford cars involved in serious accidents.[38] There was some evidence of Ford's car business being hurt by boycotts, though this scarcely mattered in 1921 or 1922, with Model T sales pushing towards the million-and-a-half mark.

The truth was simpler and, as usual, came down to Henry Ford's own ambition. At the beginning of 1922, the great carmaker was seriously thinking of running for President.

The "Draft Henry" campaigns of 1916 had never really stood much chance. They came at a time when Henry was embroiled with the Dodge brothers and starting work on the Rouge. Furthermore, they would, ultimately, have involved him pitting himself against Woodrow Wilson, the President who, of all Presidents in Henry's lifetime, stood closest to the Ford credo, particularly where war and peace were concerned.

In 1922, however, it was a different matter. The Harding administration was sinking beneath the weight of its own inertia and corruption. Even Henry Ford could do no worse than that, and some hitherto scornful voices began to give some serious consideration to his candidacy. "Why not Ford For President?" asked the *Wall Street Journal* in an editorial in the autumn of 1922. "Ford looms today a powerful and enigmatic figure on the political horizon," declared the *New York Times* early in the following year.[39]

Flattered by such encouragement, Henry was prompted to take his own presidential prospects seriously, and he even started counting votes, according to Edwin Pipp. Jewish hostility might not matter too much so far as car sales were concerned, but it could cost a lot of votes in urban areas.[40]

The great obstacle to Henry's political ambitions had

always been his total inability to speak in public. If he had had the capacity to stand on his hind legs and project himself verbally, there is no telling the position he might have commanded in American public life. William Cameron and the *Dearborn Independent* were attempts to make up for this deficiency, and in 1922 the publication of Henry's autobiography, *My Life and Work*, accomplished the purpose still more effectively.

*My Life and Work* was, in fact, the seventh book written about Henry in these years,[41] the others including such efforts as Sarah T. Bushnell's *The Truth About Henry Ford*. But it outsold all the others put together. It propagated the legends of Henry's childhood, of repairing watches and running away from home, and it punctuated the simple rags-to-riches narrative with thoughts on the present state of the nation and some homely pieces of advice as to how readers could duplicate the hero's achievements in their own lives. Written in a "let me tell you" conversational style, it read as if Henry Ford himself was sitting across the room chatting with you.

The ghostwriter had recently been seized on as a powerful and profitable tool in the field of public relations. From 1921 onwards, Babe Ruth was adding to his baseball income with syndicated writings prepared for him by others, and the *Dearborn Independent* was itself a massive exercise in ghostwriting.[42] To ghost his own autobiography, Henry picked Samuel Crowther, a journalist with an economic bent. Working from a few interviews with Henry, but largely from "Mr. Ford's Own Page" and conversations with Liebold and Cameron, Crowther crafted a masterpiece of its kind. *My Life and Work* was translated into twelve languages, and Braille.[43] It became a bestseller all around the world—particularly in Germany, where it sold alongside copies of the *Independent*'s anti-Jewish reprints—and it contributed substantially to the feeling in America that Ford was the right man for the White House.

Henry's presidential bid was linked to his attempts to

take over Muscle Shoals, the complex of dams and generating plants that were later to become the heart of the Tennessee Valley Authority. This massive exercise in regional development has come to be associated with Roosevelt and the New Deal, but it started during the First World War when the Wilson administration spent the best part of $100 million on the construction of a dam—the Wilson Dam at Muscle Shoals—and some nitrate plants. Breaking American dependence on foreign explosives had been the object of the exercise, and the plants could also be used for making fertilizer.

With peace, the nitrate plants stood derelict. The *laissez-faire* Harding administration offered them to private enterprise, and Henry Ford put in his bid in the summer of 1921. It was the perfect project for Henry: the world's most ambitious attempt to harness waterpower for electricity, and all for the benefit of the small, midwestern farmer, who would profit not only from cheap nitrate fertilizer, but from the employment and wealth that would be generated the length of the Tennessee River. Henry spoke grandly of a seventy-five-mile-long city connecting the dams and hydroelectrically powered industries that he would string along the valley. Muscle Shoals would be a new Detroit, and real-estate speculators lent credibility to his plans. They bought up land and actually staked out future communities in the Alabama countryside, including one that was named Highland Park and contained streets with familiar Detroit names, like John R. and Woodward.[44]

Muscle Shoals became a national craze for a season, another California gold rush. The entire Tennessee River system covered a vast area, some 42,000 square miles, with 4 million people living in it, most of them farmers. Its previous decay and the miraculous redemption now offered through waterpower and the genius of Henry Ford made it a symbol of hope for farmers everywhere. Rallies were held. "I Want Ford to Get Muscle Shoals" buttons were sold.[45] "He is one of the few men," wrote a Georgia farmer to President Harding, "who have acquired great wealth without lining his pathway to success with the wrecked hopes of his less fortunate competitors."[46]

Muscle Shoals was tailor-made for Henry Ford's increasingly messianic ambitions, for it enabled him to present himself to the nation playing his strongest part: getting things done, mechanical things. He might be verbally inarticulate, but his mechanical achievements spoke volumes, and here was a vast, practical project to which the Great Tinkerer could turn his talents. Henry Ford could bring solid benefits to his fellow countrymen in a way that no ordinary politician could, and he looked even further than this.

My purpose in taking over Muscle Shoals is not to benefit us or our business in Detroit or any other part of the country—my one purpose is to do a certain thing that will benefit the whole world. . . . We can here do an epochal thing—literally, I mean it —an epochal thing. We shall eliminate war from the world. . . .[47]

Muscle Shoals would beat them all: Wall Street, the gold standard, the international bankers who upheld it and who waged wars for their personal profit. Henry even had plans for a new sort of currency, an "energy" dollar, which would be based not on false metallic values, but on what the land produced. This was the "money question" he had instructed Cameron to start writing about, and although the *Dearborn Independent*'s anti-Semitic articles had stopped for the time being, the thrust of Henry's battle against the international bankers was obvious.

The problem was the price that Henry Ford offered the American government in return for Muscle Shoals. He saw his bid as essentially a personal gesture—he was offering himself, his name, his genius. Money was an incidental. But when all the figures were set down on paper and considered dispassionately, as though Henry Ford were any unknown, profit-oriented speculator, then the farmers' friend appeared to be cutting himself in on a very good deal indeed. In return for facilities which had cost the United States taxpayer some $85 million, and which were worth more than $8 million as scrap alone, Henry Ford was prepared to pay just $5 million —providing that the government found a further $68 million to renovate the derelict dams and factories that would then be his.[48] There was a complicated, hundred-year-long system of repayment proposed at a low rate of interest, but it did not amount to much. If a Jewish entrepreneur had had the nerve to make such a one-sided proposal for a major slice of the American countryside, the *Dearborn Independent* would have had material to last it a month.

"No corporation ever got a more unconscionable contract," complained Senator George W. Norris on May 10, 1922, speaking as chairman of the Senate Agricultural Committee,[49] and Norris headed a small but vociferous group in Congress determined to obstruct Henry's plan.

Through 1922 and 1923, Muscle Shoals and "Henry For President" were intertwined as the Ford bandwagon gained momentum, and as the Harding administration crumbled visibly under the impact of its successive scandals. William Cameron ghostwrote an article for *Collier's Weekly*—"If I Were President" by Henry Ford—and public-opinion surveys seemed to show that this was a real possibility. The polls showed Henry consistently beating every likely opponent. Liebold sent out one of the *Dearborn Independent* staff, Fred L. Black, to investigate the "Ford For President" clubs springing up everywhere, and Black returned with the report that the clubs appeared to have genuine local origin, and that they had enlisted reputable citizens who, with no special axe to grind, greatly favoured Henry Ford over Harding.[50]

Overflowing with proposals for currency reform, regenerating the land, and spreading hydroelectric power—while taking the occasional, knowing dig at jazz, cocktails, and Hollywood producers—the *Dearborn Independent* came to serve as a weekly campaign letter, and Henry himself started talking in presidential terms. "I'd just like to be down there for about six weeks and throw some monkey wrenches into the machinery," Black heard him say.[51] Henry Ford seemed to think that running the country would be rather like running Highland Park, wandering from department to department, while trusted aides like Liebold did all the work —a concept which certainly appealed to the self-important German secretary. Henry told Charles Sorensen he was planning on giving him, Sorensen, the War Department.[52]

But Sorensen stayed a carmaker. On August 2, 1923, President Harding died, and with the succession of Calvin Coolidge, the Republicans had a figurehead around which they were, once more, happy to rally. "Ford For President" was suddenly no longer a viable prospect, and in December 1923, Henry Ford went to the White House to inform the new President that he would be endorsing his candidacy in the coming year. In return, Coolidge appears to have promised Henry that he would put the Presidency behind the Ford bid for Muscle Shoals—which was in need of some support in the face of the stalwart opposition being organized by Senator Norris.

Henry complained that his plan to generate a great new national resource was being frustrated by sinister Wall Street influences, but this charge lacked substance, since George W. Norris was a senator from Nebraska.

In April 1924, the *Dearborn Independent* started attacking the Jews again, and the resumption of the campaign, like its temporary suspension, seems to have been prompted by Henry's national ambitions. On March 10, 1924, the House of Representatives approved the Ford bid for Muscle Shoals, which only left the Senate, and the troublesome senator from Nebraska—and Henry's second round of allegations against the Jews was well calculated to win him sympathy in the farm belt.

Aaron Sapiro had studied to be a rabbi before he turned to law, and as a lawyer he had become active in the cooperatives organized by the fruit growers of California. Sapiro refined the business and marketing procedures of cooperatives so they could take on middlemen and wholesalers at their own game, and he extended these principles from fruit to other farm produce. The aim of the "Sapiro Plan," as his system came to be called, was that farmers should control the market, rather than the market controlling them, and from 1919 onwards it spread right across the country. By 1925 the Sapiro plan had been adopted by ninety associations in thirty-two states and Canada, with a membership of 890,000 farmers,[53] and the value of farm products handled was some $600 million annually. In the farm belt, Aaron Sapiro was something of a hero.

This was the man whom the *Dearborn Independent* chose to attack in the spring of 1924. JEWISH EXPLOITATION OF FARMERS' ORGANIZATIONS, ran the headline. "Monopoly Traps Operate Under Guise Of Marketing Associations,"[54] and the opening sentence encapsulated the story. "A band of Jews—bankers, lawyers, moneylenders, advertising agencies, fruit-packers, produce buyers, professional office managers, and bookkeeping experts—is on the back of the American farmer."

Sapiro was no saint. Short-tempered and dictatorial, he had charged quite substantial fees for the advice he gave farmers; his income for 1922 had been $61,531.[55] But there was no justification for the outlandish charges of cheating and extortion that the *Dearborn Independent* now brought against him, and the lawyer sued for defamation.

In the two years which it took for the case to come to court, Ernest Liebold set a team of private detectives to work amassing material against Sapiro, and they compiled some 125 affidavits and over 40,000 pages of depositions on every detail of the lawyer's activities.[56] They also combed through the flood of correspondence prompted by the *Independent*'s articles.

Sapiro is a shrewd little Jew. . . . The Bible says Jews will return to Palestine, but they want to get all the money out of America first. . . . Sapiro should be kicked out because he is trash. . . . The sooner these leeches are given a dose of "go quick" the better. . . . Ananias on one of his best days could not have out-lied Sapiro.[57]

Most of the material gathered was like the original accusations, high on prejudice and low on fact. But since Aaron Sapiro had brought his case against Henry Ford personally, and not against the *Dearborn Independent*, the Ford lawyers were left with one loophole which they proceeded to exploit —the defence that Henry Ford himself had had no knowledge of the material that the *Independent* printed in his name. In March 1927, William Cameron went on the stand to swear to this scarcely credible proposition, and for five days Henry Ford's personal mouthpiece managed to maintain that he had never discussed any article on any Jew with Mr. Ford, that he had never sent his master an advance copy of the magazine, and that he had never even seen Henry Ford read a copy of it.

Sapiro had at least one witness who could swear to the ludicrous falsehood of this defence—which, if true, meant that the entire basis of the *Dearborn Independent* and of "Mr. Ford's Own Page" was a total fraud—but the best possible witness was Henry Ford himself, and, after some difficulty, one of Sapiro's process servers managed to get close enough to drop a subpoena, literally, into the great man's lap.

Henry had been sitting in an open car at the time, and his lawyers thought that they could evade the subpoena by claiming that the document had missed its target and fallen between his knees to end up on the floor. But the court was not impressed. Henry Ford was summoned, on pain of contempt, to appear in the witness box on Monday, April 1, 1927.

On the evening of Sunday, March 31, 1927, just a few hours before he was due to appear in court, Henry Ford appeared on foot, dazed and bleeding, at the gatehouse that guarded the driveway to Fair Lane. His normally immaculate clothes were rumpled, and he seemed confused. From what he said, he had been involved in some sort of car accident. It was a rainy evening and his Model T had skidded off the road. Doctors were called, the sixty-three-year-old magnate was put to bed, and his staff went out to look for his car.

They found it only a few hundred yards away, at the bottom of a steep and wooded embankment off Michigan

Avenue, the main road from Detroit to Chicago. It was strange that Henry Ford should have had an accident there, for it was a section of road he travelled every day of his life, almost within sight of the gates to his estate—he owned the land, in fact, on both sides of the road. His Model T, an upright, two-door coupe, had come to rest against a tree.

Henry himself blamed a Studebaker. He had been on his way home, he said, when a car driven fast by two mysterious men overtook him, to cut in sideways and force him off the road. Thinking over the incident later, it seemed to him that he could remember the Studebaker from earlier that day, and that its two occupants had been watching him suspiciously.

Friends of Henry Ford who knew his driving habits had an alternative explanation, for he did have a tendency to dawdle along towards the crown of the road, oblivious to the attempts of those behind to overtake him. Perhaps the Studebaker had sideswiped the Ford semiaccidentally, when its driver cut in early to express his exasperation.

Eyewitnesses interviewed by the police, however, failed to substantiate either interpretation. Two young men who had been driving a Studebaker in the vicinity at the time were rounded up and cross-examined by officers anxious for a prosecution, but they were released without charges. It seemed that Henry Ford had, for some reason, driven himself off the road of his own volition, run down the bank, and crashed into the tree. If he were not famous across America for his championing of abstinence, people might have come to an obvious conclusion.

The other obvious conclusion, that Henry Ford had staged the crash, even risking serious injury, in order to get out of appearing in court next day, was suspected by everyone, but never proved. Following the accident, his doctors pronounced him unfit to get out of bed, and two days later he was removed to the Ford Hospital. What really happened on Michigan Avenue would, presumably, have been the subject of inquiry once the carmaker was pronounced fit enough to appear on the witness stand—but before that could happen, another bizarre occurrence intervened.

Ford's lawyers produced affidavits from no less than fourteen witnesses who claimed that Sapiro was guilty of jury tampering. This was the very reverse of the truth. It was Ford agents, orchestrated by Harry Bennett, who had been harassing the jury, and, in the end, the harassment got results. One of the female jurors felt moved to remark to a reporter that the Ford side seemed very anxious to stop the case getting to the jury, and once this was published, a declaration of mistrial was inevitable.

A new trial date was set six months hence, but Henry Ford had had enough. On July 7, 1927, he published a retraction of the attacks on Aaron Sapiro, together with a lengthy apology for all he had said about the Jews in general, and at the end of the year he closed down the *Dearborn Independent*, on which he had lost the best part of $5 million.[58] His seven-year publishing career died as it was born—of humiliation.

Harry Bennett had been one of the agents that Henry Ford commissioned to negotiate his surrender of July 1927, and when the text was drawn up, essentially as dictated by Louis Marshall of the American Jewish Committee, Bennett telephoned his master in Dearborn.

"It's pretty bad, Mr. Ford," he said.

"I don't care how bad it is," responded Henry Ford, "you sign it and settle the thing up."

Bennett tried to read some of the statement over the telephone, but Henry cut him short. "I don't care how bad it is," he repeated, "you just settle it up." And then he added, "The worse they make it, the better."[59]

It was a replay of Henry's Oslo desertion of the Peace Ship. Obstinate in many respects, Henry Ford knew when the time had come to cut and run. There had been a moment in 1923, quite a long moment, when he had been on the very crest of the wave: running hard for the White House, on the way to acquiring Muscle Shoals, pouring out his opinions through the *Dearborn Independent* and his ghostwritten autobiography. Attacking the bankers, revered by the farmers, just about anything seemed possible for Henry Ford—and it had all come crashing down. In October 1924, faced with the continuing opposition of Norris and the Senate, Henry formally withdrew his bid for Muscle Shoals.

Henry's anti-Semitism had been the connecting thread in his jaunty venture onto the national stage, his conviction that he had discovered the secret to "how the game of rotten politics is worked"—and the basic unreality of his fantasy, the sheer intellectual unworthiness of blaming the world's problems on a nonexistent clique of conspirators, determined the dishonest and unworthy way that it all ended: the staged car crash, the jury tampering, and the apology that was not an apology at all, since Henry Ford clung to his prejudice privately, and not always so privately, for the rest of his life.[60]

Anti-Semitism has come to a particularly ugly and obscene climax in the twentieth century, and if any one American were to be singled out for his contribution to the evils of Nazism, it would have to be Henry Ford. His republished articles and the currency which he gave to the *Protocols of the Learned Elders of Zion* had considerable impact on Germany in the early 1920s—a vulnerable and, as it proved, crucially formative time. Hitler, still an obscure figure in those years, read Ford's books, hung Henry's picture on his wall, and cited him frequently as an inspiration. Hitler appears to have based several sections of *Mein Kampf* upon Ford's words as processed by William Cameron, and he accorded Henry the unhappy distinction of being the only American to be mentioned in that work.[61]

Every year makes them [the Jews] more and more the controlling masters of the producers in a nation of one hundred and twenty millions; only a single great man, Ford, to their fury, still maintains full independence.[62]

Josephine Gomon, who got quite close to Henry when she worked at Ford's Willow Run factory during the Second World War, told a story hinting at some sort of last-minute, almost deathbed repentance. Newsreel film showing the opening of the concentration camps was brought to the factory, she said, and when Henry Ford, by that time in his eighties, was confronted with the atrocities which finally and unanswerably laid bare the bestiality of the prejudice to which he had contributed, he collapsed with a stroke—his last and most serious.[63]

It is possible. Henry Ford's anti-Semitism was never the vindictive anti-Semitism of some racists, who seek power for the sake of the pain they can inflict. Without excusing Henry from the consequences of his actions, he can be absolved from that particular sin of intent. There was always an oddly detached, impersonal character to his pogrom. He was amazed when, soon after the anti-Semitic articles started appearing in the *Dearborn Independent*, Rabbi Leo Franklin, a friend and neighbour from the Fords' Edison Avenue days, returned the Model T which Henry sent him as an annual present.

"What's wrong, Dr. Franklin?" he asked. "Has anything come between us?"[64]

Henry stayed on the best of terms with the architect Albert Kahn, who, himself, remained proud of the friendship. When Henry started getting interested in antiques, it was a Jewish dealer that he used. The Fair Lane butcher was Jewish. There were never fewer than 3,000 Jews employed in the Ford work force through any of these years.[65] Henry Ford seems to have got on well with every Jew he met in his life, in fact.

Anti-Semitism was for Henry Ford a vehicle—like the *Dearborn Independent*, Muscle Shoals, and even the U.S. Presidency itself—for Henry's success had given him a conceit that was both humble and arrogant. He genuinely wished to be of service to his fellow men, and he genuinely believed he had the capacity to accomplish just about anything for them. If a moving belt could cut the time it took to make a car from twelve and a half man-hours to less than two, then he felt sure he could find similar short cuts in journalism, politics, and economics—and anti-Semitism was such a short cut.

Henry Ford genuinely believed that he had found yet another of his magical keys, an insight right into the heart of things; and if he did finally repent when confronted with the evidence which proved that he was wrong, it was probably not through remorse, nor through any belated empathy or final contact with the human feelings and suffering that he had been playing with so blithely all those years. It was more probably through blind anger and frustration. So life did not imitate cars.

# 13

## FOOD FOR THOUGHT

*I am in a peculiar position. No one can give me anything. There is
nothing I want that I cannot have. But I do not want the things that
money can buy. I want to live a life, to make the world a little better
for having lived in it.*

—HENRY FORD[1]

In 1900 there had been no more than 5,000 blacks living in
the city of Detroit. By the summer of 1920 there were 40,000,
and they were arriving, by that date, at the rate of a thousand
a month.[2] They came in search of jobs in the car factories,
and they also came to escape the oppression of life in the
South. Detroit had an open-minded, liberal reputation. In
the days of John Brown, it had been one of the northern
terminuses of the "Underground Railway" which smuggled
slaves to freedom in Canada.[3]

Dr. Ossian Sweet was one of the black, professional middle
class who enjoyed freedom and a relative dignity in Detroit.
He had built up a successful practice as a gynaecologist,
and in 1925 he bought himself an $18,000, two-storey brick
house in a predominantly white, middle-class neighbourhood on the east side of the city. As the black influx from
the South had intensified, the Ku Klux Klan had been
gathering recruits in the Motor City, and with the news that
the Sweets were moving into the area, a neighbourhood
"improvement association" was formed. Several other black
homes in the area had been harassed, so when Dr. Sweet,
his wife, and young child moved into their new home on
September 8, 1925, it was with police protection.

The police proved of little help, however, when, shortly
after dark on the second night of the Sweets' stay, several
hundred whites started massing ominously around the black
family's home. By eleven o'clock their mood had grown
ugly. Rocks and debris were starting to be thrown when

suddenly, from inside the house, there came the flash of a shotgun. Ten more shots rang out, and across the street, a neighbour who had been sitting on the porch of his home watching the demonstration fell dead. Another white was wounded.

The eight to ten police officers who had failed to do anything to control the crowd promptly arrested Dr. Sweet, his two brothers, and a group of friends he had brought in to defend his home, and all eleven blacks were charged with murder.[4]

The trial was the most controversial Detroit had known. It stirred the whole city, and it attracted national attention. Clarence Darrow, fresh from his battle with William Jennings Bryan in the Scopes Monkey Trial, came to defend the Sweets. Reporters arrived from all over America. The courtroom was packed, whites on one side, blacks on the other. As white witnesses told it, there had scarcely been anyone in the street, and there had certainly been no rock throwing when the Sweets opened fire, unprovoked. Darrow, for his part, tried to pin the shooting on a policeman with a reputation as a "nigger hater," and the trial ended with a hung jury.

In the second trial, however, Darrow changed tactics. He got Henry Sweet, Dr. Sweet's younger brother, to admit that he had fired the fatal shot, and the attorney then put the question quite frankly to the jury.

This great state and this great city . . . must face this problem and face it squarely. If eleven white men had shot and killed a black while protecting their home and their lives against a mob of blacks . . . they would have been given medals.[5]

The jury responded to his appeal. Dr. Ossian Sweet, his brother, and the other nine blacks were all acquitted.

The trial of Dr. Ossian Sweet focused Detroit's attention for the first time on a problem which was to become a consuming theme in its future. The Motor City had fared quite well through the wave of non-English-speaking immigration that its growth had stimulated. It was to cope less happily with the waves of black immigration which were to continue up to and beyond the Second World War. When Mayor John W. Smith, alarmed by the hatred unleashed by the Sweet trial, established the city's first-ever interracial committee in 1926, the committee approached Detroit's employers in the hopes of promoting more liberal employment policies towards blacks—and got absolutely no response.

No response, that is, until they got in touch with Henry Ford.

"In other factories very few Negroes were hired, and only in the most menial jobs," remembered Josephine Gomon, one of the members of the committee. "But Mr. Ford took this problem very seriously and gave it his personal attention. He tried to increase and upgrade jobs for Negroes in the plant."[6]

This was the year following the *Dearborn Independent*'s attack upon Aaron Sapiro, and Henry Ford's eagerness to demonstrate his lack of racial prejudice could be interpreted in the light of that. But there is nothing to suggest that Henry saw any connection between the two. His suspicion of Jews whom he had never met was one thing. That was a matter of fantasy, a vehicle for the insecurities and fears which haunted his spirit—and it also reflected his life-long, populist inability, or refusal, to understand that the handling of money could be a valid and creative activity.

"The Jew is a mere huckster," he told the journalist Judson Welliver in 1921; "a trader, who doesn't want to produce, but to make something out of what somebody else produces."[7]

Blacks, on the other hand, were producers. Henry Ford had seen them produce. In his tree-cutting days back in Dearborn, he had worked with a black, William Perry, who had helped him rassle the cross-cut saw. One day in 1914, Henry brought Perry into Highland Park, showed him some of the machinery, and instructed the superintendent to "see to it that he's comfortable."[8] William Perry became Ford's first black worker, and, as journalists flocked to Highland Park to report on the working of the new Five Dollar Day and on the Sociological Department, the black became something of a celebrity, cited along with the ex-convicts and tuberculosis sufferers as examples of the unconventional, progressive new Ford way.

But William Perry was no token black. By the early 1920s there were more than 5,000 blacks working for Ford, and by 1926 there were double that number—a tenth of the entire work force. The Ford Motor Company employed more blacks than all the other car companies put together.[9]

The white workers did not like it, particularly when, on Henry's orders, blacks were promoted to become foremen, with supervision over whites. This was quite unheard-of. There were fights and work stoppages, and Mayor Smith's interracial committee suggested some segregation to ease the tensions. By 1926 the Rouge blast furnaces were in full operation, and since most blacks worked in the foundry, every job in this part of the steel-making division, right up to the rank of plant superintendent, was now given to blacks. Henry Ford liked to boast that, as a consequence, the foundry was the most efficient unit in the entire Rouge complex.[10]

No other car company made its own steel as Ford did, and the unpleasant, hot, heavy chores of foundry work were traditionally—and happily—surrendered by white workers to the Negro. In later years, when union troubles started, Ford was to use its black workers as scabs and strikebreakers. But Ford never paid a man more, or less, on account of his skin. Henry Ford's black employment policy was genuinely ahead of its time. Henry believed in an equal day's pay for an equal day's work, remembering himself and William Perry among the tree stumps—"the colored man at one end of the log and white man at the other"[11]—and the measure of his colour-blindness was that he did not make much fuss about it.

"Henry Ford never posed as any special friend of any

275

race," said the *Journal of Negro History* on his death. "But he gave Negroes along with others the chance to help themselves, and in doing so he met the highest test of being a friend. . . ." [12]

Henry's unhappiness with doctors was said to go right back to Dr. Duffield, who had been the Ford family doctor when Henry's mother had died. For all her previous deliveries, Mary Litogot Ford had had a midwife in attendance, but Dr. Duffield had come for the accouchement that had killed her, and, rationally or not, Henry blamed the doctor for her death.[13] His sense of grievance was compounded by the operation which marked the end of his wife's childbearing in the 1890s, and, as young Edsel fell prey to childhood ailments, an economic resentment was added to the equation. Henry noticed that as his own income expanded, his doctors' bills tended to increase at just about the same rate.

"I am not unmindful of the large amount of time which a capable physician or surgeon gives to charity," he declared, "but also I am not convinced that the fees of surgeons should be regulated according to the wealth of the patient."[14]

It was quite easy to get medical treatment in early-twentieth-century Detroit, as in most other American cities, if you were very rich or very poor. The rich could, obviously, afford to pay for their own treatment, and they subsidized the truly indigent through charitable donations and also through the inflated fees they paid to doctors who put in a day or so every week at the charity hospitals. It was the people in the middle who lost out, who could not afford to fall ill. One of the features of the Henry Ford Hospital, which opened its doors to the general public in November 1919,[15] was a set scale of quite moderate fees which applied to everyone, rich or poor, and which were also estimated and guaranteed in advance—rather like a quotation for a car repair.

As with his other innovations, Henry Ford came at medicine somewhat sideways. When he first agreed, in 1908, to become chairman of the fund-raising committee of the institution which was to become the Henry Ford Hospital, he was putting his name to a fairly conventional philanthropic venture, a new general hospital for the city. The explosive expansion of Detroit in the first decades of the century had overwhelmed its medical facilities, and it seemed only right that one of the men responsible for the expansion should make a contribution towards putting things right.

But, largely through Henry's own inertia, the fund-raising committee failed to raise enough funds. Henry made a very generous contribution himself, but he had other things on his mind—these were the years of the moving assembly line—and he was ill at ease with his fellow fund-raisers, social bigwigs all. By the spring of 1914 it looked as if the enterprise would collapse in public scandal and mutual recrimination, for the new general hospital stood unfinished beside West Grand Boulevard, derelict and open to the weather,[16] its construction halted for lack of funds.

The fund-raising crisis came just when Henry was immersed in the excitement of the Sociological Department, and social engineering suggested a way Henry could redeem the mess he had got into. He could give Detroit "the best hospital in the world," he promised, "if you'll all get out and let me build it and run it."[17]

So in 1914, Henry paid back every dollar of contribution made to the hospital by other people, assumed liability for its debts, and made the project totally his own. Completed and opened briefly before the war came, the building was taken over by the government until 1919. Then, renovated, with its own staff, the Henry Ford Hospital set seriously to work to put its founder's theories into practice.

Henry Ford had very definite ideas about most things, and on few subjects was he more positive than health. "Pay no attention to that doctor," he said to a patient having problems with his heart. "All you have to do is get out of bed and lie on the floor for half an hour twice a day and eat celery and carrots: then you'll be all right."[18]

To their credit, the physicians whom Henry Ford recruited to run his hospital entirely resisted such crack-brain notions. They were a group of physicians enlisted largely from the Johns Hopkins Hospital in Baltimore, and their success in Detroit owed much to the professional restraint they placed upon their master's wilder enthusiasms—a restraint which the professionals of the *Dearborn Independent* catastrophically failed to impose. But the new Ford doctors did go along with Henry's innovative fixed-price list and—even more disturbing to most other doctors—they agreed to work at the Henry Ford Hospital, as they had done at Johns Hopkins, for fixed salaries, entirely renouncing any outside work for fees.

The Detroit medical establishment sneered at the Henry Ford Hospital as a "human garage," and in some ways it was. On admission, every patient was first examined by a senior physician and then moved on past three or four specialists, each of whom would make his own completely independent examination, before submitting his findings, without consultation with his colleagues, to provide the raw material for a final report. This systematic line diagnosis, now commonplace, was not the way in which most hospitals operated in the 1920s, but medical practice, rather surprisingly, proved one area which was amenable to Henry Ford's automotive principles.

"It is my shop," he said, "where I hope people can get well as rapidly as possible and have their injured parts repaired."[19]

Every patient in the Henry Ford Hospital had his own room, which enjoyed direct sunlight. Henry did practical experiments, building full-scale model rooms with adjustable walls that he shifted, in consultation with his doctors, until the optimum proportions were achieved. The rooms were then grouped together in pavilions surrounded, in the early days, by pastoral greenery in which cows grazed,[20] and the pavilions were connected by that favourite feature of every Ford building project, underground tunnels lined with pipes. Smoking was outlawed completely—a prohibition which many doctors of the period considered a gross imposition—and the Henry Ford Hospital earned the distinction of being the first general hospital in America regularly to admit and treat psychiatric patients.[21]

The entire tone of the institution was set by Henry's scorn of the conventional. "The expert is a good man to tell you what was being done down to closing time, day before yesterday," he said. "The less you know, the more quickly you can learn."[22]

He worked closely with the hospital's two principal physicians, Roy D. McClure and Frank J. Sladen, young doctors who had brought fresh ideas from Johns Hopkins. His levelling tendencies harmonized well with the essential democracy of flesh under the knife, and over the years his hospital—which treated Ford employees, but was quite independent of the company—came to establish itself as one of the foremost teaching and research institutions in the Midwest. When foreign doctors came to inspect the latest in American medical techniques in the 1930s and 1940s, they visited the Mayo Clinic, Johns Hopkins, and the Henry Ford Hospital in Detroit, and today the Henry Ford remains one of America's leading nonuniversity research and teaching institutions. Its doctors pioneered the original heart-lung machine. It was a leader, for many years, in open heart surgery—and it owed one of its medical innovations to Henry Ford himself.

In November 1932, Henry Ford was admitted, at the age of sixty-nine, to the Henry Ford Hospital for a hernia operation. It was the first medical operation of his life, and that night he went to sleep with the help of two grains of sodium amytal. Next morning, however, the patient refused to use his bedpan. He insisted on getting up to go to his own bathroom. Worse, he refused to lie in bed. Against his doctor's orders he insisted on getting up and sitting in a chair beside his bed. This was quite contrary to current medical practice, which prescribed long periods of horizontal recuperation after operations for hernia, and for virtually every other condition.

"He is more active than I should like to see him," recorded his worried doctor in his notes.[23]

But Henry Ford persisted with his own therapy. He knew what was best, and, only a week after the operation, he declared himself ready to go home. Five days later he was back at work, totally cured. When to his surgeon's amazement he remained cured, despite the strain he had placed upon his constitution, Henry Ford's doctors began to wonder whether, perhaps, the exercise he had insisted on had not been therapeutic in some fashion. Perhaps similar controlled exertion might avoid the problems of atrophy which can come from an invalid being allowed too much rest. It was not long before postoperative ambulation became one of the new features of treatment at the hospital.

Little Henry Ford II used to enjoy spending weekends in Dearborn with his grandfather. He would run up and down the pipe-lined tunnel to the Fair Lane powerhouse, he would go out into the garden to cultivate his own little vegetable plot, and on Saturday mornings he would visit the Rouge, where his grandfather had him jumping on and off trains, boarding the iron-ore carriers of the new Ford fleet, and going into the canteens to serve himself helpings of small change from the cash registers.

The problem was the food. Henry Ford II remembers carrots—pounded carrots, chopped carrots, grated carrots, carrot soup, carrot cake, carrot juice. There were even versions of the vegetable so spun, woven, and generally reconstituted that they appeared to have been knitted.[24] It was sorry fare for a chubby little boy whose principal delight was hamburger.

Old Henry Ford had always believed that we are what we eat. Dietary reform had been one of the radical new strands of thought swirling through Michigan in his youth, thanks to the Seventh Day Adventists' Western Health Reform Institute, founded in Battle Creek in 1866.[25] Dr. John Harvey Kellogg developed his new cereal-based health foods there in the 1890s—help for the midwestern farmer, and help for the human body as well—and as Henry Ford played with his steam and gasoline engines, he came to see the body as another sort of machine whose efficiency depended on the type of fuel fed to its boiler. Illness and crime, he told the *New York Times* in May 1929, are caused by "wrong mixtures in the stomach."[26] He inveighed against the evils of fresh dough: all bread stood in the Ford pantry for a full day before it was consumed. He taught that meat proteins and starches should not be consigned to the stomach at the same time—Battle Creek's dietary reformers issued dire warnings against the putrefaction of meat in the bowel[27] —and this doctrine inspired Henry, for a period, to eat his chicken at lunchtime and his potatoes at supper.

He set special store by vegetables, as distinguished visitors to the Chicago World's Fair in 1934 discovered when they were invited to one of the twelve-course banquets with which Henry Ford inaugurated the Ford exhibit. The hors d'oeuvres consisted of tomato juice with soy sauce, salted soya beans, and celery stuffed with soy cheese. The soup was puree of soya bean with soy-flour crackers. The main course was soya-bean croquettes with buttered green soya beans, while dessert consisted of apple pie with baked soy-flour crust, the whole being washed down with cocoa and soya-bean milk. As if the point needed emphasizing further, the walls of the dining room were decorated with gearshift and radio knobs, horn buttons, window winders, and distributor housings—all of them made from plastic derived from the same versatile legume on which the guests were feasting.

Henry Ford discovered the soya bean in the early 1930s. A dozen years earlier, he had started on a project especially close to his heart: a network of half a dozen small plants and factories which he set up on streams and rivers around the southeast Michigan countryside. These "village industries" brought town and country together in the way Henry had always dreamed should be possible—picturesque watermills housing clean, human-sized workshops in which local farmers and villagers could beaver away happily together, like the shoemaker's elves, producing components and accessories for Ford cars.

Henry's dream went back to his rootlessness as an oil-stained farmboy, uncertain whether he belonged in the fields or in town. One of the stranger provisions of the Five Dollar Day had been a promise that the Ford Motor Company would henceforward arrange its production schedule so that lay-offs would be made around harvest time.

"We hope, in such case," Henry had declared in January 1914, "to induce our men to respond to the calls of the farmers for harvest hands."[28]

It was an odd fancy, scheduling production in the world's largest automobile factory around the corn and how it yellowed—rural yearnings right at the heart of the measure which finished off the farm as a major dynamic in the American economy—but the village industries kept the dream alive.

"The new era will see a great distribution of industry back to the country," Henry told Judson Welliver in 1921. "This country has got to live in the country; industry must be taken back to the country. . . . The great modern city is an abnormal development. It tends to break down under its own weight"[29]

Henry had looked into the future, and decided that it would be rather like the past. The workers in his village industries could take time off in the summer to tend their vegetable plots and fields. And the whole project depended on the same magic ingredient as Muscle Shoals, waterpower.

The soya bean promised to be the final ingredient that the village industries needed for total success, since Henry's updating of the village smithy had not proved profitable in any conventional sense. Beloved of the *Dearborn Independent*, which rhapsodized almost weekly over their bucolic yet productive charms, the village industries defied virtually every law of scale and efficiency which had made Henry

Ford's other factories so profitable. The basic fallacy lay in the cost of shipping raw materials out to the countryside and then shipping finished products back—until Henry discovered the soya bean, for here was a raw material which could be grown in the fields around his plants. It could be processed on the spot in order to create the plasticlike components which were becoming more and more common in motorcars.

Henry had been thinking along these lines for some time. As early as 1916 he had formed a company with Edsel, "Henry Ford & Son Laboratories," to carry out "mechanical, botanical and chemical research."[30] Henry had a notion that alcohol could be distilled from vegetable matter for use as tractor fuel, thus making the farmer totally self-sufficient, and he had hired his old school friend, Dr. Edsel Ruddiman, away from his university researches to work on this. He set Dr. Ruddiman up in a corner of the Dearborn tractor plant, and here the chemist analysed all manner of vegetable produce from the ever-growing acreage of the Henry Ford farms. Henry had several acres put down to marijuana, which he thought might provide a base for plastics, and he also had crews roaming the local countryside with hand-operated vacuum cleaners, which they used to harvest dandelion seeds.[31]

Henry took a close interest in his old friend's experiments, bringing in piles of orange peel and kitchen garbage for him to analyse. Then one day in 1932, he unloaded outside the laboratory a consignment of *Glycine max*, the hairy annual Asian vegetable hitherto known in the West principally for the nitrogen-fixing qualities of the nodules on its roots. The soya bean had been classified for centuries as one of the five sacred plants of China—it was traditionally grouped with rice as one of the staffs of life—but it was grown by American farmers less to be harvested than to be ploughed back into infertile fields.[32]

Of the several Western prophets who popularized the diverse virtues of the soya bean outside the Orient—among them Dr. Harry W. Miller, a graduate of Western Health

Reform Institute of Battle Creek*—Henry Ford was the first to try growing and harvesting the vegetable on a major scale. As well as putting thousands of acres down to the crop in Dearborn, he had a twenty-five-acre plot which tested several hundred different varieties, while he also established a chemical plant which was soon extracting six tons of soy oil every day as part of his research into the remarkable bean. Apart from its nitrogen-fixing qualities, the soya bean contains an extraordinary proportion of protein—three times the amount in wheat, corn, or any other cereal. A pound of protein costs $9.90 when derived from beef at 1985 prices, $3.99 when derived from eggs, $2.61 from milk—and just 82¢ when granulated soya bean is the source.[34] If it also tasted nice, it would be the perfect food.

Henry Ford's primary concern with the soya bean was not particularly nutritional, however. He was interested by the potential which this farm crop held for industry, for he had grown up with the economic and social dilemma that plagues America to this day: what to do about the farmers. They were the first Americans. They made the country, they had opened it up, and yet, just about the time of Henry's birth, the changes had started which were to make them less and less central to the nation's wealth. If they had been engaged in any other form of economic activity, they would have been subject to the standard remedy—close the plant. But food is food, and, more important, the sturdy, hardworking farmer was, and remains, central to the image that America has of herself.

Henry felt the dilemma as a patriotic American, as a farmboy, and, most of all, as the giant figure who had come to symbolize almost everything that was putting the farmers out of work—hence his attempts to harmonize the harvest

---

* Dr. Miller, known as the "China Doctor," is generally credited with the perfection of the world's first meatless hotdog, as well as the development of a soy-milk-based soft drink called Vitasoy, which became so popular in Hong Kong for a period in the 1970s that it actually outsold Coca-Cola.[33]

with the Five Dollar Day. Guilt is too easy a description. Regret, nostalgia, redemption, the challenge of yet another practical problem to which a practical solution could be found—Henry Ford was not analytical in an intellectual sense, least of all when it came to the impact of his own work upon the world. Suggest to him that he was blaming the Jews for something that the Model T had done, and he would not have begun to see the connection. His remedy was action, and in the early 1930s his action centred on the soya bean and the chemurgical movement.

Chemurgy, a technological child of populism, sprang from the woes of American farmers in the 1920s and 1930s. The rich earth that supported the world's most developed farming industry continued to thrust up crops in abundance, but as unemployment grew, there were fewer and fewer customers to purchase them. Huge surpluses of cotton, wheat, hogs, and tobacco began to stockpile, and the glut sent prices plummeting. If inflation was accounted for, the price levels of certain agricultural products sank lower in the 1920s and 1930s than they had been for 300 years.[35]

As in the 1880s, the good, honest American farmer was at a loss to understand what was happening to him. He was working harder than he had ever done. He was employing scientific strains of seed and stock, as well as labour-saving devices like Henry Ford's tractors, produced first in the Dearborn tractor plant, and then at the Rouge from 1921 onwards.[36]

Yet the reward for embracing progress seemed to be ruin, and even government money did not help. In 1933 farmers were actually paid to plough in a quarter of their cotton crop. Six million pigs were slaughtered, and their carcases burned[37]—at the same time as unemployed families huddled starving on soup-kitchen lines. There was, clearly, something profoundly wrong with the system, and from the despair which this dislocation engendered came chemurgy and its hope that modern science might be able to teach farmers to produce more than just food. If the agricultural sector was producing more than people could eat, while the industrial sector was languishing, it seemed obvious that the two should get together—as Henry Ford had always said they should. Farmers should produce crops in bulk that had industrial uses, and the latest developments in chemistry suggested that this was where the future lay. Wood was providing the raw material for the miraculous new artificial fibre, rayon. Searching for a plastic or resin to replace the ivory in billiard balls, John Hyatt (of Hyatt Roller Bearing) had hit upon guncotton cellulose.[38] All manner of vegetables, from sugar beet to lima beans, could produce alcohol, or ethanol, as fuel for cars. And then there was the soya bean, whose fibrous structure promised an ideal foundation for the vegetable-based plastics that were just being developed.

Both the technology and ideology of chemurgy meshed with the causes dearest to Henry Ford's heart, and it turned out that he had been a chemurgical pioneer all the time without realizing it, since the coil cases of the 1915 Model T had been constructed from a plastic based on wheat gluten.[39] As the chemurgical movement gathered strength in the early 1930s, its champions found a ready audience in Dearborn, and in 1935 the Dearborn Inn became the site of America's first chemurgical conference, under the sponsorship of Henry Ford.[40]

The first National Chemurgical Conference—and, indeed, the second, held again at the Dearborn Inn in the following year—was, like all enterprises associated with Henry Ford, a curious blend of vision and nostalgia. There were brave, vagrant gazings into the future: "Young Man, Go Chemurgic!," "Farmward the Star of Destiny Lights Our Way!," "The Jerusalem Artichoke: An American Weed Worth a Million Dollars." The scientific delegates came from several of the country's leading chemical firms, and they represented a fair cross-section of America's more serious research chemists. But the tone of the gathering was set by a theme that went right back to Henry's years among the rural self-help societies of the 1880s. The delegate of honour in Dearborn was Louis J. Taber, Grand Master of the Lodges of the National Grange.

Taber delivered the opening oration at the first conference, and he provided the home-going valediction for the second. "Hear me!" he cried. "America stands at the cross-roads."[41] His opening address started with invocations to Ceres and Demeter, the classical goddesses of agriculture, and it climaxed with the solemn swearing, by all delegates, of a "Declaration of Dependence upon the Soil."

"The farm is the foundation of Society. . . . We have been bent on following those false gods of gold, steel, petroleum." Mankind had forgotten that the farm constituted "the key to human happiness," unrolled the catechism. But the new developments of organic chemistry would lead to a "re-birth of agriculture . . . destined to carry civilization to a higher plane."

From this emotional threshold, the delegates descended to a more matter-of-fact level, examining such topics as "Cellulose from Southern Pine," "The Industrial Utilization of Oat Products," and "The Role of Soy Bean Oil in Paint Formulation." There were papers on rayon, cellophane, and cellulose chemistry, and there were encouraging reports on the progress of alcohol gasolines. These solid, academic treatises provided a valuable summary of applied industrial chemistry to date. In the years following the conferences, Henry Ford tried to maintain the chemurgical spirit, appearing in 1939 in a silklike soya-bean tie while wearing a soya-bean suit.* Following the construction of a soy-processing plant at the Rouge in 1937, two pounds of every Ford car were made up of soya-bean products—mainly the insulating casings and the interior knobs and buttons— and Ford's chief soya-bean research chemist, Robert Boyer, developed a soy-plastic rear-trunk lid.

Henry Ford somewhat undermined the credibility of Boyer's forward-looking development in panelwork when,

* The suit was more fragile than its woollike texture suggested: its tailor gave Henry Ford firm orders not to cross his legs in public.[42]

invited to attack the plastic lid at a public demonstration, he turned around the axe he was handed and went at it with the sharp side. The trunk lid was cleft in two. But that is not the reason why motorcars today are not made of soya beans or of any other vegetable-based plastic. Twentieth-century experiments with plastics and resins had, from an early date, investigated mineral as well as vegetable sources—and minerals proved the way of the future. By the outbreak of the Second World War, it was clear that the hydrocarbons derived from coal tars and natural gas—and particularly from petroleum—provided a more flexible, reliable base for plastics technology than did bulky, seasonal farm crops.

Still, if chemurgy went the way of the Peace Ship, the village industries, and several other of Henry Ford's crusades, his campaigning on behalf of the soya bean has not been entirely in vain. Continuing experiments have demonstrated the usefulness of soya-bean derivatives in margarines and cooking oils, in paints and varnishes, and as a meat substitute—not only in pet foods, but also in hopeful concoctions placed on supermarket shelves for human consumption, from nonbeef hamburger to "bacon bits." Some people maintain that tofu, the protein-rich bean curd derived from soy milk, is really quite palatable, and physicians prescribe soy milk for infants who are allergic to mother's milk and dairy products.

As a result of this demand, U.S. soya-bean cultivation has grown so that it was, in 1984, an $11.4 billion industry, and in the national league table of cash crops, the soya bean now ranks second only to corn. Its production comfortably exceeds that of wheat, oats, rice, potatoes, and the other traditional staples of American arable farming.[43] Henry Ford would doubtless be delighted to learn that the rage among the health-conscious of Grosse Pointe in the mid-1980s is a nondairy, mock ice-cream dessert made from soya beans: Tofutti.

In the early months of 1926, Murshid Inayat Khan, a Sufi mystic, came to Detroit to deliver a series of lectures on meditation and on the life of the soul, and Henry Ford invited him out to Dearborn. Henry was anxious for some spiritual conversation, and when the two men met, reported A. M. Smith of the *Detroit News*, "each smiled at the other as though he had encountered a friend of long ago."

"I think the real power of human lives is hidden away in the soul, and farther than that," declared Henry Ford. "There are actual entities all about us, entities of force, intelligence—call them electrons, if you like. When a man is doing good, they swarm to help him. . . . We rush too much with nervous hands and worried minds. We are impatient for results. What we need, and might have, is reinforcement of the soul by the invisible power waiting to be used."

The grey-bearded mystic tried to explain how he thought that human contact with that invisible power might be made.

"It is like the artist in the painting of a picture," he said. "It is never, when finished, what he first planned. Creative inspiration comes as he loses himself in the task. Completely absorbed in his work, completely forgetful of self, shutting out the rest of the world, his finished product is, at the last, a truly creative expression of the self he has completely forgotten."

This was not a bad description of the Model T—the most truly creative expression of self that Henry Ford ever achieved.

It seemed at times during the hour-long conversation, reported faithfully on the front page of the *Detroit News* for February 7, 1926,[44] as if it was not the Sufi but Henry Ford who was the spiritual teacher.

"Do you think the souls of men are indestructible?" inquired the mystic of the magnate.

"Everything is indestructible," replied the carmaker, "nothing is ever lost. Souls come and go, and they come again, prepared by past experience for greater achievement."

The Sufi's route to the Supreme Being was by way of meditation—"periods of shutting out all of the material objectivity of the world"—and Mr. Ford said that was his route as well.

"That to my mind," he said, "is the heart of personal religion. I struggled for many years to solve the problem. . . . But I found, as you have said, that if I quietly withdrew from the nervous anxiety over things, inventions, and the business that drives from every side, there was renewal of strength in the thought of being part of the great unseen power."

Not that Henry Ford was prepared to withdraw that much from the world: "If one meditates too much," he said, "there is not likely to be much work done!"

Henry Ford had a portmanteau mind. Hospital reform, reincarnation, the relations of black and white, the soya bean, village industries—he dug his teeth into anything that caught his fancy, and he chewed right through it, oblivious to the fact that he was not supposed to be an expert on the subject.

Sometimes he got it wrong. His anti-Semitism was an ugly stain upon his record. Muscle Shoals and the *Dearborn Independent* proved ignominious episodes. But when Henry Ford kept his feet on the ground, concentrating on practical matters that were accessible to his practical talents, he was capable of great things. There were many benign impulses inside the man, genuine and sincere ambitions to be of service, and from 1914 onwards, he was able to make good use of the time and money that the continuing success of the Model T gave him.

In July 1923, Henry Ford entered his sixties, the stage of life when most people start to slow down. But Henry scarcely relaxed his hold upon the business, and he used the watershed to diversify, cutting off after lunch quite often on warm summer afternoons to drive across the dusty Michigan countryside in an open car, visiting one of his watermills or looking to see how the latest strain of beans was doing. He might well take along one of his doctors, Roy McClure or Frank Sladen, so that he could discuss the development of the hospital as he went.[45]

Judson C. Welliver, a serious and quite critical journalist who tried to encompass all the different sides of Henry Ford in a couple of articles that he wrote in the 1920s, had difficulty making sense of it all.

"As one gets closer to his innermost thoughts," he wrote, "one hardly dares be certain about the fantasies. If one didn't know the man's record of making dreams come true . . . it would be easy to smile indulgently."[46]

Welliver went through the common performance of chasing Henry Ford all around his scattered empire—Highland Park, the Rouge, the farms, the village industries—trying vainly to lay hands upon the protean genius, until finally he tracked him down to a "dingy little room," someone else's office, at the back of the Dearborn tractor plant. This, it turned out, was one of Henry's favourite hideaways, and there framed on the wall in the corner where Henry liked best to sit were some lines of poetry which, it seemed to Welliver, came closest to explaining the man that he was having such trouble pinning down.

> Back of the beating hammer by which the steel is wrought,
> Back of the workshop's clamor, the seeker may find a thought:
> The thought that is ever master of iron and steam and steel;
> That rises above disaster, and tramples it under heel. . . .
> Back of them stands the schemer—the Thinker—who drives things through,
> Back of the job the Dreamer, who's making the dream come true.[47]

# 14

# TIME MACHINE

You can see the Ford test track at Dearborn quite clearly from the upper floors of Ford World Headquarters. Off to the right it lies, across Michigan Avenue, towards the southwesterly horizon. You can just make out the small, whizzing bean-shaped cars as they skim around the circuit, their contours blurred in a haze of speed and distance, and in the far right-hand corner of the field stand the research buildings—dark and shiny space-age cubes. It is a precise and practical scene. The currency of the test track may be fantasy, but it is fantasy by slide rule, every detail calibrated and micrometer-checked to the last fraction of an inch.

Beside the test track is gathered fantasy in another vein. Spires, weather vanes, and belfries poke upwards through the greenery. A windmill raises its head above the trees. Odd puffs of smoke betray some fevered, antique mechanical activity. When, down on the ground, you go to investigate this strange juxtaposition of old and new, you can hear the plaintive calling of a steam locomotive and—can it be?— the distant clanging of a riverboat bell.

A 252-acre confection of slate, pink brick, and clapboard, Greenfield Village is Henry Ford's tribute to the past, his attempt to preserve the slow-paced, candlelit America which he, more than anyone, did so much to destroy. It is a never-never land as Norman Rockwell might have imagined it, a collection of eighteenth- and nineteenth-century buildings which have been transported from all over the United States—and, in the case of a Cotswold cottage, from even further afield—to be set together, side by side, in this grey-green corner of Michigan: the courthouse where Abraham Lincoln practised law, a stagecoach tavern, a gristmill, the Ohio bicycle shop where the Wright brothers, Orville and

Wilbur, developed their first, flimsy aeroplane. The streets are paved with gravel. The lamps are lit by gas. There is a carriage-repair shop, a cider mill, a farm.

The guides dress in period costume, but this does not slide you backwards so much as the horse-drawn omnibus that takes you down the main street. It pulls away, clip-clopping and swaying, as you would expect, but then, just as the small of your back is anticipating the move out of bottom gear, nothing happens. There is no speed-up. The bus keeps on clip-clopping and swaying at scarcely more than walking pace, and suddenly you grasp just a little of what it must have felt like to live in a world without acceleration, where things were not forever getting faster and where there were no machines to give you thrills. Speed, said Aldous Huxley, is the only truly twentieth-century pleasure, and speed is nonexistent in Greenfield Village, cut off by two high brick walls from the test track where the jelly beans zoom and brake.

From Memorial Day onwards, the cars and camper wagons line up outside Henry Ford's time machine by the hundreds. Ohio, Illinois, Wisconsin, say the license plates, for people drive to Greenfield Village from all over the Midwest. It is difficult to think of many reasons for making Dearborn the object of a pleasure jaunt, but 1.5 million visitors do come here each year, and they are all drawn by the chance of tasting the past in this complex and very particular historical reconstruction inspired by the man whose most famous saying was "History is bunk."

These are three famous words, but it is not certain whether Henry Ford ever actually uttered them. He always maintained he had been misquoted in the interview which attributed them to him in 1916.* Cross-questioned on the subject during the *Chicago Tribune* trial, however, Henry Ford did

---

* As quoted in the *Chicago Tribune* in 1916, Henry Ford said, "History is more or less bunk. It's tradition. We don't want tradition. We want to live in the present, and the only history that is worth a tinker's damn is the history we make today."[1]

agree that "bunk" accurately described his own estimate of history as presented by the average school textbook—all dates and battles and politicians' names. This sort of history left him cold, he said, and it also provoked mischief.

"Bankers, munitions makers, alcoholic drink, Kings and their henchmen, and school books"[2] lay at the root of the world's evils, he told the *New York World* in 1919, and the project which later became Greenfield Village was his attempt to battle with the last of these.

"You know," he told Ernest Liebold, on his way home from his humiliating ordeal at Mount Clemens in the summer of 1919, "I'm going to . . . give the people an idea of real history. I'm going to start a museum. We are going to show just what actually happened in years gone by."[3]

In that same summer of 1919, Henry had been prompted to start restoring the old Ford family homestead by a road-widening scheme. The increase of cars on the roads in Dearborn—most of them Model Ts—threatened the birthplace of Henry Ford, and while moving the building to safety, Henry decided to make a shrine of it as well. He gave Evangeline Dahlinger the job of searching out stoves and carpets and light fittings to match his memory, and a few years later he heard of a still larger project.

In 1923, at the peak of his presidential bid, Henry was approached by a group of Bostonians seeking contributions to save a national treasure, the Wayside Inn at South Sudbury, Massachusetts. Typically, Henry decided that rather than contribute, he would buy the inn and save it himself.[4]

The Wayside Inn had been made famous by Longfellow, who used it as the setting for an American *Canterbury Tales*, the most famous of which was the tale recounted by the landlord:

> *Listen, my children, and you shall hear*
> *Of the midnight ride of Paul Revere . . .*

George Washington had stayed there, so had Lafayette. Built in 1686, the Wayside Inn was said to be the oldest working tavern in the United States. Henry Ford spent $280,000 to shift the route of the Boston Post Road on which it stood; motor traffic was threatening the tavern's foundations, and, worse, the highway had become polluted with hotdog stands and "all sorts of catch-penny places" [5]— though catching pennies had, presumably, been the original purpose of the hostelry as well.

Acquiring some 2,500 acres around the tavern, Henry Ford decided he would make the Wayside Inn the focus of an old-time American community, a pilgrim village whose inhabitants would live and work in largely colonial style: "an idea of real history." He started to have other antique buildings from New England transported to South Sudbury, and he was delighted to discover that the old schoolhouse in the nearby village of Sterling, Massachusetts, had been attended, early in the nineteenth century, by a Mary Elizabeth Sawyer, whose pet lamb had fleece that was white as snow. This lamb would, allegedly, follow Mary everywhere, even into the Sterling schoolhouse—so Henry bought the building for his pilgrim village. Now he had two inspirations of the American poetic imagination.

Connoisseurs of "Mary Had a Little Lamb" were not convinced. They maintained that Mary's adventure with the pet that followed her to school one day had sprung unaided from the creative imagination of Mrs. Sarah J. Hale, the Boston poetess to whom the poem was normally credited. But Henry Ford had no doubts. He had Mary's little red schoolhouse dismantled and reconstructed beside the Wayside Inn as a working school for the children of the tavern's employees, and on the first day of school he occupied a desk in the front row, holding a lamb on a leash. As the great carmaker walked out at break time, waiting photographers were delighted to observe, the lamb trotted obediently in his footsteps.[6]

Henry's holidays in South Sudbury had inspired him with the idea of developing a full-scale, open-air museum of Americana. He had spent over $1.5 million on the Wayside Inn, and he was prepared to spend even more on a new project, taking the advice of a local history enthusiast, George Francis Dow, who had already started a similar enterprise at the Essex Institute in Salem, Massachusetts. The Essex Institute recreated New England colonial life in Salem through a series of "living history" tableaux staged along the lines of those that had been pioneered in the 1890s by Skansen, the Swedish folk museum.[7]

"Living history" was something of a vogue in these years. The Reverend William Goodwin of Williamsburg, Virginia, hoped he might persuade Henry Ford to make Williamsburg the site of his own new open-air museum, and he approached the carmaker as a possible sponsor in 1924. But Henry turned him down. He wanted his next project closer to home, and he left Goodwin to turn to John D. Rockefeller, Jr., who proved more responsive.

Henry's attention had been caught by the Botsford Inn, a Michigan equivalent of the Wayside Inn, a dozen miles across the countryside to the northwest of Dearborn, beside the town of Farmington. He had taken Clara there in their courting days, driving over the snow in his speedy red cutter, and he had happy memories of dancing with his sweetheart in the inn's fine, spring-floored ballroom, which he now had restored.

But the Botsford Inn also proved too far from home. To judge from what he said at the time, Henry Ford's exercises in historical preservation were originally matters of atonement—the elaborate and expensive attempts that only a multimillionaire could make to salvage his reputation from the ridicule inspired by "History is bunk." But the atonement went deeper than that. In terms of the peaceful, slow, car-free America that had existed only twenty years previously, Henry Ford had a great deal more to seek forgiveness for, and working to restore just a little of that lost world proved to yield him the finest absolution of all. It was no penance: Henry discovered that he rather enjoyed playing with history.

Now entering his early sixties, Henry Ford had, at last, found himself a hobby. For the rest of his life, the quarrying, rearrangement, and reconstruction of the past were to be his consuming passion, and scarcely a day was to pass when he did not take a stroll in Greenfield Village to inspect a new acquisition or rearrange an old one. He devoted a major portion of his energies and fortune to shifting historical artefacts from all corners of the globe to his own backyard, for he had discovered a new magic to match the thrill of engineering—objects that could recapture vanished time.

Proust savoured a madeleine. Henry Ford being Henry Ford, it took more than just a biscuit to bring the past all flooding back. Yet from the moment that he started work on Greenfield Village, Henry's life became caught up in a Proustian swirl of time in constant flux, the past and present having equal reality for him. Mornings by the Rouge blast furnaces, afternoons in an eighteenth-century labourer's cottage, tests to improve an exhaust valve, repairs to an ancient spinning wheel—it was all the same for Henry Ford. Contradictions that he had once feared now took on harmony. The music of history gave them perfect sense. By sinking back into the past instead of manoeuvring to outdistance it, Henry also discovered how to bring some ease to the heartache of the farmboy tied to the machine-shop bench. Past and present, town and country, it had all come together at last.

Henry Ford came to history not as a spectator but as a participant, for he did not restore his old homes and buildings just to look at them. He reoccupied them, climbed their stairs, sat in their chairs, and ate their food. He liked to smell the smells and listen to the creaks that brought back his own childhood in a wooden farmhouse—*the* farmhouse which his mother had loved and cared for and turned into a home.

The Ford homestead itself was not enough for him, for Henry was an old soul. Had he not lived through many previous childhoods? Who could tell, perhaps some of his lives had passed through the very buildings that were intriguing his spirit in this present incarnation.

It was a strange alchemy, and Clara brought it all back for him one evening when the couple were sitting together in their Forest Room, Henry's log-cabin-like den that occupied one corner of the basement at Fair Lane. The two of them had fallen to remembering the dances of their youth—the polka, the schottische, and the gavotte—when Clara was moved to a nostalgic rebuke.

"Do you realize, Henry Ford," she said, "that we have danced very little since we were married?"[8]

Countless thousands of husbands must have acknowledged similar remarks with a sheepish shrug. But Henry Ford did not change the subject. Holidaying at the Wayside Inn a few weeks later, he decided to arrange an old-time country dance, and, suspecting that most of the guests would prove as rusty at the steps as he was, he retained the services of Mr. Benjamin B. Lovett, who ran dancing academies in Worcester and four other local communities.

"Do you know the Ripple?" Henry inquired of Lovett at their first meeting, and was elated when the dancing master confessed that he did not.

"Stuck him the first time!" exclaimed Henry to Clara. But when, after scouring Massachusetts, New Hampshire, and Vermont, Lovett discovered that what midwesterners called the Ripple was known to New Englanders as the "Newport, Down East," he was able to report back that he was, in fact, a Ripple expert.[9]

It was the beginning of a long and fruitful relationship. For Hallowe'en 1924, Clara proposed a dance in the barn of the restored Ford homestead, and Benjamin Lovett was summoned over to Dearborn to call the steps. The evening —warmed by makeshift radiators wheezing with steam from one of Henry's old Westinghouse engines—brought the memories back in a very special way. There was canvas on the ceiling, cornstalks and pumpkins around the barn. When Lovett returned to Massachusetts shortly afterwards, it was to pack up his things and move them back with his wife to Michigan, where he was to take up a permanent position as Henry Ford's dancing master.[10]

Henry Ford was an excellent dancer. He had small, dainty feet. He moved around the floor with grace and agility, and once he had recaptured the old steps, he was anxious to pass them on. He kept Benjamin Lovett in attendance in the new engineering laboratories that he had built across Michigan Avenue from Fair Lane, and after lunch, Ford executives and guests might find themselves shepherded down for a lesson on the sprung-wood floor. The dance area was screened off by canvas from the rest of the laboratories, and it was here that Charles Sorensen was introduced to the minuet, moving around in small circles face to face with Henry Ford, guided firmly by his master's sure hand in the small of his back.[11] Dances were also organized in the evenings, with Benjamin Lovett energetically conducting a four-piece orchestra while he sang out the ho-dee-hos. Attendance was mandatory for senior Ford men and their wives.

The dances were the animated, three-dimensional equivalents of the *Dearborn Independent*, whose presses had been moved to the engineering laboratories from the tractor plant; both expressed the defiant assertion that the values of old-time, rural America were not dead. Country dancing had an ethical dimension in Henry Ford's view, and this was articulated in an illustrated 1926 offering from the Ford presses, *Good Morning: After a Lapse of 25 Years, Old-Fashioned Dancing Is Being Revived by Mr. and Mrs. Henry Ford*.

"A gentleman should be able to guide his partner through a dance without embracing her as if he were her lover," explained the manual, condemning contemporary ballroom dancing as an artificial, promiscuous activity.[12] The manual was credited to Benjamin Lovett, but its arguments were those of William Cameron and the *Dearborn Independent* ghost-writing machine, which sternly lectured readers on how the degradation of modern dancing reflected the noxious influences of city life. For cynical, profit-hungry reasons, "a form of dancing has been encouraged that enables the largest number of paying couples to dance together in the smallest space,"[13] and, as a consequence, the true focus of modern dancing was "mostly above the feet."[14] This, in Henry Ford's opinion, was not where the focus of dancing should be, or ever had been—which only went to prove how history can be just about whatever you care to make of it.

In the early summer of 1924, Fordson tractors started levelling 260 acres beside the new engineering laboratories in Dearborn. They constructed runways, flattened ground for hangars, and helped set crushed white stone into the ground so that the word F-O-R-D could be clearly seen from a height of 10,000 feet.[15] Henry Ford had gone into the aeroplane business.

In the next nine years, until the depression compelled him to concentrate on carmaking, Henry Ford pioneered several new milestones in the developing field of aviation: the first use of radio to guide a commercial airliner, America's first regularly scheduled passenger flights (between Detroit and Cleveland), and the country's first airmail service as well. Ford manufactured America's first all-metal, multiengined aircraft, the Ford Tri-Motor, built to the design of William B. Stout. All this activity was centred right beside Henry's project in historical reconstruction. The Ford test track lies beside Greenfield Village today because it took over the runways of the abandoned Ford Airport.

The juxtaposition troubled some people. They could understand the airport, but what was Henry Ford doing amassing ancient farm implements? "It is," said the *New York Times*, "as if Stalin went in for collecting old ledgers and stock-tickers."[16]

There was more paradox in store, for in 1927 and 1928 Henry Ford announced that his new historical enthusiasms were to be formalized into two sections: his historical village, which would encapsulate the essence of rural America, and, right beside it, in more conventional museum form, a collection of engines and mechanical devices which would illustrate the march of technological progress, glorifying the triumph of the modern machine. Here were the Janus faces of Henry Ford—and of America herself—set together side by side.

The resolution of the paradox came from Henry's own enthusiasms, since his twin institutions would necessitate the collecting of ancient objects on a massive scale. And it was not so much the institutions that inspired the collecting, as the collecting which had inspired the museums. Dearborn was getting so cluttered with Henry's objects that there was an urgent need of storage space.

There had been a period in the early 1920s when it was scarcely safe to drive Henry Ford past an old plough rusting in a field. If his companions were lucky enough to spy the object first, they would point eagerly at a tree or hedge on the opposite side of the road, hoping they might slip past without the mandatory stop for inspection,[17] since the task of filling the Wayside and Botsford inns with authentic furnishings had honed Henry's acquisitive instincts to a sharp edge. Never excessively materialistic on his own behalf, Henry had found that history gave him a wondrous appetite for shopping. More than one owner of an antique shop in Massachusetts had the experience of a sprightly, silver-haired gentleman, whose face looked vaguely familiar, walking into the shop with a companion, gazing around briefly, then leaving with a significant nod. The companion would then inquire if the shopkeeper cared to put a price on his entire stock—and the munificent stranger seldom haggled very hard.

The objects were unloaded in Dearborn by the railcar: porcelain, crystal, musical boxes, farmhouse dressers—all the stock needed for an exhibition of bygone lifestyles. But in addition to these conventional antiques, there were exhibits of a humbler sort: saucepans and scrubbing boards, milk bottles and sewing machines, flat irons and hip baths, a painstaking assemblage of the ordinary components of everyday life. As the railcars were unloaded around the Engineering Laboratory, it looked as though someone had been engaged in a massive attic clearing.

Today the Henry Ford Museum, destination and resting

place of this domestic potpourri, remains somehow reminiscent of Huncamunca's parlour: there are banjo clocks, cigar store Indians, a history of the humble clothespeg. Modern curatorship has wrestled the Old Curiosity Shop into some sort of academic discipline, but there still remain serried ranks of baby buggies, vacuum cleaners, cooking stoves, and endless displays of farm implements, ploughs, threshing machines, and harrows—not that Henry Ford would feel the need to apologize for any of these humble objects, least of all the harrows.

When I went to our American history books to learn how our forefathers harrowed the land, I discovered that the historians knew nothing about harrows. Yet our country has depended more on harrows than on guns and speeches. I thought that a history which excluded harrows and all the rest of daily life is bunk, and I think so yet.[18]

On September 27, 1928, Thomas Edison laid the foundation stone of the Henry Ford Museum, leaving his footprints and carving his name in a patch of wet concrete. The exterior of the museum was a full-scale, redbrick replica of three of America's most sacred buildings: Independence Hall, Congress Hall, and the Old City Hall in Philadelphia, the trio strung out together, side by side, in a long crenellated facade. Inside, the exhibits showed a strong bias towards power and transportation. There were old steam engines of the type Henry had serviced in his days as a rural mechanic, matchwood biplanes—the aeroplane, after all, was an American invention—and a full range of Ford cars going back to the historic Quadricycle.

Outside, in Greenfield Village, was laid out "the real world of folks": "that honest time," as William Cameron put it, "when America was in the making."[19] Drawn towards heroes, Henry Ford had concentrated on the early and humble homes of the great men who had contributed to this making, and in doing so he had injected his static and ultimately banal collection of structures with some of the excitement of the American dream. Walking through sections of Greenfield Village was like overdosing on Horatio Alger, every door opening on yet another rags-to-riches success story. There is the birthplace of the revered McGuffey. Here Noah Webster conceived his dictionary; across the road is the house and garden which inspired Luther Burbank's interest in seeds, plants, and hybrid technology. Two doors away was kindled the musical spark in Stephen Collins Foster, composer of "Old Folks at Home" ("Way Down Upon the Swanee River"), "My Old Kentucky Home," and "Jeanie with the Light Brown Hair"—except that, like the schoolhouse of Mary and her little lamb, the Foster house in Greenfield Village was, almost certainly, a mistake. Stephen Foster never lived there.

The choice of American heroes, of course, reflected Henry Ford's own particular view of where greatness lay. The birthplace of George Mathew Adams is in Greenfield Village for no better reason than that Henry Ford liked the newspaper columns that he wrote, and the lion's share of space in the village—occupying several acres more than Henry's own birthplace and early workshops—was allocated to the laboratories and compounds of his ultimate hero, Thomas Alva Edison. One stop on the old railway line that circled the village was Smith's Creek Depot, the wooden halt onto which the young Edison was thrown when his experiments set fire to the railcar in which he was supposed to be working as a newspaper delivery boy, and as a foundation for Edison's Menlo Park Laboratory, Henry had shipped to Michigan three railcar loads of authentic red New Jersey earth.

Greenfield Village and the Henry Ford Museum made several serious and innovative contributions to the study of history, and these stem from Henry's own peculiar genius and preoccupations. The basic populist premise of the combined institutions, that history is much more than the story of the traditional political and social elites, was salutary in itself. Social history is today its own respected discipline, and dates are very much out of fashion.

Doing homage to past technology was another useful and refreshing idea. Decades before industrial archaeology became fashionable, Henry Ford had the yards and rubbish heaps around the workshops of Thomas Edison and Luther Burbank excavated for evidence of their working techniques. Several of Greenfield Village's structures, notably a grim pair of pillboxes housing slaves on a cotton plantation, would probably not have survived if Henry Ford had not chosen to preserve them—and his sustaining confidence that this elaborate and detailed historical panoply would intrigue and entertain ordinary people has been borne out by half a century of eager visitors. Greenfield Village has set the pace for other exercises in living history like Colonial Williamsburg—and even, in more recent years, for Disneyland. Among his numerous other innovations, Henry Ford can take the credit for building America's first theme park.

But entertainment carries perils of its own. There never was a real village like Greenfield Village, so named for no better reason than the fact that Clara Ford had grown up in the Greenfield district of Dearborn. Though visitors might find it compelling to gaze upon the blood-stained rocking chair in which Abraham Lincoln was assassinated, or marvel at the glass phial containing Edison's last breath, there was a lingering, low-brow aftertaste of the fairground sideshow. The glass-cased collections of conventional museums might be elitist and unrepresentative, but the mementos preserved by Henry Ford were equally distorted reflections of his own nostalgia. Greenfield Village claimed to be history, but a lot of it was autobiography. It contained no less than three jewellery stores simply because the young Henry Ford had enjoyed playing with watches, and it was interesting what the selection of memorials did not contain: no bank, no lawyer's office, no saloon or speakeasy, and not the slightest suggestion as to how the rich had lived.

Henry Ford chose October 21, 1929, for the dedication of his grand and revolutionary historical campus. Neither Greenfield Village nor the indoor museum were quite ready to be shown to the public, but the date was the fiftieth anniversary of the day when Thomas Alva Edison had invented the incandescent bulb, and the "Golden Jubilee of Light" would provide a wide, auspicious setting for Henry's opening ceremony. President Hoover himself travelled from Washington for the celebrations. Newsreel cameras were on hand, and the guest list included such notabilities as Madame Curie, Orville Wright, and the comedian Will Rogers. Albert Einstein joined in with a contribution, made by radio, from Germany, and, across America, millions listened in as the proceedings were broadcast live. (Since the first commercial broadcast in 1920, more than 600 radio stations had gone on the air, and 10 million families had purchased sets.)[20]

The centrepiece of the entire evening was the moment when Thomas Edison, now old, frail, and overcome with emotion, went out into Greenfield Village with Henry Ford and President Hoover to fumble through a reenactment of his famous discovery in his reconstructed Menlo Park laboratory. Until this moment, the hundreds of dinner-jacketed guests in the replica of Independence Hall had been sitting in candlelit obscurity. The millions across America, listening to the broadcast ceremony, had followed Henry Ford's suggestion to switch off their own lights at home, and when Edison's carbonized fibre first broke into a tenuous glow, the word went forth. Henry Ford did not say it in so many words, but he might as well have done.

"Let there be light!"—and the switches were thrown.

It was a high point in Henry Ford's life, perhaps the highest point of all: a unique concentration of famous guests, and a massive endorsement of his own belief that it was mechanical inventiveness and practical ability that had made America the great nation that she was. If Henry Ford was ever a hero to his fellow countrymen it was now. On the night of October 21, 1929, the farmboy had all America tuned in to his own, small, native Michigan village, a demon-stration of mass, popular influence rivalled a few years later only by Orson Welles's "War of the Worlds" broadcast—

and it all unrolled just a matter of days before Black Tuesday and the Wall Street crash, which permanently shattered the "ever upwards" euphoria that the nation had come to take for granted as her natural way of life.

But Greenfield Village was not finished. Henry Ford went on adding to his creation all through the 1930s. Ray Dahlinger supervised the work of the construction teams. Evangeline was in charge of collecting the old buildings and antiques. Into the village Henry shifted the one-room schoolhouse in which he had shared a desk with Edsel Ruddiman, and he made it the focus of a working school in which the children of favoured neighbours and employees were educated in harmony with the old traditions that he thought were best.

The finishing touch came in 1937. On October 26 of that year, Henry and Clara Ford led their guests through the opening steps of a ball to mark the dedication of Lovett Hall, a grand colonial ballroom named in honour of Henry's dancing master. It was notched into the southern corner of Greenfield Village, between the historic structures and the Henry Ford Museum. Henry had been dressing up and holding parties in different buildings of the village from the beginning. He had had Edsel and Eleanor over for breakfast around the stove in the old Ford homestead. He liked to sit in with the children for their lessons in the one-room schoolhouse. He attended their early morning services in the chapel several mornings a week.

Now he finally had the setting that brought all the components of his nostalgia into place. His limousines brought guests to the pillared portico outside. Uniformed waiters dispensed sandwiches and soft drinks (no alcohol) beneath crystal chandeliers grander than any that seventeenth-century colonists could have known. Benjamin Lovett's Old Fashioned Orchestra—cymbalum, violin, bass violin, dulcimer, and accordion—took their places on the plaster-domed podium, the dancing master raised his baton, and the Motor King began to dance. . . .

**Part Four** Henry And Edsel

# 15

## HEIR APPARENT

Henry Ford recorded his early married life with a still camera. His son, Edsel, went in for home movies, and some of them survive today: faded, flickering images of white-flannelled young men making funny faces, doing silly things with dogs, and jumping off car running boards for the amusement of giggling, bobbed-haired girls. Eleanor Ford and the other young wives sit on Florida verandahs, puffing cigarettes in long holders. Edsel, slender, facetious, and energetic, is the life and soul of the party. He clowns like Charlie Chaplin. Dressed in top hat and tails, he dances like Fred Astaire.[1] He would only have to turn a cartwheel, and you would think he was Henry Ford.

Edsel Ford was twenty-five years old when he became president of the Ford Motor Company on December 31, 1918,[2] and he was to hold that position for the rest of his life. He had been working full-time for the company since he left school half a dozen years earlier, and his first responsibility as president was an important one. His father entrusted him with the task of buying out the Dodge brothers and the other minority shareholders while Henry himself remained in California, ostensibly working on his new car —and Edsel handled the job with skill. The buy-out was presented as a move initiated by Edsel, and though this was a negotiating ploy, there was reality to the notion of Ford now becoming a family firm. In the company as reorganized in 1919, Edsel Ford personally held just over 40 percent of the shares.

Edsel succeeded in many respects to the role that James Couzens had played beside Henry Ford. Edsel was in charge of the business side of the business: sales, marketing, keeping the books. He relied quite heavily on the former private secretary Frank Klingensmith, particularly where the accounts were concerned, and he also developed his own personal contribution to the Ford car: design.

Edsel knew all about engineering and what made cars tick. He had played with cylinders and spark plugs from his earliest years. Henry had equipped workshops for his son in both Edison Avenue and Fair Lane, and when Edsel went on his 1915 drive across America with some young friends, newspaper reporters were impressed that, when it came to running repairs, it was Edsel who rolled up his sleeves and stuck his head under the hood. He might be the son and heir to America's newest, most fabulous fortune, noted one journalist in St. Louis, but the lad had "a pair of well-developed forearms."[3]

Engineering at the Ford Motor Company, however, was Henry Ford's preserve. Everyone knew that, and Edsel's sense of his father's territory was precise and highly tuned. He concentrated on the more peripheral aspects of the Model T: its shape, the position of instruments on the dashboard, the configuration of accessories. These were concerns which did not matter too much in the years when the people's car was the only inexpensive workhorse on the market—when there were no instruments on the dashboard to speak of, in any case. But as cars became more complex, and as competition to the Model T increased, the look of an automobile was to become one of the key ingredients of its success.

Edsel's schoolbooks were packed with doodles and sketches of little cars,[4] and when he had the money to afford the real thing, he took pleasure in having cars built to his own specifications. In the 1920s one seldom bought a Bentley, Rolls-Royce, or Hispano-Suiza with a body. You went to a specialist coach builder to clothe the chassis and power unit with an elegant, individual skin, and Edsel delighted in ordering up special paint jobs and body finishes from carriage builders like Brewster and the Holbrook Company in New York. Long, detailed letters and telegrams survive in which he defines his preferences for special lacquers and coach stripes—as well as the adjustments necessary for him to reach the accelerator pedal.

I expect to drive this car myself a great deal, and inasmuch as I am not very tall I am anxious that the seat be as far forward as possible.[5]

Edsel Ford built up quite a stable of thoroughbred cars —a Packard, a Cadillac, a Bugatti, a Daimler, an M.G. Midget, as well as a Hispano-Suiza, at various times[6]—and his enthusiasm rubbed off on the humble Model T.

The special niche which the Model T came to occupy in America's affections has created the impression that it was just one car—and, in an engineering sense, it was. But over its eighteen years of production, the basic mechanical configuration appeared in all manner of different body shapes: no-door, single-door, two-door, four-door, closed, open, sedan, pick-up, station wagon—the variations were endless. For many years, even at the height of production, the Model T's bodies came from outside suppliers, notably the Briggs Body Company, and it was Edsel who developed, vetted, and approved all the designs. His father, who thought that it was the engineering that really counted, was content for Edsel to deal with this. "It was his custom," remembered the painter Irving Bacon, "to leave all the artistic touches and aesthetic things to Edsel Ford's judgement."[7]

As president of the company, Edsel occupied a distinguished, wood-panelled suite of offices beside his father's in Highland Park. He was in most mornings before 9:30, and he would work diligently right through the day, keeping a systematic, tidy desk. His private secretary, A. J. Lepine, could not remember seeing him once lean back, put his feet up, or read a newspaper for pleasure in all the twenty-five years that Lepine worked for him.[8]

Edsel was conscientious about seeing people. He had a little routine by which he would repeat a first and last name once or twice to himself to fix it in his memory, and, whoever his visitor might be, he would hear him out right to the end. He had no secret code or signal by which Lepine might know that it was time to call on the intercom or break up a meeting.

"He was patient with people," remembered the secretary, "never abrupt with them."[9]

Edsel's patience was something that everyone remarked on, and it went right back to his earliest years. His refusal, at the age of seven, to go out sleighing because his sleigh was too old was the last recorded instance of wilfulness in his life. He was a courteous, dutiful child. His cousin Catherine Ruddiman, the daughter of Margaret, can remember how when she was just a little girl, and Edsel was fifteen, he taught her to roller-skate, holding her up and encouraging her for what seemed like hours, without flagging.

He was "an even-tempered man," remembered Lepine. "One would practically never hear him say anything sarcastic or resentful about other people. He had a way . . . of expressing disapproval, if he did disapprove, by an attitude of silence. He kept himself uniformly under control. I never saw him do any fidgeting or show undue excitement."[10]

Nor did Lepine ever hear his master swear. "Well, hardly ever. He might come out occasionally with some apt expression . . . but he didn't use just any cheap language."[11]

Everyone was agreed, in a business not generally noted for breeding or refinement, that Edsel Ford was a true gentleman.

The marriage of Edsel Bryant Ford to Eleanor Lowthian Clay in 1916 brought a new and powerful personality into the Ford family. Eleanor Clay did not strike you as especially forceful when you met her. She was never an overbearing, bossy sort of person. On the contrary, she was rather accessible and friendly—not threatening in any way. But from the moment of her marriage to Edsel, Eleanor Clay Ford began to move her husband out of the close, smothering orbit of his parents, providing him with a context of his own, and it was Eleanor who helped Edsel Ford to stand as a Ford in his own right.

The couple moved away from Dearborn for a start. This

was clearly not what Henry and Clara had hoped for, to judge from all the expensive facilities they had provided at Fair Lane, laid out as a playground for their grown-up son. But the young Edsel Fords did not settle in Eleanor's territory either, the west-side mansions around Twelfth Street and Boston Boulevard. They moved across town to the elegant, tree-lined avenues where Grand Boulevard hit the river—Indian Village, a fashionable new neighbourhood where many wealthy young Detroiters were settling.

The couple's first address was 439 Iroquois Avenue in Indian Village. Edsel paid $60,000 for the house, a substantial but not ostentatious detached mansion, and he paid as much again to have the interior redesigned in an art deco style by the architect Leonard Willeke.[12] It was a spare, streamlined look, very modern for its time, and every detail counted. Once the young Henry Ford II, born in September 1917, was able to sit up, he took his meals in his own Willeke-designed, art deco high chair.

Detroit's newspapers had described the 1916 marriage of Edsel Ford and Eleanor Clay as the alliance of wealth with "society." This did less than justice to the financial health of the Hudson family and their department store, but there could be no doubting that, when it came to "society," it was Eleanor Clay Ford who carved out the path for her shy and modest husband. She was such a purposeful character. She had so much energy—"a lot of beans," as her friend Katie Shiell liked to put it.[13] Compact and bouncy, Ellie Ford skated in winter, hiked in spring, and swam in the summer. Edsel had travelled with his parents to fairly obvious places: New York, the Grand Canyon, England. Now Eleanor opened his horizons to fresh patterns of migration.

In 1923 the Edsel Fords bought themselves a country estate, Haven Hill, 2,422 acres of countryside to the north of Detroit near Pontiac, where they could relax in space they did not have in Indian Village. Their son Henry II had been joined in 1919 by a brother, originally called Edsel Junior, but then renamed Benson, perhaps because Benson was a Hudson family name. Josephine, born in 1923, and a baby brother, William Clay, born in 1925, completed the family, and the young Fords spent most weekends at Haven Hill with horses, a kidney-shaped swimming pool, and a quarter-mile toboggan run with a motorized lift to tow the children up the hill every time they reached the bottom.[14]

For winter and spring vacations the family moved south to Florida, to the exclusive enclave of Hobe Sound, north of Palm Beach, where they had another house; and in the summer, private railcars took them, with a retinue of horses and servants, to yet another holiday residence, an ample estate at Seal Harbor, Maine, set high on a hill overlooking the Atlantic.[15]

Eleanor Clay's own mother had taught her, as a child, to love the summer fogs and evergreens of Maine, and, not content with taking Edsel there, Eleanor tried to entice her father-in-law to the northeast coast as well.

"I am so crazy to have you come up here that I can hardly stand it," she wrote to Henry Ford in August 1918. "You would just love the forest walks revealing the mountain tops where you are unconscious of the existence of anything human."[16]

It was perhaps significant that Eleanor Clay Ford was never very fond of the curious Christian name that Edsel's parents had bestowed upon him. She always called her husband "Ned"—and he called her "Ellie." She spoke with a firm Michigan accent that accentuated her *r*s, and this was of a piece with her forthright, down-to-earth dealings with other people. Ellie Ford was a blunt person. She let you know precisely what was on her mind. Edsel was discreet, inhibited by a kindlier version of the feline duplicity that made it so easy for his father to say one thing and mean another. But Ellie expressed her feelings with a directness that could drop her hearers' jaws open on impact. Her son Henry II inherited her hooked nose and full, slightly fleshy facial features, and his bluntness came from his mother's side as well.

Like many of the Hudson family, Eleanor liked a drink, though she never overstepped the limits of what was seemly in a lady. Above all, she liked people, forming close warm friendships that lasted her life long. Most of her friends had been born into money as she was, coming from families with a certain local substance to their name. So Edsel was welcomed into a circle that had no hesitation in looking him square in the eye—a bracing change from the parochial obsequiousness of Dearborn, where Henry's success had turned him into something of a lord of the manor. For Edsel, escaping from Dearborn was, among other things, escaping from the squirearchy.

In Indian Village, the Edsel Fords' friends were young married couples like themselves, just starting families, but quite rich enough to employ nannies, cooks, and house-keepers. Eleanor did her everyday shopping at Hudson's, the family store, but her spring and autumn wardrobes were built up on three- or four-day expeditions to New York with girlfriends, and with Edsel and other husbands who might be there on business. The party would embark in the evening on a private railcar hitched to the back of the Detroiter, dine convivially on the train, and wake up next morning in New York for breakfast at the Ritz. The train home would deliver them back in time for breakfast in the leather-bound comfort of the Detroit Club on the corner of West Fort and Cass, after which the husbands would peel off back to work and the chauffeurs would ferry the girls home.[17]

There was a definite aristocracy to the comfortable life of the Edsel Fords. They certainly enjoyed their wealth, but no one suggested they did so without taste and dignity, and Edsel had the unfailing sense of noblesse oblige noted by Samuel Marquis. In 1926 Edsel and Eleanor went down to Georgia for a holiday with their friends Lynn and Elizabeth Pierson, staying in the spa at Warm Springs because Elizabeth was a polio victim. There they met Franklin D. Roosevelt, whose political career had been blighted by the polio attack that had crippled him in 1921, and as FDR drove the Detroit visitors around the spa in his old Ford with manual controls, he expounded his dream of a foundation to tackle infantile paralysis head on. When the party got back, Edsel sat down, unprompted, to write out a cheque for $25,000, momentarily striking his voluble host quite dumb. Roosevelt had never been handed so much money in his life—let alone without asking for it.[18]

Edsel Ford enjoyed a fabulous income in the 1920s, some $3 million a year on average (his father drew some $4.5 million from the company annually[19]), and, quite early in their marriage, Edsel and Eleanor started to spend some of it on art. Eleanor herself came from an arty background. Towards the end of the nineteenth century, Detroit's entrepreneurs had discovered how the acquisition of European art and antiques could provide their money with some instant social tone, and since the Hudsons operated the city's largest interior-decorating concern from their store, they played an active part in this. Eleanor, as a little girl, became quite used to paintings bearing funny French names hanging on the wall, and to the idea that old furniture could actually be more valuable than new. She had a cousin, Robert Tannahill, who had grown up with her in old Joseph Hudson's house and who was like a brother to her. At quite an early age, Tannahill had started building a collection of works by artists of whom very few people in Detroit had then heard: Seurat, Gauguin, Matisse, van Gogh.

The Hudsons did not confine their interests to the traditional fine arts. They financed the first exhibition of a new local Society of Arts and Crafts, a William Morris-like organization which sought to propagate aesthetic design in everyday life, and they were also pillars of the Pewabic Pottery,* whose exotic glazes were spearheading a midwestern revival of ceramics as an art in its own right.

Edsel enjoyed all this, for he had an artistic bent himself. Catherine Ruddiman remembers that he illustrated almost every letter he sent to her with a little drawing.[20] As a young

---

* *Pewabic* is an Indian word meaning "dark-coloured earth." Housed in a half-timbered building near the Indian Village, and still operating today, the Pewabic Pottery was founded in 1907 by William B. Stratton, Mary Chase Perry (later Mrs. Stratton), and Horace Caulkins, all friends of the Edsel Fords.

man he had made his own private collection of Renaissance masterpieces, painstakingly clipping out black-and-white reproductions of Michelangelos, Botticellis, and particularly Raphaels[21]—and among the essays that he chose to preserve from his school days were three compositions on the great painters of the world.

One of them included a poignant sentence on the young Michelangelo. "As a boy he desired to study art, but his father Lodovico opposed this because he had never heard of an artist of any kind making a good living."[22] This had the ring of real life, though Edsel's own father, Henry, seems, in fact, to have viewed his boy's artistic leanings with pride —up to a certain point.

"Shake hands with my son," said Henry Ford to the painter Irving Bacon in 1910. "Edsel is the artist in our family. Art is something I know nothing about."[23]

But then Henry turned to the Highland Park powerhouse, his pride and joy, with its burnished brass pipes on display through tall glass windows to the passersby on Woodward Avenue.

"This," he said, "is the kind of art we are now interested in."[24]

Henry and Edsel Ford had been pals all through Edsel's childhood, sharing both a love of machines and the successes that rolled from Henry's growing mastery of his field. "WON THE SELDEN SUIT," proclaimed Edsel's diary joyously on January 9, 1911, breaking briefly into capital letters to celebrate the triumph, then going on to describe the victory banquet to which Henry took his seventeen-year-old son in New York. "Bed at 2 AM."[25]

After Edsel became president of the Ford Motor Company, Henry was proud to pose for pictures alongside his son—visiting the Rouge, inspecting the cars, and, later, occupying the historic structures of Greenfield Village together. There was one photograph of which Henry was especially fond: father and son in the Village's Plympton House together, sitting thoughtfully side by side in an old, high-backed wood settle, their faces warmed and lit by a flickering log fire. Henry liked it so much he used it as a Christmas card. It showed the facial resemblance between the two men, quite striking in some lights, and it also captured the best that Henry hoped for in his relationship with his son: intimacy, warmth, partnership.

It is difficult to exaggerate the closeness that existed, in some respects, between Henry Ford and his son. Scarcely a day went past that they did not spend several hours in each other's company, talking and working together, as they had always done, on some project or other. When it was not possible for them to meet, they would talk on the telephone. A direct private line connected the study of Henry Ford at Fair Lane with that of Edsel on the other side of Detroit, and most evenings the line was busy.

"My father would call up Grandaddy every night," remembered Benson, Edsel's second son.[26]

When either Henry or Edsel travelled, they kept compulsively in touch with each other. Their personal files, as they survive today in the Ford Archives, bulge over with letters, postcards, and telegrams from one to the other, daily bulletins on the weather, the passing scenery, their state of health. The collected correspondence of Henry and Edsel Ford is impressive testimony to the need that these two men had, one for the other.

But something is missing. In all these letters and messages, so full of words and details, there is a lack of feeling. No serious issues are ever addressed. The children are well, the sun is shining, the car broke down, and the picnic was fun. But if you did not know the identities of these two correspondents, communicating so busily, you would scarcely guess that they were, between them, supposed to be running one of the largest industrial enterprises in the world. Nor would you ever guess that there were many substantial business and personal issues on which they profoundly disagreed.

To the present day, the Fords have a poor record of putting themselves or other people in touch with their deepest feelings. Angers and resentments build beneath a surface of amiability, only to explode without warning—and this proved tragically the case with Henry and Edsel Ford. They were quite often to be seen together, talking earnestly, arm in arm—or even, sometimes, embracing each other—laughing at some shared joke or discussing some practical problem that had caught their mutual enthusiasms. But alongside the love, inevitably, went more ambivalent feelings—fears, jealousies, grievances—and these the two men did not know how to express. At the heart of their affection lay the vacuum that so often exists within the complex, inarticulate fondness of father and son, the inability to talk about the really important things. Pride and rivalry, hope and disillusion— the love of Henry and Edsel Ford positively ached with contradiction, and as the two men failed to find ways to talk their conflicts out, the love grew less and the ache grew more.

If executives ever came to Henry Ford questioning decisions that Edsel had made, the old man would back his son up.

"Do whatever he says," he would say. "He's got to run the company."[27]

Journalists would quite often ask Henry exactly what he did at the company, since he had ceased to be president in 1919 and held no other official position apart from his seat on the board.

"Oh," he would reply vaguely, "I let Edsel find something for me to do."[28]

Sixty years old in 1923, Henry Ford liked to play with the notion that he was withdrawing gently from the affairs of his company, but nobody really believed this. If Edsel Ford remarked that it looked like being a clear day tomorrow, went the joke in the 1920s, "Detroit would promptly wonder if this was his own opinion or merely the second-hand observation of Henry Ford." The question would go around town, and in next to no time people would be asking, "Had Henry Ford gone in for weather predictions?"[29]

This was the first and fundamental problem between Henry and Edsel Ford. Henry could not let go, and Edsel did not know how to take over. Henry Ford was a hard act to follow, and, born in the shadow of his father's monstrous genius, Edsel's solution was to have no act at all. Dozens of tougher, more awkward characters submitted to Henry Ford's imperious demands, and Edsel did the same. He gave in. He gave in when it came to questions of his very manhood, like his draft dodging, and when it was a question of the company, he actually proclaimed his submission as a matter of considered policy:

I have not worked out a separate business philosophy for myself. It has not been necessary, for on all material points, I agree absolutely with my father's philosophy. I do not merely accept his beliefs; I feel as strongly about them as he does.[30]

Edsel made this declaration in 1929 in a ghostwritten article which Samuel Crowther had submitted for his approval and which opened with the words "Edsel Ford at thirty-six is the richest man in the world." Edsel had the opening sentence changed to read "one of the richest," but, at thirty-six, he was content to make no more claim to an identity than that of being his father's son.

The tragedy of Edsel Ford's willingness to lie down and let himself be trampled on was that his father concluded not that Edsel loved him, admired him, worshipped him—nor that he, the great overflowing Henry Ford, was responsible for the crushing of his son's spirit—but that the boy suffered from a fundamental flaw, that Edsel was weak, and that it was Henry's duty for his son's sake, and for the sake of the company, that he should toughen him up a little.

The notion may have come from Emerson. On one of the pages marked by Henry in "Compensation," the essay which he used to read and reread, was a passage dealing with weakness, and how a man could not acquire strength until he had been "pricked and stung and sorely assailed":

Whilst he sits on the cushion of advantages, he goes to sleep. When he is pushed, tormented, defeated, he has a chance to learn something; he has been put on his wits, on his manhood; he has gained facts; learns his ignorance.[31]

The "cushion of advantages" applied precisely to Edsel. "The boy is soft," Henry would complain to Evangeline Dahlinger.[32] He blamed himself for this, he told Harry Bennett. He had always "overprotected" Edsel,[33] and as a result, the boy suffered from the failings he described to Samuel Crowther in 1922:

I pity the poor fellow who is so soft and flabby that he must always have "an atmosphere of good feeling" around him before he can do his work. There are such men. . . . Not only are they business failures; they are character failures also; it is as if their bones never attained a sufficient degree of hardness to enable them to stand on their own feet.[34]

To toughen Edsel up, Henry Ford tried to follow Emerson's advice, turning his son's life into a never-ending emotional assault course, taking with one hand what he appeared to give with the other. When Edsel commissioned a line of new coke ovens at the Rouge, his father outwardly appeared to go along with the decision, while confiding in the same breath to Harry Bennett, "As soon as Edsel gets those ovens built, I'm going to tear them down."[35]

The ovens were destroyed within days of their completion. Henry Ford could, obviously, have discussed the subject with his son in the first place, arguing it out face to face, or he could simply have countermanded Edsel's order there and then. But saying nothing and waiting to destroy the project until it reached fruition increased the pain—and hence the "therapy"—for Edsel.

John R. Davis, a young member of the sales department, experienced the "therapy" firsthand when he managed to persuade Edsel of the need for new offices to accommodate the company's expanding sales and accounting staffs in the early 1920s. Henry Ford was away at the time, and in his absence a new office building was designed and commissioned. Work had already started by the time Henry Ford returned.

"What's going on there?" he asked, pointing out of Edsel's office at the workmen scurrying around outside, and Edsel explained how, with the company expanding, there was a need for more space.

"Space for who?" inquired his father, at which point Edsel made a tactical error. Davis later decided that all would probably have been well if Edsel had confined himself to stressing the expansion of the sales department, since that was the major reason for the new building. Sales were something that Henry Ford could understand. But of the several departments that were scheduled to occupy the new quarters, Edsel chose, for some reason, to start with his father's least favourite, the accountants.

Henry Ford did not wait for his son to finish.

"Come on, Charlie," he said, and swept out of the room, with Charles Sorensen in his wake.

Next morning Davis arrived at work to find the staff of the accounts department milling around the parking lot in confusion. Their cramped offices had been on the fourth floor of the old building, but maintenance men had entered the fourth floor sometime during the night and stripped it completely. Every desk, chair, filing cabinet, and rug had been removed. There was not even a telephone the accountants could call their own. Later that day it was learned that the entire department had been abolished at a stroke. Men and women who had worked loyally for Ford for years had all been summarily dismissed.

Later that morning Henry Ford called on his son with a grin.

"Edsel," he said, "if you really need more room you'll find plenty of it on the fourth floor."[36]

It was the measure of Edsel Ford that, over the weeks following his father's clearing of the fourth floor, he found jobs for every one of the sacked accountants, fitting them unobtrusively into other departments—and it was the measure of Henry Ford that he knew that Edsel was doing this. There was a twisted collusion in the sad game that father and son were to play out through the 1920s and 1930s, and its cruellest twist was that time did not heal the process, it made it worse. The more Edsel submitted, the more his father hurt him, and the more the boy was wounded, the more submissive he became.

# 16

## HARD TIMES, HARD DEALING

In October 1919, Clara Ford got in touch with an old friend she had not seen for several years. "We have built a home in the country since I saw you," she wrote, "and we love it very much, have a wonderful garden."

My son is married, and has a little son two years old and one three months old. The eldest is named Henry II and the baby Edsel Junior.\* The eldest talks and runs all over, calls Mr. Ford gadaddie. We have them out with us a great deal and could not love Edsel's wife more if we had picked her out ourselves.[1]

Both Clara and Henry Ford liked Eleanor. She was conscientious and sensible, a level-headed girl. She looked after their son. Talking to Allan Benson in 1923, Henry compared his daughter-in-law to his own mother—the highest praise he could give.[2] Eleanor might have taken Edsel away from his parents, but Henry and Clara did not feel they had lost touch. They saw a lot of the younger Fords—and they also saw a lot of Edsel and Eleanor's best friends, Ernest and Josephine Kanzler.

The Kanzlers were more than friends. They were relatives. Josephine was Eleanor's elder sister, a polished, elegant woman whom Eleanor, five years her junior, always rather looked up to. The two sisters had grown up together in their uncle Joseph Hudson's house, and after their marriages, they were neighbours in Indian Village. Ernest and Josephine Kanzler lived a few doors away from the Edsel Fords on Iroquois Avenue.[3]

Ernest Kanzler was a bright young lawyer who had risen from humble origins: his father was a country lawyer in

---

\* The Edsel Fords later thought better of calling their second son Edsel Junior and called him Benson (see page 313).

Saginaw, Michigan. Ernest had studied at Ann Arbor, then gone on to Harvard, and he had landed himself a job in one of Detroit's leading law firms, Stevenson, Carpenter, Butzel, and Backus—Elliott Stevenson being the lawyer who represented both the Dodge brothers and the *Chicago Tribune* in their suits against Henry Ford. It was Stevenson's pitiless cross-questioning which was to lay bare Henry's ignorance at Mount Clemens—and Kanzler was assigned to do the attorney's research for both cases.[4]

Henry Ford did not appear to mind this. When he first met Kanzler, the *Tribune* case was still several years from coming to court, and he used to twit the young lawyer, when Ernest and Josephine came over to Fair Lane with the Edsel Fords, by discussing the suits in great detail.

"Please, Mr. Ford," the embarrassed young attorney would protest, "don't talk about your affairs when I am here."

"You ought to be on my side," Henry would respond. "Why do you want to be a lawyer, anyway? They're parasites. Come to Highland Park and I'll give you a job."[5]

Ernest Kanzler resisted the invitation to start with. But when Henry Ford incorporated his new tractor company, Henry Ford & Son, in August 1916,[6] he offered Kanzler a chance to get in at the ground floor, and Kanzler accepted. He proved an able manager, playing an important role in getting the first Fordson tractors into production before the end of the First World War, and with the coming of peace, Kanzler stood alongside Edsel, a bright and dynamic young executive, ambitious to help steer Ford through the challenges of the postwar world.

In 1919 the Ford Motor Company moved back to full-scale production of an improved Model T, featuring an electrical self-starter. Charles F. Kettering of the National Cash Register Company had used his experience with compact motors that could deliver sharp, occasional bursts of power to develop a self-starter for Cadillac, the company which Henry M. Leland had developed from Henry Ford's original Model A. All Cadillacs had had an electrical self-starter as standard equipment from 1912 onwards.[7]

First scorned by Henry Ford as an unmanly luxury, the electrical self-starter soon established itself as an essential component in the democratizing of the motorcar, since it made the automobile truly accessible to women. Publicists had tried to make out that hand-cranking a car was no problem—"It's a knack rather than a matter of strength," wrote Miss Jean Lorimer in an article entitled "How Simple It Really Is: Any Woman Can Learn to Drive."[8] A booklet entitled "The Woman and The Ford" claimed that the Model T was "as easy to drive as the old family horse."[9]

But cranking the car required exertion, and courage as well, for wrists and arms were vulnerable to a motor that kicked back. Henry M. Leland's eagerness to use and develop Kettering's self-starter had received special impetus from the fate of a friend who, gallantly going to the rescue of a lady, had shattered his shoulder while trying to crank her stalled car. With the addition of a self-starter, the Model T became even more popular than it had been in 1917 when war slowed production. For the twelve months ending December 1919, Ford produced and sold more cars than ever before—over three quarters of a million vehicles.

Not that it was too difficult to sell cars in America in the months that followed the First World War, since automobile production had been cut back severely as the manufacturers had turned their factories over to war production. With peace, the national waiting list for a new car soon came to number hundreds of thousands, and as a general economic boom intensified this demand, Detroit discovered how pleasant life can be when America has money to spend.

But the boom ran out abruptly in the summer of 1920. Worried by inflation, the federal government cut its budget, pulling over $6 billion out of the economy.[10] Suddenly the Motor City discovered the down side, for it is amazing, when times get hard, how easy it becomes to live with the rust and rattles of the automobile that you had once been intent on trading in. Forgoing the new car is the most obvious economy to make in a time of recession, and as recession gripped America in the autumn of 1920, the cyclical nature of the car business was revealed for the first time: scaling the heights in a time of prosperity, but almost at a standstill when the economy slowed.

Ford was the giant of the car industry. By 1919, one in every three cars purchased in America was a Model T—the Ford market share for the year actually exceeded 40 percent—and no single competitor approached Ford in size. The Dodge brothers made the most comparable economy car. Buick, Oldsmobile, Chevrolet, and the other companies gathered together under the umbrella of General Motors accounted for the second-greatest total volume of business. Hudson, Studebaker, Packard, Maxwell, and Willys-Overland were all successful independents, but even in aggregate their sales did not approach those of Ford.

The sudden 1920 turndown in car sales caught Ford particularly ill prepared. The adverse judgement in the Dodge brothers' case had drained $20 million out of the company, development of the Rouge had consumed some $60 million, while mines that Henry had purchased in northern Michigan to supply coal and iron for his new blast furnaces had consumed $15 to $20 million. All these capital outlays had compelled him to borrow a large proportion of the money he needed to buy out the minority stockholders —Wall Street, apparently, was a lesser evil than the Dodge brothers—and it left Henry with a large $60 million debt to service.[11] As sales began to fall in the summer of 1920, the Ford cash flow dwindled dangerously.

Henry's solution to the problem was simple: cut prices. It had worked for him before. Instructing Edsel, William Knudsen, Sorensen, and his other top executives to work out cost reductions, he studied their list of proposed economies and informed them that they were too small.

"There, gentlemen, are your prices," he declared, offering them a sheet on which he had scribbled his own proposed price cuts, and when they protested that this would mean selling cars at a loss, he pulled the paper back and reduced the prices of two models by five dollars more.[12] The basic price of a Model T chassis, sold for conversion into a truck or van, came down from $525 to $360, the $550 runabout was to be offered at $395, and the top-of-the-line sedan came down nearly $200 to $795.[13]

These were the largest price cuts in the history of the American car business, and Henry Ford had the satisfaction of seeing them drive at least one of his competitors into serious difficulties. In 1920 the stock of the General Motors Corporation began to wilt severely under the onslaught of the Ford price cuts, forcing the company's creator, William C. Durant, to sell out to the DuPont family, who in turn mortgaged a substantial portion of the corporation to J. P. Morgan.

But Henry Ford could not, singlehandedly, stave off a nationwide recession that was assuming crash proportions. After an initial fillip in response to the price cuts, Ford sales fell as drastically as everybody else's—and Ford was taking a loss of twenty dollars or so on each car.[14] As the Highland Park plant closed for the Christmas lay-off on December 24, 1920, it was announced that work would begin again on January 5 next. But when January 5 came, the Ford gates did not open.

Louis H. Turrell, chief auditor of the Ford Motor Company, had been given the job of cutting company costs. In October 1920, he had recalled his travelling auditors from the field to carry out a comprehensive survey of the entire Ford organization, drawing up lists, preparing charts, and working out where economies could be made. By Christmas their task was complete, and on December 30 the men were called into Turrell's office to be told that their services were no longer required. The following day Turrell himself was discharged.[15]

Crisis sharpened a special cutting edge in the psyche of Henry Ford. It unleashed the sort of pugnacity he had displayed in his battle with the Dodge brothers. As Henry found himself shadowed by the prospect of bankruptcy in the winter of 1920, he found ready targets for his aggression —particularly in the bureaucracy of his company, which he had always viewed with a jaundiced eye. His office staff was cut from 1,074 to 528, the telegraph office eliminated, the tax and controller's departments merged with auditing. The desks, typewriters, filing cabinets, and paraphernalia of the surplus staff were taken out and sold, along with 60 percent of the telephone extensions—"only a comparatively few men in any organization need telephones," said Henry[16]—and the sidewalk sale even extended to the office pencil sharpeners. Members of the staff who wished to sharpen pencils in the future were required to bring their own knife to work.[17]

The world reacted to the news of the Ford fire sale with sympathy and concern. Mrs. M. D. Brown, a Detroit housewife who could not herself afford a Ford car, offered to lend Henry $100 of her life savings, and similar offers of assistance flooded in to Highland Park from ordinary people all over America.[18]

They need not have worried. Henry claimed later that he had set his face resolutely against seeking help from Wall Street, but Edsel and Liebold were certainly working out contingency plans with bankers on his behalf. In the event, he discovered another way to pay off his debts.

The scheme seems to have originated with Ernest Kanzler. While running the Fordson tractor plant during the war, Kanzler had noted how excessive supplies brought into the factory prior to production could tie up valuable plant space and money that could run into millions of dollars, and he had reorganized inventory schedules to reduce this. Raw materials and parts were purchased only as and when they were needed, with the freight cars that had delivered them being immediately employed to transport finished tractors away. After Henry Ford had acquired full control of his car company in 1919, he brought Kanzler over to work the same miracle at Highland Park.

It proved the saving of the situation in the winter of 1920, for Highland Park was stocked to the walls with spare parts. The inventory was valued by one estimate at no less than

$88 million,[19] and from this huge stockpile Kanzler carved out packages of components which were despatched as compulsory additions to every shipment of new cars, these shipments themselves being systematically increased by the factory to use up the large stocks of vehicles unsold because of the recession.

The standard terms of business between Ford and Ford dealers were payment in full upon delivery. So in the winter months of 1920–21, the 6,000 or so Ford dealers around the country began to find the trains pulling into their local station with immensely larger shipments of new cars than they had ordered, or could possibly sell—and expensive packages of spare parts as well, all of which had to be paid for in hard money on the nail. If any dealer refused to accept the consignment, he risked losing his franchise. Until the postwar boom had ended a few months earlier, a franchise to sell Ford cars had been the nearest thing in America to a license to print your own money.

Few dealers hesitated. They went to their local bank manager, borrowed the money to pay for the cars and spare parts, and hung on to their Ford franchise.

Back in Highland Park, meanwhile, the company had unilaterally changed its own schedule of payments to suppliers from sixty to ninety days, and had also used the generally depressed state of the market to cut its offer prices on raw materials and ready-made parts to the bone. By paying only a skeleton staff of executives and despatchers at Highland Park through the month of January, costs were reduced still further, and by the spring of 1921 Henry Ford could boast that he had paid off all his debts. He had an additional cash surplus in hand of no less than $20 million. Best of all, he had achieved this miracle without borrowing a penny from the bank. As they heard the news, 6,000 or so people around the country knew that they had done the borrowing for him.

Ford emerged from the postwar slump of 1920–21 leaner and more competitive than ever. In the easy boom months of 1919, the company had been employing fifteen men per car per day. When Highland Park reopened in February 1921, the ratio was cut to nine per car per day, this improvement being achieved by both rehiring fewer men and speeding up the line, and Henry Ford pointed to his increased productivity as one more argument against the bankers. "If we had borrowed," he said, "we should not have been under the necessity of finding methods to cheapen production."[20]

But Henry's cheapening had been at the expense of some of the company's most valuable—if intangible—assets, since the years 1919–21 marked the disappearance from Ford senior management of men whose wisdom and experience were not replaced. C. Harold Wills was the first to go in the spring of 1919, and his departure seems to have been linked with the buying out of the minority shareholders which occurred at that time. Wills had always been a shareholder of sorts, having a private arrangement whereby Henry paid him a proportion of his own dividends, and he left with $1,592,128.39.[21] He put his money into the development of his own car, the Wills–St. Clair, a superb state-of-the-art example of automotive engineering whose refinements totally defeated the main-street mechanics of America.

Norval Hawkins, who had supervised the marketing and advertising of the Model T for more than a decade, went the month after Wills. He had had various personal disagreements with Henry and other executives, but a more fundamental problem was the incompatibility between his own insistence on paperwork and Henry's haphazard method of doing things. Discussing car engines one day with Percival Perry, on one of the Englishman's visits to Detroit, Henry sent a clerk to collect a particular part he wished to demonstrate, and grimaced when the man returned holding out a form: "You'll have to sign this, Mr. Ford."

Ford signed, got the part he had asked for, and then took Perry to the office where Norval Hawkins's forms were stored.

"Are these all you've got?" he inquired, and on being assured that the pile in front of him represented the entire stock, he called for a can of gasoline, had the forms taken out into the middle of the testing yard, and organized a huge bonfire.[22]

John R. Lee, the recruit from Keim Mills who had helped set up the Sociological Department, completed a trio of departures in the spring of 1919. Lee left to assist Wills in his ill-starred venture. But these losses were less significant than the wholesale resignations which accompanied the shake-out of 1920–21. Frank Klingensmith, the private secretary who had risen to the rank of treasurer after James Couzens's departure, left ostensibly because he had too vehemently advocated borrowing as a solution to the company's cash-flow problems. "He was half Jewish, you know," said Ernest Liebold by way of explanation.[23] But Percival Perry later suggested that Henry had become jealous of the closeness that Klingensmith had established with Edsel, and of the way in which the treasurer had helped the young man to master the business side of the company. In the early 1920s, Henry was frequently declaring how he wanted Edsel to run the company as he saw fit, but the departure of Klingensmith was one early sign that he did not, perhaps, mean exactly what he said.[24]

The loss which was to prove most damaging in these years was the departure of William Knudsen, who left to play a vital role in the rebirth of General Motors in the 1920s, largely at Ford's expense. Knudsen's great contribution to Ford had been to get the Rouge site started with the construction of Eagle boats, and also to set up a network of Ford assembly plants around the country. It was much cheaper for Ford to ship knocked-down components in railcars rather than finished vehicles—the average railcar could only take three or four finished Model Ts, as compared to more than twenty in kit form—and Knudsen established more than a dozen regional Ford plants in different corners of America.

Knudsen's resignation in February 1921 reflected his power struggle with his fellow Dane, Charles Sorensen, who was fighting unashamedly for a seat at the right hand of

Henry. But a few years later, Henry Ford himself offered an explanation which sheds a revealing light on how he was coming to view his company now that he had rid himself of his minority shareholders.

"You see," he told the journalist Malcolm W. Bingay, "this is my business. I built it and, as long as I live, I propose to run it the way I want it run."

Henry freely admitted that Knudsen was "the best production man in the United States"—and thus, presumably, superior to Sorensen, with whom Knudsen had been quarrelling—but, he said, he found Knudsen too much to handle.

"I let him go," said Henry with one of the displays of humility at which he had become so adept, "not because he wasn't good, but because he was too good—for me."[25]

Henry Ford had never enjoyed arguments, and now approaching his sixtieth birthday, he clearly felt he had the power to eliminate them from his life altogether. There would never be another James Couzens in the Ford Motor Company. Charles Sorensen won out over William Knudsen not because he was better at his job, but because he was better at taking orders. Knudsen, among other sins, had had the presumption to question Henry's continuing reliance upon the Model T and to suggest that, after a dozen years, it was time at least to consider some sort of replacement.[26] Henry was finding it increasingly difficult to tolerate displays of independence in those around him, even from old associates who had proved their loyalty and had been with him from the earliest days.

"There is altogether too much reliance on good feeling in our business organizations," he declared a few years later. "People have too great a fondness for working with the people they like. . . . It is not necessary for the employer to love the employee or for the employee to love the employer."[27]

These Darwinian sentiments bore little resemblance to the ambitions of the man who, ten years earlier, was sponsoring the inspectors of the Sociological Department and the human face of capitalism. But ten years had wrought a change in Henry Ford. What with the Peace Ship, the Dodge

brothers, the *Chicago Tribune*, Truman S. Newberry, and
the pressure of the postwar slump, he had lived almost
continuously in the firing line, and it showed. To survive
these successive challenges, most of them of his own making,
he had developed a carapace that fitted all too well around
an ego fed with money and power in undreamt-of servings,
and his growing insistence on submission by everyone
around him reflected the tyranny of a child. As the psycho-
historian Anne Jardim has paraphrased Lord Acton, "It is
not enough to say . . . that power corrupts; power, rather,
provides the setting for regression on a massive scale."[28]

Samuel Marquis puzzled sadly over the extremities in the
man whom he had got to know so closely, but whom he still
felt, in some ways, he did not know at all. "There seems to
be no middle ground in his make-up," he mused. "There is
no unifying spirit . . . no line discernable that I have ever
been able to detect."[29]

Samuel Marquis had got closer to the soul of Henry Ford
than most men, and he had probably reflected more deeply
on the subject than any. But early in 1921 he was deprived
of the chance of further firsthand observation, for when the
new and streamlined Ford Motor Company opened up again
for business in February of that year, some 20,000 of its
70,000 employees were not rehired—among them the inspectors of the Sociological Department, judged nonproduc-
tive and therefore expendable, together with their boss, the
Reverend Doctor Samuel Marquis.

"A great business," explained Henry Ford, "is really too
big to be human."[30]

The careers of Henry M. Leland and Henry Ford had
gone in opposite directions since the two men worked
together briefly, and unhappily, in the Henry Ford Company
in 1902. Henry Ford had taken the low road, the route of
the popular car. Henry Leland had concentrated on the
other end of the market. He had become both the Rolls and
the Royce of American car manufacturing, creating first the
Cadillac, which he made a byword for luxurious, high-

quality motoring, and then, in September 1920, unveiling the car that was to bear America's other grand and prestigious marque: the Lincoln.

The autumn of 1920, however, was the very worst time to try to market a high-priced luxury car in America. Henry Ford found it hard enough to weather the storm, and Henry Leland went under completely. The Lincoln Motor Company was in difficulties from the start, and in November 1921, it was compelled to declare bankruptcy.

The age and engineering reputation of the white-bearded Henry Leland made him something of a father figure in Detroit, a town which lives or dies by the precision with which it can grind a valve, and Henry Ford always professed to share in the general respect. When Leland had left Cadillac after its acquisition by General Motors, local investors formed queues to put money into his new Lincoln Motor Company, and when that company hit the rocks in 1921, Henry Ford joined in the chorus of regret. He betrayed no indication that he might bear a grudge for the way in which Leland had eased him out of his own company twenty years earlier—on the contrary. The streamlined Ford Motor Company was producing more cars than ever before. By the autumn of 1921 it was heading for record profits, and, in the same mode in which he was offering to save Muscle Shoals in these years, Henry Ford announced he would be happy to devote some of his funds and energies to rescuing the engineer whom he acknowledged as "one of the greatest motorcar men in America."[31]

Ford homage to Leland was a family affair. Clara Ford was a friend of the wife of Leland's son Wilfred, and moved by the plight of Lincoln, she went on record with a rare public statement. "If Detroit will stand by," she said, "and see the Lelands and their men who put money into that concern lose everything they've got and not lift a hand to help them, there's something wrong with our public spirit."[32]

Edsel spoke out in similar terms. "It would be a shame," he said, "a blot on the good name of the whole community, if Detroit let the Leland Company go to ruin."

Edsel, with his love of fine cars, was a particular admirer of Leland, and the possibility of Ford acquiring Lincoln offered Henry's son a chance of developing an interest of his own. Father could keep his beloved Model T, while Edsel would work on a new, luxury, high-performance car.

"We do not need the Lincoln as an automobile venture," announced the young president of the Ford Motor Company, "but rather than see these people lose all hope for their money . . . we will buy it at the receiver's sale and continue production of the Lincoln as a Ford unit."[33]

When the Ford offer of $8 million turned out to be the only bid for the assets of the Lincoln Motor Company at the receiver's sale on January 4, 1922, it was a matter for municipal celebration. A Detroit asset had been saved for Detroit. A brass band which had, somehow, been secreted in the crowd struck up with "Hail to the Chief," an immense portrait of a smiling Henry Ford was lowered down the front of the Lincoln office building, and the general feeling around town was summed up by a cartoon in the *Detroit News* which showed a Model T pulling a Lincoln out of the mud. "Courtesy of the Road," read the caption.[34] Henry Ford was the hero of the hour.

But as Lincoln and Ford euphorically joined hands in a partnership that provided a satisfying link between the most popular car in America and the vehicle that could lay claim to being the best, there were certain ambiguities in the arrangement that people overlooked. For Henry Leland the most important of these was precisely when and how the original investors in Lincoln would be repaid, since he was now approaching eighty, and he was less concerned with profits than with his reputation.

"I didn't want to die," he later said, "with people saying that they had lost money through me."[35]

The Lelands were later to claim that they had been given a binding undertaking by Henry Ford that he would pay off all the creditors and stockholders of their company, and this was certainly the impression that Henry gave to many people at the time. It was generally assumed that ordinary

Detroiters who had invested in the company were being rescued by Henry Ford the Motor King, and the public utterances of the Fords—father, mother, and son—did nothing to dispel this illusion.

But nothing in Henry Ford's business record was disinterested philanthropy when examined closely. The Lelands had first approached him in the summer of 1921, six months before they were driven to file Chapter Eleven, and if Henry's motives had been truly disinterested, he could quite easily have helped them at that stage, when the company was still salvageable, with some sort of loan or partnership. But Henry waited, and by delaying his intervention until Lincoln had gone bankrupt, he was able to acquire for just $8 million 100 percent control of a well-equipped company whose assets were conservatively valued at $16 million. Henry had tried offering only $5 million to start with, but the bankruptcy judge rejected that.

Henry's much-trumpeted concern to help a Detroit institution paid solid dividends as well, since the publicity and the active collaboration of the Lelands provided very effective discouragement to any rival bidders who might have compelled him to pay more. It was a similar exercise, in many respects, to his attempts to take over Muscle Shoals.

Six weeks after the bankruptcy sale, a curious ceremony strengthened the general impression that Henry Ford was engaged upon an errand of mercy. February 16, 1922, was the seventy-ninth birthday of Henry M. Leland, and at a birthday celebration held in the canteen of the Lincoln plant, Henry Ford presented the old gentleman with a cheque for $363,000 in the presence of his employees.

"Show it to them, Mr. Leland, show it to them," Henry Ford was heard to urge. "Tell them that they are all going to get them just the same."[36]

The significance of $363,000, Edsel Ford later explained, was that it represented the par value of Henry Leland's B shares in the old Lincoln company, and Henry Ford's urging to make a display of the cheque seemed to carry the message

that the Lincoln employees, many of whom were also investors in the original company, could now expect some repayment as well. Reimbursing worker-investors was certainly
in harmony with the radical face of Ford business theory,
though Henry's signals on the appropriate relationship between workers and shareholders were sometimes confused.
Lunching with the Lelands in the spring of 1922, he reported
that Mrs. Ford had asked him what he was going to do
about the stockholders.

"You know what I told her?" he informed Henry Leland.
"I told her if they would come out to Dearborn we'd give
them a badge and put them to work."

Henry M. Leland apparently took this remark to be a
joke.[37]

The pledge which Henry certainly had made quite un-
equivocally—and which had inclined the Lelands to
collaborate with him to the exclusion of any other possible
bidder—was that, after the takeover, the Lelands could
continue to run Lincoln under Ford ownership just as they
had done before. Yet scarcely twenty-four hours had elapsed
from Lincoln reopening for business under Ford ownership
at the beginning of 1922 when a high-powered team of Ford
executives arrived at the Lincoln factory, headed by Charles
Sorensen and Ernest Kanzler.

Officially this delegation of Ford's brightest talents had
come to Lincoln, they said, in order to learn. Their purpose
was to study the high-quality, precision techniques of Lincoln engineering to see what could be adapted for improving
the production of the Model T. But the Lelands soon began
to feel that the Ford delegation was there not as pupils but
as teachers—and Ernest Kanzler later admitted that the
Lelands were quite right.

"We are not going to throw away any more money on
this company," he remembered Henry Ford saying, and the
Ford work-study team had taken their cue from that.

"I remember the first thing I saw," recalled Kanzler,
"was a group of workers sawing off a piece of bar steel from
which to machine a part. But they needed a number of parts,

and why saw off one piece at a time? They could have done five at once."[38]

On January 21, 1922, Edwin G. Pipp, the former editor of the *Dearborn Independent*, made a prediction about the future of the Lincoln factory. "It will become a Ford plant," he wrote, "and not a Lincoln plant. . . . There is no disposition to question Ford's intentions as to the Lelands now, but good intentions now will not be permitted to interfere with business success later."[39]

Like Samuel Marquis, another man who had got too close to Henry Ford and been hurt, Pipp retained surprising respect for the idealism of his former patron. He credited Henry with sincerity. But he had too frequently witnessed the withering of Ford altruism to believe that the Lelands could survive prolonged involvement with Henry and the man-crushing industrial machine he had created.

"It will all be made over to conform to Ford methods," he predicted. "The method of having many stop watches held on men, and push bosses speeding them up. The Lelands, if they stick, will find their desires overridden by young men placed there by the Fords for the purpose of getting production. . . . It will be the passing of the Lelands."[40]

Pipp's prophesy came to pass in less than six months. By the end of May 1922, the Lelands were so infuriated by the interference of Ford production men, and particularly by the abrasive and insulting manner of Charles Sorensen, that they wrote to Henry Ford, formally offering to buy their company back at the price he had paid, with interest.

Their letter went unanswered, as did follow-up letters on May 26 and 27, and Wilfred Leland decided to take matters into his own hands. He drove out to Fair Lane, swept imperiously past the guard at the gate, and cornered Henry Ford in his lair.

"Mr. Leland," Ford stated, according to Wilfred's later testimony, "I wouldn't sell the Lincoln plant for five hundred million dollars. I had a purpose in acquiring that plant, and I wouldn't think of letting it go."[41]

Henry did acknowledge, however, that the Lelands might have legitimate complaints over their treatment by Ford employees, and he professed himself willing to help with that.

"I'll come over to the Lincoln plant with Edsel tomorrow morning," he promised.

He was as good as his word, though Edsel did not, in fact, accompany his father next morning. Henry listened long and sympathetically to the complaints of Henry M. Leland and his son, Wilfred, and he undertook to deal with them, promising that he would henceforward spend at least two hours a day with the old man, working personally with him.

The Lelands never saw Henry Ford again—not, at least, while they were directors of the Lincoln Motor Company. Less than two weeks later, on Saturday, June 10, 1922, Ernest Liebold arrived in their office to request the departure of Wilfred Leland, and when it became clear that Liebold was speaking with the full authority of Henry Ford, Henry Leland resigned as well. By that afternoon both men were out of the factory they had created, and their personal belongings were evicted too.

It would have happened, probably, sooner or later. The marriage of Ford and Lincoln was bound to have been a difficult match, for the Lelands were demanding, perfectionist engineers, and it is not likely that, at eighty, Henry M. Leland would have responded kindly to the most diplomatic suggestions for reorganizing his operation—which certainly needed some reorganizing. One reason for the initial failure of the Lincoln was its poor and outdated styling. Intent upon mechanical perfection, Leland had clad a sophisticated and expensive postwar machine with a careless prewar body, and it was only when Edsel Ford got his hands on the car and commissioned new bodies from carriage makers like Brewster that the Lincoln started to sell in any numbers.

When the law courts came to consider the rights of the matter, they did not consider that Henry Ford had cheated or defrauded anyone. Henry and Wilfred Leland fought a succession of legal actions through the 1920s, both on their own behalf and in conjunction with their stockholders, and in every case the judges ruled that the burden of evidence favoured Henry Ford.

Still, whatever the letter of the law, Henry Ford clearly transgressed the proclaimed spirit of his Lincoln rescue—which he had presented as a rescue, and not as just another crude takeover bid. It was rather like the ousting of the Dodge brothers a few years earlier. Henry made loud declarations of moral purpose, dressing his actions with all the dignity and high-mindedness that accompanied his reputation as the small man's friend. One Detroit newspaper had even gone so far in 1922 as to compare him to the Good Samaritan. But when the smoke had cleared, there was Henry Ford in sole command of the battlefield, having struck himself a good old-fashioned, cut-price business deal.

Carmakers were not the only section of the American economy to be hurt by the recession of 1920. The art dealers of New York found their business even more severely crippled, for if anything surpasses a new car as an impulse buy, it must be an early Renaissance oil painting. Driven to a rare display of solidarity by the prevailing bad times, the principal dealers of New York gathered together under the leadership of Joseph Duveen to survey the horizon for clients, and they could only identify one whose purchasing power had survived the slump sufficiently for their purposes.

Henry Ford did not have a reputation as an art collector; by 1920, indeed, aged fifty-seven, he had purchased no significant art at all. But this only made him riper for the dealers' purposes, since Duveen's plan was to bring together and present the great carmaker with an assemblage of masterpieces which would not only represent an unparalleled instant collection for this man who was said by many to be the richest in America. Henry Ford would be offered the Hundred Greatest Paintings in the World.

Many and bitter were the disputes as the five New York dealers—Duveen Brothers, Knoedler's, Wildenstein, Seligman, and Stevenson Scott—surveyed their pooled collections to pick out the hundred paintings they would submit to Henry Ford. But finally the selection was complete, an expensive colour reproduction of each masterpiece was prepared, one hundred scholarly captions were written, and the whole was packaged into three magnificent volumes which boarded the Detroit train in Grand Central Station, together with representatives of its five creators.

Joseph Duveen represented Duveen Brothers and acted as head of the delegation which drew up, by appointment, under the limestone carport–cum–front porch of Fair Lane to meet Henry Ford. The dealers were most encouraged by the evident need for some sort of colour to enliven the dark and blank expanses of mahogany panelling, and also by Henry Ford's unaffected delight at the books they brought him.

"Mother, come in and see the lovely pictures these gentlemen have brought," he called out, as Duveen later recalled the meeting.

"Yes, Mr. Ford," replied Duveen, "we thought you would like them. These are pictures we feel you should have."

Henry Ford, now going over the three large volumes with Clara, could scarcely believe his eyes.

"Gentlemen," he said, "beautiful books like these, with beautiful colored pictures like these, must cost an awful lot!"

"But, Mr. Ford, we don't expect you to *buy* these books," Duveen hastily explained. "We got them up specially for you, to show you the pictures. These books are a present to you."

Henry Ford was overwhelmed. "Mother, did you hear that?" he asked Clara. "These gentlemen are going to give me these beautiful books as a present."

He was embarrassed. "It is extremely nice of you," he said to Duveen, "but I really don't see how I can accept a beautiful, expensive present like this from strangers."

Joseph Duveen was speechless. He had dealt with the world's richest men—Henry Clay Frick, Andrew Mellon, Bendor, Duke of Westminster—but never had he encountered such innocence. He could hardly bring himself to take the poor man's money, but gathering his faculties, he explained how these three volumes had been specially prepared in order to interest Mr. Ford in buying the originals of the treasures they displayed.

"But, gentlemen," responded Henry Ford, "what would I want with the original pictures when the ones right here in these books are so beautiful?"[42]

# 17

## FAREWELL, MY LOVELY

*It could almost be written down as a formula, that when a man begins
to think that he has at last found his method, he had better begin a
most searching examination of himself to see whether some part of his
brain has not gone to sleep.*

—HENRY FORD[1]

Edward S. Jordan, founder of the Jordan Motor Car
Company, was travelling to San Francisco in his private
railcar in the summer of 1923, when the tedium of the
Wyoming plains was broken by the sight of a beautiful
horsewoman galloping fast towards him. Tanned and athletic, the mysterious rider brought her horse racing up to
the railcar to canter alongside Jordan's window for a brief,
entrancing moment, and as she wheeled to ride away, Jordan
turned to ask a travelling companion where they were.

"Oh," came the answer, with a yawn, "somewhere west
of Laramie".—and with that answer, a new way of selling
cars took flight. Jordan, a squat, flamboyant entrepreneur
with a weakness for white spats and gaudy ties, had been
trying to off-load his latest model, the Playboy, onto the
American public for some months without success. But now,
within minutes, the new advertisement was composed, and
it appeared a few days later in the *Saturday Evening Post*:

Somewhere west of Laramie there's a broncho-busting, steer-
roping girl who knows what I'm talking about . . . the Playboy
was built for her.
   Built for the lass whose face is brown with the sun when the day
is done of revel and romp and race . . .
   There's a savor of links about that car—of laughter, and lilt and
light—a hint of old loves—and saddle and quirt . . .
   Step into the Playboy when the hour grows dull . . .
   Then start for the land of real living with the spirit of the lass

344

who rides, lean and rangy, into the red horizon of a Wyoming twilight . . . [2]

The Playboy was a rotten car. But the fantasy that Edward Jordan wreathed around it—great outdoors escapism laced with the promise of some muscular sex—extended its showroom existence magically past its natural life, and motorcar advertising was never quite the same again. Edward Jordan's copy told the would-be car purchaser nothing about the horsepower, cylinder capacity, or power-to-weight ratio of the Playboy. It was not even possible to discover from the advertisement how many seats the car had, or how many wheels. But that was not the point. "Somewhere West of Laramie" sold excitement.

Glamour and escapism had been elements in the appeal of the motorcar from the start, but advertising had never focused exclusively on these intangibles. Comfort, power, reliability, and—just occasionally—safety were the selling points. The success of the Model T revolved around its engineering virtues and value for money, and from 1914 onwards Henry Ford had not even bothered to advertise. His public role as a tribune of the people, doubling workers' pay, sailing off to end war, fighting court cases, and camping in the American countryside, provided his car with all the image it needed.

The Model T's very lack of glamour, indeed, was one of its selling points. In its original form the car was delivered in a tasteful shade of Brewster Green with red coach stripe until someone in Highland Park discovered that the resins in black paint, as then developed, dried a little quicker than those in other colours—hence the famous decree, "Any color so long as it's black."

The defiant thrift of this slogan summed up the Ford image as well as any other, but times were changing. Standing on the corner of Fifth Avenue and Forty-second Street in New York one day in 1917, Edward S. Jordan was watching the cars go by when he was struck by another of the *coups de foudre* that seem to have characterized his business style. Nearly every vehicle in sight, he observed, was painted in black or dark shades of blue. This created the strange impression, on an otherwise joyous day, that all the cars were "in mourning."

I recalled my experience in selling cars to women. It is true that while men buy cars, women choose them. I recall hundreds of women going through the same process of motor car selection. First, the quick glance at the body—it must be straight as an arrow. . . . Next, the expert eye of a woman catching the appeal of a striking color.[3]

Jordan had grasped that the motorcar was no longer just a method of transportation, any more than clothes existed solely to keep the human body warm. Fashion was beginning to shape the line of a car as much as it determined the cut of a coat—though Henry Ford was contemptuous of any such notion, and his conservatism did not appear to hamper his sales. Once it had ridden out the postwar slump of 1921, the basic Ford sold better than ever, and in 1923 Henry was able to celebrate his sixtieth birthday with a phenomenal 2,120,898 sales—57 percent of all the cars produced in America, and, thanks to a growing number of Ford agencies outside the U.S., just about half the cars produced anywhere on the face of the earth.

It was an astonishing achievement. Never before, or since, has one company so dominated world car production. The taxis of Hong Kong, the tractors of the Ukraine, most of the cars of South America—all bore the name of Ford.

The Model T kept on selling, and cautiously, it made some compromises with the times. Along with its electric self-starter, it was given a new foot accelerator on the floor (early models had been throttled by hand from the steering wheel). In 1923 the Model T became the first mass-market car to profit from the comfort and road-holding provided by the low-pressure "balloon" tyre developed by Ford's friend Harvey Firestone, and it became possible to purchase the car with a closed-in, weatherproof body.

Ford also adapted to advancing paint technology. Quick-drying pyroxylin resins and varnishes dramatically reduced the time taken to finish a car, so, from 1925 onwards, it became possible to purchase the Model T in any colour you liked so long as it was dark Arabian sand with light Arabian stripe, gunmetal blue with French grey stripe, Niagara blue with French grey stripe, dawn grey with French grey stripe —or black, if you really insisted.

It still had the same basic shape, however. "You can paint up a barn," said a New York dealer faced with the increasingly difficult task of selling the car, "but it will still be a barn and not a parlor."[4] Edsel, who brought in the new colours, did his best with it, but there was something about the spread of the wheels, the way the Model T's upright body sat, or failed to sit, upon those wide, hay-wagon springs—and the car still sounded very much as it had done back in 1908.

By the early 1920s, comparatively low-priced cars were getting smooth and quiet engines. Both Oldsmobile and Essex, a low-priced offspring of the Hudson Motor Car Company, were offering attractive six-cylinder-powered runabouts at less than $1,000. But you still heard all four cylinders of a Model T as it came up to cough at the traffic lights beside you. It was the most familiar sight and sound in the United States, spluttering its way into the nation's image of itself, so that when 1920s America looked in the mirror, she saw soda fountains, the Keystone Cops, the *Saturday Evening Post*—and the Model T, usually personalized as "Lizzie."

The very fact that the machine had a name demonstrated the special place it held in people's affections, and it was the subject of countless jokes:

*Q:* Why is a Model T like an affinity? [*Affinity* was the vogue euphemism for "mistress" in the 1920s.]

*A:* Because you hate to be seen on the streets with one.[5]

The point of this joke, as of most others about the Model T, was that being a Ford owner carried a certain social stigma. Henry Ford himself liked to boast that "a Ford will take you anywhere except into Society." He cultivated the hick, country-cousin connotations of his product, and this evidently struck an enduring chord in the American heartland since, for three full years, Ford sales continued comfortably to surpass the 2 million mark. The 1925 sales figure of 2,024,254 represented a 27 percent improvement on the sales of 1922.

But in these same three years, the sales of the low-priced automobile that was offered by the Chevrolet car division of the General Motors Corporation had increased by no less than 220 percent. Originally outsold thirteen to one by the Model T, the Chevrolet was capturing more and more of the popular car market, and Ford sales showed it. In 1925 the Ford market share was down from 57 to 45 percent, and by 1926 it was down to 34 percent—and still falling.[6]

The Chevrolet was named after Louis Chevrolet, a French-Swiss immigrant who had made his name racing cars for Buick. Chevrolet had started his own car company in 1911, but his financial backer and the moving spirit of the enterprise was William C. Durant, the mercurial architect of the General Motors group of companies. It had been Durant's inspiration to choreograph his companies so that, between them, they could offer a carefully graduated range of models that matched the diversifying purchasing power of the U.S. car market, and Chevrolet slotted into the bottom of this range. The Chevy became the conglomerate's low-priced competitor to the Model T, and GM recruited two ex-Ford men to spearhead the car's development. William S. Knudsen was able to get his revenge on Charles Sorensen by pushing Chevrolet engineering and production techniques to levels even beyond those attained at the Rouge, and he co-opted as his sales director Norval A. Hawkins, the marketing man whose paperwork had so offended Henry Ford.

The Chevrolet could not compare, in the early years, with the Model T's extraordinarily low price, and as Henry Ford felt the competition, he cut his prices still further. But Knudsen's car enjoyed advantages which counted for more and more as the decade went by. Low-income purchasers could take advantage of GM's flexible installment plan— Henry Ford refused to sell on credit—while the Chevrolet was designed to fit low inside its all-weather, closed-in body, so that it sat quite close to the modern, surfaced road. The car was noticeably more graceful and stable than the Model T, which had been designed for rutted mud tracks. Most important of all, Chevrolet engineering and styling were regularly updated in an annual model change.

Coupled with GM's graduated range of products, the annual model change was a cornerstone of the dramatic growth that General Motors started to enjoy in the 1920s, and its impact extended beyond mere marketing. Winter might take its grip on America every November and December, grey and depressing, but the promise of fresh life was offered in the window of the local car dealer, at least, for there bright lights were reflected off the shiny new colours and chrome of the models for the coming year. How rejuvenating it was to stroll inside and stroke and sniff, to revel in this glossy, leather-scented harbinger of the spring. Dealers with theatrical propensities might even keep their curtains drawn and dust sheets in place until the pre-ordained moment of the sacred unveiling.

Fashion had invaded the empire of the motorcar to stay, and along with fashion came built-in obsolescence. Brand-new showroom cars which were perfectly good assemblages of unused machinery, with scarce a speck of dust on their tyres, automatically lost 30 percent of their value if they had not been sold by the changeover day when the new models appeared—even though those new models were often little more than rearrangements of the components and chrome of the old ones. In fact, one primary function of the new models, admitted Alfred P. Sloan, who became president of General Motors in 1923, was to create "a certain amount of dissatisfaction" with the old ones.[7]

Henry Ford would have none of this. It seemed ridiculous to him that 1923's model should be rejected because it did not look like 1925's.

It is considered good manufacturing practice, and not bad ethics, occasionally to change designs so that old models will become obsolete. . . . Our principle of business is precisely to the contrary. We cannot conceive how to serve the customer unless we make him something that, as far as we can provide, will last forever. . . . We want the man who buys one of our products never to have to buy another.[8]

Copper-bottomed sentiments—but it was funny how Henry Ford was coming to sound increasingly old-fashioned.

The first serious suggestion that the Model T might benefit from some major updating had been made when the car was only four years old. In 1912 Henry Ford had taken Clara and Edsel on their first visit to Europe, and on his return he discovered that his Highland Park lieutenants had prepared a surprise for him. C. Harold Wills, Charles Sorensen, and P. E. Martin had laboured to produce a new, low-slung version of the Model T, and the prototype stood in the middle of the factory floor, its gleaming red lacquerwork polished to a high sheen.

"He had his hands in his pockets," remembered one eyewitness, "and he walked around the car three or four times looking at it very closely."

It was a four-door job, and the top was down. Finally he got to the left-hand side of the car that was facing me, and he takes his hands out, gets hold of the door, and bang! He ripped the door right off! God! How the man done it, I don't know!

He jumped in there, and bang goes the other door. Bang goes the windshield. He jumps over the back seat and starts pounding on the top. He rips the top with the heel of his shoe. He wrecked the car as much as he could.[9]

The Model T had been the making of Henry Ford, lifting him from being any other Detroit automobile manufacturer to becoming carmaker to the world. It had yielded him untold riches and power and pleasure, and it was scarcely surprising that he should feel attached to it. But as the years went by, it became clear that Henry Ford had developed a fixation with his masterpiece which was almost unhealthy.

In 1923, the all-time peak year of Model T sales, Henry Ford had grudgingly allowed Edsel to make some styling changes that his son had long been pressing for. The Model T's radiator was enlarged and slightly raised to fit into a gentle smoothing and rounding of the car's proportions, and since dealers responded to this subtle facelift with encouraging orders, Edsel took his cosmetic surgery a stage further. For the following year he managed to cut no less than four and a half inches from the Model T's ground-to-roof height, dramatically softening its top-heavy appearance.

But the change was too dramatic for Henry Ford.

"Rub it out," he commanded.[10]

In the event, some of Edsel's refinements got through, for this was the year when colour options were first provided on the more expensive, closed-body models. But it was no General Motors model change. The Model T still had the same four-cylinder power unit, which was not only noisy but failed to sustain the continuous speeds being made possible by modern highways, and Henry's beloved planetary transmission had become hopelessly outdated. It remained, as it had always been, a prodigy of engineering. It only needed the addition of a torque converter to become the modern, automatic transmission. But no one knew this at the time, and the development of hard steel alloys meant that conventional gears no longer got stripped. Compared to the simplicity of a single clutch and gearshift, the complicated system of planetary belts with its variety of pedals that needed pushing to go forward or back, fast or slow, seemed downright perverse.

Accession No. 572 of the Ford Archives at Dearborn contains a poignant selection of letters. As the beloved Model T started losing ground in the 1920s to the smooth new creations of Chevrolet, Essex, and Dodge Brothers—as well as to a sensational six-cylinder, high-compression car produced in 1924 by Walter P. Chrysler—well-wishers all over America started offering Henry Ford advice.

"It seems that we all know you so well," wrote a correspondent from Winnetka, Illinois.[11] "On every hand and from nearly every mouth," wrote a pipe-organ maker from St. Louis, Missouri, "I hear these words 'Ford is losing out, Ford is slipping.'"[12]

More or less expertly phrased, all the letters said the same thing. Fords were too noisy. They did not have the speed for "the new paved highways." Their springing was uncomfortable, and most important of all, they were in need of a simple, modern gearshift.

"Ford is a good name," wrote one of his correspondents. "So is wheat. But people won't call for wheat when they want potatoes."[13]

Middle America displayed a remarkable grasp of what was happening to itself. "Right outside my window," wrote Mr. B. F. O'Brien of Moline, Illinois, "stands a Ford, a Star and an Essex, and across the street a Cheverolet [sic] and a Pontiac. The owner of each of these cars traded in a Ford. In fact, they never owned anything else but a Ford until this year, and the fellow who still has the Ford is about to buy an Essex."[14]

Mr. O'Brien asked his neighbours why they were trading in their Fords, and their answers were all the same. They found the Model T economical and comparatively trouble-free, they said, but they were bored with it. "They wanted something different," reported Mr. O'Brien. "A change." [15]

Moline, Illinois, was trading up, and so was all America.


Henry Ford took lunch every day promptly at noon. Around 11:55 the executives chosen to eat with him would start gathering in the executive dining room, waiting nervously beside the large circular table that was covered with a fresh-pressed linen tablecloth and making small talk until the stroke of 12:00, when Mr. Ford would enter the room.

Charles Sorensen was always there. So was Edsel Ford, and business was the order of the day. Henry Ford had a horror of formal meetings. So lunch was the time when important questions of company policy could be decided, and as Chevrolet made increasing inroads into Ford sales in the 1920s, the obvious topic for table talk was the future of the Model T.

The subject rarely came up, however. Sorensen was too canny—proposing changes to the Model T, after all, had been one of the reasons for the departure of his rival, Knudsen—and most other executives followed his lead. Only Edsel had the stature personally to broach the issue of the moment, and he did not get very far. One day—having previously discussed his strategy with the company's two production chiefs, Sorensen of the Rouge and P. E. Martin, who handled Highland Park—Edsel brought up the question of hydraulic brakes. These represented a major improvement over the efficiency and safety of old-fashioned braking systems, and all new cars were adopting them. They were obvious improvements that should be incorporated into the Model T or, preferably, into some completely new Ford.

But his father would not even discuss the matter.

"Edsel," he blurted out, "you shut up!" And, rising from the table, he stalked out of the room.[16] Sorensen and Martin, who had promised to come to Edsel's aid, sat in their seats and said nothing.

The signs had always been there: the cancelled coke ovens, the evicted accountants, Henry Ford undermining and countermanding his son in sly, unpredictable ways. In the early 1920s it did not happen that often—just enough to remind everyone who was really the boss of the Ford Motor Company. But with the decline of the Model T in the middle years of the decade, the conflict between Edsel Ford and his father became a serious, day-to-day matter.

The issue was an important one for both men, since Henry Ford had come to see the car he created as central to his very identity. Attacks on his car were attacks on Henry Ford himself, while for Edsel Ford the issue was scarcely less critical. Edsel was the new generation, the future. He could see the way ahead. It was so obvious to him—as it was to most other people in Detroit—that the Model T must go.

If Edsel counted for anything to the company—or, more important, to his father—he must be able to move Ford onwards.

Other fathers and sons might have discussed this over a drink, playing golf, putting the grandchildren to bed, on the way to the bank—anywhere except in front of a group of ambitious senior executives who were, ultimately, just employees. But Edsel and Henry Ford found it impossible to communicate privately on something so loaded with emotion for both of them, and Edsel even felt the need to seek advance reinforcement from outsiders before he dared to tackle his father.

Ernest Kanzler was dismayed by the old man's tyranny. Coming to work at Ford, he had gained firsthand experience of Henry Ford's arbitrary ways, and he felt for his brother-in-law. His wife, Josephine, picked up all the resentment which her sister Eleanor felt on Edsel's behalf, and Ernest shared their anger.

"Why doesn't Mr. Ford take his goddamn fiddle," he burst out on one occasion, "and go somewhere and play, and let us run the plant?"[17]

Ernest Kanzler made no secret of his feelings. Calling one Sunday afternoon on Mr. and Mrs. Charles Sorensen, he and Josephine started talking in such terms that, more than thirty years later, Sorensen could write: "To this day my wife remembers how shocked we were at their unrestrained tirade against Mr. Ford and the way he held Edsel down."[18]

Kanzler could see that the problem was functional. The Model T was out of date, the nature of the market was changing, Ford needed a new car. But more important, Ford needed a mechanism to identify such problems, to work out solutions, and to get things done—a proper management structure, in fact. This was the fundamental reason for the rise of Chevrolet and General Motors. Ford was building the Rouge in these years, to manufacture cars. GM was building its massive headquarters on Grand Boulevard, the largest office building in the world, to manage the manufacturing. Alfred P. Sloan was running his company on the basis of systematic research, objective planning, and, above all, a logical chain of authority and decision making —everything, in fact, that the Ford Motor Company did not have.

Ford could have had it. Ford had had it, indeed, in the glory days of the moving assembly line and the Five Dollar Day. It might not have been easy to trace the precise functions of Couzens, Wills, Knudsen, Klingensmith, Marquis, and the others on one of the organization charts beloved of Alfred Sloan, but they had made up an intelligent, brilliantly balanced management team which Henry Ford had smashed to pieces on the anvil of his ever-hardening egotism —his inability to accept constructive criticism or debate, his refusal, with the acquisition of full stock control, to make do with anything less than total management control as well.

Kanzler saw Edsel as the nucleus for a new, young Ford management structure which might begin to create some rational alternative to Henry Ford's whimsical chaos, and Edsel supported his brother-in-law's plans. In 1923 Edsel successfully persuaded his father that Kanzler should be made a vice-president of the company, with a seat on the board. Kanzler reported directly to Edsel. He moved into an office close to Edsel's in Highland Park,[19] and he set about creating an integrated command structure—in modern terms, an "Office of the President."[20] The two young men were so daring as to convert Henry's Highland Park office, which he did not use anymore, into a conference suite for Edsel's new executive organization.[21]

From their new power base, the brothers-in-law hoped that Edsel might be enabled to create an independent position vis-à-vis his father—and perhaps Ford could also begin to take on just a little of the subtlety and style of General Motors.

Henry Ford saw things in simpler terms. If the Model T was not selling, it was because his salesmen were not selling it.

"Most of your trouble at the present time," he informed

his sales staff after one inquiry into the difficulties they were experiencing, "is a question of your mental attitude."[22]

Sloppiness and indolence were the reasons why Ford dealers were not doing better with the Model T, in his opinion, and from this assumption the Ford Motor Company developed a brutally simple device for punishing dealers who were felt not to be pulling their weight: the "crossroads policy," which meant that new dealers were licensed across the road from the old dealer in whom the company had lost confidence. As Ford sales fell between 1923 and 1926, some 1,300 new dealers were added to the existing network of 8,500, on the theory that all would compete more eagerly to compensate for their reduced share of the Ford pie.

This struck the men who had gone into debt for Henry Ford during his cash-flow crisis of 1921 as particularly unfair.

"We then went to the bank and borrowed to the limit of our credit," recalled George B. Carter of Petersburg, Virginia, "storing the cars until such time as they could be sold."

Carter had erected an expensive new building and purchased equipment commensurate with being Ford's only representative in town, and had then discovered that the local "roadman"—the company representative in charge of sales for the area—had decided to create "a wall" of dealerships around Petersburg. Carter was compelled to sell out to one of the newcomers in January 1926. This pattern was repeated around the country. In the twenty-one months from January 1925 to October 1926, Ford dealership changes were running at 27 percent in San Francisco, 34 percent in Seattle, and 45 percent in Salt Lake City.[23]

Quite a number of these dealers switched franchises to sell General Motors cars, since from being kings of the roadside, Ford dealers had become figures of fun in the trade. In addition to marketing the outdated Model T, they were expected to sell fertilizer, which was a by-product of smelting at the Rouge, and also to make every new Ford purchaser a subscriber to the *Dearborn Independent*—a problem they usually dealt with by paying the subscription themselves and scrapping a small mountain of newsprint every week.

New product was the only solution. But Henry Ford had not, in fact, kept his head totally buried in the sand. In between all the projects that came to occupy him in the early 1920s, he had turned his mind to some sort of complement to, if not a substitute for, the Model T. As early as 1920, Ford research engineers had started experimenting with a revolutionary new type of engine whose cylinders were not lined up side by side, but were, rather, rearranged in the shape of a cross, and Henry had come to be obsessed by the novelty and shock appeal of this idiosyncratic power unit. For more than five years he devoted the principal research resources of his company to the development of this "X" engine: eight powerful cylinders, four facing upwards and four down.

In theory, and on the test bench, the X engine was a mind-boggling piece of engineering. But it did not function well on the road. Too heavy for the Model T, it was tested in the disemboweled body of an Oldsmobile, and while the upper cylinders operated efficiently, the downward-facing spark plugs invariably clogged with dust and damp from the road. Ford's engineers had warned their employer of this discouraging practical difficulty from the beginning, and it soon became apparent that developing a conventional, straight six-cylinder power unit would be a much more straightforward, and less expensive, proposition.

But six cylinders had unpleasant associations for Henry. The large, luxurious Model K over which he had quarrelled with Alex Malcomson had had a six-cylinder engine, and Henry had had difficulty feeding fuel to it. Six cylinders, he ever afterwards maintained, represented inherently poor engineering. He nursed the ambition that his own eight-cylinder X engine would vindicate his prejudice; that it would be the revolutionary breakthrough that would give him another of his ten-year leads over the competition. When it came to arguing with Edsel, or anyone else who might dare to hint at the need for change, Henry's advocacy of the X pushed him out onto the radical flank of the argument where he always felt at ease—championing an apparently visionary innovation against a safer, but less exciting alternative.

Ernest Kanzler grasped all this in the masterful memorandum in which, on January 26, 1926, he laid out the arguments for Ford adopting a change in strategy, finally bringing the great debate out into the open.[24]

Please, Mr. Ford, understand that I realize fully that you have built up this whole business, that it has been your battle and your creation, and that all of the Company's successes, day after day, regardless by whom personally conducted, are nevertheless a direct result of your conception. . . . Any powers I may have are mostly due to the opportunities you have given me, and have not created in me any exaggerated ideas about myself. You have allowed me to play with the throttle of your engine. That's all.

The curious connotations of this last sentiment cannot have been consciously intended, but they demonstrated Kanzler's awareness that he was playing with the very manhood of his employer.

Those of us who have been privileged to follow the X development look into the future and hope for great things, BUT, and this is what worries me, I feel that there should also be other development in process on a power unit along conventional lines . . . something which will serve until you have been given a fair chance to produce the X motors to their final stages of development.

For six long, diplomatic pages, Kanzler gingerly unveiled his case, lacing each unpalatable proposition with lavish stirrings of flattery. But by the end, when desugared, his message was clear. Ford urgently needed a new car with a new engine, the X motor was pie in the sky, and the power unit that the market was coming to demand had six cylinders.

We have not gone ahead in the last few years, have barely held our own, whereas competition has made great strides. . . . There may be theoretical engineering objections to a six, but in every one

I have ever driven there has been a most satisfactory smoothness and power range, entirely different from, and far superior to, 4-cylinder performance. . . . This is not only my view, but also that of the public as demonstrated by the way they have opened their pocket-books.

Kanzler concluded his memorandum with the claim that "every important man in the Company" shared his anxiety —which was tantamount to admitting the obvious truth, that he had prepared his arguments in partnership with Edsel—and he even ventured a veiled comment on the sad state of affairs that made him the stalking horse for a debate that should really have been settled directly, between father and son.

"It is one of the handicaps of the power of your personality, which you perhaps, least of all, realize, but most people, when with you, hesitate to say what they think."

Ernest Kanzler never received a formal reply to his memorandum of January 1926, but that was hardly surprising. Henry Ford had come to loathe Ernest Kanzler. He sneered to Charles Sorensen about Kanzler sitting "on Edsel's lap,"[25] and Sorensen fostered this enmity, since the production boss rightly saw Kanzler as a challenge to his own position.

To both Henry Ford and to Clara, Kanzler was a convenient vehicle for their reluctance to admit that their only son might be trying to develop a mind of his own. "Too many people," Clara told Sorensen, "were taking advantage of Edsel, and of these Kanzler had the most influence."[26] According to Sorensen, Clara broke down in tears when she talked about it, accusing Kanzler of "creating discord between Edsel and his father and mother."[27]

The Kanzler memorandum brought matters to a head. The atmosphere surrounding the bright young vice-president took on an unmistakable chill. Kanzler was ostentatiously ignored at the Dearborn lunch table. He only went there as Edsel's guest, in any case, and his conversational overtures were abruptly rebuffed. He was receiving the medicine that Ford insiders referred to as "the silent treatment," and in August 1926, while Edsel was away in Europe on a prolonged art-buying expedition with his wife, Ernest Kanzler and the Ford Motor Company went their separate ways. Kanzler always liked to say that he "resigned," but everyone else agreed that he was sacked.

If ever there was a time for a showdown between father and son, it was now, since Kanzler's only offence had been to say what was on his brother-in-law's mind, and to argue for the good of the company. But Edsel could not face his father. It was Eleanor who went to Henry Ford on the couple's return from Europe to remonstrate on Ernest's behalf, and she cried.[28]

Ernest Kanzler did not get his job back. He probably would not have wanted it in any case. But having killed the messenger, Henry Ford was finally able to make the message his own. In August 1926, the very month of Kanzler's departure, Ford engineers were instructed to cease work on the X engine and to turn instead to the design of a new, smooth-running power unit along conventional lines.[29]

Ford was finally going to have a new car—"a car for the market."[30] But there was no more talk about Edsel's own, independent "Office of the President."

The outside world heard the news on Thursday, May 26, 1927, when the fifteen millionth Model T rolled off the Highland Park assembly line. Edsel and Henry Ford drove the car off the line together, and the ceremony marking the milestone was accompanied by the announcement that manufacture of the vehicle would soon be ceasing. The Model T belonged to the past.

The news induced a reflective mood, for having ridiculed and scoffed at the Tin Lizzie, people suddenly realized that they were sad to see it go. It marked the end of an era. The world would never be quite the same again. The obstinacies and inconveniences of the beast were forgotten, enveloped in the forgiving folds of memory, and the car became enshrined in people's minds, along with first loves, stolen kisses, and sunny springtime days, as a fond token of what was both eternal and lost forever. Were people ever moved thus by the vacuum cleaner, lawn mower, or phonograph?

"It was the miracle God had wrought," wrote E. B. White. "And it was patently the sort of thing that could only happen once."[31]

White's lyrical tribute was one of numerous elegies on the passing of the Model T, but the obituary which would undoubtedly have given greatest pleasure to the car's creator was that published in 1953, after Henry's death, by the novelist John Steinbeck, for not only did Steinbeck endow his car with a soul, he visualized that metallic yet spiritual essence surviving into a reincarnation that was especially close to the heart of Henry Ford.

I know, of course, that things do not cease to exist in some form. Metal may change its composition through rust or blast furnace, but all of its atoms remain somewhere, and I have wondered sadly about IT. . . . Maybe its essence was blasted gloriously in a bomb or shell. Perhaps it lies humbly on the cross-ties while streamlined trains roll over it. It might be a girder of a bridge, or even something to support a tiny piece of the UN building in New York. And just perhaps, in the corner of some field, the grass and the yellow mustard may grow taller and greener than elsewhere and, if you were to dig down, you might find the red of rust under the roots, and that might be IT, enriching the soil, going home to its mother, the earth.[32]

The closing of the Ford Model T production line at the end of May 1927 threw 60,000 men out of work in Detroit alone. Twenty-three regional assembly plants also fell idle, and across the country the best part of 10,000 Ford dealers had to eke out a meagre existence selling off old stock and spare parts. More than a year was to pass before Ford production resumed its full momentum and employment level, and while the shutdown scarcely provoked nationwide recession, its impact was painful—particularly in Detroit.

"That the business of one man should dominate the affairs of the fourth city of the United States," commented the *New*

*York World* on September 11, 1927, ". . . must hit the person not familiar with Detroit as remarkable."[33]

Equally remarkable was the magic which, the hiatus demonstrated, was still associated with the name of Ford. Chevrolet overtook Ford sales in 1927, as it could hardly fail to with the production line of its great competitor out of action.[34] But the overall figure for U.S. car sales in 1927 was down nearly a million on the previous twelve months,[35] and in the absence of any recession, this reflected Ford's withdrawal from the marketplace. When the news had been published—in front-page headlines across the country—that the Model T was to be superseded by a new Ford, many buyers had decided to withhold their purchases until they had seen what that fresh offering might be.

The pent-up demand exploded six months later, when Ford unveiled the vehicle which, it had been decided almost inevitably, should be named the Model A. On December 2, 1927, some 100,000 sightseers mobbed Ford's exhibits in Detroit, mounted police had to be called out in Cleveland, and in New York the crowds started gathering at three in the morning outside the main Ford showroom on Broadway. Before the day was out, the manager had hired Madison Square Garden for a week to ease the crush. Observed the *New York Sun*, "It was just exactly as if Mr. Mellon had thrown open the doors of the Sub-Treasury and invited folks to help him count the gold reserve."[36]

Within a day and a half of the Model A's first showing, more than 10 million people had taken the trouble to see the vehicle—8.5 percent of the national population. In less than a week that figure had risen to 25 million,[37] and the Ford order book showed sales to match. By Christmas 1927, dealers had taken nearly half a million firm orders, every one accompanied by a cash deposit, although scarcely anyone had had the opportunity for a test drive. There were so few Model As off the production line—and certainly not enough for every dealer—that Ford roadmen spent December driving the few available models helter-skelter around their areas, stopping for brief exhibits in each town before speeding on to the next.

The launching of the Model A was one of the great national events of 1927, rivalling the delirium with which Charles A. Lindbergh, another Detroiter,* was greeted that year after his transatlantic flight. It was an age of crazes. Nineteen-twenties America needed little excuse to get out the tickertape, and when it came to Henry Ford, it seemed that the entire country willed the regeneration of the man who had, for more than a decade, been the talisman of the nation's potency—the proof that America could outproduce and outperform anyone.

Henry himself had helped the hysteria along. From the announcement of the death of the Model T, his hints and silences on the character of his new car were masterpieces of timing. In the last few days prior to the unveiling, a $1.3 million advertising campaign had whipped up excitement still further, and the sight of Model As going into dealer showrooms in canvas bags did nothing to diminish the general fever of anticipation. Henry Ford proved he could play the model-change game as skilfully as any of his competitors, though the heart of the excitement that gripped the United States for his new creation was the touching faith the nation retained in the abilities of the people's mechanic.

The Model A did not disappoint them. The car did not have a six-cylinder engine, and, to the modern eye, it appears squat and foursquare—dumpy even. At six decades' distance, it is difficult to see what all the fuss was about. But in 1927, the Ford Model A incorporated every significant improvement in the popular car to date: strong and simple gears operated by a stick shift, hydraulic shock absorbers, and generous rubber cushioning with insulation that made for a remarkably quiet and comfortable ride.

It had balloon tyres and a reliable electrical system with

---

* Lindbergh moved from Detroit when he was a child, but was born in 1902 on Forest Avenue, the same road on which Edsel Ford was born nine years earlier.

self-starter. The heart of the car was a staunch and brawny power unit which, though it only had four cylinders, could accelerate most six- and eight-cylinder cars off the road. Compared to the Model T, the Model A went like a rocket. Its engine could push the car rapidly up to fifty-five miles per hour and keep it cruising there, and the entire mechanical package was wrapped up in a rounded body shell which Edsel had developed from a Lincoln he was working on. In 1927 the Model A represented state-of-the-art motoring with some notable innovations, like a safety glass windshield.

The car's key attraction, however, was its price. Slightly heavier than the Model T, the Model A was actually less expensive, pound for pound, than its famous predecessor, and at an average of $495, each of the variations on the basic body shell worked out over $100 cheaper than the equivalent Chevrolet. Henry Ford had stayed true. He had given the average American workingman motoring value which would have been a bargain at twice the price, and dignity as well. The Model A was a thoroughly smart and contemporary vehicle. No one need feel ashamed of driving it.

On the contrary. With the unveiling of the Model A, the Ford image swung overnight from country cousin to country club, since the scarcity of the car in the months after its first appearance suddenly endowed Ford ownership with a desperate fashionability. Douglas Fairbanks was happy to be photographed with the Model A Coupe he had given Mary Pickford for Christmas. "Mary uses new Ford in preference to all her other cars," Fairbanks telegraphed Dearborn, thanking Edsel Ford for getting him the car before anyone else in California. "It surpasses our greatest expectations."[38]

Even James Couzens, multimillionaire and U.S. senator, was not too proud to request that he should be allotted the first Model A delivered in Washington, and Edsel got the senator's car stamped with the same motor number, No. 35, that had been on the original Model A driven by James Couzens, accounts clerk, twenty-five years earlier.[39] The Ford Motor Company could afford a little sentimentality in this moment of triumph snatched—unexpectedly, in all honesty—on the very brink of defeat.

It had been a close-run thing, since Ford's facilities for testing and developing a new car were crude in comparison to those of General Motors and Chrysler, both of whom had invested heavily in sophisticated research facilities and test tracks.

Henry Ford did have research facilities. In 1925 he had commissioned a new engineering laboratory from Albert Kahn, and architecturally this was a splendid piece of work, a long and elegant exercise in perspective, faced with a seemingly endless procession of neoclassical pillars. But the interior reflected the eccentric clutter of Henry Ford's own mind. The staff of the *Dearborn Independent* had been shifted there from the tractor plant, along with the *Ford News* and a local radio station that Henry operated for a few years as a hobby. Part of the floor was cleared for Benjamin Lovett and his old-time country-dancing lessons, and a number of the laboratories were devoted to such projects as the development of a tomato juice extractor, in pursuit of Henry's growing dietary enthusiasms.

This proliferation of nonautomotive enthusiasms showed what had been going wrong with the Ford Motor Company, and Henry's refusal to delegate made matters worse. Absolute control plus divided attention was a recipe for disaster. Henry's research techniques had not developed, in many respects, from the cut-and-try experimentation of his years in Bagley Avenue, and he felt most happy placing his trust in men who operated with the same rough-hewn pragmatism that he did. The test-driving of the Model A—which was carried out on public roads, to the increasing indignation of the local police—was largely entrusted to Evangeline Dahlinger's husband, Ray, whose test reports, according to one exasperated engineer, were usually limited to one of two responses: "Goddamn good," if he had enjoyed his drive, and "No damn good," if he had not.[40]

The greatest problem with the new car lay in the area

which was supposed to be Ford's speciality: production. Charles Sorensen had assured his master that he could accomplish the change-over from Model T to Model A in a matter of months, and the transition should have been helped by the fact that the transfer involved a change of plants. The Model T would be phased out at Highland Park, while facilities for the new car were readied at the Rouge, which would finally become what Henry had dreamed of, a universal crucible, where raw materials entered at one end and finished cars came out at the other.

But Sorensen had dreams of his own. He saw the move to the Rouge as a chance finally to consolidate his control over the Ford production process, and in the transfer of personnel, he weeded out every man he suspected of being a rival. This process, mirroring Henry's purge of his senior executives following the Dodge brothers' suit, deprived Ford of manufacturing expertise at the time when the company needed it most, and it took Sorensen more than a year to get Rouge production running at full capacity.

The Model A was composed of nearly 6,000 parts, practically all of them new, and their production necessitated the refurbishing or rebuilding of some 16,000 existing machine tools, with the purchase of more than 4,000 new ones.[41] It was a minor miracle that any Model As were completed by the car's launch date in December 1927, and the production line did not get up full speed for six months or more. In 1928, three months after the Model A's first appearance, the line was still moving so slowly that Ford was losing over $300 per car,[42] and production for the year was only 633,594, much less than half the Rouge's full potential.[43]

The management of a public company could never have got away with it. Ford losses for the twelve months ending December 1927 were $30 million, in a period when Chrysler paid out $10 million in dividends and General Motors made nearly $300 million profit after tax. In 1928, additional Ford losses brought the total damage caused by the model change to around $250 million.[44]

Reasonably systematic management and planning could

have eliminated this loss almost entirely. Ford was at least two years late in abandoning the Model T, and the slow and fractured retooling for the Model A cost the company a further six to nine months of full-capacity sales. When William Knudsen produced his answer to the new Ford at the end of 1929, a totally new, six-cylinder Chevrolet, he managed to accomplish his changeover with only six weeks' shutdown—the fruit of planning and management which operated in an environment light-years distant from the warring medieval fiefdoms that surrounded Henry Ford.

Good management was the long-term reality. The sales that the Model A achieved, once its production difficulties had been ironed out, made it seem a success story. Ford eventually sold more than a million and a half of the cars in 1929, a market share of 34 percent—fourteen points ahead of Chevrolet. But the triumph was short-lived, for Chevrolet overtook Ford again the following year, and Henry Ford was never again to beat the rival that had nearly closed down in 1922 for lack of sales.[45] From 1930 onwards, the once-proud Ford Motor Company had to be content with second place.

Ford had only itself to blame. Ernest Kanzler on his own was hardly comparable to Alfred Sloan and his GM battalions, but Kanzler and his attempts to create an executive apparatus around Edsel had represented one hope that Ford might acquire some smattering of organization in the new age of corporate management. Kanzler had also represented the reinforcement that Edsel needed to stand any chance of imposing his personality on his father's company, and with Kanzler's departure, both hope and reinforcement were gone. Out of Ford in the 1920s had come a new car, with great travail. Out of General Motors had come the modern corporation.

# 18

# DEPRESSION

The Fords always liked to make the most of Christmas. As Henry Ford got older, his Fair Lane festivities grew more and more elaborate, and the celebrations that Edsel and Eleanor staged on the other side of town were equally magnificent: a tree to the ceiling, the wood panelling hung with greenery, diamonds and dinner jackets around the candlelit Christmas table. On December 25, 1930, Henry and Clara came over from Dearborn to join in the fun, and they brought a special present for their grandchildren: a working model of Henry's first Quadricycle. This prompted Edsel to reminisce about the days when he had been his children's age, and how he had sat with his parents, wedged in the front of this strange vehicle, to be smiled upon by disbelieving Detroiters.[1]

It was a rich and festive occasion, the meal prepared by the younger Fords' ample kitchen staff, with service by the full complement of their butler and maids. It was difficult to imagine that, for the last twelve months, America had been sinking into the worst depression in her history. In the year since the crash of October 1929, some 5,000 banks had failed and 6 million men had lost their jobs. The eventual success of the Model A had enabled Ford to stand the strain rather better than some other businesses: in 1930 Ford had achieved quite respectable profits of around $40 million. But this was $50 million less than profits in the previous year.[2]

Detroit was in particularly bad shape. The queues at the soup kitchens were longer than they had ever been. There were the best part of 750,000 men unemployed in Michigan, and the wages of those who were lucky enough still to have jobs had been cut by nearly 40 percent. By the end of 1931, Detroit's new mayor, Frank Murphy, had to inform the

Common Council that there were 4,000 children standing in the bread lines every day. The city's suicide rate, he said, had risen 30 percent over a previous five-year average. In the summer of 1932, the board of health was to report that at least 18 percent of the city's children were suffering from severe undernourishment, and distress was not confined to the lower classes. Fifteen private banks had been forced out of business, swallowing the savings of over 30,000 depositors.[3]

Henry Ford's first reaction to the depression had been to raise wages. Proclaiming his now-familiar economic theory that the woes of the country were caused by the men who played with money—the bankers—as opposed to those who created real wealth—like Henry Ford—he cut the prices of his cars and guaranteed a minimum wage of $7.00 a day for all his unskilled workers. Skilled tradesmen got more.

"These are really good times," he declared in March 1931, "but only if you know it. . . . The average man won't really do a day's work unless he is caught and cannot get out of it."[4]

The average man could not wait to get caught. And as critics pointed out, the price of Henry Ford's apparent generosity in paying some workers more was to employ other workers less. To maintain his seven-dollar-a-day minimum for the unskilled, he laid off tradesmen he had been employing at higher rates, and he also farmed out work to suppliers whose sweatshop wages bore no comparison to his own— notably to the Briggs Body Company, whose rates of pay, as low as twelve and a half cents an hour, were an acknowledged scandal and were soon to provoke the first major work stoppage that any Detroit company had known for half a century.*

* Walter O. Briggs, who supplied car bodies to both Ford and Chrysler (GM bodies were made by Fisher), and who was, in 1935, to become the owner of the Detroit Tigers baseball team, was notorious for one particularly pernicious labour practice. Briggs workers would only get paid for the time that the assembly line was actually in operation, so they might be required to spend ten hours at the plant, while only getting paid for two.[5]

Still, such economies were the price of survival as America's purchasing power withered in the early 1930s. The Ford Motor Company resorted to such measures rather less readily than did other manufacturers, and with the aid of his Model A profits, Henry seems to have made a genuine effort to fight the trend of recession as it started to bite. Throughout the crisis, he kept paying out large amounts of his private fortune on his own personal, labour-intensive projects. Men were employed shifting and reconstructing the scores of historic structures in Greenfield Village through all the bad years, and, in the very depths of the depression, Henry broke ground on the Dearborn Inn, America's first airport hotel, intended to service the Ford airfield beside Greenfield Village.

But it could not last. In 1931 the Model A boom broke, and Ford sales slumped as badly as those of other manufacturers. Nineteen thirty-one was the year when the Jordan Motor Car Company went out of business, along with half a dozen of the other, smaller automobile independents. General Motors and the Nash Motor Company managed to do quite well, while Chrysler actually increased its sales, thanks to an impressive new Plymouth unveiled that year by Walter Chrysler. But Ford suffered from its old problem: excessive dependence on one model. Good though it was, the Model A had been overtaken by other cars that were better— Knudsen's six-cylinder Chevrolet and Chrysler's "Free-Wheeling" Plymouth*—and in 1931 Ford had difficulty achieving more than half of its previous year's sales. The company went into the red by over $37 million,[7] and since the traditional Ford clientele was concentrated at the lower end of the income scale that had been most hit by the depression, future prospects were not promising. In 1929

* Free-Wheeling seemed the thing of the future in 1931. First introduced by Studebaker, it was a device that sprang the car out of gear, so that it could coast downhill and save on fuel. It soon became apparent, however, that fuel economy was being achieved at the expense of safety, and several states went so far as to pass laws prohibiting the device.[6]

American farmers had bought 650,000 new passenger cars. In 1932 they were to purchase only 55,000.[8]

Ford had to yield to the inevitable. Towards the end of 1931 the much-vaunted seven-dollar-a-day rate was quietly reduced to $6.00. Within a year it was further reduced to $4.00,[9] and the company's employment totals told an even sadder tale. Between 1929 and 1932, the average number of employees on the Ford payroll almost halved, from 101,069 to 56,277,[10] and as business continued to wilt, the company was forced to resort to the most demeaning expedient of all. If you had a few hundred dollars of life savings to put down, or a rich relative in need of a new car, you could obtain a job at the Rouge in exchange for the purchase of a new Ford.[11] To maintain his sales, the world's greatest capitalist had been reduced to barter.

"He thought he had the answer to depression," a journalist taunted Henry Ford's spokesman, William Cameron. "Now how does he take it?"

"I don't know," replied Cameron with rare candour. "He doesn't talk about it much. It's so terrible that I believe he doesn't dare let himself think about it."[12]

In the autumn of 1931, few communities in the Detroit area showed the impact of the depression more pitifully than the village of Inkster, a collection of shacks, mud tracks, and debris in the fields to the west of Dearborn. It was a miserable shantytown, largely inhabited by blacks who had worked in the hot and heavy foundry jobs at the Rouge and were now unemployed. Most of Inkster's families were in debt. Malnutrition was rampant. Children suffered from rickets. The local bank had closed. The electricity company had cut off power, and there was no money to pay for police protection. Inkster was a sorry spot which no sensible white visited, by day or by night, and most Dearbornites endeavoured to ignore its very existence.[13]

But in November 1931, Henry Ford moved in. For more than a decade he had been operating supermarketlike commissaries for his workers at Highland Park and the

371

Rouge,[14] and now he set up a similar store in Inkster to sell food and clothing at near wholesale prices. He reopened the school. He provided seeds for men to cultivate in their gardens. He purchased sewing machines for the women and had dressmaking classes organized for them. Within a matter of months the village of Inkster was back on its feet again, glowing with paid-for electricity and a certain self-respect, since the community was paying for its revival with its own hard work.

Henry Ford's philanthropy had always been based on the principle that people should not be subsidized: they should be helped to stand on their own two feet. In the case of Inkster, he achieved this by offering the men of the village jobs at the Rouge, for which they were paid just $1.00 a day in cash. They never saw the remaining $3.00 a day which they were owed. This money went into a fund to finance the revival of community services—the work of cleaning up the town was given out on the same dollar-a-day basis—and it also went towards the payment of the inhabitants' documented debts.

The renaissance of Inkster was an unashamed exercise in paternalism: "the Negro had not yet developed a sufficient intellect to be able to be on his own," explained Ernest Liebold later. Blacks "had to be guided and supervised."[15] Unemployed whites, who saw their jobs going to dollar-a-day blacks, interpreted the scheme as no more than an exercise in sweated labour, and one element of the project was laced with a certain anti-Semitism, since the arrival of the cut-price Ford commissary made life hard for Inkster's existing shopkeepers, who were mainly Jews.

Still, as Ford paid off the inhabitants' debts, these shopkeepers redeemed some of their losses, and Inkster came back to life. It also achieved a certain national fame, for in 1932 Henry purchased full-page advertisements in 200 newspapers to offer his fellow countrymen the benefit of his own ideas on how to combat the ever-worsening social and economic situation, and one of his remedies was self-help as exemplified by the community of Inkster. Another suggestion was a "family gardens" scheme which he had organized to help Rouge workers grow their own food, and the third was his beloved village industry project: "One foot on the land and another foot on industry. . . . America is safe."[16]

The Ford Motor Company had not advertised its cars for some time. Few companies could afford product advertising, let alone full-page reflections on the state of the nation, and Henry's three open letters—ghostwritten by William Cameron—were intended to stimulate a national debate. But America was not impressed. When Henry had announced his brave seven-dollar minimum wage in November 1929, he had created a stir comparable to that of the Five Dollar Day, attracting hopeful headlines and an almost unanimous editorial chorus of praise.[17]

But three long, hard years later, America was looking at Henry Ford with a new and jaundiced eye. He was no longer the miracle worker. The old man was nearly seventy, after all. The handwoven folk remedies that he was proposing in his three open letters were dismissed as naive and out of touch: "a confession of Ford's failure to meet the depression's problems," said the *Philadelphia Record* severely.[18] The fact that "the greatest industrialist of his age cannot care for his own employees, but must put them to work cleaning up backyards and roads of a town, and working gardens" showed the bankruptcy of his ideas.[19]

Will Rogers, who had been a guest of Henry's at Dearborn, and who, presumably, felt some gratitude for the many years of source material with which Henry had provided him, softened the disenchantment with a little humour. Since "most people got no room for a garden," he said, "what Mr. Ford will do is put out a car with a garden in it. Then you hoe as you go."[20]

Anne O'Hare McCormick caught the national mood more accurately in the *New York Times*. She came to visit Dearborn and Detroit in the spring of 1932, and she painted a sorry picture of the atmosphere there. Mass production might seem the secret of life in times of plenty, but when production slowed, she pointed out, it made for little more than mass idleness. The depression called many things into question.

"Something has happened to Ford," wrote Anne McCormick, "and perhaps through him to the America he represents."[21]

William Knudsen introduced the six-cylinder Chevrolet at the end of 1929, and a few weeks later Henry Ford stopped beside the desk of an assistant in the Dearborn engineering laboratories, Fred Thoms. "We're going from a four to an eight," he told Thoms, "because the Chevrolet is going to a six. Now, you try to get all the eight-cylinder engines that you can."[22] An engineering challenge was something that Henry Ford still did know how to cope with.

The challenge of the V–8 engine was essentially a challenge of manufacturing technique, for there was nothing new about powering a car with eight cylinders—even slanted side by side in a V-shape. Cadillac had produced a V–8 engine in 1914, and, by 1930, was offering V–12s and V–16s as well.[23] But these were top-of-the-line motors with elaborate fuel systems, individually crafted and prohibitively expensive for the mass market. Henry Ford wanted to produce the same thing at a quarter the price, and in setting himself the task of mass-producing a relatively simple, single-casting V–8 cylinder block that could go down the Rouge line at forty units per hour or more, he was raising engineering and production problems that no one had confronted before.

Fred Thoms gathered together every eight-cylinder engine he could muster, as instructed, and he lined them up side by side in the Dearborn Engineering Laboratory. All were made in at least two sections, some of them in three. Ford engineers ran them and examined them all and, by May 1930, had prepared a single-casting prototype of their own. By November they had a second model ready, and through the winter of 1930–31 they went on working to Henry Ford's orders, scrapping each version as he found fault with it. Twelve months later, more than thirty different V–8 engines had been designed, built, tested—and rejected by Henry Ford. "He sure was mad," remembered Thoms.[24]

It looked like the story of the X engine all over again, for packing eight cylinders close together into one single casting that would not crack or explode under the strain defied the then-known limits of metallurgy. Henry Ford even appears to have wavered himself in the direction of a safer alternative, ordering the delivery of 600 experimental pistons for a more conventional six-cylinder power unit.[25] But on December 7, 1931, Henry Ford went into a private conference with Edsel, and from the long meeting of father with son a definite decision emerged. Ford would go with the V–8.[26]

It was a bold decision. Henry and Edsel had decided only a few months earlier to revive the flagging sales of the four-cylinder Model A by making its body longer and lower, and by bringing it out, with a pepped-up A engine, as a Model B. Times were hard, and Ford was no longer too proud to essay a little model change. The V–8 power unit would go into the new streamlined body, so, effectively, you could buy the car with four cylinders or with eight. Charles Sorensen calculated that additional investment in the V–8 could run as high as $50 million,[27] but this was money that would speed and modernize the Rouge's manufacturing techniques, and Henry Ford never begrudged money spent on new machinery.

"Charlie," he told Sorensen, "we have too much money in the bank."[28] Cash reserves, in Henry's opinion, made the accountants and salesmen in the hated front office too complacent.

Ford gave Sorensen the go-ahead to spend money "until it hurts,"[29] and the production boss did just that, commissioning a spectacular pouring furnace which could hold two tons of molten metal as it moved alongside the conveyor belt line, tilting and filling cylinder block moulds as it went. It was the wonder of Detroit, particularly in the depths of the depression. Getting the correct alloy mix was crucial to the strength of the single V–8 casting, and Sorensen was also given a blank cheque to obtain the sophisticated electrical furnace equipment that was needed to ensure this.[30]

Ford's reinvestment in heavy machinery and manufacturing techniques at a time when the depression seemed only to be getting worse struck a more responsive note with his fellow countrymen than his advice on self-help cooperatives and gardening. One hundred thousand orders for the new B and V–8 cars were made in advance of their unveiling on March 31, 1932, and within a few days the orders had been doubled.

The V–8 engine, as originally released, proved to be less than perfect. The slant of the cylinders caused lubrication problems for, after a thousand miles, its piston rings developed a tendency to leak, turning the engine into a formidable devourer of oil. Some V–8s consumed as much as a quart of oil every fifty miles.[31] But Ford corrected this after twelve months of production, and the V–8 then went on to become the company's longest-lived power unit of all. In the early 1950s Fords were coming off the production line with V–8 engines that were, essentially, the unit that had been designed twenty-one years earlier under the demanding, personal supervision of Henry Ford.[32]

Henry had not lost his touch. The challenge of the depression might have proved too much for his political and sociological resources, but he was still an engineer. "I've got back my old determination," he told reporters, vaulting over fences and running up flights of stairs to prove that, though he might now be nearly seventy, he did not feel like it. At $460 ($650 for the most expensive version), his V–8 was another populist triumph, presenting the people with something that, previously, had been the preserve of the rich. For the first time, low-income America—and young America— had a car with real poke. The V–8 was the first hot-rod car, the progenitor of stock cars, drag races, and all the other forms of redneck motor sport which are the American answer to the daintiness of the European Grand Prix.

Gangsters found the V–8 particularly suited to their line of work. Its quick getaway left pursuers standing.

"Hello Old Pal," wrote Public Enemy Number 1, John Dillinger, to Henry Ford between holdups in 1934. "You have a wonderful car. It's a treat to drive one." And, not to be outdone, Clyde Barrow, of Bonnie and Clyde fame, sent in his own testimonial. "I have drove Fords exclusively when I could get away with one."[33]

These unsolicited tributes from the folk heroes of the era were parodies of conventional advertising, but when Bonnie and Clyde came to their gruesome and bloody end in the pine hills of north Louisiana in May 1934, they offered Henry Ford the ultimate product endorsement. Their beige-grey "Desert Sand" V–8 Fordor Deluxe, stolen 7,500 miles and twenty-three days earlier in Topeka, Kansas, had been riddled with 107 bullets from the rifles and automatic shotguns of the ambushing lawmen. But when the bloodstained bodies of the bandits were removed from the car, and the local Ford dealer was called to drive it away, the ignition was turned, the starter was pressed, and the V–8 engine started first time.[34]

# 19

## PATRON OF ART

As Edsel Ford found it more and more difficult to give expression to himself through the Ford Motor Company, he had turned in other directions, and the most fruitful of these proved to be art. In the course of the 1920s and 1930s, Edsel and Eleanor Ford became two of the most discriminating and energetic patrons of art in North America, and, right in the darkest hours of the depression, Edsel's patronage gave Detroit—and America—a masterpiece which made a powerful and compelling statement about the turmoil of those years. Edsel's commission also proved to be an enduring artistic monument to the genius of his visionary and tyrannical father.

The man who helped Edsel Ford find expression for the finest and most sensitive side of his nature—the true heart of Edsel Ford in many ways—was the bright-eyed, slightly self-important German who arrived in Detroit in 1921 to give artistic direction to the city's art museum. Dr. William Valentiner had made his name advising J. P. Morgan and the Rockefellers on the early development of the Museum of Modern Art in New York. Detroit had started its own art museum in 1885, but the museum had rather foundered, putting on exhibitions of its rich patrons' seashell and ostrich-egg collections alongside its works of art.[1] This had earned the scorn of the city's more serious aesthetes like Charles Lang Freer, the railcar magnate, who willed his priceless collection of Whistlers and Orientalia to the Smithsonian in Washington.[2] It was in the hope of giving the Detroit Institute of Arts a more professional direction that Ralph H. Booth, head of the city's Arts Commission, invited Valentiner to Detroit.

Valentiner grasped immediately the potential for patronage that was offered by the vibrant wealth of the Motor City. Money was no object in the early 1920s, with the car business riding the greatest boom in its history, and art was cheap. You could pick up a Van Gogh for little more than $4,000, and a Dufy for less than $100.[3]

Valentiner met Henry Ford before he met Edsel, at a dinner which the Society of Arts and Crafts threw in the German's honour. "There were over a hundred guests," wrote Valentiner to a friend, "among them Henry Ford and other auto kings, who were seated at small tables with candles in a festive hall with a high ceiling in Gothic style."[4]

Valentiner did not really expect great things from the auto kings. "There cannot be much hope," he wrote, "for taste or judgement in matters of art from these people." But he was agreeably surprised by Henry Ford, for the museum director managed to stimulate the mystical vein that most of the world ignored in the carmaker. Valentiner spoke frankly to Henry about the strangely solid sympathies and antipathies that people could generate at their very first meeting, and this prompted Henry to speculate, in return, that scientific research at some future date "might possibly establish that thoughts, too, are something material."

Valentiner agreed. "Possibly the reason paintings speak to us so vividly throughout the centuries," he said, "is because in them the thoughts of the artists had materialized" —and this struck Henry Ford as "very plausible."[5]

Valentiner had already set his main ambitions on Henry's son. His experience with wealthy dynasties had shown him that it was the second generation of a family that usually demonstrated more empathy with the artistic side of life, and he had consulted a fortune-teller who had predicted he would reap "all kinds of success" through Edsel Ford.[6] Valentiner manoeuvred a commission to write an article about an early Persian bowl which he knew to be in the younger Fords' possession, and when he met Edsel to inspect it, he came prepared with a condensed series of talking points that would, he hoped, stimulate the young man's interest in what he was trying to achieve at the museum.

"How lucky," he reflected, "are the mighty of this world always to have those with whom they come in contact present their best thoughts in the most concentrated form."[7]

Edsel responded well to someone trying to open up his spirit, rather than stamp on it. He invited Valentiner to his home in the winter of 1925–26 to give him and Eleanor a series of private art tutorials, and the young Fords were joined for these by the Kanzlers. Each evening Valentiner brought along a painting or sculpture from the museum as a focus for his lecture to the eager young couples, and his teaching soon showed results. Embarking with his wife on a holiday to Germany in April 1926, Valentiner was delighted to discover a basket of fruit waiting in his cabin, together with a note from Edsel and Eleanor, who were then in London, sending him the excited news that they had just purchased a unique two-canvas work, Fra Angelico's *Annunciation*, their first important acquisition as connoisseurs.[8]

William Valentiner had given a new dimension to the life of Edsel Ford, and William Richards, one of the favoured circle of local journalists that Henry Ford liked to cultivate, noticed the difference that this had made to Edsel. In the course of a discussion on the unlikely subject of Benvenuto Cellini, Edsel launched into a learned and sensitive exposition that "left everyone far behind."[9] The younger Ford became a founding patron of the Museum of Modern Art, one of the few from outside New York. He hung his office with portraits of George Washington and Alexander Hamilton that were important examples of the Early American school, and it was at his prompting that Ford branch offices across the country had their fascias covered with Pewabic tiles. The Pewabic Pottery developed a special misty, blue-green glaze for the commission: the Ford Soda Glaze.

From the acquisition of their Fra Angelico onwards, Edsel and Eleanor Ford embarked on a systematic programme of purchases for themselves, and also for the DIA, and in a few short years they brought to Detroit some Holbeins, a

Pisano, a Titian, a Perugino.[10] At the time, many of their donations were anonymous, but it has since become clear that the taste and generosity of Edsel and Eleanor Ford were a major factor in helping elevate the Detroit Institute of Arts from obscurity to the position it still holds, as one of the leading half-dozen museums in North America.

The jewel of all the many magnificent works of art that Edsel Ford gave Detroit, however, was not plunder from the Old World. It was a creation of the New. As with Edsel's more traditional purchases, it was William Valentiner who proved the catalyst for the project. Valentiner's involvement, in turn, grew out of a strange infatuation that the museum director had conceived for the Ladies' World Tennis Champion of the day, Helen Wills Moody.

Helen Wills had come to Detroit to play a tournament in 1928. (She married Frederick S. Moody, Jr., in 1929.) She had studied fine art as a student, and she had caught wind of the reputation that the DIA was just starting to establish under Valentiner's guidance, for as well as cultivating patrons like the Edsel Fords, the German director had been spending city tax money on some extraordinary modern and primitive art: the first Matisse to be acquired by an American museum, as well as tribal artefacts to fill the first-ever gallery of North American Indian art, an exhibit built up around the nucleus of Indian trophies collected by Michigan's own Indian fighter, General George Armstrong Custer.*

Helen Wills, then accompanied by her mother, knocked on the door of the DIA after six o'clock one evening, to be greeted by Valentiner, who happened to be working late, and who gave his visitors an impromptu tour around the deserted galleries.

"I am suddenly more interested in tennis than in art," Valentiner confessed to his diary in June 1929,[11] though he

---

* George Armstrong Custer (1839–76) grew up in Monroe, Michigan, and made his name during the Civil War commanding the Michigan Cavalry Brigade.

managed to rationalize his obsession. "In some way the best types of well-proportioned American women," he mused, "in their unconscious proximity to nature and art, may well come closer to the Greek ideal than their European counterparts."[12]

Valentiner devoted his Christmas holiday of 1930 to a journey to San Francisco in pursuit of his infatuation, and when he reached the West Coast he found Helen Wills posing, in between tennis matches, for a Mexican muralist, Diego Rivera, who had been commissioned to execute frescoes for the Luncheon Club of the San Francisco Stock Exchange. Rivera had immortalized the champion as the Spirit of California, her nakedness hidden by fruits, flowers, and workers symbolizing the fertility and energy of the West Coast state. Wills introduced Valentiner to Rivera: "A strange-looking heavy-set man," recorded Valentiner, "wearing a black serape and a large Mexican hat."[13] It was the start of a relationship that was to prove historic for Valentiner, for the artist—and also for Edsel Ford.

In 1930 the name of Diego Rivera was already well known on the Euro-American art circuit. Valentiner met the Mexican, in fact, only a matter of weeks before the painter was the subject of a one-man show at the Museum of Modern Art in New York.[14] Rivera was a political activist who had propagandized on behalf of the Mexican Revolution, and he was a professed, if unorthodox, Communist. In 1927 he had spent six months as a guest of the Soviet government in Moscow, where he had sketched the tenth-anniversary celebrations of the Revolution,[15] and his artistic speciality— large and dramatic frescoes on the walls of public buildings —was a political statement in itself. In Mexico he was especially famous for his murals in the Ministry of Education Building, one panel of which, *Capitalist Dinner*, showed John D. Rockefeller, J. P. Morgan, and Henry Ford, all gathered around a table, dining on ticker tape.

To the untutored eye, Rivera's work looked as though a peasant had been handed a paintbrush for the very first time; there was something caricature-like about it. His style had echoes of the heavy, primitive forms of Mayan ritual objects, so the figures he drew were distorted and lumpish.

But Rivera blended his primitivism with a paradoxical appreciation of modern machinery and manufacturing techniques, the unifying link being his empathy with the toiling masses who, ant-like, slaved to construct both Mexico's ancient monuments and the altars of modern technology. A friend of Trotsky, whom he was later to shelter in Mexico, Rivera saw himself as a people's painter, and though neither his political nor artistic qualifications would obviously have commended him to many North Americans in the early 1930s, William Valentiner could see work for the muralist to do in Detroit.

Valentiner had been reflecting for some time on a fresh use for the closed, Roman Baroque courtyard that lay at the centre of the new Detroit Institute of Arts building on Woodward Avenue. Filled with fountains, potted plants, and classical pillars, it was a refined and reverent forum— too austere, in Valentiner's opinion. The very hub of the museum should have more life to it, and Valentiner had a notion of how Diego Rivera could transform the classical courtyard into something much more jagged and native— very North American, very Detroit.

Valentiner could not commission the Mexican, however, until he knew how much money he had to offer. So, forsaking California—and Helen Wills Moody—the museum director hurried back to Detroit. His scheme was that Diego Rivera should be asked to decorate the walls of the DIA's central courtyard with murals that depicted Detroit's heavy industry—the unartistic but authentic source of the wealth that made the whole building possible—and when he put this notion to the city's Arts Commission, Edsel Ford supported him enthusiastically. Edsel offered $10,000 of his own money to commission two large murals, and Rivera agreed to come to the Motor City during the first available gap in his calendar. He was to stay for nearly twelve months.

*

Diego Rivera arrived in Detroit in the very depths of the depression, on April 21, 1932. Edsel had arranged for the artist to be shown around all the principal industries of the Detroit area: the river works, the railcar yards, the salt mines and chemical plants of the Wyandotte area, as well as the Ford factories. But it was Henry Ford's pride and joy, the massive Rouge site, that immediately captured the artist's imagination. Rivera had come to feel that the artefacts of industrial America, the skyscrapers, bridges, highways, and cars, were modern wonders of the world. "In all the constructions of man's past . . . ," he declared, "there is nothing to equal these."[16] The engineers who created them were artists, in his opinion, exponents of a plastic genius which demonstrated the creative forces bubbling inside the New World.

Americans need no longer feel inferior, that they had to go to Europe in order to secure artistic inspiration, Rivera told the *New York Herald Tribune*.

"Here it is—the might, the power, the energy, the sadness, the glory, the youthfulness of our lands."[17]

When the Mexican first arrived among the towering smoke-stacks and growling blast furnaces of the Rouge in the spring of 1932, he felt he had discovered the modern pyramids, and he fell to scribbling furiously in his sketch-book.[18]

William Valentiner's original scheme had been that Rivera should execute two murals for the DIA's courtyard, one on the automobile industry, and the other reflecting the more general story of Detroit's settlement and growth. But Rivera felt that he could say everything that he wanted to through the Rouge alone. Henry Ford's great creation embraced it all: the perfection and awesome power of the machines, the myriad crowds of men swarming around them. The Rouge was the largest single manufacturing facility that man had ever set down upon the face of the earth. What greater subject could an artist need?

After a month of sketching, Rivera invited Valentiner and

Edsel Ford to examine the finished studies for his murals. The Mexican had brought an exotic entourage with him to Detroit: an art-loving couple of English aristocrats, Lord and Lady Hastings,* and his own wife, the unconventional Frida Kahlo, who was already making a name for herself as an artist with a surrealist style. To judge from his photographs, Rivera was not a handsome man. He was unkempt and spheroid, his face rather flaccid and baby-featured. Bulbous-nosed and warty, with a prominent paunch, he could have come out of one of Brueghel's paintings—or, for that matter, from one of his own. But his succession of beautiful wives and mistresses attested to a deeper magnetism.

Lady Hastings cooked the supper. The Riveras and Hastings had taken apartments side by side in the Wardell, a residential hotel across the street from the DIA, and this evening they all crammed together into the Riveras' one-room flat. Rivera still could not speak much English. He spoke Spanish to his wife, Italian to Lady Hastings, French to Valentiner, and, presumably, smiled a lot at Edsel Ford. But when the moment came to examine his studies for the two main walls of the museum courtyard, the language barriers disappeared. Edsel Ford was carried away. The Mexican's sketches combined forceful artistic feeling with almost photographic accuracy. When Henry Ford himself later came to examine the finished murals, he was amazed at how the artist had managed to fuse operations that took place two miles apart, while keeping every inch of the picture technically correct.[19] Looking at the studies after Lady Hastings's supper, Edsel Ford had no doubt that his $10,000 would be well spent, and next day the Arts Commission agreed with him.

*

* John, Viscount Hastings (born 1901), later became the fifteenth Earl of Huntingdon. Cristina, his wife at the time of his visit to Detroit, was the daughter of the Marchesa Cassati, whose fantastic, flowing red hair was immortalized in the portrait of her by Augustus John.

"He who is not with the people," Diego Rivera liked to say, "is against the people."

As Detroit suffered through the agonies of the depression, no one could look at the car plants in the same way again. They sucked men in, chewed them up, and spat them out as remorselessly as they processed steel, iron, and rubber, and as Rivera started transferring his ideas to the walls of the DIA in the summer of 1932, his anger was plain. Henry Ford's use of the machinery in the Rouge plant had enslaved the men who worked there, and Rivera's murals were, in one sense, the story of that slavery. The workers depicted in his graphic tableaux were faceless, many of them: deadened, anonymous victims of the vast mechanical process that had been devised for the profit of somebody else.

But, in another sense, there was a lilt and grace to the choreography of the assembly line, and, as an artist, Rivera could not help being caught by that. Detroit had been hit badly by the depression, but it had not sunk to the depths experienced in other corners of America. The men still working in the Rouge in 1932 were an elite, and this showed in the liberation which they achieved through the mechanics of the production process. Man and machine together, felt Rivera, made up a new sort of collective hero, "higher than the old traditional heroes of art and legend."[20] When working in harmony with their machines, the men of the Rouge became superhuman; there was nothing they could not achieve—at least when viewed from the perspective of Rivera's own, very particular, political ideology.

"Marx made theory," declared the painter. "Lenin applied it. . . . And Henry Ford made the work of the socialist state possible."[21]

Rivera's English was, probably, not up to presenting the complexities of this sociopolitical theory to Henry Ford himself, but the artist and his wife were· by no means overawed by the great man. Invited to dinner at Fair Lane, Rivera was delighted to hear his wife's question float across

386

the table at a moment of quiet in the conversation: "Mr. Ford, are you Jewish?"*

Mr. Ford, apparently, bore no grudge. He enjoyed the company of pretty women, and, in her Mexican costume, the dark-browed Frida was strikingly attractive. Ford commandeered her to dance with him at one of his old-time evenings, and afterwards offered her the use of a brand-new Lincoln, complete with chauffeur, for the rest of her stay in Detroit. Diego declined the offer on his wife's behalf. The car, he said, was "too rich for our blood," though he did later accept a more humble Ford.[23]

The creation of the Detroit Industry frescoes was, in itself, a scientific and mechanical process, for Diego Rivera did not simply paint his images onto the surfaces of the DIA walls. He bonded them into wet plaster in the style of the classical Italian frescoists whose techniques he had studied, so that, when dried, the murals were as stone. They could not be washed off or rubbed away.

This process called for quite an elaborate team of technical assistants, to prepare walls, to mix plasters and pigments, and also to gauge the humidity of the atmosphere, since this determined how long Rivera had to paint before the plaster hardened. If he made mistakes, or had second thoughts, he could not wipe them out or paint them over. That entire section of the wall had to be chipped away and prepared afresh.

Rivera would start work around midnight. His assistants would "pounce" powdered pigment through tissue stencils to transfer the outlines of his designs onto the wet plaster, and he would then set to work with his brushes, which were

* Frida Kahlo, who suffered a miscarriage in Detroit, and who was generally less enamoured of the Motor City than was her husband, took some pleasure in shocking the local bourgeoisie, particularly the matrons of Grosse Pointe. She had quite a command of English, but she liked to make out she was only a beginner, peppering her tea party conversation with such expressions as "Shit on you!" while pretending not to understand what she had said. "What I did to those old biddies!" she would exclaim with satisfaction on her return from expeditions to the east side.[22]

tied to the ends of long wands, painting through the small hours to execute the black, white, and shade of the picture. Then, with the dawn, he would turn to his palette, using the fresh morning light to provide an accurate interpretation of the colours that he mixed onto a white enamel plate, knowing that the light would continue to improve until noon.

Edsel Ford's diary shows that he came to watch this extraordinary process at least once a week. Rivera's assistants remember that he dropped in even more frequently— every other day or so.[24] Edsel enjoyed being a participant in this living art, enlisting the buyers of the Ford windshield and window department to procure the high-quality glass ingredients that Rivera needed to give life to his pigments. Edsel had a Ford photographer working full-time to supply Rivera with pictorial reference of the Rouge as he went along, and this photographer simultaneously compiled a stage-by-stage record of the progress of Detroit's own Sistine Chapel.

Rivera confessed to Valentiner that Edsel Ford had surprised him: he was quite lacking, Rivera said, "the characteristics of an exploiting capitalist." Rivera liked his Detroit patron, for Edsel, he felt, had the simplicity and directness "of a workman in his own factories."[25] Indeed, pursuing his theory about the creators of modern industrial artefacts, Rivera came to feel that Edsel, as a car designer, was fully qualified to be considered as an artist in his own right.

Edsel had set up his own car-design studio at the Lelands' old Lincoln plant, for though Henry had, by now, largely accepted his son's responsibility for overall Ford design, Edsel needed physically to escape from his father in order to develop his ideas with freedom. Late in 1932, Rivera went to Edsel's studio and found him working there on the designs for a new aerodynamic Lincoln coupe. The drawings were on three blackboards, and the artist stood Edsel in front of them so that they formed a triptych in the background. Rivera had already included Edsel in a lower corner of his Rouge murals, along with Valentiner, following the old fresco tradition that the patron should be depicted some-where in the work he had paid for. But now the Mexican executed a full-scale portrait in oils of the second Ford.

Edsel stands in the foreground of the painting, staring out of the canvas. Rivera's rounded, simplified style has plumpened his subject's features, yet, somehow, it captures the gentleness and vulnerability of the man all the more vividly. Henry Ford's only son appears open, and quite defenceless. Is it imaginary to detect in his eyes some deep, submerged wincing of pain? He has his compass and draughtsman's implements laid out on the table in front of him, and behind him, on the blackboard, are the sweeping and beautiful lines of his car, disembodied and floating in the air, as if growing out of Edsel's head.

Diego Rivera's Detroit Industry frescoes marked a high point in the artist's creative energies, but he had scarcely started working on them when he realized that he wanted more. Valentiner and Edsel had originally asked him to execute two long panels which, as it turned out, depicted work on the V–8 assembly line, from the basic cylinder blocks to the final production of finished cars.

But Rivera came to feel that this was only half the story. Out in the wilds of Michigan lay the iron and wood; down by the Amazon, where Henry had set up his own Ford plantations, grew the rubber. The full potency of the Rouge could only be experienced in its totality when these earth elements had been incorporated into the picture. In this, the artist's vision curiously mirrored that of Henry Ford himself, who, not content with owning the Rouge, had felt that he also had to own the forests, mines, and land from which his raw materials sprang.

There were two extra walls in the museum courtyard, as well as spaces stretching above the original panels to the ceiling, and Rivera proposed to Valentiner that he should be commissioned to fill these remaining vacant spaces with additional images—at a going rate, including the wages of his assistants, of $100 per square yard.

It was a bad moment to ask anyone in Detroit for money, least of all the art institute, for the city fathers had made the museum the first object of the economies imposed by their shrinking tax revenues. Large numbers of the staff had been laid off, Valentiner had agreed to take an unpaid leave of absence to save the cost of his own salary, and, as Detroit's welfare expenses mounted, there were those in City Hall who argued for closing the costly and unproductive galleries on Woodward Avenue altogether, and selling off their collections for ready cash.[26]

Indeed, the museum would have been closed already if Edsel Ford had not personally agreed to meet the salaries of a skeleton staff for at least a year; and since Edsel had also agreed to provide $4,000 to remove some heavy plaster mouldings that obstructed Rivera's work in the courtyard, Valentiner was loath to ask him for more. Edsel's personal fortune, quite heavily committed in the stock market, had suffered like everyone else's, and he had had to pay Rivera twice over, since the bank in which Edsel deposited the artist's original $10,000 fee had gone bust.

Valentiner left it until the last minute. Due to set off for Europe on May 31, 1932, on his leave of absence, he went to a farewell dinner in his honour the night before, then drove on to the home of Mrs. William Clay, Eleanor Ford's mother, where, he was told, the family would be gathering to celebrate Mrs. Clay's birthday. The lights were still on when he arrived, and inside he found the Fords and the Kanzlers, gathered at card tables, playing games.

Valentiner sat down at a table with Eleanor and her sister, Josephine, and started to talk nervously and intensely about Rivera's work. The museum director did not dare broach what was really on his mind, but Eleanor could sense it, and she brought it straight out.

"William is very nervous," she called across to Edsel. "Can't you take him into a corner and find out what he wants to tell you?"[27]

Rivera got his money—and the Detroit Institute of Arts got a complete and unique work of art, covering every spare inch of its once-classical central courtyard. The originally commissioned panels that showed the V–8 workers at their tasks ran around the centre of the walls, while above them Rivera painted vast, primeval landscapes in which earth giants lolled, their huge hands sifting the salt, sand, and rock that made possible the frenzied mechanical activities in the panels below. These giants, Indian, Negro, Asian, and Caucasian, represented the four races that had shaped North America, and their heavy, impassive features strangely echoed the shapes of the machinery below, so that, one realized, the machines themselves had faces. You could look at the sculptured metalwork and just see stamping presses—or you could see towering Mayan idols, with the cloth-capped Detroit workers doing homage to them, human sacrifices prostrate at their feet.

Henry Ford, the inspiration of it all, was in the frescoes. So was his henchman, Sorensen. Henry appeared to be lecturing a class of apprentices on his V–8 engine, which bore a curious resemblance to a mechanical poodle, while Sorensen, grim, humourless, and rather sinister as he watched over the line, was the obvious figure of authority. A frieze of panels showed grey-blue workers, male and female, picking up their wages from an armoured car and filing home across the Miller Road overpass. Other panels showed the peaceful and destructive uses of technology side by side, passenger planes contrasted with war planes, chemical warfare with medical research, while deep below the soil, a human baby took shape in the seed germ of a plant. "The unity of all life," declared Rivera, "is derived from the earth."

When Detroit finally laid eyes on the extraordinary explosion of images that was Edsel Ford's gift to it, the city was outraged. There had been murmurings for months at the vast sums of money that were being paid to an artist—and a foreign artist at that—to blotch crude and garish colours over the whited walls of the city's principal claim to gentility, and when Rivera attended a private preview for the museum's more affluent patrons, the hostility was palpable. Sipping cocktails, the denizens of Grosse Pointe bemoaned the loss of their peaceful, plant-lined garden court, for Rivera had painted the walls with the very things they wanted to escape. Why come to a museum to be confronted by the grime and ugliness they could see in Wyandotte any day of the week?

Could not Señor Rivera, someone asked, have chosen images that presented a more pleasant aspect of Detroit— a concert, say, an open-air festival, or an art exhibit?

Rivera replied bluntly that he considered any factory superior to such a suggestion.[28]

The discreet enmity of Grosse Pointe was nothing to the storm which broke a few days later when the murals were put on display to the general public, for as the average middle-class Detroiter looked at Rivera's handiwork, he did not require much instruction to realize he was being got at. There were little things: a red star painted on a worker's glove, a compass pointing northeast, towards Moscow. More intangibly, there was a subversive spirit that transfused the entire enterprise, a defiant vitality which exuded from the collective sinews of the workingmen, who both buoyed and threatened the process in which they participated. The toilers of the Rouge kept the behemoth going, but they were also the men who, in these years, were stirring with the first signs of organized labour resentment. This double-edged message was the reason why, in later years, union organizers would bring new recruits to the central courtyard of the DIA to gaze and drink in the lurid, teeming images that swarmed across its walls. Commissioned by a son of capitalism, Rivera's frescoes had turned out to be a powerful exercise in consciousness-raising for the proletariat.[29]

"I painted these walls," said Comrade Rivera, "out of my heart."[30]

Most opponents of the Rivera courtyard preferred to skirt around its political message. The social issues involved were too close to home, and communism had not become the target it was to be in later years. Critics concentrated on more easily graspable religious and moral objections: the full breasts of the various earth goddesses, which were judged to be "pornographic," and the tableau in which Rivera had depicted the peaceful uses of technology. In this panel a little baby was shown being vaccinated by a white-coated scientist, attended by the horse, cow, and sheep whose bodies had provided testbeds for the life-saving vaccine being used. The pose of the child and its mother was clearly modeled on a nativity tableau, and this, said its detractors, was a blasphemy.

An Episcopal minister, the Reverend H. Ralph Higgens, wrote a letter of protest to the papers, and this touched off a chorus of indignation from other ministers, ladies' clubs, and politicians anxious to get in on the campaign. Within a matter of days, more than 20,000 visitors entered the museum to inspect Rivera's work—the largest crowds the DIA had known at any time in its history—and the verdict was distinctly hostile. Not a single local public figure spoke up for the frescoes, and the general consensus was that they should be whitewashed, or chipped away.[31]

But Edsel Ford was unmoved. Confrontation was not his style, but he stood by Rivera.

"I admire Mr. Rivera's spirit," he said. "I really believe he was trying to express his idea of the city of Detroit"[32]

As president of the Arts Commission, Edsel totally refused to countenance the notion that the frescoes should be screened or obscured in any way, and aided by an energetic campaign mounted by the DIA's professional staff, Edsel Ford prevailed. Diego Rivera's Detroit Industry murals survive to this day, the living centrepiece of the art institute in which they stand, and also, arguably, the finest native celebration of North America's industrial power and genius to have been created in our times. Edsel Ford did not know how to stand up to his father, but to his eternal credit, he did know how to stand up to Detroit.

When Diego Rivera had finished his work in Detroit, he travelled to New York City, where he had been commissioned to paint murals in the cathedral-like lobby of the new Rockefeller Center, just going up along Fifth Avenue. The artist discussed the progressive theme of the frescoes with the Rockefellers, who agreed with him, and by early May 1933, the work was well advanced.

As in Detroit, however, New York public opinion took against the radical tone of Rivera's imagery, which included a portrait of Lenin. An indignant outcry arose, and the response of the Rockefeller family proved rather different to that of Edsel Ford. On May 9, 1933, security guards ordered Diego Rivera down from his scaffolding and removed him, with his assistants, from the lobby of the Rockefeller Center. Screens were hurriedly thrown up to conceal his work from the public gaze, and shortly afterwards, every square inch of the frescoes that he had painted was methodically chipped away.

# 20

## BANK HOLIDAY

*Detroit's financial institutions have been a silent but vital force in its almost magical growth.*

—GUARDIAN GROUP BROCHURE[1]

In 1929 the Edsel Fords became Grosse Pointers. Henry Ford had never got rid of the 3,000 feet of Lake St. Clair shoreline, Gaukler Point, which he had acquired when he had planned to make Grosse Pointe his own home, and in 1926 his son purchased the land from him,[2] commissioning Albert Kahn to design a manor house upon it in Cotswold style.

Albert Kahn was a schizophrenic architect. His factory buildings were strictly functional, employing prestressed concrete and glass to create stark and unashamedly utilitarian structures which won him deserved international renown. But when it came to private commissions, Kahn went chintzy, and his design for the Edsel and Eleanor home was whimsical in the most deliberate fashion. Touring the Cotswolds on a reconnaissance, the architect noticed how many of the buildings had had additions tacked on to them across the centuries. Most of these picturesque, "added on" buildings were, in fact, inns, cottages, and farmhouses. The traditional Cotswold manor house is usually a unified, rather severe piece of work. But this did not prevent Kahn from elaborating his Ford manor house by the lakeshore into a cascade of higgledy-piggledy roofs, chimneys, and quaint dormer windows from which Snow White might have popped her head at any moment.

It was a great improvement on Fair Lane, however, and the Edsel Fords grew very fond of their new lakeshore estate. The children could play in the ninety acres of grounds without the security problems they had had in Indian

Village, and by the end of the 1920s most of Eleanor and
Edsel's friends were living out in Grosse Pointe as well.
George Fink, president of Michigan Steel, Howard Bonbright, president of the General Securities Corporation,
Carlton Higbie, president of Keane Higbie, Alger Shelden,
president of the Shelden Land Company—the Edsel Ford
circle was moneyed and influential, the very sort of people
that had helped Henry Ford decide that Grosse Pointe was
not the place for him. Edsel's closer acquaintances even
included Phelps Newberry, son of the hated Truman Newberry, who had defeated Henry Ford in his bid for the
Senate.

Their closest friends of all remained the Kanzlers, Ernest
and Josephine, who also came to Grosse Pointe and moved
into a grand lakeshore home. One of Ernie's enthusiasms
was tennis. He filled his life methodically with a series
of hobbies and accomplishments which he would study,
practice, and master with infuriating thoroughness—golf,
sailing, the violin—and in Grosse Pointe he applied himself
to tennis. With Edsel, Kanzler built an indoor tennis court
—the Tennis House—which became the basis of an exclusive little winter club for themselves and their friends.

Ernest Kanzler's next stage after motorcars was high
finance. The American economy was picking up momentum
in 1926, the year of the memorandum that marked the end
of Kanzler's career with the Ford Motor Company. It was
a good year to invest, and Kanzler had been investing for
some time with two other Grosse Pointe friends, George
Fink and Carlton Higbie. They called their investment
syndicate KFH, and Edsel Ford had come in on some of
their deals.[3] Edsel used KFH as a channel for his own
investments, and he made money. Kanzler made money.
Fink and Higbie made money. It was difficult not to make
money in these years, borrowing it, lending it, playing the
stock market.

The partners decided to expand, to get into the banking
business themselves, and so was formed the Guardian Detroit Company "to transact every phase of banking, trust

and investment business for individuals and corporations."[4]
It was the practice in the 1920s—and sometimes it was the
law—for banks and finance houses to create fresh companies
as they expanded rather than opening branches, so the
Guardian Detroit Company soon started to spin off new
entities—the Guardian Trust Company, the Guardian Detroit Bank, the Union Guardian Trust.

The names were slightly different, all variations on the
same, solid-sounding Guardian theme, but each company
offered essentially the same financial services as the next—
"under unified ownership and with coordinated management"[5]—and as the group grew, existing banks joined it,
or were taken over. The German-American Bank, whose
then president, John Gray, had advanced the crucial capital
that had enabled Alex Malcomson to get the Ford Motor
Company started in 1903, joined the group and became
the Guardian National Bank of Commerce.[6] By 1929 the
Guardian Group comprised no less than twenty-five associated banks and trust companies, and its list of directors
made up a who's who of Grosse Pointe: Howard Bonbright,
Ralph Booth, Roy Chapin, George Fink, Carlton Higbie,
Alvan Macauley, Phelps Newberry, the Sheldens, and, of
course, Edsel B. Ford.[7]

The moving spirit of the Guardian Group was Ernest
Kanzler. Tall, dark, and owllike with his steel-rimmed spec-
tacles and his smartly trimmed moustache, the onetime
lawyer, onetime car executive proved to be best of all at
making deals. He worked hard, he took quick decisions—
and he had a wealthy brother-in-law. As Ernest Kanzler got
started in the banking business in 1927, everyone knew that
he had Ford money behind him, and his deals multiplied
the faster. In only two years the Guardian Group grew to
be the largest financial conglomerate in Michigan. Ernest
Kanzler was chairman of the board of the holding company,
Edsel Ford was the largest stockholder, with 50,000 shares,
and their biggest single deal was with the Ford Motor
Company itself, for, faced with the task of selling the new
Model A, Henry Ford had finally consented to installment

sales. The Universal Credit Company was formed, a partnership between the Guardian Group and Ford, and in 1928 UCC started offering credit to both Ford dealers and Ford customers. Swelling the volume of Model A sales, and benefiting from it, UCC arranged over 400,000 loans in its first year of business.

The Guardian's other line of business was mortgages, to domestic customers, and also to the growing throng of developers buying up downtown Detroit. This made even more money than cars. In the late 1920s, America's real estate market was booming, and the directors of the Guardian Group decided they should do some real estate developing of their own. Detroit's youngest, brightest bank should have a headquarters to match, and thus was born the Guardian Building, quite the most exotic skyscraper in downtown Detroit. Pale terracotta tipped with orange and white, it still looms above Griswold Street, tiled with vermillion, cream, and green stripings like a cigarette packet, epitomizing the jaunty spirit of an era when making money was just plain fun.

When the Guardian Building opened its doors at the end of March 1929, the *Detroit News* declared it to be a very "Cathedral of Finance."[8] Thirty-six storeys above the street, an aurora of moving, coloured lights shone out at night. With its lobby of fiery Pewabic glazes and stained-glass windows, the building was surpassed in gaudiness only by the new Fox movie theatre on Woodward Avenue—and in the years that followed, the adventures that unrolled inside its offices took on not a little of the drama of Hollywood.

Edsel Ford's involvement in the Guardian Group represented a bid for freedom. It was an attempt to do something as a business-man in his own right—and it also represented, in just about the most direct fashion that Edsel could manage, a gesture of defiance towards his father. In financing Ernest Kanzler, Edsel was publicly backing a man who had dared to question the great carmaker's judgement; and by becoming a director of the Guardian Group, he could scarcely have registered a clearer disagreement with his father's well-known views on bankers, moneylenders, and financial speculators.

The Wall Street Crash of October 1929, however, proved the wisdom of Henry Ford's financial conservatism, for the Guardian Group, like so many other enterprises that had mushroomed in the late 1920s, soon felt the strain. The Guardian's rapid expansion had been based upon the assumption of easy money, on the cleverness of living on credit. The group was in difficulty from the moment that people stopped borrowing; and when existing borrowers started delaying or defaulting on their repayments, the trouble grew really serious, since the Guardian had itself borrowed quite heavily from insurance companies and other banks, and without money coming in, it had difficulty meeting its own repayments.

The customary remedy, foreclosing on its debtors to recover the lost capital, offered little relief, since real estate values had collapsed with the crash. If the Guardian Group compelled its clients to sell up, they could only hope to get a fraction of their money back.

By the end of 1930, Ernest Kanzler's banks were starting to suffer major cash-flow problems, and Kanzler turned to his brother-in-law for help. Edsel drew on his own reserves in other banks to increase his deposits with the Guardian, and he bolstered the group's balance sheet with Ford Motor Company funds as well. There was nothing improper in this. It was a question of Edsel and the company putting their money in Guardian banks rather than in others, and between December 1930 and January 1933, Edsel made no less than $12 million of such deposits.[9] In 1932 the Guardian Group also borrowed $15 million from the RFC, the Reconstruction Finance Corporation, established by President Hoover to help banks that found themselves in temporary difficulty.

Borrowing alone, however, was not enough. The stock of the Guardian Group, which had been traded in August 1929 as high as $350 a share, fell with every other listing on Wall

Street. By the autumn of 1930 it was down to $75, and in October that year a stock pool was formed to try and bid up the shares. The plan was to push the share price over $100 by the purchase of 60,000 shares that would be held for a year. One hundred and ten directors of various Guardian companies, including Edsel Ford, made up this buying syndicate, which operated through a committee headed by Ernest Kanzler and Roy Chapin. Junior employees of the group were encouraged to mount similar schemes, and, flattered to be in the know, young executives with growing families borrowed heavily to acquire Guardian shares, confident that if they bought at $75, they would soon be enjoying the guaranteed profit of selling again at over $100.

The shares, however, did not rise, for the financial history of America in the early 1930s was a series of false dawns. There seemed no end to the depression. Newspapers regularly agreed that the bottom had been reached, only to discover there was a still deeper trough into which to sink, and the Guardian Group sank along with everyone else.

The problem was more than just cash flow, for in order to bank-roll the share-boosting activities of its directors and employees, the Guardian Group began, effectively, to lend itself its own money. By 1932 the Guardian National Bank had loaned its own officers and directors $3,481,000—34 percent of its capital[10]—while another bank in the group had loaned 122 junior officers and employees over $1 million against collateral that subsequently turned out to be worth less than $15,000.[11] By the end of 1932 the group was holding 149,574 of its own shares as security for loans[12]— a practice which, in any regular bank, state or national, was just plain illegal. Officers who knowingly engaged in such artificial self-financing were liable to go to prison, and the Guardian was sailing on the narrow edge of legality when it channelled these transactions through its holding company.

The fine line was crossed when federal auditors arrived in Michigan to investigate whether the Guardian Group could be entrusted with the funds it was requesting from the government's Reconstruction Finance Corporation. In the

1850s Michigan bankers had outwitted official examiners by transporting kegs of nails, topped with thin layers of silver coin, from bank to bank just ahead of the travelling teams of auditors. In 1932 it was possible to do this on paper, and in May 1937, Herbert L. Wilkin, assistant receiver of the Guardian Detroit Union Group, was fined $5,000 for a false bookkeeping entry in the 1931 ledgers of one bank in the group. The case was long and complex, but it boiled down to the bank—which was in Flint, sixty miles northwest of Detroit—showing the federal auditors $600,000 which was not really there.[13]

There is no evidence that Ernest Kanzler or Edsel Ford was personally aware of Wilkin's fraud. They were not involved in such day-to-day details. But these were stressful, difficult days, the era when respected businessmen threw themselves out of skyscraper windows. There was great pressure on junior employees in organizations like the Guardian to cut corners, and, at the Guardian, this pressure came, ultimately, from Ernest Kanzler and Edsel Ford as they manoeuvred desperately to keep their leaky ship afloat. Sharp bookkeeping was the price of survival. When the ledgers of the Guardian group were finally opened for scrutiny in 1933–34, no less than thirty-three of its officers were indicted for improper financial procedures—though, in the event, Herbert Wilkin was the only one to go to trial.

Edsel and Kanzler's strategy had been to maintain public confidence until such time as the American economy took an upturn. Between 1930 and 1932 they declared dividends of $9 million that bore no relation to the conglomerate's underlying health[14]—and then they ran out of time. In January 1933, a major insurance company which had lent the Union Guardian Trust Company funds to finance real estate mortgages started pressing for repayment.[15] The Union Guardian Trust Company was one of the weaker units in the group, and lacking the cash, it was compelled to turn to the Reconstruction Finance Corporation for yet another loan, this time of $50 million.[16]

The RFC agreed to put up $37 million of the money the

Union Guardian Trust was requesting, provided that Edsel Ford and the group's other main depositors found the $13 million balance. Edsel and Kanzler put the rescue package together in the last weeks of January 1933, and salvation seemed to have been quietly assured, when, out of the blue, old antagonisms reared their heads. James Couzens, a senator for Michigan and also head of a subcommittee of the Senate Banking and Currency Committee, took it upon himself to denounce the proposed RFC intervention. He was already angered by previous RFC rescues—Charles Dawes, the RFC president, had lent his own Central Republic Bank of Chicago $90 million[17]—and, when it came to Detroit, the Union Guardian Trust Company, said Couzens, was "Mr. Ford's baby."[18] If a Ford-financed bank had got itself into difficulties, then that was the Fords' problem. They should bail it out themselves, 100 percent. It was not a proper object for taxpayers' money, and if any such public rescue went through, Couzens promised, in a phrase for which Detroit was never to forgive him, that he would "shout against it from the rooftops."[19]

The intervention of James Couzens in February 1933 drew Henry Ford's attention to the problems of the Guardian Group for the first time in a serious way. Until Couzens publicly linked Henry Ford's name and reputation with the manoeuvrings of Kanzler's banking empire, Henry had not been aware of the difficulties, nor had he pondered very much on the Guardian connection. The Ford Motor Company had to put its money somewhere. Better in Edsel's bank than in the rival Detroit Bankers' group financed by GM and Chrysler—and anyway, Henry left that side of the business to Edsel, Ernest Liebold, and the company treasurer, B. J. Craig.

As the depression deepened, Henry had been engrossed by his own projects—Inkster, Greenfield Village, the problems of his aeroplane company, which he decided to abandon in 1933, and, above all, the V–8. The V–8 had been an engineering project in the old style, Henry working late, coming in early, getting his fingers dirty as he directed the research of Fred Thoms and his team. Banking was the least of his interests, and Edsel had had no reason to enlighten his father as to the very real problems of Ernest Kanzler's banking group. If the RFC rescue had gone through quietly, all might have been well.

But Couzens's outburst transformed the situation. Edsel could no longer hide the Guardian's problems from his father. He would have to explain himself, go into embarrassing details—and also ask his father for help.

Edsel was already under considerable strain. The fall in the value of the Guardian stock had wiped nearly $14 million off the value of 50,000 shares that he owned, and William Valentiner estimated that his patron's total losses could amount to as much as $20 million. "Edsel Ford," Valentiner wrote in his diary in the spring of 1933, ". . . is more depressed than I have ever seen him."[20] "Art" Backus, one of the clerks in Edsel's office at Ford, remembered his master becoming snappish and grumpy, quite unlike his normal self.[21]

Edsel was cornered. He had chosen to associate with friends of whom his father did not approve, in a business venture which flouted his father's most cherished principles —and he did not know how to confide in his father at the best of times. So desperate that there were tears in his eyes, it was to Ernest Liebold that he went to confess his failure, and it was the private secretary, not Edsel, who told the truth to Henry.

"You don't take very good care of your son," the German told him abruptly.[22]

Liebold himself was overwrought. His many duties included the supervision of two Ford-supported Dearborn banks, which were having difficulties of their own meeting payments. But the underlying finances of both the Ford Motor Company and Henry Ford himself were fundamentally strong, since Henry had long ago laid down his basic financial policy: spread savings around, and avoid the stock market like the plague.

"We've got plenty of business now," he had declared with satisfaction in September 1930, "because we didn't go dabbling in stocks."[23]

The Ford Motor Company had kept $50 to $100 million in safe government securities all through the 1920s, with a further $100 to $250 million on short call in various banks.[24] So Henry met the depression cash-rich, in a much stronger position than most. He certainly had the funds to help his son—if he felt inclined to.

Edsel's Grosse Pointe connections had become a further source of grievance for Henry Ford, since Henry seems to have nursed the hope that his son might, one day, bring his family back from Indian Village to Dearborn. He had kept a large plot of land reserved for Edsel right beside Fair Lane, and when Edsel opted for Grosse Pointe in 1926, it was this Dearborn estate which Henry gave to the Dahlingers.[25] If Henry could not have one son living beside him, he would have another.

Ernest Kanzler, of course, was an old bogey, and the prestigious Grosse Pointe names who were Edsel's friends and business partners in the Guardian excited Henry's mistrust still more. Henry suspected Edsel of favouring them with Ford supply contracts,[26] and he had still deeper suspicions about their lifestyles. These were the years of Prohibition, but Grosse Pointe was particularly nonchalant in its disregard of the law, and Edsel kept his bar as well stocked as any of his neighbours. According to Harry Bennett, Henry Ford bribed one of the Edsel Ford servants to give him information about what went on in the house. And one day, while Edsel and Eleanor were away, Henry Ford drove across to Gaukler Point with Bennett.

It was his intention, he said, to break up a stock of whisky and champagne which he had heard that Edsel had, and although Bennett, by his own account, refused to cooperate, remaining in the car, Henry Ford did get out and go into the house. When he came back, according to Bennett, "his clothes smelled of liquor."[27]

On the face of it, Edsel Ford's difficulties with the Guardian Group provided his father with a golden opportunity to humble his son. But this had never been Henry Ford's deliberate, conscious intention. It might seem to be the message emerging from the successive humiliations, great and petty, with which Henry dripped acid, drop by drop, upon his son's manhood through the 1920s and 1930s. But Henry needed Edsel beside him. Without Edsel, how else could Henry prove his strength? He continued to rationalize his bizarre treatment of his son in terms of his perverse therapy through pain, but the transparency of that was becoming obvious. Edsel weak was more valuable to Henry Ford than Edsel strong—and Edsel cast adrift just made no sense at all.

We do not know exactly what transpired between Edsel Ford and his father in February 1933. This was one moment of truth which father and son did keep to themselves. But Henry wasted no time in bailing Edsel out. He instructed B. J. Craig to transfer several million dollars of company money to Edsel's personal account at once.[28]

Rescuing Ernest Kanzler and his banking empire, however, was another matter. In the second week of February 1933, Roy Chapin, a director of the Guardian Group at the same time as being Secretary of Commerce—such were the ethics of the Hoover administration—travelled to Detroit to bring Henry Ford a personal appeal from the President. James Couzens's outburst had made the Guardian rescue a national affair. If Henry Ford would underwrite the Guardian banks just one more time, promised Hoover, then the government would do all it could to save them.

It was a last-ditch appeal in every sense. Hoover was due to step down in two weeks' time for the recently elected Franklin D. Roosevelt, who was promising such a radical array of solutions to the country's problems that, some feared, he might even nationalize the banks. But having made sure his son was safe, Henry Ford felt no responsibility to the Guardian Group, and he was evidently piqued by the public challenge that had been thrown in his face by his onetime partner.

"I am not likely," he declared sharply, "to leave my money in a bank in order to prevent Jim Couzens from spouting on the floor of the Senate."[29]

Henry was not willing to put up a penny to save the Guardian, or any other Detroit bank. If a crash had to come, said Henry Ford, then "let the crash come."[30]

On February 10, 1933, the leading industrialists and bankers of Michigan filed through the mosaic arches of the Guardian Building on Griswold Street for an emergency conference. Summoned to the "Cathedral of Finance" by Alfred P. Leyburn, national bank examiner for the Fourth Federal Reserve District, their mission was to save the Guardian Group—and hence the banking system of all Detroit.[31]

For three days they argued in the building's top-floor "gingerbread" suite, a long, narrow sequence of luxurious rooms set, like a club car, between the crenellated arches at the skyscraper's summit. But at 1:32 on the morning of Tuesday, February 14, after a day when the banks had been closed for Lincoln's birthday, and only hours before they were due to open again to what, it was confidently expected, would be total mayhem, all concerned confessed defeat. The governor of Michigan, William A. Comstock, was requested to call a bank holiday, and after this unusual expedient had been explained to him, he signed the administrative order. All the 436 banks and trust companies of Michigan closed for a week, and when no solution was found at the end of that time, they stayed closed.

It was an eerie, ominous time in the life of the Motor City, which older Detroiters still recall with a shudder. Detroit was almost totally without money. The city itself had to default on its bonds. There was a food panic. People fortunate enough to have gone to the bank before the holiday, cleaned out grocery stores while there were still supplies to be had, and then dollar bills vanished as well, since anyone who had hard cash hoarded it. To keep paying its bills, the city government issued its own money, $42 million worth of

Detroit scrip—paper undertakings to pay hard cash when cash again became available—and for months the entire community survived on this homemade Monopoly money. Some companies had been prudent enough to bank a proportion of their funds out of town, and in February and March of 1933, the road from Chicago became thronged with armoured trucks and their gun-toting escorts. Fortunate were the employees who could queue up on payday at one of these trucks and receive their money in genuine green dollar bills.

Dr. Conrad Lam, then a young intern at the Henry Ford Hospital, remembers coming into the operating theatre in the spring of 1933 at the moment when the hospital's chief surgeon was just making the first incision in a patient.

"Sir," said young Lam, "you asked to know when the armored car had arrived."

The surgeon looked up and took off his mask—which was how Conrad Lam came to perform his first gall bladder operation.[32]

The Detroit bank collapse of February 1933 permanently shattered the Motor City's bid to become the financial capital of the Midwest. There had been a time when Griswold Street seemed set fair to take over from Chicago. But the Bank Holiday made clear the narrow and vulnerable economic base of the Motor City. Detroit was a single-product town, and the three days of inconclusive squabblings in the gilded summit of the Guardian tower seemed to suggest that the local tycoons were, ultimately, just car-makers, obsessed by their own private balance sheets and incapable of realizing that the willingness to make the occasional sacrifice is a crucial ingredient in building the reputation of a successful money mart.

Detroit has never quite recovered. The city today, even at its very heart, has a depopulated, empty feeling. Whole blocks lie vacant, used as parking lots if they are lucky but, more often, derelict and scrubbily vegetated, dotted with whorls of what looks like tumbleweed. The inexplicable gaps between high-sided buildings are reminiscent of a British city after the Blitz—and some of them have been that way for more than half a century now.

When Frida Kahlo, Diego Rivera's wife, arrived in 1932 and laid her horrified eyes upon the automobile metropolis, which she had expected to find bustling and packed with life, she described Detroit as "a shabby old village,"[33] and that is a pretty good description of how it still looks today. Its rambling and diluted character dates back to the 1920s when land speculators bought up block after block in anticipation of the building boom that stopped almost as it started. In 1926 construction was running at $183 million per year in Detroit. Following the bank collapse of February 1933, it fell to $4 million, and uncompleted buildings were to stand like skeletons on the skyline for more than twenty years.

When the financial establishment of Detroit came to weigh up responsibility for the debacle of February 1933, they displayed considerable self-pity, but little evidence of self-blame. Grosse Pointers still recall the Bank Holiday as the time when "everyone lost their money," though, in fact, the upshot of the crisis was that every single account holder in a Detroit or Michigan bank eventually got his money back, one hundred cents on the dollar. It was the bank owners and stockholders, most of whom came from Grosse Pointe, who lost their money because they were legally compelled to make all lost deposits good from their own personal funds, and this double liability intensified the bitterness with which the barons of Griswold Street attempted to identify the cause of their woes.

With few exceptions, they settled on James Couzens. When the senior senator for Michigan seated himself two and a half years later, and only a few months before his death, at a luncheon table in the Detroit Club, the members beside whom he had sat down picked up their plates and removed themselves from the senator's presence.[34] The man was a traitor in the eyes of Griswold Street, for Couzens had been mayor of Detroit before he went to the Senate, and he was supposed to represent the interests of the city and state in Washington, right or wrong. Chicago had got its money from the RFC, thanks to Charles Dawes, who resigned his Washington post to save the Central Republic Bank. But Couzens had played dog in the manger.

The animosity stirred up by his old partner helped Henry Ford and his son emerge from the Detroit banking fiasco with their reputations less damaged than they might have been. For a time, indeed, they seemed set to be heroes. On February 24, 1933, ten days after the Bank Holiday had begun, the father and son issued a joint letter offering to take over not only the Guardian Group but most of Detroit's other closed banks as well. The Fords identified bad management as the cause of the collapse, and they proposed to create two new banks to be staffed by "the men whom we all believe will merit public confidence. . . . The institutions so established will be of the type of financial structure that will merit public faith in the ability of industrial Detroit to rehabilitate itself."[35]

Edsel and Henry offered to back these new banks with $8.25 million of their own money,[36] and the local newspapers at first considered this a magnanimous offer. Outside the Dearborn Town Hall some 3,000 demonstrators paraded with banners bearing the slogan "Bank with Hank."[37]

But the Ford offer was in the Muscle Shoals tradition. It amounted to a cut-price takeover bid for the entire banking system of Detroit, and their remarks about mismanagement were pretty cheeky, in view of Edsel's involvement with the Guardian. Not surprisingly, General Motors and Chrysler had ideas of their own. Working with the RFC, General Motors put up the money to form their own banking network, the National Bank of Detroit group, a conservative and well-funded enterprise which became the city's largest banking group, leaving Ford, a few months later, to found and fund its own bank, the Manufacturers National Bank of Detroit, which opened in August 1933.

The price of Henry Ford bailing Edsel out was Edsel severing his business relations with Ernest Kanzler. In the spring of 1933, Ford withdrew from its partnership in Kanzler's brainchild, the Universal Credit Company, and UCC was sold to the Commercial Investment Trust of New York. CIT became the Ford credit arm. No car company could hope to survive through the hard years of the mid–1930s without some sort of mechanism for installment selling. But now the car company itself had no direct involvement in the deal. After Edsel's flirtation with the wicked world of finance, Ford was clean again.

The Detroit Bank Holiday of February 1933 was a chilling demonstration of the power that the Motor City had come to exercise in the American economy. On February 23 the banks in Indiana closed; on February 25 those in Maryland; on February 27, Arkansas; February 28, Ohio; March 1, Alabama, Kentucky, Nevada, and Tennessee; March 2, Arizona, California, Louisiana, Mississippi, Oregon. By March 4, 1933, there were only a handful of banks open anywhere in the United States,[38] and two days later Franklin D. Roosevelt was compelled, in one of his first acts as President, to confront the nationwide crisis by declaring a general Bank Holiday.

There were clearly structural weaknesses in a system that could be brought down by the imprudence of just one bank, but the dominoes ran right back to the ornate Guardian Building on Griswold Street. Edsel Ford's excursion into high finance had had wider consequences than could possibly have been imagined when he first struck out on his own with Ernest Kanzler.

In personal terms, the consequences were even sadder. Henry Ford reached his seventieth birthday in July 1933—the occasion, by any standards, for him finally to hand over the reins of the Ford Motor Company to his son. But the great carmaker had always had difficulty pretending that he seriously intended to surrender real power to Edsel, and with the Guardian fiasco, the pretence ceased altogether.

# 21

# OVERPASS

> *They put me to work on the assembly line,*
> *My clock-card number was 90–90–9.*
> *Those Fords rolled by on that factory floor,*
> *And every fourteen seconds I slapped on a door.*
> *Those Fords rolled by all day and all night,*
> *My job was the front door on the right.*
> *Foreman told me the day I was hired,*
> *"You miss one door, Mr. Jones . . . you're fired."*
> *I slapped those doors on, always on the run,*
> *Every fourteen seconds, never missed a one.*
> *And I staggered home from work each night,*
> *Still slappin' 'em on—front door right.*
>
> —JOE GLAZER
> "YOU GOTTA FIGHT THAT LINE"[1]

Tool-and-die men are the aristocrats of the assembly line. They make the machines that make the cars. Every metal component of an automobile has to be shaped, and that shaping is done by a die, which either provides a mould for the component or stamps it out into its final form. The craft of fashioning the die is the speciality of the tool-and-die man.

Tool-and-die leaders, the men who coordinate and supervise groups of tool-and-die men, are veritable princes of the production process—the elite of the elite. In any car factory they are the elders of the tribe, and they usually have fifteen to twenty-five years' craftsmanship to their credit.[2] So it was hardly surprising, when an apple-faced twenty-year-old from West Virginia presented himself for a tool-and-die job at the entrance to the Ford hiring department one morning in the spring of 1927, that the guard should turn him away.

"Get on your way," said the Serviceman, "you're just a kid."[3]

Ford was hiring die leaders for the massive retooling

needed to accomplish the change from Model T to Model A, and it seemed inconceivable that this youth from hillbilly country could have the experience to be a tool-and-die man, let alone a tool-and-die leader. But the boy thought otherwise—and he proved rather argumentative.

"How can you look at me," he asked the guard, "and tell what qualifications I have?" The Serviceman, he argued, could not possibly have the knowledge to make judgements about who was, or was not, able to handle the special skills of tool-and-die making. He should allow the eager young applicant inside to talk to the employment manager face to face.

"How did you get in?" asked the employment manager, and the youth went through the same arguments again. The boy's experience was not, in truth, extensive. He had come north to work at Briggs Body after a machine shop apprenticeship in West Virginia, and his tool-and-die experience was limited to a period watching die makers cut patterns in a glass factory. But he insisted that his abilities should be tested by a supervisor who really knew about tool-and-die work.

The supervisor arrived with blueprints under his arm and asked some technical questions. Receiving some reasonably informed answers, he agreed to a two-day trial. The boy passed with flying colours and was given a job. For $1.05 an hour the Ford Motor Company had acquired the services of tool-and-die leader Walter P. Reuther.

On March 7, 1932, three weeks before the public unveiling of Henry Ford's new V–8, 3,000 men waving red banners marched upon the Ford River Rouge plant. Their demands included a six-hour day, free medical care, the abolition of all manner of labour grievances, from "speed-up" to favouritism in hiring and firing—and also the right to form unions. The march was organized by the local Communist party, whose Detroit following had increased significantly through the years of distress, and the Communists were making the most of the dramatic possibilities offered by a confrontation at the gates of the factory owned by the world's most famous capitalist. But the majority of the demonstrators seem to have been quite ordinary men who had been unemployed for months, who had few prospects of finding work, whose families did not have enough to eat —and who were, quite simply, desperate.

There had been previous demonstrations outside other Detroit factories, and even, on a small scale, outside the Rouge itself,[4] but the organizers of the Ford Hunger March of March 7, 1932, had not applied for a permit to march in either Detroit or Dearborn, and while the Detroit Police prudently turned a blind eye to this, content to escort the marchers along their way, the Dearborn Police decided to show that they were made of sterner stuff.

In 1932 the Dearborn Police were little more, in many respects, than a branch of Ford's own company police force, the Ford Service Department. Dearborn was a company town. Ford property accounted for 62 percent of the city's tax base, so it was only appropriate that the Dearborn Police Chief, Carl Brooks, should be a former Ford Serviceman. Brooks's qualification for this public office was that he had previously served as head of the Ford plant police at Highland Park, and when he came across to Dearborn, he continued to take his orders from Harry Bennett, the head of the Service Department.

As the 3,000 hunger marchers reached the Detroit-Dearborn city line, they were met by forty armed Dearborn policemen under Brooks's command. Brooks ordered the marchers to turn back, and when they refused, he had tear-gas canisters fired into the crowd.

The demonstrators scattered, breaking into small groups, which continued to make their way across open fields and along side streets in the direction of the Rouge plant. The police went after them, wielding truncheons to turn them back, and the marchers retaliated with whatever lay to hand: rocks, lumps of slag, fence posts. Newspaper reporters on the scene were unanimous that the marchers had brought no weapons with them.

The Dearborn Fire Department were waiting in Miller Road, outside the plant, ready to turn their hoses on the demonstrators, but their fire engines were overrun. Up on the metal overpass bridges which ran across from the plant to the parking lots on the other side of Miller Road, Ford Servicemen unrolled hoses of their own, and they sprayed the freezing water down onto the crowds.

As demonstrators massed against the wire fences of the Rouge, Harry Bennett himself decided to intervene. A personally courageous man, whatever else might be said against him, he rushed out through the front gate to argue with the leaders of the march. The man he happened to buttonhole was Joseph York, a nineteen-year-old organizer of the Young Communist League, and as the crowd saw the short, bow-tied executive arguing with York, they turned upon him. A lump of slag struck Bennett on the side of his head. He grabbed at York, blood streaming from the wound, and both men fell to the ground wrestling.

It was York who got up first, and as he did so, a hail of machine-gun fire rang out. York went down again, dead, his body landing on top of the still-prostrate Bennett, and three other men went down as well, mortally wounded in the same fusillade. By the time the demonstration was dispersed, there were twenty more men wounded, five of them seriously.[5]

The Dearborn Police and Ford Servicemen tried hard to seize film from the cameras of all the photographers at the scene. The *New York Times*'s photographer claimed that he actually had his camera shot out of his hands.[6] Reporters were driven away and threatened. But the next day the Rouge massacre was on the front page of every major newspaper in the country, and the verdict was almost unanimous.

"The Dearborn police are to be condemned for using guns against an unarmed crowd, for viciously bad judgement and for the killing of four men," declared the *New York Herald Tribune*. "Such action must arouse resentment among the unemployed everywhere and accentuate class antagonisms so alien to our American life."[7]

Four days later, 15,000 mourners gathered to bury Joseph York and the three other martyrs of the Rouge in a four-mile procession that wound through the streets of Detroit. The coffins of the four dead were draped in red. Many of the mourners wore red armbands or waved red banners, and as the men were laid in the ground, a band played the "Internationale" and the funeral march of the 1905 Russian revolutionaries.[8]

The name of Ford had come to stand for yet another strand in the complex fabric of American capitalism.

The Ford Hunger March of March 1932 shot an ugly hole in the mantle of Henry Ford, the worker's friend. America had come asking for help, in frayed trousers, cracked shoes, and with belts tightened over hollow bellies, wrote John Dos Passos, and "all they could think of at Ford's was machineguns."[9]

"The legend of high wages, good conditions [and] contented workers," declared the pamphleteer Robert L. Cruden, "was riddled by the bullets which killed four unemployed workers."[10]

As March 1932 drew to an end, certain Rouge workers who went to the checkout clock at the end of their day's work started finding that their time card might be missing. The time clerk would refer them onwards to the employment office, and there they would be handed a pink slip: notice to quit. Since many of these men had been among the 15,000 mourners who had walked behind the coffins of the men shot dead in Miller Road, the rumour soon went around the factory that Ford cameramen had been among the press photographers recording the ceremony. Their negatives, it was said, were screened at special gatherings of Ford Servicemen, who picked out faces they recognized and then arranged for their dismissal.

It was not unlikely. One of the saddest sets of files in the Ford Archives at Dearborn is labelled "Labor Relations-Es." The "Es" stands for Espionage, and the box is filled with the intelligence dossiers of the spies—known as "spotters"—who worked, ostensibly, on the Ford assembly line, but whose real job was to keep a careful note of their fellow workers' badge numbers, and then to tittle-tattle on them in detailed reports.

11:03 I noticed all the men in this Dpt. washing their hands in oil getting ready for lunch, which we eat at 11:15.

11:09 I saw E–4282 leave the Dpt. and purchased two sausage sandwiches. I saw him do it. . . .

Here is an accurate report on E–3349 time that he killed in the toilet today:—

| | | | | |
|---|---|---|---|---|
| 8:12 to | 8:29 | —17 | Min. | |
| 9:03 | — 9:21 | —18 | " | |
| 9:57 | —10:16 | —19 | " | |
| 10:52 | —11:02 | —10 | " | |
| 1:15 | — 1:27 | —12 | " | |
| 2:07 | — 2:20 | —13 | " | |

89 Minutes stolen.[11]

J–6347, who, the records showed, was Frank F. Conner of 10 Highland Avenue, got into especially hot water.

At about 7:45, location, Aviation Field, J–6347 while in the course of an argument about capitalists passed the remark to J–6993 in presence of J–5990 that Mr. Ford was a G--- d--- son of a b---. . . .

Affidavits by J–6993, Robert Anderson, and J–5990, Louis B. Deneweth are hereby attached.

LIEUT. 2814.[12]

These Ford espionage records date back as far as the First World War, and a number of their dossiers do focus on possible sabotage and enemy sympathizers. But their main concern is with time-keeping, factory discipline, and, above all, monitoring attempts at organization among the workers. Big Brother was very much alive and well at Highland Park in the same years that the Sociological Department was still endeavouring to make Ford a model of compassionate and sun-strewn human relations—and the spying extended outside the factories. Pretending to have radical sympathies, Ford spotters infiltrated meetings of the local Communist party.

Operative—15.

Report on Joint-meeting; English branch No. 1 and Russian branch No. 2.

7:30 P.M. I entered The Fraternity Hall, 140 First St. There were sixty-one members present. . . .

Comrade Green was elected Temporary Chairman. . . .

Schachinger, Johnson, Elbaum, Bolt, Jones, Weiss, Rushton and myself was named for the committee . . . (Weiss and Rushton are both employees of The Ford Motor Co. Highland Park, Rushton is a toolmaker on the 1st. floor A Bldg. and Weiss is working on special Die work in the same bldg. on second floor.)[13]

Going home afterwards with Weiss and Rushton in Rushton's Ford touring car, Operative 15 tried to trumpet his radical ardour—and nearly came unstuck. He did not mind if he got dismissed for his progressive activities, he boasted to his companions, because he had invested $500 in War Bonds.

The two comrades were horrified. "You invest your money," they asked, "in a Capitalist proposition?"[14]

The spy had to do some quick talking to reassure his Socialist brothers-in-arms, but, reviewing his performance afterwards, he reckoned that he had put up a convincing display, since, before the men split up for the evening, Rushton confided to the spotter that 90 percent of the toolmakers at Ford were "Socialists and pretty good Bolshivic."[15]

This, undoubtedly, was an overestimate. As unions started forming in Detroit in the 1930s, most of the car workers showed themselves to be pretty solidly anti-Bolshevik. But it suited the spies, as much as the comrades, to exaggerate the menace they were being paid to investigate—and the most patriotic American could not pretend that the fruits of the free enterprise system were being evenly distributed at Ford.

In his novel *Journey to the End of Night*, the French writer Céline described the experience of filing through the Ford hiring gate. New recruits were stripped and examined, wrote Céline, as if they were being required to cast off their own identities.

417

They gazed at one another distrustfully, like animals used to being thrashed. A urinous, sweaty smell rose from their ranks, like at the hospital. When they talked to you, you avoided their mouths, because the poor already smell of death inside.[16]

Céline (whose real name was Louis-Ferdinand Destouches) was a snob, an anti-Semite, and a fascist, and it is not always easy to separate fact from fantasy in his highly coloured genre of autobiographical writing. Still, the Frenchman certainly came to Detroit and worked for Ford for a period after the First World War—he claimed that he spent most of his leisure time and pay at a brothel which he discovered hidden in a back street of the northern suburbs —and his description of the trauma of life on the line has firsthand authenticity.

The whole building shook, and oneself from one's soles to one's ears was possessed by this shaking, which vibrated from the ground, the glass panes and all this metal, a series of shocks from floor to ceiling. One was turned by force into a machine oneself, the whole of one's carcass quivering in this vast frenzy of noise, which filled you within and all around the inside of your skull and lower down rattled your bowels, and climbed to your eyes in infinite, little, quick unending strokes.[17]

This din echoed inside Céline as he headed for freedom beyond the factory gates. Nothing he could do would shake it from his head—not even the pleasures of the northern suburbs. The noise stuck in the Frenchman's ears all night long, he complained, and when he puzzled over the bowed and broken posture of his fellow workers, he came to realize that he was wrong to think in purely psychological terms. They did not bow their heads in shame: it was, quite simply, the unremitting physical impact of noise that had broken them.

You give in to noise as you give in to war. . . . You've become old, all of a sudden—disgustingly old. Life outside you must put away; it must be turned into steel, too, into something useful.[18]

In 1936 Charlie Chaplin graphically portrayed the deadening grind of mass production in *Modern Times*. He had visited

Highland Park in the 1920s as a guest of Henry and Edsel Ford, but his film demonstrated evidence of some additional research. When the Little Tramp takes refuge in the washroom of the factory where he is working, he finds that he is being scrutinized by a television camera—and he is then sternly ordered by his boss, electronically manifest in a screen on the lavatory wall, to get back to work and stop shirking.

Twenty years after the Ford assembly line had first started to move in Highland Park, its deadening impact on the human spirit became a fashionable object of concern for writers. In *Brave New World*, Aldous Huxley satirized the totalitarian aspects of Ford production techniques, imagining a religion whose god was "Our Ford" and whose symbol was a cross with the top cut off, since it was the Model T which had inaugurated the brave new era.

Upton Sinclair, who, like John Reed, had been one of the progressive writers to idolize Ford at the time of the Five Dollar Day, now turned on his idol with all the anger of a convert deceived, writing and financing his own publication of *The Flivver King*, a compelling and painful fable that was half novella, half call to arms. When the Rouge Massacre was set in the context of the sustained and permanent exploitation inside the Rouge's walls, declared Sinclair, it was surely true to say that Ford cars now came in any colour, so long as it was "Fresh Human Blood."[19]

Poets, novelists, and film stars, of course, seldom have temperaments that empathize readily with the monotony of regimented manual labour. They tend to make the same complaints about factories as they do about armies. As the organizers of the 1932 Hunger March had shrewdly perceived, Henry Ford provided a ready-made symbol of the entire economic system whose deficiencies had been laid bare in the hard years since 1929—and in reality, conditions were no better inside the factories of General Motors or Chrysler than they were inside the Rouge. If anything, they were somewhat worse.

But Henry Ford could hardly complain at being selected as the target for the growing disillusionment with mass production, since he was one of its architects. And had he not, once upon a time, promised that he could transfuse it with humanity?

If the moment were to be named when the idealism of the Five Dollar Day was buried—or, at least, consigned in the direction of the cemetery—it would have to be the departure of the Reverend Samuel Marquis on January 25, 1921.[20] The Dean had been the conscience of the Ford Motor Company, brought in by Henry Ford's humanitarian ambitions and working hard to keep them alive, even when his employer's interests started straying towards politics and waterwheels. But with Marquis's disappearance at the beginning of the 1920s, moral considerations gave up the uneven battle with speed, efficiency, and the quest for sheer profit.

In retrospect, it is easy to see that the Ford Sociological Department could not possibly have survived in its original and idealistic form, since it owed its existence to Ford's initial monopoly of the moving assembly line. For a few brief, magical moments, the development of this accelerated production process gave Henry Ford a competitive edge that was almost unique in industrial history—he was a Dark Ages scribe who had stumbled upon the word processor—and the profit-sharing system administered by the Sociological Department was a response to the incredible riches which had flowed from his special, but temporary, advantage.

Once the other car companies had discovered the secret, however—and Henry Ford, to his credit, laid bare every detail of his innovations, making no effort to patent or conceal his industrial techniques—there was nothing very special about any Detroit car worker getting paid $5.00 a day. Everyone working on a moving line anywhere in the Motor City was soon remunerated at around $5.00 a day, and during the First World War inflation meant that the real purchasing power of the once-extraordinary Ford wage actually sank below pre-1914 levels. Five dollars a day proved over the long haul, in the words of Allan Nevins and

Frank Ernest Hill, official historians of the Ford Motor Company, to have been no more than "fairy gold."[21]

In 1919, $6.00 was set as the Ford daily minimum wage —and now it was just that, a minimum wage that workers could compare with the similar base rates being offered by the other car factories. There was no more talk of profit-sharing. In good years the Ford Motor Company distributed bonuses to its work force, but the Sociological Department had become a personnel department like any other. Sociology inspectors visited employee homes in order to investigate absenteeism or particularly drastic family problems, but Ford take-home pay was no longer dependent upon good behaviour. Henry had abandoned his bid for Utopia in Detroit.

Ford factories, however, remained models of enlightened working conditions—in their physical aspects, at least. They were bright, clean, and well ventilated, and they had safety records that were exemplary by the standards of the time. Henry's obsession with cleanliness showed itself in a cadre of 5,000 men with mops and buckets who did nothing all day long except keep the Rouge clean and polished. These cleaners and painters emptied rubbish cans every two hours, washed the windows once a week, and every month they got through more than 5,000 gallons of grey-blue paint and 11,000 gallons of egg-shell white—these particular colours having been determined after elaborate testing to discover what was most compatible with the working eye.[22]

In 1918 Ford had installed a special suction mechanism to syphon iron dust from the air in the making of piston rings—almost certainly the first such device in America, or anywhere else in the world—and similar Ford systems of climate control, using blowers and exhaust fans, set the pace for industry as a whole. Company nutritionists laid down standards whereby the box lunches brought into the factory and sold by outside contractors never contained less than 800 to 900 calories. The water temperature in the Rouge's 2,900 drinking fountains was controlled between fifty-five and sixty degrees. Salt pellets were provided in summer;

telephones, eye goggles, and respirators were sterilized every twenty-four hours. Even the coat racks were disinfected regularly.[23]

The pity was that, amidst all these admirable material surroundings, the spirit was quite, quite dead. There was a form of ventriloquism known in Detroit as the "Ford Whisper," a technique by which workers conversed with each other without the spotters noticing, and also a complaint known as "Ford Stomach," a nervous dyspepsia which stemmed from the tension of working too long in such conditions.

Ford's was no fun. The place had a tautness about it. Whether you worked in management, or whether you worked on the line, you could never quite be sure of anything. Henry liked to boast that he kept the executives around him perpetually off balance, and this spirit seeped right down to the factory floor. It might be a spotter, it might be a general lay-off, it might be the whim of a vindictive foreman, but, somehow, there was always the possibility that you might find yourself going home in the evening with a pink slip in your hand.

One thing you could be quite sure of when you worked at Ford was that you worked. Walter M. Cuningham, who published his own aggrieved account of his experiences as a Ford employee in the 1920s, suggested that it was the one linkage that could be most accurately predicted in mental association tests. People usually respond "dog" to "cat," and "chalk" to "cheese," but "Ford," said Cuningham, could never fail to elicit the reflex "work."[24]

Henry Ford, of course, had never denied or apologized for this. The ethos of the Five Dollar Day had always been a matter of industriousness and productivity. Work was the heart of the matter. But in those early days at Highland Park, with production records getting broken and new techniques being discovered, there seems to have been genuine excitement—exhilaration even—and clear evidence of self-motivation on the factory floor. Workers would cluster around to study the output figures posted on the notice board and resolve that, next week, they would do still better.[25]

But by the end of the 1920s this enthusiasm and spontaneity was long past. Work was just a grind at Ford, the same joyless tedium that you could find on any other factory floor. The burdens created by Henry's poor product decisions, furthermore, were being laid directly on the backs of his work force. As he had cut the price of the Model T in his desperate efforts to prove that the vehicle was not behind the times, the only area for economy had been in "speed-up" —more cars per man-hour. Sorensen set the increased production schedule, and everyone below him had to run that much faster to keep up.

"We were driving them, of course. We were driving them in those days . . . ," remembered Bill Klann, the production assistant. "Ford was one of the worst shops for driving men."[26]

Just plain hard work, however, was tolerable. The poison at Ford came from the arbitrariness and injustice that was created by the driving spirit. There was hypocrisy. When Ford introduced the Five Day Week in 1926, the first in the motor industry, William Cameron attempted to present it as a matter of labour reform, talking of the need for the workingman to have more leisure, as well as an extra day to spend his week's wages, and thus fertilize the economic cycle.

But the Ford Five Day Week of 1926 was no more than short-time working. Ford was first with it in the industry because Ford could not sell its cars. It was the alternative to mass lay-offs as the sales of the Model T inexorably declined. The men now got paid for only five days' work instead of six. It was the particular genius of Henry Ford to present a compulsory cut in his workers' weekly take-home pay as a gesture of enlightened generosity. Then, soon afterwards, came the massive, across-the-board lay-offs that were created by the shutdown of Model T production.

The lay-off was the bottom line, and it was not confined

to cataclysms like the changeover from Model T to Model A. On a lesser scale, it was an annual event. "Along about June or July it started," recalled one man.

The bosses would pick the men off a few at a time, telling them to stay home until they were notified to come back. . . . The foreman had the say. If he happened to like you, or if you sucked around him and did him favors—or if you were one of the bastards who worked like hell and turned out more than production—you might be picked to work a few weeks longer than the next guy. . . .

In October and November we began to trickle back into the plants. Again, the bosses had the full say as to who was rehired first. Years of service with the company meant nothing. . . .[27]

There were no guarantees. Men who had worked their way up to $8.00 or $10.00 a day could find themselves rehired at the basic rate. Older men might find themselves not rehired at all—one sad phenomenon noted by Detroit and Dearborn drugstores as rehiring time drew near was an increase in sales of hair dye—and workers did not even enjoy the dignity of a definite recall. They were given a date to report back to Miller Road with their lunch boxes, ready for a full day's work. But they might find themselves hanging around for several days before they were told that they were definitely needed. Until that happened, they were to be seen sitting aimlessly, opening their lunches, and eating them in the café across the street.[28]

"If I had been one of the men in the shop, and this had been done to me," said Harry Bennett, whose Service Department helped administer these arbitrary arrangements, "I'd have been in sympathy with the union myself."[29]

When compared to workers in Britain, or in almost any country in Europe, American workers were remarkably un-unionized at the moment that the depression came. In 1926, the year of the British General Strike, less than 4.5 million American workers belonged to unions—some 22 percent of those eligible for membership—and the proportion was falling.[30]

American employers had fought hard to keep labour organizers out of their factories, and on the whole, the courts and government had supported them. In 1921 a group of prominent industrialists had met in Chicago to promulgate the "American Plan," an aggressive campaign to preserve the open shop, and until depression came, they had met with considerable success.

Henry Ford never formally subscribed to the American Plan. He did not believe in joining anything. But he could fairly argue that the rational and relatively generous wages policy that he had pioneered in Detroit had played a major role in keeping unions out of American factories—and certainly out of the well-paid factories of the car industry. Detroit car workers might be afflicted by speed-up and unpredictable lay-offs, but they ranked as the most highly paid group of workers in the country—and, therefore, in the world. Where else on earth in the 1920s and 1930s were ordinary workingmen to be seen driving themselves to the factory in their own cars? The prevalence of bribery on the car industry's employment lines—outsiders and newcomers paying money to foremen who promised they could slip them into the system—was a reminder of how, for all its problems, Detroit was, relatively, Fat City.

Labour organizers had not helped their own cause. As wage cuts and lay-offs started stirring Detroit to the anger that exploded in the Ford Hunger March of 1932, the established labour organizations were still dominated by old-fashioned guilds and craft unions. These looked down on the workers of the mass-production industries. The generally accepted mouthpiece of the average worker was the American Federation of Labor, a body which was dominated by the craft unions, and attempts to establish labour organizations inside the car factories in the 1920s had foundered on the factionalism of the AFL's component guilds. The carriage makers, blacksmiths, painters, and upholsterers had all competed to swell their own memberships at each other's expense, and their recruiting was further handicapped by the mixture of scorn and envy that the traditional craftsman felt for the unskilled, but highly paid, toilers on the line.

The AFL played no role in the Ford Hunger March, nor in the almost spontaneous putting down of tools with which workers had rebelled, in January 1933, against the appalling wages and conditions at the Briggs Body Plant. But Roosevelt's coming to power and the provisions of Section 7A of his National Recovery Act of June 1933 gave the AFL the encouragement to reorganize in the Detroit area. Riding on the tide of militancy that the depression had provoked, strikes were organized in Flint, at the Fisher Body and Buick plants, and also in Detroit, where the Hudson Motor Company was the target.[31] Ford, it was generally agreed among labour organizers, would be a hard nut to crack, and the strategy was to pick off weaker plants before attempting to assail the Rouge.

The Roosevelt administration was alarmed by the novel threat of major strikes in the car industry. It seemed to jeopardize the two-sided industrial cooperation that was the basis of the New Deal, and in the spring of 1934 the President intervened, inviting the AFL leadership for confidential talks in the White House. Flattered by the invitation, the AFL leaders agreed to call off the strikes, securing in return the creation of an Automobile Labor Board, which would supposedly keep a special eye on their interests, and also a system of workers' voting rights, which appeared to offer a chance for the unions to gain recognition in the car factories.

But the effect of this complex system of proportional representation was, in fact, to enable employers to create their own tame "company unions." The AFL had been duped by the employers—or, worse, had sold out—and in the autumn of 1935, grass-roots dissatisfaction with the craft-union domination of the labour movement finally exploded. In a celebrated confrontation in Atlantic City, John L. Lewis, the charismatic mineworkers' leader, punched the leader of the Carpenters' Union in the face, thus making clear what the mass-production workers had come to feel about their craft-union brethren. Lewis headed the walkout of mass-production workers which led, later that year, to the formation of the Congress of Industrial Organizations, and a new, more militant phase in American industrial relations had begun.[32] Meeting at South Bend, Indiana, in April 1936, car workers' representatives agreed to affiliate with the CIO, and the United Auto Workers Union of today was born.[33]

The UAW's leadership continued the strategy of leaving Ford until last. They identified General Motors as their most vulnerable target, and in a series of aggressive sit-in strikes in the early months of 1937, they achieved their objectives with remarkable speed. GM recognized the UAW in February 1937, agreed to negotiate with the union for increased wages, granted seniority rights that would regulate the arbitrariness of lay-offs and rehirings, and started a study of speed-up in order to eliminate its abuses. When the UAW turned its attention to Chrysler, that company scarcely bothered to fight. On April 8, 1937, Walter P. Chrysler agreed to UAW terms which were very little different to those conceded by General Motors. So in May 1937, Ford suddenly stood alone.

The union wasted no time. Early in May 1937, it applied to the Dearborn City Council for a license to hand out pamphlets at the main gates of the Rouge plant on the twenty-sixth of the month, and since this right had been well enshrined in the Wagner Labor Relations Act of 1935, and had survived challenge in the courts, the council had little choice but to consent. Not surprisingly, however, someone made sure that May 26 was heavily ringed, well in advance, on the calendar of the Ford Service Department.

As union demonstrators started gathering on the morning of May 26, around the overpass which connected the parking lot on one side of Miller Road to the Rouge factory on the other, they were struck by the number of long black cars parked underneath the overpass, and by the number of behatted, heavy-set men inside them. There was no mistaking their sinister appearance. One was a noted local boxing champion, two were professional wrestlers, and some were even recognized as members of Detroit's more violent riverside gangs.[34]

But it was the middle of the day. Leaflet distribution had been scheduled for the early afternoon, when the changeover of shifts took place, and there were press reporters and photographers on hand. No one was prepared for what happened next.

The union-pamphlet distributors were led by a quartet of local activists, Richard Merriweather, Ralph Dunham, Richard Frankensteen, and Walter P. Reuther, the apple-faced young West Virginian who had argued his way into a job at Ford as tool-and-die leader in the spring of 1927. Reuther had soon argued his way out of his job at Ford, and virtually everywhere else in Detroit, as a result of his attempts to organize and raise the consciousness of his fellow workers. He was given his pink slip from the Rouge, and discovered that his name was on the blacklist which Ford and the other car companies distributed amongst each other.[35]

But Reuther had gone abroad for a period—he actually secured work as a tool-and-die leader in the Ford-assisted factory at Gorky in the Soviet Union—and he had used an alias to find employment when he got back to Detroit. Using the rumble seat of his Model A as a motorized soapbox, he had participated eloquently in the dramatic progress won by the UAW in the early months of 1937, and as he strode up onto the Ford overpass on May 26, 1937, he displayed every sign of expecting another victory.

A press photographer captured the moment as Reuther, Frankensteen, and their two bespectacled union colleagues watched the approach of the plug-uglies of the Ford Service Department. The four union men are all smiling, as if marvelling that such a collection of B-movie heavies should actually be gathered together in real life. Reuther looks particularly jaunty, with his hands on his hips and a gold watch chain slung across the waistcoat of his dark three-piece suit.

An instant later he felt a sharp crack across the back of his head. He went down, to be picked up, pummelled, thrown back down on the concrete, and picked up again. He counted eight different times when this happened to him, and each time, as he lay on the overpass footway, his assailants kicked him hard around the face and body.

Frankensteen, who was, if anything, a better-known union figure than Reuther at this time, found his coat pulled up over his head to form a strait jacket, and he was held helpless, with his arms above his head, as kicks and blows rained down upon him. Dunham received similar treatment. Afterwards he required ten days in hospital to get over his injuries. Merriweather's back was broken.[36]

When the attackers had finished their work, they pulled and dragged the four bleeding and semiconscious union men to the end of the overpass and dumped their bodies over the edge. There were thirty-nine steel steps leading down to the parking lot, and Walter Reuther later recalled, "The end of my spine hit every one."[37]

# 22

## DARK ANGEL

*Labor, like Israel, has many sorrows. Its women weep for their fallen.*
—JOHN. L. LEWIS[1]

The Battle of the Overpass was violence wielded by the Ford Motor Company in a fashion that was unashamed, exuberant almost, and this was no accident. In 1932 the Ford Hunger March had ended in bloodshed more by mishap than by design. The shootings at the Rouge gates do not seem to have been part of any company plan. But the intimidation which was openly deployed on the overpass against Walter Reuther, Richard Frankensteen, and their union colleagues in May 1937 represented a deliberate and calculated policy worked out by the director of Ford labour relations appointed by Henry Ford himself.

A few weeks before the confrontation, Edsel Ford had been summoned to his father's office, along with Charles Sorensen, to be briefed on the policy that Henry Ford wished them to adopt, now that General Motors and Chrysler had both recognized the UAW. The old man was obdurate. No matter what his competitors might consent to, Henry Ford was not willing to meet personally with any union official. He severely instructed the two men to follow his example, and he further forbade them from discussing labour relations with anyone, and certainly not the press.[2]

"If things get too warm for any of us," he said, "we should take a trip and get away from the plant. I've picked someone to talk with the unions. I want a strong, aggressive man who can take care of himself in an argument, and I've got him."[3]

Describing the episode later, Charles Sorensen said that he was not particularly surprised to discover that the strong,

aggressive man who was now being given total responsibility
for Ford's dealing with the unions should be the man who
had been behind all the thugs and spotters of the Ford
Service Department. But he could see that this further
extension to the powers of Harry Bennett came as a nasty
shock to Edsel.[4]

Legend traces Harry Bennett's relationship with the Ford
Motor Company back to a brawl in the streets of New York
sometime in the months before America's entry into the
First World War. Bennett was a sailor, just off his ship, and
he was saved from being thrown into the nearest police
station by Arthur Brisbane, the Hearst newspaper columnist, who had happened to see the fight develop. Brisbane
was able to persuade the police that Bennett was not to
blame, since, as the journalist saw it, Bennett had only gone
to the rescue of a friend.

By further coincidence, Brisbane was on his way to an
appointment with Henry Ford, who turned out to be more
interested by the tale of the street fight and by the pugnacious
young sailor than he was by the scheduled subject of the
meeting. Brisbane had brought Bennett along with him, and
Henry promptly offered the young hero a security job at the
Rouge.

"Can you shoot?" he asked Bennett.[5]

If this story is true, it is difficult to understand why
Harry Bennett's first recorded position at the Ford Motor
Company should have been as an artist in the photographic
department.[6] But many aspects of the ex-sailor's improbable
character and career are overladen with myth. It suited both
Bennett and his detractors to play up the tale that his origins
were rough and violent—when, in fact, he started his youth
in the tranquil university town of Ann Arbor, where his
stepfather was a professor of engineering. In his teens
Bennett spent several years studying at the Detroit Fine
Arts Academy[7]—hence, presumably, his start in the Ford
art department—and his claims that his pre-Ford career
included Secret Service work, underwater sabotage, a sabre

through his forearm, and a bullet through his side have never been substantiated.[8]

What is certain is that Harry Bennett knew next to nothing about cars.* He was not a mechanic or an engineer, not a designer, an accountant, or a lawyer even. It was a comment on the enterprise which Henry Ford had created by the middle of the 1930s that Harry Bennett's very lack of car-making experience should be the qualification he needed to rise to the top of it. The Ford power structure was so ill defined, as more than one journalist discovered:

It is a little difficult to sort out the Ford executives for the reason that Mr. Ford does not believe in titles. . . . Ask any of the executives what their job may be, and after a few minutes' thought, they may admit that they look after this or take care of that. But never say they: "I am the Sales Manager" or "I am the Chief Engineer."[9]

In later years Harry Bennett's empire of darkness was to be interpreted as an alien growth which overwhelmed Ford from the outside, seizing control of a great industrial corporation through arm twisting, violence, and bribery, and Harry Bennett certainly employed these weapons to full effect. But the power that the man acquired was all Ford—the logical, inevitable consequence of what the Ford Motor Company had become by the middle of the 1930s.

It had started two decades earlier with the departures of John Dodge and James Couzens, two independent minds who were never overawed by Henry. Then had come the executive shake-out in the early 1920s—the elimination of Wills, Knudsen, Klingensmith, Marquis, Lee, and a number of others who had all played their part in the glory days. With the exception of Wills, these men had never quite been

---

* "I wasn't a car man," he told David C. Smith in the lengthy series of interviews he granted Smith towards the end of his life. "I drove a Franklin most of the time I was there."

"At Ford?" responded Smith. "You didn't drive a Ford?"

"No," replied Bennett. "I liked this car [the Franklin]. It didn't have water in the radiator or anything. . . ."

partners, but each had a stature of his own that derived from the contribution he had made to the greatness that was Ford; it was because of their stature, ultimately, that they were frozen out. Every business enterprise, said Emerson, is "the lengthened shadow of one man," and the shade cast by Henry Ford was wide and chill.

Edsel Ford had been the one possible source of an alternative line of command inside the company, the only player with the guaranteed tenure around whom some rational network of authority might have been developed. But Edsel's bid for his own power structure, aborted with the departure of Kanzler, had been crushed completely with the Guardian fiasco. So that left just Sorensen, "Cast Iron Charlie," keeping the line moving, getting the cars out, doing what the Ford Motor Company was supposed to be doing; and Bennett, Harry, the ultimate henchman, helping Mr. Ford do what Mr. Ford wanted to do.

Soon after Bennett had started working for Henry Ford, the carmaker had given the ex-sailor some advice.

"Harry," he said, "never try to outguess me."

"You mean I should never try to understand you?" Bennett responded, unsure of what his master was getting at.

"Well," replied Ford, "that's close enough."

Asking the same question a few days later, and receiving the same answer, Bennett worked out that Henry Ford usually had two motives for everything he did: the motive that he gave, and the real one.[10] Henry Ford was telling him, Bennett decided, never to probe the difference between the two, to execute his master's will without raising questions or difficulties, and he bent himself single-mindedly to this task, becoming the executive arm of Henry Ford's increasing egotism and whimsicality. If Harry Bennett had not existed, the great carmaker would have had to invent him.

Harry Bennett liked bow ties. He always wore one, and it was typical of the man that he should explain this habit not in terms of sartorial preference, but as preventive strategy in the event of getting into a fight. Conventional neckties, he would explain, can be used to strangle you; bow ties come undone. In retirement he was to live in a shapeless orange jumpsuit and slippers,* but while working at Ford, he took his cue from the boss and was invariably turned out in a well-cut and -pressed suit. With his reddish, slicked-down hair and bright blue eyes, Harry Bennett was an engaging character. Though short—he was an effervescent five foot six—he had kept in good shape since his boxing days in the Navy. He spoke fluently, and he could tell a joke well. Even people with every reason to dislike the man had to admit that he was amusing company.

These personable qualities advanced Harry Bennett rapidly through the early stages of his Ford career, in which he seems to have been no more burdened with formal job titles than anyone else. He gained control of the Rouge Service Department sometime in the early 1920s when he suggested that workers were better employed making cars than spying on each other,[11] and, following his purge, the department became effectively his own private army. He staffed it with superannuated boxers and football players, together with thugs whose legal work experience was ill defined, but its ranks were not manned exclusively by spies and storm troopers. They also included a good proportion of dogsbodies who could turn their hands to just about anything.

Arriving at the Michigan State Fair one year to inspect the Ford exhibit, Henry Ford was disappointed by the array of machines and motorcars with which his company had filled its space.

"This isn't the way I remember State Fairs when I was a boy," he said plaintively.

Next day Harry Bennett brought his master back for a second look, and this time Henry Ford stepped out of his car to find himself surrounded by a field of waving wheat, a field of soya beans, cows mooing, sheep baaing, the crops growing to their full height, and the livestock tended by venerable rustics sucking straws.

* He was photographed in this curiously toddler-like costume by both Jim Dunne (with David C. Smith) and by David Lewis in 1974.

"That's nice, Harry," said Henry Ford.[12]

Getting things done was the secret of Harry Bennett's success. His employer had only to ask, "Can you take care of that, Harry?" and the problem, whatever it might be, was taken care of, from the spiriting away of serving girls to getting the jury in the Sapiro trial dismissed.[13]

This notable coup had coincided with the closing down of Model T production, and since the shutdown ended the regular pattern of Henry Ford's visits to Highland Park, Harry Bennett took the trouble during these months to drive over to Fair Lane every morning, wondering if there was anywhere in particular that the boss wanted to go that day. By the time Model A production had gathered momentum, the morning rendezvous had become a regular habit, and for the best part of twenty years thereafter, Harry Bennett either picked up Henry Ford in the morning or spoke to him on the telephone. He often took him home as well.

Harry Bennett liked to talk tough—and to act tough as well. He had a target box standing on one of the green metal filing cabinets in his office, and he would whip an air pistol from his desk for impromptu sessions of target practice. Visitors waiting in his outer office were puzzled by muffled ringing sounds coming through the door which did not sound quite like a telephone. It was the target box, which struck a bell every time Harry hit the bull's-eye.

Nor did Bennett confine his shooting to the paper target. He boasted that he had once shot an evil-smelling cigar from the mouth of a visitor impolite enough not to extinguish it before entering the room. Prince Louis Ferdinand Hohenzollern, the Kaiser's grandson, who came to work at Ford for several years in the 1930s, had firsthand experience of the little man's marksmanship when he ushered in a visitor who inadvertently failed to remove his hat. Bennett shot a hole through it.[14]

He fortified his tough-guy act by keeping lions and tigers as pets. They roamed the Wild West-style ranch that he constructed on the Dearborn side of Ann Arbor, and occasionally he would bring the animals to work, walking them around the Rouge on leashes, or even slipping them into the backseats of visitors' cars as a joke. One such lion, left to slumber, woke, according to Dearborn lore, to find himself being driven through the city streets, and roused himself to place his paw affectionately upon the driver's shoulder.

After the driver had fled, the beast disembarked to inspect the neighbourhood, ending up at the Dearborn Police Station, where the duty officer took matters into his own hands. His official report recorded that the lion had "hanged himself"—this being the world's only known case of leonine suicide.[15]

Henry Ford just loved stories like this. Bennett's appetite for danger gratified the violence in the carmaker's own character, the aggression that had torn the doors off the would-be replacement to his Model T. Harry Bennett was the tough, strong son to Henry Ford that Edsel was not—and Harry never disagreed with the boss or showed signs of wanting to lead a life of his own.

Harry loved intrigue and melodrama. He had a house on Grosse Ile, down the Detroit River from the Rouge, where he would press a button to swing back a wall of shelves and reveal a winding staircase going down to the speedboats in his boat well below. He also catered to the old man's irresponsibility. Never fond of using his own office, Henry Ford got in the habit of meeting visitors in Bennett's because, he said, he could always get up and walk out whenever he wanted to.[16]

Many great men feel the need for a court jester to handle the anarchic and irresponsible currents that flow through their soul, and Harry Bennett played this role for Henry Ford—while also feeding his master's fantasies of omnipotence. Was there anything at all that the fixer could not fix?

"Put it this way," replied Harry, when a journalist once asked him this question in the presence of Henry Ford. "If Mr. Ford told me to blacken out the sun tomorrow, I might have trouble fixing it. But you'd see a hundred thousand sons-of-bitches coming through the Rouge gates in the morning all wearing dark glasses."

Mr. Ford thought that was a marvellous joke.[17]

Detroit's car production slumped dramatically during the depression years, but the Motor City remained the nation's principal source of a commodity for which demand did not flag: booze. Chicago gained its reputation for gangster activity during Prohibition, but Detroit was the place that most of Chicago's liquor came from. It was just a few yards away from Canada, by car, boat, or train, and Detroiters could look out across the Detroit River to the towers of the Hiram Walker distillery, which enjoyed record sales during the years that America went "dry." In the mid1920s, Windsor's liquor shipments to Detroit increased at an annual rate of 25 percent, to exceed a million gallons in 1928—and the Canadian authorities charged duty on every bottle.[18]

Henry Ford was, from the first, a temperance crusader. There is some evidence that his father, William, had a drinking problem[19]—often a spur to teetotalism in a son. Henry had imbibed temperance along with the other puritanical radicalisms of his youth, and in this he was similar to a majority of the inhabitants of Michigan. In May 1918, by popular referendum, the state went "dry" on its own initiative, twelve months before the rest of America.*

Conferring illegality, however, upon a pleasure which many people persisted in considering harmless proved disastrously counterproductive. The Prohibition experiment transferred some $2 billion a year from brewers, distillers, and their shareholders into the hands of murderers and crooks,[20] making possible the extraordinarily embedded role that organized crime plays in modern American life. In Detroit the gangs thrived with particular vigour.

---

* Michigan was the first state to adopt the amendment repealing Prohibition on April 10, 1933, but corners of the state remain abstemious to the present day. The city of Grosse Pointe Park did not repeal prohibition for its restaurants until November 1984, and the city of Temperance, in the southeast corner of the state, remains quite dry.

They organized on an ethnic basis. The Black Hand—predecessors of the Mafia—were of Sicilian and Neapolitan origin. The city's fruit and vegetable markets had long been dominated by Italian syndicates. There were black gangs and Polish gangs. Bootlegging, which often involved doing business with the city's most respected names, provided obvious "upward mobility" for the bright children of immigrant families, and few were brighter than the young Jewish immigrants on Detroit's west and northwest side, many of them worshippers in the congregation of Rabbi Leo Franklin at Temple Beth El.

Detroit's Jewish gangs seem to have started in self-defence, protecting the ghetto's shopkeepers against hoodlums from Highland Park and Hamtramck. But Prohibition, and the ease with which supplies could be obtained from across the river, provided too good an opportunity to miss. Canadian coast guards and customs officials positively refused to cooperate with U.S. liquor agents; the Detroit Police were easy to bribe.*

When the Windsor-Detroit roadway beneath the river was opened in November 1930, it was promptly christened the "funnel." Ferries sped to and fro on the water above, openly transporting liquor in bulk. And when the *Detroit News* published photographs illustrating all the details of this traffic,[22] it simply diversified for a few weeks, using the innumerable creeks and mud flats of Lake St. Clair. In winter bootleggers could choose any route they pleased, motoring freely across the lake, with their car doors open for rapid escape in the event of the ice giving way.

Harry Fleisher, Irving Milberg, Harry Altman, and other Jewish youths living in Highland Park got started on Oakland Street, three blocks east of Woodward Avenue, where they set up their own distillery in a building that became known as the Oakland "Sugar House."[23] They soon joined

---

* The city's police force reached such a low ebb in these years that the recruited intake of 1928 averaged 83 on a mental test equivalent to the modern I.Q. The Detroit Fire Department required a minimum score of 100 in this test, but the police department was satisfied with 65.[21]

forces with Sammy "Purple" Cohen and the Bernstein brothers—Abe, Isadore, and Ray—who, like the Sugar House Gang, had progressed from shoplifting and minor extortion to serious bootlegging. By the middle 1920s the Purple Gang dominated crime in Detroit, supplying Old Log Cabin whisky from Canada not only to the city, but also to the Capone organization in Chicago. It was Buggs Moran's highjacking of a shipment of Old Log Cabin from the Purple Gang which led to the St. Valentine's Day Massacre of the O'Banion brothers and other members of the Moran gang in Chicago in 1929.[24]

Henry Ford was both fascinated and terrified by the lawlessness that Prohibition had helped provoke. Dressed in flashy clothes, the Purple Gang swaggered openly into restaurants and box seats at baseball games like royalty. They acted as if they owned Detroit. When a popular, campaigning broadcaster, Jerry Buckley, a former Ford employee,* dared openly to denounce the gangland warlords, he was shot down, machine-gunned as he sat in the lobby of the La Salle Hotel.[26]

Henry Ford, of course, did not see any connection between the spread of lawlessness and the principles he held dear. He blamed not the law, but the people who broke the law by continuing to drink, thus supplying the gangsters with their marketplace. He threatened, in the event that Prohibition were repealed, to shut down his production line—which, as the *New Yorker* remarked, would neatly secure the destruction of Detroit's two leading industries at one blow.[27] He proposed that the dead capacity of shutdown distilleries might be used to produce denatured alcohol—"a cleaner, nicer, better fuel for automobiles than gasoline"[28]—but he had no comment on the observation that bootlegging was, essentially, a motorized crime.

Henry Ford was implicated in all the developments he

---

* Buckley had been one of the agents employed by Ford to investigate Truman Newberry's expenditures in the disputed 1918 election for the Senate.[25]

deplored. Prohibition led to gangsterism, and when the gangs were not shipping drink, they developed sidelines like kidnapping, which became an epidemic in the 1920s. Kidnapping was a frequent topic of Ford's conversations with Harry Bennett, for though conspicuously nonchalant about his own safety—the carmaker walked and drove around Dearborn with a remarkable lack of escorts or protection—Henry Ford was terrified on his grandchildren's behalf. He felt sure they were the object of sinister kidnapping plots, and he encouraged Harry Bennett to cultivate contacts with the underworld of Detroit, and of other major cities, in the hope of gathering advance intelligence of such conspiracies.

There were realistic grounds for his concern. In March 1924, the Detroit Police arrested racketeers who had threatened to blind the Ford grandchildren unless Edsel paid protection money,[29] and there had been at least one previous kidnapping attempt. But implicit in Henry Ford's anxiety, which amounted at times to a neurosis, was the old man's assumption that Edsel was too weak, that he could not be trusted to protect his own family.

Edsel, in fact, had organized very thorough security arrangements both in Indian Village and at his Grosse Pointe home. All the guards and chauffeurs of the estate were permanently armed.[30] They were licensed by the Grosse Pointe Police to drive straight through red lights if they felt that a halt might endanger their passengers. They patrolled the house and lakeshore of Gaukler Point constantly, and if one of the family ventured out into the grounds for the briefest walk, their promenade was monitored through binoculars.[31]

None of this impressed Henry Ford. He insisted that two of Harry Bennett's Servicemen, Frank Holland and Jim Brady,[32] should ride extra shotgun on all major trips away from home by Henry II and the other grandchildren, and that Edsel himself should be shadowed wherever he went—which provided a convenient excuse for Henry being supplied with regular and detailed reports on all his son's movements. Most pernicious of all, however, Henry Ford allowed Harry Bennett to develop the relationships that led to one of the more extraordinary chapters in modern industrial history: the establishing of day-to-day working links between the Ford Motor Company and organized crime.

In his ghostwritten memoirs, *We Never Called Him Henry*, Harry Bennett accused Henry Ford of having "a profound morbid interest in crime and criminals."[33] This was the reason, Bennett claimed, for the much-vaunted Ford policy of rehabilitating convicts. The carmaker, according to Bennett, derived a perverted thrill from meeting these jail-birds, and liked to cross-question them, when they arrived at the factory, about the details of their criminal lives.

The accusation reveals more about Harry Bennett than about Henry Ford. The carmaker had many ugly sides to his character, but they do not justify the theft from him of his genuine idealism. By Bennett's own account, in fact, Ford's interviews with ex-convicts were frequently limited to the observation "I'll bet a woman got you into it"—this comment usually being delivered before the man had had a chance to say anything—while Ford's recorded interest in practicing criminals was confined to one peevish query as to why, in view of all the company's "contacts around town," it was not possible to discover the details of a particular kidnapping case.[34] There is no evidence that Henry Ford ever knowingly met with anyone pursuing a career in crime, and he certainly never cultivated such men as friends.

The same cannot be said, however, about Harry Bennett. He positively revelled in making personal contact with the underworld, and his memoirs are a boastful catalogue of the murderers, racketeers, and extortionists whose friendship he purchased with the funds and influence of the Ford Motor Company.

There was Chester LaMare, a short, bull-necked Sicilian, leader of the Italian mobsters who challenged the Purple Gang's preeminence in the late 1920s, and who managed largely to eliminate them by the end of the decade in a series of bloody ambushes and gangland executions.[35] This made LaMare the effective boss of organized crime in Detroit. Federal agents estimated his bootlegging income for 1928 at $215 million.[36] Bennett gave LaMare a car agency, the Crescent Motor Sales Company, whose premises became the gang's headquarters,[37] and he also granted the gangster the profitable concession for supplying fruit to the canteens and lunch stands of the Ford factories. This was a particularly notable manoeuvre in view of the fact that the concession for supplying box lunches to the Rouge—a license to print money—was granted at this time to the family of a local judge, His Honour Leo J. Schaefer.[38]

Joe Tocco was another of the Italian warlords who, like LaMare, would consort with Harry Bennett, deferentially referring to him always as "Boss." In his memoirs, Bennett describes Tocco showing him how he had wired dynamite to the walls of a restaurant that refused to pay him protection money.[39] Bennett actually invited Leonard Cellura, a mobster known as Black Leo, to lunch at Dearborn at the same time as the governor of Michigan, and he got Lou Colombo, an attorney who specialized in representing Black Hand/Mafia chieftains, retained as a legal adviser to the company. Touring other major crime centres at Henry Ford's suggestion, Harry Bennett made contact in the East with Murder, Incorporated, and two of its gangster members, Joe Adonis and Tony D'Anna, were given franchises to truck Ford cars to dealers on the eastern seaboard.[40]

Social reformers liked to claim that it was sometimes difficult to tell the difference between crime and big business in the 1930s, and that was graphically the case for any visitor who paid a call on Henry Ford's right-hand man during these years. Harry Bennett ruled his empire from the Administration Building that the company had opened on Schaefer Road overlooking the Rouge, but his office was not on one of the upper floors. It was located in a corner of the basement, right beside the garage, so that his visitors could be driven straight in to see him without anyone being aware of their identity.[41]

The door to Bennett's inner office was controlled by secret buttons beneath his own desk and that of his secretary, a burly ex-linebacker from one of the University of Michigan's toughest squads. The lock clicked heavily before and after you had entered,[42] and anyone lingering in that corner of the building uninvited was likely to be approached by one of the heavy-set gentlemen who were fixtures of the local scenery, and whose jackets bulged below one armpit. You would be hard put to recognize you were at the nerve centre of a major American industrial enterprise, what with the pool-hall clientele, the air thick with menace, the odd ringing sounds coming through the door. By the middle of the 1930s, Harry Bennett had woven the Ford Motor Company into a network of underworld connections with hoodlums of largely Italian origin, and the unholy alliance came into its own in the battle which Ford fought against the unions with increasing ferocity as the decade went by.

Arnold Freeman, a reporter on the *Detroit Times*, recognized one of the thugs lying in wait for Walter Reuther on May 26, 1937, as a suspect who had been questioned recently at the Detroit Police Headquarters in connection with a holdup, and when tackled, the man freely admitted what he was doing loitering that afternoon in Miller Road.

"We were hired," he said, "as far as I know, temporary, to take care of these union men that are to distribute these pamphlets," adding that the hirings had been carried out by the Ford Service Department, who were allocating four recruits to take care of each UAW pamphlet distributor.[43]

Confronted with such allegations, Harry Bennett just laughed. The beatings handed out to Reuther, Frankensteen, and the others, he said, came from ordinary Ford workers, and they demonstrated the feeling of the average man on the line, who wanted nothing to do with union agitators or their works.[44]

*

Harry Bennett's reign at Ford has often been compared to the regime of some late medieval potentate—a Sforza or a Borgia. But if Bennett matched such tyrants in ruthlessness, he dispensed hospitality with equal grace and prodigality. Anne Morrow Lindbergh went to one of the summer rodeo parties that Bennett gave on his Ann Arbor estate—her husband, Charles, had been hired by Ford as an aeronautic adviser—and she found him a delightful host, "a compact little man" who gave her "the impression of youth and taut trigger health."[45]

Mrs. Lindbergh was amazed by the lengths to which Harry had gone for the entertainment of his guests—false illuminated trees lit the way through the fields to a picturesque "log" cabin that was, in fact, made of metal—and the host himself was dressed in cowboy costume, serenading the assembled company with tuneful ballads. Mrs. Lindbergh wondered whether the notorious chief of the Ford Service Department might not nurse "a hankering to be a troubador."[46]

It was the Godfather syndrome. A lot of people liked Harry Bennett. By his own, twisted standards, he operated to a strict code of honour, and he liked to preside personally over hearings into disciplinary infractions. If the offenders were young, he would have their parents summoned to hear the justice that he proclaimed.[47]

"God knows how many college graduates and professional men—doctors and dentists and lawyers—there are in the state of Michigan thanks to Harry Bennett," the writer Booton Herndon was told in 1968. "College students were given easy jobs, like night watchmen, night drivers, with time to study. He paid the tuition for a lot of guys."[48]

College football players were special recipients of Bennett's benevolence. The University of Michigan squad worked en bloc at Ford during the summers of the late 1930s, reporting every day at the Rouge for light duties, but spending most of the time training under their coach,

Bennett's drinking companion, Harry Kipke.* U. of M. teams enjoyed unrivalled success in these years, but this brought little joy to the Ford workers who witnessed the annual arrival of the football players.

"Married men with families were getting laid off for the summer," remembers a union activist from those years, "and here were college kids coming in and getting paid for doing nothing."[49] The injustice of it proved the final push needed to persuade quite a number of men to join the UAW.

Harry Bennett knew how to deal with unions, however. The Battle of the Overpass was only the opening salvo in his campaign against labour organization inside Ford, and to serve as his storm troops he assembled semipermanent gangs of thugs similar to those who had beaten up Reuther and his friends. Known as "outside squads," these drew heavily on Bennett's underworld contacts. They were specially recruited combat groups whose mission was to identify and neutralize labour activists in every aspect of Ford activities, and—thanks to the organizer of one such outside squad who turned state's evidence in 1939—we have a vivid idea of how the outside squads worked.

"Fats" Perry was given the job of coordinating anti-union activities in Dallas, Texas, where Ford had an assembly plant. The plant's champion tug-of-war team were relieved of their ordinary duties to form the core of an outside squad, and this was armed with pistols, whips, blackjacks, lengths of rubber hose called "persuaders," and a variety of other weapons, some of which were made up by a department in the plant itself.[50]

"If it takes bloodshed," announced the plant management to two mass meetings of the work force, "we'll shed blood right down to the last drop."[51] They proved as good as their

* When the University of Michigan, unhappy at Harry Kipke's style and methods, dismissed their football coach, Harry Bennett gave him a concession to purchase parts and accessories, on commission, for Ford. He also had Kipke nominated for the university's Board of Regents, and financed the campaign which got the ex-coach elected to the same governing body which had dismissed him.

word. Fats Perry estimated that his squad handed out some twenty-five or thirty beatings to union organizers in the summer months of 1937—and the beatings were brutal. W. J. Houston, an attorney representing the union, was felled to the pavement, kicked mercilessly in head, groin, and limbs, and lapsed into unconsciousness just as his assailants started to jump up and down on his stomach.[52] The beating was so savage that Houston decided to give up the struggle, and actually moved his law practice to another city.

Fats Perry's proudest achievement was the disruption of a union meeting held in a Dallas park to show a new labour film, *Millions of Us*. The gathering was organized by the Textile Workers' Union and the Socialist Party, but this did not prevent the Ford outside squad going in, demolishing the projection equipment, destroying the film, and kidnapping the projectionist, who was deposited some hours later in a newspaper office, naked, beaten, tarred, and feathered.

Perry's outside squad was assisted in this attack by the local park rangers. Official cooperation was a feature of all Ford's anti-union activities in Dallas. When the police got word of labour organizers arriving in town from another city, they would pass the details on to the company.

The authorities in Kansas City were less cooperative—to start with. In the spring and summer of 1937, the UAW made major progress at both the GM and Ford plants there —thanks, in no small part, to the local police, who were reasonably gentle with the union pickets. GM surrendered quite quickly, as it had done in Detroit, reaching an agreement with the UAW, but in October 1937, Ford announced that it was not willing to compromise. Rather than surrender to the union, it was going to close down its Kansas City plant and move its operations to Omaha.

The response was immediate. The transfer of the Ford facilities would mean the loss to Kansas City of some 2,500 jobs, and the city manager, H. F. McElroy, urgently telegraphed Harry Bennett, then flew to Dearborn for negotiations which proved to be little less than surrender. In return for Ford agreeing to reopen its Kansas City factory, the authorities pledged that "men who wished to work" would, in future, be "permitted to do so without interference"—which was another way of saying that the police would, henceforward, break up picket lines and assist strike-breakers. When, just before Christmas 1937, an overzealous sheriff from Jackson County, which was not party to the agreement, arrested a Ford outside squad whose twenty-eight members were armed, between them, with twelve shotguns, fourteen revolvers, and sixty assorted other weapons, the prosecuting attorney declined to prefer charges, declaring that the city was quite happy for the men to be released without bail.[53]

"A striker caught with a slingshot was sentenced to the municipal farm," telegraphed Homer Martin, the UAW leader, to the Kansas City authorities in protest, "but, with company backing, thugs can carry an arsenal fit for the army and you release them until you decide whether you will issue charges. . . . On the lighted cross of the magnificent City Hall hangs the broken body of Justice."[54]

Modern sentiment would tend to endorse the indignation of Homer Martin. Intimidation stretching from routine, daytime pavement sluggings to the blackmail of an entire city seems scarcely possible in a twentieth-century democracy. But Ford's intransigent stand against labour found many supporters in America in the late 1930s. Professor David Lewis has demonstrated the remarkably consistent endorsement Ford received in these years from public-opinion surveys: one poll conducted by the Curtis Publishing Company in May 1937, the very month of the Battle of the Overpass, showed that 59.1 percent of Americans believed that the Ford Motor Company treated its labour force better than any other company. The second-ranked company, Bell Telephone, received only 14.1 percent, and General Motors, who had recognized the UAW three months earlier, got only 6.3 percent.[55] The legend of the Five Dollar Day died hard.

"We have no sympathy with the persecution of Henry

Ford," ran a syndicated editorial carried by many small-town papers. "Let persecution be confined to the men who have not done as much for working men as he has. Ford has kept his money at work making more and more jobs instead of hoarding it as he might have done."[56]

There was a solid band of sentiment in middle America which genuinely believed that union organizers were sinister manipulators who were misleading the ordinary honest American working-man—and this was certainly Henry Ford's belief.

"Labor unions are part of the exploitation scheme," he had told the *Christian Science Monitor* in 1923. "The men probably don't know it, and maybe their leaders don't even know, that they are really but tools in the hands of the master exploiters."[57]

Henry Ford classed the likes of Walter Reuther and Richard Frankensteen along with Wall Street, the Jews, and his other populist bogies. "All wars, labor unions, strikes, by an insidious conspiracy group of war mongers and mongrelds," ran one typical entry in his notebooks.[58]

There was a sense in which, after his seventy-fifth birthday in 1938, Henry Ford ceased to inhabit the twentieth century. One source of Harry Bennett's influence over the old man was the illusion of potency he gave him, the chance to deny what was happening to his body and mind. But those who endorsed the Ford war upon the unions included some very prominent figures indeed. One staunch supporter of Harry Bennett was J. Edgar Hoover, director of the FBI.

"Dear Harry," ran a letter from Hoover to Bennett in 1943. "I wanted you to know how much I appreciate your fine cooperation."[59]

A study of FBI papers obtained under the Freedom of Information Act makes it clear that Harry Bennett worked very closely with the FBI in the late 1930s and early 1940s, and also explains why the Ford Service Chief was able to operate so long outside the law. The country's principal law-enforcement agency gave him a license to do so. Having dealt initially with local Detroit FBI officers, Harry Bennett met Hoover for the first time in January 1939, and the FBI director sent the Ford Service Chief autographed photographs of their meeting to commemorate the occasion.[60]

The relationship started in the mid-1930s with understandable distrust on the FBI's part when Bennett presented agents with evidence of petty corruption in the Michigan governor's office. "Bennett is no friend of the FBI," scrawled Hoover on the bottom of a report of November 1, 1935.[61] But an unceasing flow of information—together with active personal assistance on Bennett's part—began to alter this. "On numerous occasions when serious crimes occurred in Detroit and elsewhere in the state," ran a report of March 30, 1939, "he has personally entered activities of the investigation and been of considerable assistance."

By 1939 John Bugas, head of the FBI's Detroit operations, was endorsing the Ford Service Chief as "a very valuable friend of this office," and Bugas got in the habit of visiting Bennett's basement office regularly for an exchange of tips. Obviously enamoured of Bennett, Bugas described him to Hoover as "without question one of the best sources of information along practically any line in this area."[62]

One line that Bugas found particularly helpful was the data which Bennett had collected on local labour agitators, and which he made available to the Bureau, according to a report of October 1939.

This office has contacted the Ford Motor Company for the past several weeks to obtain pertinent data from their vast files on Communist activities. This office has been able to procure a great abundance of important data along this line from the Ford Motor Company.[63]

The FBI's faith in Harry Bennett does not appear to have been shaken by its subsequent discovery that Bennett had purchased many of these Communist names from Gerald L. K. Smith, the local Fascist leader, at one dollar per head.[64]

Henry Ford's grandchildren had graduated beyond playing with the cash registers in the Rouge canteen. They spent occasional months working quite seriously in the plant, and one day Benson Ford asked Harry Bennett if he had been listening to the propaganda that the UAW had been broadcasting recently.

"You should listen to them some time," he said.

The union had set up its own little radio station in a downtown Detroit office building, but the transmitting signal was weak.

"How the devil do you get it?" inquired Harry Bennett.

"Easy," replied Henry Ford's second grandson. "You just push one of the selector buttons on a Ford car radio."

One union sympathizer in the radio department had evidently been tuning the preset buttons before the sets were installed[65]—a more elegant expression of grass-roots grievance than the strategy adopted by workers in the body assembly, who deposited dead rats behind the panelling of hollow car doors.

The real battle was fought in the courts, however, where the union brought charges through the National Labor Relations Board against Ford. Based largely on testimony relating to the Battle of the Overpass and the activities of the outside squads, including the confessions of Fats Perry, they made up an unanswerable case. Ford's violations of the Wagner Act had been many and flagrant. It was clearly only a matter of time before the company would be compelled to come to some sort of compromise with the unions, and preparing for that day, Harry Bennett showed that his politicking was as good as his street fighting.[66]

He was aided by dissension within the union ranks, for, confronted by Ford intransigence, UAW leaders had been divided on tactics, and their disagreements were intensified by personal rivalries. Ambitious Young Turks like Frankensteen and Reuther, who was by now president of the UAW's Detroit West Side Local, soon grew restive at the more moderate leadership of Homer Martin.

Harry Bennett saw his chance. He invited Martin to the Rouge to talk over their differences, flattered the union leader with a private luncheon and a meeting with an attentive and conciliatory Henry Ford, and then showed him around the factory. Martin, a former preacher, had never been inside the Rouge and was both surprised and impressed, as all visitors were, by the brightness and cleanliness of the plant which had become, for union propagandists, the archetype of dark, satanic mills.[67] The UAW leader cautiously agreed to off-the-record negotiations. He seems to have cherished the hope that Henry Ford's old interest in the workers might be rekindled, and he knew that Edsel Ford, generally assumed to represent the future of the company, did not share his father's intransigent views.

Playing on this, Bennett led Martin into what proved to be a fatal trap. In late December 1938, it was announced that the Ford Motor Company and the UAW had, through Martin, come to a tentative agreement. The details were never spelled out, but they involved the union's withdrawal of all the lawsuits it had launched against Ford through the National Labor Relations Board.

The consequence was uproar, for it was already clear that Ford was facing almost certain defeat in the courts. The legal cases were the union's long-term hope of victory, their most significant bargaining tokens, and in return for their surrender, Martin had negotiated little that did not depend upon the good faith of Henry Ford and Harry Bennett.

Activists like Reuther denounced Martin as a traitor, and within three months the UAW had disintegrated into a cloud of ill-tempered recriminations and proliferating acronyms. The activists reaffirmed the militancy of the old UAW as affiliated with the CIO, while Martin and his supporters formed a new UAW in affiliation with the old craft-working unions of the AFL. It took the car workers more than a year to regroup after the split, and Harry Bennett took advantage of the time to do some further work on Homer Martin.

Knowing that the UAW–AFL leader was short of funds, Harry Bennett offered him a couple of purchasing accounts for Ford, as well as a fully furnished home in Detroit.[68] Martin was so foolish not simply to accept the bribes, but to write Bennett a fulsome letter of thanks for them.[69]

His web finally woven, Bennett then intensified his outside squads' attacks on the hard-core UAW–CIO, while financing recruiting drives for Martin's UAW–AFL.

Bennett knew that he could not hold off the inevitable forever. One day, somehow, Ford would be compelled to grant recognition to a union inside its walls. But when that day came, Harry Bennett's intention was that the union in question should be the one whose leader had sent him the thank-you letter that he had in his pocket.

Armageddon did not go quite according to plan. The Supreme Court's definitive upholding of the UAW and NLRB suits against Ford in February 1941 provided the context for a final show-down. Now buttressed indisputably by the law, the hard-core UAW–CIO canvassed and pamphleted openly around the Rouge. Employees even sported their union buttons as they walked to work across the overpass, and the most that the Service Department dared do was pull them off —only to see them defiantly pinned back on again.

On April 1, 1941, a dispute in the Rouge rolling mill led to 1,500 of Ford's steelworkers refusing to work. The stoppage spread quickly to the other buildings of the Rouge, and early that afternoon Walter Reuther and the officers of the West Side Local made the strike official. There were machine guns sited over all the plant gates, but the Service Department knew it could not use them. Bennett had prepared against a union sit-in by organizing squads of largely black procompany workers, who occupied the plant on full pay. But the strategy misfired when his garrison smuggled in alcohol and started drunken races through the plant machinery, driving new cars. Valuable drafting-room blueprints were used by the strikebreakers as mattresses.

Bennett telegrammed appeals for help to both the White House and Michigan governor Van Wagoner, but received cold comfort.

"It is strange to see Henry Ford call frantically for Government help," commented the *Louisville Courier Journal*, "because no American industrialist has so often defied the Government in connection with labor disputes. . . . [He] has asked for what he is getting."[70]

Edsel Ford had been on holiday in Florida when the crisis broke. He travelled back immediately to Dearborn, to be ordered by his father to stay right out of the problem and leave everything to Bennett, who was, on April 3, 1941, refusing even to discuss the terms which the UAW–CIO offered for settlement. But this time Edsel did have some impact on events. He stood up to his father. He argued that negotiating with the UAW–CIO was the only way ahead, and, as Bennett subsequently told it, "Mr. Ford gave in to Edsel's wishes. I don't think the CIO would have won out if it hadn't been for Edsel's attitude."[71]

A return to work was agreed, pending a full contract to be negotiated after elections that would determine which union would represent the work force, and the Service Department set to work canvassing for the final outflanking that Harry Bennett hoped to accomplish. The election of May 21, 1941, however, showed only 27.4 percent of the ballots in favour of the AFL faction, as compared to 69.9 percent (51,868 of the 78,000 workers) for the hardcore CIO.

It was a measure of Henry Ford's contact with reality at the age of seventy-eight that he appears seriously to have cherished the expectation, in the spring of 1941, that his men would, in a gesture of confidence and gratitude for his lifetime of labouring on their behalf, reject both of the union options and vote instead to make Ford a non-union shop. He could then, legally, administer the benevolent autocracy which, in his mind, he had exercised most of his life. But only 1,958 votes, 2.7 percent of the total, were cast in support of this optimistic proposition, and the old carmaker could hardly believe it. It was, wrote Charles Sorensen later, "perhaps the greatest disappointment he had in all his business experience. . . . He was never the same after that."[72]

*

The contract negotiated between the Ford Motor Company and the UAW–CIO in the weeks following the election of May 1941 bore the mark of Harry Bennett.* You were either a friend of the man or a deadly enemy, and if you were a friend, you had to be his accomplice. Harry Bennett was never just content to like people, or do business with them. He had to place them in his debt. This proved spectacularly the case with the contract he negotiated with the UAW in the spring of 1941. When its terms were published in June, American industrial leaders were outraged. It was the most generous labour contract ever granted by a major industrial enterprise—a partnership, almost— and Ford's competitors in the car industry disbelievingly denounced it as total surrender.

Ford granted the UAW an almost totally closed union shop. Only a few job classifications, such as foreman, were exempted. Chrysler had refused to grant the union sole bargaining rights, but now, at Ford, you could only get a job if you were a member of the UAW. Ford agreed to pay back-wages to more than 4,000 workers discharged in the course of its long struggle with the union. A procedure for adjudicating grievances over seniority and speed-up was put into effect almost exactly as the UAW proposed it, and it was agreed that the Service Department would henceforward wear distinguishing uniforms, caps, or badges to eliminate spying.

The wage rates conceded were astonishing. Ford agreed to match the highest rate paid by anyone else in the industry, and, most significant of all, the company agreed to deduct all union initiation fees and monthly dues from workers' pay on the UAW's behalf—the "checkoff." No other car company had granted anything like this. From being the UAW's bitterest foe, the Ford Motor Company had swung, in a matter of weeks, to become its accounts clerk and dues

* In the negotiations, which started on June 1, 1941, between Ford and the UAW, the Ford team was headed by Harry Mack and the company's legal counsel, I. A. Capizzi. But Bennett took part in some of the negotiating sessions, and supervised the Ford position in all of them.

collector, and the agreement of June 1941 was to become the model for labour agreements in the postwar American car industry.

Henry Ford had taken no part in the negotiations, and when Harry Bennett showed him the terms finally agreed on June 18, 1941, his first reaction was to reject them as abject surrender. But when he got home to Fair Lane that night, Clara wanted a report on the union question, which she had been following quite closely. She knew that Edsel had always favoured an agreement, and she also knew that Bennett's thuggery and influence over Henry had been upsetting her son deeply.

"Who is this man Bennett," she had cried out in distress to Charles Sorensen on one occasion, "who has so much control over my husband and is ruining my son's health?"[73]

Clara had made her mind up about the union. There had been enough bloodshed and violence already, and the battle could never be won. If Henry did not agree to the contract, she said, then she was leaving him.

"What could I do? . . ." Henry said later when he told the tale. "Don't ever discredit the power of a woman."[74]

It was more complicated than that. With America gearing up for war, Ford had defence contracts which the government would certainly take away if the company did not change its labour policies. Several thousand pro-union workers had lodged claims for wrongful dismissal which the courts were now certain to uphold, and the back-pay bill for those was going up every day that Ford did not settle. The mood of America was changing—and then there was the old demon in Henry which loved to surprise. He phoned Harry Bennett to tell him to sign, and next day Ford was a union shop, in the vanguard of labour relations again for the first time since the Five Dollar Day.

"We have decided," said Edsel, "to go the whole way."[75]

"During the thirty years I worked for Henry Ford," runs the revealing first sentence of Harry Bennett's autobiography, "I became his most intimate companion, closer to him even than his only son."[76]

Harry Bennett's violent and prolonged battle with organized labour in the late 1930s proved totally futile in terms of its obvious and declared motive, to keep the union out of Ford. But in terms of the secret intentions that Harry Bennett had learned to look for in his master, it had proved eminently satisfying for Henry Ford. For four long and bitter years, Henry had been able to enjoy the sensation of having a rough, tough, forceful son battling against the world on his behalf, breaking heads, getting up to mischief, plotting, conniving, double-crossing, and generally doing all the things that Edsel would not or could not do.

When Henry Ford had invited Edsel into his office to inform him that he had found a strong and aggressive man who could "take care of himself in an argument," he had been administering a none-too-subtle rebuke to his son— and Edsel had done little to prove that the analysis was incorrect. The boy who had come running to his father when the bank crisis got rough had not shown much more grit with the unions, one way or the other.

Everybody knew that he cared. You could tell it from his deep, dark, wounded eyes. "His soul bled . . . ," remembered Walter Reuther many years later. "He was a decent man and he cared. I felt sorry for him. I still do."[77]

Decency alone, however, was not enough. Though now in his mid-forties, Edsel Ford still found it painfully difficult to confront his father directly on any subject that really counted. Henry Ford found out from Ford Hospital doctors, and passed on to Harry Bennett, that Edsel was so wrought up that he would go home after work, throw himself on the bed, and sob with frustration.[78]

It was scarcely surprising. One day in 1939, John R. Davis, who had been general sales manager of the company since 1937, came to Edsel complaining at the behaviour of Harry Mack, a henchman of Harry Bennett's, who had broken up a sales meeting the previous evening with a group of carousing companions. The meeting had been held at the

Dearborn Country Club, built by Henry on Ford land and at Ford expense in order to prove that golf courses, tennis courts, and luxurious clubhouses need not be the monopoly of Grosse Pointe. The only differences between the Dearborn Country Club and the most exclusive in the land were that the members were forbidden from smoking, and that not a drop of alcohol was consumed there. So Harry Mack had had the Service Department send over a truckful of liquor for the sales meeting, and in the course of the subsequent carousing, he had provoked a fight which had landed him in hospital.

Edsel was overjoyed, since Harry Mack was one of the more obnoxious cronies in the coterie surrounding Harry Bennett. As manager of the Ford Dearborn branch, Mack was the conduit for the free cars which Bennett distributed as favours and payoffs to his dubious associates, Mack camouflaging their disappearance with elaborate lists of travel and entertainment expenses which Edsel's accountants regularly queried, and which Bennett invariably approved.[79] Mack's smuggling of liquor into the Dearborn Country Club was a transgression which, Edsel felt sure, would arouse Henry Ford's ire.

"Fire Harry Mack," he told Davis, confident that he would, for once, have his father foursquare behind him. "You can do this with my personal authority"[80]

But Edsel underestimated his adversary. Harry Bennett summoned Jack Davis to his basement office for a meeting in the presence of Henry Ford, and there he flatly contradicted the sales manager's version of events. It was not Harry Mack who had smuggled liquor into the Country Club, he said, but Jack Davis, and when Davis retorted that that was just a lie, Bennett responded by threatening to punch Davis on the nose—at which point Henry Ford ducked under Bennett's arm and made a rapid exit.

The old man went straight to his son's office.

"That Davis is a liar," he said.

Edsel remonstrated with his father, defending his sales manager, for Jack Davis was an ally of Edsel's. He had been on Edsel's side ever since the day in the early 1920s when he had seen Henry Ford clear the fourth floor of accountants. Other executives observed humiliations like that and kept their distance from Edsel. But Davis had stayed true, and now Edsel made the issue a matter of confidence, supporting his own man against Harry Bennett's, going to the wire for Davis in the way that he had not dared defend Ernest Kanzler.

Jack Davis was worth a million of Harry Mack, said Edsel. As president of the company he had listened to the arguments. He had come to a decision, and now he expected his father to back him up.

"If Jack Davis goes," he said, "I go too."

Henry Ford looked at his son long and hard.

"Get the man out of my sight," he said.[81]

# 23

## BROKEN HEART

When Edsel Ford later tried to describe his confrontation with his father, he found it difficult to speak.

"There is nothing I can do," he told Jack Davis, almost in tears. "This is the saddest day of my life. You only did what I told you to."[1]

But Jack Davis was not fired, because that was not, in fact, precisely what Henry Ford had ordered Edsel to do. He had said, "Get the man out of my sight," and Edsel did that, transferring Davis to California to supervise West Coast sales. It was like the accountants cleared out of their fourth-floor offices, then redistributed by Edsel to other departments. There were rules to the game. As Henry grew older, Edsel did more for him, travelled more, issued public statements. But every so often, unpredictably, the old tyrant would stamp his feet, and then the boy would have to go through the liturgies of appeasement.

For the Ford family, ambivalence had become a way of life. Henry would throw nighttime skating parties on his lake at Fair Lane, memorable, spellbinding occasions for which the cars were driven out onto the ice to form a great semicircle, their headlights blazing.[2] Blowing the steam off his oyster soup, Henry would seem in the best of spirits, laughing and joking in the bosom of his family. Then, a few nights later, he would sidle up to Benjamin Lovett conducting the orchestra at an old-time dance. Henry had seen Edsel arrive with some Grosse Pointe friends, detected liquor on their breath, and ordered his dancing master to speed up the tempo.

"Afterwards," according to Harry Bennett, "Mr. Ford would report with glee how he had danced Edsel and his friends until they were all in, and how they 'sweated until they stank.'"[3]

Henry continued to spy on his son. "You would think Edsel was working for someone else," commented John Dahlinger later.[4] In an attempt to gain some privacy, Edsel took to spending more time at the Briggs Body Plant, in the studio where he had worked on Briggs designs for the Model T. He was a friend of Walter Briggs, and Briggs's treasurer, Howard Bonbright, was a very close friend indeed. Here Edsel could relax a little, playing with design concepts for the Lincoln, the aristocratic car that he loved so well.[5]

"Father made the most popular car in the world," he once said. "I would like to make the best."[6]

He hired John Tjaarda, a designer who had worked on some of the most beautiful Duesenbergs and Packards, and Tjaarda built prototypes for Edsel's personal use. In 1935 Lincoln produced the Zephyr, hailed by the Museum of Modern Art as "the first successfully designed streamlined car in America,"[7] and in 1939 Edsel produced his most beautiful car of all, the Lincoln Continental. Long and low, with its rear trunk scalloped around its spare tyre, the Continental was a classic car in the age of the classic car, Edsel's finest achievement. With a smooth twelve-cylinder engine, the Lincoln offered "glider-ride."[8]

But Henry Ford was not too impressed. He had little interest, he said, in "motors that had more spark plugs than a cow has teats."[9]

Henry Ford's final decade in charge of his own company was the Roosevelt years, and Henry had started them with enthusiastic support for the new President.

"A great thing has occurred among us," he declared in a series of personal messages, ghostwritten by William Cameron and inserted in company advertisements in May 1933. "We have made a complete turn around and at last America's face is to the future." Americans had looked backwards for too long, said Henry, but now there was a new spirit in the country, and "thanks for that belongs to

President Roosevelt. Inauguration day he turned the Ship of State around."[10]

Henry liked the idea of a people's President who would attack the existing establishment. But he soon discovered that he was a major pillar of the establishment that the President wanted to attack. Roosevelt's National Industrial Recovery Act started the tradition of government involvement in industry that has lasted to the present day, and Henry did not like it.

"I was always under the impression," he commented tartly on the day the act was signed, "that to manage a business properly you ought to know something about it."[11]

Aware of how important Henry Ford could be to the New Deal, Roosevelt invited him to the White House in the autumn of 1933, but Henry was already suspicious of the degree to which the President was intervening in industry. It took five years for the appointment secretaries of Henry Ford and President Roosevelt to arrange a face-to-face encounter, and by the time that the two men did finally get together, in May 1938, the gloves were off. Ford had declined to cooperate with the NIRA. The Ford Motor Company had made no secret of its support for Alfred Landon in the election of 1936. Rouge workers found slips with their pay warning them of the dangers of voting for Roosevelt.[12] And the Battle of the Overpass had issued the clearest defiance of Roosevelt's labour policies, and, indeed, of the entire social welfare drift of his administration. For the first time in his life, Henry Ford found himself a hero in Grosse Pointe.

It takes one news manipulator to recognize another, and as he prepared for his momentous White House summit conference in the spring of 1938, Henry Ford grew understandably apprehensive at the briefing which Roosevelt's staff might be expected to hand out at the end of the encounter. He therefore decided to enlist the services of the hometown newspapers and arranged to have Jay G. Hayden, the political correspondent of the *Detroit News*, and Clifford

Prevost of the *Free Press* waiting for him outside the White House afterwards. Henry Ford wanted to be sure of getting his own version of events firmly and rapidly on the record.

The meeting itself does not appear to have been of any great consequence; indeed, it is difficult to see why either man should have agreed to it. Henry delivered his standard homily on farm and city and the village industries. Roosevelt manoeuvred vainly for some sort of endorsement of his own industrial policies, and the two men withdrew to their respective press secretaries.

In Ford's case the mouthpiece was William Cameron. But Cameron sat silent in Ford's private railcar, the Fair Lane, as his master gave Jay Hayden and Clifford Prevost his firsthand account of his conversation with the President. After the White House, Henry had an appointment in New York, and he brought the two Detroit reporters along with him for the ride, dictating his thoughts and memories to them nonstop for the best part of four hours.

Neither reporter understood a word that he said. Henry's tendency to concertina his logic and leap from one thought to another, without bothering to explain the stages in between, was supercharged that day, and although both Hayden and Prevost had books full of notes by the time they reached New York, they had very little idea what they meant.

Arriving at the station, Henry Ford, now a few weeks away from his seventy-fifth birthday, caught sight of a long flight of stairs, and swiftly detached himself from the party to sprint up one side and down the other. "Haven't had a bit of exercise all day," he explained.

Clifford Prevost, filing for the *Free Press* next morning, now made his farewells and went off to telephone his story to Detroit. But Jay Hayden had a less urgent deadline. The *News* was an afternoon paper, so Cameron took the young reporter aside and offered to help him make sense of all the notes he had gathered. Hayden would read out a sentence or so that he had written, and Cameron would then embark on an interpretation—which usually seemed to Hayden to be completely at odds with what Henry Ford had said.

Still, at least Cameron's version had the virtue of making sense, and so, next day, the two stories appeared in the rival Detroit newspapers, Prevost's version directly from the lips of Henry Ford, Hayden's very different account as modified by William Cameron, though Cameron was not mentioned in it. All of his statements were put between quotation marks and attributed to Henry Ford.

Anxious to read both stories, Henry Ford scanned them eagerly next day—and exploded in fury. He went to the extraordinary length of having Clifford Prevost banned from all Ford plants until further notice, on the grounds that the reporter had misrepresented the entire story and put words into his mouth. As proof, Henry Ford held up the story in the *Detroit News*.

"Jay Hayden," he said, "quoted me just right."[13]

On July 30, 1938, Henry Ford celebrated his seventy-fifth birthday in Dearborn, and the inhabitants turned out in force to celebrate with him. The town's most famous son had presented twenty acres along a southern branch of the Rouge River to be used as a municipal park—on condition that alcoholic beverages should not be served there[14]—and the grateful community had christened the resort Ford Field. Here Henry sat in splendour, decked out in an immaculate white suit and straw boater. As an indication of the world-wide stature attained by the man who had put Dearborn on the map, he had been honored that day by the presentation to him, by Detroit's German Vice-Consul, of the Grand Cross of the German Eagle, the highest award to a foreigner that Hitler could bestow.

Henry Ford professed surprise at the widespread outrage that greeted his acceptance of a Nazi honour. The medal came, he said, from the German people, who "as a whole are not in sympathy with their rulers in their anti-Jewish policies. . . . Those who have known me for many years realize that anything that breeds hate is repulsive to me."[15]

But this was disingenuous. Though Henry Ford had

maintained his support for pacifist causes throughout the 1920s and 1930s, it was remarkable how often these seemed to have a pro-German tincture. At Clara's urging he provided support for the "moral rearmament" campaign of Frank Buchman's Oxford Group—until Buchman failed to pay a bill incurred by the group at the Dearborn Inn[16]— and he also endorsed the "America First" lobby of Charles A. Lindbergh, who had himself accepted the Order of the German Eagle in 1938, from the hands of Hermann Goering.

After Hitler's invasion of Poland and the outbreak of war in Europe in September 1939, Ford joined Lindbergh in opposing U.S. aid or arms sales to Britain and France. "If we start shipping that stuff over there we'll be in the war right away," he warned,[17] and he latched onto newspaper reports about the "Phoney War" as a means of sidestepping questions as to which side might be in the right. "If I were put on the stand," he said, "I'd say there isn't any war today."[18]

Off the record, however, it was clear that Henry Ford's old prejudices were as strong as ever. "You know, John," he told the twenty-year-old John Dykema, whom he used to see at the Huron Mountain Club, "there hasn't been a shot fired. The whole thing has just been made up by the Jew bankers."[19]

Henry Ford never seems to have been totally clear on the distinction between deploring all war on ethical grounds, and the more politic anxiety to keep America out of whatever mess the rest of the world might get itself into. If America was safe, in his view, there could not be too much wrong with the rest of the planet Earth. So when the Nazi engulfment of Europe provoked a flurry of military preparedness in Washington in the summer of 1940, he proclaimed himself happy to help with the defence of the nation. The Ford Motor Company stood ready, Ford declared on May 28, 1940, to "swing into a production of a thousand airplanes of standard design a day."[20]

This was a ludicrous claim. Modern companies, even the producers of quite simple aircraft, do not turn out that number in a year. Henry appears to have been piqued by the news that morning that his former employee, William S. Knudsen, who had risen to the presidency of General Motors and who had, for more than a decade, been directing that corporation in its systematic outclassing of Ford, had just been appointed Commissioner for Industrial Production by President Roosevelt. The Ford Motor Company, said Henry pointedly, would produce its thousand planes a day "without meddling by Government agencies."[21] Still, when the War Department sent a pursuit plane to Dearborn so that Ford could examine the possibility of producing it in bulk, Henry consented to Edsel travelling to Washington to discuss the production details with Knudsen.

The old man appeared agreeable to the proposal which Edsel brought back from Knudsen, that Ford should not so much make planes, to start with, as concentrate on the manufacture of aeroplane engines. With the Battle of Britain reaching its perilous climax, Whitehall had approached Washington for help with the urgent production of 6,000 Rolls-Royce Merlin engines for its Spitfire fighters, and Knudsen thought Ford was the company to do the job.

Edsel and Sorensen were fired with enthusiasm for the project. The Rolls-Royce Merlin represented an ultimate in motor engineering, and quite apart from guaranteed profit, the invitation to produce the engine in bulk provided the finest possible endorsement of Ford manufacturing techniques. Henry Ford allowed Edsel to make the Rolls-Royce project public.

But then Lord Beaverbrook, Minister for War Production in London, hailed the Ford deal as a major step forward in the British war effort, and within hours the phone rang in Knudsen's Washington office. It was Edsel Ford calling from Detroit.

"Bill," he said, "we can't make those motors for the British."

"Why?" asked Knudsen.

"Father won't do it."

"But you are president of the company."

"I know, but Father won't do it, and you know how he is."[22]

Knudsen got straight on a plane for Detroit. "Mr. Ford," he said as he walked into Edsel's office, where Henry and his son were waiting with Charles Sorensen, "this is terrible about those motors."

"What motors?" inquired the seventy-seven-year-old car-maker, with one of his innocent, little-boy looks.

"Those motors for the British. Edsel telephoned me and said you wouldn't make them."

"Nor will we," snapped Ford.

"There will be a hell of a stink about it if you don't," said the Industrial Production Commissioner.

"I don't care," responded Henry Ford, explaining that he was willing to make the motors for Britain if his contract was channelled through the American government, but that he would not sign a contract with the British direct. It was against his principles to provide war materials directly to a foreign belligerent.

This argument might have carried more weight if the Ford Motor Companies of Britain and Germany had not, at that very moment, been producing cars, trucks, and armaments flat out for their respective national war machines. Like General Motors and several other multina-tional American companies, Ford derived profits in the Second World War from both sides. But logic had never featured prominently in Henry Ford's thinking, and William Knudsen, of all people, understood that.

"Mr. Ford," he remonstrated, sticking to basic principles. "We have your word that you would make them. I told the President your decision, and he was very happy about it."[23]

The mention of Roosevelt ended whatever chance Knudsen might have had of salvaging the Rolls-Royce en-gine deal.

"Withdraw the whole order," barked Ford, suddenly tense.* "Take it to someone else. Let them build the engine; we won't."[24]

As Knudsen got up and left the meeting, he was—according to Sorensen—"purple with rage." The GM man had started his Washington assignment by offering this job to Ford as a gesture of his good faith and impartiality, and it was a major embarrassment in his first important government venture.

But Knudsen's embarrassment was nothing compared to that of Edsel. Having publicly committed Ford to the contract, he was compelled, three days later, publicly to contradict himself. There was some sort of logic to the about-face which derived from Henry Ford's isolationist principles, but it was too complicated to explain. The only reason that the forty-seven-year-old company president could give for his reneging was that he was doing as his father told him.

It was soon after Pearl Harbor that the strain of it all started to show on Edsel's face. Fit and healthy—regular tennis and sailing kept him in good shape—he had always looked composed and comparatively unflustered. Rare were the days when he did not confront the world with a good-humoured smile. But in the early months of 1942, Edsel Ford seemed to people suddenly drawn and harried. "Art" Backus in his outer office noticed that Edsel would shut the door to his private washroom, where he had a leather couch, and say that he did not wish to be disturbed.[25]

It looked as though the trouble was ulcers. Edsel had a stomach-ulcer operation in January 1942;[26] his staff had to ferry glasses of milk for him from the canteen. But milk made the problem worse—the milk that Edsel drank when he was at home, at least, because that milk came directly from the Ford farms. Henry Ford did not allow the past-

---

* In addition to the 6,000 engines for Britain, the contract had also carried an order for 3,000 engines to be manufactured for the American government.

eurizing or sterilization of that milk, because he liked it to taste as he remembered milk tasting in his childhood: fresh, untreated, straight from the cow. The Ford herds and dairies were spotless, so there was no suggestion, ever, of the milk carrying tuberculosis. But one batch that Edsel swallowed must have contained the less pernicious brucellosis bacteria, for later in 1942 Edsel came down with a severe attack of undulant fever: chills, painful joints, and high temperatures at night. Today the treatment of undulant fever is by broad-spectrum antibiotics, but in the early 1940s the doctors of the Ford Hospital could prescribe nothing better than rest, and, with the outbreak of war, Edsel did not have time for that.

The Ford Motor Company was America's third-largest defence contractor in World War II—General Motors was the largest, Curtiss-Wright, the Wright brothers' Ohio plane-making company, second.* Detroit prided itself on being the "arsenal of democracy," and Ford's contribution included jeeps, armoured cars, troop carriers, trucks, tanks, tank destroyers, Pratt and Whitney aircraft engines, and gliders. But the project that won the company most fame was the construction in the countryside beyond Dearborn of Willow Run, a huge purpose-built aircraft factory that was nearly a mile long. At the time of its opening early in 1942, Willow Run was the largest single industrial structure in the world under one roof, and when completed, B–24 Liberator bombers were scheduled to roll from its production line and take off for the front at the rate of one per hour.

Willow Run took its name from a willow-lined stream which meandered through woods and farmland that Henry Ford owned outside Ann Arbor. Not far from Harry Bennett's cowboy ranch, the fields had been put down to soya beans for most of the 1930s. The idea that Ford should build the B–24 in bulk had come from the U.S. Army Air

* GM's prime war supply contracts totalled $13.8 billion between 1940 and 1944, Curtiss-Wright's $7.09 billion, and Ford's $5.26 billion. Chrysler ranked eighth in the league table of defence contractors with $3.39 billion.[27]

Force, which was worried that the designers of the bomber, Consolidated Aircraft Corporation of San Diego, could not produce the plane in sufficient quantities. When first suggested at the end of 1940, the challenge of Ford creating what would, in many respects, be the world's first integrated aircraft assembly line had enthralled Charles Sorensen even more than the mass production of Rolls-Royce engines, and Henry Ford had no objection to working for the American government.

It was the biggest adventure facing the Ford Motor Company since the changeover to the Model A, though with Henry now close to his eightieth birthday, it was Edsel and Sorensen who had to supply the drive needed to turn the audacious dream of Willow Run into reality. Henry Ford had suffered a slight stroke in 1938, from which he had recovered. But he did not fare so well following a second stroke in 1941. Displaying strange lapses of memory, he moved and spoke noticeably more slowly, though he was not willing to admit that there was anything wrong with him —and he was certainly not prepared to surrender control of the company. Edsel, like Sorensen and Bennett, remained just a lieutenant.

Willow Run was Albert Kahn's largest single project, and also his last. The architect was to die in 1942. Kahn designed the seventy-acre structure—"the most enormous room in the history of man"—in an L shape, which was not a logical configuration for a continuous assembly line, particularly one which had been specifically located in the open country-side so that form could follow function. The obvious shape for Willow Run was a long straight line, but that would have meant the building running out beyond the boundary of Washtenaw County—a conservative, rural, generally pro-Republican community—into Wayne County, which levied heavier taxes and had a nasty tendency to elect sympathizers with Franklin Delano Roosevelt. Henry Ford's second stroke had surrendered much of his mind to his darker impulses, and his suspicion of the President had grown to paranoid proportions. Harry Bennett, furthermore, had close links with Earl Mishner, the vehemently anti-Roosevelt Washtenaw congressman.[28]

Henry Ford's other contribution to the bomber plant was his insistence that the stream of Willow Run itself should not be diverted but should be housed, at considerable expense, in a concrete conduit that followed the waterway's wandering course. So, thus confined, the stream flowed on beneath the buildings, across the site, and its hidden presence was the generally received explanation as to why, once the factory was erected, birds continued to nest in its girders as if the willow trees were still there. They chirped and fluttered, blithely oblivious to the heavy planes taking shape below them, and they swooped down to make birdbaths of the huge circular fountains in which the workers washed up.[29]

The building of Willow Run captured the imagination of America. Dismayed by Japanese progress in the early months of 1942, the country was desperate for any token of some eventual victory, and Ford's bomber plant supplied it.

"It is a promise of revenge for Pearl Harbor," enthused the *Detroit Free Press*. "You know when you see Willow Run that in the end we will give it to them good."[30]

Superplant was the proof that, despite appearances to the contrary, America had not lost what had made America great. She could still make things. Willow Run was "the damndest colossus the industrial world has ever known" (Westbrook Pegler),[31] "a sort of Grand Canyon of a mechanized world" (Charles Lindbergh),[32] and once again, it was Henry Ford who had given expression to the American industrial genius. People did not care that the old man was only a figurehead. Though newsreels and newspaper stories made clear that Sorensen and Edsel Ford were the backbone of Willow Run, it was the fact that old Henry Ford himself was involved, however tenuously, that gave people real reassurance.

"When Ford tools up he tools up . . . ," declared the *Manchester Leader and Evening Union*, a New Hampshire paper.

"The old fox has never failed to have the last laugh."[33]

For all his faults, Henry Ford had become a national talisman. The country wanted to make him a hero as much as he wanted to be one, and though General Motors was producing nearly three times more war material than Ford, it was Ford, and Willow Run, which came to represent the domestic war effort in the national imagination. Opinion polls consistently showed Ford being favoured for its contribution to the war effort over GM—by 31 to 21 percent in one poll, by 28.1 to 25.1 in another[34]—and though Chrysler was, in 1943, to open an aircraft-engine plant near Chicago that was even larger than Willow Run, it did not excite America as the Ford plant did.

"The Pyramid of Cheops or the hanging gardens of Babylon may have satisfied the ancients . . . ," declared a reporter for the *Christian Science Monitor* towards the end of the war. "But for me, I'll take a today's phenomenon to top my list of wonders. Willow Run. . . . It is, horizontally, what the Empire State Building is, vertically, to American industry. . . . It is a promise of American greatness."[35]

The creator of Highland Park and the Rouge had done it one last time. When it was announced, on May 14, 1942, that Willow Run, open countryside only twelve months earlier, had begun the "actual production of bombers,"[36] patriotic enthusiasm knew no bounds. "In the future," declared the *Detroit Free Press*, "it will be written that the shadows cast by the flight of Willow Run's bombers in the spring of 1942 portended the coming doom of the enemies of humanity."[37] By late summer, promised Charles Sorensen, Willow Run would be producing one B–24 per hour. "Bring the Germans and Japs in to see it," he boasted, "hell, they'd blow their brains out."[38]

Not for the first time, however, Sorensen promised more than he could perform. Willow Run was, in time, to turn out to be the superplant it was planned to be. But, just as it had taken time to iron out the retooling difficulties of the Model A in 1927, so the challenge of reshaping plane making into the disciplines of automobile production proved complex and time-consuming. Mass production looks a great deal easier than it really is, and Sorensen had let himself be deceived by his own wizardry. By the end of September 1942, Willow Run had, in fact, produced just two planes: one "knockdown," a collection of parts that were sent, by land, to Tulsa for assembly there by the Douglas Aircraft Company, and one complete, bolted-together B-24 that did actually take off and fly.

"You cannot expect blacksmiths," sneered J. H. Kindelberger, president of North American Aviation and a consistent critic of the government decision to give plane contracts to the car companies, "to learn how to make watches overnight."[39]

Continuing manufacturing tie-ups meant that the grand total of B-24s produced at Willow Run by the end of 1942 amounted to fifty-six—less than three days' production at the vaunted plane-an-hour rate—and as the truth became public, the great Ford plant was transformed from a source of inspiration into a national disgrace. "The March of Time" newsreel burrowed into "the truth about mis-management and lack of morale in Detroit that is slowing U.S. war production to the danger point."[40] *Life* magazine analysed the high turnover of Willow Run workers, who found their wages consumed by the expensive, and rationed, gasoline needed for the two-hour journey from Detroit and back. The Ford Motor Company was losing more skilled men than it could hire, reported the *New York Times* in December 1942,[41] and newspapers across the country ran similar complaints. In February 1943, *Flying* magazine ran a story headlined WILL IT RUN?[42]

It was Edsel Ford who took the national scorn and disillusion hardest, for his father was, by now, drifting off into a world of his own. When Roosevelt came to inspect Willow Run in September 1942—after his inspection the President conceded, off-the-record, that the plant was not yet in production—it was suddenly noticed that Henry Ford was not standing in the welcoming lineup. Harry Bennett despatched his Servicemen on a five-alarm search which located the old man playing with a new machine tool in a corner of the plant,[43] and though Ford drove, seated between the Roosevelts, in their limousine through the factory, he remained withdrawn and uncommunicative, glaring ferociously at Edsel and Sorensen whenever he caught them being gracious to the hated visitors.[44]

Henry was failing visibly, and it looked as if the moment of transition might finally have arrived. The crown prince could come into his inheritance—as many Ford employees had so long and fervently hoped.

"You always figured there was one person who was a perfect gentleman," said Harold Hicks, the engineer who developed the Model A engine, "and that some day he was going to run the place, and that it would be a fine place to work when he was running it. You stuck around because of him."[45]

But by the autumn of 1942, with national criticism of Willow Run reaching its height, it became clear that Edsel Ford himself was unwell. Sorensen, not a young man, had found the strain of pushing Willow Run into production the greatest test he had ever experienced—he fainted twice while working in the plant, and had to be hospitalized— and for Edsel, debilitated by his stomach operation and by undulant fever, the strain was just too much. He struggled in to work because he felt that he had to, but he was operating, much of the time, on painkillers and sedatives. He could not keep his food down. He retired to the leather couch in his washroom more and more often, and each time, his secretaries noticed, it was longer and longer before he came out.

When Edsel had first reported his stomach problems to his doctors in the late 1930s, they had organized the most thorough battery of tests that the Ford Hospital could devise. But Edsel, a fastidious man, found the programme of barium meals and enemas both painful and humiliating, and as his stomach pains got worse, he shied away from a repetition of the distasteful ordeal. In November 1940, Dr. John

Mateer, the hospital's gastrology specialist, wrote to him urging the need for some thorough examination and promising there should be no need "for any tube swallowing this time."[46] But Edsel procrastinated, and it was more than a year before the surgeons found out what was really wrong with him.

They might possibly have stopped the cancer if they had found it earlier, but it was vicious and deep-seated, and when Edsel went on the operating table for the removal of half his stomach in January 1942, it had already spread elsewhere. Before long it reemerged in his liver.[47]

The doctors never told Edsel Ford what was making him suffer so. When he was readmitted to hospital in November 1942, the official diagnosis was his undulant fever—and certainly that draining infection never left him. As he struggled with all the problems of Willow Run—early in 1943 he had to face a grilling from Senator Truman's Special Committee Investigating the National Defense Program[48]—Edsel Ford was demonstrably an ill man. "Doesn't look good to me," noted Charles Sorensen in his diary.[49]

Sorensen was struck by how unsympathetic Henry Ford seemed towards his son's ailments. Henry had often said it before, and he said it again: there was nothing wrong with Edsel that a change of lifestyle would not cure. The boy was too fond of cocktails and decadent east-side living.

"If there is anything the matter with Edsel's health," he told Sorensen, "he can correct it himself."[50]

Henry Ford frequently preached that Edsel should learn to live right and eat right—"right" meaning life lived according to the principles of Henry Ford, which was particularly rich, with Edsel laid low by the milk that Henry's principles had declined to have sterilized. The boy was suffering from the ultimate case of Ford Stomach.

Edsel went on working. "I spent all day yesterday at Willow Run," he wrote dutifully and mundanely as ever to his parents, who were wintering in Georgia in the early months of 1943. "Talking manpower, work incentives, trying to make plans to reduce absenteeism, now over 10% per

474

day."[51] But the real problems facing Edsel Ford were the wilfulness of his father and the sponsored mischief-making of Harry Bennett.

In February 1943, Edsel Ford had yet another Jack Davis-like confrontation with the Service Chief. A. M. Wibel, an upright character who had started his Ford career as a machinist in 1912 and had risen to the rank of director and vice-president, was in charge of company purchasing. Wibel had succeeded Fred H. Diehl, who had resigned in vain protest at the contracts Bennett had given to known gangsters like Chester LaMare, and for more than a decade Wibel wrestled with corruption in a department vulnerable, in the best-run companies, to favouritism and the kickback.

Wibel and Bennett operated almost constantly at daggers drawn, and in the winter of 1942–43 their conflict came to a head when Wibel refused to deal with a supplier that Bennett favoured. Edsel supported the purchasing chief, telling Bennett "to keep his nose out of purchasing" and "stick to personnel and union negotiation"[52]—and Bennett went to Henry Ford.

On April 15, 1943, the phone rang on Charles Sorensen's desk. The production chief was due to leave for Florida on vacation the following day, but, before he left, Henry Ford wanted him to arrange a meeting with Edsel "and change his attitude on everything."[53] Henry Ford then proceeded to dictate over the phone a list of the grievances he nursed against his son, from Edsel's friendship with Ernest Kanzler to his disagreements with Harry Bennett. As the old man talked, Sorensen noted the points down, a, b, c—"Discord over handling labor unions . . . Wibel is through . . . Bennett in full accord with Henry Ford. Henry Ford will support Bennett against every obstacle. . . . Change relations with Bennett. Kanzler relationship—wants it broken up." And the last point of all was the most important. "Regain health by cooperating with Henry Ford."[54]

When Edsel saw Sorensen's list next morning, he broke down in tears. "The best thing for me to do," he said, "is to resign. My health won't let me go on."[55]

It was not the first time that Edsel had talked to Sorensen of resignation, nor the first time that the production chief had seen Edsel cry. Sorensen sat down on the couch beside Henry Ford's weeping son. He had not always been close to Edsel. Taking his cue from his master, the Dane had been openly contemptuous of Edsel's weakness on occasion. But the rise of Harry Bennett, and the increasing capriciousness of Henry Ford, had inclined the production chief to mend his fences. Sorensen dissuaded Edsel from his resignation threat.

"If you go, I go too," he said. "I've had enough of people resigning."[56]

The most important issue for the moment was Wibel, for the smooth running of the government defence contract depended on Washington retaining confidence in the honesty and competence of Ford's purchasing department. Later that day Sorensen spoke directly to Henry Ford in support of Edsel's rebuke to Harry Bennett.

"Is Harry Bennett immune to correction by Edsel?" he asked.[57]

Sorensen left on holiday, confident that trouble had been averted for the time being and that A. M. Wibel, in particular, was safe. But five days later he got a phone call in Miami instructing him to secure Wibel's resignation, and when he got back to Detroit at the beginning of May 1943, he found that Edsel was at home in bed.

The Ford family today shy away from remembering this sore, exposed time in their history. The pain seems to have wiped clean the memories of Edsel's two surviving sons. They were not there in any case. Henry Ford II was in Chicago, undergoing naval training. William Clay Ford was at Yale. Henry Ford II can remember that his father's disgust and unhappiness with what had happened to the family firm was such that Edsel had, at some time, seriously discussed leaving the company, disassociating himself from the sordid chaos, making a complete break.[58] But now it was too late.

Eleanor Ford had been trying for months to persuade her husband to give less of himself to the company and to conserve more of his energies at home, to enjoy himself a little. But the time for enjoyment was past. As he lay bedridden in his upper room at Gaukler Point, Edsel had little energy for anything. He was sinking visibly. There were nurses in attendance, injections, bottles, tubes. There was a doctor permanently in the house, administering the morphine to deaden the pain.

His mother came to see him once or twice a week.

"Well," Clara would say after lunch at Fair Lane, sending for the chauffeur, "I'll go and see my son."[59]

Ernest Kanzler rang most days from Washington, trying to cheer his brother-in-law up. But Ernie would stay on the telephone too long chattering, and Edsel did not know how to cut him off.[60]

By the end he was scarcely conscious, drifting in a sad, darkening haze from the drugs and his inexorable physical breakdown. There was no point in taking him into hospital. The doctors knew there was nothing they could do for him there. When Henry Ford was told, on May 18, 1943, that his son was dying, he refused to believe it. He insisted that the doctors at his hospital must be able to bring Edsel back to health.[61]

But he was wrong. Eight days later at 1:10 A.M. on May 26, 1943, the duty doctor came out of Edsel Ford's bedroom at Gaukler Point to inform Eleanor that her husband had just passed away. Edsel was five months short of his fiftieth birthday.

The cause of death was difficult to specify—stomach cancer, liver cancer, undulant fever, ulcers, there had been so many afflictions. Closest was the diagnosis of the dead man's friends who knew how love and torture had intertwined in Edsel's life. Edsel Bryant Ford died, they said, of a broken heart.

**Part Five** Henry II

The Ford International Weekly

# THE DEARBORN
# INDEPENDENT

By the Year $1.50          Dearborn, Michigan, August 6, 1921          Single Copy Ten Cents

And Now Leprosy
Is Yielding to Science
Years of experimenting brings a remedy

Fountain Lake, the
Home of John Muir
A story of naturalist's wilderness abode

## Fighting the Devil in Modern Babylon
First of a series of articles on New York by Rev. Dr. John Roach Straton

# Jewish Jazz—Moron Music—Becomes
# Our National Music

Story of "Popular Song" Control in the United States

## The Chief Justices of the Supreme Court
Only ten men have held this post since the tribunal was first organized

Teaching the Deaf to
Hear With Their Eyes
How Chicago is educating afflicted children

Many By-Products
From Sweet Potatoes
Recent discoveries prove great possibilities

*Chronicler of the neglected truth*

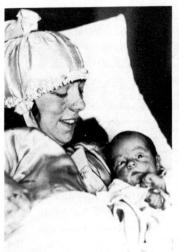

*Evangeline Dahlinger with John in 1923 and in period costume at Greenfield Village*

*From left to right: Henry Ford, Benson Ford, John Dahlinger, and Evangeline Dahlinger, December 1931*

*Roughing it. Henry Ford,* **right,** *and* **above** *with the Vagabonds: Thomas Edison* **left,** *John Burroughs and Ford on the wheel, Harvey Firestone (right)*

*No stockholders. Money the root of all evil. One of Henry Ford's notebooks*

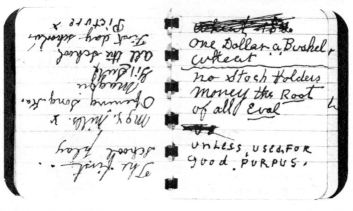

*The mighty bean. Henry Ford with soya-bean suit* **above** *and testing soya plastic body panel* **right**

*Henry Ford II*

*Benson (left), Henry II, and seed potatoes*

*Henry Ford and his grandsons at Fair Lane*

*Memories. Henry Ford enjoys a* McGuffey Reader **above** *in the restored McGuffey homestead in Greenfield Village, and* **below** *rocks his own cradle in the restored Ford farm*

**Above** *Mowing, 1922*
**Below** *The Ford Airport, Ford Tri-Motors at front left. In the background, the Henry Ford Museum*

*Henry and Clara Ford,*
*c. 1940*

*Eleanor Clay Ford. Her wedding photograph*
*November 1916*

*From left to right: Edsel, Eleanor, Henry II, Benson, Josephine, and*
*William Clay Ford on the terrace at Gaukler Point, Grosse Pointe, c. 1935*

*Father and son.* **Above** *Henry and Edsel camping in 1921;* **below** *in the Plympton House, Greenfield Village, in 1941;* **opposite, top** *beside Henry's first lathe in 1928;* **opposite, below** *introducing the Model A in 1928*

**Left** *Edsel Ford and Dr. William Valentiner as depicted by Diego Rivera in the Detroit Industry frescoes*

**Below** *Diego Rivera (right) with Frida Kahlo and Albert Kahn*

**Right** *The Rouge as photographed by Charles Sheeler in 1927*

**Below** *The Detroit Industry frescoes by Diego Rivera, north wall. The gods, the earth, the cylinder blocks. In the top corner panels, the abuse and use of science – chemical warfare (left) and vaccination (right)*

The Battle of the Overpass,
May 26, 1937, before,
during, and after. **Above**
Union organizers, including
Walther Reuther and
Richard Frankensteen in the
centre, watch the Ford men
approach. **Left** The attack.
**Opposite, top** Reuther
and Frankensteen (holding
his head). **Opposite,
lower left** Tarred and
feathered, a victim of the
outside squads. **Opposite,
lower right** Harry Bennett

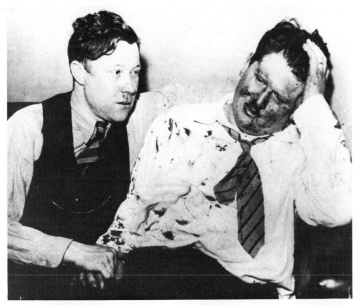

*Bonnie Parker, gun, and Ford V-8*

*William Knudsen*

*Charles Sorensen*

*Ernest Kanzler*

# 24

## YOUNG HENRY

*There are so many people here it is easier than if there were just a few. There are some who Edsel and I have known and it is always my greatest pleasure to talk about Edsel and find people who love to talk about him too. I do miss him so terribly that at times it seems impossible to go on, and yet I feel so very close to him that that gives me comfort. I brought down so many pictures so that everywhere I look I can see him.*

—LETTER FROM ELEANOR FORD
HOT SPRINGS, VIRGINIA, AUGUST 1943[1]

Eleanor Ford had let few people see what she really felt about her father-in-law's treatment of her beloved Edsel. She never discussed it directly with her children. It hurt too much. In later years Henry Ford II, Benson, Josephine, and William Clay could only talk of clues given meaning by the things that other people told them.

Eleanor did share her anger with the Kanzlers, and with one or two other very close friends, but her outward demeanour remained reserved and loyal. In the first moments of her grief she sat down to write a letter of rare comfort and thanks to her dead husband's parents.

DEAR MR. AND MRS. FORD,                    SUNDAY NIGHT

*Somehow I have a rather difficult time sleeping at night, so I am writing you a line to thank you for giving me the most wonderful husband and father God ever made. I don't mean to be emotional, but I realize the formative years were yours and your son and my husband is our greatest treasure in the years to come. . . .*[2]

It was significant that after nearly thirty years of marriage Eleanor had never, and could not now, refer to her in-laws by their Christian names, let alone as Mother and Father. It was significant too that she should arrange Edsel's burial not in the Ford Cemetery at Dearborn, but in the Woodlawn

481

Cemetery in Detroit, close to the Hudson family crypt, where Edsel lies today beside such friends of Henry Ford as James Couzens and the Dodge brothers.

Eleanor was distraught. Her youngest son, William Clay Ford, who spent his summer vacation in 1943 consoling his mother and trying to make the mansion at Gaukler Point seem a little less empty, recalls her breaking down in unpredictable fits of weeping. She would talk quite frequently of suicide.[3] It would take only one thing to push her over the edge—and this was supplied when the question of Edsel's successor as company president arose. Henry Ford wanted to give the job to Harry Bennett.[4]

Being interviewed by a magazine writer in the early years of the war, Henry Ford I was asked who he considered the greatest man he had ever met, and he replied by jerking his thumb across the car in which he was seated. The magazine writer was confused, because the carmaker seemed to be pointing at his short, bow-tied sidekick, who appeared a brisk enough character, with a certain charm, but who was not obviously on a par with the Presidents, captains of industry, and other great men with whom Henry Ford must have rubbed shoulders in the course of his life.[5]

It turned out, however, that the man who had once idolized Thomas Edison and John Burroughs could now imagine no one in the world who was finer than Harry Bennett—and inasmuch as Bennett represented the faithful reflection and busy realization of Henry Ford's own ego, it was a logical choice. Of Henry Ford's principal executives in the summer of 1943, Charles Sorensen and Harry Bennett were the two obvious contenders for the position of president after Edsel's death, and only one of them could be relied upon unquestioningly to execute his master's bidding.

The news that Harry Bennett was Henry Ford's candidate to succeed her husband, however, was for Eleanor the final straw.[6] Bennett had been Edsel's nemesis, the villain against whom he had pitted his life's energy. Both Eleanor and Edsel found it easier to focus their hatred on Bennett than on the true source and sustainer of Bennett's troublemaking.

Making Bennett president of the family company was tantamount, for Eleanor Ford, to saying that Edsel's life had been lived for nothing, and the bitterness which might otherwise have been restrained came welling out.

"Mrs. Ford called me," runs Charles Sorensen's diary for May 31, 1943, "asked me to see Mrs. Edsel [who] is rowing with Henry Ford."[7] Sorensen did not elaborate on the subject of the rowing, but Harry Bennett related, in a section of his memoirs that was deleted prior to publication after pressure from the Ford Motor Company,[8] "When Edsel died, Edsel's wife told Mr. Ford in a fit of anger that he had killed his son. That came as close to breaking Mr. Ford as anything."[9]

At Edsel's funeral Henry had displayed a conspicuous lack of emotion. "Well, there's nothing to be done," he said. "Just work harder. Work harder."

But the recriminations of Edsel's widow—probably delivered, thinks her son William Clay, in the course of various telephone conversations—made Henry Ford consider his treatment of Edsel for the first time in his life.

"He couldn't keep away from the subject," recalled Bennett. "He'd bring it up with me, and we'd discuss it a while, and then he'd say: 'Now, we aren't going to talk about it anymore.' But then he'd come back to it, again and again."[10]

"Harry," Henry Ford asked Harry Bennett on one of these occasions, "do you honestly think I was ever cruel to Edsel?"

Harry Bennett temporized. "Well," he replied, "if that had been me you'd treated that way, it wouldn't have been cruelty."

Bennett was presumably saying that his own hide was tough enough to have survived the treatment that Henry Ford had handed out to Edsel. But the old man did not catch his meaning.

"Why don't you give me an honest answer?" he insisted.

So Bennett replied, "Well, cruel, no; but unfair, yes. . . . If that had been me, I'd have got mad."

"That's what I wanted him to do," said Henry Ford, seizing eagerly on his henchman's answer. "Get mad."[11]

Six days after Edsel's death, on June 1, 1943, Henry Ford met with his grandsons Henry II, now twenty-five, and Benson, twenty-three, who represented the 41.9 percent of shares that had been held by their father, and, for the first time in the company's history, a major batch of nonfamily working executives was elevated to board status. Since the recent resignation of Wibel, the purchasing director, Charles Sorensen was the only non-Ford member of the board. Now he was joined by the company treasurer, B. J. Craig, an Edsel man, by Mead L. Bricker, a production manager loyal to Sorensen, and by Ray S. Rausch, a production manager who was very definitely one of the Bennett crowd. Harry Bennett himself made it to the board, but his presence was balanced by the election of Mrs. Edsel Ford—and when the new board of directors met later that day, with Henry II and Benson holding their mother's proxy, it was decided that the new company president should be not Harry Bennett, or any other executive who might disrupt the family succession, but old Henry Ford himself.

The vacuum left at the top of the Ford Motor Company by the death of Edsel Ford caused grave alarm in Washington. With all the production difficulties at Willow Run, there had already been whispers that the Ford management just was not up to the job, and alternative options had been canvassed, from the blending in of some fresh line management—Studebaker had been mentioned as a possible source—to an even more drastic alternative. J. K. Galbraith, then deputy director in the Office of Price Administration, has recalled suggestions that the government should get rid of Ford entirely and run the plant itself.[12]

Faith in Edsel—and Roosevelt's friendship going back to their meeting in Warm Springs, Georgia—had blocked this drastic option. Washington respected Sorensen and the other nonfamily director, A. M. Wibel. But now Wibel and

Edsel were gone—and it soon became obvious that, without allies, Sorensen himself was being undermined. On June 18, 1943, less than a month after Edsel's death, Harry Bennett got himself appointed Sorensen's "assistant" for administrative problems, and flanking his rival's other side was the newly elevated Ray Rausch, who was given powers of his own in the production domain that had, hitherto, been Sorensen's alone.[13]

"We could tell Sorensen was slipping," recalls the Ford test-track manager, Al Esper. "It was just the way the orders started coming down."[14]

The prospect of a major component of the American war effort being surrendered to a senile old man and the collection of hoodlums and semicriminal fixers surrounding Harry Bennett was not to be contemplated, and it was fortunate for the Ford family that Ernest Kanzler, who had been working as director general inside Knudsen's Office of War Production, had cultivated some high-level contacts in Washington. Kanzler had flown back to Detroit to confer with Eleanor at the time of Edsel's funeral. Two months later, he and Josephine took Eleanor to spend some time with them in Hot Springs, Virginia.[15] Kanzler's solution to the problem at Willow Run was that the young Henry Ford II, now approaching his twenty-sixth birthday, should be brought out of the Navy, where he had enlisted in 1941, to play an active, perhaps even a dominant, role in the Ford management.

Henry II was just completing his studies as an ensign at the Great Lakes Naval Training School near Chicago, and he had hopes of joining the U.S. Mediterranean Fleet on the staff of Admiral Hewitt.[16] Well aware of the controversy attending his father's draft deferral in the First World War, he was by no means receptive to the idea that he should leave the service.

"He wanted," recalls one of his friends, "what you English call 'a good war.'"[17]

But the worsening situation at Willow Run represented a melding of national and family duty that was difficult to resist. With old Henry off in an orbit of his own, and Sorensen fast losing ground to Bennett, there was no one who could save Willow Run for Ford—and Ford for Ford —except Edsel's eldest son. Early in August 1943, the U.S. Secretary of the Navy, Frank Knox, issued a personal authorization for Ensign Ford's honourable release from the armed services, and Henry Ford II came back to Detroit.

In October 1924, the Prince of Wales had come to Detroit, and the Edsel Fords entertained him in their Indian Village home beside the river. Great was the excitement among the elder Ford children, Henry II, just seven, and Benson, now five, and their mother promised them that if they were well behaved in their nursery, the prince might be brought up to see them for a brief minute.

Traffic was heavy, however, in Detroit that day. When the prince did finally arrive, he was an hour and a half late, and the strain proved too much for one of the family, Eleanor Ford's mother, Mrs. William Clay, who ran upstairs to take refuge in the nursery with her grandchildren, not knowing that the nursery would be the prince's first port of call.

His Royal Highness strode in, extending his hand to young Henry Ford II.

"How is everything?" he inquired.

"Well," replied the seven-year-old, pointing across the nursery at his younger brother Benson, "he just threw up, and Grandmother is hiding behind the screen."

Blunt speaking was one of the qualities that the second Henry Ford was to bring to the task of rescuing the family firm from the mess that his grandfather had made of it. But when Ensign Ford came back to Detroit in the summer of 1943, he was not obviously qualified in any other respect for the immense task facing him. "Dissolute" may be too strong a description for the youth of Henry Ford II, but "indolent" certainly is not.

A tale of Henry Ford II's student days relates how, confronted with the deadline for a Yale end-of-term paper on the novels of Thomas Hardy, he paid Rosenberg's, a local cramming agency, to prepare the paper for him, and then submitted the paper with Rosenberg's bill inside.

Henry Ford II today rather scornfully denies that he was ever so foolish as to leave the bill inside the paper—"I may be stupid," he told Booton Herndon, "but I'm not *that* stupid"[18]—and, from his later eminence, he has managed to extract a little humour from the episode.

"I didn't write this one either," he remarked in the spring of 1969, opening the typescript of the speech which he had been invited to deliver before the Yale Political Union.

The young man's failure to graduate from university set a disappointing seal on twenty-three years of only mediocre achievement. Like his namesake and grandfather, Henry Ford II has stimulated the most wildly divergent reactions, from those who would die for him as a warm, loyal, and straight-talking friend, to those who consider him a tyrannical oaf—and this divergence goes back to his childhood.

There are those who remember an overweight, somewhat overbearing little boy at Detroit University School in the late 1920s, altogether too conscious of what his name was and what that meant. "Lard-ass" is the nickname that his youngest brother, William Clay Ford, rather unkindly recalls.[19]

John Dahlinger, Evangeline's son, who came between Benson and Josephine Ford in age, remembers all the Ford grandchildren as "spoiled, nasty little kids."[20] Young Dahlinger would be brought over by old Henry to play with Henry II and Benson when they came to stay at Fair Lane, and it seemed to him that the two elder boys' principal object in life was to wreck the expensive toy cars that were presents from his fairy godfather.

"They would ride them around," he complained in later years, "and 'accidentally' bump into everything possible, leaving them scratched and dented."[21]

John Dahlinger was not, perhaps, a totally objective witness. A more balanced view is provided by Donald Thurber, who was one year behind Henry II, and one year ahead of Benson, at the Detroit University School. Thurber played in football games with Henry II and remembers one afternoon when Henry was playing centre—the player who, on the signal, snaps the football back between his legs. This play should start with the ball dead on the ground, but Henry II was picking up the ball and fingering it, so that he had a split second's advantage.

Aggrieved, Thurber crossed the line and pushed Henry back. Both teams froze, aghast at his gesture.

"What do you mean by that?" asked the teacher.

"He was juggling the ball," complained the righteous Thurber. "Well, he can't do that," replied the teacher, awarding a penalty against Henry, and for the rest of the game young Ford started all his "downs" with the ball dead on the ground.

What Thurber recalls from the episode is the docility with which Henry Ford II responded to being corrected: "He didn't sulk or bear malice, as many boys might have done." The most telling thing was the horror with which Thurber's fellow classmates, and his teacher, regarded his *lèse majesté*.

"The whole school—boys as well as teachers—was always, somehow, in awe of him," remembers Thurber. "People might pretend otherwise, for the best of reasons, and they might try to treat him normally. But no one could ever quite forget that he was Henry Ford II. Boys picked up the attitude from their parents, who were just delighted that their son was in the same class as Henry Ford II—and teachers, well, you could tell they would never rebuke Henry, or put him right quite as naturally as they treated everybody else."[22]

Detroit University School was followed by Hotchkiss, one of the East Coast boarding academies which prepare the young rich for the Ivy League, and there Henry II drifted through four amiable but far from brilliant years. "You've got something there," counselled his graduation handbook in 1936, "if you handle it right"[23]

"Chauffeur Frank will call for you," runs a typical telegram from Edsel Ford to Hotchkiss around holiday time,

"at front porch main school building 1:00 P.M. tomorrow
Saturday, and drive you to Ritz Carlton. Love Father."[24]

A boy cannot help developing a certain outlook on life if
he regularly gets telegrams like that. Young Henry Ford II
wanted for nothing. Records of the Edsel Fords' summer
holidays in Europe show Henry's pocket money running
into the thousands of dollars.[25] Does he remember being
spoiled?

"I don't know what spoiled means," he replies[26]—and
that is the precise truth, for what standard of comparison
did he have?

In adult life Henry Ford II was to display a happy
aptitude, when not working, to enjoy himself 200 percent.
He developed this knack at quite an early age, and it reached
its apogee in a summer-long vacation on which he embarked
in his twenty-first year, driving round Europe in a streamlined Lincoln Zephyr with two Grosse Pointe friends, George
"Bud" Fink and Jerry DuCharme.

"You are Henry Ford," said their hotel manager in
Vienna, where they arrived in the summer of 1938, only a
few weeks after Hitler's storm troopers had effected the
union of Austria with Germany, "and I know what you
want. Please don't go out into town to pick up a girl. Since
the Nazis came they all have syphilis."[27]

The Ford entourage heeded this considerate warning—
though, when they got to Paris, they did pay the statutory
young American courtesy call on the famous House of All
Nations, where the girls came in every colour and language.
Their odyssey finished in the south of France. Henry Ford
II had been intrigued by the French custom of having female
attendants in male lavatories—a sorry fate, it seemed to
him, for any self-respecting woman—and at dinner one
night his travelling companions suddenly noticed that his
absence from the table had been rather overlong. In forsaking them he had also, apparently, taken the champagne
bottle with him, and when they eventually tracked him
down, it was to the gentlemen's lavatory, where a merry
young Henry II was sitting on the tiled floor, serenading

the washroom attendant, while that confused but happy lady toasted her minstrel in Dom Perignon.[28]

A document in the Ford Archives at Dearborn gives a less cheery glimpse of youth as enjoyed by the third generation of America's principal automobile dynasty. Transcribed from the papers of Edsel Ford, it records how, while driving through the small Connecticut town of Oxford on November 18, 1937, Henry Ford II, now a Yale sophomore, had struck and injured a twelve-year-old girl as she came across the road from behind a school bus. The $25,000 case brought by the girl's family was settled out of court, with little publicity. "It was a tragic thing," says Henry II today, "and it was my fault."

Edsel Ford, whose surviving correspondence files contain a particularly strained and salty collection of letters between Edsel and the various long-suffering tutors, headmasters, and doctors charged with the care of his self-willed children, had few illusions about his eldest son. Informed from Yale late in 1939 that Henry II was really doing quite well at his studies, his father responded: "It is almost time for him to do so, having but a few more months left."[30]

The hope of Henry II's parents was that marriage might settle him down, and this was why they raised fewer objections than they might otherwise have done to their son's friendship with a stylish, blonde Long Island girl whom he met soon after he went up to Yale, Anne McDonnell.

Anne McDonnell was a serious girl, and there was nothing wrong with her parents' financial resources. In Southampton the McDonnells owned a fifty-room mansion whose green and manicured acres rolled down impressively to the Atlantic. When the McDonnells summered on Long Island, they were looked after by sixteen servants, one for each member of the family.[31] In New York they made do with twenty-nine rooms spread over three floors on upper Fifth Avenue. Their credentials filled pages of the *Social Register*, and no breath of scandal had ever attached to Mr. James Francis McDonnell's handling of his very profitable business, a Wall Street stockbrokerage specializing in the traffic of rights options. The problem was that the McDonnells were Catholic.

They were the most refined sort of Catholic. They had their own chapel, and when Mrs. McDonnell went to Lourdes every summer to give thanks for her latest delivery, she never failed to visit the couture houses of Paris, bringing home a useful selection of $10,000 dresses which New York customs inspectors, usually Irish, tended to let through duty-free.[32]

The McDonnells saw no cause to apologize to the Fords for their religion—indeed, they insisted that young Henry Ford II should become a Catholic as a precondition to marrying Anne. The McDonnells set high standards for their daughters. At about this time, Anne's sister Charlotte McDonnell was being courted quite seriously by the young John Fitzgerald Kennedy, and many years later Senator Kennedy reminded Mrs. James Francis McDonnell of this when he ran into her in a New York lift.

"Did you know," inquired the senator from Boston in a friendly fashion, "that I almost married your daughter?"

"Yes, I did," replied Mrs. McDonnell, "and I am very glad that you didn't."

Edsel and Eleanor Ford were low on prejudice of any kind. The important thing for them was that their son should enjoy the sort of marriage that they had had. But Rome featured high in the demonology of Henry Ford Senior. He came from Irish Protestant peasant stock, and he knew what he thought about Catholic peasants. He was not happy at the prospect of his eldest grandson getting involved with a Catholic family—especially one whose wealth came from Wall Street—and he was particularly put out that Henry II should have taken his religious instruction from Monsignor (later Archbishop) Fulton J. Sheen, the leading Catholic propagandist of his day. Henry Ford II was welcomed into the Roman church in a private ceremony on July 12, 1940, the day before his marriage, and Pope Pius XII sent the young couple his personal blessing.

Old Henry put a good face on it at the wedding, held on

Long Island and featured by the society pages as the Wedding of the Year. He managed to chat politely with Fulton Sheen, and he was much taken with the pretty young bride. Chic and attractive in her hollow-cheeked, East Coast way, the latest Mrs. Ford looked exactly how a rich girl should, and the old carmaker danced enthusiastically with her.

He was enraged shortly afterwards, however, when Walter Winchell suggested on his radio programme that, with the younger Henry Ford now secure in the ranks of the Catholic church, there was a possibility of his grandfather joining him. This was based on the misunderstanding of a private joke that old Henry always enjoyed when a clergyman grew too heated on the subject of his own particular religious convictions.

"Well now," he would say, "you've got the best religion in the world,"[33] and move on to another conversation.

Henry Ford had used this ploy when he met Fulton Sheen on Long Island, and the remark had evidently raised the monsignor's hopes. So to demonstrate what he really felt, Henry Ford renewed pledges of Masonry he had taken sometime in his youth, and went down to the huge Masonic Temple in Detroit to go through the liturgies that would take him to the thirty-third degree—the highest and most difficult rank to obtain.

"I'm going down to take care of Winchell," he would remark with relish as he set off for the latest batch of rituals.[34]

The old man's gesture hardly hurt young Henry Ford II, but its spite and childishness did not augur well for the prospects of grandfather and grandson working happily together. Old Henry Ford had never been willing to surrender his company to Edsel, and now caprice, old age, and Harry Bennett made it still less likely he would cooperate in any smooth transition to Edsel's son. The hitherto unexceptional young Henry II would have to dig into himself and locate somewhere the courage and resources to attempt what his father had never been able to accomplish.

Harry Bennett had no intention of letting anyone but Harry Bennett control the destiny of the Ford Motor Company. In later years he was to claim that his ambition did not stretch beyond serving Henry Ford I.

"I always said," he told David Lewis in 1974, "that when Mr. Ford left, I would go."[35] He never doubted, he maintained, that the old man's departure would mean the end of his own career at Ford, and he had hopes of nothing more.

But these claims are clearly contradicted by the facts. The man who reckoned that he had half of Michigan's political establishment in his pocket—and most of the Detroit underworld as well—had grand and long-term plans for his future.

He started off by getting rid of Charles Sorensen. The production chief did not survive the death of Edsel by even a year. Part of the fault was Sorensen's. Though his memoirs make clear his awareness of Henry Ford's ever-sensitive ego, and the need to handle it with care, the production chief did not shrink from the limelight in the months when Willow Run was still impressing America as an eighth wonder of the world. He became the subject of a number of adulatory articles. *Time* wrote admiringly about him, as did *Newsweek*. "Cast Iron Charlie" became quite a national celebrity in the summer of 1942, and that did not sit well with his employer.

Sorensen had also fallen foul of Clara Ford, who, as her husband weakened, was coming to occupy a more and more pivotal role in the power play. Clara had decided, with her daughter-in-law, that Henry II represented the future of the company. United in their grief and anger over Edsel's death —there is evidence that Clara engaged in some recriminations of her own over Henry's treatment of their only son[36]—the two women were coming to form an alliance that was to prove decisive in the struggle ahead.

Clara had interpreted Sorensen's recent taste for publicity as a bid for personal power at the expense of her grandson —and the fact that Sorensen went to some length in his memoirs to disavow any such ambition suggests that Clara may well have been right.

With Bennett also working energetically against him, Sorensen did not have a chance. Bennett now held such thrall over Henry Ford that the old man was taking everything he said as gospel. He interpreted criticisms of Harry as criticisms of himself, and Sorensen, by his own account, does not seem to have done much in his final months except fight Bennett. The circle was complete.

Early in January 1944, Sorensen, who had already submitted a formal letter of resignation, bumped into Henry Ford in the Dearborn engineering laboratories and told him he was leaving for Florida the next morning, and that he would not be coming back. Henry Ford was unmoved.

"I guess there's something in life besides work," he remarked, followed Sorensen to his company car, shook hands with him, and never saw him again.

Thus ended the forty-year relationship that had accomplished some of the mightiest deeds, in peace and war, in the history of American industry—except that, while Sorensen was in Florida, some representatives of the Service Department went over to his home in Dearborn and took his company car away.

When Henry Ford II arrived at the Rouge on August 10, 1943, he concentrated, to start with, on keeping his head down.

"I just moseyed around on my own," he recalled later.[37]

The young man could tell that Harry Bennett was no friend of his. But he had no idea of the lengths to which the Service Chief was going, behind his back, to exclude him from what might have seemed the inevitable family succession.

Henry Ford I's suspicions of the ties his grandson had formed with the McDonnell family were not confined to his anti-Catholic prejudice. Taking the Ford Motor Company public would be just about the biggest coup that any stockbroker could pull off, and old Henry had no doubt that his grandson's Wall Street father-in-law would soon start pushing the boy in that direction.[38]

The carmaker had already developed a mistrust of his elder grandsons, in any case. Sometime in 1941, before Pearl Harbor, when Henry II and Benson were both working at the Rouge, their father, Edsel, had come to Sorensen in some distress one day with the news that his father had demanded the banishing of the boys to California.[39] It was a repetition of the Jack Davis situation—the old man wanted Henry II and Benson out of his sight. So far as anyone could tell, the problem stemmed from injudicious comments that had been made by both young men. Less restrained than their father, the boys had made no secret of their dislike of Bennett and his "goons," as they referred to the Service Department, and one of these goons had evidently carried the message to his superiors.

The incident was smoothed over, and the grandsons stayed on at the Rouge until their enlistment. But they continued to be outspoken in their dislike of what they saw going on—especially as they saw it damaging their father's health. In one outburst, Benson exploded to Charles Sorensen with the accusation that was evidently the Grosse Pointe Ford refrain, that his grandfather was responsible for his father's sickness and that he, Benson, was through with him.[40] After the death of Edsel and the company board rearrangement that followed, Benson made his feelings apparent by declining to attend any further board meetings at which Harry Bennett was present.[41]

Old Henry Ford was clearly failing. "Let's go over and see Charlie," he would quite often say to Bennett after Sorensen's departure.[42] He spent more and more time retreating into the bygone world of Greenfield Village, and he seemed at his happiest among the children in the grade school there. But the devil in him was not yet dead, particularly with Harry Bennett on hand to apply the jump-start cables from time to time, and another source of information added mischief of its own to the pot.

One day Ray Dahlinger came to Henry Ford with the news that Henry II had "unloaded" to him.

"Grandad killed my father," Dahlinger reported young Henry saying.[43]

"That's Ernie Kanzler," exclaimed the old man at once. "He's back of that, telling the kids that."[44]*

The "Office of the President," the credit company, the Guardian Group, and now poisoning the mind of the next generation—would Kanzler's scheming never cease? Henry Ford I determined he would foil the man once and for all, and sometime in 1943, quite soon after Edsel's death, I. A. Capizzi, the attorney whom Bennett had selected to succeed Louis Colombo as Ford's chief legal adviser, was summoned to a meeting at Willow Run.

As Capizzi recalled the meeting some years later to the researchers for Allan Nevins and Frank Ernest Hill's official history of the company, both Bennett and Sorensen were present—which means that the meeting must have taken place sometime before Sorensen left at the beginning of 1944. Capizzi could sense the rivalry between Ford's two lieutenants. It was evident to him that they both saw themselves as contenders for the succession, and the succession was the subject of the meeting.

"Mr. Henry Ford was concerned," Bennett informed the lawyer, "that Henry Ford II would come too much under the influence of Kanzler in the operation of the company and that therefore Mr. Henry Ford was interested in setting up a means whereby the operation of the company would vest in others until Henry II and the other grandchildren were old enough to manage the company themselves"[46]

Capizzi's legal advice was that Henry Ford I's purpose could be accomplished if a board of trustees was set up to operate the company after his death, and that such a board

* According to the painter Irving Bacon, young Henry made similar remarks to Charles Sorensen who "bawled him out about it." Referring, presumably, to young Henry's battle with Bennett, Sorensen told him, "I won't do a thing for you to help you, as long as you talk about your grandfather that way."[45]

could be established by means of a codicil to Mr. Ford's will. Bennett instructed Capizzi to draw up such a codicil, and later listed the men who were to serve on the board of trustees: Bennett himself, who was to act as secretary; Capizzi; Sorensen; the former private secretary Liebold; Liebold's successor, Frank Campsall; old Henry's school friend and soya-bean researcher, Dr. Edsel Ruddiman; Charles Lindbergh; and Clara Ford's brother, Roy Bryant.

There are several ambiguities surrounding this list. According to Bennett, Henry Ford later erased Liebold's name and replaced him with Carl Hood, the administrative director of Greenfield Village. Dr. Edsel Ruddiman died in 1943, while John Bugas, the FBI man, who saw the codicil sometime in 1944, did not think that Lindbergh's name was on it.

The purpose of the document, however, was quite clear. The trust committee was to hold power for ten years following the death of Henry Ford. Capizzi and Campsall were both firm allies of Bennett. With Bennett as secretary of the board, the codicil ensured that the old regime would survive long past the death of Henry Ford—with one further twist, which Bennett described in the original version of his memoirs. Old Henry Ford had grown so disenchanted with his two elder grandsons, said Bennett, that he wished the trustees to hold power until their younger brother, William Clay, was old enough to start work at the company.

"Harry," he would say, "can't we get Henry out of here, and Billy in instead?"[47]

When you visit the twelfth floor of Ford World Headquarters today, the power centre, the floor where the chairman and the president have their offices and where the vice-presidents line up in ranks, you will see oil paintings of Henry Ford I and Henry Ford II, the two great heroes of the company's history—the grandfather and grandson between whom the baton passed, you would assume, in warmth and trust and family feeling. You would not guess that sometime in 1943 old Henry Ford so disliked and distrusted his grandson and namesake that he actually plot-ted to exclude him from the succession. His affection for William Clay was based on little more than the boy's youth, and the presumption that the eighteen-year-old had been less poisoned than his elder brothers by the bitterness surrounding Edsel's death.

The codicil and board of trustees which would have denied Henry Ford II taking over the Ford Motor Company are one of several incidents on which Henry II's memory today draws a blank. He has a paper shredder in his mind when it comes to the difficulties in his past. He cannot remember the details. He does not want to talk about them. But John Bugas, the man to whom young Henry went early in 1944 when he discovered the threatening codicil's existence, remembered that the young man's first reaction was to throw in the towel. He would quit the company, he told Bugas, sell his stock, and write to Ford dealers all over the country advising them to cut their links with Ford.[48]

Bugas was by this time a Ford employee. He had been invited to join the company in November 1943 after a series of investigations had revealed theft and trafficking in Ford spare parts exceeding $1 million a year.[49] This winked-at corruption was the way in which Service Department stooges were remunerated, and Bennett appears to have hoped that he could make Bugas his own man by bringing him inside the company, at double his FBI salary.[50]

In the event, the FBI man had decided to throw in his lot with Henry II, and now, in January 1944, Bugas, nine years older than Henry II, calmed the young man down. He should not do anything drastic, he said. He would go and talk to Bennett personally—and when he did so, he found the Service Chief somewhat alarmed at Henry's discovery of his plot.[51]

"You come in here tomorrow," he told Bugas, "and we'll straighten the whole thing out."[52]

Next day Bennett had the codicil ready, and he showed it briefly to Bugas. He then placed it dramatically on the floor, lit a match, and set fire to it. When the document was just ashes, Bennett swept them up, placed them in an envelope, and handed them to Bugas with the words, "Take this back to Henry."[53]

When the lawyer, Capizzi, later heard of this bizarre and casual end to his carefully drafted legal instrument, he asked Bennett what he had been playing at.

"It wasn't any good anyway . . . ," the Service Chief replied. "Mr. Ford had carried the instrument around in his pocket for a long time and had made a lot of scribblings on it, including verses from the Bible."[54]

Born of the senile wanderings of old Henry Ford's mind, the mysterious codicil had been destroyed by them.

Until the discovery of the plan to alter his grandfather's will, Henry Ford II had been digging himself into the Ford Motor Company without any obvious sense of urgency. He had taken his grandfather's death or retirement for granted. The old man's eventual disappearance seemed to be the one certain point in a very uncertain and difficult scene—the moment when the young prince could claim his birthright.

But the codicil had called that in question. It made clear the extent of Harry Bennett's ambitions and the danger that Bennett represented to young Henry so long as his grandfather was alive. The young man's first reaction to the plot had not been impressive. But faced with a clear and identifiable challenge, he started to fight back. Nothing was going to fall into his lap. If he wanted the company, he would have to do battle for it.

On April 10, 1944, Henry II got himself named to the position of executive vice-president, which gave him paper authority over Bennett, and he worked to give the position real effect. John Bugas was one useful ally. Mead Bricker, Sorensen's former production assistant, was another. Henry organized strategy sessions with these lieutenants in private rooms on the upper floors of the Detroit Club, out of sight of Bennett's spies. Touring the dealers on the West Coast in the first half of the year, the new executive vice-president added a third recruit whose reinforcement was both helpful and symbolic.

"Get Jack Davis," his mother had told him,[55] remembering Edsel's old ally, exiled after the showdown with Harry Bennett, and when Henry II got to California he asked the former sales manager if he would come back with him to Dearborn. Davis refused. He liked West Coast life and he doubted, frankly, whether young Henry could protect him against Bennett any more effectively than Edsel had.

But Henry II insisted. "If I stay, you stay," he told Davis. "If you go, I go. . . . We shall share the same fate."[56]

How could Davis refuse? Edsel had said the very same thing, but, as Davis put it later, Henry Ford II "had the drive that Edsel lacked. He would win if it killed him. . . . We'd do it for Edsel, but he never asked us to. Henry asked us."[57]

The return of Edsel Ford's friend and lieutenant was a clear message to the Bennett faction. They had a war on their hands. The old regime gave young Henry II a nickname, "The Tooth," which seemed to indicate a certain grudging anxiety and respect—and the anxiety proved to be justified as the young man started picking off Bennett sympathizers and firing them. When the Service Chief, with whom the young Ford still maintained a veneer of cordiality, asked the reason why a particular man had been let go, he was given an answer that would be heard on more than one occasion in the next thirty-five years: "I just don't like his looks."[58]

Harry Bennett's customary response to attacks upon his empire was to turn for help to old Henry Ford. But the old man was becoming an increasingly unreliable reinforcement. He would drift off for days at a time in reveries of his own, and Clara, who was assuming more and more authority over him, gave the Fair Lane telephone operator a decisive instruction. If Mr. Bennett called, Mr. Ford was not in.[59]

Bennett later claimed that this prohibition was to do with commissions he had undertaken on his master's instruction connected with old Ford girlfriends, including the memorable Wantatja.* But Clara's intention was more serious than that. Sometime in 1944 or 1945, she and her daughter-in-law, Eleanor, had discussed problems like the codicil and had come to the conclusion that the family company would not be safe for Henry II until he had actually taken over the presidency from his grandfather. The time had come for the women of the family to make a stand.

"He killed my husband, and he's not going to kill my son" is the sentiment frequently attributed to Eleanor Ford at this climax in the affairs of the Ford family. She wanted her son made president, and, according to Nevins and Hill, the official historians of the Ford Motor Company, she was prepared to go to drastic lengths.

"If this is not done," they report her saying, "I shall sell my stock."[61]

Henry Ford II today cannot remember his mother making any such threat. But he cannot remember his own threats to Bugas to sell his shares either. It is clear from every other source that feelings were running very high indeed inside the Ford family—and it seems most likely that it was Clara Ford who eventually accomplished the impossible. Working on her husband through the summer of 1945, she slowly induced the old autocrat finally to relinquish his power and hand it not to Harry Bennett, his alter ego, but to the family's choice.

On September 20, 1945, Henry Ford II was summoned to the gloomy halls of Fair Lane for a momentous interview. There his grandfather beckoned him into a chair and informed him that he was, finally, ready to step aside and let the young man take over the presidency of the company.

According to his own recollection, Henry Ford II was less than gracious in victory.

---

* According to Bennett, his mission was to make sure that the ladies were not in any special need, and most of them, apparently, were not particularly flattered by his inquiries. Asked whether there was anything Henry Ford could do for her, one of them sharply replied that she had got on perfectly well without his help for most of her life and saw no need of it now.[60]

"I told him I'd take it," he later recalled, "only if I had a completely free hand to make any changes I wanted to make. We argued about that—but he didn't withdraw his offer."[62]

From Fair Lane young Henry drove immediately to the Administration Building on Schaefer Road. There he informed Frank Campsall what had happened, directing the private secretary to draw up his grandfather's letter of resignation and call a board meeting next day to ratify it. Knowing Campsall's sympathies, he was not surprised to receive a phone call a short time later.

"Henry," Harry Bennett informed him, "I've got wonderful news for you. I've just talked your grandfather into making you president"[63]

Next day Bennett was less genial. As B. J. Craig, the treasurer, started to read old Henry's resignation into the minutes, the Service Chief got up bitterly to leave the room. He knew what was coming. Prevailed on to stay, he sat through the resignation and the vote that confirmed it.

There was one last act to the drama. Henry Ford II walked down to the basement to inform Harry Bennett that his services to the company would no longer be required. Henry Ford II does not today recall the details of this final encounter, except that, beforehand, he "might have been a little scared."[64] Bennett recalled that the young man was "nice as hell with me. Cripes, you could cut butter . . ."[65] —which did not inhibit him from delivering a bitter parting shot.

"You're taking over a billion dollar organization here," he informed Henry II, "that you haven't contributed a thing to!"[66]

The basement office was filled with smoke for the rest of that afternoon as Harry Bennett burned his records, and that evening the new president of the Ford Motor Company drove over to Fair Lane to inform his predecessor of his first executive act.

"I went to him with my guard up," Henry II recalled later. "I was sure he'd blow my head off."[67]

But old Henry Ford was strangely uninterested in the news that the man he had once called the greatest in the world had been given his marching orders.

"Well, now," he murmured, "Harry is back where he started from."[68]

# 25

# THE WHIZ KIDS

The company which Henry Ford II took over in September 1945 was not dying, in the opinion of Jack Davis. "It was already dead," he said later, "and *rigor mortis* was setting in."[1] The Ford Motor Company had performed less and less impressively through the 1930s. Edsel had designed some classic cars for Lincoln, and a new, intermediate nameplate had been devised for Fords that were sold with upgraded, middle-range features: the Mercury. This had been an attempt to take on Buick and Pontiac, the heavyweight midrange divisions which yielded the bulk of General Motors' profits, but it had not sold well.[2] With less than 19 percent of the prewar U.S. market share, Ford had consistently finished a poor third to Chevrolet and Chrysler. In 1945 the company was by no means as close to ruin as has since been claimed by the detractors of Harry Bennett—and Jack Davis, it must be remembered, was one of those. But the calibre of the surviving management, engineering, and financial staffs was patchy, to put it kindly, and if it had not been for the $5.26 billion of guaranteed income yielded by government war-supply contracts, the company would have been in a parlous state.

In 1946, the first year of new car sales in America after the war, the list of U.S. manufacturers included such names as Nash, Hudson, Kaiser-Fraser, Willys, Packard, and Studebaker.[3] If Ford was to escape the fate which overtook all these companies in the next dozen years or so, it would have to discover something that had been eluding it for more than a decade. Because it was a private family company, the key to its survival was the man on whom the family now pinned its hopes, Henry Ford II. In the autumn of 1945, *Life* magazine despatched a writer, Gilbert Burck, to weigh up the young man whose role would be so important as the company readied itself for postwar car production, and Burck was impressed by the twenty-eight-year-old's "blunt frankness and intolerance of pretence." Burck also remarked, however, after lengthy observation of the new Ford president, that it was possible "to imagine his becoming as arbitrary as his grandfather when he got as experienced and confident."[4]

The article, which appeared in *Life* for October 1, 1945, was read by Arjay Miller, a young officer on the lookout for a job after he left the U.S. Army Air Force. "I've still got a copy of it," he says today.[5]

Miller was not quite any Air Force officer. Before he enlisted, he had lectured on business at the University of California, Los Angeles. More significantly for the subsequent history of the Ford Motor Company, Miller was one of a group of ten young Air Force officers who had developed particular planning and financial skills during the war, and who had decided to stick together and hire themselves out, in peacetime, as a ready-made management team. Unapologetic about their talents, they had produced a brochure explaining how their Air Force expertise could be transferred to industry, and they had sent this to a hundred major corporations[6]—which did not, until publication of the *Life* feature, include Ford.

The young officers' expertise was considerable, for they had served together in the Office of Statistical Control, the administrative pivot that had helped make the U.S. Army Air Force the massive and dominating power it had become by the end of World War II. It was one thing to train fliers by the thousand and to produce flying machines in bulk— though, as Charles Sorensen had discovered, it was not that easy. It was quite another to get fliers and machines together on the same Pacific atoll or East Anglian airbase with the correct amount of fuel, ammunition, flak jackets, nylons, and Hershey bars. This demanded cost analysis, price control, and management skills developed to a rare degree. When the need arose, for example, to shift 100,000 tons of equipment from San Francisco to Australia, the Office of Statistical Control could show precisely how it would take 10,022 planes and 120,765 air crew to duplicate the task already being performed by forty-four surface vessels and 3,200 seamen.[7] On the basis of such data are modern wars won and lost.

In 1945 the head of the Office of Statistical Control was Charles Bates ("Tex") Thornton, aged thirty-two and one of the youngest colonels in the U.S. Army Air Force. The notion of packaging the OSC's expertise and putting it out to tender had been his brainchild, and he had handpicked a high-powered team: Robert S. McNamara had been on the faculty of the Harvard Business School; J. "Ed" Lundy had served in the economics department at Princeton; Francis C. Reith, like Thornton, had established a record of business success before joining up; and the remainder of the group had skills which ranged from law to federal government responsibility.* Aged between twenty-six and thirty-four, they thought they were just what the Ford Motor Company needed, and Thornton fired off a telegram to Henry Ford II which did not so much solicit his interest as demand his consent: "We have a matter of management importance to discuss with you."[9] The tone of the telegram, recalled one of the cadre later, did border on the impudent, but the group had already received an offer from the Allegheny Corporation, who had given them one week to decide.[10]

Henry Ford II wasted no time. The very next day Thornton got a phone call inviting him and his friends to

---

* Besides Thornton, Miller, Lundy, McNamara, and Reith, the group included Wilbur R. Andreson, Charles E. Bosworth, Ben Davis Mills, George Moore, and James O. Wright. By the time all ten had completed their business careers, six had become Ford vice-presidents, two had served as president of the company, three had taken chief-executive jobs in other companies, one had held cabinet office—and one had dreamed up a car called the Edsel.[8]

Detroit, and the ten men got ready for the journey—with the exception of Robert McNamara, who had been invited to return to Harvard as a full professor and had decided that the lure of Dearborn was not for him. He wasn't interested.

"Well," snapped Thornton, "you'd better get interested." He knew that McNamara's wife had been hospitalized for some months with polio, and he pointed out that a college professor's salary would hardly pay the bills.[11]

McNamara was stationed at Wright Field in Dayton, Ohio, at the time, and he drove up to Dearborn, through Toledo, with Lieutenant-Colonel Charles Bosworth, another member of Thornton's handpicked group. Bosworth remembers both of them being struck breathless by the great looming mass of the Rouge. It was the first time either of them had seen it.

What impressed them most, however—and this was the same for all of the group—was Henry Ford II, whom they met up with that day. He was "a gleaming figure," remembered Tex Thornton, "a young man with determination."[12]

Henry II was about the same age as these thrusting, self-assured young men. He could not match them in terms of brainpower, and he met them without an entourage, just one against ten. But when the crown prince entered the room and started talking, Bosworth remembers, everyone felt smaller, just a little less cocky. They had come to be courted, and suddenly they were selling themselves.

"There was something heroic about him, the way he held himself, with his crew cut," he says. "He was so upright, so erect. We sensed sincerity in him, something genuine."[13]

There was an edge of danger in the air. It was only a few weeks since Harry Bennett had been fired, and no one knew for sure that he was going to stay fired. There were many of his henchmen still around. Old Henry Ford was in Fair Lane, failing, as everybody knew, but still a factor to be reckoned with. The challenge of it all appealed to the desktop officers.

That evening they went for dinner with John Bugas in a private room at the Detroit Athletic Club, a venerable downtown institution which had, for three decades, been combining the wood-panelled virtues of a gentlemen's club with hot tubs and workout facilities. Henry II had delegated the detailed grilling of the would-be recruits to the ex-FBI man—somewhat to their resentment. They felt that Bugas was interposing himself, that he was jealous of the closeness he had built with Henry during the tense days of the show-down with Bennett.[14]

But in reality, Bugas liked the team. When he spoke to Henry II next day, he gave them his blessing. His only reservation was the money they were demanding: ten salaries ranging from $8,000 to $15,000, depending on a scale drawn up by Thornton. Bugas thought this was ridiculous.[15]

Henry Ford II disagreed. Ernest Kanzler had arranged for his nephew to have a confidential conversation with Robert A. Lovett, the Assistant Secretary of War for Air,[16] to whom Thornton and the others had reported, and Lovett had nothing but good to say. The young officers were worth their price ticket. One of the undeniable strengths of the Ford Motor Company in 1945, thanks to old Henry's financial conservatism, was money in the bank—$697 million cash in hand on June 30, 1945[17]—and Ford had always paid its top executives well. Charles Sorensen's quarter million dollars a year was fabled in Detroit in the 1930s as by far the highest salary paid to any car executive, while Harry Bennett had benefited from even more handsome remuner-ation. He had access to a safe containing several million dollars in cash, to which he appears to have helped himself quite liberally. Whatever his meanness in other directions, Henry Ford I was generous to executives whose talent he respected, and his grandson has maintained that policy to the present day. Ford middle management gets remunerated on the same scale that it does in the other car companies, but if you are at, or near, the top of the Ford Motor Company, you get very rich, very fast.*

Next day the team were taken on a tour of the Rouge, the entire operation. It left them in awe but also feeling quite confident, for, as they went around, there were problems they could see, even at a first glance—and it excited them. The coking ovens, the rolling mill, the glass plant, the line itself —it was all there just waiting for their touch. That night Bosworth and McNamara drove back to Dayton, talking Ford all the way, the cool, adding-machine McNamara seeming, for once, excited, like a kid. His old Model A Ford coupe was giving them trouble, fluttering and sputtering with some problem in the carburettor, but Bob pulled the choke out and kept on going, telling Charlie that things were going to be okay. The future looked good.

It was agreed that Thornton, McNamara, Miller, Bosworth, and the others would report for work at Schaefer Road on February 1, 1946, and they all arrived a day early. It was not long before the group were dubbed collectively the "Whiz Kids."

The Whiz Kids have popularly been credited with the remarkable revival achieved by the Ford Motor Company in the years after the Second World War. It makes such a good story, and they, certainly, arrived in Dearborn intending to tell it that way. But even as they were arranging the furniture in their new Michigan homes—Robert McNamara, never totally a car executive in his own mind, moved into Ann Arbor and drove an hour east and an hour west each day for the sake of the campus atmosphere—the true saviour was on his way.

* The important comparison here is with General Motors. League tables of the salary, bonus, stock options, and other benefits enjoyed by top car executives show Ford men consistently equalling or outdistancing their equivalents at GM, although Ford is half the size, with its managers supervising, in gross terms, half the revenues. Lee Iacocca's salvation of Chrysler has produced its own crop of instant millionaires, but this is largely a matter of stock-option schemes (see pages 512–14 below).

Ernest R. Breech was not a Whiz Kid. He was an old-fashioned, dyed-in-the-wool accountant who had been in the car business for more than twenty years when he came to Ford in 1946—and he had started out in life, forty-nine years earlier, as an Ozark Mountain blacksmith's son. In the small community of Lebanon, Missouri, which boasted no less than seven churches, the Breech family were religious enough to earn a special reputation for their piety: they were born-again Baptists. Young Ernie was taught to say his prayers regularly, and he was proud in later years to claim that he had not let a day of his life go by without a conversation with God.

As a boy, Ernie Breech persuaded his father to transform his village smithy into the local Dodge dealership. Ernie worked his way through college by setting up and operating a clothes-pressing shop in an empty basement. He spent his vacations as a door-to-door salesman peddling books and Victrolas. In the evenings he studied to gain his professional qualifications as an accountant, and, not surprisingly, in the few moments he had left for pleasure, his favourite books were the tales of Horatio Alger.[18]

Breech's career took an upward swing in 1925 when, aged twenty-eight, he caught the eye of John Hertz, a Chicago entrepreneur in the taxi business who was diversifying into car rental. Hertz's Yellow Cab and Driv-Ur-Self System was swallowed up in that year by General Motors, and Hertz's figures man was swallowed as well.

Figures were Ernie Breech's strong suit. His speciality was the then little-known science of cost analysis, and as GM pursued its voracious programme of acquisitions in the early 1930s, his skills were in high demand. He was the corporation's cleanup man. He was brought in to straighten out the finances of Frigidaire, and when Bendix, one of the conglomerate's plane-making subsidiaries, got into difficulties in 1937, GM sent for Ernie. By 1939 he had turned Bendix around. A monthly loss of $250,000 had become an annual profit of over $5 million,[19] and as it became obvious what war was going to do for the plane-making business,

Ernie Breech was given the job of making sure that GM got a good share of it. On February 24, 1942, he was elected president of the Bendix Aviation Corporation[20]—and Bendix happened to be one of the many pies that contained the finger of another Ernie, Ernest Kanzler, who was serving as a director on the board of Bendix as World War II drew to an end.

William Gossett, the New York attorney who was then general counsel for Bendix, can remember the night late in 1945 when he was travelling back to New York with Kanzler, after a Bendix board meeting, and the two men fell to discussing Breech's future career prospects. The next logical step for the blacksmith's son, after his success at Bendix, was the presidency of General Motors itself, but this had already been conferred upon Charles E. "Engine Charlie" Wilson—soon to win fame for his immortal, but often misquoted, testimony to the Senate Armed Forces Committee: "I have always thought that what was good for the United States was good for General Motors, and vice versa."

Wilson's assumption of the GM presidency had deeply wounded William Knudsen, who had returned from his war-production duties expecting a warm welcome, only to be shown the door as a working executive, and it had also blighted Ernie Breech's younger, and more realistic, ambition.

"They're going to regret that," Gossett told Kanzler, as the Detroiter carried the two men eastwards through the night. "Breech is much abler than Wilson, and if any other company is looking for a power-house as chief executive officer, then they are going to pick him up."[21]

Breech himself, however, cannot have been looking all that hard for another job, because when, forty-eight hours later, his secretary informed him that Henry Ford II was on the phone, he assumed that the Ford Motor Company wanted to do some business with Bendix. Breech had made no special study of Ford as it stood at the outset of the reign of Henry II, and he shared the general GM view of their ailing Dearborn rival—a mixture, as he later described it,

of pity and contempt.[22] He turned down the job offer that
Henry II made to him, but he liked the young man, and he
was sufficiently touched by Ford's sincerity and openness to
offer some help and advice. At the end of 1945, Breech was
approaching fifty and Henry II was just twenty-eight.

"Here's a young man," Breech told his wife, "only one
year older than our oldest son."[23]

He agreed to cast an eye over the Ford books, and the
moment he got into the figures, Ernie Breech was hooked.

"The company was really a mess," he later recalled. "Not
only did it need help, it had to have help or the Big Three
would surely become the Surviving Two."[24]

This was the type of challenge that GM's cleanup man
had been handling all his accounting life. It seemed to have
the Breech name written all over it, and early in 1946, just
as the Whiz Kids were signing on, Henry Ford II got himself
a new first lieutenant, who would watch over them. It was
agreed that Ernest R. Breech would join the Ford Motor
Company in July 1946. When asked later what had overcome his initial misgivings, Breech replied, "I said a few
prayers for guidance."[25]

It was not quite that simple. During the negotiations that
led to Ernest Breech leaving General Motors for Ford in the
summer of 1946, the question of stock options arose, the
chance for Breech to purchase equity which had, for more
than a quarter of a century, been among the most jealously
guarded private stock in North America. Since the buy-out
of Couzens and the Dodge brothers, no one outside the Ford
family had held shares in the Ford Motor Company.

Henry II's willingness to cut Ernest Breech in showed
how serious his offer was, and it also showed how well the
young man understood the realities of the big league to
which he wanted Ford to regain admission. War had saved
capitalism in America. The massive government supply
contracts of the early 1940s had proved to be the salvation
that the free enterprise system had been vainly seeking since
1929; and as American business rode the postwar boom,
it was the stock-option scheme, which sidestepped many

current tax regulations, that was the only game in town when it came to hiring real management talent.

Stock-option schemes are not, on the face of it, a secret. Their bare essentials are fully reported, as the law now requires, in the accounts and reports of all public companies. But it is perhaps worth spelling out, for the ordinary worker or middle manager who labours a lifetime for a set salary, precisely how the managers at the very top can get quite so rich so quickly. A stock option is an option to buy a specified amount of company stock at a specified price—usually the quoted share price prevailing on the day that the option is given. The option usually lasts for at least a year, so if, twelve months later, the quoted price of the company stock has risen, the option can be exercised for a guaranteed profit. If the share price has fallen, however, then the option holder says thanks, but no thanks, and has lost nothing.

Stock-option schemes enrich managers in every segment of modern business, but they hold particular attractions for executives in the car industry, so much more vulnerable to general upswings and downswings than other sectors of the economy. Automotive stocks can be something of a gamble for the ordinary outside investor, veering wildly between spectacular peaks and troughs. But the stock-option scheme means that car executives do not lose when the stock goes down—it can even be to their benefit. In a bad year they choose not to exercise their old option, and they can usually take out a fresh option at the trough price, which makes their private profit all the more spectacular when the peak comes. In 1984 Lee Iacocca, Gerald Greenwald, and Hal Sperlich, all former Ford executives who moved to Chrysler, exercised Chrysler stock options that realized them net profits of $4,315,012; $2,419,104; and $2,040,238, respectively. At Ford, in the same year, executives Philip Caldwell, Harold "Red" Poling, Thomas C. Page, Will M. Caldwell, and Donald E. Petersen, who all stayed loyal to Ford, realized stock option profits of $2,485,221; $2,291,025; $1,460,241; $1,386,357; and $1,184,291, respectively. All eight executives, in both companies, also received routine

salaries and bonuses at or near the level of $1 million each
—in addition to having their country club memberships
paid for.[26]

In the course of the Ford Motor Company's recovery
between 1946 and 1956, no less than sixty-seven of its
senior executives became millionaires thanks to stock-option
schemes, and Ernest R. Breech was the first of these.[27] The
scheme which Ford originally offered him in 1946 did not,
in fact, work out, but a more elegant solution was arrived
at. One obvious area into which the Ford Motor Company
might hope to expand in the postwar years was bus manufacture; old Henry's obstinacy had allowed General Motors to
gain a near monopoly in this field in the 1930s. Another
area of expansion would be tractor distribution, since Henry
II had determined to end the relationship which his grandfather had formed with Harry Ferguson, the Irish tractor
and farm-implement manufacturer.*

So in 1946 two new companies were formed: Michigan
Motors, which would hold the exclusive distribution rights
to Ford buses,[28] and Dearborn Motors, which would enjoy
a similar monopoly of Ford tractor distribution. As things
turned out, the plans for Ford bus manufacture came to
nothing, but the company already had its tractors in production, and in January 1947, Dearborn Motors started
distributing the machines—to the considerable profit of its
stockholders. Ernest Breech was the chief of these, with 20
percent of the shares.[29] Jack Davis, who appears to have
dreamed up the scheme, was rewarded with 12 percent, and
10 percent each went to four new executives brought in by
Ernest Breech: William T. Gossett, the ex-Bendix general
counsel who had helped negotiate Breech's own terms of
employment and had been brought in to create a new,
professional, Ford legal department; Lewis D. Crusoe, an
accountant who had been Breech's principal assistant at
Bendix; and two engineers, Harold T. Youngren and Delmar

* Ferguson invented the hydraulic linkage which solved the problem of
tractors tipping backwards, and Henry Ford had gone into partnership
with him at the end of the 1930s.

S. Harder, who had made their names at Borg Warner, the manufacturer of parts for car transmissions.[30]

Smaller shareholdings of 6 percent each went to John Bugas and Mead Bricker as rewards for their loyalty in the battle with Bennett. It would not have been right if Uncle Ernie Kanzler had gone without his 6 percent slice of the action, while a fourth 6 percent share went to Albert J. Browning, a onetime merchandising manager for Montgomery Ward, who had been director of War Department buying and had been recommended as a tough purchasing director by Secretary Lovett. (It was a mark of the relatively junior status of Lovett's other protégés, the Whiz Kids, that none of them was included in these private financial schemes.) The final 4 percent in Dearborn Motors went to a solitary survivor from the Henry I days, Herman L. Moekle, a veteran accountant who had resisted the blandishments of Bennett when dozens did not.

When Ernest Breech arrived at Ford in the middle of 1946, he found that things were even worse than he had first suspected. The chief engineer, he later recalled, "knew as much about designing cars as a pig did about Christmas. . . . They had financial statements like a country grocery store."[31]

"In one department," Henry Ford II told *Look* magazine in 1953, "they figured their costs by *weighing* the pile of invoices on a scale."[32]

Such anecdotes cannot be taken at quite their face value. Like Jack Davis, Henry Ford II and Ernest Breech have had obvious reasons for exaggerating the plight of the business which they steered to such triumphs in such a short time. Harry Bennett may have been a crook, but the Ford Motor Company had not fared that badly under his stewardship to find itself, in the middle of 1945, with over two thirds of a billion dollars in the bank.[33]

The extraordinary tale of the weighed invoices, however, does appear to be true. Given the shortage of clerical staff allowed by Henry Ford I's unending war on the accounts

department, and the need, nevertheless, to get the paperwork done, Ford chief accountants had worked out a system
whereby paid invoices below a certain amount were stacked
by category—engine parts, body parts, etc.—and then
weighed when tallies of itemized costs were required.[34] With
a little sampling and some ingenious calculations, quite
accurate results could be obtained. In its rough way, this
system represented a sophistication of Henry I's basic
accounting philosophy, which was to compare the bank
balances at the beginning of the month with those at the
end. If the figure went up in the course of the four weeks,
then there could not be, in his opinion, too much wrong
with the business.

Ernie Breech, the apostle of cost analysis, was flabbergasted.

"But how do you know," he asked the treasurer, B. J.
Craig, with horror, "whether a steering wheel is costing you
a dollar or a dollar fifty?"

"What's the difference?" replied Craig, pointing at the
undeniably substantial figure in the black. "There's the
profit."

Breech's official title was executive vice-president, placing
him second in the hierarchy to Henry Ford II. In the employment contract negotiated for him by William Gossett, he had
demanded sweeping powers to go with his position, and this
worried the Ford family lawyers, as Ernest Kanzler discovered one evening driving home along Woodward Avenue.
Woodward is the road which gave drag racing to America, as
young men gunned their V–8s down its straight, two-lane
stretches apportioned by traffic lights into convenient half-
mile segments. As he picked his way through the traffic,
Kanzler became aware of another car driving hard to catch
up with him. It turned out to be his nephew, Henry, anxious
at the power he was about to surrender.

"My lawyer says," he worried, "I'm abdicated [sic] when
I make Ernie Vice President."[35]

"You can't give him the power," replied Kanzler, "you
must make it understood that you are to retain the power."

Both Henry II and Breech, recalled Kanzler later, "were awfully afraid of what they were doing. . . . Both had very important futures to protect."[36]

Within months of the Breech-Ford partnership going into action in 1946, however, it became clear that the two men were operating as a team.

"He knew a lot more than I did," recalls Henry II today, "and so the major operating decisions, he made them. . . . He was really the chief, and I was watching and learning, hopefully."[37]

Outsiders remember how the normally assertive and cocky Ernest R. Breech was always very careful to defer to Henry II in public. He never contradicted the younger man, and there seemed at times an almost uncanny degree of shared knowledge and agreement between the two—though this stemmed from nothing more mysterious than a connecting washroom between their adjacent offices, which they used to facilitate meetings that the outside world knew not of.[38]

Henry Ford II's brief to Ernest Breech in the summer of 1946 was to make Ford more like General Motors. The dream of Edsel Ford and of Ernest Kanzler could finally come true.

Henry Ford II had never really known the Ford Motor Company as a dominant, successful enterprise. From the moment he had become aware, around the age of seven or eight, of what his family name stood for, the story of the family firm had been one of caprice and incompetence—and, increasingly, of corruption and chaos as well. Ford's successes like the Model A had been won at the expense of traumatic, debilitating battles, as if progress itself was something to be viewed with suspicion. It was General Motors and its management skills which had set the pace for the car industry.

"I had great admiration for General Motors, always have had," says Henry Ford II today, "and I thought that with the experience that Ernie Breech had gained working for

Mr. Sloan, or whoever else he worked for at General Motors, that he could bring an insight and knowledge and ways of doing business that we didn't have."[39]

Ernie Breech did not disappoint him. Peter Drucker had just completed his historic *Concept of the Corporation*, the study which enunciated the role that the modern corporation had come to play in twentieth-century American life. Drucker had got to know Breech in the course of his researches into the management practices of GM, and when Breech arrived at Ford, Drucker became required reading for everyone who wanted to appear on their toes—including Henry Ford II.

"Sure I read it," he told Booton Herndon later. "I didn't have any choice."[40]

The senior managers that Breech brought in with him, Crusoe, Youngren, and Harder, were all ex-GM men, and GM management practices became the order of the day at Ford: decentralized administration, organization charts, and, Ernie Breech's special jewel, the "profit centre." The idea of the profit centre was that it should be possible to tell precisely how much each steering wheel added to the value of a car, and whether it saved money to have it with three spokes instead of four. By spreading profit centres through the company, it became possible, for the first time, to identify which areas of activity were making money for Ford, and to analyse closely what was wrong with those that were not.

The GM management philosophy also stressed the importance of communication between different sectors of the company. So, for the first time, all Ford senior managers met together at regular meetings in which one would explain exactly what he did in his department, while, at a lower level, efforts were made to eradicate the "fear complex" that was the legacy of the Service Department.[41] The face of authority at Ford, it was decreed, should henceforward wear a smile, and junior managers were given crash courses in human relations, which were, inevitably, known as "charm school."[42]

But a system could only accomplish so much. The Ford Motor Company existed to sell cars, and if the final product was no good, the cost-effectiveness of the organization producing it counted for little. When Ernest Breech first arrived at Ford, his most urgent duty was to sit through the product-planning conferences examining the specifications of the company's postwar cars, and as Breech looked at them, he knew that the engineering was out of date. The V–8 engines still had cooling problems. Ford had next to no work done in the area of automatic transmissions, where GM's Borg Warner was establishing a commanding lead. A legacy of Henry I's insistence on the old Model T transverse springing was a total absence of Ford patents in modern coil-spring, front-end suspensions.[43] The changes in all the mock-ups and clay models being presented to Breech for 1948 and 1949 were essentially cosmetic. They were tartings-up of the last prewar Ford, whose mechanical specifications went back to the 1930s. When, at a Policy Committee meeting in September 1947, Breech raised the possibility of a totally renovated car, he was told that this would take three years to complete.[44]

Driving home to Bloomfield Hills along Telegraph Road that evening in his executive Lincoln—itself a prewar model —Ernest Breech was deeply depressed, and as was his wont in times of trouble, he bowed his head, mentally, and said a little prayer.

"Show us the right way to go," he asked—and next morning, on his way back along Telegraph, the answer came to him. "Start afresh!"

"I have a vision," he informed the Policy Committee that day. "We start from scratch."[45]

There was no point, Breech said, in spending more time and money "phoneying up" the old Ford. The market was going to judge the company on the next car it produced, and that would have to be a new one. If crash programmes were possible in wartime, they were possible in times of peace.[46]

The product of Ernest Breech's prayer on Telegraph Road was the 1949 Ford, which, thanks to the production and materials difficulties that afflicted all the car companies in

1947 and 1948, turned out to be the first truly new car exhibited in the popular price range in the postwar years. Low and light when compared to its predecessors—the car had no running board—it featured smooth, aeroplanelike styling and an almost totally new mechanical specification which included, for the first time, overdrive, available as an optional extra. The car's champagne launch at the Waldorf-Astoria recalled the public interest in the unveiling of the Model A. Crowds mobbed the hotel's baroque ballroom, and the company's order book was soon filled. In 1947 and 1948 Ford sales had been in the region of half a million. In 1949 they soared to over 800,000, and, with the addition of Mercury and Lincoln sales in that year, Ford passed the million mark for the first time since 1930. The company still occupied third place in the league table of American carmakers, but the low, stylish lines of the 1949 Ford brought it within less than 5,000 vehicles of Chrysler,[47] whose legendary fedora-wearing president, K. T. Keller, obstinately clung to the prewar styling principle that a car's roof should be high enough to accommodate a man wearing a hat.

"We build cars to sit in," Keller would say, "not piss over."[48]

In 1946 Ford's profits had been just $2,000. In 1947 the company managed $64.8 million, and in 1949 they were nearly three times that.

The success of the '49 Ford was very much the success of Ernest Breech. On his arrival at Ford, with plans to bring in his own team of GM-trained helpers, Breech had not been willing for the Whiz Kids to remain a unit on their own, and Tex Thornton, who, according to Jack Davis, "wanted to be President practically the first day,"[49] did not stick around once his power base had been removed. Thornton left Ford in 1948 to work for Hughes Aircraft, and, later, to found his own immensely successful conglomerate, Litton Industries.

George Moore and Wilbur Andreson also left around the same time, but the seven survivors provided a powerhouse in Ford middle management. Breech deployed them around the company, reporting to himself, and to Crusoe, Youngren, Harder, and the rest. It made for good chemistry, the thrusting Young Turks working for the older men. Miller, McNamara, Lundy, and Reith proved particularly effective, and it soon became clear that they offered Ford something the company had never had: a trained cadre of management who could take up the reins when the existing group of managers retired.

The entire management team, old and young together, also provided an unparalleled faculty to coach Henry Ford II in the skills of running his own company. Ernest Breech understood from the start that he was hired as a mentor. He had to save Ford, but he also had to teach Henry II how to manage the company. Everyone else understood that as well.

"If I had to do a briefing," remembers Arjay Miller, "I liked, if I could, to brief the two of them separately. Breech was a real pro. You could shorthand a lot of stuff for him. But with Henry in those early days, well, you'd lay a background, you would try to fill in."[50]

Henry Ford II was a good learner.

"He did not try to conceal his ignorance," remembers Miller. "He knew what he didn't know. He was never afraid to ask questions."[51]

The new Ford management team were crammed together in the old Administration Building on Schaefer Road overlooking the Rouge. They had small offices, cubbyholes almost, separated by clear-glass partitions, legacies of the days when Henry I liked to run his eye down a corridor to make sure that all the bureaucrats were working—and that no one was playing with a cigarette.

Henry II was one of the team. "You might well bump into him," remembers Miller, "in the john." As problems appeared, impromptu task forces were formed—Jack Davis coping with the sales or distribution aspects, Crusoe or one of the Whiz Kids tackling the finance, and old Del Harder, gentle and smiling, taking care of the manufacturing. When

Harder opened his mouth about manufacturing, people listened.[52]

Everybody mucked in. There was so much to do, so many challenges to tackle, more than enough jobs to go around, and Henry II's best learning came by doing. He was the new figurehead of the company, the corporate spokesman, and everybody worked around that, boosting him, grooming him, because if Henry looked good, then the company looked good too. The young man's need was to find some particular identity within himself, some contribution he could make beyond being a personable young fellow who happened to be called Ford. Henry II found it in the field of "human engineering."

The phrase came from Walter Reuther. The ending of war had brought a renewal of labour trouble in the car industry. Grievances set aside as part of the drive for victory suddenly exploded in a rash of wage claims and work stoppages, and union leaders blamed the bosses.

"It is time management realized," Walter Reuther declared on October 19, 1945, "that human engineering is just as important as mechanical engineering."[53]

"Human engineering" struck a chord in Henry Ford II. It expressed what he was trying to do at Ford—what he had to do if the company was to survive—and there was a very personal challenge in the phrase.

"I think Henry always wanted to compete with his grandfather," says Arjay Miller, "but he didn't want to compete head on. He knew he could not invent something—and this 'human engineering' offered him the way. He was going to do to people what his grandfather did to machines."[54]

"Human engineering" had been the weakness of Henry Ford I as he grew older. His failure in the area which had once been his triumph had nearly wrecked the company. Now Henry II's ability to pick the right people and engineer a new management team was proving Ford's new way ahead. Faced with the labour disturbances at the end of the Second World War, Henry Ford II decided to address himself to some grass-roots engineering as well.

He already had a ready helper in John Bugas, effectively the number-two man in the company until the arrival of Ernie Breech. Personnel and labour relations were to be Bugas's speciality in the new scheme of things. Henry II recruited another adviser, Earl Newsom, a smooth publicity man from New York.

Newsom was one of several men who helped fashion the science of public relations from the old craft of press agentry in the 1930s. Working for the oil industry, he had helped educate America as to the attractions of a grime- and dust-free cellar, persuading people to switch from coal heating to oil, and removing fears that oil-fired boilers might blow up. He was thus the father of the rumpus room.[55]

Newsom helped Henry Ford II frame a letter in response to the wage claim that the UAW made against Ford at the end of 1945. Feelings were raw and bitter in Detroit. The UAW had struck General Motors, and the easy response for Ford would have been to give in. Instead Henry II pointed out that his company had suffered no less than 773 work stoppages in the years since the very generous settlement that had been granted the union back in 1941. Ford requested, he said, "the same degree of security as we have given the union itself,"[56] and the promise of such security was his precondition for opening talks.

Though measured and statesmanlike, Henry II's letter constituted a tough negotiating stance, and it elicited a sharp retort from the union.

"There is a very simple way to avoid work stoppages," replied Dick Leonard, director of the UAW's Ford department. "That is to stop provoking them."[57]

This riposte, however, lacked meat in the wake of Harry Bennett's recent departure, which showed that Ford was turning over a new leaf. In the purge that followed the sacking of the Service Chief, more than 1,000 Ford employees were abruptly let go, and Henry Ford II had personally directed this energetic spring cleaning. For all the apparent severity of his bargaining response to the UAW, the young man was clearly cast in a very different mould from the other leaders of the car industry, many of whom were still fighting the old battles of the 1930s. This became clear on January 9, 1946, when the clean-cut young Henry II spoke in Detroit to the 4,000 members and guests of the Society of Automotive Engineers—just about everybody who was anybody in the car business.

This was Henry Ford II's first public appearance as head of the Ford Motor Company, and he addressed himself to the theme that was worrying everybody in the Motor City. Today his words sound like common sense, but in 1946 they appealed to his hearers as both radical and inspiring.

Men who in their private lives would not think of entering into a brawl on the street have over the years found themselves blasting each other in the public press by colorful name-calling. . . . There is no reason why a grievance case should not be handled with the same dispatch as a claim for insurance benefits. There is no reason why a union contract could not be written and agreed upon with the same efficiency and good temper that marks the negotiation of a commercial contract between two companies.[58]

No major industrialist had ever spoken out in such a conciliatory and constructive fashion. "Labor unions are here to stay," said Henry Ford. "We of the Ford Motor Company have no desire to 'break the unions,' to turn back the clock."[59]

Henry II had been scared stiff before he made the speech. It was his debut and he knew the doubts the Motor City had about him. "He looks little like his frail, sharp-eyed grandfather," said *Time* magazine. "Nor has he seemed in the past to have any of the old man's genius."[60]

Earl Newsom's office prepared no less than eighteen drafts of the original speech, and Henry II rehearsed each one of them. Whenever he stumbled over a word, it was changed, for the young man was not much more of a natural orator than his father and grandfather had been. The Ford voice had sounded oddly high-pitched in the earlier generations, and Henry II worked hard to bring it down.

The day before the speech, Earl Newsom was walking

down from his Madison Avenue office to catch the Detroiter at Grand Central Station when he bumped into Henry's wife, Anne, in New York on a shopping trip.

"Are you coming out to Detroit to hear the speech?" he inquired.

'I scarcely need to," replied Mrs. Ford II. "He kept me up nearly all night reading it aloud. He practically knows it by heart, and so do I."[61]

Henry II's nerves did not show on the night, and his command of his material meant that when he rose to his feet, he was able to speak not just with fluency but with feeling. He spoke, reported the *Detroit News*, "with a sincerity that held his huge audience. . . . Several times during his speech there was barely a sound from it."[62] His remarks were quoted at length in front-page stories and editorials by every American newspaper of note. Even the White House had a reaction—"We've been saying it all along"[63]—and the young man himself was the subject of coverage in which words like *courage, candor*, and *statesmanship* featured prominently. Professor David Lewis, the definitive quantifier of the impacts that both Henry Ford I and II have had upon the American media, reckoned in 1976 that Henry II's "Human Engineering" speech was the most publicized of his entire career.[64] It made the latest Ford a figure of national stature overnight—as was proved on February 4, 1946, when Henry Ford II appeared on the cover of *Time* magazine.

The UAW settled with Ford within a few days of Henry II's speech, setting a tone for Ford's labour relations which has, broadly, been followed ever since.

"Whenever the union wanted just money," remembers Victor Reuther, Walter's brother, "it would put the screws on General Motors. But when it came to points of principle —the first guaranteed pension, supplemental unemployment benefits—it always went to Ford first."[65]

"We knew," says Douglas Fraser, UAW leader in the late 1970s, "that Ford policy was ultimately and decisively controlled by a man who was willing to break new ground and who was sensitive to human considerations."[66]

Henry II's enlightenment has paid dividends for Ford since 1945. The company has suffered some strikes, most painfully in 1967, but its open-mindedness to union initiatives has usually yielded benefits—most notably in 1950, the year in which Chrysler's K. T. Keller obdurately refused to grant his workers the pension rights which Ford had agreed to in 1949. The ensuing strike cost Chrysler over $1 billion in lost production, led to the retirement of Keller—and also provided Ford with the chance to leap past Chrysler and occupy the number-two ranking in the U.S. car industry which it has held ever since.

Henry II did not bring special financial skills to the Ford Motor Company. He was never a great wheeler-dealer—his younger brother Bill has proved rather more crafty in that respect. Nor has Henry II ever laid claim to any technical expertise. But in "human engineering" he located a theme which he could develop in his own way, and which also continued a family tradition that both his father and his grandfather (at his best) had associated with the name of Ford.

Henry Ford II is not at ease discussing family continuity. He had a job to do when he took over the company, as he tells it, and he went about it in the most obvious way. His view of life—the view of life, at least, that he is prepared to reveal to the world—is that you take one step after the other. Things just happen. People do what they have to do. He has little truck with historic sweeps, grand connections, or psychological rationalizations. He is particularly short with suggestions that, in saving the family company in the late 1940s, he was trying to outdo his grandfather or to win the battles that his father lost.

But the people who worked with him in those years remember it quite clearly: the drive, the edge, the itch under the collar, the impulse to prove something, which he usually managed to conceal, but which would surface every so often in the most surprising ways. William Gossett, preparing the company's case for the legal battle which followed the breakup of the Ford-Ferguson tractor partnership, thought it might be helpful to enlist the help of the retired Charles Sorensen, and he arranged a meeting between Henry II and Sorensen at which the old production chief offered all the help he could.

"I'll think about it," responded Henry II ungraciously, at the end of a conversation throughout which he had been distinctly offhand and abrupt.

"He killed my father," said Henry afterwards to Gossett, by way of explanation for his behaviour. Sorensen, he said, had been an accomplice in the frustrations and embarrassments with which old Henry Ford had made Edsel's life hell, and as such he was implicated in Edsel's death.[67]

"I think Henry's always had to prove something," says Joan Bugas, the second wife, and widow, of the ex-FBI man who became Henry II's closest confidant in the company. She can remember "red wine" evenings in the 1970s when her husband and Henry II would sit together into the small hours drinking and reminiscing about the old days, about their battles with Harry Bennett, telling stories of how for a period they had actually carried guns to work because they were worried about the Service Chief and his henchmen: two old comrades in arms looking back over a quarter of a century and reliving all the excitement, the risk, the danger.

"Henry, why did you bother?" Bugas asked suddenly. "You didn't have to do it. Why didn't you just go out and play?"

Joan Bugas can still remember the power and vehemence in the response of a man who seldom permits himself to show emotion.

"My grandfather killed my father in my mind," said Henry Ford II. "I know he died of cancer—but it was because of what my grandfather did to him. I remember my father."[68]

It is strange the passion of carmaking, the way in which the manufacture of a metal box on four wheels has, over the years, provided an outlet for some of the most ardent drives of the human spirit: ostentation, jealousy, rivalry, revenge. Creating new vehicles, particularly from companies which people thought would never create new vehicles again, has proved an especially satisfying way for carmakers to get even with each other, and in the years after 1945, the plumpish crown prince whom nobody had taken very seriously went about getting even in his own way. He proved that he had what it took to be a true Henry Ford.

# 26

## CANDLELIGHT

Henry Ford I did not, perhaps, in his heart of hearts, really believe that he would live forever, but he does seem to have expected that he would make a hundred. From his middle years his obsession with diet and exercise had been directed to that end. "I exercise my eyes," he told Ralph Waldo Trine in 1928. "You can exercise your eyes, you know, the same as any other part of the body."[1] To the fury of Dr. Mateer and his other physicians at the Henry Ford Hospital, he delegated more and more of his personal medical care to his Mack Avenue chiropractor, Lawson B. Coulter,[2] who came across town every day to give the carmaker a massage and manipulations. Henry Ford also, in his later years, developed a curious interest in one of the great painters, Titian—because, he found out, that artist was still producing masterpieces at the age of ninety-nine.[3]

But Henry Ford did not make it. The strokes he suffered in 1938 and the early 1940s took their toll. For much of the time he remained lucid and spry. But there were black, withdrawn periods as well, and, as he got older, these lasted longer—sometimes for days at a time.

Mrs. Renville Wheat, a member of the Huron Mountain Club, remembers a journey with Henry Ford during the wartime years.

Founded at the end of the nineteenth century, the Huron Mountain Club lies in Michigan's Upper Peninsula, a collection of log-built cabins on the shores of Lake Superior. Henry Ford's own wooden palace in the compound contained no less than six modern, fully plumbed bathrooms,[4] and his neighbours, the cream of the Midwest's oldest families, shacked among the pine trees in similar splendour. Henry Ford and Clara had been admitted to this privileged enclave in the late 1920s, and they would travel up to spend the hotter weeks of each summer there, sailing to Marquette on one of the ore boats of the Ford navy. Each of these vessels boasted, in addition to the crew's quarters, two or three luxurious staterooms beside the bridge, as well as a dining room where the captain entertained in style. The captain's table on a Ford ore boat was the Great Lakes' equivalent of Cunard's Verandah Grill, and Harry Bennett liked to use ore-boat excursions as a luxurious perk for his network of clients.

One summer towards the end of the Second World War, Clara Ford invited Elizabeth Wheat and her children to join the Fords on their return voyage from the Huron Mountain Club to Detroit, and, happy to avoid an overland journey which took the best part of two days, Mrs. Wheat was delighted to accept. As he always did, the captain of the ore boat speeded and slowed the vessel so that it passed through the most picturesque portions of its voyage, the locks of Sault Ste. Marie and the journey down the St. Clair River, during the hours of daylight, and Mrs. Wheat found the trip a most agreeable experience—not least because her young children were on their best behaviour.

Henry Ford I, however, was not. Clara Ford was gracious-ness itself, chattering and caring for her guests solicitously. But Henry Ford was sullen and withdrawn, oddly vacant, a dumb malcontent glowering at the head of the captain's table at every meal. As Elizabeth Wheat got off the ship inside the Rouge basin, she realized that her host had not said one coherent word to her throughout the voyage.[5]

Harry Bennett thought it was Edsel's death that did it. "After that," he wrote, "he wasn't anti-Semitic or anti-Catholic or anything else. He was just a tired old man who wanted to live in peace."[6]

At times the old man took solace in his notions of reincarnation.

"Well, Harry," he would say, "you know my belief—Edsel isn't dead."[7]

Henry Ford took to spending more and more of his days in Greenfield Village, the never-never land where he had given physical shape to his own second childhood, and his special interest was the school he had founded there in the reconstructed version of his own, one-room schoolhouse. Since 1929 the school had grown from one to twelve grades, overflowing to occupy other structures in the village, and every morning the children would assemble in the white-painted church Henry had built to the memory of his own and Clara's mother, the Martha-Mary Chapel.

"If you want to keep up with the time," he told William Stidger, "learn from the children and from youth. They are the last product of destiny—and the best."[8]

Henry Ford was driven early every morning to the Martha-Mary Chapel so that he could sit at the back of the church to listen to the children's voices pipe their hymns. He always kept a Jew's harp in his pocket, and he would gather the children around him under a tree, sit down on the grass, and play them the songs he remembered from his childhood.

"It is a good thing for a man to keep close to the children . . . ," he told William L. Stidger, "they have faith. They are the dawn; and through them you catch its gleams."[9]

Pursuing his interest in his own childhood, Henry had his court painter, Irving Bacon, embark on a series of tableaux recreating the episodes that floated most strongly through his memory—the walk into the meadow with his father to look at the bird's eggs beneath the fallen tree, his beloved mother presiding over the homestead that she kept so neat and clean—and, as models for these paintings, the carmaker picked out people he believed to be reincarnations of the subjects in real life. The model for the young Henry Ford I was easy to find—John Dahlinger, who, as everyone agreed, bore a certain physical resemblance to young Henry I, and more so to the dead Edsel. As the model for his mother, he picked out a young cousin from the Litogot side of his family, Dorothy Richardson.

Struck by a resemblance between Dorothy and his dead mother, Henry Ford I came to believe that his niece was the reincarnation of Mary Litogot, and he told Dorothy so, presenting her with a copy of *Reincarnation, the Hope of the World*. The little girl does not appear to have shown much interest in this theosophical treatise, but she enjoyed the special attention that Henry Ford paid her. He took his reincarnated mother for rides in the countryside, teaching her to drive when she reached the age of sixteen, so that she could experience the creation that had made her son famous, and he asked Dorothy to reenact some of his childhood memories in a film, which he personally directed. He had two dresses made for Dorothy to wear according to patterns that he remembered his mother making, and the film opened with the scene that was now a fixation, the Ford family walking through a rough field dotted with stumps in the direction of a fallen log. . . .[10]

It did not take Irving Bacon long, working on his eerie commissions, to realize that his years of Ford patronage had to be drawing to a close. The painter still worked at his easel in the studio that was curtained off for him on the main floor of the Engineering Laboratory, but after the advent of young Henry II, the building was getting used more and more for its originally designated purpose. It actually started to fill up with engineers, and visiting Bacon one day to inspect the progress of a commission, Henry Ford turned around and started to walk back to look at all the new drawing boards that had been set up on the main floor.

"What are all those people doing?" he asked.

"They are engineers," he was told, "making drawings, Mr. Ford."

Clara ran forward and pulled her husband away.

"Making automobiles with a pencil!" sniffed the old man as he was led off in the direction of his car.[11]

Charlotte Ford, the oldest of Henry I's great-grandchildren, can remember something of her great-grandfather from these years. Charlotte was born in 1941, shortly before her father, Henry II, enlisted in the Navy, and her sister, Anne, was born just under two years later in Chicago, where the young Fords lived during the months that Henry II was training at the Great Lakes Naval School.

Charlotte can remember her great-grandfather as a papery old presence, who shook hands with her. He felt boney. She had been driven over to Fair Lane with her younger sister just before Christmas, and the two little girls were wrapped up in blankets and put on a sleigh that was pulled through the snow by real reindeer. They were dragged for what seemed like hours through the dark Fair Lane woods, until they came to a little clearing in which stood a log cabin, and as their sleigh drew to a halt, the door opened and out came Father Christmas.

At the time this apparition did not really surprise Charlotte Ford. Any little girl taken for a sleigh ride by reindeer would naturally expect to meet Santa Claus—and Fair Lane's Father Christmas was no bit-part actor in false beard and whiskers. His beard was real, and in some ways his act was also, since, sometime in the 1930s, Henry Ford gave one of his estate workers, who already boasted an impressive white beard, the job of living full-time in the Fair Lane woods, working through the summer months as a Christmas elf getting presents ready for December 25, and then, when the festive season came, serving as Henry's resident Father Christmas.

The new regime at Ford made occasional use of the company's founder, wheeling him out from time to time to give new models a touch of history, but he was clearly not the Henry Ford he was. His lean features were puffy with drugs, the once-keen expression was fading from his eyes, and the old man was not so stupid that he was unaware of his deterioration. "Here we are," he told George Holley, developer of the Holley Carburetor, at a 1946 dinner celebrating the fiftieth anniversary of his own, and Charles King's, introduction of the automobile to Detroit. "Two old buddies growing old, and drinking milk together."[12]

That winter Henry and Clara went south to Georgia on what had become an annual pilgrimage. On one southerly excursion with the famous band of travelling companions, John Burroughs had pointed up the Savannah estuary and

said, "Good bird-watching country." Henry had accordingly bought land on the Savannah estuary, in the vicinity
of Ways, Georgia, and had built himself an estate there,
Richmond Hill.

It was a swampy, unpromising natural habitat. When the
landscaping was completed, one of the sights at Richmond
Hill was the rattlesnake segments flying through the air as
the gardeners mowed the lawns. But the creation of the
estate provided an outlet for the same enthusiasms Henry
had indulged in Dearborn. Hundreds of acres were put down
to experimental cultivation, and he built special schools for
the children of his estate workers, white and black. The
schools were segregated, as was the way in Georgia, but the
facilities of the black school matched those of the white in
every respect, and when his grandchildren had come to stay
in the early 1930s, it was to the black school that Henry sent
them. "Time they learned something," he said, "that they
won't learn from those damn' stiff-necked Grosse Pointe
sons-of-bitches."[13]

With the departure of Harry Bennett, the Dahlingers,
Ray and Evangeline, had got closer to the Henry Fords
than ever. They chauffeured and nannied the old couple,
arranging all the practical details of such projects as the
annual migration to Georgia, and Clara Ford appears to
have put whatever had happened in the past behind her.
She and her husband did not have that many friends left
from the old days.

The Fords got back from Georgia in the spring of 1947
on Easter Sunday, April 6. The weather in Michigan was
atrocious. It had been raining for days, and the Rouge River
was rising to levels it had never reached before. Soon after
dawn on the morning of Monday, April 7, John MacIntyre,
one of the engineers in the powerhouse that still supplied
Fair Lane with all its light and heat, came up to the house
to tell Rosa Buhler, Clara Ford's personal maid, that the
power plant was flooded.[14] He had had to switch all the
turbines off.

Rosa went up to the Fords' bedroom and, hearing the

couple talking, knocked on the door to tell them the news. Henry Ford didn't seem to hear what she was saying.

"What's wrong, Callie," he kept saying. "What's wrong?"

Rosa's idea was that the couple should go over to the Dearborn Inn for breakfast, but Henry thought that was ridiculous.

"My gracious," he said, "we have fireplaces! In Scotland or in Ireland they cook everything on the fireplace!" and he burst out laughing.[15]

Rosa went downstairs to get the fires going throughout the house, and when Henry Ford came downstairs he summoned Rankin, his chauffeur, to drive him around Dearborn and show him the flood damage. They went to Greenfield Village, where Ray Dahlinger showed Henry Ford his Suwanee Riverboat under water, and there the old man had a telephone call put through to New York, where his grandson Benson was to sign an endorsement contract that day with Babe Ruth. He decided he would like to visit his other grandson, Henry II, down at the Rouge, since he had not seen him for several months, but the roads were all flooded, so he went instead to the Ford family cemetery on Joy Road, where his father and mother were buried.

Back at Fair Lane, the fires were all roaring in the hearths, filling the house with flickering light, supplemented by candles.

"Buhler," said Henry Ford, "I'd like to have a cup of warm milk."

He asked how repairs were going in the powerhouse.

"I'll sleep well, tonight," he said. "We're going early to bed."

Later that night, the maid was woken from her own sleep by someone knocking on her door. It was Clara. "I think Mr. Ford is very sick," she said.

Rosa went upstairs with her, and together the two women sat and watched Henry Ford, who was sleeping only fitfully. Clara had lit two candles, but her husband was restless, and motioned her to put them out.

With the telephone not working, Rankin, the chauffeur,

had been sent to find a phone booth to summon Dr. Mateer from Grosse Pointe.

Henry Ford wanted to get out of bed, so Clara helped him to his feet.

"Henry, talk to me," she kept saying.

When she realized he could not stand, she helped him back to bed again, propping him upright with pillows, then went to her dressing room to get ready for the doctor's arrival.

Rosa Buhler sat on her own in the room, looking at her master. "I could see the change, you know, on his face." She called to Clara's dressing room. "You'd better come out," she said. "I don't know. I don't like the looks. . . ."

"What do you think it is?" asked Clara.

"I think," the maid replied, "Mr. Ford will be leaving us."

When Dr. Mateer reached Fair Lane around midnight on April 7, 1947, Henry Ford was already dead. Henry Ford II, also summoned by Rankin, arrived soon afterwards with his wife, Anne.

"Feel him," said Clara to Anne. "Feel how cold he is."[16]

The young Fords had just got off a train from New York and had come straight to Fair Lane from the station.[17] But they did not arrive sooner than another visitor, summoned by Clara to pay her own farewell. Evangeline Dahlinger was already waiting at Fair Lane when Henry II got there.[18]

So, aged eighty-three, Henry Ford I left the world, lit by candles and warmed by log fires, as he had entered it. In one sense the great carmaker had been forsaken in his final hours by the twentieth century, but there was another sense in which Henry Ford I had long since forsaken it.

They laid him to rest in his Village, in the pillared hall that lay beneath his beloved ballroom, and for a whole day, on Wednesday, April 9, 1947, the people filed by. The *Detroit Free Press* thought there could have been as many as 100,000 who walked through.[19]

They were plain folk most of them, local people, a lot of workingmen with open shirts and hands in their pockets while they waited for an hour or more in line, people who were touched, people who were weeping, people who had brought their children to witness the passing of history. Many of them knew Henry Ford—or felt they did, at least. Americans like their heroes plain and simple, said Tocqueville. It is the democratic, levelling instinct. They do not like the idea that a great or successful man may actually possess superior qualities to their own, and Henry Ford had never worried his fellow countrymen in that respect.

Irving Bacon, the painter, came to take one final look at his subject. But he was disappointed. "He did not resemble the Henry Ford I had known," he said, "the iron-gray hair having bleached to white, the muscular cheek and jaw covered with soft-puffy flesh, and the chiseled nose more shapeless."[20]

Ernest Breech came, along with his team: Crusoe, Harder, Gossett, Browning. But you could tell that it did not mean much to them. Only Gossett, the lawyer, had thought to wear a black tie.[21]

The obituaries were kind—eulogistic, even. New York's *P.M.* described Henry's mind as a "jungle of fear and ignorance and prejudice in social affairs,"[22] but most writers remembered the good things. Even B'nai B'rith found it in its heart to be magnanimous at the end. Richard E. Gutstadt expressed "deep admiration" for Ford's "great contribution to the American economy and to social relations."[23]

Sigmund Diamond has remarked on the almost universally positive obituaries that Henry Ford received from the American press, as compared to the very mixed notices handed out to J. D. Rockefeller, Cornelius Vanderbilt, J. P. Morgan, and other businessmen-heroes of the era.[24] But Henry—as he would have pointed out himself —had actually produced something. He had not played with money or cornered a market. He had not even cornered an invention. He had manufactured a car that people could afford, that took them where they wanted to go, that gave them a great deal of fun. It was so simple. If you were not Jewish, had not been beaten up by an outside squad, and were not a friend or relative of Edsel Ford, you felt that your own life had been touched directly by Henry Ford and had been touched for the better, on the whole.

Next day more than 20,000 people gathered outside St. Paul's Episcopal Cathedral on Woodward Avenue for the funeral.[25] It was raining, and their umbrellas formed a dark, sombre framing to the scene. The service started at 2:30, and as the church doors closed, so all Detroit came to a halt. Buses stopped for a minute, and as motorists and other traffic did the same, bells started to toll in every corner of the city.

It was a memorable demonstration. Henry Ford had not counted for much inside his company—inside his family, even—for the last couple of years. But the world had a longer memory. Detroit's City Hall was draped in black, with a thirty-foot-high portrait of the greatest carmaker hanging down the front. All city offices had closed at noon. In Dearborn they were closed all day. The newspapers had published the route that the cortège would take to the cemetery, and people stood along the way, often dressed in black—except outside the Henry Ford Hospital, where the nurses were on parade in their white uniforms, a great cloud of swans, waiting to say farewell to their very particular founder.

It was a pity that his final ride should have been in a Packard, but it was appropriate too. Ford still did not make cars grandiose enough for limousine or hearse work. In Henry Ford's pockets on the day of his death had been found just a comb, a pocket knife, and a Jew's harp, the paraphernalia of a little boy; and when the lawyers came to draw up the inventory of his assets, they discovered they included $26.5 million kept in a personal bank account, cash on hand. Going through the debts owed to the carmaker, they also found there was a payment owing of $20—due to Henry Ford from a sale he had made of one load of hay.

\*

Henry Ford does not appear to have worried greatly about what would happen to his company after his death. It had always been his own creation, existing primarily for his own enjoyment. If he cared to devote his engineering laboratories to newspaper publishing or to old-time country dancing, then that was his prerogative, and there was even a sense, as the 1930s progressed and as the company was surrendered more and more to Harry Bennett's bully-boys, in which Henry Ford was destroying his own creation.

He certainly had no strong impulse to preserve his enterprise for future generations. The enacting in 1916 of America's first permanent inheritance tax prompted America's rich to start concentrating on the foundations and philanthropic devices that do the world good while also, conveniently, enabling family fortunes to remain in family hands. But Henry Ford was not so undignified. He disapproved of lawyers and of the crafty legal mechanisms needed to sidestep the inheritance levy, and he did not, in any case, contemplate the possibility of his own death. He had never accepted charity, and he could imagine few things worse than his fortune becoming a reservoir for handouts, which he deplored.

"I have no patience with professional charity or with any sort of commercialized humanitarianism," he told Samuel Crowther in 1922. "The moment human helpfulness is systematized, organized, commercialized, and professionalized, the heart of it is extinguished, and it becomes a cold and clammy thing. . . . It hurts more than it helps."[26]

But the wealth tax proposed by President Roosevelt in 1935 changed the old man's mind. Preparing for his reelection campaign of 1936, Roosevelt called for an attack on the "unjust concentration of wealth and power" in America, and the result, at the end of August 1935, was higher income tax—and increased inheritance tax as well. Fortunes over $4 million were liable to a 50 percent assessment, and from $50 million upwards, the tax levy rose to 70 percent.[27]

The Roosevelt wealth tax made dramatically explicit what

had, in fact, been the case ever since 1916. The death of either Henry or Edsel Ford would seriously jeopardize family control of the company, while the death of both would wipe it out completely, since their heirs would have to sell major blocks of shares in order to meet the tax bill. This possibility seems to have worried Henry Ford rather less than the prospect that, under Roosevelt's plan, the bulk of his hard-earned fortune might end up providing a major source of finance for the New Deal, and in 1935, a few months after his seventy-second birthday, he told Edsel to talk business with the lawyers. Within a matter of weeks Ford's legal advisers had made a study of the new inheritance-tax pro-visions, and by the autumn of 1935 they had worked out how to outwit them beautifully.

The first step was to convert all the company's existing shares into two new classes of paper: Class A stock, to which was allocated 95 percent of the old shares, and Class B, which represented the remaining 5 percent. None of these shares was to be publicly available, and they were all to remain in the hands of the family—Henry, Edsel, and Clara —during their lifetimes. Class A was to be the sacrifice stock, so it carried no votes. Voting power was confined exclusively to the Class B shares. This meant that it would be possible, in the future, for the Ford family to lose as much as 95 percent of its shareholding in the company (the Class A shares) and still retain the voting control which went with the Class B stock. The family would obviously lose the capital value of any Class A shares it was compelled to surrender, but so long as it could hang on to its 5 percent Class B holding, it would still retain its absolute, 100 percent voting control.

The next step was the establishing, on January 15, 1936, of the Ford Foundation, "to receive and administer funds for scientific, educational, and charitable purposes, all for the public welfare and for no other purpose."[28] By American law, donations to recognized charities are exempt from tax, so now, if the Fords were to will their Class A stock to this new foundation, they would not only retain their voting power, they would completely escape the payment of tax on 95 percent of their wealth.

Early in February 1936, Henry and Edsel signed wills to accomplish just this. They had already split the new Class A and Class B shares between themselves in proportions that corresponded to the family share-out which had prevailed since the buy-out of Couzens and the Dodge brothers: 55 percent to Henry, 42 percent to Edsel, and 3 percent to Clara.[29] Now Henry bequeathed all his Class A stock to the Ford Foundation, and he divided his Class B stock equally between his son and his four grandchildren. Edsel similarly surrendered his Class A shares to the family charity, while dividing his vote-holding B shares between his wife and children.

Without these arrangements, the deaths of the founder and his son within a few years of each other would have marked the end of the Ford Motor Company as a family business. But thanks to the Class A and Class B shares, and to the Ford Foundation, the company had a whole new lease on life—and the family were spared the payment of some $321 million in tax.[30]

Not long before the death of old Henry Ford I, according to Jack Davis, the great carmaker had been confined to his bed for a spell, suffering from an unwonted depression that quite baffled his doctor. The old man seemed to have lost his will to live, and speculating that some contact with the outside world might revive his patient's spirits, the physician arranged for a newspaper reporter to pay a visit, since nothing ever galvanized Henry Ford like the chance to utter some words for publication. So it proved when the journalist was ushered in.

What, inquired the newsman, were the possibilities of the Ford Motor Company going public?

The reaction was instantaneous, and displaying energy not seen for weeks, Henry Ford rose up from his sickbed to lift his voice in passion.

"I'll take my factory down brick by brick," he declaimed

stoutly, "before I'll let any of those Jew speculators get stock in the company."

"I think," said the doctor hurriedly, "that will be enough questioning for today," and the newspaper reporter was spirited smartly from the room.[31]

Even before Henry Ford II had taken over the Ford Motor Company from his grandfather, he had realized that the family business could not remain private forever. If it was to offer serious competition to General Motors—or, indeed, to survive at all in the long run—it had to have the capital that only the open market could supply, and one measure of the achievement of young Ford, with Ernest Breech and his associates, would be the eventual willingness of the American public to invest in the company. Large family-owned corporations were things of the past, and there was never any doubt, once Henry II took over, that the Ford Motor Company would go public. The only question was when.

It was the Ford Foundation which supplied the answer. Endowed with the A shares of Henry and Edsel Ford, as well as of Clara, who died in 1950, the Foundation opened its doors as a major national philanthropy in the early 1950s. The Ford Foundation was, indeed, the largest American foundation of all, far outdistancing Rockefeller and Carnegie, its second- and third-place rivals in the national-league table of charities —a whale among a school of tuna fish, as Dwight MacDonald described it in the *New Yorker*.[32] In 1955 a survey of its holdings showed that the Ford Foundation was in possession of no less than 3,089,908 shares of Class A stock in the Ford Motor Company, some $417 million at the 1947 estate-tax valuation of $135 a share;[33] and since the company had prospered greatly since 1947, the Foundation was probably worth well over a billion dollars.

The Foundation had no effective control over this immense wealth, however, because none of its shares in the Ford Motor Company held votes—which meant that America's principal philanthropic foundation, with a spending budget comparable to that of some of the smaller states, was almost totally dependent upon the fortunes of a commercial enterprise in whose management it had no say. It could not stop the Ford family voting all of one year's profits back into the business, if it wanted to, thus denying the Foundation any income for that year; and, aside from the question of control, the Foundation's revenues were totally dependent upon one company in an industry whose fortunes were notoriously cyclical.

It was not a satisfactory situation. There was a clear duty for the Foundation's trustees to diversify out of their dependence on Ford Motor Company stock, but it was difficult for them to do this while the company shares were not traded in the open market. So, early in November 1955, the Ford Foundation announced its preparations to sell a proportion of its Ford Motor Company shares. This offering would be the first chance for outsiders to purchase stock in the Ford Motor Company, and since more than 7 million shares were to be offered, it was, in effect, a public flotation.

The family's problem in going public was how to preserve family control. The clever wills of Edsel and Henry had saved them tax and had preserved their voting control so long as the company remained private, but the essence of the scheme had been to give away the bulk of the family's capital in the company. Following the death of Henry Ford, his heirs owned just 5 percent of the company, thanks to their Class B stock, and they also owned about 7 percent of Class A stock which they had not surrendered. But any shares offered to the general public would have to carry votes, and if those shares were offered on a normal basis, one share one vote, then the Fords would end up with just 12 percent of the votes—which was a very long way short of control.

Fifty-one percent of the votes, obviously ideal from the family's point of view, was quite out of the question. But 40 percent was pretty close. In the event of a takeover challenge, the family would only need to buy a further 11 percent to be safe. Studying the regulations of the New York Stock Exchange, Ford's lawyers took a hard look at a rule permit-

ting the trading of shares which represented 60 percent of
the capital in a company.

"We put it to them this way," remembers Alan Gornick,
the Ford tax counsel at the time. "Okay, your rule provides
that the shares must represent sixty percent of the equity.
Let's interpret that to mean sixty percent *control*."[34]

Forget about the capital, in other words. Don't look at
the deal as the Ford family getting four votes for every dollar
invested, while the rest of the world gets just one—a 40
percent vote for just 12 percent of the money. Concentrate
on the 60 percent say in the company that your customers
will be able to buy. The New York Stock Exchange, anxious
to secure for itself the largest stock offering in the history of
Wall Street, agreed.

From that point onwards it was easy. The existing distinction between Class A and Class B shares was maintained:
Class A for the public, Class B for the Fords. Both types of
share would be worth exactly the same amount, and they
would receive the same dividend. But when it came to votes,
the shareholders would vote in their separate classes, and
the Class A votes would only count for 60 percent. It was
like the French Estates General: nobles and commoners
voting separately to preserve the nobility's power.

One angry voice was raised in protest. "The small stockholders of America," complained Senator Joseph C.
O'Mahoney, chairman of the Senate subcommittee on monopoly, "are surrendering their economic freedom to big
business management."[35]

But from the moment the Ford Foundation announced
its plans to sell its shares on November 7, 1955, it became
obvious that the small stockholders of America were only
too happy to surrender their economic freedom for a slice
of the action—even a small slice. They could not wait.
Switchboards were jammed. Seven hundred underwriters
specially enlisted around the country were swamped,[36] and
turmoil on the day of the offering itself, January 17, 1956,
was even worse. Plain folk who had never bought a share
in their lives wanted a piece of Ford. Here was a chance to

buy into something that helped make America great. People saw it as a nest egg for their children and grandchildren. Inasmuch as they thought about the disproportionate voting power of the Fords, they evidently liked the idea. The offering was many times oversubscribed. By the close of trading on January 17, the stock had risen from $64.50 to $70.50, and the Ford Foundation was $640 million better off.[37]

People had not been buying shares in a car company. Nine years after the death of Henry Ford, the national stampede to buy into his company was America's final, colossal tribute to the magic in his name—the sincerest tribute of all, since it was expressed in terms of dollars— and the way in which his descendants managed to preserve their own private power in the process of "going public" was surely a deal of which the old man would have approved.

# 27

# THE NEW MR. FORD

Anne McDonnell Ford made her mark on the Motor City with
the very first dinner party that she gave. The guests were assembled around the table, just ready to start when Mrs. Ford
closed her eyes, bowed her head, and said grace out loud.

It was not so much her prayer that struck people, as the
sight of her husband devoutly joining in. The new president
of the Ford Motor Company had mentors at the office, and
he evidently had one waiting for him when he got home.
Anne McDonnell took her religion seriously, and the willingness of Henry II to share it with her was a tribute to Anne
as much as to the instruction of Fulton Sheen.

The happy-go-lucky young "lard-ass" had become a very
serious Henry Ford. He was to be seen every Sunday without
fail at St. Paul's beside the lake. He did not exhibit quite
the personal devotion of his wife, who was up and at Mass
every single morning by 6:00 A.M., but he did accompany
her to the dawn worship throughout the forty days of Lent,
and, when Anne was in hospital for an operation on her
feet, he went to Mass on his own, and he was seen to stay
on afterwards, kneeling for a time in prayer.[1]

During the course of the operation itself, the anxious
husband paced the waiting room outside for more than three
hours, refusing all offers of a seat, and he did not stop pacing
until he could join his wife again. He had decided to keep
walking, he told her later, as a penance. He was so worried
about her. Pacing up and down was his offering to God until
he could be quite sure that she was all right.[2]

They made a handsome couple. He was still rather overweight, always looking, somehow, more like a butcher than
a captain of industry. But he had a commanding presence,
muscular and powerful, with piercing blue eyes, while she

was commanding in a different way, spare and thin, with the fierce, superior look of someone who is rather shyer than they would like the world to know. She was a stylish woman, was Anne McDonnell Ford. She had inherited her mother's weakness for haute couture clothes, and she could spot a designer dress at a thousand yards.

Like her husband, Anne McDonnell had grown up accustomed to the best. She had a taste for French furniture, and she was able to indulge this when the couple moved into Grosse Pointe. In 1943 they had settled on Provencal Road, a private avenue protected from the world by uniformed guard and sentry box, but once Henry II was firmly in the saddle at Ford, they moved, as befitted an auto baron and his lady, to one of the stately mansions beside the lake: 421 Lakeshore. Here Anne McDonnell Ford set about creating a context for eminence. She scoured the sale rooms of New York and Europe for classic pieces, and before she went to an auction she would take the advice of Paul Grigaut, the DIA's Curator of European Art, who, in the tradition of Valentiner, made himself available as an unpaid adviser to rich local patrons who might be expected, every so often, to drop the odd treasure the DIA's way.

"Bronzes," Grigaut would say, "are very important in a house."[3]

Anne McDonnell Ford built up one of the finest collections of signature furniture west of the Hudson—as you could tell from the humidifiers puffing out vapour in every room. The desk in her bedroom was Marie Antoinette's. The Henry Ford II wine coolers had once cooled the wine of Catherine the Great, and the carpets had that colour-drained, threadbare look which you either find at garage sales or in the palace of Versailles.

Anne McDonnell Ford was a connoisseur, and she educated her husband in her tastes. Henry II had grown up surrounded by beautiful things. A son of Edsel and Eleanor Ford could not help but have good taste. But he was not obviously an art lover until his wife took him with her on her pilgrimages around the galleries buying furniture, and buying art as well. Anne had a good eye, and she helped her husband develop his own as they went hunting together —Cézanne's *Paysan en Blouse Bleue*, some van Goghs, an unusual Gauguin, an outstanding Renoir.[4] In the late 1940s and early 1950s, the young Henry Fords were known, in the tradition of Edsel and Eleanor, as two of the most active— and discriminating—collectors in the market.

There were those who said that Anne had the taste and Henry had the cheque book, but this was not true. Henry soon knew exactly what he wanted. Anne once got on the trail of a Holbein which cousin Bob Tannahill judged the finest outside a museum, and she had it shipped to Detroit for Henry's perusal.

"I hate it," said her husband firmly when he got home from work, and the Holbein went straight back to New York.

Henry Ford II had a taste of his own. He knew the sort of collection that he wanted, and he built it—an integrated, well-thought-out selection of the best French impressionists, with a preference for nudes.

Mr. and Mrs. Henry Ford II built themselves an opulent gilt and walnut-panelled lifestyle after the fashion of third-generation grandees, but without third-generation frivolity. Their affluence was disciplined within a sense of purpose, their European yearnings tethered to Midwest roots. Taking "human engineering" outside the Ford Motor Company, Henry II had got involved with local philanthropy. Frustrated by the waste and duplication of Detroit's principal fund-raising campaigns, he proposed that they should amalgamate their drives, and after a month or so of lobbying he persuaded three of them to take his advice. In 1949 the Detroit branches of the Red Cross, the American Cancer Society, and the Community Fund came together in what is today known as the United Foundation, and they raised more money, with less cost, than the charities had ever raised when working separately. The experiment was extended. The charities have worked together ever since, and Henry II's better idea is today the way in which funds are raised in almost every major American city.

Mrs. Henry II matched her husband and outdid him. Her days were crammed with useful and worthy activities while her husband was at the office. She had a big, thick engagement book which sat beside the phone, and every hour of it was filled: Mass before dawn, the decorator, the hairdresser, charity benefits, fund-raising galas, innumerable philanthropic breakfasts, lunches, and teas. Doing good works could be a full-time job in Detroit. People in the East were more nonchalant, somehow, about civic duty. Perhaps they had less to prove. But in the Midwest an auto baron's lady was expected to put in a day's work to match her husband's, and Anne McDonnell Ford did her duty without complaint.

The pinnacle of her achievement came when she raised the funds to help bring the Metropolitan Opera to Detroit for the first time in nearly half a century. It had not been at all certain that Detroit could muster the audiences to pay for the visit, but Anne McDonnell Ford went into battle with her engagement book—plus a couple of P.R. men on loan from Ford—and when the opera arrived, every performance in the 4,600-seat Masonic Temple was sold out. Not only that, the Met's annual visit to Detroit became the high point of the city's social year, a week-long round of glittering parties and receptions, presided over by Mr. and Mrs. Henry Ford II, whose handsome combination of style, taste, and social purpose made them the obvious figureheads of the community.[5]

The couple had a chance to work together on a philanthropic problem in the early 1950s, when the newly established Ford Foundation started becoming an object of controversy. Trying to hew its own path away from the scientific drift of many other foundations, the Ford Foundation had set itself objectives in the fields of economic development, education, the fostering of peace and democracy—more "human engineering." Its early projects—encouraging agriculture in India and Pakistan, helping displaced persons, trying to get more education on TV— were not obviously radical or subversive.[6] But this was a bad time for foundations. The recently convicted Alger Hiss had allegedly organized his Communist activities while on the payroll of the Carnegie Endowment for International Peace. The Cold War was at its height. In November 1952, Congress felt impelled to set up a committee, under Rep. Edward Eugene Cox of Georgia, to ascertain "whether the foundations have used their resources to weaken, undermine or discredit the American system of free enterprise . . . while at the same time extolling the virtues of the Socialist State."[7]

A number of right-wing newspapers and columnists thought this precisely described the direction being taken by the Ford Foundation. A fortune built up through red-blooded capitalism was being dissipated on pinko, do-gooding projects outside America, and the attack focused on the professional "philanthropoids" chosen by Henry II to run the Foundation day to day: Paul G. Hoffman, a sometime administrator of the Marshall Plan, and Robert Hutchins, a former chancellor of the University of Chicago. These were the most forceful members of an executive direc-torate which had started work on the immense task of giving away the Foundation's money in January 1951, and which had set up headquarters in the luxuriant, palm-fringed habitat of Pasadena, California—soon nicknamed, inevi-tably, "Itching Palms."

Late in 1952 Anne and Henry Ford flew out to Pasadena to discuss the problem with Hoffman and Hutchins. The controversy had actually started to affect business. "Do you own a Ford, Mercury, or Lincoln?" ran pamphlets being distributed by the Constitutional Education League. "If you do . . . then you are unwittingly giving support to the Communist cause through Ford Company profits being spent by the leftist-leaning Ford Foundation."[8]

The liaison between Henry II and the Ford Foundation was a P.R. man formerly with Earl Newsom's office, W. "Ping" Ferry, and as Ferry prepared for the confrontation between the Fords and the philanthropoids, he was particu-larly worried about Anne McDonnell Ford. She had a chilly side, he had discovered. When displeased she could display a smile "almost as warm as that microphone," as he later put it, "and a mouth about as wide as one of those blue lines," pointing to the lines on his interviewer's notepad. She could be "a very, very frosty lady."[9]

In Pasadena, however, Ping Ferry decided that Mrs. Ford was trying. He got the impression that, prior to her journey, she "had been fed an awful lot of stuff by the Parish priest or somebody about what an awful place the Foundation was," and how Hoffman and Hutchins, in particular, were bad men—Communist sympathizers. But when Mrs. Henry Ford II met Robert Hutchins, she betrayed no sign of this.

"How nice," she said, flashing her brightest smile, "to meet somebody who knows something about education. Henry certainly doesn't."[10]

She was very hopeful, she said, that thanks to the presence of Hutchins at the Foundation, "we'll get some attention to the thing that I'm interested in . . . the problems of Catholic education, mainly in the city of Detroit."

Ping Ferry had tried to warn Hutchins before the Fords' arrival that the young couple had taken public criticism of the family foundation greatly to heart, and how it would be important for Hutchins to make an effort to charm Anne. But the Hutchins way was not the way of compromise. The former chancellor of the University of Chicago knew what he thought about education, and he launched into a lecture on all the failings of the Catholic school system, and how it was not the job of the Ford Foundation to bail it out. Anne Ford was rich. If she was worried, she could take care of that sort of thing herself.

"I told her . . . ," Hutchins would later recount with glee, "to hell with it—no business of ours." And for good measure he treated the young Catholic mother to a lecture on the virtues of birth control.

"It was the kiss of death for Bob and Paul," remembered Ferry.[11] A few months later, in February 1953, Paul Hoffman abruptly submitted his resignation from the Ford Foundation, while Robert Hutchins was sidelined to a charity which did not actually carry the name of Ford. "Itching

Palms" was closed down. The Foundation's headquarters were shifted to its New York office, and, as president of the trustees, Henry II transferred the family foundation to less contentious hands—though despite all the public pressure, which was to provoke yet another Congressional inquiry, this one aimed specifically at the Ford Foundation,* he steadfastly declined to repudiate the pattern of giving which Hoffman and Hutchins had initiated in his name.

"Goddammit . . . ," he burst out on one occasion, "we're good Americans and we've got a right to our position."[13]

Henry II's own patriotism could hardly be impugned. In 1953, as America's best-known young businessman and a generous supporter of the Republican party, he was invited by President Eisenhower to serve on the U.S. delegation to the United Nations for a session. The high point of his brief career as an international diplomat came on Thanksgiving morning 1953, when the leader of the Soviet mission took advantage of his opponents' preoccupation with their national holiday to launch an onslaught on American imperialism, using Henry Ford II as a symbolic target.

Ford, an alternate delegate, was not scheduled to speak that day, but there was, clearly, only one man who could reply to the attack that the Russian was making. So aides shuffled together some figures, handed them to Henry II, and the young man rose to his feet to speak for ten minutes —cogently and lucidly, according to those who heard him.[14] After his triumph, he was seen anxiously scouring the holiday streets for a taxi.

"I'm going to catch it from my mother-in-law," he said. "I'm an hour late for Thanksgiving dinner."

There was a freshness and charm about Henry Ford II —a great modesty, people thought. By the middle of the 1950s, he and his purposeful wife were shining examples of the best that inherited wealth can produce: they were dedicated to the production of more wealth, and to its

* In the summer of 1953, Rep. B. Carroll Reece of Tennessee started investigating "important and extensive evidence concerning subversive and un-American propaganda activities of the Ford Foundation."[12]

enjoyment, but aware and sensitive, never losing sight of their duties to their fellow man. People started comparing young Henry to his namesake. Like his famous grandfather, he had that reassuring quality of not being too brilliant, and, unlike his grandfather, he seemed poised and balanced, down-to-earth in a noneccentric way. He was credited with idealism, but he was also credited with common sense. The Ford Motor Company was faring better under his stewardship than it had fared for thirty years, scaling new heights every year. Chevrolet was getting worried. It was really quite remarkable how, by the middle of the 1950s, when people talked about Henry Ford, it was the new Henry Ford that they meant.

People were impressed with the Ford family as a whole. During the lifetime of Henry I, the Fords had not often been thought of as a clan, nor did they act as one. There was always that friction, the distance—and the old man was so overpowering. Edsel may have been president of the company, but people did not really know what to make of him. How much had the son really contributed to the success of Ford?

The revival of the family business in the years following the Second World War, however, was clearly the work of a new generation. There must be something in the genes. By 1953, the year of the company's fiftieth anniversary, the Ford family was starting to be seen as one of America's backbone dynasties, worthy of mention in the same bracket as the Vanderbilts or Rockefellers, and Earl Newsom played up the theme. The company's Golden Jubilee was marked by a *Time* magazine cover showing the three brothers, Henry, Benson, and William Clay, driving together in the front of a car, and Newsom also got the clan to sit for special portraits by *Life*.

The appeal of the *Life* pictures, with all the male Fords assembled in one group portrait, and all the females grouped together in another, was given extra impact by the fact that Dodie—Henry II's only sister, Josephine—had managed to marry a man who bore the same surname. Old Detroiters identify at least two other local Ford dynasties who have no connection with the carmaking Fords—the "chemical" Fords, who owe their prosperity to the salt beds of the Wyandotte area,* and another clan known as the "banking" Fords, although the original source of their wealth lay in lumber and real estate. Both of these Ford families are judged socially superior to the descendants of Henry Ford I—their money is older. It was from the ranks of the "banking" Fords that sprang Walter Buhl Ford II, a young architect and industrial designer of talent, who courted and married Josephine Ford in the early 1940s. As a result of this marriage, Josephine and the four children that she bore between 1943 and 1950, are, technically, the "Ford" Fords.

In the early 1950s the management of the Ford Motor Company seemed to be taking on an especially dynastic character. Henry II's younger brothers were not only directors and vice-presidents, they were given their own divisions to run. Benson was in charge of the Mercury Division from 1948 onwards, and the company's Jubilee was marked by plans for a new prestige car which was entrusted to William Clay Ford: the Continental Mark II. The idea was to resurrect Edsel's triumph, the graceful, hand-built Lincoln Continental of 1939, and create a truly exclusive, limited-edition car which would carry even more prestige than a Cadillac. The Continental Mark II would be an American Rolls-Royce.

In the late 1940s, Ford publicity photographs had shown Henry II surrounded by the Breech team and the Whiz Kids—the new team. Now, with his brothers running their own divisions, the pictures were of Henry with Benson and Billy beside him, a dynamic triumvirate of brothers. The normal rule for the sons of rich men, said *Time* in May 1953,

---

* The "chemical" Fords built up the Wyandotte Chemical Company, and they are the Ford in Libbey-Owens-Ford, a major U.S. manufacturer of glass (one of whose principal ingredients is soda ash from salt beds).

was "shirt sleeves to shirt sleeves in three generations." But it looked as if the Ford boys were proving that wrong.[15]

Young Billy Ford seemed especially dynamic. Of all the brothers, he was the one who looked most like Edsel, trim and short. He was the best sportsman—an amateur tennis champion, a golfer who could do the Greenbrier in seventy-one. He put together a 165-man special-projects department for his Continental Mark II, and he saw himself carrying on the styling traditions of his father. To this day there are just two pictures on the wall behind the desk of William Clay Ford in Ford World Headquarters: his father's Continental, and his own graceful updating, the Continental Mark II, which was unveiled in 1955.

Billy Ford's Continental Division died, however, at almost the moment that it produced its new car, just a few months before the company went public—and it was the public flotation that was the reason for its killing. The car had originally been Ernest Breech's idea, a "loss leader" to enhance the Ford image. The Mark II was never intended to make money.[16] But as January 1956 approached, and the company was due to go public, Breech started having second thoughts. Financial statements would have to be disclosed and meetings of shareholders confronted, and when Breech came to contemplate the figures that would show the world the result of his ten years' stewardship of Ford, the disciple of cost analysis decided that he did not want red ink appearing on them anywhere. The way to deal with the losses of the Continental Division was not, in his opinion, to explain them as a form of image enhancement, as first intended, but to hide them in the figures of another, more profitable division—which meant, effectively, the end of Bill Ford's private empire. The Continental should be merged into the money-making Lincoln Division, proposed Ernest Breech, and Henry Ford II agreed.

The death of the Continental Division was one of a number of changes stimulated by the company ending its fifty-three years as a private concern, and the most important of these was the enhanced status now taken on by Henry Ford II—chief executive officer overnight of one of America's major public companies.

Going public might have been expected to remove or diminish family involvement in the management of the enterprise, and it did mark the conclusion of corporate brotherly love, since a company that was now answerable to outside shareholders could tolerate neither loss-leader cars nor family figureheads. Benson Ford, affable, but never fit, stepped down from running Mercury in 1956 to take over less-demanding duties in dealer relations, while William Clay Ford also removed himself from active day-to-day management in that same year.

Henry Ford II could theoretically have stepped down at the same time as his brothers. He had saved the company, he had created a team of managers that was the equal of any in the industry, and he could have let his managers get on with the job without a qualm.

But the notion never crossed his mind, nor the mind of anyone else. This new public trust was the job for which the new Mr. Ford—his wife, his family, his tutors—had been preparing. What had ten years of mentorship been for, if not for Henry to run his own show? He was just cresting the summit of his thirties. He had found his stride, he was enjoying his job—and 40 percent of the shareholder votes had "Ford" stamped indelibly upon them.

Since taking over the Ford Motor Company in 1945, Henry II had been guided by two objectives: the urge to modernize the enterprise, and his own pride in the name of Ford. Rational and irrational, these two impulses had moved him and the company forward hand in hand, and the public flotation which paid such homage to the memory of his grandfather was also a vote of confidence in Henry II's own abilities to lead the company through the years ahead. His name offered no other destiny. Henry Ford II had been the crown prince long enough, and now the time had come to claim his kingdom.

*

When little Anne Ford, aged twelve in January 1956, travelled abroad, she took it for granted that she and her family should always get off the plane before anyone else, and be greeted at the bottom of the steps by a bouquet of roses. Her parents would take her and her sister, Charlotte, to Europe on one of the big, double-decker Stratocruisers which had bunks upstairs, and after the reception on the tarmac, they would be whisked away in a long limousine. It made perfect sense to little Anne to be treated as royalty abroad, because that was how she was treated at home.[17]

By the time the Ford Motor Company went public, Mr. and Mrs. Henry Ford II and their children were the royal family of Grosse Pointe. When Henry II was growing up there, he had lived very grandly, but so had a score of other families: the Newberrys, the Joys, the Sheldens, the Ferrys. By the 1950s there were comparatively few families living in the old style, and the grand mansions were already starting to come down. Nineteen fifty-six saw the demolition of the Newberry house. The Sheldens' Deeplands estate had already disappeared.[18] As the subdivisions crept along the lakeshore, Grosse Pointe was on its way to becoming just another suburb, and the inhabitants found solace in the chandelier-hung grandeur of the young Henry Fords.

The Ford children were raised to a sense of their own importance. Anne McDonnell Ford had been brought up never to make her own bed, and she brought up her daughters, Charlotte and Anne, never to do the same. Bed making, she said, was the maid's job.[19] As a consequence, Charlotte, a strong-willed girl, has made her own bed ever since.

Other prohibitions, however, were harder to circumvent. Just after Christmas in 1947, Anne McDonnell Ford presented her daughters, then aged six and four, with a new baby brother, and Charlotte vividly recalls the arrival home from the hospital of little Edsel Bryant Ford II.

"I can remember as if it was yesterday," she says. "I was so excited I could hardly stand it. And I wasn't allowed to do anything"[20]

The little girl had anticipated holding the baby, mothering

557

it, giving her brother his bottle at feeding time, perhaps. But the new baby's nurse, whose name was Letty, would not let Charlotte close.

"She'd let me stick the bottle in," recalls Edsel's big sister. "Then she would take it away again."[21]

Charlotte got her revenge on Letty though. The Christmas following Edsel's arrival, she asked if *she* could have a nurse's uniform, complete with white stockings and cape, and her mother got the outfit made up by the household seamstress who worked, full-time, on the third floor. Mrs. Ford had gone to some trouble to procure the correct accessories from the Henry Ford Hospital, so she was rather upset, a few days later, when she saw that Charlotte had got blue ink on her brand-new white stockings.

"That's not ink," replied the little girl, smiling innocently. "That's Letty's varicose veins."[22]

Life at 421 Lakeshore Road was a formal affair. When Edsel Ford II went to school, his best friend was Billy Chapin, the scion of another automobile dynasty.* Billy would come over to 421 quite often in order to spend the night with his friend Edsel, and his memory today is of "Mademoiselle," the French governess who was then Edsel's supervisor and constant companion. Mademoiselle sat with Edsel in the breakfast room where his breakfast and evening meal were served. She made sure he went to bed early. She taught him his manners, and she taught him perfect French, so when the Fords were in Rome and dropped in at the Vatican, little Edsel was able to chat quite fluently with the Pope.[23]

The children who came around to play with Charlotte and Anne Ford found it difficult to reconcile their friends' father with the important figure their parents pointed out to them in the newspapers. When Charlotte and Anne started dating, Henry II would shuffle downstairs late at night to share a beer with their boyfriends.

"Daddy," the girls would say, embarrassed by his pyjamas. "Go upstairs to bed again."[24]

* William R. Chapin is the son of Roy Chapin, Jr., chairman of American Motors in the 1960s, and the grandson of Roy Chapin.

The Fords encouraged their children to invite their friends home. It was much safer than the girls going out. There was always beer and Coke and the butler on hand, with sandwiches for the teenagers who dropped in. During vacations the circular drive in front of the lakeshore house could be lined by eight or nine old clunkers, nose-to-tail, while the kids staged drag races with motor scooters, or climbed over the latest Ferrari or Maserati brought home by Henry II to test for the weekend.

There were barbecues. Henry II made a very good steak sauce, its secret ingredient being the best part of a pound of butter.[25] These youngsters did not see the chilly side of Anne McDonnell Ford, nor the temper Henry II could unleash when he got angry. The two parents were away a lot—too much, perhaps—but when the whole family was at home together, a good time was had by all.

Billy Chapin remembers how one night in the kitchen— a Thursday night, which was the cook, Gertrude's, night off —Henry II started flicking pieces of cake across the counter at Charlotte and Edsel. The children had a cake on their side of the kitchen, and within minutes a full-scale food fight had developed, which finished with the main constituents of two very expensive items of patisserie splattered all over the walls, cupboards, and ceiling.

Gertrude the cook was a formidable lady, and Henry Ford II left very early for work the next day.[26]

The family was on its best behaviour when Mrs. Eleanor came to visit. A call from the gatekeeper gave the butler time to put on his white gloves, and the family would line up in the hall to greet Granny, the children dressed in their latest outfits from Rowe's. The entire gathering was carefully time-tabled, and when you returned the call you did not just "pop in." You had to phone 1100 Lakeshore in advance to fix a time—though once you got there, remember the children of Henry II, Granny was always marvellous fun. After tea she would play "hide-and-go-seek" around the house.[27]

In Grosse Pointe's royal family, Mrs. Eleanor was the Queen Mother. The lakeshore boasted flashier matrons, notably Mrs. Anna Dodge, widow of Horace, whose 230-foot yacht loomed out in the lake like an ocean liner. But the subdued lifestyle of Mrs. Edsel Ford was much more in keeping with local canons of taste. Grosse Pointe did not worry greatly whether your money was old or new so long as it was quiet.

"Now, there's a lady," everybody would agree. Through the thirty-three years by which she survived her husband, she was escorted by numerous hopeful beaux, but no breath of scandal ever attached to Mrs. Eleanor Ford. She patronized the DIA, the Merrill-Palmer teaching institute, the Pewabic Pottery, the Artists' Market, which gave a start to promising local artists, and her charitable sorority, Tau Beta. There seemed no end to Mrs. Eleanor's generosity and good works—though most of her donations were made under the strictest conditions of anonymity. She was unfailingly smiling, courteous, and punctual. If you invited her for 7:30, she would drive up on the dot, and she was always good fun at a party—dancing, laughing, pleased to see everybody, never cold.

Mrs. Eleanor's one slight ostentation was a singular, upright limousine with running boards, in which she travelled around the neighbourhood. It was a curious hybrid, a 1953 Lincoln, into which her son had had the company design studio graft a tall, coach-built passenger compartment, which his mother could enter and alight from without stooping her head. Parked outside the hairdressers or one of the shops, Mrs. Ford's limousine was the unmistakable signal of her presence, and when they spotted it, her grandchildren would get off their bikes and go inside in search of her.

Christmas was the occasion that brought all the Fords together once a year, for the brothers did not socialize amongst themselves very much. Christmas lunch was a command performance, as was dinner on Thanksgiving Day. Mrs. Eleanor expected all her children and their spouses on parade, in black tie. The grandchildren ate separately, and, afterwards, they would be shunted along to the barrel-vaulted music gallery, where a 35 mm projector would crank out the latest feature release.

Outsiders might imagine these gatherings to have been hotbeds of family plotting, strategy sessions in which the clan's business progress was mapped out for the months ahead. There was even a pervasive myth, doubtless stimulated by Mrs. Eleanor's rebellion after Edsel's death, that the true leader of the tribe was the matriarch. Young Henry, it was rumoured, submitted all the company's major business decisions—and personnel choices—to his mother for approval.

This was pure fantasy. Mrs. Eleanor was no businesswoman, and she had no pretensions to the role. From the day he took full command of the company, Ford family business planning sessions went on inside Henry Ford II's own head.

A whole way of life for the Ford family reached a pinnacle on December 21, 1959, when Mr. and Mrs. Henry Ford II presided over the debut party of their eldest daughter, Charlotte. Planning for the event had lasted more than a year. In homage to their preeminence in Grosse Pointe, the Country Club was surrendered to the Fords for the night— and for the several previous nights which it had taken Jacques Frank, the Parisian decorator who did debuts for the Rothschilds, to transform Albert Kahn's mock-Tudor clubhouse into a passable imitation of the Petit Trianon. Frank ordered 2 million fresh magnolia leaves to be stuck painstakingly, one by one, to the walls of the main reception rooms in order to create a fish-scale effect, and an elaborate pastoral bower was thrown up in the parking lot to serve as a welcome arch.

The small army of staff in attendance included sixteen security men, one plumber, and one electrician, all camouflaged in black ties and dinner jackets, while a promenading hairdresser patrolled the corridors, hairspray in hand, ready to freshen the locks of ladies in need of roadside maintenance. The ceremonial route to the reception line actually went through the men's locker room, but the way was so beribboned and beleaved that no one realized.

"It was like walking into fairyland," remembers Lloyd Semple, who was the escort that night of Charlotte's younger sister, Anne.[28] Along with a dozen or so other young ushers, he wore a red and white enamelled medallion on a ribbon below his white tie, as if newly elevated to the Légion d' honneur.

The cabaret was Nat "King" Cole. The guests included Lord Charles Spencer-Churchill, the Gary Coopers, the Nicholas DuPonts, and the Ernest Kanzlers, as well as the current presidents of both Chrysler and General Motors. The music was supplied by the Meyer Davis society orchestra, who had flown in from New York with a song, "Charlotte," specially composed in honour of the belle of the ball:

> *Five foot five, delectably sweet,*
> *Ambitious, delicious, de-loveliest treat.*[29]

Newspaper reporters present were lost for words and fell back on statistics: 1,270 guests, 5,000 finger sandwiches, 2,160 scrambled eggs, 100 pounds of corned beef hash (for the dawn breakfast), and 480 bottles of Dom Perignon '49.[30] The Hearst columnist Cholly Knickerbocker had no hesitation pronouncing it "The Party of the Century."[31]

The evening started with Henry II taking a solo turn around the dance floor with his blonde-streaked daughter while the band played "The Most Beautiful Girl in the World," and the dancing continued until 6:30 next morning, enlivened by Henry II jumping on the bandstand from time to time to lead choruses of "Hey-Ba-Ba-Re-Bop," the "Whiffenpoof Song," and his special favourite, "When the Saints Go Marching In."

The tab for the entire affair was conservatively estimated at $250,000, and the binge is still recalled with fondness along the wooded boulevards by the banks of Lake St. Clair

—the memory of a happier, more carefree time before riots and emission controls, when there were still staff in the servants' quarters, and nobody had heard of Ralph Nader, Toyota, or Martin Luther King.

Two million fresh magnolia leaves, can it really have been?

"Yes," reply Grosse Pointers, smiling with proud melancholy. "It really was like that."

Charlotte Ford's debut party was headlines all over the country. It was the wonder of the news magazines. It marked the apogee of the modern Fords as America's first family of business, the Mid-west's answer to the just-emerging John F. Kennedys: the dynamic, youngish man of affairs, the polished wife with a flair for style, the handsome, well-dressed, submissive kids.

But the pinnacle was also a conclusion. Life in the Ford family was not quite what it seemed. There were the tensions between the brothers, for one thing. It was no coincidence that the clan only gathered when their mother summoned them, for Henry II, Benson, and William Clay Ford liked each other less than they claimed.

It was the brothers' attempt to work together as a triumvirate that had brought it out into the open. Henry intended to run the company his own way. William Clay Ford had found that out when his beloved Continental Division was killed. He argued with Henry quite bitterly, but Henry backed Breech—and that was that so far as William Clay was concerned. He had put so much of himself into his project, and he never made the mistake of being so generous to the company—or to brother Henry—again.

The problem was aggravated by drink. William Clay Ford had snapped his Achilles tendon in the same winter his Continental Division was axed, and the injury affected him, if anything, even more than his corporate defeat. Sport meant so much to him, and when the tendon snapped for a second time he sought consolation in the bottle. Never an early riser, he got into the office later and later, and was soon being absent for weeks at a time. He was a director of the company and his executive title was Vice-President, Styling. "W. C. Ford," said the label on his parking place outside the Design Center, right at the head of vice-presidents' row, but, said the wags, if you were having difficulty parking your car in Dearborn, that was one space you could always be sure of finding free.

Benson Ford adjusted more readily to the monocracy of brother Henry. He was such an easygoing man, affable and good-humoured. Everybody liked Benson. His assignation in the shake-down that dislodged the younger brothers from their control of corporate divisions was to take charge of Lincoln-Mercury dealer relations, and this proved a responsibility admirably suited to his gregarious talents.

Benson could remember a name—and a wife's name, and where the children went to college as well. He liked to travel. He liked to drink—he was at his best swapping jokes with a bourbon in his hand. Grassroots representatives of a family company do like it when they can meet up with some members of the family; it is satisfying, after all, to let slip how "Benson Ford was saying to me. . . ." So Benson became the Ford who pressed the flesh, and he pressed it very well.

His wife, Edith McNaughton Ford, was not so happy with her husband's role. Edie was the daughter of a General Motors executive, a vice-president of Cadillac, Lynn McNaughton, who had carved out a social swathe for himself in Grosse Pointe. Edie had made a good marriage, people said, when she landed young Benson, but the McNaughtons had no cause to feel beholden to the Fords. Edie could be touchy, at times. She had demonstrated her independence by leaving Benson, for a month or so, at an early stage of their marriage, and she felt that her husband was unfairly overshadowed by her elder brother-in-law.

Not that Edie made her unhappiness public. Ford family tensions are seldom the subject of outright conflict. Bill had had a good shout at Henry over the mercy killing of the Continental Division—"I was pretty outspoken about it," he says today. "I didn't think I'd really had a fair shot at it"[32]—but the Fords, in general, have always had some difficulty putting themselves, or anyone else, in touch with their deepest feelings. Edsel Ford I had stumbled all his life through an emotional mist, understandably confused by the alternately loving and vindictive messages that his father was sending. He kept up appearances to the outside world. He protected himself inside an armour of reticence, and he endowed his children with the same courteous carapace. Unhappiness and disagreement in the family were kept hidden, their presence being conveyed by code—an unexplained mood, a silence, a change of subject, anything in preference to a face-to-face row.

Alcohol was a route that many of the Fords took to their feelings—including Henry Ford II. Oddly shy in some respects, he found it difficult to relax without a few drinks inside him. His father-in-law, James Francis McDonnell, thought this a dangerous trait in so young a man.

"Just be careful," he would warn his daughter.[33]

The Ford ambiance did not, however, encourage sobriety.

"She *did* insist on such a long cocktail hour" is just about the closest that any of Mrs. Eleanor Clay Ford's friends will come to casting aspersions on her sainted memory. Her grandchildren retain fond recollections of the family Christmases at 1100 Lakeshore, but they took it for granted that all of their parents would go home drunk.

"The grown-ups got so *loud*," remembers Charlotte Ford. "I think it was their way of being able to have a good time within the confines of the family, and nobody knowing about it. They could just let it rip."[34]

Alcoholism is a family disease. Modern research seems to indicate it is a biochemical imbalance that is inherited. The diabetic's metabolism cannot cope with sugar, the alcoholic's cannot cope with booze—though this malfunction can show itself in unexpected ways. Young alcoholics are often the best drinkers of all, the ones who win the chug-a-lug contests and display no ill effects. William Clay Ford, today a pillar of Alcoholics Anonymous, having taken the cure in the late 1960s, can remember how at Yale he could line up fourteen empty martini glasses and still be drinking when everyone else was under the table.[35] When you discuss Henry II's drinking with his colleagues and friends, they hasten to produce tales of how he can carouse until dawn, then turn up at an 8:00 A.M. meeting bright-eyed and bushy-tailed, as if, somehow, this makes him less vulnerable to alcohol. His brother Benson was to die an alcoholic. His nephew Alfred has chosen the way of Alcoholics Anonymous, however, and so has Benson's son, Benson Junior.[36]

It might seem strange this formidable collection of drinking problems should have descended from a famous teetotaller like Henry Ford I, but fanatical dislike of alcohol can often be a sign that someone, sometime, has had an unhappy experience with the demon drink. William Ford, Henry's father, brought a heavy drinking habit with him from Ireland. It was one of the things that Dearborn folk most remembered about him.[37] Perhaps it was one element in his son's unexplained hostility towards him. Henry himself had a strange curiosity about alcohol. He used to test out its impact on his own metabolism. Grace Prunk, a niece of Clara Ford's, can remember how Uncle Henry would sometimes come down to meals from his workshop over the garage, looking rather green.

"It just makes me ill," he would say. "It's a poison for me."[38]

The great carmaker had been dosing himself from bottles of liquor that he kept in his workshop, and his experiments proved, to his own satisfaction, that the human body had a natural antipathy to alcohol. What he actually proved was that alcohol was antipathetic to his own particular Ford body—and, thus, perhaps, to that of other Fords as well.

Drink released a Henry Ford II that was very different from the tasteful, sensitive, churchgoing exponent of "human engineering." It unleashed the dark side of his soul. Just aglow, with only a few drinks inside him, Henry II could be wonderful company. He cracked jokes and generated fun, the proverbial life and soul of the party.

On one memorable occasion, he led an entire dance band through the shallow end of a swimming pool, fully clothed, to the strains of "When the Saints Go Marching In"—and the band did not miss a beat.

As an evening progressed, however, Henry could turn very nasty. He could say such hurtful things when he was tight. Frank Donovan, chairman of the Detroit Grand Opera Association, remembers how, at the white-tie reception held to celebrate the first successful visit of the Met in May 1959, someone congratulated Henry Ford on his wife's great achievement, and expressed the hope that she would chair the opera again next year.

"Well, *I* hope not," bellowed Henry Ford II to anyone who cared to hear. "This goddamn opera is ruining my sex life."[39]

Anne McDonnell Ford did not, perhaps, react as well as she could have to her husband's earthy side. Her immediate successor would just laugh at Henry when he made a fool of himself. The third Mrs. Henry Ford II just goes up to bed and leaves him to get drunk without her.

Anne McDonnell Ford, however, would get mad. Her mouth would tighten, and her shoulders hunch.

"Henry," she would say, "it's time for us to be leaving now," and she would frog-march him to the door. She was not afraid to walk out onto a dance floor to haul him off a partner with whom, she felt, he was getting rather too intense, and onlookers were always surprised by how meekly he would go.

"That Anne Ford," people would say. "She knows how to handle him." But people were wrong.

The wild boy was particularly in evidence on the June night in 1961 when Henry II's younger daughter, Anne, celebrated her coming-out.

The decor for the occasion was entrusted once again to Jacques Frank, who decided that the only thing better than magnolia leaves was 50,000 red and white roses, each in its own small separate container, and these flowers were all shipped in by a convoy of refrigerated trucks from Long Island. Since Charlotte's debut, the family had moved from 421 to 457 Lakeshore Road, an even grander mansion, and it had been agreed that its gardens would provide the perfect setting for the coming-out of Anne. On the night and day before the party, the beefy shapes of the University of Michigan football squad were busy all around the estate, planting the roses to the instructions of Jacques Frank.

Meyer Davis and his orchestra flew in again, their song for the occasion reflecting the developing character of the new hip decade, "Man, That's Anne." The cabaret was Ella Fitzgerald, and the overall theme for this celebration was Venice—which turned out to be an ill-fated choice in that, on this one night in an otherwise unbroken month of beautiful Michigan summer evenings, the skies chose to open. The rain started falling shortly before the guests arrived, and the downpour did not let up until they had departed, cold and bedraggled, the following dawn.

One particular problem that evening was the lack of lavatories. Queues formed outside the two powder rooms in the main reception area, and, in desperation, guests dashed outside in the pouring rain to the Portaloos which had been erected for the servants' benefit.

Even these were occupied, however, and surrounded by a milling crowd, when Neil Brown, one of the medallioned band of ushers, arrived outside. Rather than fight his way through, he continued his desperate way on towards the rhododendron bushes, and there, in the dark, his dress shoes squelching in the sodden soil, he was finally finding relief when, to his horror, he heard footsteps behind him.

"It's Mrs. Brossy," he thought with horror. "She's going to strike me off her list"—Mrs. Brossy being the formidable matron who supervised the guest lists for local deb parties, and who made it her business to patrol hidden nooks and crannies on the lookout for young couples carried away by the excitement of the occasion.

But it was not Mrs. Brossy, for as the footsteps got closer, and as Neil Brown stood miserable and helpless in the pouring rain, the downpour above him mysteriously stopped, and he looked up to see a large black umbrella being extended courteously above his head. The umbrella remained there, motionless, while not a word was said, and then, when young Brown had finally completed his transactions in the shrubbery, and turned to head back towards the party, the umbrella followed, suspended above him, keeping him dry all the way back to the house.[40]

After the party everyone agreed that the rain had not helped things, but that something more fundamental had been wrong. The Fords had been so on edge.

"Henry really was awful that night," recalls one of Mrs. Eleanor's friends. "Something turned him very ugly."[41]

People had been noticing how, with Henry II entering his forties, the wild boy had been surfacing more and more. Perhaps it was a certain ennui with his marriage. Perhaps it was just his time of life. Something was complicating his existence, and the refuge he sought from it was drink.

At his daughter's debut Henry's drunkenness had been embarrassing. "I don't know who the hell half of you are," he had shouted, jumping up on the stage to try and create some calm before the appearance of Ella Fitzgerald. "But, dammit, shut up."[42]

His wife had looked ghastly all evening. It had been hard for her to raise a smile. As for her daughter, little Anne, you would not have guessed that the entire extravaganza had been organized to give her fun. There was clearly something amiss in the house of Ford.

# 28

## GRADUATION

*We want our friends to understand,*
*When they observe our car,*
*That we're as smart and successful and grand*
*As we like to think we are.*

— EDSEL PRESENTATION SHOW LYRIC,
AUGUST 1957[1]

Tail fins, whitewall tyres, and the two-tone colour scheme —the mid-1950s marked a baroque climax in the history of the American motorcar. With the Korean War over, the United States surrendered herself to an orgy of consumer indulgence: 33⅓ r.p.m. records, dishwashers, television sets —and the acquisition in 1955 of 7,169,908 brand-new automobiles, the first time that the 7 million mark had ever been passed, and only the second time the U.S. car industry had got past six.*

Cars had long since ceased to be mere methods of transportation. They were expressions of the ego in an increasingly ego-conscious world—vehicles for status, escapism, dreams. If you lacked an exciting personality, you could at least possess an exciting automobile. General Motors' hit of 1953 had been the Corvette, a finny, two-seater sports car. Ford responded in 1954 with the even finnier Thunderbird —its roofline based on Bill Ford's ill-fated Continental— and the atmosphere of excess spread across the Atlantic. In Britain, Nora, Lady Docker, the wife of a Birmingham small-arms manufacturer, became a national celebrity on the strength of her Daimler, whose every exposed piece of metalwork, from front bumper to exhaust pipe, was gold-

* In 1950 U.S. new car registrations had totalled 6,326,438, but had then fallen to 4,158,394 in 1952.[2]

plated, and whose flanks were adorned with a galaxy of 7,000 six-pointed gold stars.

Ford rode this consumer boom even more exuberantly than either of its rivals. With Chrysler overtaken, Ford set its sights on General Motors, whose postwar expansion had been equally dramatic, and though the giant proved too nimble to let the competition get anywhere within sniping range, by 1954 Henry Ford II and Ernest Breech could proudly contemplate sales which were better than anything Ford had achieved since the heyday of the Model T—a market share of no less than 30.83 percent.*

Market share, however, is not the only name of the carmaking game. Two million cheap cars will give you the same market share as 2 million luxury sedans. But the profit on the former can be a fifth—or even a ninth or tenth—of the profit on the latter. Big, luxury cars are where the money is. Detroit has often been criticized for its failure to develop a significant range of small, economy cars in the years since the Second World War, but, except when squeezed by the worst of fuel crises, Americans have displayed a distinct lack of appetite for economy vehicles, while company share-holders have never appreciated the drain which small cars represent on the balance sheet. Down-sized cars mean down-sized profits—or worse. In the late 1970s Chrysler stole a march on all Detroit with the introduction of its compact Omni-Horizon, but the Omni-Horizon could not generate the cash to save Chrysler. At the time of writing, Ford's best-selling car in the United States is another compact, the Ford Escort—over 400,000 were sold in 1985 in its various incarnations[4]—but the car barely makes money for Ford by the strictest rules of accounting, and, over five

---

* Market-share figures for 1946 had been GM, 37.78; Ford, 21.97; and Chrysler, 25.74. In 1954 the equivalent figures were 50.7, 30.83, and 12.90. The remaining—and dwindling—market share (14.51 in 1946 and only 5.57 nine years later) was divided between struggling independents like Studebaker and Packard, who merged in 1954, and Hudson and Nash, who also amalgamated in that year to form American Motors.[3]

years, it has represented a net drain on the company's resources.

This was the problem facing Henry Ford II and Ernest Breech as they contemplated their best-ever sales figures at the beginning of the 1950s. Chevrolet had been their target since 1946. "Beat Chevrolet" read signs posted at the end of every Ford assembly line. Double agents would secure advance models of the new season's Chevys, then rush them to the Ford Design Center, where they would be gutted and spread out on the floor, piece by piece, so that every one of the car's 13,000 or so components could be tested, compared, and priced against its Ford equivalent. As a result of such efforts, Ford was neck and neck with its rival by 1954, losing the annual battle of new car registrations that year by only 1,400,440 to 1,417,453[5]—amid angry accusations that Chevrolet had unfairly swelled its figures by getting its dealers to register inventory that had not, in fact, been sold.[6]

But whereas Chevrolet was partnered at General Motors by the corporation's four medium-priced and luxury divisions—Pontiac, Buick, Oldsmobile, and Cadillac—each of which sold fewer cars than Chevrolet but yielded higher profits, Ford had only its Lincoln and Mercury lines, neither of which sold particularly well. In 1952 Jack Davis, just recovering from a heart attack, was set the task of examining this problem, and he came up with the obvious conclusion —that the Ford Motor Company should immediately start developing plans to introduce another car in the medium-priced field.

The Davis report was handed to the Lincoln-Mercury Division, since this was the home of Ford's medium-priced-car experts, and Benson Ford, then running the division, passed it on to his assistant general manager, Richard E. Krafve. True to the way in which Ford now operated, Krafve, a bespectacled ex-management consultant, formed a study group to analyse the proposal, and in September 1954 the Krafve task force came up with plans for a new medium-priced car that would be produced and sold within the existing Lincoln-Mercury Division and its dealers.

But this safe and obvious proposal did not fit in with the grand vision of at least one senior Ford manager. Lewis D. Crusoe had come to Ford with Ernie Breech. His chubby, cherubic features belied a capacity for tough political infighting—it was Crusoe more than anybody who had run Tex Thornton out of the company—and by 1955 Crusoe had established himself as number three in the Ford hierarchy, with more day-to-day power in some ways than either Henry II or Ernie Breech. Fifteen years a divisional controller at GM before he came to Dearborn, Crusoe was a fervent exponent of the GM way, and he now saw the chance for Ford to take one final step in its postwar cloning of its great rival. Ford needed more than a new car, in Crusoe's opinion: it needed an entire new division—a new nameplate, a new network of dealers—and he set up a task force to work this out under the direction of a special protégé of his, Francis C. "Jack" Reith.

Fast-talking and highly strung, Jack Reith was one of the original 1946 Whiz Kids, and in 1955 he was the blue-eyed boy of the Ford Motor Company, for he had just returned from Europe, where he had pulled off a spectacular coup. Ford of France had long been the lame duck among the company's European subsidiaries. Overshadowed from the first by France's great native carmakers, Citroen, Peugeot, and Renault—as well as by Ford of England, which had owned 60 percent of its stock—French Ford had been saddled by Dearborn after the Second World War with the designs for a small car, originally developed for the U.S. market, then abandoned. This "Vedette," which was anything but a small car by French standards, had helped drive the company towards bankruptcy. In October 1952, the Ford Executive Committee in Dearborn learned that their French subsidiary would go into receivership if they did not guarantee some of its loans, and Jack Reith had been sent to Poissy, the Ford factory outside Paris, to perform emergency resuscitation.

Reith succeeded with remarkable speed, managing not

only to improve the Vedette as a product but also to institute financial reforms which soon showed Poissy operating at a profit. Seizing the moment, he entered into negotiations with the Simca Car Company (Société Industrielle de Méchanique et Carrosserie), and he succeeded in off-loading Ford of France onto Simca, lock, stock, and barrel, in return for 15.2 percent of Simca stock (later sold by Ford to Chrysler at a handsome profit).[7] At one bound Jack Reith had extracted Ford from what had appeared to be an endless and depressing financial morass, and he had achieved this through knowing both how to handle money and how to develop cars. As the Whiz Kid returned from France trailing clouds of glory, it seemed obvious that Crusoe's ambitious new venture—christened the "E" car project—was for him.

On April 15, 1955, Jack Reith appeared in front of the Ford board of directors, and he presented his own recipe for the company's entry to the medium-priced-car market in lucid and dramatic terms. Ford commanded 43.1 percent of sales in the popular, low-priced field, he demonstrated, but only 13.6 percent, through its Mercury and Lincoln cars, in the middle and upper price range. Reith further identified a $700 market gap between Mercury, whose prices stopped at $2,400, and Lincoln, which started at $3,100. When basic Ford buyers "traded up" into this gap, he pointed out, they were getting captured by General Motors, who had three cars in this price bracket, and even by Chrysler, who were managing to sell two. Here was the target that Ford should aim for, argued Reith, and his proposal was that Ford should attack the gap in the same way that General Motors did, with a distinct and calculated brand image for that market sector—not Ford, not Lincoln, not Mercury, but something different, something new.

The Ford directors—Henry II and his brothers, senior executives like Breech, Davis, and Crusoe, a representative of the Ford Foundation, and Jim Webber, Mrs. Eleanor's cousin, head of the J. L. Hudson Company—listened to Reith's proposals, and approved them unanimously. Not all of them can have been versed in the arcane Detroit theology which instinctively sniffs out the distinction between a high-priced Buick and a low-priced Oldsmobile, but the ambitious and hardworking Reith had, with Crusoe's help, prepared the ground carefully in advance. All the directors had been visited and briefed before the meeting by either Reith or Crusoe, and when it came to the vote, the result was a foregone conclusion. As William Clay Ford put it later, the skids were "pretty well greased" under the car that turned out to be the Edsel[8]—and Reith was certainly saying what both Ernie Breech and Henry II wanted to hear. They had got their cost analysis and their profit centres. They had developed their corporate organization, and now Ford was going to go seriously multidivisional as well.

In 1964 the Ford Motor Company was to introduce the Mustang, a car whose phenomenal success was exceeded in the company's history only by the Model T, and Ford executives have fallen over themselves ever since to claim credit for its parentage—Lee Iacocca heading the pack. The Edsel, somehow, has provoked more modesty. Ernest Breech went so far in his memoirs as to claim that he argued against the car when Reith first proposed it.

But the record shows that Breech voted for Jack Reith's proposals in the spring of 1955, and any other red-blooded businessman would have done the same. The moment seemed so ripe. As the Ford directors listened to Jack Reith's persuasive presentation, after a decade of almost unbroken success and only nine months before the company was due to go triumphantly public, the entire American car industry was performing better than it ever had before. Sales were flowing at a phenomenal rate. Every successive set of ten-day figures seemed to demonstrate the inevitability of the market expanding on a perpetual basis. Inventories were at record lows. It was hard to keep almost any car in stock. New segments of consumer demand were continually opening up: the business car, the runabout car, the teenager's car. The possibilities were endless.

The only suggestion of caution came from Jack Reith

himself in the restructuring that followed the creation of the new "E" car division in the summer of 1955, for, curiously, Reith did not appropriate this exciting responsibility for himself. With the help of his mentor, Crusoe, he was now elevated to the rank of vice-president in charge of the newly independent Mercury Division, which meant that he could always take credit for the new car, if it should prove a success. If the car should turn out to be a lemon, however, Reith had distanced himself sufficiently to dodge the fall-out. By an irony of corporate politics, the real hot seat—command of the new "E" car division itself —was given to the man who had first studied the original Jack Davis proposal on behalf of the Lincoln-Mercury Division, and who had argued against its conception as an expensive and independent entity, the ex-management consultant Richard E. Krafve.

Krafve's new division was initially assigned to a collection of wooden huts lying to the east of Fair Lane, and to the west of Ford World Headquarters, an impressive chrome and green-tinted structure just taking shape beside Michigan Avenue and due for completion in 1956, when it was immediately christened "the Glasshouse." The "E" division's command post-like huts had formerly been the home of William Clay Ford's short-lived Continental Division, and as Dick Krafve assembled his staff there in the summer of 1955, one of his first priorities was to select a name for his "E" car, since this could prove the key to the new product's success. The name had to excite the public, while not alarming it unduly. It had to distance the new vehicle from the existing Ford, Lincoln, and Mercury labels, while remaining reassuringly part of the same great family of automobiles. It had to satisfy all manner of other requirements, from starting with a letter that would look good on a front hood ornament, to not rhyming with anything rude.

Emmett Judge, the product planner, gave the job of reconciling these requirements to David Wallace, a sociologist who had earned a Ph.D. at Columbia University—and who was later, after his bruising contact with the cruel, hard

and minimizing their weaknesses. When he got to the end of the list, he informed his hearers that tests showed the Corsair as having the highest public acceptance of all.

The Executive Committee listened unimpressed. It was clear they were not greatly excited by any of these proposals, which had taken twelve long and arduous months to research and analyse, and Ernest Breech, chairing the meeting in the absence of Henry II, said as much. If that was the best selection available, he declared, looking around slowly at every member of the committee, then he had to say that he did not like any of them.

"Why," he asked, "don't we just call it Edsel?"[12]

Edsel had been the name that several newspapers had suggested as soon as the formation of Ford's new car division was announced in the summer of 1955. "E" car seemed to point in that direction, and Richard Krafve himself rather liked it. It fitted well, somehow—an old family name for a brand-new product, just as Ford was becoming a public company.

When Krafve had passed the idea of "Edsel" on upwards, however, he was firmly informed that the family were not pleased by the idea. Henry II sent down the strictest word that his father's name should not even be considered—and when, following Ernie Breech's decision to go with the name, Charlie Moore, vice-president in charge of public relations, took the news to Mrs. Eleanor Ford at 1100 Lakeshore, he reported that she slammed the door in his face.[13]

It must have been a windy day. Mrs. Edsel Ford was a lady at all times, not least in her dealings with the employees of the company. But she was certainly unhappy about the use of her dead husband's name, and so were her children. It took all of Ernie Breech's persuasiveness to overcome Henry II's instincts that the name was just wrong, and in order to convince him, Breech had to stretch the truth, overstating both the enthusiasm felt by the Executive Committee for Edsel as a name, and also its evolution out of the 18,000 name selection process.

The decision was a classic example of the growing isolation of Detroit from mainstream America. People in the Motor City knew who Edsel was and what he stood for— the Lincoln Continental, patronage of the DIA, charm, style, humanity, an instinct for progress. But to the rest of America Edsel was just a funny name. When David Wallace sent out market researchers to discover the "immediate associations" that Edsel produced when fired at people in the street, they had come back with the answers "Schmedsel," "Pretzel," and "Weasel"—while 40 percent of their respondents had just reacted "What?"[14]

When Krafve brought back the news of Breech's decision to his eager and anxious "E" car lieutenants, his P.R. director, C. Gayle Warnock, responded with an angry one-sentence memo which he typed out himself and laid accusingly on Krafve's desk.

"We have just lost 200,000 sales."[15]

Ford car design in the age of the tail fin was in the manicured hands of George W. Walker, famous for his description of his life's "finest moment," in an interview with *Time* magazine. "There I was in my white Continental," he said, fondly recalling a trip to Miami, "and I was wearing a pure-silk, pure-white, embroidered cowboy shirt, and black gabardine trousers. Beside me in the car was my jet-black Great Dane. . . . You just can't do any better than that."[16]

Walker laboured in the shadow of Detroit's preeminent dream maker, General Motors' flamboyant and meticulous Harley Earl,* who had stunned the Motor City as long ago as 1927 with his spectacular LaSalle, the first mass-production car to be self-consciously "styled," and who had developed the use of sculptors' modelling clay, laid over a wooden frame, as a method of designing cars. Clay modelling

* Earl was one of the sights of Detroit, driving around the city in his futuristic prototypes, and, like Walker, he extended his styling to his own clothes. His underlings used to marvel at the fact that his footwear was not only polished but totally crease-free, so that as he walked around the design studio, it looked as if his shoes still contained the trees.[17]

was the technique which led to Detroit's smoothed and rounded dream machines, with their wraparound windshields, aircraftlike fuselages, and, of course, the tail fin, whose inspiration was the twin-tailed Lockheed P-38 fighter, which Earl glimpsed in 1948 on a visit to the Selfridge Air Base just up Lake St. Clair from Detroit.

George Walker had nothing to be ashamed of when his work was set beside that of Harley Earl. He had been hired by Ford in the late 1940s on the strength of the streamlined designs which became the 1949 Ford. His studio had the Thunderbird to its credit. Walker's own styling work on the basic Ford range had earned him the nickname "the Cellini of Chrome."[18] For the design of the Edsel he selected one of his assistants, Roy A. Brown, Jr., who had caught his eye while supervising the final detailing of the Futura, an exercise in motor-show fantasy dreamed up by Lincoln-Mercury's chief stylist, William Schmidt. The Futura was later to earn immortality, through television, as the runabout of Gotham City's caped crusader: the "Batmobile."

From all these beginnings something extraordinary should surely have emerged—and it did. Roy Brown's original clay model for the "E" car is still treasured in the minds of the few admitted past all the guards, passwords, and locked doors of the Ford Design Center. Brown had photographed the front end of every current Detroit offering, reduced the designs to their bare essentials, and then pinned up the pictures to demonstrate that the configuration of all the competition was essentially horizontal. Smiling, snarling, honeycombed, or betoothed, all Detroit's grilles had the same basic "Band-Aid" look, and Brown proposed to take his car in the opposite direction by giving it a single, vertical, bladelike structure at the prow.[19] With concealed airscoops below the bumpers, this first version of the "E" car was original and dramatic—a dream-like, ethereal creation which struck those who saw it as the very embodiment of the future.

But then the compromises started. The engineers pointed out that the dramatic prow design would provoke ventilation problems for the engine, so the swordlike blade was hollowed out into an egg shape, later to be variously compared to a horse collar or toilet seat. The product planners had their say, and then the accountants came in—the "bean counters"—and they started analysing the production costs of all Brown's curves and scallops.

"Take a buck out of here," they would say. "Take a buck out of there."[20]

Brown was a designer, not a corporate guerrilla. He lacked the skills to defend his own turf strongly—and none of the proposed corrections was misguided in itself. The car's power unit obviously needed air intakes so that it could be cooled efficiently. But the "E" car's design-correction process, as it developed through the winter of 1955–56, was a classic example of the way in which Detroit could take a good idea and improve it to death. The Edsel as it finished up—horse-collar grille, doubled headlights, a gull-winged rear deck, and scallops below—represented a logical solution to every problem that had arisen during the course of its design. But the car's midwives had got so close to their anxieties they did not realize that their final collection of solutions added up to a package they would never have chosen in the first place.

It has to be said that this is all wisdom after the event. The Edsel was regularly unveiled to Henry II, Breech, and Ford's other senior managers as it went through the design process, and it was invariably greeted with gasps of delight and a standing ovation. Roy Brown selected a striking hue of turquoise to show off his clay models, and, when deployed with lashings of chrome and bright white, this had a dazzling effect. When the car was finally unveiled, auto writers joined in the chorus of praise, and it was only later that people started making unkind jokes about the egg-shaped grille—when other, more substantial faults had started to become apparent.

The most fundamental of these was that the Edsel was not really a new car at all. It had its own name, its own division, its own set of dealers, and its own body shape, together with a few gimmicks, like automatic gears which operated from buttons in the centre of the steering wheel, instead of by a conventional gear-shift lever. But underneath all this, the vehicle was a basic Ford or Mercury. It was due to appear as four variations on the same basic theme, the two least expensive constructed on the standard Ford chassis with a 118-inch wheel base, the two top-of-the-range Edsels on a longer, 124-inch Mercury platform. David Wallace's year of market research had borne some fruit in the names that were given to these four models: the Edsel Ranger, the Edsel Pacer, the Edsel Corsair, and the Edsel Citation.

There was a very real sense, however, in which the whole enterprise was a massive confidence trick. Striking an elaborate pose of reticence, Gayle Warnock had masterminded a two-year P.R. campaign of carefully contrived leaks whose bogus secrecy gave the impression that Ford was desperate to hide something totally new—and the media had taken the bait. "The new car," stated *Life* magazine in September 1957, is the "first big new car to be brought out by a major U.S. manufacturer in almost 20 years," while *Time* magazine even swallowed and propagated the company falsehood that the vehicle was the result of "10 years of planning."[21]

This was just ridiculous. The 1949 Ford had been a big new car. GM's Corvette was an original, as was Ford's Thunderbird and William Clay Ford's expensive Continental. It was possible that someone, somewhere at Ford might have begun thinking about a new medium-priced car sometime in 1947, but serious planning had not started until the Krafve study of 1954. The Edsel was only an elaboration of Detroit's annual model change with more hoopla attached —the same shell game GM played, shuffling bodies and chassis between its various divisions, but a shell game for all that.

If the American consumer had been satisfied with the new Ford product, none of this might have mattered, since the morality of P.R. and advertising extends no higher than the bottom line. But the speed with which the Edsel went from concept in the spring of 1955 to sales in the summer of 1957 created problems of quality from which the vehicle never recovered.

So few people at Ford really loved the car. After much manoeuvring, Krafve won his division a small, outdated assembly plant of its own, dedicated to nothing but turning out Edsels. But most of the car's crucial first-year production was farmed out, to be put together on existing Ford and Mercury assembly lines. Every hour an "E" car body would be lowered onto a Ford or Mercury chassis, in place of the standard body shell that characterized the other sixty Ford and Mercury units for that hour's production, and the lonely Edsel would then trundle its way down the line—an irritation and inconvenience, from that point forward, for everyone who encountered it along its route through the production process. Ordinary assembly workers had to break their routine to scoop different components from their bins—and they only had fifty-nine seconds, instead of sixty, to carry out the work of their station, since Ford and Mercury did not cut their existing sixty-units-per-hour schedule to accommodate the new vehicle. The new Edsel became an extra unit, number sixty-one, that had to be completed inside that hour, and it bore the brunt of all the stress and impatience that a speed-up always produced.

Quality inspectors and managers harboured no more affection for the cuckoo in their nest. The Edsel Division paid the Ford and Mercury divisions for each finished "E" car they produced. It was as if Ford and Mercury were outside suppliers—and it might have been better if Krafve had been dealing with outsiders when the inevitable problems of quality started to arise. He could have refused to pay an outsider who delivered an Edsel with defective brakes. But inside the company, he could only complain.

Worried about quality, Krafve went to Robert McNamara, who had taken over Crusoe's responsibilities for cars and trucks, to request the right to install his own quality inspectors on every Ford and Mercury assembly line that was producing Edsels. But the division chiefs of Ford and Mercury defended their territories with ire. They would not open their assembly plants to "E" car men, and, as a compromise, McNamara instituted a tally system whereby defects were analysed numerically: a missing part cost twenty points, a chip in the paintwork, 0.1. It was agreed that if a sampling of any half-dozen cars resulted in a tally of more than thirty-five points per car, then every Edsel in that production batch would be held back from delivery and made good at that particular factory's expense—which made Ford and Mercury regard their demanding and unwelcome guest as still more of a nuisance.

"It was sometimes difficult," says one "E" car man, recalling the production-line warfare of 1957, "to remember that we were all supposed to be working for the same company."[22]

The assembly plants' reaction to McNamara's tally system was the proof of that. To keep up deliveries, they would identify and correct sufficient defects to ensure a thirty-five-point average, but then they stopped bothering, so that, by the law of averages, some Edsels were shipped out with only five or ten points against them, while others went to dealers with defects totalling seventy or more—and, quite often, with repair instructions taped to the steering wheel for the dealer to cope with himself.

Gayle Warnock's publicity plans for the car's debut included the loan of seventy-five Edsels to journalists attending the launch. The plan was that these specialist auto writers would drive the cars from Dearborn to their local Edsel dealerships, generating publicity along the way. It was obviously imperative that these vehicles should not be afflicted by the quality problems that were becoming apparent by the spring of 1957. But when a special mechanical unit was set up to test and prepare these seventy-five demonstration vehicles, it took two months to get them all in shape—and only sixty-eight cars emerged from the vetting process. The other seven had to be cannibalized to supply spare parts, and the average repair bill for each vehicle came to $10,000, more than twice the sticker price on a top-of-the-line Edsel.

None of these problems was apparent at the end of August 1957, when the sixty-eight identical turquoise and green two-door Edsel Pacers, plus seven new ones, lined up to show off their qualities to an expensively assembled crowd of dealers and newsmen on the Dearborn test track beside Greenfield Village. Quality was pronounced to be the watchword of the day, and quality was demonstrated in a fashion with which every ordinary motorist could identify, as the seventy-five white-coated test drivers stepped from their vehicles and slammed their doors shut in one satisfyingly rich-toned and unanimous *clunk*.

The general public was introduced to the Edsel by a television spectacular starring Bing Crosby, an event which show business judged historic because it marked the crooner's rather late transition from radio to TV. Behind-the-scenes tension centred on whether the toupees of Crosby and his principal guest, Frank Sinatra, would stand the test of live television scrutiny—they did—and whether Rosemary Clooney's Edsel would start—it didn't. Longer-term advertising for the car was centred on an untried, but promising new cowboy series, *Wagon Train*, and from the point of view of general publicity, the auguries for the new brand name seemed encouraging.

"By dusk next Wednesday, September the 4th," promised *Fortune* magazine in September 1957, "every American whose sight and hearing are not badly impaired will have learned three things: the Edsel is here, it is made by Ford Motor Co., it is a medium-priced car. . . ."[23]

The trouble was that by September 1957, the average American was not nearly so interested in buying a medium-priced car as he had been when the Edsel was conceived, for the U.S. economy had turned sharply downwards. Car sales slumped. In August 1957, *Automotive News* reported that American car dealers held the second-highest inventory of unsold vehicles in history. More worrying still, the mix of small and medium-sized cars within the reduced sales figures had turned severely in the Edsel's disfavour. Between 1950 and 1956, the years of the "E" car's gestation, medium-priced cars had accounted for 40 percent of the market. By 1958 that proportion had fallen to 25 percent— and it has never really risen since.

The year 1957 did not, in any case, prove a very happy one for the American psyche. On August 27, the very day of the Edsel's launch, the Soviets announced they had a missile that could drop a bomb anywhere in the U.S.A., and they proved it two months later by launching the *Sputnik*— not that that stopped the *Detroit Free Press* from running "First Pictures Of Edsel" in a banner line above the bad news from Moscow.[24]

One new car did sell well in 1957. Introduced at the same time as the Edsel, American Motors' Rambler sold nearly 100,000 in the year of its launch, and doubled that in 1958. It was a small, economy car, and the Rambler's success catapulted its handsome progenitor, George Romney, to the governorship of Michigan and even, for a time, to serious consideration as a presidential contender. What the success of the Rambler proved from Ford's point of view was that the general U.S. recession was not sufficient alibi in itself for the failure of the Edsel—people would still buy the right car if they were offered it. Reith's financial projections of 1955 had called for a 3 percent market share. Krafve's more modest analysis when at Lincoln-Mercury had called for 1.2 —and, in the event, the new car only managed .83 of the shrunken market.[25]

When Robert McNamara went to Washington in the 1960s, his political opponents delighted in tagging him with the failure of the Edsel. Barry Goldwater took special pleasure in tying the car, like an albatross, around the Defense Secretary's neck, and people at Ford who knew the inside story all said that this was unfair. It was true that as Group Vice-President, Cars and Trucks, McNamara was given the job of trying to save the Edsel, and that he had to clear up the mess when salvage proved impossible. But everyone knew that it had never been his sort of car.

McNamara was a puritan—a hair-shirt, bread-and-butter breed of car man, who obstinately persisted, for the fifteen years that he spent in the Motor City, in regarding the automobile as a method of getting from A to B. No tail fins and chrome filigree for him.

"He wore granny glasses," said the automotive writer Charlie Barnard, "and he put out a granny car."[26]

McNamara's pride and joy, the triumph which bore him out of Detroit and into Kennedy's 1961 administration, was to be the 1960 Ford Falcon, a foursquare, no-nonsense, compact car—basic family transportation. If old Henry Ford's spirit was ever subjected to the ordeal of reincarnation among the fanciful confections of Detroit in the late 1950s, it surely found a refuge in the utilitarian lines of McNamara's economic and reliable Falcon, developed in 1957 and introduced in 1959.

After the departure of Tex Thornton in 1948, Robert McNamara had become his acknowledged successor as leader of the Whiz Kids. He was clearly the brightest and pushiest—though not in the flamboyant, political style of Jack Reith. McNamara's politics were not a matter of buttonholing and premeeting lobbying, but simply of getting things done. He had such reserves of power beneath the hood, sheer incisive brainpower, which he would unleash without scruple when he wanted to get his way.

"Even when you knew he was wrong," said one of his underlings, "he would plow you under."[27]

The McNamara task-force studies reported earlier, argued harder, and, somehow, left no room for disagreement —a plan to coordinate the assembly plants, a reorganization to put profit back into the supply of spare parts.[28]

Jack Reith's "E" car plan of 1955 was an unmistakable challenge to McNamara's run at the top. If the four new types of Edsel, together with the now separate Lincoln and Mercury divisions, managed to get Ford up and well established on the medium-priced and luxury-car plateaux,

Reith could plausibly present himself as the obvious successor to Ernest Breech, who reached sixty in 1957, and with whom, people were noticing, Henry Ford II was venturing more and more to disagree.

But McNamara knew better than to oppose the "E" car publicly, and when the question of corporate reorganization arose, he kept his head down.

"Leave me out of it," he said. "Count me out."[29]

"Bob was against it, really against it," remembers Arjay Miller. McNamara could see the need for Ford to enter the medium-priced market, but he saw no need for the risk and expense of doing that with a new car, a new division, and a new set of dealers. Why not upgrade the top-of-the-line Ford?

"Let me put fifteen bucks in it, and make it seventeen inches longer," he said. "That's the second string to the bow. Give me that and then count me out."[30]

The price of counting Robert S. McNamara out was the 1957 Ford Fairlane (released at the end of 1956), a glamorous stretching of the Ford's basic Mainline series, which had made its debut in 1954. With radio, whitewalls, tinted glass, an electric clock, and a two-tone finish, the Fairlane was distinctly un-McNamara-like—except in price.

"Put in value, not cost" was one of McNamara's favourite instructions to his product planners, and the 1957 Fairlane overflowed with value. It was quite the most lavishly equipped car that Ford had ever offered, but it arrived in the showroom at only $2,556—and it proved to be the Ingredient X that Henry Ford II and Ernest Breech had been searching for since 1945. In 1957 the Ford Division, under Robert McNamara, finally achieved the long-sought goal of beating Chevrolet: 1,493,617 Fords to 1,456,288 Chevrolets.

Amid all the celebrations, however, people lost sight of what this 1957 triumph meant for the new Edsel, since Ford had achieved its Fairlane victory essentially by invading the medium-priced-car market—and the lesson was not lost on Chevrolet. The top-of-the-line Chevy for 1958 (released within a few weeks of the Edsel in the autumn of 1957) was a package to rival the Fairlane in extras and price, and Chrysler stepped into the ring with an upgraded Plymouth. In addition to this competition, the Edsel had to match up, at a time of recession, with the offerings of the second-hand market. The very cheapest new Edsel had a sticker price, stripped, of $2,519, while a motorist could get last year's used Fairlane, with its full complement of extras and only 30,000 miles on the clock for just $1,876.[31]

Richard Krafve and his lieutenants had thought they could give their new car a head start by introducing it in August 1957, a month or so ahead of the traditional new-season's launch, and when their first depressing sales figures started coming in, they consoled themselves with the thought they were having to compete with the price cuts of dealers clearing out their old season's stock. But even when the Edsel started taking on its full-price competitors, it continued to perform poorly.

The car's faults of quality did not help, of course. Nor did the jokes which became an avalanche as the news of the car's failure percolated.* Desperate marketing ploys, like stabling a pony at every Edsel dealership to entice families to come in for test drives, only made the catastrophe more abject and ridiculous. Ford bought back defective Edsels and attempted to repair them, at enormous expense, in the old workshops of the Continental Division—Detroit's only known example of an assembly line in reverse—and the horse-collar grille was redesigned as quickly as retooling would permit.

The new front end was unmistakably "Band-Aid." But even as the restyled Edsel came off the assembly line in the autumn of 1959, Henry Ford II announced that, after little more than two years in the marketplace, the car, together

* The earliest published reference to the Edsel as a synonym for failure appears to have been a 1960s cartoon showing the SST, America's answer to the Concorde, attempting to take off with an Edsel horse-collar grille. More recent comparisons have been with the Susan B. Anthony dollar, Dupont's miracle leather Corfam, and 1985's New Coke.[32]

with its division and dealer network, was to be scrapped. The Reith plan to take on General Motors at its own multidivisional game had been a failure.

The Edsel died because it was ugly, because it tended to go wrong, and because it was introduced in the depths of a recession. But it also died because Ford—and hence Chevrolet—had invaded and reduced the very market at which the new car was aimed. So there was a sense in which Robert McNamara deserved his albatross.

The failure of the Edsel was more than the failure of a motorcar. It deprived Ford of a whole way ahead. From 1955 onwards, the company's progress had been based on the assumption it could become ever more like General Motors—and now it stood on the brink of the 1960s without a strategy.

Henry Ford II could hardly be blamed for the debacle. Ford had had to get into the medium-luxury market somehow, and only in retrospect was it obvious that McNamara's way was the right one and that the grandiose Crusoe-Reith approach had been wrong. Still, the failure of the Edsel had to prompt some rethinking. If the new car, the new division, and the new dealer network had all worked out, then the flowering of the Ford Motor Company in an ever more GM-like structure would have created its own momentum. But perhaps Ford now had to face up to the fact that it could not beat the great market leader at its own game— that the end of a stage had been reached.

Henry Ford II felt he had outgrown Ernie Breech in any case. There had been a period in the late forties when the two men operated as one—by osmosis, almost. There were other big players in Dearborn in those years, but they all deferred to Henry and Ernie, and everyone knew that you could not play the old game of outflanking one by going to the other behind his back. The two men thought the same and spoke the same, and, if they did not, then they would work out a joint line quickly and amicably. Henry Ford II today recalls Ernest Breech as the executive he got closest to, the one he remembers most warmly as a friend, and even more.

"I wouldn't say a father, but almost. . . ."[33]

As the 1950s progressed, however, it was clear that the son was growing up. Henry II would contradict Ernie more often at meetings, and people soon discovered that if Breech said no to a project, then it might still be possible to keep it flying by going straight to Henry.

"When Henry was a child, he had been a little fat boy with no macho," recalls one of the Ford executives of the middle fifties, "and, in the beginning, something of that still lingered. If you argued with him, he would always back down. He was hesitant. He was extra-courteous. But the success of the company and going public gave Henry more swagger, a sense of himself—and you could not help noticing it."[34]

Ford started to become more corporate. There had been an atmosphere of teamwork in the locker-room jumble of the old Rouge Administration Building on Schaefer Road —jackets off, shirt-sleeves rolled up, much popping in and out of offices. But with the 1956 move to the new World Headquarters building, life became more stratified. Eleventh-floor executives were entitled to a potted palm and a Monet reproduction. On the twelfth floor you got a sofa and a conversation area as well. Life became more formal. Secretaries and personal assistants held more sway—and there was no popping in and out now, unless you had an appointment.

The change of environment had its effect on the chain of command. Henry and Ernie did not share a bathroom anymore—and, somehow, there was less of the "Henry" and "Ernie" in any case. In the Schaefer Road dining room they had presided together over the single, long lunchtime table. Now, in the executive penthouse of World Headquarters, with its own roof garden and its spectacular view to the distant spires of downtown Detroit, they often ate at separate tables.

It was not that there were special rules about who ate

with whom. But as you studied the seating patterns over the weeks, you could see the cliques form. There was nothing so crude or obvious as corporate warfare—yet. Rather, it was a softer, sadder question of drift and distance, like a marriage going sour.

The design studio is a traditional arena where underlings in a car company get to see who is currently on top.

"Take off that trim," says the chairman.

"Put it back on," says the president, as he passes through a day or so later, and from the final fate of just a few inches of chrome you can gauge the way that the boardroom wind is blowing.

By the late 1950s Henry Ford II and Ernest Breech were regularly indulging in that sort of skirmish, and, down in the studio, Eugene Bordinat, an ambitious young designer with well-developed political instincts, was making a careful note of how annoyed the skirmishing made Mr. Ford—and of how often Mr. Ford won.[35]

Company legend has it that Henry II ended all the fencing one day with the graceful words, "Ernie, I've graduated." The time had come, he said, to drop the pilot. At the time of the company going public, the two men did agree that Henry II would henceforward play a more predominant role.

"My job was to teach Henry," said Breech, "and he was a good learner."[36]

But others remember a more brutal quietus, at a meeting of senior managers held at the Greenbrier Hotel in West Virginia. These retreats were part of the company's new postwar management style—time out every year or so for some reflection. Chief executives from the Ford enterprises all around the world would be summoned to West Virginia. Trains were chartered to ferry the upper echelons from Dearborn overnight—a red train and a blue train, each with its own bar, lounge, dining car, and a baggage car for golf clubs.[37]

All the senior executives, including Ernest Breech, were required to submit their presentations to Henry Ford two days prior to the meeting. It was at one such meeting, down at the Greenbrier, after all the papers had been delivered, that Henry II himself rose to present his own view of the future—a view which turned out to be well pondered, and to differ, in several significant respects, from the way ahead which had been charted, just a few moments earlier, by Ernest Breech.

The pause that followed was awkward and painful, like that moment of truth when the manager says he is quite pleased with the team's performance, and when the owner of the club makes it clear that he isn't. Everyone knew that Henry could quite easily have liaised with Ernie in advance if it had been his intention to present a combined front. That is how he would have handled it in the old days. But the boss's speech was a personal manifesto, his own vision of what Ford would do next, with more "I's" and fewer "we's" than the team had grown accustomed to. In one sense the disagreements that it enunciated were honest and forthright, but in another, the sideswipe which Henry delivered at his guardian angel seemed inconsiderate, to say the least.

"Ernie blanched," remembers Alan Gornick, who was at the meeting. "It was clear that he had not had an inkling of what Henry was going to say, and he did not stick around when the session was over."[38]

Arjay Miller remembers the moment. "Henry had his ways," he says, "of letting you know he was ready to take over."[39]

In July 1960, Ernest Breech submitted his resignation as chairman of the Ford Motor Company.

Chairman, vice-chairman, president—the titles do not always mean quite what they seem. Analysing the hierarchies at the top of American public companies can be a little like working out where real power lies in the Kremlin. The man officially ranked at the top of the pecking order may, indeed, be the big potato, but it is just as likely that he counts for nothing at all.

The title of president in the Ford Motor Company had

always been afflicted with this ambiguity. The very first president was the banker John Gray. Henry Ford himself held the title from 1906 to 1919, but then Edsel took it over, and for more than twenty years it became a cruel joke played out at his expense. Henry II fought to secure his father's position and to give it real substance, but when the company went public in 1956, Ernest Breech, executive vice-president until that moment,[40] was made chairman of the board of directors—which meant that it was Breech, and not Henry Ford, who acted as company spokesman at the annual meeting of shareholders.

Henry II had to sit dumb beside his voluble and cocky lieutenant, and the subordination evidently irked. For the first three years of the company's public history, the proxy statement to shareholders was prefaced by a bloodless note from the company secretary. But in 1959 the proxy statement was introduced by a personal letter from the president, who signed off, "Cordially, Henry Ford II," and the same went for 1960, the year in which Ernest Breech resigned. Henry Ford II held the positions of both chairman *and* president for a few months after that, so no one could have any doubt who was really in charge. Then, on November 9, 1960, he named his new number two, and also ended the confusion as to which title counted for most—Chairman Ford was to be assisted by President McNamara.

Forty-three years old in November 1959, and only one year older than Henry Ford II, Robert Strange McNamara owed his precocious eminence to intellect and sheer hard work. When he had become group vice-president in charge of all the car and truck divisions, he had offered the position of executive assistant to Paul Lorenz, then working in the same capacity for Jack Reith.

"What size of staff will we have?" inquired Lorenz, who had seventy-five people working directly for him under Reith.

"Just four," replied his new boss crisply. "You, me, and our two secretaries."[41]

The programmer who wired up the circuits beneath the

slicked-down cranium of Robert S. McNamara might have missed a connection or two when he reached the sense-of-humour zone—but McNamara's earnestness had the common touch. The group vice-president always chose his own airline reservations. If he had to go somewhere, he would leaf through the airline guide on his desk and make up his own itinerary—and he was furious when, arriving once in Switzerland for a vacation, he was met by the managing director of Ford Switzerland, who offered him the use of a company car. Company perks were not for personal jaunts.[42]

There was method, however, in this mortification, for when the spurned Swiss executive shadowed McNamara out to the Hertz parking lot, he was horrified to crane around a corner and see his boss getting into an Opel station wagon —a General Motors car. Back in Dearborn a week later, Robert McNamara revealed himself a master of what the competition was up to in Europe, and he also came home with some well-tested ideas about the product requirements for the station-wagon version of his beloved Falcon.

The McNamara years could have created a whole new style at the Ford Motor Company. In 1957, dealers' wives at the Edsel launch had been treated to a fashion show and a speech from a female impersonator, who marked the climax of the proceedings by triumphantly flinging his wig in the air. When Marg McNamara had the task of entertaining dealers' wives, she gave the girls a tour of the new University of Michigan cyclotron.[43]

Bob represented such brainpower. Ted Mecke, a P.R. man who started work in Dearborn in the Schaefer Road days, remembers coming in every morning to see McNamara through the open door of his office, his desk clear already, his chin in his cupped palm, staring concentratedly into the middle distance, just thinking. . . .[44]

McNamara had thought out the way to catch Chevrolet. He had thought out the way to invade the medium-luxury market. He had thought out a way to beat the troublesome numbers of imports—and some of the chrome dinosaurs too

—with his curved little Falcon. There was no knowing what he could not achieve for Ford. He was the next stage of the rocket that had been blasted off so solidly by Ernest Breech —"a new go," as Henry Ford II puts it today.[45]

Yet hardly had Robert S. McNamara become president of the Ford Motor Company than he was gone. November 9, 1960, the date of his elevation, was also the day on which John Fitzgerald Kennedy won his narrow electoral victory over Richard Nixon, and the talent scouts soon latched on to the new man at Ford.

McNamara was not a political creature, nor were his political loyalties set. He had a record of giving to the Republican party—although, significantly, his money was coupled with a plea for the party to espouse candidates of the moderate persuasion.[46] He refused Kennedy's offer of the Treasury, accepted the Secretaryship of Defense, and, on January 3, 1961, went off to fight on the New Frontier.

The sigh of relief around the Glasshouse, remembers one of his staff, was audible. Robert S. McNamara was a demanding boss who did not suffer fools gladly. You would work for him on a presentation, slaving for weeks and dredging statistics from a cast of thousands. He would listen to it, and then, without pausing, apparently, for a moment's reflection, he would snap into action. "You are wrong," he would say, peeling off the reasons why you were wrong across his hand, a, b, c, often running out of fingers, and by the time he had finished, you had to admit that he was right. Some took it as McNamara's judgement on his former colleagues that, when he left for Washington, he did not invite a single person from Ford to join the handpicked team he was recruiting to help him subdue the Pentagon.

But the new Secretary of Defense was, perhaps, only being realistic. He forfeited over a million dollars in stock-option profits on his departure for government service,[47] and he may well have concluded that few others on the twelfth floor were willing to make a similar sacrifice. Robert S. McNamara was not, in any case, built quite like other men —as his old friend and colleague Charlie Bosworth had occasion to notice at the funeral of Jack Reith, father of the "E" car.

It was one of the sadder moments in the late 1950s, the end of Jack Reith, destroyed by his own hand, by accident or by intention, nobody quite knew. He was found dead from a shotgun blast through the chest, and it could well have been a mistake while he was cleaning the weapon.

But Reith was a highly strung man. Though no one had tagged him directly with the failure of the "E" car project, he had not performed that well in the niche he had chosen for himself at Mercury, and in 1957 his mentor, Crusoe, had suffered a heart attack that led to his early retirement. It all helped put the block down on the high ambitions which Jack Reith had nursed at Ford, and he had gone off to a company that did want him in the number-one spot, the Avco Corporation in Ohio.

But Avco was not quite the same as Ford—and there had been problems in his personal life. So it was a sad group who went to pay their final respects in Cincinnati. It was the first major loss the Whiz Kids had suffered since the departure of Tex Thornton, and all the survivors were there in the church together, marshalled by McNamara, who had arranged the logistics of the trip—and who also spent part of the service, noted Charles Bosworth, leafing through a pack of three-by-five note cards. He had an important presentation to deliver next day.

The departure of McNamara meant that the Ford Motor Company was rudderless for the second time in twelve months. At the end of 1959 the death of the Edsel project had left the company looking for a strategy. Now the man most likely to supply that strategy had disappeared as well.

When Henry Ford II had "graduated" from Ernie Breech, it was not with the intent of running his company as an autocracy. That would have made nonsense of the teamwork and corporate structure he had worked so hard to construct between 1945 and 1960. Henry II had grown up with the ghastly example of the havoc that autocracy could wreak, both on a business and on a family. His contribution to Ford had been to take the company away from that, and if he had wanted a rubber-stamp president, he would scarcely have selected the tough-minded McNamara as his partner for the next five years or more.

"You couldn't run it your own way," says Henry II today, "if McNamara was around."[48]

But now McNamara was gone, and with no one obviously ready to succeed him, what was the alternative to autocracy?

**Part Six** Henry and Lee

# 29

# MUSTANG

On October 15, 1924, four months after the Ford Motor Company had produced its ten millionth car, Nicola Iacocca, the owner of the Orpheum Wiener House in Allentown, Pennsylvania, had cause for celebration. Nicola's wife, Antoinette, gave birth that day to their first and only son, and, in memory of a happy trip to Venice in their native Italy, the Iacoccas named their son Lido.*

Nicola Iacocca thought highly of Fords. As he made money from his hotdog joint, he diversified into car rentals. He purchased the Allentown franchise for the U-Drive-It car-rental agency, and he invested in Model Ts and Model As as the staple of his fleet.[2]

Young Lido was a quiet and studious boy—"A little shy, too much reserved for his young age," remembers one of his eighth-grade teachers. "He was all business."[3] The only son slaved long hours at his homework, ignoring all distractions, and his studiousness has inspired biographers to repeat anecdotes which could have sprung straight from the pages of Horatio Alger:

Often his friends would stand outside his window and call, "Lido! Lido! Come on out!" Lido ignored the voices, and when they would continue calling he finally would get up and shout from the window: "Go away! I've got to study."[4]

The purposeful tone of Lee Iacocca's boyhood was set by his restless and hard-driving father, a first-generation immigrant from southern Italy who had embraced the

---

* Lee Iacocca was not conceived on his parents' visit to the Lido, as legend has it, since, as he points out in his memoirs, his father went there alone, while still unmarried. Young Lido was not born, in any case, until three years after his parents had arrived in America.[1]

American dream with enthusiasm, but who had not, perhaps, mastered quite all of its subtleties. After he had hit off
his ball on the golf course, Nicola Iacocca would immediately
set off after it at a run.[5]

Allentown is a drab, grey, hilltop city in eastern Pennsylvania with streets of small frame houses following the contours of the slope, like a mining village. Its weaving mills
drew Italian immigrants in the nineteenth century, and
many went on to the steel mills in nearby Bethlehem,
Pennsylvania. It was a tough environment, and when the
Detroit journalist Kirk Cheyfitz went to investigate the
Allentown background of Lee Iacocca in 1978, he discovered
that Lee's father had displayed a toughness to match. Nicola
Iacocca had appeared in the local papers on charges of
violating state liquor laws, operating as a realtor without a
proper state license, assault, and reckless driving. A number
of the businessmen with whom he had dealings ended up
suing him.

In 1957 he appeared in court for having driven through
the warnings of a school crossing guard, narrowly missing
running down a little girl.

"Look, I got money . . . ," he told the protesting guard.
"You can have me arrested, but it ain't gonna be a damn
bit of good. . . . You whore. Why don't you go home and
work in your kitchen?"

"I think," remarked Bennie Rizzoto, the magistrate who
found Nicola Iacocca guilty of reckless driving, "the fact is
he resented a woman telling him what to do."[6]

This imperious man, who played the game unapologet-
ically by his own rules, had high ambitions for his son, and
young Lido bent himself dutifully to their accomplishment.
The boy earned his industrial-engineering degree at Lehigh
University in Pennsylvania, in three years instead of four,
by going without any summer vacations, and he then went
straight on to Princeton for his master's.

Towards the end of Lido's time at Lehigh, the Ford
recruiter arrived on campus. It was the late spring of 1945,
and the Ford personnel department was discreetly carrying

out the orders of the recently arrived Henry Ford II to ignore his grandfather's wishes, and to hire more college graduates. Lehigh lay in the bailiwick of one Leander Hamilton McCormick-Goodheart, a talent scout who carried out his recruiting expeditions in a car to match his name—a long, low, black, and polished Lincoln Continental. The twenty-year-old Lido, already attracted by the idea of working for Ford, was totally won over by Edsel Ford's streamlined masterpiece.

"That car really turned my head," Iacocca was later to say. "One glimpse of it and one whiff of the leather interior were enough to make me want to work at Ford for the rest of my life."[7]

Lido started work at Dearborn in 1946 only a few months after the Whiz Kids, but at a considerably lower level. The new recruit was placed on a programme for trainee engineers, and it did not take young Iacocca long to realize that designing clutch springs was not going to accomplish his ambitions in a hurry. While at Princeton, he had already announced his intention of becoming a Ford vice-president by the age of thirty-five, and that meant that he had a lot of ground to cover before October 15, 1959. Looking at the car boom of the postwar years, when a dealer's principal problem was not selling cars but keeping his customers happy during the months that they languished on his waiting list, Lee Iacocca decided that his fastest way ahead would be out in the field, and he got himself a job in Chester, Pennsylvania, working in sales.

It was a brave decision for a shy and awkward youth, still living in the shadow of his forceful father—Chester was only a few hours' drive from Allentown. Iacocca's job was to negotiate with car fleet purchasing agents, notoriously tough and hard-bitten hucksters, and he would get a sinking feeling every time he picked up the phone.

"Before each call I'd practice my speech again and again," he later recalled, "always afraid of being turned down."[8]

Lee Iacocca spent the best part of a decade as an obscure provincial salesman, doing deals, polishing his patter, talking ever faster, tracing through his weekly sales books why some cars live and some cars die. He got to know the dealers, the hardbitten men who know how to turn thirty-five "I'm just looking"s into solid, cash-down handshakes every week. He got so good at selling that he was promoted to teach the sellers—he wrote a little handbook, *Hiring and Training Truck Salesmen*—and then in 1956, the same year in which a number of ambitious young executives in Dearborn were congratulating themselves on assignation to the "E" car project, Lee Iacocca had his bright idea.

Fords were going slowly that year. Robert McNamara had made safety the theme of the 1956 Ford—a deep-dish steering wheel, crash padding on the dashboard, and dramatic films that showed corpselike dummies thudding into the windshield. The campaign was a disaster. Car advertisements are supposed to promote love, life, and a fast getaway from the traffic lights. Ford's attempts to persuade customers that the purchase of a Ford could save them from a grisly death had the very opposite effect. Ford sales slumped, and Chevrolet widened its sales advantage that year by nearly 300 percent[9]—all except in Pennsylvania, where the Philadelphia district sales manager had been doing some sums.

Subtract a 20 percent down payment from the price of a new '56 Ford, calculated Lee Iacocca, and that would leave thirty-six monthly payments of $56, a sum that just about anyone could afford. "56 for '56" became the Ford slogan in the Philadelphia district, and Iacocca coupled it with two additional gimmicks: a packet of potato chips, and a card known as a "wujatak," which was pronounced "would-ya-take."

Iacocca's idea was for Ford salesmen to drive around supermarket parking lots, "would-ya-takes" in hand. Whenever they saw a well-cared-for used car, they were to look up the car's value in their secondhand-car price guide and write this price on their "wujatak," so that when the shopper got back to his or her car, there, taped to the windshield, would be a "wujatak" offer of x dollars for the vehicle in exchange for a new Ford—plus Iacocca's packet of potato chips bearing the motto "The chips are down. We're selling cars for $56 a month."[10]

Corny and complicated, the fifty-six-dollar-chips-and-wujatak campaign met with instant success. Within a few weeks the Philadelphia district was number one in the Ford sales league table, and Robert McNamara decided to extend Iacocca's sales approach to the whole country—minus the giveaway potato chips. "56 for '56" became a late shot in the arm for Ford sales that year, and McNamara later calculated that the campaign helped move 75,000 extra units that he would not otherwise have sold.

Lee Iacocca had made his mark. In the autumn of 1956 he was transferred from Philadelphia to Dearborn to take charge of Ford truck marketing, and soon after his arrival the company sent him to the Dale Carnegie Institute to improve his public-speaking skills. Dale Carnegie, author of *How to Win Friends and Influence People*, had turned his best-selling book into a franchised system of encounter groups designed to help introverted business executives come out of themselves, and the system had a remarkable effect upon the shy young salesman who had been afraid to pick up the phone.

Shyness was not to be a problem for Lido Anthony Iacocca again.

Henry Ford II says today that the first time he can remember meeting Lee Iacocca was in November 1960, when he summoned the young salesman to his office to tell him he was giving him command of the Ford Division.[11]

"It was like being summoned to see God," remembers Iacocca.[12]

The two men had shaken hands a few times before, but this was the first time they had had a real conversation. The job carried with it the rank of vice-president, and Iacocca was mildly disappointed that he had not made it by his target date. His thirty-fifth birthday was already a year behind him.

Everyone else in the company, however, was amazed at

such a major responsibility going to someone so young. Ford was the elite of divisions. Created in 1949 to coordinate the development, production, and selling of cars carrying the Ford label, as opposed to Lincolns or Mercurys, the Ford Division had been entrusted to the company's highest fliers.[13] Crusoe and McNamara made their reputations there—and it was McNamara who had recommended Lee for the job. The new president wanted the architect of "56 for '56" on his team, and when McNamara left for Washington, Iacocca stayed in place, suddenly responsible for the major portion of the company's car turnover and profits in the 1960s.

Ford would need some extra drive and originality at divisional level because the company presidency, vacated so abruptly by McNamara, was given to a pleasant but unexciting production manager, John Dykstra, a onetime GM man whom Breech had recruited back in 1947.[14] Dykstra was not the brightest of the topmost echelon—the Whiz Kids Lundy and Miller were that—nor did his length of service compare to that of John Bugas, who had run industrial relations from 1945, and who had been on the board since 1950. But Dykstra was safe. Square-jawed and silver-haired, he looked like a president. He was the competent, inoffensive cardinal pulled from the college to be Pope until younger, fiercer talents had matured.

The history of the Ford Motor Company in the years after 1960 was, in many ways, a story of increasingly erratic and wilful autocracy on the part of Henry Ford II. But this was not by design. Henry II knew his limitations. That was why he had flooded the company with abler talents in the years following the Second World War. His personal impact on the company, the contribution praised by all the business magazines when they came to write about Henry Ford II, was the reforming and rationalizing of Ford—and unwilling to admit how much he was acting out the frustrated ambitions of his father, he expressed this drive to modernize as an almost exaggerated respect for General Motors.

"He really envied GM," remembers Ted Mecke, "and

particularly the way in which GM had developed a system of management succession."[15] For fifteen years Henry II had laboured to create a mirror image of GM at Ford.

But that part of Henry II's spirit which was Ford to its very essence, that corner of his heart with the blue oval stamped upon it, knew that Ford was not General Motors. It was warm-blooded, impulsive, prone to hunches— human, in fact. For Ford to be truly Ford, there had to be a Henry at the head of it—and the partnership with Robert McNamara had offered that prospect within reasonable limits. It was hypothetical now how it might have worked out, but all the right ingredients had been there—McNamara was so close to Henry in age and ambitions, so safely separate in taste and style. Looking at the subsequent histories of the two men, both of them to be battered roughly by their now-disparate destinies, it was a might-have-been with some poignant overtones.

Whatever autocratic impulses had been present in Henry II's dumping of Ernest Breech had been counterbalanced by the choice of McNamara as a successor. But Dykstra was no McNamara, and the real import of his appointment in April 1961 was the enhanced management role it gave Henry II. Dykstra did not pretend to know about finance. His speciality lay in making the cars, in managing the assembly plants. He knew how to get the product to market inside the budget and on time, and while he concentrated on this, Henry II turned his mind in other directions—and towards diversification in particular. In a flurry of expenditure in 1961, Henry II spent $368.1 million on repurchasing the publicly held shares in Ford's European companies, $28.2 million to take over the spark-plug business of Electric Autolite, and $83 million, by an exchange of stock, to take over Philco, makers of radios, TV's, and other domestic electrical appliances. Now Ford had its nonautomotive equivalent to GM's Frigidaire.

Lee Iacocca meanwhile concentrated on the selling of motorcars in the way that he knew best. Soon after dawn on New Year's Day, 1963, two chartered aeroplanes touched down in the south of France to disgorge more than 200 assorted journalists, photographers, and Ford executives. The group had been toasting each other in champagne all night, and when they reached their ultimate destination, the palace of Prince Rainier and Princess Grace of Monaco, there was still more champagne waiting for them, this time served in beer mugs.

The purpose of the expedition was less to do homage to America's own homegrown princess, who duly appeared at ten o'clock that New Year's morning to shake hands with the by-now weak-kneed pilgrims from Detroit, than to inspect the latest range of Ford Division cars—in particular, a limited "Monaco Edition" of the Thunderbird, along with a decapitated version of the Ford Falcon, which was to be offered to the U.S. public as a "European-style" convertible. Robert McNamara is said to have sworn out loud at the sight of what Lee Iacocca did to his no-nonsense people's car.

Still, the Falcon convertible sold well, as did the Monaco T-bird with white leather interior and its special numbered brass plate. As the years went by, Lee Iacocca was to prove the master of this sort of thing—"packaging," the art of taking a sound basic product and adding the quick, easy trimmings which not only increased the car's attractiveness, but added real profit to the vehicle. It was an axiom of the auto business that the dealer made his living less from the basic product than from all the extras he could persuade the customer to add on to it, and Lee demonstrated how the manufacturer could get in on the same game: body stripes, vinyl roofs, walnut panelling—all the fripperies that sidestepped the cost of serious tooling and long production time, but gave the product a different flavour. For 1963 he restyled the Falcon's "greenhouse"—the roof and window section of a car, which is always the easiest to change—and he also offered a V-8 engine option to whet the growing appetite for muscle cars identified at GM by Pontiac's jazzy young John Z. DeLorean.

It was in 1964, however, that the salesman from Allentown

presented America with his greatest package yet. The 1960s already had its own music, and it was developing its own particular genre of clothing, leisure, and lifestyle. On April 17, 1964, Lee Iacocca was to wrap this all up, place it on wheels—and stake his own claim, in the process, to being the new carmaker at Ford.

In the early days, Detroit did not take the imports seriously. The Volkswagen looked so funny. The Big Three's research staffs regularly did surveys into public perceptions of the European cars that started trickling into America in the 1950s, and they concluded that Detroit had nothing to worry about.

"To the average American," ran one such report by the Ford Division in 1952, "our present car and its size represent an outward symbol of prestige and well-being."[16] It seemed obvious that as America became more prosperous, she would express her prosperity in terms of a bigger and better car, and the Edsel was a reflection of such a philosophy. Nobody with a decent job and education could possibly choose a European car for its own sake. Beetle-buyers were people who could not afford a real car—a challenge to the used-car market, perhaps, but not a phenomenon that domestic manufacturers need concern themselves with.

"What they sell in a year," said Ernest Breech dismissively of Volkswagen in 1956, "is not one day's production here."[17]

These words were already untrue when Breech uttered them, and they became increasingly misleading as Volkswagen doubled its sales in each successive year. By 1958 the German manufacturer was selling 104,000 vehicles in North America, and in that year Japan's answer to the Ford family, the prolific and talented Toyoda [sic] clan, made their first venture into the U.S. market. For 1958, imports as a whole totalled nearly half a million cars.[18]

Robert McNamara's response had been his Ford Falcon, and General Motors rushed in with the Chevrolet Corvair, an ungainly looking rear-engined vehicle whose ill-tested rear suspension could derail the car when cornering, thus providing the basis for Ralph Nader's momentous 1965 exposé, *Unsafe at Any Speed*.

Neither car really addressed the root of the problem, however. What Detroit did not yet realize was that European cars like the Volkswagen and, to an increasing extent, the Volvo, were selling well in the United States not just because they were cheap, but because they were better made. They were engineered to hold the road. When you turned the wheel, you did not plough through marshmallow. There were fewer rattles. Their flanks did not honeycomb so rapidly with rust, and though foreign parts were expensive and hard to get hold of, these foreign cars did not seem to break down so often. A dozen years of a seller's market had made Detroit sloppy.

Ford was particularly vulnerable in this respect, for the great achievement of rebuilding the company and catching up Chevrolet had been at the cost of quality. Something had had to go. Ford cars were notorious rust traps and rattlers in the 1950s, and this was reflected in their secondhand value. New Fords might sell at around the same price as a new Chevrolet, but on the used-car lot they commanded prices $200 or more below that of their equivalent competitor.

The Falcon did well despite this. It was a light, simple car. It did not contain too much that could go wrong, and it was quite gracefully styled. General Motors' offering, however, aroused suspicions from day one. The Corvair's engineering was unusual. Its rear engine made its styling look peculiar, and within a matter of months it was clear to the GM sales department that their new economy compact was dead in the water.

Enter Harley Earl's successor in the GM styling studio, William Mitchell, and a new Chevrolet account executive at Campbell Ewald Advertising Agency, David E. Davis, a car fiend whose very features, stitched together after a racing crash, were a patchwork tribute to his life's enthusiasm. Mitchell had just produced a customized version of the Corvair for his daughter—a special paint job, mean-looking wheels, bucket seats—and when this car was put on a stand

at the Chicago Automobile Show of February 1960, it was
an overnight success. Bearing the name "Monza," the prototype violated all the rules of the Corvair to date. Instead of
providing low-priced competition to the Volkswagen, the
Monza went upmarket, with a fancy package that turned it
into a little Thunderbird, a sort of family sports car—and
David E. Davis saw the way ahead.

"Put it on the market," he said. The Monza would
generate sales in its own right, but more important, it could
transform the overall image of the Corvair. By emphasizing
sportiness, it could make some sense of the new, unconventional rear-engined technology. Campbell Ewald could run
Corvair-Monzas up Stone Mountain in Georgia, leap across
great chasms in the West, drive through swamps, and do
all the things which, Ralph Nader later claimed, the Corvair
was particularly ill equipped to do—but, no matter, it would
all add up to excitement, youthfulness, and fun.

The result of this creative outpouring was a production
version of Bill Mitchell's styling exercise, which did everything Davis had promised for it. The Monza sold well.
Customers paid dealers a premium to get hold of one—and,
on the rebound, Corvair sales improved as well.

None of this was lost on Ford. "The damn thing had
beautiful red bucket seats and good-looking wheel covers,"
recalls Hal Sperlich, one of Iacocca's product planners who
saw a prototype Monza. "I remember seeing it sitting there
and thinking, son-of-a-bitch, the bastards have turned defeat
into victory!"[19]

The Ford product planners went into action to see how
they might match the Monza, and the Ford design studio
was already thinking along the same lines. Gene Bordinat,
just taking over Ford's design vice-presidency from George
Walker, had been discussing the sporty-type Corvair with
Don DeLaRossa, his chief of advanced design, and the two
men decided to try putting Ford's 289-cubic-inch V-8 engine
of the day into the light and resilient platform of the Falcon.
They then devised a totally new body shell to give this car
a power-packed appearance in the traditional way—"lotsa

hood"—and they rounded the two-seater off with a squared roof and a low, flat rear deck. "Di-noced" bright red,* the clay model was the Mustang, and when Lee Iacocca saw it, he knew it—though the car was, at that stage, named the Allegro. Bordinat and DeLaRossa presented the car to Lee Iacocca in the autumn of 1961.

In his authorized version of the Mustang's creation, Lee Iacocca makes much of the market research which had, he claims, helped him to identify the new and immensely profitable youth sector of the market—the baby boomers coming of age, and the explosion in the incomes of college graduates and comparatively young people. But two members of his team do not remember this. The Mustang's chief designer is adamant that the car came out of his department, not from market research—while Donald Frey, who, as Iacocca's manager of product planning, would have been responsible for such research, agrees.

"Most of the market research stuff was done after the fact," Frey told *Mustang Monthly Magazine* in May 1983. "They made it all up afterwards—somebody did—in order to sanctify the whole thing. . . . The market research that you read [of] is a bunch of bull."[20]

The market research was needed to persuade Henry Ford II and Arjay Miller, who was now in charge of finance, to commit to the expenditure of producing a new car. The wound of the Edsel still smarted, and Henry II had abruptly walked out on Iacocca's first attempt to sell him on the Mustang. The chairman had been out of sorts that day. Inspecting the prototype had been his last appointment before leaving for six weeks in bed with mononucleosis.

"The guy was sick as a dog," remembers Bordinat.[21]

The second presentation, held in the spring of 1962, was more carefully staged. An example of every current Ford product was set out beside the Design Center, paired off against its equivalent Chevrolet competitor—except that

* Di-noc is a patented plastic film which is placed over the clay model of a car to give the impression of paint.

there was a gap opposite the Monza. Ford had no offering in the sporty youth market which, Frey's hurriedly assembled figures showed, was expanding rapidly, and for which Iacocca now proposed the bright red Bordinat-DeLaRossa prototype—with one very important amendment, which, all agree, was Iacocca's own idea: the addition of a rear jump seat, which turned the vehicle from a pure sports car to a cramped four-seater.

Henry Ford II was impressed. His own particular contribution was to add an extra inch to the car, thus making its rear seat a little less cramped. Arjay Miller decided that the car was worth risking money on, and its name became "Mustang"—though the origin of the name was not, in fact, the wild horse, but the legendary World War II fighter plane.[22] Unveiled at the New York World's Fair in the spring of 1964, the Mustang proved a sensation. With its chunky yet graceful lines, it became an instant classic. The car cost only $2,368, basic, but it looked, and drove, as if it was twice the price. It exuded excitement. It racked up record sales and it created, virtually on its own, a major new sector of the U.S. car market: the so-called "small-sporty."* Lee Iacocca well deserved the rare accolade of simultaneous cover stories in both *Time* and *Newsweek*.

Lee Iacocca was not the father of the Mustang—not the natural father, at least. The car itself, the long, low alchemy of line and steel that was the source of all the magic, sprang from the loins of the Ford design studio, who first gave it form, while the original seed was planted by the Corvair-Monza, Chevrolet's injection of youth and sportiness into its ailing compact car. It was even possible to argue that, as with virtually every other new direction taken by the Ford Motor Company in the years since the Second World War, the original idea for the Mustang came from General Motors.

---

* In both 1965 and 1966 the Mustang alone sold more than half a million units: 549,400 in 1966, its best year ever. This represented 6.1 percent of all cars sold in North America and no less than 78.2 percent of the small-sporty segment.[23]

But General Motors did not make the Mustang. Ford did —and the credit for that went to no one but Lee Iacocca. Once Lee saw the car, he knew that he could sell it, and he got it out. He built the figures around it, and he commissioned the survey data he wanted to prove his point. He fought doggedly through the Ford hierarchy for a totally new, youth-oriented car at a time when his superiors, including Henry II, were trying everything they could to avoid spending real money: a Falcon convertible, a V-8 package, anything rather than a decisive, Edsel-like commitment to a brand-new car—though the Mustang, of course, as fresh sheet metal on an established platform, was no more a "new car" than the Edsel had been.

"Lee was so inspiring," remembers Charles Bosworth, the Whiz Kid who, frankly, was overtaken by the dynamic young man from Allentown. "He had the ability to switch on, to light up. In a group he might appear awkward. But then you put him on a platform, and he came to life, swelling with his feeling about the car. You would hear him talk at one of those meetings, and I remember the feeling, it was quite extraordinary, we all felt it, that we wanted to go back to the office and work some more, to put in another couple of hours that night if we could."[24]

Iacocca built a Mustang team that was dedicated to him. They would not only work late, they would come in early on Saturday mornings as well, to iron out the production and quality problems that had been the death of the Edsel, and they crashed through a thirty-month programme in less than twenty. They would meet for breakfast at seven on Saturdays at the Fairlane Motel on Michigan Avenue: Frey (today chief executive of Bell and Howell), Hal Sperlich (today president of Chrysler under Chairman Iacocca), and Donald E. Petersen (today chairman of Ford). The group also included Joe Oros and Dave Ash, the designers who had developed the original Bordinat-DeLaRossa prototype to its final form, and Walter Murphy of the company P.R. department, who, said the envious, was taking on the role of Iacocca's personal publicity agent.

There were many who envied Iacocca, many egos that got bruised as he brushed them aside with his go-getting style. Lee knew how to intimidate and manipulate. He could scare you to death. He tolerated fools no more kindly than had McNamara, and he listened less than he should have to arguments that threatened to complicate or slow down his own headlong progress to the top. He swore a lot, he wore loud suits, and he took to waving a big fat cigar. He had all the grace and sophistication of the East Pennsylvania car dealers who first taught him his trade. He seemed pretty obnoxious to the people who did not adore him—but he got results. He got his car out on time, and, when early demand proved so strong, the Iacocca team got a second and then a third assembly plant switched to the Mustang, doubling capacity.

Lee Iacocca could deservedly claim the adoption papers on the Mustang—and the success of the car placed him in a grand and honourable Ford tradition, since the great victories of the company, its true character, had always lain in its cars. The Thunderbird, the '49 Ford, the V-8, the Model A, and, most seminally of all, the Model T—these were the triumphs. They were the essence of Ford's history, the combinations of glass and steel and rubber that people liked to drive. What did the general public care about management organization charts or proliferating corporate divisions? Perhaps Lee Iacocca had found the new way ahead for Ford: not to let corporate theorizing get in the way of the basic business of making cars.

Henry II was delighted by the success of the Ford Mustang. It redeemed the failure of the Edsel, and it did so with a special Ford flair and style. It also suggested a recipe for success in the future that owed nothing to outsiders. GM had had the Monza-Mustang idea originally in their pocket, but they had not had the imagination or flexibility to know what to do with it.

Ford might have let the idea slip too if it had not been for Lee Iacocca, and in January 1965, the young vice-president, still only forty years old, was rewarded by promotion to the position of Vice-President, Cars and Trucks, with overall responsibility for Lincoln-Mercury as well as Ford—the grand supervisory position held by Robert McNamara before he became president. Lee had been given the Ford Division in 1960 because he had been McNamara's nomination. But he got his new job because he had now won the confidence of Henry Ford II.

# 30

## MEDITERRANEAN PHASE

One hot June evening in 1961, Mrs. Anne McDonnell Ford paused outside her husband's bedroom as she walked to her own room. Their daughter Anne's coming-out party would be the following night. Tired by all the last-minute arrangements, Mrs. Ford was going early to bed, and she was just about to say goodnight to her husband when she heard his voice raised through the door. Henry II was evidently engaged in a long-distance telephone conversation, and wondering who he could be talking to so late at night, his wife lingered to listen.

"Yes," she heard her husband saying. "Yes, I will marry you."[1]

Looking back on it all, the friends of old Mrs. Eleanor are inclined to trace the beginning of the trouble back to the influence of Ernie Kanzler—or, rather, of his second wife.

Josephine Kanzler, Ernie's first wife and Eleanor Clay Ford's beloved elder sister, was found dead at the bottom of the Kanzler swimming pool in Hobe Sound in 1954.[2] She had been drinking heavily, and she had either suffered a heart attack while at the pool's edge, or had just stumbled in drunk. Alcoholism, unfortunately, sometimes came packaged with the Hudson genes. Cousin Jimmy Webber died an alcoholic.

Ernest Kanzler worked hard, and he liked to play hard too. Alfie Ford, the second son of Dodie and Wally, remembers holidays in Maine with Great Uncle Ernie. Kanzler would organize elaborate paper chases through the woods in his thorough and detailed way, Hansel and Gretel-like trails that went up hill and down dale, and just when you were getting really sick of it, when you thought that your legs could not carry you another yard, you came out into a clearing, and there was Uncle Ernie beaming, with a butler beside him in tailcoat, setting a silver tray and white linen tablecloth down upon a tree stump, with hampers full of food and ice buckets full of Coca-Cola and champagne.[3]

Ernest Kanzler did not mourn his wife for long. In 1954 he met Rosemarie Ravelli, a thrice-married Swiss-born beauty, and he became her fourth husband within a year of his first wife's death. The glamorous Rosemarie helped Kanzler add luxurious homes in St. Moritz, Mexico, and Cap Ferrat to his existing residences in Hobe Sound, Grosse Pointe, and Maine. Jetting first-class between them, Uncle Ernie applied himself, with his customary thoroughness, to getting the most out of each exotic locale.

"He was like a man transformed," recalls his business associate George Reindel[4]—and Kanzler confided to his nephew Henry that he felt like a new man. He had had his "batteries recharged," he said.[5] Yes, there was life beyond Grosse Pointe.

In March 1960, Ernest Kanzler threw a dinner party at Maxim's in honour of Princess Grace of Monaco, and he invited Henry II and his wife, Anne, who were in Paris at the time with their daughters. Rosemarie extended an invitation to her old friend Maria Cristina Vettore Austin, a vivacious thirty-four-year-old divorcée then living in Milan, and Cristina flew up to Paris. She sat beside Henry at the dinner—and suddenly the carmaker felt that *his* batteries had been recharged. Ford told his daughters afterwards that he found Princess Grace a crashing bore, but it was obvious to everyone that he was impressed by the lady seated on his other side.

Anne Ford saw her husband falling all over the pouting blonde Italian with the seductively fractured accent, and she decided that Henry had had too much to drink. When the couple entwined around each other on the dance floor, Anne stalked out to separate them, dragging Henry back to their hotel, and she did not think about the woman again, until, just about a year later, she heard her husband, through his bedroom door, talking long-distance on the telephone.

The affair between Henry Ford II and Cristina Vettore Austin had gathered rapid momentum in the months following Ernest Kanzler's party at Maxim's. It blossomed in the same spring and summer of 1960 in which Henry II got rid of Ernie Breech, thus becoming chairman of his own company—and the timing was not coincidental.

"Henry has a way of deciding things," says one of his old friends. "He gives no sign of it, but the wheels are going round in there. He's unhappy about something, going back to basics, working out a new way. And then, bang, when he's decided that the new way is the right way, he goes through with it, just like that. Nothing can stand in his way."[6]

Three years into his forties in the spring of 1960, Henry Ford II was set upon breaking new ground. For more than a decade, his very closest relationships had been with Ernest R. Breech and with his wife, Anne. He shuttled between them every day, without diversion. He left early for the office every morning, and when he set off for home at night his secretary would phone, without fail, to let Anne know that Mr. Ford was on the way.[7] Henry II was devoted both to his family and to his business. He gave them of his best, and the styles of Breech and Anne McDonnell had each shaped his own style in their respective spheres.

But now, for Henry Ford II, all that was at an end. Both of his mentors were expendable—and Anne Ford found the hemlock pushed in front of her in the same oblique fashion that it had been proffered Ernie Breech.

The doses were small to start with. Anne McDonnell Ford had an aversion to the press. She shied away from interviews. But when she had started her work on behalf of the opera, the Ford P.R. department had suggested she might loosen up her style a little, and Anne began allowing journalists into the family home. It made for a less exclusive image, and the columnist Shirley Eder reported, after one such interview, that the Henry Fords would be sitting down that evening to a dinner of hamburger and fries.

Henry Ford was furious. He posed happily for photographers in nightclubs and restaurants—even calling them over, on occasions, to instruct them what poses they should snap. Like his grandfather, he rather prided himself on his ability to get along with the press. Yet the scandalous revelation that he ate hamburgers for supper stung him on a raw nerve. Perhaps it was his finely developed sense of privacy, whose limits he could not, in his inarticulate way, define. Perhaps it was just jealousy. *He* could tell the world what he ate for dinner, if he wanted to, but that was not a secret that his wife was at liberty to reveal. Humble in so many ways, Henry Ford II could unexpectedly stand upon his dignity like a pasha—and when he did so, he had a moodiness to match.

Inside the family, Henry II's confidante was his younger daughter, Anne. Charlotte was a little too abrasive—"forty years old when she was fourteen," remembers one of her friends. She had the Ford bluntness. She did not like to drink. But Anne was prepared to sit up with her father when he got into his cups, and sometimes, late at night, when she was up in her bedroom, fast asleep, she would be wakened by the pressure of his hand on her shoulder. Then Henry Ford would sit there on the side of her bed, talking for hours, pouring his soul out, a sometimes sad, sometimes happy— but always, somehow, lonely—man, rich and successful, with no one to share his deepest thoughts.

That was how Anne Ford, at the age of eighteen, came to hear, out of the blue, the night before her debutante party, that her father was planning to divorce her mother. Henry II had brushed off his wife with an excuse when she confronted him about the woman he was talking to over the telephone, but his teenage daughter was awakened from her sleep with the brutal truth.

"Your mother has just caught me speaking to my girlfriend," confessed Henry Ford II. "I love her, and I am going to marry her, no matter what."[8]

This was the reason why the Ford women had looked so strained at young Anne's Venetian party. It was nothing to do with the rain. Anne McDonnell Ford had got up at five that morning for an urgent session with her priest.

"How I kept going," she says today, "I just don't know."

Her daughter Anne seems to have forgotten all the lavishly arranged details of the occasion that was supposed to mark the high point of her youth—and sister Charlotte's comment is characteristically sardonic.

"My father," she says, "has a marvellous sense of timing."[9]

They tried to make a go of it. They had loved each other, after all, for so long. There were the children. There was their religion—not to mention the image of the company. And then there was Mrs. Eleanor, who was deeply distressed when friends explained the "blind," no-name gossip-column references to the problems in the marriage of a "prominent industrialist."

Henry made an effort. In the summer of 1961 he stopped seeing Cristina for a time, and for nearly two years he and Anne tried to recapture what they had lost. They gave up their separate bedrooms. Anne moved in with Henry. There were more family holidays. Henry had recently got himself a boat, the 125-foot-long *Santa Maria*, built to his specifications in the Netherlands, with air-conditioned suites for six and quarters for a crew of seven.[10]

But the family cruises were to the Mediterranean—not to Maine or Martha's Vineyard.

"I just assumed," remembers Charlotte, "that we had done all the American spots, and now it was time to 'do' Europe."[11]

And it was strange how Henry II insisted on supervising his new boat's decor himself. Colour schemes and furnishings had always been his wife's province, but this yacht was evidently to be his own private toy.

"It was meeting Gianni Agnelli [owner of Fiat] that did it," remembers one of the family. "Here was this man, who

was just about the same age—handsome, macho, sun-
tanned, dynamic—running a successful major business, but
also jetting from St. Moritz to St. Tropez, with hot and
cold running blondes. And suddenly Henry Ford realized,
'Christ! *This* is what running a family car company is all
about.'"

Henry Ford II had long ago proved to himself, and to
Detroit, that he could make it, that he was more than just
a fat little rich kid, lucky enough to be born in the right
place and at the right time. But there is only so much
satisfaction to be derived from the praise of the local
Chamber of Commerce. Henry Ford II wanted some fun,
and though he made a manful effort to have it with Anne
McDonnell Ford, the attractions of his wife for twenty years
proved no match in the end for the fresh appeal of Cristina
Vettore Austin.

Cristina was so uninhibited. Henry started taking more
and more trips to Europe, sometimes in the company of his
old Grosse Pointe drinking companion, Bill Curran, who
was excellent company, and who also served as a convenient
escort for Cristina in the eyes of the world.

"We were in a boutique together," remembers Curran,
"and one thing I must say for Cristina, she was no gold
digger, no matter what the world might say. She never asked
for expensive things. It was always Henry who insisted on
buying them. And one day, there he was in this cubicle with
her, somewhere in Italy, I think, when he suddenly stepped
out and whipped back the curtain, so there she stood,
bare-ass naked for all the world to see. She just stood there
and laughed at us. She thought it was a wonderful joke."[12]

Cristina Vettore Austin made a welcome change from a
lady whose engagement book weighed a pound. The
"Austin" came from a British businessman to whom Cristina
was briefly married in the 1950s. Some gossip columnists
hinted that she was a contessa, but Cristina herself only
claimed to be a physician's daughter, while those who knew
the Vettores said her origins were even humbler than that.

Cristina had made her way in the world on the strength of her own personality. She was an exotic creature, wild and untamed. Show her a Louis Quinze settee, and she would leap up and perch herself on the arm of it, talking excitedly, waving her arms in the air—and displaying her girllike slender legs to great advantage. She exuded animal magnetism, and Henry Ford II was not the only mogul to be ensnared by her.

Bumping into Cristina in New York one day, and failing to catch her name, Charles Revson, king of Revlon, was so struck by her beauty that he had one of his artists draw her picture from his memory. The cosmetics tycoon then had this sketch circulated around Manhattan's smarter restaurants, with the offer of a thousand dollars for the maître d' who could come up with the name of the Italian beauty.

Cristina had recently moved into a new apartment, and one day 300 roses were delivered to her door, followed by 300 the next day, and the next day, and the next day. . . .

A fortnight, and several florists' shops, later, a note finally arrived that revealed the identity of Cristina's mysterious admirer. The Revson courtship happened to coincide with the period when Henry II was trying to patch things up in his marriage, and Cristina felt free to accept her new suitor's invitation to spend some time on his country estate.[13]

When later recounting the course of her romance with Henry Ford II, Cristina would cite the Revson interlude as one of the turning points in the relationship. Having a rival —and a rich one—really got to Henry.

Back in Grosse Pointe, Anne McDonnell Ford would come downstairs to catch Henry engaged in yet another of his long-distance telephone calls. She was not forgiving, and he fought back. The atmosphere grew more and more rancid.

"You could see her wilting before your very eyes," remembers one of her friends.

The lawyers were called in. It was a crabbed, bitter, unhappy time which, for Anne Ford and her daughters, has permanently drained all the savour from the memories of their Grosse Pointe years.

Coming home for the holidays at the end of a term at Hotchkiss, Edsel Ford II, now a teenager, was surprised to find that both his father and mother had come to accompany him on the company plane. Flying back to Detroit, they broke the news that his sisters knew already. On December 26, 1964, young Edsel flew out with his mother, his friend Billy Chapin, and his sister Anne for a skiing holiday in Sun Valley, and when the time came for Edsel and Billy to fly back to school, Mrs. Ford stayed on. She completed the requirements of Idaho residence, and then, in February 1965, six weeks to the day after her arrival, it was announced that Mrs. Anne McDonnell Ford had sought, and had been granted, an uncontested decree on grounds of mental cruelty.

The financial details of the divorce were not made public, but it was estimated that the settlement cost Henry II the best part of $16 million. There was no argument over custody, and as for the goods and chattels, Henry kept the paintings and Anne got the furniture—which she took to her new headquarters, a large and elegant apartment in New York, facing the park at Fifth Avenue and Sixty-fifth. Her children moved in with her.

"And that was the end of it," says her daughter Anne, as if recalling a vanished world. "I never really went back to Grosse Pointe again after that."[14]

It seemed rather strange, when Henry Ford II and Cristina Vettore Austin got married on February 19, 1965, that the happy couple should choose to go off on their honeymoon with the groom's two grown-up daughters, Charlotte and Anne. But then the Henry Ford family did seem to be getting rather strange. Young Edsel, hitherto an average and moderately persevering student, had managed to get himself thrown out of Hotchkiss. Mother Anne, who once said grace at dinner parties, was now to be seen at jet-set resorts in the company of Ted Bassett, a notoriously racey socialite whose only visible means of support was a sharp game of cards.

It made wonderful material for the gossip columnists, but

it was all, in truth, rather sad. The Fords were a family who had lost their way. They might have appeared prim and conventional five years earlier, praying together every Sunday in St. Paul's beside the lake, but at least they had been together. Now their glossiness hid loneliness and confusion. Beneath all the jet-setting there was a certain desperation —and this showed itself particularly in the two daughters, Charlotte and Anne. They were the lost girls.

In Grosse Pointe the Ford girls had been noted for their propriety. They had been brought up on a pedestal, and they intended to stay there. Lloyd Semple, Anne's escort at Charlotte's coming-out party, still remembers the indignation with which he was pushed off the sofa when he ventured on his first tentative advances.

"Don't you ever do anything like that again," she exclaimed.[15]

Fords were not as other girls. Charlotte had talked for a time of becoming a nun. But now, in the early 1960s, based with her mother in New York, she amazed an old Grosse Pointe girlfriend by casually remarking that she had decided it was quite all right if she went to bed with men.[16]

Charlotte and Anne's staid convent upbringing was knocked sideways by the breakup of their parents' marriage, and it caused their grandmother particular distress. Mrs. Eleanor Ford had been deeply wounded by her eldest son's divorce. It did nothing for the name of Ford. But she was still more concerned by the impact that Henry's new wife and lifestyle seemed to be having upon her eldest granddaughters. Henry thought that taking the girls on his honeymoon would help them get to know Cristina. It would be fun for them, a change. But Mrs. Eleanor did not approve. St. Moritz was not the right sort of place, she felt, for girls who were now approaching a marriageable age.

"What sort of husbands can they hope for," she would worry, "if they only know the sort of man you meet at resorts?"[17]

If Mrs. Eleanor had been asked to give shape to her

nightmare, she might well have imagined one of the girls falling for an aging playboy, filthy rich, a Greek shipowner, perhaps, much married and much divorced—what other type do you find in St. Moritz?

Stavros Niarchos was eight years older than Henry Ford II, fifty-five to Charlotte's twenty-three, when they first met —and she knows everything there is to be said on the subject of father complexes. She has spent several years, and a good few thousand dollars in analysts' fees, in the process of working them out.

"Yes," she says today, "I am sure it was a reaction to the divorce. But I can't blame Daddy for that. I was a big girl."[18]

Charlotte Ford is elegant and feminine. "When she's in the blue jeans, and you're in the $500 silk dress," says one of her girlfriends, "*she's* the one who looks chic." But Charlotte has always known what she wants. The standard line, not always delivered with total admiration, is that if Charlotte had been a man, she would be running the company by now.

Her weakness has been her choice of male companions. She has specialized in the ego-centred—Henry Kissinger, Frank Sinatra, Anthony Newley, David Frost—and there is no need to labour the father complex about that either. Charlotte Ford seems to have taken it for granted that the man in her life should push her around, and the pattern started with Stavros Niarchos in the spring and summer of 1965.

The romance started on her father's honeymoon in the Alps, then moved on through the summer to Niarchos's private island in the Aegean. By the autumn Charlotte was pregnant.

"I remember sitting with her," says her sister, "waiting for the results of the test, and the doctor put his head around the door and said, 'Positive.'

"'Oh, oh,' said Charlotte, 'what do we do now?'

"'Call Daddy,' I said."[19]

Henry Ford was in New York within hours.

"I'll never forget it," says Charlotte today. "I was desperate. He just dropped everything, flew from Detroit and
stayed with me 'til we'd got everything sorted out."[20]

Henry II put his daughters on a plane and flew with them
across the Atlantic for a summit meeting with Niarchos
in London—and also with Anne, his divorced wife, who
happened to be in England at the time.

"Daddy didn't shout, or twist his arm, or anything,"
remembers Charlotte. "In fact, he said that Stavros mustn't
marry me unless he really wanted to."[21]

It was not quite as simple as that. Stavros Niarchos had
tax problems with the U.S. government—$25 million of
problems, according to some reports.[22] He could not safely
set foot in the United States until they were settled, and one
of the incidental benefits for the Greek when he married
Charlotte Ford was that his young father-in-law might be
able to have a quiet word with his good friend President
Johnson.

On December 14, 1965, Eugenie Niarchos, nee Livanos
(sister of Tina Livanos, then Marchioness of Blandford,
formerly Mrs. Aristotle Onassis), appeared in a courtroom
in Juarez, Mexico, and requested that her eighteen-year
marriage to Stavros Niarchos be terminated on grounds
of incompatibility. She got her decree. Two days later her
ex-husband and Charlotte Ford both arrived in Juarez,
in separate, Ford company planes, and they met to go
through a brief civil ceremony in a hotel room, Stavros
presenting Charlotte with a forty-carat diamond ring,
today referred to by Charlotte's intimates as "the skating
rink."

The couple then flew across the Atlantic for Charlotte's
second St. Moritz honeymoon in less than twelve months—
this second idyll having an even more curiously family
flavour than the first, since the previous Mrs. Niarchos
happened to be staying in the resort at the time with her four
children, ensconced in the family chalet. Since Charlotte's
condition precluded her from skiing, it was Eugenie who kept
Stavros company on the slopes, and one evening Stavros,

Eugenie, and Charlotte were even to be seen dining together at the Palace Hotel. The most hardened St. Moritz sophisticates were shocked.

Meanwhile, back in New York, Charlotte's younger sister, Anne, was getting married to an Italian, Giancarlo Uzielli, a roguish companion of Ted Bassett, Mrs. Anne Ford's playboy friend. Uzielli had only been divorced once in his thirty young years, but Mrs. Eleanor Ford did not attend the wedding. Guests at the premarriage party in Delmonico's included Truman Capote and Douglas Fairbanks. With the recently eloped Charlotte on everybody's mind, Henry Ford proposed a double toast to his sons-in-law "Gianni" and "Stavros."

Mrs. Brossy would never have believed it. At the reception following the wedding, Henry II forwent the "Saints" for music with an "Italian" flavour—"Arrivederci Roma" and "Ciao, Ciao, Bambina"—and beside him the new Mrs. Ford, looking radiant, kissed everybody in sight on both cheeks.

Contrary to the assumptions of the monogamous, people who marry frequently think highly of marriage, and this has certainly been the case with Henry Ford II. The clear pattern emerging from the apparent fickleness of his three ventures in matrimony is the wholeheartedness with which he has, successively, thrown himself into each of them, for Henry II is no run-of-the-mill Don Juan. He does not sweep his women up like some marauding buccaneer, heading for his own horizon. Rather, he has let each of his partners dictate his course—Mass and art galleries with his first wife, "Ciao, Ciao, Bambina" with the second. It is extraordinary the degree to which this apparently forceful cock-of-the-walk has submitted his own lifestyle—and even, to some extent, his own personality—to the very different interests, friends, families, and characters of his successive women, so that he has, in some respects, led three lives in one.

It speaks to an underlying insecurity which belies his apparent stolidity. Henry Ford II is evidently not so sure of who he is. Beneath the bluster lies a deep urge for comfort.

the sensual surrender of the little boy burying his face in his mother's lap. For years on end he seems quite happy to submit. He takes it for granted that his woman of the moment should be able to lead him by the nose, and this odd docility has made for three separate phases in the personal life of Henry Ford II—these phases changing with his women, as one in-law puts it, "from class, to brass, to ass."

After she had been married to Henry Ford II for a few years, the former Maria Cristina Vettore Austin was looking around her palatial Grosse Pointe home one day when she realized, to her surprise, that there was not a single picture of the founding father, Henry Ford I, anywhere around the house. She had done her homework on the history of the company, and she knew something of the hostility that had existed between her husband's father and the old man. But the omission seemed strange to her, and she set about correcting it.

A few weeks later, Henry Ford II came home from work to discover some carefully selected black-and-white photographs of his grandfather set in silver frames in strategic positions around the house. He was furious.

"Take those damn things outside," he said, "and throw them away."

"No, no, no, no," protested Cristina. "He was a great man, he was your grandfather"—and, in her fractured English, the second Mrs. Henry Ford II launched into a defence of Henry Ford I which owed more, probably, to passion and gesticulation than it did to history, but which did manage to coax her husband into grudging acceptance of the pictures' presence.

"Maybe you are right, Bambina," said Henry Ford II. "It takes a European to teach me these things."[23]

Henry Ford II had felt Europe had a great deal to offer him from the moment he first came down a Cunard gang-plank with his parents to find a Rolls-Royce waiting at the bottom.[24] The Edsel Fords had summered quite often in Europe, buying art, searching out furniture for their lake-shore home, and they took their children with them. Everywhere they went their way was smoothed by the attentive local acolytes of Ford, and Henry II got to know the sweet taste of that reverence which Europeans reserve for their elite. Auto barons' sons were not uncommon in Detroit, but in London and Paris his name seemed to carry an extra magic. So this was what being a Ford was all about.

Cristina Ford ministered well to this side of her husband. She was European and exotic, but she had not been born into the grand hotels and salons to which Ford wealth now admitted her, so she, like her husband, was a little overawed. Basically Cristina was a peasant, and since this matched the earthy side of Henry's nature, the two of them were quite comfortable together.

Europe gave Henry II the chance to escape from the hayseed aura which had always clung to Ford—the small-town, hick image which went back to the firm's founder and had been so carefully cultivated by old Henry I. Henry II's homage to this was his own blunt, no-nonsense side, a very necessary coloration for a car man in Detroit. But in Europe Henry II did not need to apologize for being a gentleman. He could shoot grouse, live in a manor house, have a London pied-à-terre, party at Annabelle's.[25] Henry did all these things. He cultivated upper-crust British friends like David Metcalfe, son of Fruity, aide-de-camp to the Duke of Windsor. He went to Broadlands to shoot with Lord Mount-batten, and Dickie was so taken with Cristina, he gave her a couple of Labradors to take back to Grosse Pointe.

Today, retired from day-to-day involvement in the Ford Motor Company, Henry II spends a lot of his time in England—more time now than he spends in Detroit. He lives outside Henley, in a house that was once the home of Julie Stonor, King George V's true love,[26] and there he pursues the life of an English country gentleman. He drives a Range Rover and he tramps the countryside in a flat tweed cap and Wellington boots. Old Henry Ford searched for his soul in Greenfield Village, his grandiose exercise in Americana. His grandson seems to find heartsease on the other side of the Atlantic.

This European strand in the persona of Henry II has given a very special character to the Ford Motor Company under his stewardship. His first project after he had got the Breech team and the Whiz Kids established in Dearborn was to cross the Atlantic and revive the Ford enterprises in Europe. Ford became a market leader in Germany, as it had long been in Britain.[27]

In June 1967, Henry Ford II invited four of his principal European executives to the Plaza Athenée in Paris.[28] Twenty years after the war, Europe was finally putting itself together again. Britain was still outside the Common Market, but integration was clearly the way ahead, and Ford should be part of that. John Andrews, the tall, fluent chief of Ford Germany, had been arguing coordination for some time. He had a particular project, a medium-sized van, the Taunus-Transit, which he thought he could sell in both Britain and Germany. Henry II was thinking in grander terms, and in one of the fits of business vision which illuminated his career, as they had done his grandfather's, Ford of Europe was born.

To start with, it was little more than a dozen executives in a corporate jet shuttling between Ford's various European enterprises—and between Germany and Britain in particular. But after a year or so, the product started to come: engines from Germany, transmissions from France, electrics from Enfield, Middlesex. The Ford Cortina was no longer just a British car. It had a German incarnation as well, and in 1976 came the finest fruit of the integration process, the Ford Fiesta, a small car researched and designed from the ground to fit the requirements of every European market.[29]

Like all the best ideas, it seems so obvious in retrospect. But General Motors' European executives did not think of it. GM's European subsidiaries, Vauxhall and Opel, continued to go their separate ways until the early eighties, and General Motors is still endeavouring, at great cost, to achieve the coordination which Ford acquired painlessly more than a decade ago. Ford of Europe has helped make Ford far and away the most profitable European manufacturing company of any sort in the post–World War II era[30]—and it also gave Henry II himself an international statesman's stature. He was better than a statesman, in fact, because, unlike the average politician, he had real money, to give or to take away. When he dropped a remark in March 1971 suggesting that Ford of England's labour troubles might incline him to invest elsewhere in Europe, he was received obsequiously by Edward Heath and his senior cabinet colleagues in Downing Street, wined and dined and treated like a visiting head of state.[31]

Ford of Europe became the way ahead for ambitious young go-getters in Dearborn. "Overseas" is Siberia, the kiss of death for executives in most American corporations, but Henry II personally made sure that managers who went to Europe received dramatic promotions when they got home, and the Glasshouse soon got the message. The men at the top of Ford today have all served apprenticeships in Europe, and this shows in the cars which Ford is finally producing after the disasters of the 1970s: tough, stream-lined, thoroughly engineered machines which hold the road and are the first products from Detroit to stand comparison with Audi, BMW, or even Mercedes.

It has all worked out very well. Ford of Europe became the great profit centre of the Ford empire in the late seventies and early eighties, the crutch on which Ford of North America leaned during the dark days following the Iranian energy crisis. A training ground for managers, the inspiration of better product, Ford's European dimension has turned out to be a crucial component of its modern corporate identity.

But this did not come from corporate study groups or developing organizational structures. It owed nothing to GM. It was a hunch in the grand old Ford tradition. Ford of Europe sprang essentially from the mind and tastes of

Henry II himself, from the international dimension in which he had grown up, from his idea of what it meant to be a Ford. Henry II's European venture in matrimony did not, as it turned out, prosper very well. But Ford of Europe ranks as an achievement second only in his life to the extracting of the company from the hands of Harry Bennett.

# 31

## TROUBLE ON TWELFTH STREET

*The future, I believe, will see a very wide removal of people from the cities. . . . Big cities had a purpose, but they have served their purpose. With very few exceptions they are all now shabby and run down and too far gone to make over.*

—HENRY FORD I[1]

At 10:00 P.M. on the night of Saturday, July 22, 1967, shifts changed in the Tenth Precinct, Detroit Police, and the precinct's plainclothes "Clean-up Squad" drove out of the station to start on their evening's work. Sergeant Arthur Howison and his three patrolmen were investigating "blind pigs," the unlicensed, and usually black, liquor establishments which often doubled as gambling, dope, and prostitution operations in inner Detroit. Howison was particularly interested by one establishment on an upper floor in Twelfth Street. It called itself the United Civic League for Community Action, but Howison had raided it as long ago as February 1966, and had discovered that it was, in fact, the front for a blind pig.[2]

At 10:30 P.M. that summer's night, Patrolman Charles Henry knocked on the door of the blind pig in Twelfth Street, to be refused admission. But five hours later, at 3:34 in the morning, the United Civic League for Community Action was being less selective, and the patrolman got inside. Waiting around the corner in the squad car for the ten minutes he needed to be sure that his man had ordered and paid for his illegal drink, Sergeant Howison radioed for help, then went into action, smashing down the door of the blind pig with a sledgehammer.

Howison had expected to find a score or so of drinkers inside. Instead, he discovered no less than eighty-two, who appeared to be engaged in nothing more nefarious than a

636

party in honour of a group of servicemen, two of whom had just returned from Vietnam. It took over an hour, and four paddy-wagon trips, to ferry all the revellers to the Tenth Precinct police station, and by the time the last consignment left, quite a crowd of spectators had gathered.

A college student was whipping up the crowd. "Mother-fuckers!" he was shouting. "Leave my people alone!"[3]

The onlookers were all black, the police all white, and a rumour spread that one of the patrolmen had manhandled a black woman while carrying out the arrests. As the last squad car left Twelfth Street, an empty bottle was thrown and smashed against its rear window. Someone heaved a litter basket through the window of a store, and when the police came back to the scene of the commotion, a lieutenant was struck by a flying brick. By 6:30 A.M. burglar alarms set off by the broken windows of Twelfth Street were awakening all the residents in the area, and, down in the Detroit Police Headquarters on Beaubien Street, officials were meeting for a council of war.

The city police chief had already informed the mayor, Jerome P. Cavanagh, of the trouble on Twelfth Street, and at seven o'clock on the morning of Sunday, July 23, 1967, Cavanagh decided to take no chances. He requested that the FBI, the state police, the Wayne County Sheriff's office, and the Michigan National Guard should all be put on alert. The situation was looking dangerous, and, in the mayor's opinion, there could be real unpleasantness in Detroit.

Detroit's race relations had made little progress since the trial and acquittal of Dr. Ossian Sweet. The Second World War had prompted a large influx of blacks from the South, and poor whites had come too, both groups drawn by the job opportunities offered by the Arsenal of Democracy. Crammed together in the tired old wooden homes and apartment blocks around the downtown area, the new-comers were soon at each other's throats. Working long, hard, forced-production shifts, wartime Detroit was a city with frayed nerves, and the tensions had exploded in June

1943 in a race riot that was the worst in American history to that date. Thirty-four people died, twenty-five of them black, over 1,000 were wounded, and the police made 1,883 arrests.[4]

For forty-eight hours Detroit had been surrendered to total lawlessness. "We killed eight of 'em . . . ," bragged one of the teenage whites who cruised the ghettoes shooting indiscriminately from cars. "I saw knives being stuck through their throats and heads being shot through, and a lot of stuff like that. . . . They were turning cars over with niggers in them, you should have seen it. It was really some riot."[5]

The barbarity appears to have prompted no remorse, and very little reflection in Detroit. On the contrary, feelings hardened along racial lines, and local politicians started running for office on overtly racist platforms—the most notorious being Dearborn's mayor, Orville Hubbard, who was first elected to run the Ford company town in 1943, and who built a political career lasting more than a third of a century on the well-understood and thoroughly redeemed pledge to "Keep Dearborn Clean."

Hubbard was considered an embarrassment by Southeast Michigan politicians of all persuasions in the 1940s, 1950s, and 1960s. But this was only because he insisted on advertising, in his loud, redneck way, the same policies that everyone else was trying to camouflage. In Grosse Pointe the real-estate agents quietly kept up the tone of the neighbourhood with a "points system" which screened would-be residents according to such criteria as their race, religion, education, and general approximation to the American way of life. Fifty points was the pass mark, unless you were Greek or Italian, in which case you needed sixty-five points. Jews needed eighty-five—and if you were nonwhite, nobody bothered to start counting.*

* Grosse Pointe realtors today deny there was ever such a thing as the "points system," and, not surprisingly, there is no documentary evidence of its existence. But the title deeds to quite a number of Grosse Pointe homes still contain the original, but now illegal, exclusion clauses prohibiting the sale of the property to anyone of non-Caucasian origin.[6]

By the late 1950s it seemed strange to recall that Detroit had once been considered a centre of racial enlightenment, the libertarian northern terminus of John Brown's Underground Railway. In 1959 blacks made up more than a quarter of the city's population. Their numbers had grown in a few years from some 300,000 to nearly half a million.[7] But most of the city's bars, restaurants, and hotels were restricted to whites. The Detroit Bowling Proprietors' Association barred blacks from almost all of their alleys.[8]

The most effective segregation of all was migration. Between 1950 and 1959 more than 350,000 whites moved out of inner Detroit for the suburbs[9]—families, businesses, whole communities. It was quite common for the congregations of Detroit's white churches and synagogues to find themselves meeting in the 1950s to discuss and vote on a proposal to move, usually out to the suburbs to the northwest.

The new freeways made it so easy. You could drive in and out and all around Detroit on two-lane, three-lane, four-lane highways, spiraling over and under each other in cloverleafs and underpasses. You could travel, said the city planners proudly, four times faster on one of the brand-new freeways than on one of the old-fashioned city surface streets, and people did—away from Detroit as fast as they could go. The freeways were routes of escape.

In 1950 J. L. Hudson's department store decided to open a branch out near the northwestern suburbs. So many of their customers were living out there now. They invited other varieties of store to come out and cluster with them in the same, purpose-built site, and there, at Northland, a few convenient yards off the ramp from the John C. Lodge Freeway, America had her first comprehensive, regional shopping mall.[10]

Made by the car, the Motor City was unravelled by the car in the 1940s, 1950s, and 1960s, its identity stretched and spun ever outwards in unending subdivisions and new housing developments: Eight Mile Road, Nine Mile Road,

Ten Mile Road, Eleven—the signposts went past like the ribs on an ever-expanding corset, and as the people went, the peddlers followed them, throwing up their chains of plastic-clad shanties: pizza stands and muffler shops, late-nite bars and veterinary hospitals. Tarmacadamed and neon-lit, these four-lane alleys became centres of existence for more and more inhabitants of the Motor City. All that life had to offer was laid out here, from motels to carpet bargains. The temptations stretched side by side for mile after mile, and people learned how to cruise the unending roadside supermarket shelf, eyeing the goods and pulling in to pick off their fancy.

It was a new way of shopping, a new way of living—a new way of constructing a city, if such undisciplined sprawling was worthy of that name. In Europe the space is too precious. Cities have green belts around them, girdles to restrain their expansion—and their basic shape and identity has, in any case, usually been determined centuries before the onslaught of the automobile.

But in the 1950s and 1960s there was nothing to stop Detroit expanding ever outwards across the flat Michigan countryside—nothing except the Detroit River to the south, and that only served to double the rate of the expansion northwards. What was left in the middle, by the early 1960s, was getting perilously like a vacuum, and its character was becoming more and more black.

The new black reality was dramatically displayed in the city elections of 1961. The incumbent mayor, Louis Miriani, was opposed by Jerome P. Cavanagh, a liberal young Democrat who favoured equal rights, and the mayor defended himself with armour of the 1950s. He accused his idealistic young opponent of running as a Negro candidate—and he lost the election. By 1961 blacks made up nearly a third of Detroit's population.

Youthful, charismatic, and Irish, the thirty-three-year-old Jerry Cavanagh had much in common with the recently elected inhabitant of the White House. The mayor knew how to put Detroit's problems into stirring words, even if he was not able, in reality, to do that much about them, and his dynamic style helped focus national attention on a problem that America was just starting to worry about: the decay of her inner cities. Treating the American Municipal Association to a stirring address on the subject of urban decay in 1962, Cavanagh began to attract a celebrity that extended far outside Detroit. Here was one young man, it seemed, who knew the answers—and the health of the Motor City, just enjoying the cyclical upswing of the affluent early sixties, seemed to bear out Cavanagh's promise.[11]

In the summer of 1963 Cavanagh welcomed Dr. Martin Luther King to Detroit for a "Freedom March" commemorating the twentieth anniversary of the 1943 riots, and the marchers heard Dr. King's soaring, resonant voice proclaim, "I have a dream." (Later that summer King gave the same speech, and made it famous, in Washington.) In 1964 President Johnson chose southeast Michigan, where he was welcomed by Jerry Cavanagh, to proclaim his "Great Society," and when, in January 1965, Johnson presented his message to Congress on the cities, many of his ideas came from advice and study papers he had received from Detroit's articulate young mayor.[12]

The first of the 1960s' great ghetto riots was in Watts, in Los Angeles, in the summer of 1965. But, said Detroiters, it could never happen here. Mayor Cavanagh was on top of the problem, integrating the police force, syphoning major —and, yes, disproportionate—amounts of federal funds into the city through his friendship with the President.

Above all, ran the conventional wisdom, Detroit had a black middle class. The ghetto would police itself. Right in the heart of the city there were 3,000 blacks enrolled in Wayne State University, more black students than in the entire Ivy League. There were black lawyers and doctors and politicians—Detroit was the only U.S. city with two black congressmen—and the pride of black Detroit was manifest in the city's own unique black music, the Motown Sound, not blues, not protest, but a slick, chirpy, upbeat, very sixties sort of rhythm. Motown radiated the self-confidence and optimism of its black performer-composers —and it also made them a lot of money. The founder of the Tamla Motown record label, Berry Gordy, once a Ford assembly-line worker, had recently bought himself a Louis Napoleon-style palace on Boston Boulevard, just a few doors along from the mansions once inhabited by the Dodge brothers, Uncle Joseph Hudson, and young Miss Eleanor Clay.

The mansions of Boston Boulevard lie just five blocks away from the intersection of Twelfth Street and Clairmont, and by lunchtime on July 23, 1967, a pall of smoke hung over the entire neighbourhood.[13] At ten past four that afternoon, Mayor Cavanagh put in a telephone call to the governor of Michigan, George Romney, who was home for the weekend on his Bloomfield Hills estate, and before the sun started to go down, the state troopers were out on Twelfth Street, flak-jacketed and helmeted, their submachine guns at the ready.

The crowds were just coming out from the baseball game. The Yankees were in town for the weekend, and Tiger Stadium had been packed. Around five o'clock that afternoon, the best part of 50,000 spectators drove home through and around the developing battle on Twelfth Street, without being really aware that their city was becoming a combat zone.

That was the wonderful thing about the freeways. You could just zip along the concrete canyons in the comfort and privacy of your car, concentrating only on the eight-track and on the bumper ahead of you. You need never be aware that, just up there beyond the crash barrier, only a few blocks away from General Motors—the largest, richest corporation in the world—were trash cans poisoned to discourage derelicts, twelve-year-old black girls waving flashlights at passing motorists, or, on this warm and muggy afternoon in late July 1967, tanks, troop carriers, and armoured cars, with blacks and whites who were shooting at each other, to kill. The final death toll was 43, with 347 serious injuries and over 7,000 arrests.[14]

The various postmortems, conducted by a national commission, by the city, and, endlessly, by the media, put the blame on a long catalogue of ills: unemployment among young blacks, the economic downswing of 1967,[15] the long, hot summer—and the disillusioning discovery that Detroit's black middle class had no more or less interest in the problems of the ghetto than the middle class of any other colour.

The most obvious scapegoat of all was the media, the television news bulletins which, nightly through the previous weeks, had covered riots in other cities, providing bored young blacks with a graphic course of instruction in how to walk up to a shop window, smash it, and walk away with a colour television set. But what made the kids so bored and hostile in the first place? Why did they have no skills? And why, skilled or not, could they not find jobs in this great American city where, thanks to Henry Ford I, the high-paid, unskilled job had been born?

Whatever the reason, most whites did not stay to find out. The exodus to the suburbs hastened from a measured trot into a headlong gallop. The riots of July 1967 put an end to Mayor Jerome Cavanagh's once-lustrous political career. Indeed, the disaster appeared to call the whole political process into question. For what could one mayor do? Politics alone was clearly not enough. Detroit called for some new saviour—and he turned out, rather unexpectedly, to be Henry Ford II.

Less than a week after the Detroit riots, the survivors met to find out what had gone wrong. An emergency conference of all the leaders of the city was summoned—white industrialists, black militants, union leaders, social workers—and of all the many speeches and declamations, by far the most organized and coherent came from Walter Reuther. Avoiding rhetoric, the car workers' leader had prepared a detailed list of diagnoses and specific cures for the problems of Detroit's inner city, and Henry Ford II listened to them, very impressed.

"That's what we should have done," he said when he got back to the Glasshouse later that day, "had some real ideas ready, not just sat there and wrung our hands."[16]

Three months later, one of his staff placed some very specific ideas in Henry Ford's hand. Levi Jackson was a black executive who had been at Ford since the late 1940s. Ford had been the only company to offer Jackson an interview when he left Yale, and Jackson often thought that he owed his job, in a strange way, to the Ford family, since he had been a football star at university—the captain of the team, in fact—and, while training, he had made the acquaintance of William Clay Ford, who shared his sporting enthusiasms. Arriving in Dearborn for his interview in 1949, the young black found himself being interviewed by a personnel officer who kept his feet up on the desk throughout the meeting—until Levi happened to see, through the glass partition, his old varsity friend walking by. He turned to wave "Hi, Bill," and by the time he turned back, his interviewer's feet were on the floor.[17]

Jackson's ideas of October 1967, set out in a ten-point memorandum, addressed the problem of unemployed and marginally employed young blacks—most of them illiterate, many of them with police records, and few of them knowing how to try to get a job in a Ford factory, even if they wanted to. Bored, angry, and frustrated, these alienated youngsters had been at the heart of the riot—indeed, to all intents and purposes, they themselves had been the riot. Trapped inside a vicious circle, they were Detroit's number-one problem, but they were already lost to Detroit's number-one industry —unless, argued Jackson, that industry was prepared to take a chance and go out to them.

Thus began the Ford Motor Company's Minorities Hiring Program, the first to be implemented in Detroit—or anywhere else in the United States. Jackson's idea was that Ford recruiters should go into the ghetto and be prepared to set aside their customary hiring criteria like literacy tests.

They should be willing to overlook minor police records—which usually involved arrests, not convictions—and they might even offer to loan new recruits some of their first week's wages to keep them out of trouble until they got paid. Jackson proposed this programme to Henry Ford II at lunchtime on October 11, 1967. He developed its details at a meeting Ford called later that day, and the plan was approved by the evening. When the chairman really cared about something, it happened quickly.

"Equal employment opportunity," declared Henry II when Ford made the plan public a few weeks later, "requires more than the elimination of deliberate racial discrimination. Opportunity is not equal when people who would make good employees are not hired because they do not know of the openings, because they lack the self-confidence to apply, or because formal hiring criteria screen out potentially good employees as well as potentially poor ones. . . . Management should be willing to go directly into the city, to seek out the unemployed, to make sure that hiring standards are not unnecessarily or unrealistically restrictive."[18]

The company set up recruitment desks in two community-action centres near Twelfth Street. Written tests, previously compulsory for Ford hirees, were eliminated. A special bus service was instituted to the Rouge plant from the ghetto. In a strange echo of 1914, more than 1,500 job applicants began lining up outside the recruitment centres before dawn—and that was not the only reminder of the glory days at Highland Park. In 1967 and 1968, Ford recruiters soon discovered that men just out of prison, on parole, made better workers than men hired off the street—they were in sounder physical shape and more disciplined—while personnel officers found themselves, like so many sociological inspectors, counselling new recruits on the usefulness of purchasing an alarm clock, advising on the benefits of opening a savings account, and helping to create "buddy" systems, so that if someone started slipping, his comrades could help him back on track.

Quite a number of the new young Ford workers did indeed

slip off track. In 1969 Henry II reported a failure rate of 40 percent in his minorities hiring scheme. There had been a noticeable increase in fights, dope peddling, and thefts during the months that followed the arrival of the recruits from the ghetto, and there was also a tendency for some of the new workers to show up drunk in the mornings. On Monday mornings, a number did not show up at all.[19]

Still, 40 percent failure meant 60 percent success. Turnover in the hot, uncomfortable conditions of the foundry, where many of the young blacks were put to work, had traditionally been over 30 percent, while dope peddling, theft, and absenteeism were then—and are today—part of the everyday story of carmaking folk.

"If they weren't working," commented Henry Ford with pride in 1969, "they'd be scrounging for a buck here or there, or on relief. Maybe both. Relief carries with it no dignity, no pride. These men can hold their heads up. People talk about the matriarchal society of the Negro. Well, this is the way to break it down."[20]

"These men can hold their heads up." The words could have come from the lips of the old Motor King himself. "Relief carries no pride." That is pure Henry Ford I. The 1946 commitment which young Henry Ford II made to "human engineering" in his very first public speech had held many echoes of his grandfather, and now the 1967 crisis of Detroit evoked a similar response.

"Henry always professes that he doesn't know very much about anything," says his friend Max Fisher, who was to be one of Henry II's principal allies in his attempts to revitalize post-riot Detroit. "But that's always the first put-down. In reality, he is a very caring and studious fellow."[21]

Henry Ford II has often enjoyed striking a curmudgeonly pose, and the affectation has increased as he has got older. Under the influence of drink he is a curmudgeon, and no mistake. But when his finer side is really caught by a problem, then he focuses on it with a rare intensity. He reads and he studies and he canvasses expert opinion. His intellect is a sharp one. He has an eagerness to learn. This is the open, inquisitive, idealistic face of Henry Ford II that made Bosworth, McNamara, and the other Whiz Kids want to work for him in 1945, which created Detroit's United Foundation—and which also tried to do something about the racism of Dearborn's mayor, Orville Hubbard.

Embarrassed by the fact that the Ford Motor Company supplied more than 50 percent of the tax base that enabled the mayor to enforce his discriminatory policies, Henry II lent his discreet support to Hubbard's opponents in one election year. Dearborn's politics were temporarily enlivened by the activities of a mysterious and high-powered professional from out of town who tried desperately to generate a groundswell of popular opposition to the "Keep Dearborn Clean" platform—and who met with a predictable lack of success.

The mayor considered it a great joke. He had won his first election victory back in 1941 opposing a Harry Bennett–sponsored candidate, and he had named his son Henry Ford Hubbard. "My motto is Be Nice To People," he said of the Ford-inspired attempts to unseat him, "and that includes young Henry."

Henry Ford II did not return the compliment. "I've about given up on the whole thing," he growled with resignation in 1969. "I can't lick him, and I'll be damned if I join him."[22]

In 1966 Bill Curran, who worked for Time-Life, helped arrange the participation of Henry Ford II in a fact-finding tour of eastern Europe, and after the tour he asked a Time-Life colleague who had accompanied the group how his friend Henry had fared.

"I don't understand him," came the answer. "At the meetings he was one of the best participants—serious, well-informed, sensitive. He was very impressive. Then afterwards he was like another person—'Where's the booze? Where's the pussy?' That sort of thing."[23]

The war against racial injustice has brought out the finer

side of this complex man. Henry Ford II's record on race
has proved energetic and courageous, for he seems to have
sensed how the particular era of urban decay and racial
disharmony in which he found himself living did not get
that way by accident. Its tragedy stemmed from the same
genius, drive, and wickedness that had made his own family
so rich and famous. If ever the sins of the fathers were
graphically visited upon a community, it was upon downtown Detroit in the late 1960s, and, contemplating the
devastation, the grandson of the great carmaker saw his
destiny, for a season, in doing what he could to redeem
them.

Money was never a problem. Donald Thurber can remember how, when he was fund-raising for the United Negro
Colleges, not then the fashionable philanthropy that it later
became, he could always count on a generous contribution
from both the Ford Motor Company and from its chief
executive. Whitney Young, Jr., the black director of the
National Urban League, recalls receiving a handwritten
note from Ford and a cheque for $100,000 one Christmas.*

But Henry Ford II's crusade against prejudice extended
well beyond cheque writing—and also beyond the battles
of black and white. In the mid-1960s he had been one of the
moving spirits in a campaign to get his friend Max Fisher
and two other prominent Jewish businessmen elected to the
venerable Detroit Club, which had, previously, blackballed
all Jews.

Henry Ford first made Max Fisher's acquaintance
through Anne McDonnell Ford's work for the opera. Among
the regular dates in Anne's big engagement book were
lunches on the other side of town, for with the exodus to the
suburbs, Detroit's centre of wealth had started to swing
away from Grosse Pointe. You could identify one ethnic

* Henry Ford II met Whitney Young, Jr., on the 1966 fact-finding tour
of eastern Europe, and he took pleasure, as the most famous capitalist in
the party, in disappointing the expectations of his Communist escorts by
carrying the briefcase of his new black friend when they got on and off
buses together.[24]

group who was not short of cash by counting the proud and expensive new synagogues rising on the green ramparts overlooking the northwestern freeways, and it was towards the northwestern suburbs that Anne McDonnell Ford headed in the late 1950s when she started to raise funds for both the DIA and the opera. She shocked some older Grosse Pointers by inviting her Jewish friends from Bloomfield Hills to her daughter Charlotte's debutante party. Among these new acquaintances, Henry II got on particularly well with Max Fisher, a genial, heavyset financier who had made his fortune in oil and in real estate.

When Max Fisher first met Henry Ford II, he was already a name to reckon with in Detroit, and he became truly high-profile in 1962 when he and his partners purchased the soaring, twenty-eight storey, gothic office block built on West Grand Boulevard for the Fisher brothers (of "Body by Fisher"). The Fisher Building was, arguably, the most prestigious edifice in all Detroit—and when Max Fisher made it his own headquarters in 1962, he saved himself the expense of putting a new nameplate on the door.

Max Fisher has got closer to Henry Ford II than have many men, and he is generous in praise of his best friend's strengths—which he has seen as few others have.

"Henry," he says, "honestly does things from his heart. There's a lot of feeling deep down inside of him."

Fisher is also quite candid, within the bounds of loyalty, about other aspects of the Ford character.

"He finds it very hard, quite often, to express his emotions. I say, 'Come on, Henry, why don't you let it go?' But really, he finds that side of things pretty difficult."[25]

When Max Fisher came to Detroit in 1930, a bright but impoverished student from Ohio State University, the name Ford was, for him, synonymous with prejudice. He found none of it in Henry Ford II.

"I've organized a couple of trips for him to Israel," he says, "taking him around to meet all the right people"—by which Max Fisher, North America's leading fund-raiser for the State of Israel, means the likes of Golda Meir, Moshe

Dayan, and Shimon Peres. "But it wasn't a question of converting him. I've always found Henry an open, liberal-minded sort of guy."[26]

In 1966 the Arab League responded to Ford plans to let a Jewish entrepreneur assemble Ford trucks and tractors in Israel by threatening a boycott, and Henry Ford II went ahead with the plan. "Nobody's gonna tell me what to do," he told Max Fisher[27]—and as a result of his defiance, all Ford cars and Ford trucks were banned from the Arab market for nearly twenty years.

"It was just a pragmatic business procedure" is Henry II's comment on the subject, trying to downplay the principles at stake—and sidestepping the fact that the Ford Motor Company has, in the last twenty years, lost far more in sales to Arab countries than it has made from the relatively small Israeli market. "I don't mind saying I was influenced in part by the fact that the company still suffers from a resentment against the anti-Semitism of the distant past. We want to overcome that. But the main thing is that here we had a dealer who wanted to open up an agency to sell our products —hell, let him do it."[28]

When Max Fisher and Henry Ford II embarked side by side on the endeavour to redeem something from the misery of Detroit in 1967, the enterprise at first generated more heat than light. New Detroit was a forum where black and white could sit down together to hammer out their differences, but its problems were indicated by the response to the announcement that Joseph Hudson, Jr., would act as the forum's chairman. Several hundred Hudson's customers turned in their charge cards rather than shop in a store whose president had dealings with blacks.[29]

The feeling was reciprocated. Through the autumn and winter of 1967, Detroit's white business establishment dutifully trooped along to the campus of Wayne State University, across Woodward Avenue from the DIA, for meetings at which they were, usually, subjected to the rancour of sunglassed militants who harangued them bitterly with the modish insults of black power.

"There was a lot of ventilating in those days," remembers Max Fisher.[30]

Henry II soon stopped attending the meetings. He had more practical use to make of his time. But he was not averse to listening if a real dialogue was involved. One of the black community's most inflammatory activists in the late 1960s was the Reverend Albert Cleage, pastor of the Central United Congregational Church, at the junction of Dexter and Grand boulevards. It had been a chilling, symbolic moment for white Detroit when the face and hands of the Virgin outside Cleage's church had been painted black, and the building renamed the Shrine of the Black Madonna. Cleage had invited black militants like Rap Brown to speak there.

"Motown," Brown had declaimed less than a month before the riots, "if you don't come around, we are going to burn you down!"[31]

In the frightened, strained atmosphere that followed the riots, most whites considered Cleage the devil incarnate. Grosse Pointers had had the uncomfortable experience of waking up to the sound of gunfire during those hot, humid days. They lived in fear that militants like Cleage would provoke a renewal of the violence, and the conservative elements of New Detroit were unwilling to let the pastor of the Black Madonna become a member of their committee. Considering himself snubbed, the black militant retaliated by refusing to come and meet with New Detroit, threatening the direst consequences.

But Henry II wanted to talk to Cleage. He was curious. He wanted to make his own judgements about the man and what he stood for. "I'll meet him anywhere he wants me to meet him," said Ford[32]—and he went into the very heart of the ghetto, to sit in the basement of the Shrine of the Black Madonna itself, listening and talking to the Reverend Cleage for three hours. On another occasion Henry II spent an almost equal amount of time alone with Norvel Harrington, a high school militant who was later to lead the Detroit chapter of the Black Panthers.[33]

"Henry has no sense of fear, so far as I can see," says Larry Doss, a black accountant and activist who refused—and still refuses—to describe the disorders of 1967 as "riots." He calls them "the rebellion" on the grounds that they represented legitimate black protest at exploitation by the white power elite.[34]

"Henry's an explorer, he loves adventures of the mind," says Doss. "I think he found it a tremendous challenge to meet people and deal with concepts that almost everybody else was scared to death of. And his response was always in terms of action. 'Well,' he would say, 'what are we going to *do* about that?'"[35]

Like his grandfather, Henry Ford II approached this social problem as a practical, solvable issue.

"Some of us who thought we knew Henry Ford almost had the feeling we were seeing a stranger during those days," said Allen Merrell, a friend of Henry II's since boyhood and later a Ford Motor Company vice-president. "The way he sought out people with whom we thought he had so little in common, and the way he accepted them and understood them and interpreted them to us—well, he was like another man."[36]

For someone who had failed sociology at Yale, Henry Ford II conducted some pretty original and courageous research in the autumn and winter months of 1967. He hired his own personal consultant on racial affairs, a social worker from Pittsburgh whom he placed on a running Ford study group with Levi Jackson and Larry Washington, another black Ford labour-relations man. Henry would meet with them every other week or so and listen to the findings of their latest research—his own private race-relations seminar.

"There's a side of Henry," says Max Fisher, "that is very much the student."[37]

From Henry Ford's studies emerged enough practical new initiatives to occupy half a dozen sociology schools. He had all the company's outside parts suppliers surveyed. White-owned businesses were encouraged to start minority hiring programmes. Black-owned businesses were given bigger contracts. Top Ford managers were seconded to oversee some of the community reconstruction projects created in the aftermath of the riots. Arjay Miller, president of the company since 1963, was given charge of a new Economic Development Corporation, Henry II's own idea, with the job of supplying seed capital for the creation of new inner-city businesses—particularly businesses that were minority owned and run. ICBIF, the Inner City Business Improvement Forum, started by Larry Doss and other blacks, was a particular recipient of EDC funds, and Henry II was one of the prime movers in ICBIF's creation, meeting with Doss and his partners within days of the riots.[38] As a counterpart to the scheme to give unskilled blacks employment on the factory floor, Ford started an affirmative-action programme to recruit more blacks into the company's senior management—and when it came to the creation and funding of new black banks and financial institutions, it was Henry Ford II who could always be counted on to provide the crucial, initial, cornerstone guarantee.

"How can minorities hope to operate in a capitalist society," he asked, "without their own capital?"[39]

Henry Ford II's contribution to the redemption of Detroit was thorough, generous, and all-embracing.

"I think that for a period," says one of his friends, "it was quite the most important thing in his life."

"Henry Ford was not the only white businessman to get involved with the problems of black Detroit," says Larry Doss. "It was a cooperative effort. But there is no doubt that Henry was the leader, and everyone will tell you that. From 1967, for more than a decade, he had the most extraordinarily consistent, involved, and distinguished commitment to this issue. He really moved Detroit forward. He was the one who showed the way"[40]

As Henry Ford II had worked to clear up the mess left by his grandfather in the late 1940s, the Ford farms had seemed a particular example of the old man's eccentricity.

What an irrelevant and unproductive use of investment capital to cover half of Dearborn with soya-bean fields!

By the late 1960s, however, it was clear there had been method in the old man's madness. Henry Ford I had consistently predicted the drift of population out of big cities towards the countryside, and when it happened in the 1950s, his farms turned out to have been a most profitable real estate investment—the value of Ford land in Dearborn being still further increased by Mayor Hubbard's much-scorned racial policies. It might pain Henry II that his company paid the taxes which helped, effectively, maintain Dearborn's colour bar, but keeping the town white had a wondrous effect on local property prices. By 1971 one of the Ford Motor Company's smaller but solidly prosperous divisions was the Ford Motor Land Development Corporation, which administered and developed the rural empire so fortuitously put together in the Dearborn area. In that year, Ford Land's energies were concentrated on the creation of Michigan's grandest shopping mall yet.

The plan was to develop some soya-bean fields just across the Southfield freeway from Ford World Headquarters. So promising was the site that Hudson's, Sears, J. C. Penney, and Lord and Taylor all bought in as anchor stores, while Hyatt signed up for one of their shiny greenhouse hotels, complete with glass-bubble elevators and a futuristic railway on stilts, a "People Mover." Since the development involved stealing the bottom of Henry Ford's old garden, it was christened Fairlane—and when you mention Fairlane today to the average Detroiter, it is the shopping mall he will think of, not the auto baron's old mansion, which lies hidden in the woods beyond.*

---

* Fairlane conjured up only unhappy memories for Mrs. Edsel Ford, and after the death of Clara Ford in 1950, the family lost no time selling it to the company, who first used it as a home for the Ford Archives, then presented it to the University of Michigan. The university has constructed a Dearborn campus in the grounds and has also used the mansion itself as a conference centre. Under its present director, Donn Werling, Fairlane has become a centre for the practice of interpretive history.

The Fairlane shopping centre, however, precisely illustrated what was wrong with Detroit. It was the latest example of valuable development being syphoned out of the downtown, and it was in strange contradiction to Henry II's ghetto hiring programme, his encouragement of minority suppliers, and all his other efforts to inject life into the inner city. If Henry II was really serious about urban renewal, argued Larry Doss, just taking over the presidency of New Detroit, then he should ease up on his investment in the suburbs, and put some of his money where he said that his heart was: into the physical development of downtown Detroit.

"We were meeting in Henry's office," remembers Doss, "at the top of the Glasshouse, and from it we could see all the way to the river and to downtown Detroit. Perhaps we even walked over to look at the view, I don't know. But I said to Henry, 'Look, the time has come for action, a real centrepiece, something to show the people who live down there that you seriously mean what you say.'"

Larry Doss knew, better than most, that Henry Ford II had already done a great deal.

"More than anyone else, in fact—and that was why I was pushing him. Because when blacks looked at the Fairlane development and all the other offices and shops going up in the suburbs, you couldn't blame them for feeling cynical about what the white business establishment said they believed in when they came to the meetings of New Detroit. It was for Henry to provide still more leadership.

"I wasn't angry with him, or confrontational. It's not my style to exhibit rage. I was laying a challenge on him—and when I did, I remember, he smiled a little."[41]

Larry Doss got more than he—or anyone else—bargained for.

"That sort of pricked my brain a little bit," admits Henry Ford today, remembering Doss's challenge. "It got me thinking."[42]

Henry II did not ease up on Fairlane. With A. Alfred Taubman, a shopping-mall magnate whose acquaintance he had made through Max Fisher, he turned a profit on his suburban development in record time. But the chairman of the Ford Motor Company also came to town and there, on the site of an old grain elevator and derelict warehouse beside the Detroit River, he caused to be thrown up, right beside the tunnel to Canada, the biggest shopping mall you ever saw: shops, offices, restaurants, clubs, parking garages, a hotel. It was a ready-mixed downtown, complete with its own skyscrapers, all packaged in fashionably dark and shiny glass. Today, however you approach the Motor City, by air, by river, or cruising up over some undulation in the glacier-worn flatnesses of Michigan or southern Ontario, it is the shining new towers of Henry Ford II's 740-foot-high Renaissance Center which tell you where the heart of Detroit is. Or is supposed to be, at least.

Robert McCabe, an urban-development expert picked out by Ford headhunters, and hired by Max Fisher, to spearhead the business community's efforts to kick some life back into downtown Detroit, remembers going to Henry II in the spring of 1971 to broach the possibility of Ford sponsoring a Fairlane-like development on the old warehouse site beside the Detroit River.

"My people say there's no market for it," reported Henry after putting the project to the staff of Ford Land.

"I know," replied McCabe. "It's for us to force the market."[43]

Max Fisher remembers a discussion beside his swimming pool that same summer of 1971 on the edge of the Franklin Hills Country Club.

"I told him that the name Ford was part of Detroit," says Fisher, "how important it was, how he could do so much—and how only he could do it. I just told him that he *ought* to."[44]

It can be an elusive item to locate, the sense of social obligation in a Ford. Trying the "ought" trick on either Henry Ford I or II has all too frequently produced consequences akin to those of Russian roulette—try again or sudden death. But the incentive for taking the risk, and asking just the same, is that, when the right button is pressed, the noblesse oblige has sometimes proved to flow very free, in both men. The first Henry Ford was truly prodigal with his time and money on behalf of any cause that caught his fancy—often at the expense of his carmaking —and the same has proved true of Henry Ford II.

Whether it was the challenge of Larry Doss, the specific riverbank project proposed by Robert McCabe, or the lecture from his friend Max on the obligations of being a Ford, Henry II was stung into an extraordinary personal crusade to build the Renaissance Center and help regenerate downtown Detroit. For nearly six years, from the autumn of 1971, when the project was first announced, to the spring of 1977, when the complex was officially opened, Henry Ford II devoted considerable energy to marshalling company money and the funds of fifty other local corporations—including Chrysler and General Motors—to raise the $357 million needed to complete the development.

"I sat beside him and saw him operate at some of those meetings," remembers A. Alfred Taubman, "and it was an extraordinary performance. No one, basically, wanted to risk their money. They knew they could lose it—and unfortunately they have. But Henry would say to them, 'Look, gentlemen. We have taken an awful lot out. We have got to put a little back.' And the people paid up."[45]

It was not simply a matter of charm and a just cause. In Henry II's early Eisenhower days, members of the Ford clerical staff found themselves being bussed down to Cadillac Square to welcome Ike to Detroit[46]—though Henry II today insists he gave no orders to this effect—and twenty years later Ford suppliers felt that their hearts, minds, and bank accounts were being similarly dragooned in support of Henry II's riverside project.

On the top floor of one of the Renaissance Center towers —so tall that, on a clear day, you can look out from it across both lakes St. Clair and Erie, and feel the whole tower sway under you on a windy one—is the Renaissance Club. Henry II built it when the Detroit Club politely declined his invitation to shift their lodgings to his new mini-city, and on a plaque by the entrance is a list of the individuals and companies who, at his request, got out their cheque books to make this part of the complex possible.

"That guy makes the fanbelts for Ford," explains your local interpreter. "That one makes the seatbelts. There are the speedometers. And that's the insurance. It was a simple question of survival. Everyone knew the score—you either chipped in your cash, or you said goodbye to your business with Ford."

The Renaissance Center was the largest single building project ever in Detroit's history, and it was more than a matter of shops. One of the problems with the downtown of the Motor City had always been the lack of office workers, the tens of thousands of clerks in green eyeshades who, in the days before computers, had kept the banks and insurance companies operating—and had also, in the process, helped generate the infrastructure of flourishing downtowns like Manhattan or Chicago's Loop.

In Detroit, however, the high wages offered in the car plants had tended to pull white-collar workers out of the heart of the city, making it difficult for other employers to compete. The Motor City's sidewalk crowds had always, somehow, been thin and weedy, even along Griswold Street, so in the early 1970s the towers of the new Renaissance Center were designed as offices that would draw several thousand new white-collar workers daily into the heart of Detroit.

All that the new towers needed was someone to rent them. Well, how about, for starters, Manufacturers, who happened to be the Ford Motor Company's bank, and, later, J. Walter Thompson, the major Ford advertising agency?

"One of the things you learn to do well if you are brought up as Henry was," says one of his older friends, "is how to kick ass. And when it came to getting the RenCen built, Henry kicked ass very well indeed."[47]

And so it stands, soaring up from the riverbank, right

beside the tunnel to Canada, an undeniable centrepiece, a massive and truly impressive monument to one man's commitment and energy. If you have seen the Peachtree Center in Atlanta, or the Trump Tower, or any of the concrete-and-glass big tops that are the vogue in modern American cities, you have seen it before: the waterfalls, the full-size trees, the toweringly enclosed indoor space dramatically crisscrossed by moving staircases. It is futuristic. It has something about it of a space station—and, say its critics, it has proved just about as relevant as that to the real problems of downtown Detroit.

When the Renaissance Center opened in April 1977, you would scarcely have guessed from its shops that it was catering to the tastes of a blue-collar town: Cartier, Gucci, Mark Cross, an Oriental art gallery run by Henry's aesthetic nephew, Alfie. That is not what gets Detroiters out in their cars by the thousands. Try a basketball game or a football match—and it did seem rather unhelpful that, just as Henry II was straining every muscle to draw people into the middle of Detroit, his brother Bill should be moving his Detroit Lions, the football team he purchased in 1963, out of the city to the very remotest of the northern suburbs. Bill's ass, evidently, was not for kicking.

Still, it was not the exodus of sports fans that kept Detroit's Renaissance Center resolutely in the red for the first eight years of its existence. The retail heart of the development could never attract one key anchor store. Its geography proved baffling, its size intimidating. Its architect (John Portman) was said to be the best in the business, but no one could call his Detroit creation very warm, or welcoming, or even very friendly. The strange, rampart-like service buildings that separated the great fortress from Jefferson Avenue actually created a barrier, cutting the whole complex off from downtown Detroit. Seen from Bloomfield Hills or Grosse Pointe, it was rather a long way to drive for some complicated and expensive parking—and wasn't it rather close, in any case, to all those downtown murders and muggings that one heard about on the news?

Within a couple of years the carriage-trade stores of the Renaissance Center had vanished in a welter of closing-down sales, leaving depressing gaps and whitewashed dead windows—while its grandiose central hotel ("the world's tallest") never proved able to command more than 60 percent occupancy. When Ford Land had said that there was no market for such an ambitious development in the heart of a mouldering manufacturing town, they had not even counted in the catastrophic recession that hit the Motor City soon after the RenCen's opening. Built right through the mid-seventies energy crisis and soaring interest rates, the construction of the development went $100 million over budget. In 1980 Ford and its other fifty partners were compelled to renegotiate their mortgage. In January 1983, they defaulted even on their renegotiated payments, and they finally wrote off several hundred million dollars by surrendering the building to their mortgagees, the insurance companies, who are now the owners of the Renaissance Center in partnership with Ford Land.

The profit and loss columns, of course, do not tell the whole story. Max Fisher, Robert McCabe, Joe Hudson, and the other whites who work so hard to generate life in what is now a 70 percent black city, argue that Henry Ford's Renaissance Center has achieved far more for Detroit than any balance sheet can express—and they are correct. In the height of summer, swarming with the crowds who come to watch the Detroit Grand Prix (another Ford-inspired bid to pull life into the city), the RenCen generates all the fun, pride, community spirit, and revenue that it was intended to. Fisher and Taubman, who have put up a successful pair of apartment blocks a few hundred yards along the river, say they could never have risked such residential development if Henry had not gone before. The Renaissance Center has proved a catalyst for all manner of new buildings and plans for downtown Detroit, and the great glass complex rises proudly beside the river, bloodied yet unbowed, a massive and defiant statement that the Motor City has not lost its faith in itself.

"We would be nowhere without it," says Larry Doss. "It's an investment, in the very long term, in the destiny of the city. It's a statement that we intend to make it—physically, economically, and spiritually. And if Detroit can't make it, where else in North America can?"[48]

It is a good question, an important one, and the spirit is there, all right—at the very top, at least. You have never met such a group of cheerleaders as those who trumpet the renaissance of Detroit. But in economic and physical terms the news is not so good, not for the downtown of the Motor City—nor, if Detroit is truly a model, for the other tired old inner cities of the North American rust bowl.

Drive out of Detroit on a warm summer's evening, out along Northwestern Highway, past Ten Mile, towards the grey wood and landscaped developments that have names like Hunters Ridge or Pebble Creek, and you cannot fail to see where the wealth of the Motor City is really flowing—and will continue to flow. How pleasant it is out here, how very pleasant, as the sun catches the angles on all the high rises and the new centres and the geodesic gallerias. Motown has got money all right, real money, but it is out here in the Perrier belt, among the atriums and the weeping figs, not in downtown Detroit.

Henry Ford II accomplished a near miracle. His Renaissance Center has helped preserve the original city, the spot where Cadillac first landed, and where his grandfather, the first Henry Ford, trudged to start work, over a hundred years ago now, as an apprentice at Flower Brothers. Henry II's efforts have helped maintain old Detroit as one viable focus in the vast metropolitan conglomeration of proliferating townships and villages which still bears Detroit's name. But the old downtown is little more than that now, just one more exit on the freeway system, as Los Angeles has become an ever-proliferating sequence of hubs without a heart. The city that gave the world built-in obsolescence, and made a fat living from it for many years, is finally paying the price.

HENRY AND LEE

It is sad to see, the gap-toothed streets, the weeds, the burnt-out cars, the empty lots. How can a whole cityful of people do this to themselves? The problem remains basically one of race. Inner Detroit is today a black city. The whites have given up on it, and the blacks are not too sure they would have them back in any case. Crime and drugs are the growth industries. Handguns rank in inner Detroit as a domestic appliance—there were, at the latest count, 300,000 more of them than inhabitants[49]—and as Detroit children enter school, it is routine for them to pass through metal detectors and get body-searched, as if they were boarding El Al. The number-one crime, appropriately, is stealing cars. One goes every nine minutes.

Hawkins Ferry, the historian of Detroit and its buildings, explains it primarily in economic terms. "There is something in the raw, unfinished scene," he writes, "that reflects the mobility of the industrial process itself"[50]—and if you look at Detroit in terms of shifting patterns of wealth, then it all makes perfect sense. With the help of its own miraculous, four-wheeled product, the Motor City has spun itself to pieces, as in a centrifuge, and the heavy stuff has stuck to the outside. In a society where everything is disposable, Detroit has become the ultimate convenience, the throw-away city.

Henry Ford II has endeavoured to stop this process. On the face of it, you could liken his work to the efforts of his grandfather to redeem Inkster in the 1930s, but there is an apter comparison. In Greenfield Village Henry Ford I tried to put up his hand and make time stand still, and in the aftermath of the Detroit riots Henry II attempted an even grander and more romantic gesture. He tried to halt the atomizing of Detroit, to preserve the jumping downtown, the city, the community that he remembered from his childhood. Attempting the impossible, he could hardly be blamed if he failed. In his battle he took on the motorcar and racism, two of the most dynamic and formative influences in modern American life, and if, ultimately, he had no more success fighting

662

them than his grandfather had defeating war, his crusade remains a monument to his humanity, courage, and vision. Henry Ford II has his Peace Ship.

# 32

## BUNKIE

When Henry Ford II got out of bed on the right side in the morning, according to one of his wives, he would look into his shaving mirror and award himself a little smile.

"I am the king," he would announce with satisfaction. "And the king can do no wrong."[1]

Over the years, Henry Ford II's chief executives have learned the truth of this—many of them the hard way. In February 1968, Arjay Miller, who had taken over the company presidency from John Dykstra in 1963, arrived back in Detroit one evening, at the private Ford terminal to the east of Metro Airport, to find a message waiting. Would he please go immediately to World Headquarters? The chairman wanted a word. And there, at the top of the dark and otherwise deserted building—for it was a Sunday night —the jet-lagged Ford president received the news that he was president no more.

February 1968 was a time for surprises. John Bugas was shown the door. Henry II had already come to terms with the fact that the ex-FBI officer was not a particularly brilliant businessman. In 1965 he had shunted his old comrade-in-arms sideways after half a dozen years' undistinguished work directing Ford's International Operations. Bugas had gone to Washington, still on the Ford payroll, and had done a good job representing Ford, and the other car companies, in the battles with government which were the new reality of life in the age of Ralph Nader. But now, in the spring of 1968, the king decided that Bugas's tenure had finally expired.

"Don't degrade him," said Henry's Italian wife, Cristina. "Put him in Australia."

"No," said Henry II, "he's got to go."

So Bugas went. But Cristina Ford did notice that her husband was taking painkillers of some sort for the two days before he had to give his old friend his marching orders—and headaches were not usually one of his problems.

The clean-out came at the end of five years in which Ford had done quite well—but, somehow, not quite well enough. Henry Ford II did not actually fire Arjay Miller. He wanted to shift him sideways, to a new position as vice-chairman.

Arjay had not done anything wrong. In his five years at the top he had presided over some notable successes. He had had the vision to try to get Ford started in Japan, and he had had the prudence, like the good accountant he was, to stop Ford of England buying the Rootes Group: Hillman, Humber, and Singer.[2] Chrysler bought it instead and wrestled with its losses for a decade.

But Ford had not got any closer to Chevrolet during the Miller years—even in Lee Iacocca's year of the Mustang. Lincoln-Mercury still stood no comparison with Buick, Oldsmobile, Pontiac, and Cadillac, the GM profit centres —and when it came to cars, Arjay the bean counter had no real solution to offer. That was not his field. Finance men cannot be expected to generate new product. *Vroom, vroom* means nothing to them. Put them in a Ferrari, and they worry about the fuel consumption.

Henry II sensed the drift, and he knew that he himself could not do much about it. His marital problems had not helped his concentration in the early years of the decade, and now that he was settled down with Cristina, the question of Detroit had arisen, a question that really gripped him. Henry Fords were more than just makers of motorcars. They were public figures, local institutions—American institutions indeed, and the lead that Henry II was taking in tackling the burning social issues of the day was making him a national figure of some note.

Early in January 1968, Henry II received a phone call from the White House. President Johnson wanted the carmaker in Washington. In pursuit of his Great Society, Johnson was proposing a major cooperative venture between government and industry. The aim was to create at least 500,000 new jobs for the nation's hardcore unemployed, and since Henry II had blazed a trail in the creation of jobs for the hardcore unemployed of Detroit, he seemed the obvious man to head LBJ's new creation, the National Alliance of Businessmen.[3]

Henry Ford II took the job. It was an honour, a duty. Besides, he had a high regard for Johnson. Under Johnson's spell Henry II had surprised Detroit—and rather surprised himself—by abandoning his lifetime Republican loyalties in 1964. He liked the President's earthy, belly-to-belly style. One summer the resources of the Ford organization were set to discovering a Model T of the year in which Johnson had learned to drive, because, the President had let slip to the chairman, he had first learned to drive on a Ford.

Henry II presented the car personally at a party on the LBJ ranch.[4] Henry and Cristina stayed with the Johnsons more than once, flew to Washington for White House dinners, exchanged birthday greetings with the first family. Henry II, the President told the carmaker in more than one letter, could consider himself a "friend"—and also a "belwether in the nation. Where you go, less courageous souls are willing to follow."[5]

Henry II's appointment to head the National Alliance of Businessmen seems to have been LBJ's personal decision. The President's chief of recruitment, John Macy, was not overly impressed with Henry II's intellectual abilities. "Ford is not extra bright . . . ," runs a note in Macy's files. "Not a contributor to a policy-making committee."[6] But Macy did allow that Henry II had "the ability to hire excellent staff personnel," and he rated the businessman "good to have from a political standpoint."[7]

That was certainly true. Henry Ford II was loyal. He had stoutly supported every one of Lyndon Johnson's political positions—including the war in Vietnam, about which Henry II had serious private reservations. It was agreed that running the NAB would be a three-year assignment for the Ford chairman, starting in this, LBJ's reelection year. So the question that arose at the beginning of 1968 was, who was going to run the Ford Motor Company while its chairman was occupied elsewhere?

The answer presented itself almost miraculously, tying together the diversion of Henry's energies towards public life and his feeling that he wanted a real car man at the head of the firm. In the same weeks that Henry was approached by the White House, he came to hear that Semon E. "Bunkie" Knudsen, the top car man at General Motors, was discontented and looking around for another job.

The windfall had a satisfying symmetry to it, for Bunkie was the son of William Knudsen, the Dane from the Keim Mills, who had helped Henry I build his local assembly plants and the Eagle boats, and who had been sacked for his pains—Knudsen of the six-cylinder Chevrolet, and then, later, of the plan for Ford to build Spitfires for Britain in 1940. The threads intertwined in so many ways. Bunkie Knudsen had risen, in his father's footsteps, to within one step of the summit of General Motors, and having been passed over for the presidency in favour of a rival, Ed Cole, whom he particularly disliked, he would welcome the chance to get even. In the 1920s a Knudsen had led Chevrolet to victory over Ford. Perhaps, now, a Knudsen was the person finally to regain that long-lost supremacy.

Henry II had long admired the abilities of Bunkie Knudsen from a distance. He was not a close friend, but Henry did know him socially. Thanks to his lineage, Bunkie was one of the few car executives listed in the Blue Book. He and Henry would meet and compare notes at auto shows. In the mid-1960s Henry had even put out some tentative feelers to try to lure Bunkie across to Ford. Knudsen was that rare thing—and perhaps this was why Henry was so intrigued by him—an aristocrat who really knew about cars. People talked about the youth market, and how Iacocca had tapped it. But half a dozen years before the Mustang, Bunkie Knudsen and the hip, young engineer he had hired away from Packard, John Z. DeLorean, had taken GM's Pontiac Division by the scruff of the neck and transformed its image from fuddy-duddy to hot rod.

Until Bunkie and DeLorean hit Pontiac in the late 1950s, the division's market profile had been symbolized by the mascot on all its cars, an antique, moulded death mask of old Chief Pontiac, which, thanks to a little light bulb behind its eyes, glowed eerily in the dark. Bunkie scrapped the Indian.

"Why," he asked, "should I advertise a dead race?"[8]

He put spacers on the wheels of the sedate Pontiac sedans, fitted them with fat, wide tyres to make them look mean and low, and entered them in drag races.

"You can't sell an old man's product to a young person," he would explain, "but you can sell a young person's product to the old. There are plenty of sixty-year-olds who fancy themselves in blue jeans."[9]

With this philosophy, Knudsen had taken Pontiac from sixth place to the brink of third in overall U.S. car sales—and, in 1959, right to the top of the medium-price field in which Ford sought to thrive. His division gathered 30 percent of that market,[10] and he continued his success in the 1960s at the head of Chevrolet. The Monza came out during his time there—though Bunkie was never very keen on the original, nor on any of the derivatives of the ill-fated Corvair, which, as he delighted in telling everyone, was the brainchild of Ed Cole.

With Cole's victory in the race for the GM presidency, Knudsen decided he did not need to live with being number two. He was already a multimillionaire in his own right, thanks to his father buying up large areas of Bloomfield Hills when it was still farmland. Bunkie also owned, in 1968, General Motors stock worth over $3 million.

On the day after Knudsen told James M. Roche, the GM chairman, of his intention to resign, his phone rang at home.

"This is Henry Ford," said a voice.

Knudsen had a friend who specialized in making phone calls with funny voices, and, to start with, Bunkie thought that the joker was at it again. But it soon became clear that this call was for real.

Someone had told him a story, said Henry Ford, and he wanted to know if it was correct.

That depended, replied Knudsen, on what the story was. "Do you want me to come to your office?" he asked.

Henry II did not think that would be such a good idea. "Your house?"

Henry II was not keen on that notion either, because, he said, Cristina had some houseguests, and they were "talking Italian all over the place."

So it was arranged that Henry Ford II would drive over next day, a Saturday, at 10:00 A.M., to Knudsen's forty-acre Bloomfield estate, with its twin tennis courts, on the other side of town. Next morning, at five to ten, Bunkie looked out of the window to see an Oldsmobile coming up the drive.

"Oh, oh," he thought, "I'm really in a pickle. Here comes somebody from GM."

But it was not a colleague who would stumble across the embarrassing fact that GM's number-two man was entertaining the head of the enemy for morning coffee. It was Henry Ford II himself. If he had come in his own Ford or Lincoln, with its company plates, he might as well have sent a brass band on ahead.[11]

When Bunkie Knudsen took command of Ford in the spring of 1968, he found, to his surprise, a company that, far from being lean and hungry, appeared to have grown quite happy with its number-two position in the industry, and that seemed content to stay that way. Bunkie had heard the stories about all the rivalry and the "Beat Chevrolet" signs at the end of the assembly lines, but he never saw any in all the time he was at Ford.

"It was a feeling I had when I got there," he says, "that there was no real desire on the part of anybody to really go out and charge and take over from Chevrolet."[12]

Knudsen—broad, muscular, and handsomely clean-cut in a Scandinavian way that was more reminiscent, really, of Charles Sorensen than of his father—went bullheaded at the problem. One particular discipline he had acquired from his General Motors days was getting in early to the office, and he set about establishing the same regime at Ford. Ted Mecke, Ford's chief P.R. man since 1962, and himself an earlier bird than most, liked to be at his desk by eight. But from the morning that Bunkie arrived, Mecke would get in to discover the new president's light burning fiercely in the squawk-box on his desk. Knudsen was already up there, in the boss-corner of the twelfth floor, with the papers read, wanting to talk.

Mecke decided to show willing, and came in next morning at 7:45—to find the light on. Next morning he aimed at 7:30, and his welcome was the same. When, with a supreme effort, a seven o'clock arrival yielded the same result, the Vice-President, Public Affairs, decided he had shown willing enough.[13]

Bunkie's early-morning ways were not, in fact, totally typical of GM.

"J-J-Jesus Christ, Bunkie!" Harley Earl would respond to the seven o'clock meetings Knudsen liked to call at the GM styling studio. "Goddamnit, you get up with the b-b-birds!" And the great designer would come in to work when he pleased.[14]

But Knudsen's new underlings at Ford were more intimidated.

"Holy shit," he exclaimed one morning to Lee Iacocca, who had turned up at one dawn meeting in a royal blue suit. "I know I got you up early, but where the hell did you drag out that goddamn old suit?"[15]

Bunkie, apparently, had meant the dig kindly. The remark could even have been interpreted as an oblique sort of compliment, since the new president was virtually colour-blind. You had to wear a very blue suit indeed to catch Bunkie Knudsen's eye.

But Lee Iacocca did not see the funny side. His wife, Mary, liked to relate how Lee kept a little piece of paper at home on which he would map out his career through the years ahead, with his future promotions, and salaries, all listed with their target dates.[16] Bunkie's arrival had set this timetable back by eight to ten long years at least.

By the beginning of 1968, Lee Iacocca was already working on the assumption that Henry II would not leave Arjay Miller in the presidency for another five years—and Lee saw himself as the next man in line. He had made several end runs around Miller, boosting himself and undermining Arjay with projects that he took directly to Henry II, and he had not been discouraged.

But now, out of nowhere, Bunkie had appeared. Knudsen was fifty-five in 1968, which meant that the new chief executive could spend as long as a decade at the top of Ford. That meant, in turn, that Lee would not get his shot at the presidency until he was nearly fifty-five himself. For a man disappointed not to have been a vice-president before he was thirty-six, the delay was unacceptable.

"Lee had chewed through ten layers of management to get where he was," said one of his colleagues later[17]—and to get through to the very top of the final layer, Lee had no hesitation in chewing through Bunkie too.

Soon after Knudsen's arrival, John Nevin, a relatively obscure executive who had been elevated, through Iacocca's special care, to the position of marketing vice-president, found himself travelling with his patron in the privacy and comfort of a corporate jet.

Had Nevin read, inquired Iacocca, a recent article in *Sports Illustrated* about Vince Lombardi, the great football coach? What impressed him most about Lombardi, explained Iacocca, was the love that his players had for their leader, so that they would stick by him, and fight for him, against all odds, through thick and thin.

By the time Lee had told the same story a few more times to those he considered his loyalists, the point had been taken. There was to be no compromise, no halfway house. You were either for Lee or against him, and in the summer months of 1968 the battle lines took shape.

\*

Bunkie Knudsen was no corporate virgin. You do not spend thirty years clawing your way up the GM ladder without learning a trick or two, and within weeks of his arrival in Dearborn in the spring of 1968, he had moved to establish his authority in that most visible arena, the styling studio. The 1970 cars were supposed to be ready for tooling —"locked up," in the designers' parlance—but Bunkie picked on the 1970 Thunderbird, chopped five inches off the front, gave the car a pronounced snout, and redesigned the taillights. By the time he had finished, the Ford looked remarkably like a Pontiac.

Bunkie Knudsen was acting as though he were Mister Ford—and, in a way, he was. Part of his brief had been to take the chairman's place when Henry II was away, particularly when it came to the product, the cars that would determine Ford's fortunes in the marketplace, and the powers he had been given as president exceeded those of any previous holder of the post. Knudsen was the first Ford president ever to be paid at Grade 28, the same salary and bonus level as Mr. Ford. That meant he was paid $200,000, with a $400,000 bonus, in his first year, and, under a new corporate organization chart, the senior vice-presidents who used to report to Henry II now reported directly to Bunkie himself. Chief among these was Lee Iacocca, who, in his post-Mustang position as Executive Vice-President, Cars and Trucks, had already given his own final approval to the Thunderbird which Knudsen had so drastically cut about.

Lee bided his time. He knew he was a match for Bunkie as a car man. He had just produced Detroit's first answer to the imported compact, the Maverick, which was selling, in its initial months, at a rate not much slower than that of the original Mustang.* He was hard at work on a subcompact, the Pinto, which was targeted, in the best Iacocca tradition, at a "2,000:2,000" objective. The car should weigh less than 2,000 pounds, and also cost less than $2,000. Best of all, in answer to the objection that small cars do not make

---

* In its first six months the Maverick sold more than 150,000 units.[18]

*Henry and Clara Ford with Henry Ford II at Gaukler Point, April 1943*

*Fords old and new. Henry I, Henry II, and the Quadricycle at Greenfield Village, c. 1945*

*Wedding Day. Henry Ford II and Anne McDonnell, Long Island, July 13, 1940.* **Below and opposite, top** *on holiday at Southampton.* **Opposite, below** *As ordered. "Take my photo," Henry instructed at the Knickerbocker Ball in 1952, and the photographer obeyed*

*"Human engineering". Henry II, aged twenty-eight,
at the Rouge*

*Henry Ford II and Ernest Breech*

*The Whiz Kids, in the first row, of a group of Ford executives left to right: Arjay Miller, F. "Jack" Reith, George Moore, James Wright, Charles "Tex" Thornton, Wilbur Anderson, Charles Bosworth, Ben Mills, J. Edward Lundy, Robert McNamara. Jack Davis is in the second row between Wright and Thornton*

*Henry II with Harry Bennett*

**Left** *John Bugas*

**Right** *William Clay (left),
Benson, and Henry Ford II
drive out a winner*

**Below** *A loser*

*November 1960. Robert McNamara with Henry Ford II*

*Coming out. Anne, sixteen, Charlotte, eighteen, Edsel, eleven, Henry II, and Anne McDonnell Ford at Charlotte's debut, December 22, 1959*

*Coming out: Henry II and Anne Ford at her debut party, June 20, 1961*

*Lee Iacocca with his Mustangs I (rear) and II*

*December 11, 1970. Henry Ford II announces the appointment of Lee Iacocca to the presidency of the Ford Motor Company*

**Left** *Anne Ford (left) with her sister Charlotte in London, July 1962*

**Below** *Charlotte with her daughter, Elena Niarchos, Henry II, and Cristina Ford, May 1968*

**Right** *Honeymoon. Henry II and Cristina Ford, St. Moritz, February 1965*

**Below** *Edsel Ford II on his wedding day in 1974 with his father*

**Left** *True friend,*
*Max Fisher*

**Below** *Little brother.*
*William Clay Ford with his*
*Detroit Lions*

*After the battle. Bunkie Knudsen and Henry Ford in 1984*

*Office of the Chief Executive. April 14, 1977. Henry II explains his plan
with Lee Iacocca and Philip Caldwell (right)*

*Edsel II and Cynthia Ford at the Detroit Grand Prix, 1984*

**Left** *Benson Ford Junior*

**Right** *Alfred Brush Ford and Dr. Sharmilla Bhaktivedanta on their wedding day, December 26, 1984*

**Below** *Anne (left) and Charlotte Ford, 1980*

**Right** *New model. Kathy DuRoss, a Ford, and the Renaissance Center*

**Below** *Henry and Kathy Ford, April 1985*

money, Lee had just unveiled a confection which, far more than the Mustang, he could truly claim as his own creation.

Unable to sleep one night in a Canadian hotel, Iacocca had had a vision which he transmitted instantly, by telephone, to Gene Bordinat in Detroit.

"Put me a Rolls-Royce grille on the front of a Thunderbird," he commanded, and the result was one of the most farfetched, vulgar, and profitable fancies ever fashioned in Detroit, a two-door sports car stretched to the length of a limousine.

The vehicle was christened the Lincoln Continental Mark III. The Mark I had been Edsel's creation. The Mark II was the aborted beauty produced by William Clay Ford, and the Mark III claimed a family resemblance by virtue of a rococo, false spare-tyre cover, moulded like a cartwheel onto the rear. It made no pretence at performance. It had the weight of a hearse, and it drove like one. With its endless front hood and its oval opera rear windows, it was pure Las Vegas, Ronald Searle's idea of the type of chariot that octogenarians might select for cruising around Palm Beach —and they did, in their thousands and tens of thousands. Within twelve months of its introduction in April 1968, the Mark III had outsold the Cadillac Eldorado, which had, hitherto, dominated the two-door luxury field.*

The most attractive thing of all about the Continental Mark III was that it scarcely cost Ford more, in terms of engineering and production expense, than had been first suggested by Iacocca's phone call to Gene Bordinat. Lee had proved his forte again—laying clever sheet metal over a proven and existing base. Tooling and manufacturing for the Mark III came to less than $30 million, an unheard-of bargain for something presented as a brand-new car, and, since it was at the top end of the market, Lincoln could pull in a pure profit of around $2,000 per vehicle. In 1968 Lincoln actually made a profit for the first time since Henry I had

---

* In its first thirteen months the Lincoln Continental Mark III sold 22,306 units.[19]

wrestled the company away from the Lelands in the early 1920s, and within a few years it was contributing almost $1 billion to the overall Ford balance sheet.[20]

Devised, styled, and manufactured before Bunkie Knudsen's arrival in Dearborn, the Lincoln Continental Mark III suddenly and dramatically achieved one of the most important things that Knudsen had been brought from General Motors to accomplish: getting Ford established in the medium-priced and luxury car market. Small wonder that Lee Iacocca chose to drive the baroque Mark III, or one of its ever-more-stretched and Disneyfied successors, as his personal car for the remainder of his time at Ford.

Bunkie Knudsen's greatest mistake, in terms of boardroom strategy, was not to bring any allies to Dearborn with him. He dived into the Ford shark pool virtually unprotected. Nor was his arrival on the twelfth floor marked by the classic sign that an imported executive has taken charge, a basket full of severed heads. When Lee Iacocca went to Chrysler, he fired more than thirty vice-presidents. When Bunkie went to Ford, he fired just one. Somebody had to carry the blame for all the losses at Philco.

Knudsen today defends his moderation. "I have never done things that way," he says. "I cleaned out a few people at Pontiac who weren't doing their job. That's why I brought in DeLorean. But there was no trouble at the Ford Motor Company. See, that's Lee's method of operating: throw 'em out, and bring in your own gang. That means you have a difficult time getting along with people, if you ask me."[21]

Bunkie did bring in one old GM associate, Robert Hunter, to try to get to grips with Philco-Ford, and into the styling studio he infiltrated Larry Shinoda, a tough, streetwise Japanese-American who had made his name designing hot rods and racing cars. Shinoda's greatest claim to fame was his work on the torpedolike '63 Corvette. He had also had a hand in Chevrolet's pre-Mustang youth car, the sporty Monza GT.

This last qualification did not endear him to the resident

team of designers at Ford, and Shinoda did not go out of his way to be particularly nice. Soon after his arrival, he gave an interview to the auto press announcing his ambition to be the first Japanese-American vice-president in Detroit —an ambition he could only achieve at Ford by displacing the existing styling vice-president, Gene Bordinat.

Shinoda set out to accomplish in the styling studio the same sort of shake-up that Bunkie was trying to administer to the company as a whole.

"It was design by country club," he remembers.[22]

Shinoda was a hustler. When Bordinat quietly ignored him, or sidetracked him onto dead-end projects, Shinoda would go out into the company to make contacts of his own —the parts division, the glass division, the vinyl plant— collaring a few thousand dollars from this budget and a few thousand from that. He even got Ford Aerospace to put up some cash for a drag racer.

In this fashion, Shinoda scavenged and reworked a discarded fibreglass model of the 2,000:2,000 subcompact that Ford was working on in 1969, the Pinto, and, at an early-morning design show of the offerings prepared by Bordinat's protégés, he announced that he had prepared an offering of his own.

"Well, let's see it," responded Knudsen.

The viewing of Shinoda's own prototype Pinto was set for a reconvened meeting at 1:30 that afternoon. But when Knudsen arrived in the styling auditorium, after lunch, with Iacocca, there was no sign of Bordinat, nor of his associate, Don DeLaRossa.

"Larry," said Knudsen, "call up Gene's office"—which Shinoda did, to be informed that Mr. Bordinat was in conference, and could not be disturbed.

"Gimme the goddamn phone," spat out Knudsen, and he let the girl know, in no uncertain terms, that Bordinat was required in the auditorium. Now.

A few minutes later a limousine was heard to go roaring across the courtyard outside, in the direction of the Dearborn Inn, and ten minutes later it came roaring back.

"You could always tell," remembers Shinoda, "when Gene had been drinking pretty heavy. He would walk very stiff, and he would kind of cock his head a little bit, so he could line up on something, and then he could walk very straight. But Don DeLaRossa couldn't almost stand up straight at all."[23]

By the etiquette of the styling studio, the company president, and all the vice-presidents, could watch design presentations from chairs. Everybody who was not a vice-president had to stay standing up—and to preserve his equilibrium, Don DeLaRossa leaned against the wall.

When the lights went up at the end of the show, however, it became apparent that DeLaRossa had slid downwards somewhat, and he was now in a sitting position on the floor.

"What the hell happened to him?" inquired Knudsen.

"He's drunk," Shinoda informed him helpfully.

Knudsen walked over to investigate, and as he loomed into DeLaRossa's vision, the designer looked up at him from the floor.

"How's yer ass, Bunkie?" he asked.

Lee Iacocca, who was to take Don DeLaRossa to be his chief designer at Chrysler, bit on his cigar and said not a word.*

Bunkie Knudsen's alterations to the 1970 Thunderbird had been after the gun. But he had plenty of time to impose his thinking upon all the models of the 1971 range, and as he did so the conflict between him and Iacocca became less and less disguised.

"Lee resented Bunkie telling him how to style cars," one Ford executive later told the *Wall Street Journal*,[24] and the feuding in the styling centre became more and more bizarre. Knudsen would make his rounds, known to the designers as the "dawn patrol," and shortly afterwards Iacocca would

* Neither Bordinat nor DeLaRossa today remembers this incident. Bordinat denies it occurred. DeLaRossa, who recalls his long "business lunches" with Bordinat with mingled fondness and regret, acknowledges the possibility.

follow along the same route, questioning and altering the decisions made earlier.

"They were literally re-doing each other's work," said one of the stylists. To protect themselves, stylists would show Knudsen things they were not showing Iacocca, and vice versa.

The conflict broadened beyond the design area. Soon after his arrival, Knudsen commissioned Shinoda to go on a familiarization tour, visiting and checking odd corners of the Ford empire on his behalf, and what Shinoda discovered horrified him.

"I went through a stamping plant outside of Chicago," he remembers, "and they were complaining to me. They said, 'Well, you're from the big office, and we've got a real problem. We've got a roof that leaks, and we can't get any money to fix the roof. The water's dripping on the stamping dies, and then they rust, so we have to waste hours just to clean them off.'"

Shinoda discovered that that year's maintenance budget had been slashed and diverted to the profit column to help make Iacocca's balance sheet for the year look good. It was scarcely a heinous crime, a matter of business judgement, really. It was quite possible that Iacocca himself knew nothing about it, because that was his style, to snap out objectives at his team, really tough objectives, and then tell them to damn well get the job done, and not bother him with the details. That was how the figures for Iacocca's divisions always came to look so good.

But the healthy black ink was at the price, Shinoda discovered, of niggling inconsistencies—like Glasshouse washrooms being maintained and repaired if they were on senior-executive floors, but being neglected if they were not.

"You'd go inside some of the men's rooms," remembers Shinoda, "and one urinal would be broken off the wall, with one of the doors gone off the crappers. And this was World Headquarters!"[25]

"Jesus Christ!" said Knudsen when Shinoda showed him

his findings. "What are you trying to do?" Knudsen shelved the report.

"Bunkie's problem," says Shinoda today, "was that he had never been down the alley with an alley fighter."[26]

Bunkie Knudsen was not quite as green, however, as he allowed his aggressive subordinate to imagine. Broken urinals were no issue to go to war over. But the new president had started to pick up some disturbing rumours about Lee Iacocca's increasingly lordly ways and, in particular, about his friendship with an ambitious New York travel agent/ limousine operator, William Dennis Fugazy.

Iacocca had met Fugazy in the early 1960s when Fugazy had come to Ford bidding on the company's travel business. It was guaranteed profit, 10 percent of the annual multimillion-dollar travel bill incurred by Ford executives flying to every corner of the company's worldwide empire —and staying in first-class hotels when they got there. Even more profitable was the business known as "incentive" travel, organizing the jaunts which Iacocca loved so well, filling up planes with press, and dealers, and crates of champagne, and jetting to exotic locations in order to launch a new car—or, sometimes, to reward dealers for selling an old one. The calendars at Ford, GM, and Chrysler were ringed with the dates. Luxury hotels would be requisitioned and filled to the roof with dealers and executives for days on end, all expenses paid, with lavish buffets, banquets, and floor shows to provide relief between the conference sessions.

These ritual durbars marked the passage of the seasons for car men. By the early 1960s, the packaging of this gaudy mixture of work and play, from charter planes to dancing girls, had become a profitable business for a small group of original and enterprising suppliers to the automobile industry, and Bill Fugazy wanted to become one of them.

It turned out that Bill and Lee had family connections. Fugazy's grandfather, Luigi, had been a father figure to the Italians landing on Ellis Island. They called him Papa. He helped arrange steamship packages from Genoa, and he lent money to the new arrivals to get them started. Luigi Fugazy had extended a helping hand to Nicola Iacocca when he first reached the New World, and one good turn deserved another. Nicola's son, Lido, suggested that Bill Fugazy might care to bid on the introduction he was planning for his new youth car, the Mustang, in the spring of 1964. It would be Ford's biggest incentive package yet.

The launch, of course, was a great success. It was at the New York World's Fair, Fugazy's own territory, and the long Fugazy limousines (Lincolns, not Cadillacs) shuttled to and fro, carrying the dealers, their wives, and the senior company executives. It was difficult to pander too much when trying to make that sort of affair go with a real swing. Ford had file cards showing what brand of booze every senior executive and dealer favoured, and the drink had to be waiting for him in his hotel room—along with the right flowers or perfume for his lady. The Fugazys had always made a speciality of personal service. In the 1930s, Bill's father had got the steamship contract for MGM. He would book the staterooms for the stars: Mary Pickford, Douglas Fairbanks, Louis B. Mayer himself.

"Other kids had autograph books for classmates to sign," remembers Bill's sister, Sister Irene, a member of the Sisters of Charity. But Irene and Bill filled their books with the signatures of real celebrities.[27]

Having Ford as a client helped Bill Fugazy expand dramatically in the 1960s. He leased himself a cruise ship, the S.S. *Independence*, and Lee leased it from him, at a cost of $44,000 a day,[28] in order to launch his autumn offerings for Lincoln-Mercury in September 1966. Lee Iacocca recalls the cruise in his memoirs as one of the high points of his career at Ford:

At sunset on the second day, we assembled all the dealers at the stern of the ship. At a predetermined moment we released hundreds of helium balloons, which floated skyward to reveal the 1967 Mercury Marquis. . . . Two nights later, on the island of St. Thomas, we unveiled the new Cougar. At a beach lit by clusters of brilliant torches, a World War II landing craft pulled up to the shore and lowered its ramp. The audience was breathless as a shining white Cougar drove out onto the sand. The door opened, and out stepped singer Vic Damone.[29]

That was the touch Iacocca really liked. Bill Fugazy knew everybody—bishops, baseball players, Howard Cosell—and he introduced Lee to them. The boy from Allentown began to spend more and more time in New York. The gossip columnists still could not pronounce his name, let alone spell it correctly, but they could not fail to note how the pushy, young vice-president from Detroit had been admitted to the oddly assorted aurora of celebrities around Fugazy: Bob Hope, Cardinal Spellman, and Fugazy's old childhood friend Roy Cohn, the lawyer who had made his name as a red-baiter, doing Senator Joe McCarthy's dirty work in the early 1950s, and who was now representing several reputed Mafia chieftains in New York.

Bunkie Knudsen had seen all this once before. His sober, hard-working chief engineer John DeLorean had gone right off beam when he realized the power and perquisites that his patronage could bring. Bunkie had been tempted himself.

"I mean," he remembers, "the first time I got to be a general manager, it wasn't three days before I got the call, 'C'mon out—we'll have a big party for you. We've got the girls, and the booze, and everything else.' You know what I mean?"[30]

In DeLorean's case, the temptations had been of the West Coast variety: sun, sand, long sideburns, and plastic surgery to give his chin a sharper edge.

"It's the advertising," explains Knudsen, "because, you see, they make all those commercials out there, and all that stuff, and advertising is a big business. Those guys want to keep the accounts so, when you get to be a general manager . . . You can't blame them. If a fellow is subject to that kind of thing, why not?"[31]

Knudsen is talking about girls, the vivacious, leggy, attractive girls with a weakness for fur coats and private jets, who are just so *interested* to talk to middle-aged men about, say, their projections for the new car season.

"A young guy goes out there," says Bunkie, "and he's married a nice girl, and she's taken good care of him all that time. Then he sees one of those broads, and he goes a little crazy."[32]

The girls were pretty at Bill Fugazy's parties, the champagne of the best, and there was no harm in Lee enjoying himself in Fugazy's company. But the travel agent also had a business relationship with the Ford Motor Company, and Bunkie was getting disturbing feedback in that respect. Fugazy's competitors in the incentive business were complaining at the way in which they were getting cut out. They would put in their bids to the Ford marketing department, and it seemed to them that they were hitting a brick wall every time.

The annoying thing, confided one of the chief executives at E. F. MacDonald, the leading company in the business, to Gene Bordinat, when the designer was himself hosting an incentive jaunt to Hawaii, was that Fugazy's winning packages always seemed to outclass the very best ideas submitted by everyone else. There are two things that get you contracts in the incentive business: the right price, and an interesting plot. The best dealers, the ones you really want to reward and encourage, are rolling in money anyway: Maui, Acapulco, Rio de Janeiro, you name it, they've been there, and you have to offer them something extra—a new idea, status they cannot buy. The best incentive men cogitate for weeks to come up with a new angle.

So how was it that Fugazy's schemes for Ford so often managed to cover all the angles—and also came in just a tad below the price that anyone else could offer?[33] E. F. MacDonald himself went to see Knudsen in 1969 with the accusation that someone at Ford was giving Bill Fugazy the inside scoop.[34]

Knudsen was worried by another problem. He had Fugazy's invoices to Ford audited and discovered that the travel agent had been charging Ford considerably more than his original estimate, some $300,000 more. He took the figures to Henry Ford, and Fugazy was ordered to pay the

$300,000 back—which he did. But Bill Fugazy continued to receive Ford business, and Henry Ford II did not seem too worried by that, for in the early months of 1969 he was more concerned with getting himself back in charge of his own company. Things had not worked out as planned at the National Alliance of Businessmen. At the end of March 1968, Lyndon Johnson had decided not to run for reelection after all, and the arrival of Richard Nixon in Washington in 1969 meant an end to Henry Ford II's role in the NAB after just one year instead of three.

As Henry II contemplated the guerrilla warfare being waged inside his company by the early months of 1969, his view was quite simple. He had put Bunkie in charge, and if there were problems, it was for Bunkie to sort them out—or answer for them himself.

Knudsen had, in fact, summoned a summit conference in January 1969 in an effort to patch up his differences with Lee Iacocca, but the truce had proved short-lived. The wrestling continued over the new cars. Having two opinionated car men in such senior positions was, evidently, not such a good idea. When the Ford line for '71 was finally, and acrimoniously, put to bed, the battle moved on to the offerings for '72—and Lee knew how to handle Henry so much better than Bunkie did.

"If Henry called Bunk in," said one observer at the time, "and told him to move some plant down in Indiana, let's say, Bunk would argue. He'd say, 'Let's keep that there, and move the one in Ohio.' If Henry would tell Lee to move the plant, Lee would go move the goddam plant."[35]

Lee might be getting lordly, but he had not forgotten how to play the courtier. Bunkie, on the other hand, was behaving as if he were sitting on the throne himself—and that was not a mistake to make at the Ford Motor Company. Henry II got particularly upset when Bunkie "signed off" on the cars going into production for 1971, for giving the final O.K. on the latest product line-up had been Henry's personal prerogative since 1945. When the chairman was away on a

Mediterranean cruise in the summer of 1969, however, and the production people told the president that they were ready to go ahead with the '71 line, Bunkie told them they could press the button.

At the time Knudsen did not think twice about it. "When I was at Pontiac," he says, "and when Mr. Curtice [GM president in the late 1950s] was off in Europe somewhere, I just okayed the car and went ahead with it. That was my job there."[36]

That was Knudsen's job at Ford as well—on paper. But Bunkie did notice that when Henry II got back from his cruise, he was several degrees cooler towards him than he had been previously.

Knudsen interpreted the change in terms of the death of Sidney Weinberg, the Wall Street man who had helped the company go public and who had since become Henry Ford's chief confidant and mentor. Weinberg had died in that summer of 1969, while the *Santa Maria* was in the Greek Islands, and Henry II, visibly upset, had cut short his holiday to attend the funeral of his friend.[37] Since Weinberg, as a senior and much-respected member of the Ford board, had been something of a Knudsen partisan, Bunkie could not help seeing Weinberg's death as weakening his own position at the company.

But Bunkie signing off on the '71 cars without consulting Henry weakened the president's position far more, and when Lee Iacocca tried one of his end runs, going behind Knudsen's back to complain directly to Henry II about the president's plans for the 1972 line, he found that he received a surprisingly sympathetic hearing. A committee was established under Henry Ford himself to reassess the decisions that Knudsen had thought were final.[38] No one could remember such a publicly delivered snub since the days when Henry II had been edging out Ernie Breech.

Soon after six o'clock on the morning of September 1, 1969, Bunkie Knudsen received a phone call at home from Ted Mecke. It was Labor Day, when most people sleep in late, but Mecke's phone call was not revenge for eighteen months of morning greetings from a glowing squawk box. The Ford Vice-President, Public Affairs, knew that Bunkie's body clock did not acknowledge weekends or national holidays, and he had important news.

"I've got to come out and see you," he said.

"Fine," replied Knudsen, and soon after seven, Mecke, a Grosse Pointer, was parking his Lincoln in the Knudsen drive.

"I've got a sad tale to tell you," said Mecke, getting straight to the point. "You're not going to be with the Ford Motor Company any more after tomorrow."

"Did Mr. Ford send you over here?" responded Knudsen.

"Well, no," replied Mecke. "I came over primarily as a friend to tell you."

"Now don't give me that stuff," replied Knudsen. "You don't come out at six o'clock in the morning to tell a friend he's being fired."[39]

When Henry II confirmed Mecke's message next day, the best explanation he could come up with was "It just didn't work out"[40]—and that was his official line when, two weeks later, the news was made public, following its confirmation by the Ford board of directors.

Knudsen's dismissal was announced at a news conference on September 11, 1969. Henry II had wanted to present his president's departure as a "resignation," but Bunkie had insisted on the embarrassing truth—and, sitting beside Henry II, Lee Iacocca made the truth still more apparent. As his chairman tried to fend off the endless questions about the skulduggery and politics involved, Iacocca puffed contentedly on a big black cigar, reported William Serrin in the *New York Times*, "smiling the faint, tight smile of a Mafia don who has just consolidated control over Chicago."[41] When the press cornered the triumphant vice-president afterwards, and a reporter asked him if he was sad to see Mr. Knudsen go, Iacocca smiled still more broadly. "I never said no comment to the press yet," he declared, "but I'll say no comment now."[42]

Bunkie Knudsen today is similarly noncommittal. He just laughs at the preposterous suggestion in Lee Iacocca's memoirs that his dismissal in 1969 was the consequence of his walking into Henry Ford's office too often without knocking, and he declines to discuss the politicking that brought him down. "It is a foolish man," says one of his partisans, "who gets into a pissing contest with a skunk."

In the reorganization that followed Knudsen's departure, Iacocca was made one of three "presidents" reporting directly to Henry Ford II.

"I did not know him well enough," says Henry II today, explaining why he fitted Iacocca into his three-cornered arrangement. "He was the leading contender. But I had never worked with him directly. There had always been somebody in between."[43]

Iacocca was to supervise all Ford's North American Automotive Operations. Robert Stevenson, previously head of Foreign Operations, was given a grander international title, and the third member of the triumvirate was Robert J. Hampson, in charge of Philco-Ford and tractor operations.

In theory, all three executives were equal. It would not do to let Knudsen's departure appear too much the triumph of any one man. But some presidents are more equal than others, and it was not without significance that, after the autumn of 1969, in the shower room of the corporate gymnasium, the hairbrush holder of Lee Iacocca was now directly next door to that of Henry Ford II.[44]

Only two other executives left Ford with Bunkie Knudsen: Richard Johnson, marketing manager at Lincoln-Mercury, and, inevitably, Larry Shinoda, whose departure from the styling studio was marked by a designerly farewell of gleeful malice. The designers who worked for Gene Bordinat, the vice-president over whom Shinoda had promised to vault for the honour of Japanese America, had a huge red sun painted and raised on wires inside the styling studio, and as Shinoda left the building, the sun was lowered with derisive ceremonial to the floor.[45] Inside Ford, such jokes were the

way people dealt with the sad futility of the Knudsen episode, one of the better witticisms being based on the famous
aphorism of the company's founder—"Bunkie," said the
Glasshouse wags after September 1969, "is history."

In 1973, the Harvard Business School organized a study
programme to analyse the Bunkie Knudsen episode and
what it meant for Ford and for other corporations. Professor
Ralph Hower assembled sixty-nine sheets of closely typed
and detailed material from the business press, and the weight
of evidence bore out Professor Hower's suggestion that the
fall of Bunkie Knudsen was a "classic demonstration of what
can happen when an outsider is placed at the helm of a
vast, established organization with power centers jealously
guarded by men who have spent their professional lives
developing them."[46]

But the Knudsen episode carried more lessons for Ford
than that, for it illustrated a growing weakness in Henry II:
his regal impulse for the quick fix. Knudsen in, Knudsen
out. In the early years Henry II had built patiently, but as
he grew older he was falling prey to the same weakness as
his grandfather, the autocrat's illusion that the most decisive
action must necessarily be the best. His first wife and his
children had already suffered from it, and the same failing
was about to be demonstrated by his railroading of the
Renaissance Center. It was brave and generous, but might
not a little more reflection and a little less impatience have
produced something more organic, something which grew
more directly out of the needs of the situation?

Knudsen had been grafted artificially onto Ford. This
indicated a curious lack of confidence on Henry's part in
the organization he had spent more than twenty years
building up, and it also betrayed his enduring obsession
with General Motors. Knudsen had been imported in the
tradition of Ernie Breech, another miracle worker from the
office on West Grand Boulevard.

"I'd like for my epitaph," said Henry II in some confused
thoughts delivered at the time of Knudsen's departure,
"—but I don't think I've accomplished it yet—an organiz-

ation arrangement that will be stable enough and good enough—I'm not talking about individual people now, I'm talking about an organizational arrangement that anybody can fit into. That's the big thing General Motors has."[47]

There were those at Ford who thought Henry II had only made one mistake. Bringing in Knudsen was a not-unreasonable experiment, in their opinion, and it might actually have worked if Henry had tried a little harder to "shove Bunkie down Iacocca's throat,"[48] since Lee's ego was the only reason why the two executives had not proved able to work together harmoniously, if not lovingly, for the good of the company. Ford was a business, not a kindergarten.

This was the most worrying aspect of the Knudsen episode: the sheer destructive anger of Lee. Corporate manoeuvring was part of the game, but there were certain rules. The business was ultimately more important than the battle, and in his obsessive drive to win, Lee Iacocca sometimes seemed to lose sight of that.

Until 1968 the Ford Motor Company had benefited from the positive energies of Lee Iacocca. But the importation of Bunkie Knudsen, a talented car man who could have helped Ford as he had helped Chevrolet and Pontiac, had revealed another side: the tough, domineering side of his father, Nicola Iacocca, throwing his weight around in the streets of Allentown. There was something Iago-like about Lee when he was crossed. His ego was so demanding, and although Henry Ford II had surrendered to what was, effectively, an ultimatum on Iacocca's part in the summer of 1969, the lesson was not lost on him.

Henry II still thought highly of Lee Iacocca's many talents. "But," he would ponder to his friends, "the trouble with Lee is that he is not a team player."[49]

# 33

## THRIFTING

Lee Iacocca got his "2,000:2,000" subcompact car. His Pinto came out at the end of 1970, miraculously weighing only 2,030 pounds and, even more miraculously at a time of inflation, costing less than $2,000.*

Unlike the Edsel, the Mustang, and the Continental Mark III, the Pinto could fairly be called a new car—a brand-new platform as well as new sheet metal—and, somehow, Lee had managed to get the whole job done in only a few weeks more than three years. Designing and producing a totally new car usually took forty-three months or more, but the Pinto was knocked out in six months less than that—and it sold. In its first twelve months, the new subcompact racked up more than 250,000 sales.

Lee had had to fight Bunkie Knudsen to get Ford initially committed to his subcompact, while Henry II had also taken some convincing. Unlike his wiry, almost sparrowlike father and grandfather, Henry II was hewn out, physically, on a major scale. He was built for those great American boats whose power steering means you can drive them one-handed, with your other arm flopped out sideways, across the top of the bench seat. Henry II liked the ride of a big car, the classic, spongy, made-in-Detroit, magic-carpet sensation, and he also liked big-car profits. But Lee's snappy

---

* This account of the Pinto and its problems is based on outside evidence described in the source notes for this chapter, and also upon data supplied by the Ford Motor Company. Ford has faced a total of 117 lawsuits alleging improper fuel-system design in the Pinto and in its Mercury equivalent, the Bobcat. Nine of these suits are still open, and the company position is that the Pinto was no less safe than any comparable small car, and that it was designed and produced with all due consideration for its occupants' safety.

little subcompact, with its oddly sloping, truncated back, seemed to promise profits too once it started to sell in bulk. The Pinto only confirmed once again what a sure touch Iacocca had when it came to cars.

But soon after the new car's launch, one day in May 1972, Mrs. Lily Gray,[1] a California housewife and mother, pulled out onto a highway near Santa Ana in her brand-new Ford Pinto, to have the car's engine suddenly fail and stall under her, as she entered the merge lane. Coming up behind her, another car, also a Ford, could not manage to stop in time, and it rear-ended the Pinto, causing serious damage.

The fuel tank of the Pinto, sandwiched between the rear bumper and the axle, was ruptured. Gasoline vapour mingled with the air in the passenger compartment, and a spark exploded the mixture. Lily Gray died horribly a few hours later, in a nearby hospital's emergency room, her entire body having been charred and incinerated in the explosion. Her less fortunate passenger, Richard Grimshaw, a thirteen-year-old schoolboy, lingered on, scarred inhumanly, his features literally melted away. Richard Grimshaw's teenage years were destined to be spent in operating theatres, where surgeons would work vainly to graft a new ear and nose for him from the few unscorched portions of his atrociously tortured body.

This was when making cars became more than a game. In the months that followed the death of Lily Gray, more and more Pintos suffered accidents that trapped and burned their occupants. Most makes of small car had vulnerable gas tanks like the Pinto, wedged between the bumper and the axle, and, by their nature, they had comparatively fragile body frames which tended to crush around the doors, trapping their occupants inside. But, adding to the problem, the Pinto also had a filler neck to its gas tank that seemed prone to get ripped out if the car was involved in a collision. By conservative estimates, fifty-nine Pinto drivers and passengers were burned to death[2] in collisions from which they might otherwise have walked away comparatively unscathed. Trapped inside their cars with a lethal mixture of gas and air, they suffered the same horrible death as Lily Gray.

In his memoirs, Lee Iacocca accepts responsibility for the Pinto, though not quite as prominently as he takes credit for the Mustang and for the Continental Mark III. He also defends himself against the charge that he knowingly made a dangerous car. "The guys who built the Pinto had kids in college who were driving that car," he writes. "Believe me, nobody sits down and thinks: 'I'm deliberately going to make this car unsafe.'"[3]

That is not quite the point. Nobody has accused Lee Iacocca and the Ford Motor Company of deliberately manufacturing machines that would burn people to death by the dozen. The question is whether Ford and Iacocca exhibited all due care for their customers' safety when balanced in the complex carmaking equation that involves cost, time, marketability, and profit. Confronted with the facts of how Lee Iacocca and Ford actually built the Pinto, a number of juries across the United States concluded that they did not.

When Bunkie Knudsen arrived at Ford, he was horrified by the seat-of-the-pants attitude he discovered to both the production and engineering of cars. "I was appalled," he says, "when I first got there to find a high percentage of the new models being made on temporary tools. I never saw that before."[4]

This practice stemmed from the fact that Ford management—which, as Knudsen discovered, effectively meant Henry Ford II—was almost always late in giving the final "sign-off" to cars.

"They just didn't have time to make the permanent tools," he remembers. "The normal way to do it is to make a flow chart, you know—here is day one, right here, and you go through here, and you show how long you have got to design this thing. Then, when you get to here, you see how long you have got for your engineering releases to go out. Then there's an overlay chart showing what percentage of the tooling is ready, what percentage has been tried out, and so on—until you get out here, to the day you're supposed to be running the thing. Well, at Ford in those days, they just couldn't do anything like that. It was a hit-and-miss deal."[5]

The up side of this home workshop state of affairs was that there were some extraordinarily innovative production engineers at Ford who could jerry-rig just about anything in record time. "I don't think," says Knudsen admiringly, "that you could ever have gotten General Motors to have pushed a car out with as little lead time as they gave them over there. It was unbelievable."[6]

The down side was that in all the haste and improvisation, mistakes could creep into the final car—and in the case of the Ford Pinto, these mistakes were to prove serious. Evidence produced in the law case following the death of Lily Gray, and in other cases, showed that Ford had carried out rear-impact tests upon the Pinto before and after the car was launched, and that the gas tank had ruptured in several of these. But such were the constraints of time, cost, and weight upon the project that the significance of the problem was not realized.[7]

The crash tests which, prior to production, were carried out on European Capris whose rears had been modified to simulate Pintos, indicated several ways to protect or strengthen the Pinto's gas tank. Tyre husking was placed between the gas tank and the car's rear axle so that, on impact, the bolts on the axle could not perforate the thin tank metal.[8] Other tests explored the possibilities of lining the gas tank with some sort of rubber bladder.

Very much aware of the dangers of gas-tank fires, Ford had been developing this sort of protective inner lining for some time. Several years earlier, in July 1965, Arjay Miller had given testimony on the subject to a U.S. Senate subcommittee, and he had spoken with a special enthusiasm about a fabric gas tank which Ford engineers were testing at that very moment. "If it proves out," he promised, "it will be a feature you will see in our standard cars."[9]

The fabric gas tank, however, did not work out. Nor did various other rubber bladders which proved vulnerable to extremes of heat and cold. Tyre husking could scarcely provide a permanent, nonperishable barrier between the thin metal of the gas tank and the bolts on the transmission bulge of the rear axle.

Did no one draw Lee Iacocca's attention to the problem and the urgency of solving it?

"Hell, no," a senior Ford engineer told the San Francisco investigative magazine *Mother Jones*. "That person would have been fired. Safety wasn't a popular subject around Ford in those days. With Lee it was taboo. Whenever a problem was raised that meant a delay on the Pinto, Lee would chomp on his cigar, look out the window and say, 'Read the project objectives and get back to work.'"[10]

The project objectives of the Pinto were set out in the Pinto "green book," the top-secret sequence of monthly manuals containing the engineering specifications for the product, which did not address themselves to safety.[11] That did not loom high on Lee Iacocca's list of priorities, except when he was publicly corralled in a safety-conscious forum —and not always even then. Ford executives still wince at the memory of how, addressing the Society of Automotive Engineers in Detroit's Cobo Hall in March 1978 with Joan Claybrook, President Carter's car-safety chief, on the podium beside him, Iacocca departed from his set text to launch a scornful attack upon the lady and her safety policies.* It was the voice of the salesman whose big opportunity had come in 1956 when Ford sold safety and Chevrolet sold cars.

But times had changed since 1956. Ralph Nader's campaign against the GM Corvair in the mid-1960s had pro-

---

* Since World War II, the speeches of senior Ford executives, including those of Henry Ford II, have, almost invariably, been prepared by company speech writers, who are part of the public relations department. Speeches on sensitive issues are vetted by committees, and all speaking texts, together with marginal notes and annotations to show the degree to which the original text was departed from, are carefully filed for future reference. The agreed text of Lee Iacocca's speech of March 1, 1978, is on file at Ford, but the "speaking text" and notes which show what he actually said have disappeared from the file.[12]

duced some ugly revelations—among them the fact that
Ford engineers had examined the Corvair in the course
of their routine testing of the opposition's products, had
discovered the same oversteering fault that Nader identified,
and had done nothing about it. In September 1966, the
National Traffic and Motor Vehicle Act became U.S. public
law number 89-563, the National Highway Safety Board
opened its doors as a government agency in January 1967,
and the following January the NHSB started issuing the first
national automobile safety standards. Largely in response
to Ralph Nader's disclosures, the U.S. government had
got involved in carmaking, and running the Ford Motor
Company was never to be quite the same again.

Henry Ford II has been forthright on the subject of car
safety and on its greatest advocate in North America.

"Look," he told the author Booton Herndon in 1969, "I'll
tell you what I want you to put in your book about Nader.
You say, from me, he's full of crap."[13]

The obedient Herndon wrote it, and published it, just as
Henry II told him to, and since Herndon's entire book was
vetted and sanitized before publication by the Ford P.R.
department, we can assume that the other thoughts on safety
attributed by Herndon to Henry II accurately reflected the
Ford chairman's views.

"Look," said Henry Ford II, "we could build the safest
car in the world. We could build a tank that would creep
over the highways and you could bang 'em into each other
and nobody would ever get a scratch. But nobody would
buy it either. We'd last about two months putting out stuff
like that. The American people want good cars, good looking
cars, fast cars, cars with power and styling, and that's the
kind of cars we build. We spend a hell of a lot of time trying
to make them better and safer, and then some pipsqueak
who doesn't know a thing about the industry, comes along
and tries to tell us how to do what we've dedicated our lives
and billions of dollars to doing."[14]

This is a slightly more elaborate version of the Iacocca

693

"our own kids in Pintos" defence. Ralph Nader, who did overstate his case on occasions, and who encouraged his own cult of personality with the assiduousness of a Ford or Iacocca, never suggested that Ford should build and market armoured cars. He was calling for a greater role for safety in the traditional carmaking equation, together with the injection into the process of environmental considerations like pollution. If Detroit had shown the slightest willingness genuinely to police and regulate itself when it came to questions like crash-worthiness or the amount of lead in exhaust fumes in the early 1960s, it might have enjoyed a smoother entry into the consumer age. But the car companies, with Henry Ford their most recognized spokesman, resolutely refused to admit they had a problem. As a consequence, they were, by the beginning of the 1970s, being subjected to government regulation of the most detailed and, in their view, most hindersome sort.

The 1971 Pinto, as launched in the autumn of 1970, conformed, in fact, to all the federal standards for car construction then prevailing. The government regulations which addressed the problem of rupturing fuel tanks did not become effective for several more years. The Pinto was never an illegal vehicle. But conforming to the letter of the law was hardly a defence for those executives inside Ford who discovered what a hazard to life the Pinto gas tank represented soon after the car was launched. The need to meet future government safety standards and the reports of fuel-tank fires prompted further testing of the vehicle, and the lack of protection for the fuel tank, and for the fuel-tank filler neck, was confirmed. The question was how much that protection should cost.

Quite early in their negotiations with the officials of the National Highway Traffic Safety Administration (as the NHSB became titled after 1970), Ford pushed the federal regulators to put some price on auto safety. What was the cost-benefit analysis of all these improvements they were suggesting? How much, in basic terms, was a human life worth?

Cost-benefit analysis had, ironically, been something of a vogue in Washington ever since the arrival in 1960 of Robert McNamara. McNamara had brought with him the cost-analysis techniques he had practiced in the USAF Statistical Control Office under Robert Lovett, and then at the Ford Motor Company. Working on the same principle, the accountants at NHTSA came up with a price for a human life in the early 1970s—$200,725, the sum of twelve "societal components":[15]

| Component | 1971 Costs |
|---|---|
| Direct productivity losses | $132,000 |
| Indirect productivity losses | 41,300 |
| Hospital costs | 700 |
| Other medical costs | 425 |
| Property damage | 1,500 |
| Insurance administration | 4,700 |
| Legal fees and court costs | 3,000 |
| Employer losses | 1,000 |
| Victim's pain and suffering | 10,000 |
| Funeral | 900 |
| Assets (lost consumption) | 5,000 |
| Miscellaneous accident cost | 200 |
| Total per fatality | $200,725 |

Pain and suffering, $10,000. It was an agency of the U.S. government which arrived at this blood-chilling calculation, not the Ford Motor Company. But the way in which Ford then took this government figure and used it for its own purposes carried a chill all its own. Working on a different but related problem, the tendency of fuel systems to leak when a car is turned upside down in a crash, two members of the Ford engineering department, E. S. Grush and C. S. Saunby, attempted to assess the cost of installing a fuel "rollover" valve in all Fords, and they set out their conclusions in an internal 1972 company memorandum entitled "Fatalities Associated with Crash-Induced Fuel Leakage and Fires."[16] The fuel valve, they calculated, would cost $11 per car. Add $11 in modification costs per unit to the price of 11 million cars and 1.5 million light trucks, and you get a total cost of $137 million.

Then look at the benefits, the dollar value of the lives saved and the injuries avoided by the $11 per car modification. Assume, say, the avoidance of 180 burn deaths per year at a rounded-off cost of $200,000 per death. Assume the additional avoidance of 180 serious burn injuries, at $67,000 per injury, plus 2,100 burned vehicles that will not now be burned, at a saving of $700 per vehicle. If these are your figures and your assumptions, you end up with a total benefit cost of just $49.5 million—which falls short of your investment in fire prevention by some $87.5 million.

In the final paragraph of their report, Grush and Saunby pointed out that their study concerned "only rollover consequences and costs." They were not examining the expense of preventing Pinto-like rear-impact fires. But, they concluded, "similar analysis for other impact modes would be expected to yield comparable results, with the implementation costs far outweighing the expected benefits."[17]

Car-safety experts have several quarrels with the Ford figures. Twenty-two dollars per vehicle was too high an estimate, they say, for the modifications proposed. Grush and Saunby calculated one burn injury per burn death, where some estimates set the rate of injuries to deaths as higher. Sixty-seven thousand dollars is a low figure for burn-injury compensation when compared to the millions routinely awarded by juries in U.S. courts.

In other words, Ford could quite easily have altered their calculations as to the cost-effectiveness of the proposed safety measure by counting in a greater number of burn injuries saved, and/or a higher rate of compensation per injury, and if they had done that, they would have arrived at total benefits valued at *more* than the cost of their rather expensive fire-prevention modifications.

But they did not, and their conclusion, wrapped up in dull, toneless prose spread over seven typewritten pages, is quite simple. If burn-death protection costs $137 million, and it yields only $49.5 million in benefits—save the money, not the lives.

Was it really as callous as that? The jury trying the case of Richard Grimshaw versus the Ford Motor Company thought that it was. They awarded $3.5 million in compensation to Grimshaw, but, on top of that, having heard testimony as to how Ford saved costs and increased profits by "thrifting" fuel-tank protection on the Pinto, they added a further $125 million to the settlement in punitive damages. If Ford had made that amount of profit from producing the machine that killed Lily Gray and destroyed Richard Grimshaw's face, ran their plain-man thinking, then that was the amount that Ford should pay.

The judge in the case disagreed. Accepting the $3.5 million compensatory award, he reduced the punitive damages from $125 million to $3 million. Ford appealed against this, but they lost the appeal, and also a request to take their arguments to the California Supreme Court. In the end, the Ford Motor Company paid Richard Grimshaw some $6.5 million with interest.[18]

In the years that followed, Ford had to pay out many millions more in settlement of over a hundred Pinto suits, including one that involved charges of reckless homicide—the first time that Ford, or any U.S. carmaker, had ever been charged with a criminal offence.[19] Ford was, finally, acquitted on this criminal charge, but the grand jury hearings in Elkhart, Indiana, and the subsequent court case at Winamac, Indiana, made headlines in 1978 and 1979. Ford's burning cars became a regular item on the nightly TV news.

The fundamental problem with the Pinto was that Lee Iacocca, who was its moving spirit, had only once before worked on a new car that was really new. Ford's basic 1965 sedan offering, the LTD/Galaxie, had been new from the wheels up, and it had been developed over a proper, full-length, forty-month or more testing and production programme.[20] But the Mustang had been based on the Falcon, the Continental Mark III had been based on the Thunder-bird, while the Maverick, a fine example of the layers-on-layers technique that makes up the metal archaeology of Detroit, was an adaptation of the Mustang-Falcon base.[21]

It makes good sense, in fact, for a carmaker not to produce too many truly "new" cars, even though he may tell the customer that everything is "new." Working with existing engineering systems means lower costs, and it also means that you are fitting together components which have, over the years, had most of their "glitches" ironed out of them.

More than many Detroit cars, however, the Pinto did make a stab at some sort of originality, for Lee Iacocca's 2,000-pound weight objective aimed at the essence of compact carmaking. Long or short, broad or slender, a compact car is *light*. The Pinto—along with its sister car, the virtually identical Mercury Bobcat—was an attempt to introduce some low-weight, European engineering into traditional U.S. carmaking practices. But the rush programme for the car's testing, production, and launch simply underestimated, or refused seriously to consider, the time, cost, and technical problems involved in such an ambitious undertaking.

New engineering means new tooling—and hence money—as well as a great deal of testing, which can only be done with time, and if you are thinking seriously about safety and quality, then you make allowance for those things.

But Lee Iacocca's eyes were set on his "2,000:2,000" target. As the best car salesman in Detroit, he knew the value of the magic $2,000 marketing figure, and the Pinto was "thrifted" to meet this price. For some of the most crucial months of the car's development, Lee was locked in battle with Bunkie Knudsen, and the Pinto was one of the pawns in that. Another Mustang-like triumph could administer Bunkie the coup de grace. The Pinto was pushed through on a Mustang-like schedule, and the consequence of these impossible demands was revealed by the substantial modifications which Ford was compelled to make to the car in subsequent years.

The trick whereby the Pinto came in at less than 2,000 pounds weight was achieved, basically, by cutting off the car's rear end. The Pinto was the first modern U.S. Ford produced without rear subframe members, the solid steel skeleton which both carries the sheet metal of a conventional rear trunk and also protects the fuel tank in the event of a rear-end collision.[22]

Ford soon realized its mistake. Partly in response to government regulations, and partly to protect the Pinto fuel tank, it started putting steel—and hence weight—back into the rear of the car. But as you add weight to a vehicle, you need to add more power to the engine, which means still more weight. A more powerful engine calls for a heavier transmission, and as your poundage increases, you need bigger tyres and bigger brakes. By the time that the 1976 and 1977 Pintos were being put on the market, they were weighing as much as 2,600 pounds.

Some of these weight increases came from the addition of creature comforts. But some represented the difference between life and death. By the end of the Pinto's production life, Ford engineers had made it a reasonably safe and roadworthy vehicle, but they had achieved this by totally abandoning Iacocca's original 2,000-pound target.

"Lee really did not bother himself with engineering," says Gene Bordinat. "He sort of disdained the engineers. When it came to confrontations, he liked to say, 'Hey, look, I've got a degree in engineering.' But I don't think he really knew diddley-damn. He just let the engineers get on with it."[23]

What about the suggestion that an engineer might be scared to confront Iacocca with the news that protecting the Pinto fuel tank would add weight to the car—and, worse, might delay the launch of the vehicle by weeks, months, or even a year?

"Well," says Bordinat, "Lee had a tendency to intimidate people, and I'm afraid that they may well have thought, 'He'll kill the messenger, he'll say, "Hey, don't bug me with bad news!"'—particularly if it was going to have any effect on shifting introduction dates."[24]

Tom Feaheny, who was chief systems engineer at Ford during the development of the Pinto, and who was closely involved in the diagnosis of the fuel-tank problem, disagrees.

"If I had discovered something which was seriously wrong and which needed correction," he says, "I would not have been afraid to stand up to Lee and tell him. The truth is that, at the beginning, we just did not know."[25]

Feaheny is talking about the very earliest days, before the Pinto went into full production, and he can be believed—so far as he personally was concerned, at least. A tall, broad, and fiery Irishman, he carved out an irascible reputation for himself at Ford, and he was eventually fired for, among other things, arguing too heatedly with his superiors. Feaheny does not believe that he helped design a defective or unreasonably dangerous vehicle, but, no admirer of Henry Ford II, he blames confusion and indecision stemming from the very top for the shortcomings of the Pinto. He also feels that the car was given insufficient time for thorough research and development.

"Work should have started a year earlier or more," he says. "We just did not know about rear-impact problems in those days. The crash tests we conducted, which were not just on Pintos, were to find out how to conduct crash tests, as much as anything else."[26]

This bears out a more general point made by Gene Bordinat, a friend and ally of Iacocca's when the two men were at Ford together, though subsequently somewhat estranged.

"I think we have to admit," says the stylist, "we were not very good, in those days, at taking weight out of cars. It's an art. But, over the years, there had been a tendency in America not to be concerned with weight, because, frankly, we weren't concerned with fuel—and that generated one hell of a lot of bad habits so far as the American engineer was concerned. He really didn't understand that you have to go and fight for ounces in every little component of the machine—and that means that the finance people have to face up to the cost of retooling a lot of components that had been carried over in the same way through the decades."[27]

Historically, the Pinto was caught in a time warp. The ideal car for the fuel-conscious era which started with the Arab oil embargo of October 1973, it was designed and engineered back in the age of twenty-cents-a-gallon gas, and that was hardly the fault of Lee Iacocca, Henry Ford II, or of the men who took their cue from them.

Still, let us not feel too sorry for the innocent and confused Ford engineers. In February 1974, the Ford Motor Company was fined $3.5 million for cheating on the emission-control test required of all cars under the requirements of the 1970 Clean Air Act.[28] Three hundred and fifty criminal counts were brought against the company, to all of which it pleaded guilty, and it agreed to pay a further $3.5 million in civil penalties. Ford engineers had been keeping two separate sets of emission-control reports, coded "Us" and "Them," and when "Us" showed that a number of Ford's regular production cars were polluting above legal limits, a set of special cars had been illegally doctored to produce "Them" readings that were within the limits.

Henry Ford II apologized, insisting that every detail of the wrongdoing be disclosed to the government and acknowledging that the trouble may have stemmed from his own vocal opposition to the Clean Air Act.[29] But things were awry in a company where the chairman's disagreement with a law could be taken by his staff as a license to break it.

# 34

## STREGA

The Mediterranean marriage of Henry Ford II appeared
to get off to a very good start. With her exotic Italian manners and her mane of streaked blonde hair, Cristina
Ford took Detroit by storm. She brought glamour, if not
grammar, to the Motor City. Pretty enough to be a
model, she posed beside some of the new Ford offerings
when autumn came around, and her unceasing stream of
flamboyant new outfits kept the fashion writers busy for
weeks.

But there was also a simple, Italian mama, pasta-cooking
side to the new Mrs. Ford. This had been part of her original
appeal for Henry II, and when she arrived in Grosse Pointe,
Cristina worked hard to cultivate it.

"He must be encouraged, he must be comforted," she
said in 1968, ". . . I must help him. This is my responsibility.
This is why I stay home and do not run around getting my
picture in the papers. I could be chairman of this, chairman
of that. But Henry tell me that he is doing enough for both
of us, and I should take care of *him*. So I do. I want to be
ready for him when he comes home."[1]

The dig about being chairman of this and chairman of
that was, of course, aimed at the first Mrs. Ford, and her
successor set about establishing a very different lifestyle for
herself—and for her husband. Although the world saw the
Fords in the late 1960s as the epitome of a glossy and
jet-setting couple, they spent a surprising number of their
evenings quietly at home, in front of the television, with
trays on their laps—and Cristina set special store by Henry's
health.

"When I meet him, he is like Louis Quatorze," she said
later, "chins, one, two, three, four. He weigh two hundred

forty pounds. But I say, 'Enery, you must eat better, walk more, not drink so much.'"

Cristina Ford recognized from the first the fruitlessness of weaning her husband completely away from alcohol, but she did manage to cut out the early-evening cocktails, and she also restricted his consumption fairly closely to wine: "Just two bottle a night, with dinner. That, for Enery, you know, really is not very much."[2]

Her campaign to cut out his smoking was not successful. The Ford chairman continued to smoke when he was at work, requesting photographers at car launches and receptions not to snap him while he had a cigarette in his hand. "I'll catch hell from my wife," he would explain. He also searched out secret smoking dens around the home, as Cristina discovered when she opened the door to the downstairs cloakroom one evening to find Henry II inside, puffing furiously.

Cristina Ford was on the brink of forty when she married Henry II, but you would scarcely have guessed it, she looked after herself so well. She went for long walks with her dogs along the lakeshore. She had her own private masseur, as well as her own dance teacher, who came five or six times a week.[3] She tried to get her husband to take more exercise, and she liked to whisk him away at least once a year to the exclusive California resort of La Costa, where Henry II would relax and lose weight on a regime of controlled eating and regular daily swims.

Benson Ford Junior, who was in college in California, came across the athletic couple swimming together one day when he drove over to La Costa with a college friend. The surprising thing was that, although Benson and his friend arrived by invitation, they found Aunt Cristina topless as a mermaid in the pool. While Uncle Henry hurried off, mumbling that he wanted to put on some clothes, Cristina got out of the water welcomingly and sat beside the boys, politely making small talk until her husband reappeared.[4]

Fiery and unconventional, Cristina had something about

her that was reminiscent of Diego Rivera's wife, Frida Kahlo. The new Mrs. Ford liked to shock, and life in Grosse Pointe provided her with the perfect occasion. She taught her husband some particularly obscene Italian swear words which he could exchange with her, as mock terms of endearment, at dinner parties which they judged to be rather boring—though they played this game on one occasion apparently unaware that one of their fellow guests, Tina Hills, the wife of the *Detroit Free Press* publisher, spoke perfect Italian.[5]

In the early years of their marriage, Cristina gave some thought to the circumstances which had made her the second Mrs. Henry Ford II, and she endeavoured to follow through on their implications. One of her husband's problems, she felt, that was little appreciated by the world, was his lack of self-confidence. He was such a mixture of things. He was capable, she had discovered, of being extraordinarily considerate and sensitive. His delicacy was displayed in his taste, in his eye for art, and in the neatness of his personal habits, but, desperately mistrustful of the world—as though life had, at some time in the past, scarred him cruelly for revealing his gentler side—he would so often mask his finer qualities behind his crude, roaring-boy façade.

It was difficult to escape the conclusion that Henry Ford II suffered from an inferiority complex.

"He did not know himself," Cristina later said, and she did her best to bolster his self-esteem.

"You are a Ford," she would say to him. "You must behave like one."[6]

Discovering at an early date how touchy Henry was about his failure to graduate from Yale, she took advantage of an encounter with Kingman Brewster, then president of Yale, to press for the awarding to her husband of an honorary degree. She enlisted the services of the actress Merle Oberon to charm Brewster over lunch in New York. To the campaign she recruited McGeorge Bundy, the former national security adviser who had become president of the Ford Foundation in 1966, and she also called on the firepower of Robert

McNamara, who was now president of the World Bank, and who nursed a specially soft spot for Cristina.

Henry Ford II finally got his Yale degree, an honorary doctorate of law, in 1972.[7]


The Mediterranean marriages of Henry Ford II's two daughters came to grief rather more rapidly than that of their Italian stepmother. Charlotte Ford divorced Stavros Niarchos on March 17, 1967, only fifteen months after she had married him, and though she declines today to discuss the particular reasons for the separation, she was more outspoken at the time.

"He drove me nuts," she said.[8]

Two years later, she opened up a little more to *Look* magazine. "Greeks don't like to see you dead," she said. "They like to watch you dying."[9]

Anne Ford Uzielli's marriage ended in separation at the end of 1973, and divorce little more than a year later, after some rocky years, not always smoothed by her father. In the autumn of 1968, when Mr. and Mrs. Uzielli came to Detroit as Henry II's guests to watch the Tigers win that year's World Series, he took the couple to celebrate after the game in the Bronze Door, Grosse Pointe's closest approximation to a fashionable restaurant, and there the party happened to encounter Lloyd Semple, Anne's teenage escort whom Henry had always rather favoured as a possible husband for her. Henry II had tried, on one occasion, to offer Semple a job at Ford.

Semple, now married and doing well as a lawyer in his own right, came across with his wife to sit with the Fords for a while, until Henry II was suddenly struck by the implications of his presence, and all it said about what might have been.

"Semple," he suddenly bellowed, "I know why you're sitting here! You've always wanted to fuck my daughter."[10]


One February night in 1975, California Highway Patrol officer Gene Hunt noticed a red and white 1975 Ford sedan going the wrong way on a one-way street, not far from the University of California at Santa Barbara. The driver appeared to be intoxicated, and sure enough, when the patrolman invited him to leave his car and to recite the alphabet, he could not get to the end. A blood test at the Santa Barbara Hospital confirmed the diagnosis, and, after four hours behind bars in one of the cells of the county jail, Henry Ford II pleaded "No contest" to a charge of drunken driving, and was put on probation for two years.

Subsequent accounts of Henry Ford's misadventure on the road to Santa Barbara have talked darkly of Chappaquiddick-like phone calls to the high and mighty, and of attempts to enlist friends inside the FBI. But the officers who arrested Henry II remember no such thing.

"He only made one phone call, as he was entitled to," says Milton Turner, the sergeant who was on duty that night. "He called his lawyer. There was no threatening stuff, no bullying. In fact, he was a very affable gentleman."[11]

Henry Ford complimented the police on their brand-new jail: "A nice-looking place," he said, "I'd like to buy it."[12] He did not complain at being handcuffed, or at any of the other indignities involved in his conviction. The only trouble came from the police officers who crowded around their celebrity captive, using the station's mug-shot machine to take instant photographs, which he autographed most cheerfully.

Henry Ford's comment on the entire episode, a Disraeli quotation provided by his English friend and public-relations officer, Walter Hayes, was of a piece with this insouciance. "Never complain, never explain," he said to the reporters who besieged him a few days later at a meeting of the Economic Club of Detroit in Cobo Hall, and the several hundred businessmen in the audience rose to their feet, as a man, to offer Henry Ford II a prolonged standing ovation.

Henry had scar tissue, wounds of honour and dishonour. That was what the Motor City liked about him. He drank too much, he got into trouble, and he offered no apologies —not to the world at least. But when he got home it was a different story, for travelling in the car beside Henry Ford II at the time of his arrest had been a blonde model, Kathy DuRoss, twenty-three years his junior.

Confronted by his outraged wife, who had been away on a trip to the Far East while her husband was motoring in California, Henry II went down on his knees, telling a complicated story which involved offering a lift to the escort of his English friend, David Metcalfe. Henry Ford swore that nothing improper had occurred between himself and Mrs. DuRoss.[13]

But he was lying. Henry II had known Mrs. DuRoss very well indeed, and for some time. For the previous five years, in fact, and for the second time in little more than a decade, Henry Ford II had constructed for himself a most thorough and elaborately organized double life.

Kathleen Roberta DuRoss, née King, thirty-five years old in 1975, was a widow who had not got off to the best of starts in life. Pregnant at fifteen, she had dropped out of school to marry her teenage sweetheart, David DuRoss, a Chrysler worker who moonlighted as a trombone player in local dance bands. By the age of seventeen she was the mother of two daughters and was living in a small upstairs flat on Phillip Avenue, a street of frame houses in one of the poor but respectable Detroit neighbourhoods which were white in the 1950s and are black today. At 11:45 on the evening of Sunday, December 12, 1959, her husband, David, was killed on his way back from band practice when his car skidded on a patch of ice entering the Lodge from the Edsel Ford Freeway, and Kathy was a widow at nineteen.

Kathy DuRoss had talent. Cass Tech, the school she had left at fifteen, was noted for the facilities it offered for gifted city children to pursue their artistic specialities.* Kathy DuRoss had been majoring in music. She was an excellent

---

* One of Kathleen King's fellow students at Cass Tech, and a cheer-leader with Kathy for the football team, was Mary Jane Tomlin, who later carved out a show-business career for herself, having changed her Mary Jane to Lily.

violin player, and when she was widowed, her first thought
was to try to make a living as a music teacher.

Modelling, however, proved an easier and more
remunerative path to follow, and for the next fifteen years
Kathy DuRoss worked to support herself and her two daughters, as well as her mother and her mother-in-law, who were
both widowed in the 1960s, through her proficiency on the
runway.

For a drab blue-collar town, Detroit has a surprising call
for models—not the hollow-cheeked, remote, high-fashion
models who parade clothes in *Vogue* and in the glossy magazines, but the rounder, more cheerful, accessible girls who
look so good inside, outside, and alongside a highly polished
motorcar. There is some photographic modelling in this line
of business—exciting dawn encounters with mysteriously
shrouded cars, which are briefly unveiled for the photographer to do his work—but most of the assignments are "live,"
and this was how Kathy DuRoss got started, handing out
brochures. You can do "runway work" (walking around the
cars), "spieling" (walking around them with a microphone),
and "convention work" (which means, essentially, handing
out carnations to the visitors), and Kathy DuRoss applied
herself to every discipline. Shapely, vivacious, and unpreten-
tious, she was popular with her employers and with her
fellow models. She had an uncomplicated nature which
shrugged off difficulties—of which, on the face of it, she had
many.

She had a family to raise, two children to support, and
she had to dress well enough to keep getting jobs. When
work was slack she lived on Social Security.[14] Her rent
was reasonable, because her apartment was the top half
of her parents' house. She took jobs in supermarkets handing out Seven-Up samples if that was the best she could
get.[15]

Kathy DuRoss was one of a group of elegant, amusing
girls who were often to be seen on the arm of prominent
local bachelors and men-between-marriages, and it was in
this capacity that she came to a couple of parties at the

Henry Fords' in the winter of 1969–70—the second time in the company of one of Detroit's consular corps. Mrs. Henry Ford had had some contact with this diplomat in the course of her charitable work, and she did not care for him greatly. He had bad breath, she remembers, and she nicknamed him "Halitoxi."

Cristina Ford's enmity towards "Halitoxi" may not be unconnected with the fact that the gentleman appears to have brought about the fateful meeting of Kathy DuRoss with Henry Ford II. Something about the consul's companion evidently caught the carmaker's eye, for when, a few months later, Max and Marjorie Fisher were arranging a dinner party in their Farmington Hills home, Henry II asked if they could invite, and if he could be placed beside, a model called Kathy DuRoss. In the spring of 1960, Ernest Kanzler's second wife, Rosemarie, had phoned Turin for Cristina. Now, in the autumn of 1970, Marjorie Fisher phoned Kathy DuRoss in Toronto, where she had gone for the weekend.[16]

Cristina was out of town. After a few years of being Mrs. Henry Ford, she had grown somewhat less home-bodied and pasta-cooking. She travelled with her husband, but also, increasingly, she travelled by herself. She went to New York to do her shopping, to London, Paris, or Rome even. In later years this was to become a grievance that her husband threw against her. Henry Ford II came to feel, after the first domestic years of marriage, that his second wife, just like his first, had got far too fond of the perks of her position, and that she deserted him unreasonably on her foreign jaunts. Cristina Ford, for her part, counterattacks with the allegation that her husband actively encouraged her to go away as often as she did, because, from 1970 onwards, it gave him license to pursue his illicit affair with the woman whom she refers to as "Miss Porno."

The affair between Kathy DuRoss and Henry Ford II was certainly well established long before the Santa Barbara incident brought their friendship out into the open. Kathy Ford today refers to the B.C. years—"I always say Before

California and After California"—when she was "sort of like underground."[17]

The B.C. years ran from 1970 to 1975—a long enough stretch in anyone's life. Kathy bought herself a small townhouse in Grosse Pointe, where Henry would visit her, after dark. He had a radio phone installed in her car, so that he could contact her wherever she might be. Friends provided the couple with secluded settings where they could meet. John Bugas, who had suppressed the hurt he felt from his "early retirement" in 1968, had a ranch in Wyoming which he made available for weekends, or even for whole weeks at a time[18]—with the couple always travelling, prudently, on separate planes. When it came to a fur coat for Christmas, Kathy picked out what she fancied, Bugas put it on his credit card, and Henry refunded him in cash.[19]

Afterwards, Cristina realized what had been going on, why her husband would encourage her to go off a few days early before a trip to London, "so you can get the house ready, Bambina, and do some shopping," why, on one cold evening in the middle of winter, when she was packed and all ready to go off to New York for a few days' shopping, he got so angry and frustrated by her last-minute decision to stay at home with him by the fire.[20]

"Think about it," she said some years later. "When married men court women, they tell them their wives don't understand them, that there is no communication, that they've drifted apart because their tastes have become so different. The man is the victim of the *strega* (witch) at home. . . . Time goes by, and history repeats itself."[21]

What is going through the mind of a man who, having made excuses to his wife, or having packed her off on some pretext for a day or so, drives through the darkened streets to another woman, not just on some casual, short-lived fling, but regularly, month after month, year after year—for five years, in fact—so that the deception, the sidestepping, the constantly looking over his shoulder, the saying one thing in one of his lives, and another thing in the other, becomes in itself a way of life? Is he a happy man? Can he operate efficiently at work? What does it say about his ability to cut through day-to-day, real-life confusion to arrive at sharp, unequivocal business decisions?

The 1970s was a turbulent period for the Ford Motor Company. It went through some very dark years in this decade, and it did not emerge from them well prepared for the still darker years of the early 1980s. It was a period of drift outside the company, and of conflict within, when analysts and competitors started sniffing the wind and wondering if the great enterprise might, perhaps, be floundering.

There was certainly reason to flounder, and the next car company down the ladder, the Chrysler Corporation, got into very serious trouble indeed. It was not an easy decade in which to be a carmaker, especially if you were making cars in Detroit. There was the intrusion of government—safety regulations, emission controls, compulsory recalls. There was the challenge from abroad, first from Europe, and then, far more threateningly, from Japan. Most crippling of all, there were the two energy crises, one in the middle and one at the end of the decade.

Inside Ford there were also the special, growing tensions between Henry Ford and Lee Iacocca. There were the safety disasters, the exploding gas tanks—emotionally harrowing and financially such a drain. None of these problems helped Ford's senior management create a long-term strategy for the 1970s or for the years beyond. They soldiered on from crisis to crisis, as best they could, but after a while the weariness began to show—and right at the heart of it all, right in the centre of this company which was so different, yet not so different, from the imperious old autocracy of Henry I, was a man divided, a man who was more lonely and torn than he would admit even to himself.

It is clear from his bitterness, and from the stories that he subsequently spread about Cristina, that Henry Ford II really did believe that his wife was the *strega*, a malign

711

influence who had bewitched him. It was not in his character to ponder his own responsibility for the unhappy situation which he, more than anyone, had created. Nor was it his nature to work through the complicated mechanisms of putting things to rights.

Henry Ford II had painted himself into a corner. After the scandal and comparative messiness of his first divorce, it would be difficult to get rid of his second wife after only half a dozen years or so of marriage, just like that. It could not help but raise questions about his judgement, his assessment of character. As the chairman of a public company, he had to pay some attention to what the share-holders, and the directors, would think. Worse, as head of the family, he was burdened with the Ford name—and, in particular, with the high standards that his mother set for it.

Mrs. Eleanor Ford had been moved to tears by watching the investiture of Prince Charles on television in the summer of 1969.

"It was so beautiful," she told one of the family, "the moment when the mother placed the crown on her son's head—just like me with Henry. Except," she said, and here she frowned, "Henry is not really the same as Prince Charles, is he?"[22]

Still very much alive and the presiding matriarch until 1976, the year of her death, Mrs. Eleanor Ford had gracefully adjusted to her new Italian daughter-in-law. She had even become quite fond of Cristina, and there could be little doubt as to what she would think about her Henry deserting a second wife for the sake of a motor-show girl who came from the wrong side of the tracks.

Faced with different—but not that different—pressures, Henry Ford's grandfather had opted for a double life with Evangeline Dahlinger in the 1920s, and the climax of that double life, the birth in 1923 and early childhood of John Dahlinger, had exactly coincided with the company losing its way in the changed conditions that led to the death of the Model T. Henry Ford I was fifty-nine when John

Dahlinger was born. Henry Ford II was fifty-eight when he decided to leave Cristina for Kathy DuRoss.

No marriage ever breaks down prettily, but the collapse of the relationship between Henry Ford II and his second wife was a particularly ugly affair. Cristina did not prove the answer to Henry II's mid-life restlessness. When Kathy DuRoss started seeing him in the early 1970s, she felt sure that her boyfriend had already indulged in some other extramarital flings.[23] Even while encouraging his wife's absences for the freedom it gave him, Henry II came to brood upon them resentfully. Cristina was spending a lot of time in the company of Imelda Marcos, wife of the then president of the Philippines, and Henry became suspicious that the two women's relationship went beyond mere friend- ship.[24] He was said to have accused his wife of lesbianism, a charge which Cristina indignantly denies.

It was resentment and bitterness beyond measure, and at the root of it lay Henry Ford's feelings that, just like Anne before her, Cristina had got far too fond of being Mrs. Henry Ford. In 1974 Cristina Ford acted as hostess at a high-society benefit at Lincoln Center, New York, in honour of the eightieth birthday of Sol Hurok, the impresario who had done so much for American ballet, and who had, in particu- lar, helped promote exchanges between the leading ballet companies of Russia and America. It was a glittering, black- tie occasion, with television lights and flashbulbs reflecting off all the diamonds that New York can muster on a good night, and Cristina Ford was the centre of attention, over- shadowing even the Onassises, Aristotle and Jackie, who were present.[25]

Afterwards, Cristina realized the awful similarity which the gala could not help but have to the glossy celebrations which her predecessor had worked so hard to organize as the queen of Detroit—chairman of this, chairman of that. But, at the time, Cristina did not reflect unduly on why her husband, standing in the background, should be looking quite so strained and pale, coldly furious.

Henry II sat through the first act with his wife, in the box of honour, but sometime before the end of the performance he vanished.[26]

"Where is Henry?" people asked at the gala party afterwards, and Cristina, who had no more idea than they did, said that he had been taken a little ill and had had to go to his room.

Henry Ford II had, in fact, left the gala and had himself driven straight to the airport, to be flown back to Detroit—and when Cristina finally rejoined her husband in Grosse Pointe, she found that he was still seething.

"Remember you are nothing," he shouted. "You are only somebody because of me. I can throw you out tomorrow."[27]

Early in December 1975, ten months after he had been caught with Kathy DuRoss in Santa Barbara, Henry Ford II phoned his physician, Dr. Richmond Smith of the Henry Ford Hospital, to inquire what the doctor was planning to do over Christmas. Agreeably surprised by his patient's solicitude, Dr. Smith told him he was planning to stay in Grosse Pointe.

"That's good news," replied Henry Ford II.

A week or so later, just a few days before Christmas, Henry II and his wife were packing, ready to go away. They had planned quite an extensive trip, which was to include a visit to Lord Mountbatten, at Broadlands, and Cristina had been looking forward to the holiday as an opportunity for reconciliation. Her husband had vowed to make amends for his misbehaviour in California, and, as he went through her travelling wardrobe with her, Cristina reflected on how well things were going. Henry seemed so attentive, so concerned that she should take the right dresses, and make the best possible impression.

"No, Bambina, I don't like you in that colour," he was saying. "How about this one, or this one?"

When the selection was completed, Henry II considerately suggested that his wife must be tired, and that she should, perhaps, go upstairs to sleep in preparation for the strain of travelling tomorrow. Cristina had gone upstairs, and was getting ready for bed, when she remembered that she had left a newspaper downstairs which she wanted to read. Going downstairs to retrieve it, she was astonished to find her husband dressed to go outside, with a little travelling bag packed, apparently ready to leave the house.

"Henry," she exclaimed, "where are you going at this hour? Is the company burning down?"

Cristina thought, for the moment, that her husband's apparent departure without her must be part of some elaborate joke. But it was not—for having first ventured, half-heartedly, into a feeble excuse, Henry Ford II abandoned pretence, and told his wife the brutal truth, that he was leaving her, then and there, and that he would not be coming back again—ever.

Cristina Ford, a highly strung woman at the best of times, collapsed in hysterics at the news, and her husband went over to the telephone.

The doctor was there in no time.[28]

# 35

## KEYS TO THE KINGDOM

When it was over, Henry explained it all in one of those sayings of his that told so little, and yet so much. "Well," he told Lee Iacocca, "sometimes you just don't like somebody"[1]—and, in one sense, there is really not much more to be said.

Most people have difficulty with this. The world believes —that part of the world, at least, which declines to endorse Lee Iacocca's caricature of Henry Ford II as a total megalomaniac—that there must have been *something*. Henry Ford cannot actually have done what he did, to the mind of any reasonable outsider, unless he had uncovered some discreditable goings on. He must have had *something* on Lee, something so enormous that it just could not be said. It all must be documented, runs this sensible line of thinking, all stashed away somewhere in a top-secret file. It must have been a scandal that implicated other people in the company, that wounded the honour of the company itself, perhaps. Indeed, the honour of the company was one thing which might have caused Henry Ford II to hold his tongue.

But there was no smoking gun. The top-secret file does not exist, because there is no single, easy explanation that can take care of it all in a neat sentence or so. It was, rather, a mass of things, little things which had been building for a long time until they became big things—little things that you can now, with hindsight, look back upon and piece together as parts of an inevitable pattern. It had all the momentum, the sheer inexorability, of a Greek tragedy.

Sometimes you just don't *like* somebody, and if you are Henry Ford II, thinking about who you would choose to carry on the reputation and traditions of your family name, you really do not have to offer anyone a better reason than that.

On December 10, 1970, just fifteen months after the firing of Bunkie Knudsen, Henry Ford II had walked into the office of Lee Iacocca with some very good news. He had decided to put an end to the complicated three-man Office of the President which he had set up in the wake of Bunkie's departure, he told Lee, and he now wanted Iacocca to be the sole and undisputed president of the Ford Motor Company.

"This is the greatest Christmas present I've ever had!" thought Iacocca to himself.

"We just sat there for a moment or two," he was to write in his memoirs fourteen years later, "he with a cigarette and me with a cigar, and blew smoke at each other."

The moment Henry Ford had left the office, Iacocca put through two telephone calls, one to his wife, Mary, and the other to his father, Nicola, down in Allentown.[2] Lee's new promotion left only one position to be crossed off on his little sheet of paper.

Franklin D. Murphy, the affable Irish physician who was chairman of the Times Mirror publishing group in Los Angeles, and who had been one of the outside directors on the board of the Ford Motor Company since 1965, remembers Lee Iacocca once confiding in him about his ultimate ambition.

"You know," he told Murphy, "my only dream back there in Allentown was someday to be the president of the Ford Motor Company."

"Lee," responded Murphy, who liked Iacocca, and who could remember him saying the same thing on at least three occasions, "do you really mean that? You just want to be president, or would you want to be chairman? You are president now, and you don't seem to have achieved what you want."

"I think when I said president," replied Lee Iacocca honestly, "I meant 'run the company.'"[3]

It was by no means an unreasonable ambition—not for someone who had reached Iacocca's position, at least. Even if Henry Ford II did work out his full term, until his sixty-fifth birthday, that would still leave Lee seven or eight years to enjoy the chairmanship—and there was no one else around to do the job.

The newspapers liked to talk about Henry's son, Edsel II, succeeding his father, but everyone knew, Henry II most of all, that that was out of the question, for the time being at least. Edsel had managed to graduate from college with a degree, which was more than his father achieved. But his college career had not been brilliant, and though Edsel might, or might not, make it to the top one day, it would certainly not be by the age of thirty-three, which would be his age in September 1982, the month of his father's sixty-fifth birthday.

Henry had been younger than that when he took over the company, but in those days it had been a private, family enterprise, a totally different situation. Now the Ford Motor Company was one of America's great public corporations, answerable to its shareholders, who had billions of dollars invested in its fortunes, and even if the family did control over 40 percent of the votes, they could not easily force family striplings into executive positions which carried serious power.

Brother Benson, two years younger than Henry, was out of the running by reason of inclination, health, and drinking habits. Brother Bill just was not interested. Bill might take a ceremonial position, so there should always be a Ford on the notepaper or on the podium at shareholder meetings— and that was a very proper status for him. Prudent and canny with his money, Bill had built up his investment in Ford. By 1959, within three years of the company going public, he had had a larger shareholding than Henry,[4] and by 1970 he was, spectacularly, by far the largest individual shareholder in the company, with 1,800,708 Class B shares to Henry's 1,116,292.[5] But Bill had had it with Ford and with serious carmaking. The fate of the Continental Division had killed it for him. Besides, he had his football team.

If Charlotte Ford had been a boy, or if she had come of age in the era of women's lib rather than in the age of debutante parties, she might have been a plausible family candidate, since she was old enough to take over from her father in her mid-forties. But this was all just speculation —might-have-beens. From the moment that Lee Iacocca became president of the Ford Motor Company in December 1970, he was clearly in line to succeed Henry II one day as chairman, the first non-Ford ever to hold the reins of power undisputedly in his hands. The line of the kings would read Henry I, Edsel I, Henry II, and then Lee—with Edsel II, perhaps, resuming the succession thereafter.

The problem was that Henry Ford II did not see things quite this way. In 1972 Lee Iacocca suffered an odd little check to his empire building when his nomination of Hal Sperlich, the talented product planner, to run Ford of Europe, was turned down by Henry II. The chairman preferred Philip Caldwell, a grey, cold-blooded bean counter who had brought the company some success in the unglamorous, but profitable, world of trucks and commercial vehicles, and whose principal distinction was finally to have sorted out the mess at Philco. Henry Ford teamed Caldwell in London with Bill Bourke, a marketing executive who had been on assignment with Ford of Australia, since 1965 and who had, thus, had little opportunity to get infected by the special enthusiasms of Iacocca's own fiercely loyal team.

At the time no one read much into this. Sperlich, an abrasive and erratic character, was by no means the most obvious candidate to run a complex operation like Ford of Europe. Caldwell and Bourke were scarcely Knudsen-sized challenges to Lee Iacocca, and there was no doubt that it was Iacocca who ran the company day to day. Still, it was strange that Henry Ford II could not work up more enthusiasm for his president's future career prospects when the chairman was interviewed, on May 26, 1974, on the Lou Gordon television show on Channel 50 in Detroit.

No one went on the "Lou Gordon Show" just for fun.

HENRY AND LEE

You submitted to the ordeal if you had a public-relations
need to prove that you were tough, or, as was the case with
Henry Ford II, if Gordon cornered you socially, and you
felt that you could not refuse. Gordon was an independently
wealthy man who appeared on television as a hobby, not to
make a living, and this showed in the way he took a meat-axe
to his guests. His special claim to fame was having pressured
George Romney to admit that he had, on a visit to Vietnam,
been "brainwashed"—that single remark bringing Romney's hitherto promising bid for the White House to an
immediate and final halt. When Gordon wanted the answer
to a question, he would go after it like a terrier in pursuit of
a bone, and so it proved when the question of Henry Ford's
possible retirement came up.

"Will Lee Iacocca be the man who will succeed you?"
asked Gordon.

"Well," replied Henry II, sidestepping smartly, "that's
up to the board to make that decision. I can't make that
decision."

Lou Gordon was not buying that.

"I think," he responded drily, "you have a pretty good
amount of influence with the board, haven't you?"

Henry II tried to inveigle his interviewer into a discussion
of the family block vote, ignoring and talking over a repetition of the question about Iacocca. But when he had
finished, Gordon came back at him for a third time.

"I think," responded Henry stoutly, still not giving a
direct answer, "Lee Iacocca is a great fellow. He has done
an excellent job for the company."

Gordon moved in for the kill, and at this, the fourth time
of asking, it just was not possible to sidestep again.

"And you would like to see him succeed you?"

"Yes," responded Henry Ford II weakly. But he did not
look very happy about it.[6]

Lee was just so damn lordly. Everyone remarked on it.
He just could not wait. Anyone would think he was chairman
already to see him arrive at the car show—a line of people

720

to meet him, long limousines full of aides, men in raincoats mumbling mysteriously into walkie-talkies. Even the stewardesses noticed it on the company planes. Mr. Ford was usually happy with just his sandwich and the fruit basket. In fact, he seemed to prefer it like that. But for Mr. Iacocca it had to be the best linen, the china, the silverware.[7]

It was partly a matter of history, of cultural background —the difference between a first-generation American, the son of immigrants, and a scion of the third generation, who was born into money and could look back on his family's getting off the boat from the relative comfort and distance of 130 years. When Lee went to the Chop House, he had to have table number one. Henry II was quite content with one of the less prominent banquettes around the side— which sounded modest and unassuming, but which said nothing at all, in fact, about the relative sizes of the two men's egos. It just showed that Henry had learned to hide his better.

Lee Iacocca has come to be quite candid about his love of the good life, the fine wines, the big cigars. "I enjoyed being president," he wrote in his memoirs. "I liked having the president's perks, the special parking place, the private bathroom, the whitecoated waiters."[8]

In fact, the waiters who minister to the needs of Ford's senior executives and outside directors on the topmost floor of Ford's World Headquarters in Dearborn wear black coats, not white. It is rather difficult for an outsider to distinguish them from the executives they serve—and there are a number of other discrepancies in Lee Iacocca's memories of his life at Ford.

He tells a tale, for example, of luxury hamburgers, ground up especially for Henry Ford II from an inch-thick New York strip steak, and he gives the impression that this was a particular and unique indulgence of the Ford chairman.[9] But, in reality, the strip steak was routinely ground whenever an executive requested a hamburger on the thirteenth floor —and his colleagues remember that Lee Iacocca requested one more often than most. Indeed, it was precisely so that he could have the same hamburgers prepared for him at home that he requested the chef to reveal his recipe.

Slightly more costly for the Ford balance sheet was the saga of the 727. In his memoirs, Iacocca alleges that this plane, a Boeing acquired from a Japanese airline, was converted by Henry II into a personal luxury cruiser for his trips to Europe, and that he was so annoyed by Iacocca using it on company business that he had the jet sold, at a loss, to the Shah of Iran.[10]

In reality, the plane was earmarked for Iacocca's use, rather than Henry II's. Rationally or not, Henry II always refused to cross the Atlantic on anything less than four engines, and the 727 only had three. Gene Bordinat, who was given the job of redesigning the aircraft, remembers working specifically to Iacocca's instructions, so that the plane ended up a very definite reflection of the president's own taste—from double bed to the gold-plated plumbing.[11]

Just the thing for the Shah of Iran.

"Henry got rid of that aeroplane," says his English friend David Metcalfe, "because it was the only way he could stop Iacocca going round the world in the bloody thing."[12]

People who have worked with Lee Iacocca will regale you with countless stories like this. In the thirty-nine boxes of correspondence which Lee Iacocca left behind on his departure from Ford can be found letters requesting Philco television sets and air conditioners to be despatched cheap to his friends, the commissioning of special Mustang cufflinks, letters to accompany autographed covers of *Time* magazine, and a thick file regarding Mr. Iacocca's personal desires for his presidential office—a large number of these being requests that he should be provided with comforts and styling touches which he had noticed in Benson Ford's office down the corridor.[13]

This is petty stuff. Company executives have been known to award themselves more lavish perks. In August 1975, the Ford Motor Company was to commission a most thorough and costly inquiry into the expenses of its senior executives, and, as Lee Iacocca correctly states in his memoirs, "the investigation failed to turn up a single damaging item about me or my people."[14]

The point is that it got under Henry Ford's skin. He had always been extremely generous to his top executives—high salaries, big bonuses, no quibbling about expenses. No car man in Detroit got a better deal than Lee. Iacocca was paid more, even, than the president of General Motors,[15] and by 1973 he was, like Bunkie Knudsen, being remunerated at exactly the same level as Henry II himself ($275,000 salary with a bonus of $590,000). But Iacocca had to push it—get his Mark III "personalized," take his wife and daughters on that plane, fly down to Allentown to see his parents— act like a Ford, in fact. And a Ford was something that Lee Iacocca could never be.

Henry Ford II might not have worried so much about the imperial style of the Iacocca presidency if it had not been for the friends that Lee chose to share it with. It placed a question mark over Iacocca's judgement, in his opinion, and Henry Ford had particular reservations about Bill Fugazy.

"Aren't you afraid of Fugazy?" Henry one day asked Paul Bergmoser, Ford's chief of purchasing, who handled the details of Fugazy's travel deals. "Aren't you scared of ending up in the East River with a pair of cement boots?"[16]

He was still more outspoken to Iacocca himself, who even recalls Ford as saying, "I think he's mixed up with the Mafia," brushing off Iacocca's vigorous denials. "He's got a limousine company. Limousine and trucking companies are always Mafia fronts."[17]

Henry Ford II had a thing about the Mafia. He got most upset on one occasion when he suspected that a girlfriend of his son Edsel's might come from a family with Mafia connections.[18] Many of the gangsters with whom Harry Bennett consorted had been Italians, members of the Black Hand, precursor of the Cosa Nostra. Cleaning Bennett and the gangsters out of Ford had been one of Henry II's great achievements, and it would not be much of a climax to his career to hand the company back to a similar sort of setup.

Given the troubles that Henry II was also having with his Italian wife in the early and middle 1970s, Lee Iacocca's ethnic origin was no help to him whatsoever as he sought to convert his presidency into the eventual chairmanship of the Ford Motor Company—and his cause was not advanced by a friendship with another Italian whom Henry II grew to dislike as much as he disliked Fugazy: Alejandro de Tomaso.

De Tomaso was the owner of the Ghia car-design studios in Turin. Faced with the challenge of imports from Europe in the 1960s, all the Detroit companies teamed up with European "skunk works" who could throw out ideas, get prototypes built in a hurry, and generally ginger up the design studios back home. Today the Motor City has forged similar links with car customizers and designers on the West Coast, which is, geographically, just about as close as Americans can get to Japan, and where designers might also be expected to be in tune with the latest trends in California, the marketplace of tomorrow.

De Tomaso was an Italian who had grown up in Argentina—hence the spelling of his Christian name—and his company, Ghia, had other Latin American links. The design studio had come to prominence in the early sixties while financed by Leonidas Ramadas Trujillo,[19] son of the dictator of the Dominican Republic, and it developed a profitable sideline in armour-plated limousines, some of which it sold to Generalissimo Franco.[20] Alejandro de Tomaso fitted neatly into this scheme of things by employing, for his private plane, the onetime personal pilot of Benito Mussolini.[21]

De Tomaso was a racing driver who had started making it as a businessman in the early sixties after his marriage to Elizabeth Haskell, a handsome blonde from Red Bank, New Jersey, who stood a head taller than Alejandro, and who was both a racing driver and an heiress. Elizabeth, his second wife, changed her name to the more Italian-sounding Isabelle, and she persuaded her family company, Rowan Controller Industries, of Oceanport, New Jersey, to stake de Tomaso in Ghia. When two directors of Rowan, one of them a Haskell, died in a private plane crash in 1970, de Tomaso went to Ford and got them to take an 84 percent interest in Ghia and the other enterprises he had pieced together, including the Turin coach builders Vignale.

Lee Iacocca seems to have got to know de Tomaso through Carroll Shelby, the Texan racing driver who had himself built up a thriving motoring business through spicing up standard production cars—notably the Ford Mustang and the handsome British A.C. Roadster. Powered by a Ford V-8, much breathed upon and tweaked by Shelby, the A.C. Cobra became a classic in its own time, and de Tomaso decided to match the Cobra with a car of his own, named, with Rikki-Tikki-Tavian echoes, the Mangusta, or Mongoose.

Mid-engined, which means that the exhaust manifold is roaring somewhere just behind your left ear, the Mangusta was a beautiful car: sleek, graceful, long, and low. Straight out of a James Bond fantasy, it was one of the archetypal cars of the 1960s, worthy of visual comparison with a Lamborghini. Its engineering, however, was appalling. The clutch was heavy, the windows would not wind right down, the handling was treacherous, the braking was poor, and the rear vision almost nonexistent.[22]

The Mangusta was a fine example of why so few of the beautiful "concept cars" that you see revolving on stands at motor shows ever actually make it into full production on the road. Turning an attractive design concept into a machine which is safe and reliable for an ordinary member of the public to drive without a crash helmet is a great deal more complicated than might be imagined—and it is, of course, what the serious automobile business is all about.

It is not certain whether Alejandro de Tomaso has ever fully realized this, and in the late 1960s Lee Iacocca also appears to have been blinded by the sheer beauty of the Mangusta. Shrugging off the car's engineering deficiencies, he agreed that de Tomaso would build a similar car, to be known as the Pantera (or Panther), to be sold through Lincoln-Mercury dealers in the United States. It would be an exotic, two-door sports car to compete with GM's Corvette, and it was anticipated that sales could be as high as 10,000 units per year.

Iacocca seems to have imagined, or to have picked up the idea from de Tomaso, that a quick reworking by a handful of Ford engineers could turn the Mangusta into a "Ford-Ferrari" which would meet all the engineering standards implied by those proud names—not to mention the U.S. Federal Safety Standards. Iacocca visited Ghia in August 1969, and less than six months later, at the New York Motor Show of January 1970, Ford was displaying a prototype of the Pantera that it was planning to market in 1971. Looking very similar to the Mangusta, the car had, in theory, been completely reengineered beneath the skin—and it boasted an exotic-looking power unit, though this was, in fact, the standard Ford 351 V-8 engine, shipped from its Cleveland engine plant to Turin, where mechanics removed the blue Ford-embossed tappet covers from the top and screwed down black and magnesium replacements that bore the de Tomaso name.[23]

The Pantera went from prototype to production in less than nine months—and it showed. The car was crash-tested in California, and, remembers Tom Tjaarda, its designer, "the front wheels ended up under the driver's seat."[24] The photographs of these tests are today missing from the Ghia archives in Turin, but the files of the National Highway Traffic Safety Administration, Office of Defects, in Washington, do contain some interesting data on the de Tomaso–Ford Pantera:

—Possibility that crossmember at steering gear mounting may crack. If not corrected, could eventually cause separation of gear mounting, resulting in possible loss of steering. . . .
—Possibility that front brake hose is incorrectly located and may chafe against small lip in front fender well. If condition exists, could result in loss of hydraulic pressure in one of two hydraulic systems, and impair braking efficiency. . . .
—Possibility that brake pedal stop was omitted in production, which could lead to progressive build-up of hydraulic pressure. . . .

May cause over heating which could impair braking performance. . . .
—Possibility that fuel tank could develop cracks in seams, permit-
ting fuel leakage. If condition develops could present possible fire
hazard. . . . [25]

Alejandro de Tomaso seems to have been less concerned
with details like these. Questioned by Ford engineers during
one visit to Dearborn about the Pantera's rear suspension,
which had the ugly habit of hitting the road, de Tomaso
replied, "What do I know about that? I'm just an artist."

That afternoon he met with the artists of the design studio,
who complained at the deficiencies of the interior layout.
"What do I know of that?" the Italian responded. "I'm only
an engineer!"[26]

When cornered by the press about the Federal Safety
Standards which were, eventually, to remove the Pantera
from the U.S. marketplace, de Tomaso shrugged his
shoulders.

"If a guy has the money to afford to pay the insurance,"
he said, "he should be allowed to buy such cars."[27]

If the de Tomaso Pantera had sold in North America in
anything like the numbers of the Pinto, it would have been
another disaster for Ford. But it was, fortunately, aimed at
a smaller market, and the problems which the car caused
for itself had a self-containing effect. In 1971 Ford sold 130
Panteras, in 1972 just 1,552. The peak year for the car which
had been scheduled to sell 10,000 units annually came in
the twelve months of 1973, when Lincoln-Mercury dealers
managed to off-load 2,033. In 1974 the car sold 712, and
that was the end of it. Since the vehicle could not possibly
meet the five-miles-per-hour bumper-impact standards
about to come into effect, the car was taken off the market
before 1975, when Ford, keeping the Ghia studios for itself,
had already severed its connection with de Tomaso.

Which was not quite the end of the story. "Ghia" remains
the name for the top-of-the-line trim package on English
Fords. Alejandro de Tomaso was, later, to intervene in a
surprising fashion in Lee Iacocca's battle with Henry Ford

II—and when Iacocca went on to Chrysler, one of the first things he did, once his cash flow permitted, was to sign an agreement with his old friend Alejandro, which enabled de Tomaso to take control of Maserati and build specialty sports cars for Chrysler.

The Pantera, meanwhile, still produced in small quantities in Europe, lives on in the memory of automobile aficionados as the sporting motorist's Edsel. David Benson, the motoring correspondent of the London *Daily Express*, recalls driving a Pantera at 125 miles per hour on one occasion in Switzerland, with Jackie Stewart, the racing driver, and his wife, Helen, when the entire airconditioning system of the car dropped into the front passenger compartment, thus misting the windows and making driving somewhat hazardous.

And David Benson's favourite memory is of driving, again with Jackie Stewart, in a Pantera along the Corniche, in the south of France, with Alejandro de Tomaso himself driving in a car behind. Suddenly all the electrics of the Pantera failed—the lights, the electric windows, and even the electric door locks, which were a futuristic feature of the car. With a great deal of effort, working from the outside, it took de Tomaso nearly an hour to get Benson and Stewart out.[28]

Shortly before Henry Ford II had raised Lee Iacocca to the company presidency in December 1970, he had taken the young executive along to 1100 Lakeshore to meet his mother.

"She never really got directly involved in the affairs of the company," says Bill Ford, who was present at the meeting. "It was a pretty broad-brush approach, mainly to do with the tradition of having a family member at the helm."[29]

Mrs. Eleanor had arranged a cocktail party for Iacocca —though he was not informed that it had been staged specially in his honour. There were some members of the Ford board and some old-time executives whose histories went back to the time of Edsel I, and Mrs. Eleanor greeted the would-be president glowing at full wattage. That was her speciality.

Lee Iacocca was quite bowled over by it, and the experience seems to have inspired in him the belief that he had, from that moment onwards, a particular and very important ally upholding his cause at the heart of the Ford family. He confided this to the author Victor Lasky,[30] and in his memoirs he even ventured to suggest that it was only after the death of Mrs. Eleanor, in 1976, that Henry Ford II had dared to move against him.

He was quite mistaken. Mrs. Eleanor was surely very polite to the would-be president that day on Lakeshore Road. She was warm and charming to everybody. It was her way. But no one in the family or among her friends can remember her ever afterwards acknowledging any special interest in the bright Italian-American—or even much awareness of his existence. He was Henry's responsibility, and William Clay Ford, who was Iacocca's strongest supporter among the Fords, remembers his mother being faintly disparaging about the aspiring chief executive.

"You don't have to worry," she said to Bill, taking his arm and drawing him aside at one stage of the party. "He'll take the job."[31]

The misunderstanding goes to the heart of the ambiguity on which Lee Iacocca's ambition was to founder—the particular ambiguity of working for Ford—for his story is not a simple tale of business ambition first encouraged and then thwarted. If the young Iacocca had simply wanted to be a senior executive in a car company, he could have gone to General Motors or to Chrysler—which was bigger than Ford at the time that Iacocca was recruited.

But Iacocca chose Ford. He chose it because the name meant something special to him, and he rose to be president because, until he became president, Mr. Ford had liked him.

Having made it that far, however, Lee Iacocca had reached a stage where his next move involved more than a simple promotion. To take over Ford as chairman, 100 percent, he either had to become Ford-like in some way himself, or else avoid being any threat to the firm's Ford identity—and it was this final hurdle that he suddenly faced in the early weeks of 1976 when Henry Ford II started getting chest pains.

Marian Heiskell, nee Sulzberger, a member of the family owning the *New York Times*, of which she is herself a director, joined the board of the Ford Motor Company in the spring of 1976, just a few months after Henry II's angina pectoris was diagnosed. Mrs. Heiskell was the first woman ever to be elected to the Ford Motor Company board. The token black, Dr. Clifton R. Wharton, Jr., had gone on in 1973.

Charlotte Ford had been nagging her father for a long time to name a woman director—she did not want the job for herself—but her father, an unapologetic male chauvinist, had taken some convincing. In the end it was board pressure which compelled Henry II to yield, and that raised all sorts of practical questions.

Henry Ford II had given some thought to his directors and their comfort when he had been planning Ford's twelve-storey World Headquarters in Dearborn in the early 1950s. Right up on top of the building he had a long, low penthouse constructed, in effect a thirteenth floor, and into it went the top-executive dining room, with roof garden and view to Detroit, and various entertaining facilities. Squeezed right up into the roof of the penthouse on a further, mezzanine, fourteenth floor, was a row of little bedrooms in which the visiting directors could stay.

It was more a matter of convenience than expense. Putting the outside directors into the Dearborn Inn when they came on the second Thursday of every month would involve cars, drivers, fetching, and carrying—inevitable delays. It made much more sense to have them all sleep in above the shop. So, right up in the roof of the Glasshouse, the outside directors' sleeping cubicles and built-in bathrooms were lined up together, side by side, along the length of a dark, narrow, muffled corridor—rather like the sleeping compartments on the Orient Express.

The imminent arrival of Mrs. Heiskell in this previously all-male preserve provoked some anxious questions. Would it not, perhaps, be more proper if she slept across the road, in the recently constructed Hyatt in the Fairlane development? In the end, sense prevailed, and Mrs. Heiskell was welcomed up, with her toothbrush, to the fourteenth floor—though she does remember, from her very first visit, a floral centrepiece in the dining room, which does not seem to have been repeated since.[32]

"Ford looks after you very elegantly," she says. "Cars to meet you at the airport, people to make sure that you never get lost. I have never been more cared for in my life than when I go out to Detroit."[33]

Mrs. Heiskell was struck by the almost collegial atmosphere of life on Ford's thirteenth and fourteenth floors. Having directors fly in the night before board meetings to eat together and then to relax and talk after dinner made for an intimate, integrated sort of camaraderie. The committee meetings started about five—Organization Review, Finance, Compensation, and Option, all finalizing proposals for the main board meeting next day. Then the evening became more informal, with directors sitting down together to carry on their discussions, share their worries, or just gossip.

It was in this wood-panelled, armchaired setting on Ford's thirteenth floor that was played out, from 1976 to 1978, the dramas that were to decide Lee Iacocca's fate.

"I think," remembers Marian Heiskell, "that Henry wanted to get rid of him from the first time I ever set foot in the place."[34]

As she took her seat for her very first meeting as a director of the Ford Motor Company, Marian Heiskell was surprised to hear the company chairman proposing to fire the famous and dynamic president whom the outside world generally credited with some of the company's most notable successes. Not quite sure of the etiquette of the thirteenth floor, Marian Heiskell had wandered into all the committees that were meeting that evening in March 1976, even those committees to which she did not belong, and the sitting directors were too polite to turn her away. She was, however, a member of the Organization Review Committee, and here she found herself listening to Henry Ford, who, as committee president, was reporting on his recent heart trouble and the questions which that raised about his succession. If he was mildly incapacitated, the top ranks of the company could be reorganized in such-and-such a way. If his health problem proved more serious, then perhaps a different set of arrangements should be tried.

Listening to all the hypothetical arguments, the new member of the board tried to inject some womanly common sense into the debate.

"I found myself saying, 'Well, why don't we talk about your health first, and then worry about the rest of the things after that?'" she remembers. "I guess I sort of instinctively felt that first things came first."[35]

It was clear to Mrs. Heiskell that Henry Ford's heart trouble had scared him quite considerably. He did not seem to be thinking or talking as a man who had very long to live. "He was worried that he was going to drop dead tomorrow," she remembers.[36]

One of her fellow directors, Dr. Franklin Murphy, who had known Henry II for more than a decade, got the very same impression. "It scared the hell out of him," Murphy remembers, "it really did"[37]—and as an old friend and confidant, Murphy fancied that he understood the background to the trouble.

"Problem number one," he says, "was the woman problem. The Italian girl to whom he was married was a very difficult person, to say the very least, and he'd been getting some rather unsavoury stories back about her, and some of her friends, and some of her travels, and this and that. He had, apparently, simultaneously fallen in love with his current wife, Kathy. So he was going through this difficult kind of business knowing that he would have to go through a divorce, and that this divorce would be a messy

divorce. . . . And then, right in the middle of all this, the
company started losing tons of money. The industry is in
chaos. The company is being criticized for making shoddy
goods, with all these lawsuits. And then, he learns he has a
heart problem. Well, you can imagine, these things just all
came down on him like a ton of bricks. . . ."[38]

Franklin Murphy greatly admired Lee Iacocca. He knew
that his fellow directors felt the same, and today Murphy
has no doubt, looking back on those early months of 1976,
that if Henry Ford II had indeed dropped dead as he feared,
then the board would have turned to Iacocca by a 60:40
vote, and probably 70:30, to make him chief executive officer
of the company.[39] The idea of getting rid of the talented
and visible president at the very moment that Henry II was
incapacitated struck Murphy, and all the other directors, as
he remembers, as quite out of the question.

"Lee was a strong and vital person," says Murphy "very
visible in the industry. . . . We all felt that the last thing we
needed was a public explosion where the president is either
fired, or quits, or there's a lot of acrimony, and so on."[40]

As the outside directors on the Organization Review
Committee defended Lee Iacocca, Henry Ford II was notably short of specific complaints he could make against his
president, and he was already falling back on the form of
words that was later to become his refrain.

"No," says Marian Heiskell today in response to a specific
list of grievances which Henry Ford might have raised
against Iacocca in the spring of 1976. "He did not go into
that, he did not. . . . He just bluntly said, 'I don't really like
him. I don't like him. I don't want him working for me.' It
was his gut feeling."[41]

In view of the momentous step he was proposing, it was
strange that Henry Ford II could not actually come up with
any concrete reasons for dismissing Lee Iacocca—and it
was dismissal, board members remember quite distinctly,
that the chairman had in mind. When Marian Heiskell
arrived in Dearborn in March 1976, Henry II was not
talking about demotion or shifting his president sideways.

He wanted Lee Iacocca right out of the company—and this was because he had seriously come to believe in the imminence of his own death. Plain retirement was not a problem. He could have kept control of things from a seat on the board and membership of a few key committees. But Henry Ford II knew that if he died, then Ford would be Lee's.

In his memoirs, Lee Iacocca portrays the outside directors of the Ford Motor Company as a troupe of puppets, dancing as their master twitched the strings. He even goes so far as to suggest that Henry Ford II bribed his directors by increasing their fees, thus securing their compliance in his removal of Iacocca.

Like a number of other statements in Lee Iacocca's autobiography, this gives too much importance to Lee Iacocca. Ford's non-employee directors did receive pay rises in the years when Henry II was trying to get rid of Iacocca, but these were intended to keep pace with the sharp inflation of those years, and did not even accomplish that. In the thirty years since the company went public, the total pay rises to Ford's directors have worked out at $500 per year—a simple annual rate of 2 percent.[42]

The more serious accusation, however, is against a group of men, and one woman, who appreciated and sincerely admired Lee Iacocca's finer qualities—if not all his qualities —and who worked systematically to defend his cause.

"I think," says Marian Heiskell, "that we did slow Henry for a couple of years ... from knocking Lee off right away. . . ." She can remember working with a group of three or four other directors to defend Iacocca and to preserve his talents for the company. "You can't take away the fact," she says, "that Lee is an exceedingly fine automobile man."[43]

Dr. Franklin Murphy rated Iacocca particularly highly, and amid the general anxiety about Henry II's health, he felt that the Ford president was worthy of some concern as well. Murphy had been noticing how badly Lee Iacocca had been reacting to the vibrations he could sense coming from his boss. The president knew that something was up. He was becoming very tense, and as the two top men in the company started to jar on each other more and more obviously, Franklin Murphy felt it was his duty, as a senior director, to try to heal the breach.

Since he was trained as a physician, Dr. Murphy also felt that he had some special skills that he could bring to the job, so, as he now remembers it, he started including a little counselling and mediation in his monthly duties in Dearborn.

"I took it upon myself," he says, "with the encouragement of most of my fellow directors, to be a kind of psychiatrist to some of the residents. . . ."[44]

On April 14, 1977, Henry Ford II summoned a news conference to explain an important reorganization he was undertaking at the head of the Ford Motor Company. He revealed that, on the advice of McKinsey and Company, the management consultants, he had decided to create a new, three-man Office of the Chief Executive to run the company. Henry II would remain chairman, and Lee Iacocca would remain president. But now they were to be joined at the top by Philip Caldwell, who was back from a most successful tour of duty with Ford of Europe. Caldwell, announced Henry, would henceforward hold the freshly created position of vice-chairman, and as he made this announcement, Caldwell and Iacocca sat on the podium on either side of him.

Asked whether this new arrangement had been his own brainchild, Henry II replied that the three-man device had been the result of the research of McKinsey in pursuit of better management. But this was disingenuous. Henry's last triumvirate after the fall of Bunkie Knudsen had been a political device, and so was this. If he did not want Iacocca as a successor, Henry had to produce an alternative, and his Office of the Chief Executive was his way of doing this.

What would happen when Henry II was away? the reporters wanted to know. Who would be captain of the ship?

The question did not arise, replied Henry Ford, because he could be contacted wherever he was in the world.

But what if he was ill? the questioners persisted.

Well, came the response, in that situation the Office of the Chief Executive would contain just two men, for the time being, instead of three.

And which of those two men, for the time being, had final authority?

Henry Ford II could evade the issue no longer.

"Philip Caldwell," he responded.

The sudden elevation of Philip Caldwell in the spring of 1977 brought the battle between Henry Ford II and Lee Iacocca out into the open.

"It was a real crack in the face," remembers Lee Iacocca in his memoirs, selecting a singular example of how it really hurt. "Every time there was a dinner, Henry hosted table one, Caldwell hosted table two, and I was shoved down to three. It was public humiliation."[45]

The boardroom psychiatrist found his work cut out for him. Franklin Murphy would arrive in Dearborn to find desperate notes from Iacocca waiting for him. "Please come and see me. What's happening here? They're trying to crucify me!"[46]

Murphy would find Iacocca pacing up and down in his office—"I mean, his fists on the table, and almost in semi-hysteria."[47]

This was the other side of the driving ego which had accomplished so much for Ford, and for Lee Iacocca. His subordinates had learned to live with it, to find ways around their boss's pride. Whenever Gene Bordinat disagreed with Iacocca, he never voiced his dissent in front of others, or even in typewritten memorandum form.

"If it was typewritten," he says, "Lee knew that someone, my secretary, had to have seen it. So I would write my thoughts down, in my own handwriting, on sheets from a yellow legal pad. Then he could tell it was private, and if there was no risk of losing face he might just be prepared to bend."⁴⁸

The Iacocca ego, first laid bare by the killing of Bunkie, had come to lie at the heart of Henry Ford II's doubts about his one-time protégé. Today Iacocca himself likes to discourse long and learnedly on the difference between a "strong" ego, which is constructive and healthy, and a "large" ego, which is destructive and sick.⁴⁹ He claims to know the difference, and he is quite confident that his errs on the side of healthiness.

Others are not so sure. In a bizarre aftermath to the murders of Sharon Tate and her friends in Los Angeles in 1969, the FBI circulated a hit list of other possible victims selected by the Manson cult, and a number of Ford senior executives happened to figure on it. This had caused general merriment in the Glasshouse, since the list seemed to have been culled indiscriminately from a business directory. But Lee Iacocca took the list seriously and shortly afterwards disclosed that there was another, more exclusive list of really important victims, on which his name also figured—and on the basis of which, he decided it would not be prudent for him to attend a forthcoming Ford sales meeting in San Francisco. In the end, after much executive time had been consumed discussing the dangers of the president visiting California, Iacocca went. But the walkie-talkie men were out in greater numbers than ever, and Iacocca's speech to the assembled Ford dealers was not, finally, delivered by him personally. He got an aide to stand up on the podium and read it for him.

Lee Iacocca's paranoia went into overdrive in the latter months of 1977. Telling Marian Heiskell a story about how once, by accident, he had bumped his head on a car door, he informed her that, at the moment the accident happened, he had assumed he had been shot.⁵⁰

On the other hand, there certainly was somebody persecuting Lee Iacocca in the mid-1970s, and it was a pretty big somebody at that. Henry Ford II wanted to drive his president right out of the Ford Motor Company, and

737

Iacocca's accusation in his memoirs, that his employer was engaged in "salami-slicing"[51]—cutting off one part of his body after another until Iacocca would finally be driven to admit defeat—is not that far from the truth. The elevation of Philip Caldwell was part of that.

"I think," says Franklin Murphy, "Henry's theory was Lee would get mad and quit, and [that] this was an easy way of firing somebody."[52]

It did not prove so easy, however, since Lee Iacocca fought back. He had got rid of Knudsen in 1969, and compared to Bunkie, Philip Caldwell was pretty small beer. Caldwell did not even possess the total confidence of Henry Ford, for celebrating *his* elevation, the hitherto modest bean counter put in requisitions for a magnificent new office that would have cost the best part of $100,000.[53]

Guerrilla warfare escalated to open confrontation as 1977 advanced. By the end of the year, Iacocca and Caldwell were scarcely speaking to each other, and their staffs took their cue from that.

"It was hell," remembers Tom Feaheny, then vice-president in charge of engineering. "There were Iacocca's men and Caldwell's men. They would come to you separately, trying to advance their own projects, trying to get ammunition."[54]

It was like the Bunkie Knudsen battles all over again—except that this time Henry Ford himself was entering the fray. He picked off lieutenants of Iacocca's: Hal Sperlich, his product planner, fired in 1976, and Paul Bergmoser, in charge of purchasing, who was given "early retirement" in 1977. Bergmoser did all the Ford business with Bill Fugazy, and Henry II attacked in that direction as well. He ordered that all Ford contracts with Fugazy should be terminated.

It was open war, and Lee Iacocca had no illusions as to who his real enemy was. He could skirmish with Philip Caldwell as long as he liked, but if he wanted to come out the serious and ultimate victor, he would have to set his sights higher than that. Lee Iacocca would have to take on Henry Ford II himself.

# 36

## SAY IT ISN'T SO

It started in quite a small way, an obscure case in New York County: Clayton H. Donnelly and others versus Fugazy Continental, Fugazy All-City RentaCar, and the Ford Motor Company.*

Clayton H. Donnelly and others were limousine drivers, and the case stemmed from Henry Ford II's severing of connections between Ford and William Fugazy. This had hurt Bill Fugazy, but it had also hurt the limousine drivers who operated under his franchise. They had, in particular, lost the insurance cover which Ford had once provided for their rented Lincoln and Mercury limousines, and on January 31, 1978, the drivers brought suit against both Ford and Fugazy.

In theory, Ford and Fugazy stood accused together. But Ford's Wall Street attorneys, Hughes Hubbard and Reed, soon got an uneasy feeling about their supposed partner. Bill Fugazy might be listed on Ford's side in the case, but somehow the papers submitted by his attorneys contained statements whose net effect was to embarrass Ford.[2] As for Clayton H. Donnelly and others who had, through mechanisms unspecified, spontaneously abandoned the traditional individualism of the taxi and limousine driver to bring this joint suit, it was surprising that they should have had the contacts and the funds to retain the services of a prominent Manhattan law firm, Saxe Bacon and Bolan —whose dynamic senior partner was Roy M. Cohn, the childhood chum and best friend of Bill Fugazy, whom the limousine drivers were suing.

* Also named in the suit as codefendants with Ford and Fugazy were Liberty Mutual, the insurance company involved, and Country Lincoln-Mercury, the dealership through which the limousines were rented.[1]

The limousine case petered out early in May 1978, but by that time the attack had become more direct. On April 24, 1978, Roy M. Cohn himself lodged papers with the Supreme Court of the State of New York, County of New York, against Henry Ford II, the Ford Motor Company, and the entire Ford board of directors accusing them of "an illegal and fraudulent conspiracy . . . to divert to themselves or to persons with whom they were or are associated, the assets of the Company, and wrongfully, illegally, and fraudulently to use the said assets of the Company for their own selfish, personal interests, advantage, and profit."[3]

Roy Cohn had cut his legal teeth as an aide to Senator McCarthy in the 1950s when, only a few years out of law school, he had become nationally notorious as the baleful young man who whispered conspiratorially into the senator's ear. McCarthy's witchhunts in the 1950s had been masterpieces of smear and innuendo, but in April 1978, Cohn appeared to have some very detailed evidence to justify the sensational allegations he was bringing against Henry Ford.

The opening paragraphs of his first complaint, front-page news in both the *New York Times* and *Wall Street Journal* at the end of April 1978, accused Henry Ford II of boasting that he had all the outside directors of the Ford Motor Company "in his pocket," and that he bought their loyalty and obedience "with large pay . . . and with Dom Perignon champagne."[4] Henry II, Cohn alleged, had compelled the company to pay more than a million dollars towards his occasional residence in "a six room duplex cooperative apartment at the Carlyle Hotel, New York, New York," and the attorney had some telling details to indicate he might know what he was talking about. This apartment, he alleged, was unavailable and off-limits to ordinary Ford officials, and was lavishly furnished with Louis XV antiques, which included "a tulip wood desk valued at $82,000 and a chest of drawers valued at $31,000."[5]

Picking on Henry II's friendship with Pat de Cicco, a businessman who was a duck-shooting companion of the

Ford chairman, Cohn alleged that Henry II had given de Cicco's catering company, Canteen Corp., "an exclusive concession to provide food and beverages at the Company's various offices and factories, in exchange for approximately $750,000.00 in illegal and improper 'kickbacks'"[6]—and Cohn made similar allegations against Henry II's brother-in-law, Walter Ford, whose design company had been given contracts by the Ford Motor Company. According to Cohn, Walter Ford had paid for this business favour by supplying furniture and furnishings for Henry II's private homes.[7]

The damaging thing about all Cohn's accusations—none of which he was ever to prove in open court and which he was, in fact, to drop less than two years later—was that they all contained elements of plausibility. Henry Ford II had maintained an apartment in the Carlyle Hotel for his use while he was in New York, and the company reimbursed him when he stayed there on company business. Pat de Cicco's company did have some catering contracts with Ford—they supplied vending machines—and Walter Ford's design partnership had quite often carried out design work for the Ford Motor Company. Among their commissions had been the remodelling of Lee Iacocca's office.

The important question was whether Henry Ford II had had improper involvement in any of these transactions, exploiting them for his own private profit. The thrust of Cohn's attack against Henry II was exactly that of Henry II against Iacocca and Bill Fugazy: favouritism, the abuse of company power, and the warping of business judgement through friendship.

Cohn's attack on the Ford chairman, however, went a stage beyond Henry II's campaign against Iacocca. Henry had launched his inquiry into Iacocca's business dealings, and, having discovered nothing criminal, he had made no accusations. Cohn took suspicion and gossip and formalized them into allegations just the same. He produced no solid documentary evidence for his charges, but in these post-Watergate years he did not need to. If Henry II was powerful, he must be wrong.

On May 2, 1978, Henry Ford called a press conference in Dearborn to answer Cohn's allegations, and he was visibly angry. The Ford chairman threw "Never Complain, Never Explain" to the winds.

"I have been criticized for a lot of things in my life," he said, "and most of the time I just don't pay any attention to what is said or printed about me. . . . But I am not going to wait for court processes to clear my name. I have nothing to hide and that's why I'm here to meet this personal affront head on."[8]

The gist of Henry II's defence was that, having established his reputation by cleaning corruption out of the company when he took it over, and having run it ever since as a matter of personal and family pride, he was hardly likely to indulge in relatively petty improprieties that could only sully his own name. He was the man who had chosen to take the company public and to make his own conduct publicly accountable in 1956. Friends did sometimes ask him for business favours, he said, and when they did, he told them that he could not offer them any special deals. It would make nonsense of a lifetime's work to do otherwise. Answering every question from the assembled journalists fully and without evasion, Henry Ford II could fairly be judged to have cleared his name.

The problem was that Henry II was up against no ordinary adversary in Roy M. Cohn. With his hooded eyelids and scarred face set in an almost perpetual scowl, Roy Cohn looked a tough character—and he was. He had amply demonstrated his mastery of legal infighting in the defence of such clients as "Fat Tony" Salerno and Carmine "Lilo" Galante, the reputed boss of bosses.[9]

"Roy symbolizes viciousness in protecting a client," his friend Bill Fugazy told Ken Auletta when Auletta was preparing a profile of Cohn for *Esquire* magazine in 1978.[10] Cohn was the ultimate lawyer—he would do just about anything to win. If an estranged wife wanted to give her ex-partner a really hard time, it was Roy Cohn she would call, and when the victim received the threatening letter from Saxe Bacon and Bolan, he knew that he might as well open up one of his arteries on the spot.

"Hey, mister. This is now the eleventh hour before the monster strikes!" was how Cohn himself paraphrased his legal missives.[11]

"I must have had fifty men call me over the years," said Bill Fugazy, "and ask, 'We hear Roy Cohn is going to represent my wife. Would you make sure he doesn't rough us up?'"[12]

A few days after Henry Ford's press conference, Roy Cohn flew to Detroit to rough the Ford chairman up publicly at the Ford shareholders' meeting scheduled for May 11, 1978.

"I realize," he declared as he rose from the floor, "that I'm in the Ford kingdom and that I am not a subject."[13] Cohn crossquestioned Henry II as if he were in a court of law, and as he developed his charges, he added some surprising new questions to the allegations which he had already filed in New York. He had received disturbing information, he said, about expenses incurred by the refurnishing of the office of Ford's new vice-chairman, Philip Caldwell. Was this further evidence of financial impropriety?

Lee Iacocca and Philip Caldwell sat impassively on either side of Henry II as their chairman responded to Cohn's questions from the floor, and when Cohn reached the high point of his attack, a demand that Henry Ford II should step down as chairman of the Ford Motor Company while his charges were investigated, neither man betrayed by a flicker what was going through his mind.[14]

Henry Ford II survived. Indeed, the general verdict on his contest with Roy M. Cohn in the Edsel and Eleanor Ford Auditorium on May 11, 1978, was that the Ford Motor Company chairman had given as good as he got. In his gravelly and oddly impassive voice, Henry II had presented solid factual rebuttals to Cohn's charges. He had shown himself undismayed by the Cohn invective that had made other brave men run for cover—and there had been no

response at all from the audience to Cohn's suggestion that
Henry II should step down.

But the battle had just begun. Roy Cohn had embarked
on a campaign that was being accorded mini-Watergate
status by the reporters of several reputable newspapers. He
was not a man to quit while he was winning—or losing—
and the publicity was doing no harm at all to his reputation
as the meanest attorney in North America.

More worryingly, Roy Cohn had clearly been supplied
with information that came right from the heart of the Ford
Motor Company. His suit was nominally filed in the name
of clients who held a small number of Ford shares—relatives
of his law partner Bolan. But although their names were
listed on the legal documents, Cohn never made any pretence that they were the moving parties in the suit. His real
client was someone else, someone who wanted to get Henry
Ford II very badly indeed—and who was managing to
supply Cohn with information on a continuing basis, since,
evidently unhappy with the outcome of the shareholders'
meeting, this source, or sources, rapidly came up with some
fresh material. Just a few days after Cohn's inconclusive
confrontation with Henry II in the Ford Auditorium, the
lawyer released another batch of disclosures, and these were
so inflammatory that he would undoubtedly have made
them public if he had known about them when he came to
Detroit on May 11.

On May 16, 1978, Cohn filed an amendment to his
original complaint in New York, stating his initial allegations
all over again, and adding to them the charge that Henry
Ford II had compelled Ford's advertising agencies to pay
"wrongful" and "unlawful" fees to the Leslie Fargo model
agency "in which one Kathleen DuRoss of 394 Rivard
Avenue, Grosse Pointe, Michigan, a person in a close personal relationship with the defendant Ford, has an interest."[15] Max Fisher and Alfred Taubman were also dragged
in, their names misspelt as Max "Fischer" and "Morris"
Taubman. The two developers were accused of conspiring
with Henry II to buy land which they knew to be affected

744

by the Fairlane and Renaissance projects, and of then splitting the profit with their friend.[16]

In January 1980, Roy Cohn was to admit that he could not substantiate these or any of his other charges against Henry Ford II. Just off a plane from Acapulco, and still wearing his floral beachwear, he arrived in the Wall Street offices of Ford's lawyers, Hughes Hubbard and Reed, cheerfully to sign an admission that "it now appears that there was no wrongdoing by Henry Ford II or the others who were involved in the suit."[17]

As part of this settlement, Ford agreed to make a contribution towards Cohn's legal expenses, together with those of other lawyers associated in the suit, of $230,000. But in June 1985, a New York court ordered that Cohn must now repay even this money to Ford, since, ruled the judge, his suit had been entirely without benefit to the shareholders.[18] This final judgement was the result of action brought against both Cohn and Ford by a Washington public-interest group which was concerned at the dangers of lawyers holding public companies and their shareholders to ransom by getting publicity for scandalous charges that were high on sensation but low on solid and provable fact.

In the spring and early summer of 1978, however, nobody could guess at this eventual vindication. The Ford Motor Company appeared trapped in a ghastly maelstrom of adverse publicity. Detroit was alive with rumours of the bitter conflict being waged inside the Glasshouse. The lawsuits provoked by the flaming fuel tanks of the Pinto were coming to a head. Gossip columnists were having a field day with the messy legal skirmishes that were leading towards the eventual divorce of Henry II from Cristina.

Scarcely a day seemed to pass without the name of Ford being linked to some damaging headline or other, and on May 16, 1978, Roy Cohn added to the misery with his most serious accusation of all. Henry Ford II, he alleged, together with some of the directors, and certain of the employees, had "authorized and caused to be paid a 'bribe' in the sum of approximately One million ($1,000,000.00) dollars of

Company funds to an official of the Indonesian Government in connection with a contract between Philco, the Company's Overseas Services Subsidiary, and an agency of the Indonesian Government to build ground stations for said country's domestic satellite communications systems."[19]

As usual, many of the circumstantial details of Cohn's accusation were correct. Ford-Philco had bid on a contract to build ground stations in Indonesia, and the comparatively junior Ford executive negotiating the contract had, without telling his superiors, agreed to pay an Indonesian general a "commission" which he was planning to conceal in other transactions.

Ford's financial-control procedures, however, were stringent. They had been established by that expert in financial control, Ernie Breech, working in the late forties with the likes of Arjay Miller, and in August 1975 the system identified an unauthorized million dollars heading for a Singapore company that was a channel to the general. When word of this reached Paul Lorenz, the executive vice-president with responsibility for Philco, he stopped the payment and ordered an immediate inquiry. No commission was paid, and Ford-Philco got the contract in any case.

An inquiry into the incident by outside lawyers retained by Ford's Audit Committee confirmed that the problem had been a comparatively low-level thing. No senior Ford executives had been involved. They had stopped the bribe the moment they found out about it—and when, as a result of Roy Cohn's allegations, the U.S. Justice Department made an inquiry of its own, it came to the same conclusion, as did the Securities and Exchange Commission. There was no case to answer.

Lee Iacocca, however, in his memoirs, repeats the charge made by Roy Cohn. He asserts that Henry Ford II personally authorized Paul Lorenz to pay the $1 million bribe, and he gives his own account of a conversation between himself and Lorenz in which, he says, Lorenz admitted his own complicity, and that of Henry II.

"The chairman sort of winked at it," he quotes Lorenz as saying.[20]

Lorenz, today a director of Texas Instruments and of a number of other public companies, all of whom carefully investigated his role in the Indonesian affair before inviting him onto their boards, says that he is not willing to dignify Iacocca's version of events with discussion.

"Neither I nor Mr. Ford in any discussions with me," he says, "ever condoned or 'sort of winked at' any such payments, and I made that quite clear in my discussions with Mr. Iacocca at the time."[21]

Lorenz told the investigators of the U.S. Justice Department everything he knew, he says, and he testified to them under oath. He is content to be judged by that verdict.

The months of May, June, and July 1978, in which Roy Cohn's attack on Henry Ford II reached its climax, were the very months in which Lee Iacocca and Henry Ford II came down to what Henry II would later describe as "the rumbling point." Ford World Headquarters was a battlefield. Iacocca's men and Caldwell's men were sniping at each other ceaselessly. Caldwell and Iacocca could hardly be constrained to address a civil word to each other, and as for Iacocca and Henry II himself, there was now no pretence.

"Things were enormously tense around here," remembers Franklin Murphy. "In fact, I used to hate to come back to the meetings."[22]

Murphy found Lee Iacocca was getting more and more on edge. "Lee was not sleeping well. It was just a bad scene. It was a very bad scene. . . . I would go in and talk to him, and he would pour it out. It would be like to a priest."[23]

The headlines being generated by Roy Cohn's recurrent and proliferating attacks upon the reputation of Henry II might be helping Lee Iacocca in his week-by-week battle with the Ford chairman, but the publicity generated by the Pinto affair was not. Three months earlier, the record-setting award of $127.8 million to Richard Grimshaw had provoked a flood of other suits against Ford. The National Highway

Safety Administration had started pushing for the recall of all 1971–76 model Pintos, and finally, on June 15, 1978, right on the eve of a public hearing that seemed certain to force Ford to recall the car in any case, the company announced the "voluntary" recall of 1.37 million Pintos and 30,000 Bobcats (the Mercury version of the subcompact).[24] The cost of this recall was $40 million, and what it amounted to was a modification of the gas-tank filler neck and cap, together with the insertion, between the tank and the rear axle, of a high-density plastic shield, protection at last against the tank splitting open on the nuts of the transmission housing.

The Pinto had been Lee's baby. He had said so himself. He had taken all the credit for the car when the subcompact had sold so well in its early, successful years. But now the car was a public-relations disaster, and it was prompting serious questions about the quality of all the Ford cars built under Iacocca's stewardship.

In 1977 Ford had had to offer an extended warranty on 2.7 million cars with four- and six-cylinder engines which had suffered from excessive wear in cold weather. The problem had been caused by the removal of two small oil holes from the cylinder blocks—part of a cost-cutting exercise. An additional 1.3 million cars had been called back for faulty fans, though this was a problem of design rather than of "thrifting." Ford led the industry in recalls. By midsummer 1978, no less than 18.163 million Ford vehicles were the subject of recalls or official probes for safety, mechanical, or emissions defects,[25] and even in a city self-protectively tolerant of transgressions in this area, eyebrows were being raised.

"Our quality was so bad," said one Ford executive, "it was getting embarrassing to go to cocktail parties and tell them where you worked."[26]

This sort of thing worries outside directors very much. Quality and safety are just two among the wide range of concerns that keep a car executive busy—but they are quite predominant anxieties for the men and women whose names are on the letterhead. Outside directors only come into the hothouse atmosphere of headquarters one day a month, and for the other twenty-nine they have to live out in the ordinary world, going to cocktail parties, reading newspapers, and receiving angry letters from shareholders whose six-cylinder Mercury has just given up the ghost.

After more than two years of fairly consistent resistance to Henry Ford's wish to be rid of Lee Iacocca—proof, in itself, that the directors were not in the chairman's pocket —some of the outside board members were beginning to wonder whether Henry II might not be right. Perhaps Lee was not such a great automobile man after all.

"He was the man, who, they said, had gasoline in his veins," recalls Murphy, "who'd done the Mustang. And yet here was the company losing money in great amounts and not able to penetrate, to do anything about the small car market, a company in which morals seemed to be rather bad and in which, among everything else, in the most humiliating way, product quality had gone to hell."[27]

Lee Iacocca has boasted of the record profits that were being enjoyed by Ford in 1977 and 1978, after the bad years following the 1973 oil crisis. But, as is the pattern in Detroit, the prosperity was spread. General Motors was also enjoying record sales in 1978—70 percent more than Ford's[28]—and when the Ford figures were analysed, it was clear that much of Ford's profits were not actually coming from the divisions under Iacocca's most direct control. It was Ford of Europe, Henry II's creation and Philip Caldwell's recent fiefdom, which was making the most substantial contribution to the Ford treasury in 1978: no less than 40 percent of total company profits.[29] Ford's U.S. cars—Iacocca's special area of expertise—had been a disaster. Between 1972 and 1977, General Motors had managed to increase its profits from its North American automotive operations by 46.5 percent. But in this same period, Ford's equivalent earnings had actually fallen by 4 percent.[30]

"The fact that we were sinking," remembers Franklin

Murphy, "that Ford of North America was getting less profitable all the time, was something that was sort of camouflaged by how well we were doing overseas. . . . There was great confusion in the management as to what should happen to Ford of North America."[31]

Lee Iacocca has blamed Henry Ford for this, citing, in particular, Henry II's opposition to small cars, and Henry Ford, for his part, has acknowledged his own failure to see the way things were going. But, at the time, Lee Iacocca does not seem to have argued that strongly for the course that now seems so obvious. In 1976 the Ford president had proudly unveiled his range of new cars with the boast that Ford was still the home of the "whopper," as if the energy crisis had never been. General Motors was down-sizing its model range that year, but Iacocca made fun of GM with a relish which did not suggest that Henry II was twisting his arm very much. WRONG MOVE? ran a headline in the *Detroit News* in February 1976. "Ford's Iacocca believes GM erred in deciding to downsize big cars."[32]

Nor were Lee Iacocca's more recent ventures in carmaking that impressive. He seemed to be losing his touch. In 1974 he had brought out a successor to the car that had made him famous, the Mustang II, based on a prototype by Alejandro de Tomaso. Oversculpted and toylike, as though lifted off a fairground carousel, the Mustang II was a travesty of its famous forebear. In 1977 the Mustang II had sold only 170,700 units, less than 14 percent of the sporty market sector which had come to be dominated by GM's Firebird and Trans Am—the very sector in which the Mustang I had once proudly controlled as much as 78 percent of the market.[33]

Marian Heiskell remembers discussing cars with Lee Iacocca, and, in particular, the practice of "thrifting"—the shaving of pennies from the cost of components in order to save millions of dollars overall. This was the conversation that had provoked Lee's strange story about imagining himself to have been "shot." Having ordered the removal of some trim from around a window, the Ford president had run into the untrimmed glass door because he did not see it while getting into the production version of the car.

"You see, it really doesn't pay to save nickels" was the moral that Iacocca drew from the incident.[34] But this item of wisdom did not appear to have been very deeply assimilated by the carmaking divisions under Iacocca's command, and as the company's U.S. and Canadian operations continued to perform poorly, concern mounted on the topmost floor.

"There was no question," recalls Marian Heiskell, "about the fact that we had to build up North America."[35]

A wider question was of Iacocca's mastery of Ford's international dimension, and of Ford of Europe, in particular. One specific objection that Henry Ford II had to Lee Iacocca was that Lee did not know enough about Europe —and, on this point, he had been able to secure the fairly general agreement of his directors. Many of them had travelled to Europe with both Henry and Lee, and they had observed the two men operate.

Lee Iacocca made much of his Italian origins, but his was an Allentown interpretation of what being Italian was all about, as authentically European as pizza pie—spicy, but definitely made in America. Bill Fugazy had a photo of his friend in his office inscribed, "*Al mio carissimo amico Bill con i migliori augori, Lido,*"[36] but when Walter Hayes travelled in Italy with Iacocca in the late 1960s, he noticed that Lee never ventured once into the local tongue.[37]

Henry II the Europe lover had always seen his family empire as an international one. It was part of its Ford-ness, and he was very conscious that the company he must now hand on was, outside North America, the largest car company in the world. In 1978 Ford produced almost 20 percent of the new cars, trucks, and tractors sold anywhere on the face of the earth.[38] Its chief executive had to have many of the qualities of an international statesman—and Henry Ford II felt that these qualities were lacking in Lee Iacocca.

"Why," remembers one European Ford executive,

"Iacocca actually came to see me once wearing velvet shoes."[39]

The shoes did not worry Henry II. The profanities did. Henry Ford II could swear with the best of them, and he did so quite unpleasantly when in his cups. But he had never made four-letter words the habitual currency of his business conversation, as Lee Iacocca did.

Franklin Murphy tried to give Iacocca some friendly advice on one foreign trip.

"Lee," he would say, "you must, you don't understand how your use of profanity, your nonuse of proper English, really reflects discredit on you as a person."[40]

Henry Ford would wince visibly, remembers Murphy, at some of the obscenities Iacocca would let drop at board meetings.

"Some of our other directors would wince," says Murphy. "There are very few boardrooms in which this kind of talk goes forward. . . . Henry knows as many four-letter words as the next fellow, but never in those board meetings. To him a Ford board meeting is a holy experience . . . a very important, serious, consequential thing."[41]

Perhaps it was just a question of style. But style counted for much in an equation which was, ultimately, to be all rolled up in terms of whether one powerful man liked another.

Late on the afternoon of June 26, 1978, a messenger set off from the East 68th Street offices of Saxe Bacon and Bolan on what had become quite a routine errand: the delivery of yet another legal missive to the Wall Street offices of Ford's lawyers, Hughes Hubbard and Reed. It contained still further allegations of corruption in the Ford Motor Company, this time that Henry Ford had accepted no less than $65 million from "the highest officials of the Philippine's [sic] Government," and that in return for this payment, Henry II had directed Ford to build a stamping plant in the Philippines at a cost to the company of $50 million.

The accusation was as wild as Cohn's previous ones. For the Philippines' government to lay out $65 million to secure an investment of $50 million did not make sense by anyone's system of accounting, and, having reduced the amount of the alleged bribe to $2 million by a subsequent filing, Roy Cohn was, in due course, to abandon the charge altogether, along with all his others. His friend William Safire wrote a column based on the accusation in the *New York Times*, which he was also, later, totally to withdraw.

"*Henry Ford II:*" Safire wrote on April 14, 1983. "I took a sneaky, oblique pop at him based on unproven charges, am ashamed of myself, and take this occasion to apologize. That was my worst column."[42]

Safire's apology appeared in a retrospective column in which he either withdrew or reaffirmed a potpourri of insults he had flung, in the course of the previous decade, at such public figures as Henry Kissinger, Edward Kennedy, and Frank Sinatra, and Safire's two sentences are remarkable for being the only retraction ever printed by any of the journalists who had so gleefully propagated Cohn's charges against Henry Ford II without bothering to check their factual basis.

In June 1978, the significance of Cohn's accusation about the Philippines was that it enabled Henry Ford II to exclude one possible candidate who might have been behind the campaign which he had already publicly identified as a "personal vendetta."[43] Until this point it had been plausible to imagine that all the poison could be coming from his estranged wife Cristina. She was just the person to have supplied Roy Cohn with details like the $82,000 price tag on the tulip-wood desk in the Carlyle apartment—and she was certainly angry enough. Only a few months earlier, in February 1978, Cristina Ford had forced her separated husband into court to give four hours' testimony[44] in defence of his wish to sell off some antique furniture and a valuable collection of snuff boxes to which, she said, she had come to feel a deep "emotional attachment."[45]

"I was under Librium, what they give crazy people,"

she testified,[46] describing the nervous breakdown she had suffered after her husband's departure, and she was clearly very bitter.

Early in 1978 Cristina Ford had been seen in a New York restaurant talking to Roy Cohn,[47] and there were even rumours that he was going to represent her in her divorce —a double scourge for Henry.[48] But Cristina could hardly have been the source of Cohn's allegation about the Philippines. The last thing she would have wanted was to embarrass her friend Imelda Marcos with talk of kickbacks. On May 5, 1978, Cristina had issued a statement through her lawyer, Carl Tunick, stating that whatever her domestic quarrels with her husband, she was "completely out of sympathy" with Roy Cohn's lawsuit. So far as she knew, she said, Henry II's business conduct was "beyond reproach."[49] While this did not totally rule her out as one possible source of all the details that were getting to Cohn, it strengthened the argument that other sources must be involved.

When questioned as to where all their detailed inside information was coming from, members of Roy Cohn's law firm had referred to "disgruntled former employees" of the Ford Motor Company who had been "fired and humiliated" by Henry II,[50] and Roy Cohn himself, when pushed, gave *Esquire* magazine the name of Paul Bergmoser, the Ford executive who, as chief of purchasing, had handled the details of contracts with Bill Fugazy, and also with Pat de Cicco. Bergmoser, said Cohn, had "absolute proof of the kickback"—and Bergmoser himself confirmed that he had talked to Cohn, though only in general terms.[51]

Bergmoser was a close associate of Lee Iacocca. So long as he had been on the Ford payroll, "Bergy" had operated as one of the campaign managers for the Iacocca forces in the Glasshouse. He was Iacocca's contact man with Bill Fugazy, and Fugazy was the logical person to have put Bergmoser in touch with Cohn. That was what Fugazy was so good at, putting people in touch with one another, and as the Cohn assault on Henry II's honesty mounted to a crescendo in June 1978, the obvious question was whether Bill Fugazy was acting as the channel between his old friends Roy Cohn and Lee Iacocca.

The question has several times been put to Fugazy, and he has always, categorically, denied it. But Henry Ford II thought otherwise.[52] He was convinced that Bill Fugazy was deeply implicated in Roy Cohn's attacks upon him, and he also felt sure that the network stretched further than that. By the end of June 1978, in fact, Henry Ford II had come to believe that his own president, Lee Iacocca, a serving officer in the Ford Motor Company, was at least one of the sources—and was certainly the overall inspiration—of the public campaign dedicated to Henry Ford II's humiliation and removal.

Carter L. Burgess, Chief Executive Officer of the American Machine and Foundry Company, onetime U.S. Ambassador to Argentina, and a director of the Ford Motor Company since 1962, worked on the staff of General Eisenhower for a period during the Second World War. In his desk drawer Burgess used to carry a stock of colonel's eagles, and whenever Eisenhower decided that one of his generals was not commanding right, he would send the general along to Burgess's office to pick up the insignia of his new, lower, rank.

"So, you see," says Carter Burgess, "I've been raised with total understanding that I'm an expendable quantity in the business world ... and I think we all have to enter life with some understanding that if our superior, for good and sufficient reason, doesn't think that there's a compatible forward relationship, we pay the price."[53]

Carter Burgess, who, along with Arjay Miller, had been one of Henry II's most stalwart supporters in the two years of boardroom arguments over the future of Lee Iacocca, believes that the Ford president had had a very simple choice in April 1977, when Henry Ford's elevation of Philip Caldwell had, effectively, handed Iacocca his colonel's eagles.

"He should have quit at that point," says Burgess, "or laid down his pistol and gone to work."[54]

That apparently simple and logical choice might have been appropriate in the Army, or for almost any other executive in the Ford Motor Company, but Lee Iacocca was one person to whom it could not apply. The man did not know how to be anything other than number one—and he did not know how to quit either. He did not want to quit. There was nowhere else but Ford for the only son of Nicola Iacocca, the U-Drive-It Ford man, for it was one of the more poignant ironies in the unfolding drama that Lee Iacocca identified with the Ford Motor Company only slightly less than did Henry Ford himself. Lee had had his heart set on that corner office on the twelfth floor for so long that he found it difficult to think of anything else.

He was never going to get it though, not while Henry Ford had breath in his body, and in June 1978, a month after the Cohn-haunted shareholders' meeting, Henry II made another, determined attempt to bring the question to a head. After just over a month of Roy Cohn's mysteriously well-informed attacks, Henry had had enough. When his outside directors arrived in Detroit on June 7, 1978, he was waiting for them with two surprise items of news. The company was about to recall the Pinto—the recall notice went out three days later—and Lee Iacocca was definitely going to be fired.

On Iacocca the outside directors' reaction was unanimous.

"We said, 'Don't do it!'" remembers Franklin Murphy. "It was at a committee meeting before dinner. 'Don't do it! Let's try to patch this up. Let's see if we can't build a bridge.' I realize now we were naive. But we were so desperately wanting to prevent an explosive episode."[55]

Later Murphy went downstairs on one of his peacemaking missions to Iacocca's office. "I said, 'Lee, now look, things are quieting down. . . . You're not going to be fired.'"[56]

According to Lee Iacocca's memory of the conversation,

Franklin Murphy reported Henry II as having declared, "I lost my board today."[57]

"But that's Lee's interpretation," says Murphy. "I can't imagine my saying that he 'lost his board,' because Henry never lost his board. . . . We didn't say, 'We're going to vote you down.' We simply said, 'Postpone it,' as it were."[58]

As some sort of compromise, the oddly assorted Office of the Chief Executive was now stretched from three members to four by the inclusion of William Clay Ford—proof, if there had ever been any doubt of it, that the OCE was a political device, not a serious management mechanism, since Bill Ford had not managed anything at the Ford Motor Company for at least twenty years.

At the end of June 1978, Henry Ford II departed with a number of senior executives on a trip to the Far East, together with Kathy DuRoss, who was now being treated as Mrs. Henry Ford in everything but name. The journey had been planned for some time—Ford was negotiating a stake in the Japanese car company, Mazda—and putting his brother Bill into the OCE had reflected an anxiety on Henry's part as to what Iacocca might get up to in his absence.

His anxiety proved fully justified. Within days of the chairman leaving the country, Iacocca was also on a company plane, heading to Boston and New York to see the two outside directors who had, he thought, over the months, proved most sympathetic to his cause: George F. Bennett, an investment banker from Boston, and Joseph F. Cullman III, chairman of the board of Philip Morris, the tobacco company.

Neither Bennett or Cullman will discuss what actually happened at those meetings in any detail. "He wanted to point out his position," says Joseph Cullman. "He wanted to seek the support he was entitled to."[59] Cullman had been at the core of the directors who were supporting Iacocca. "I admired him then," he says, "and I admire him now."[60]

But when Henry Ford II got to hear of his president's travels, he had no doubt at all what was going on. Lee was evidently not intending to go quietly. He was building up support. Both men knew that the battle would be decided in the boardroom, and Lee, as usual, was aiming to be the one who finished up on top. In 1969 Iacocca had managed to bring down Bunkie Knudsen, and now he was planning to do the same to Henry Ford.

You could compare him to the young David, vaulting in his ambition. You could compare him to Icarus, daring to brush his wings against the sun. Or you could just say that Lee Iacocca had taken leave of his senses—and that was the conclusion that the outside directors of the Ford Motor Company came to when they gathered together on July 12, 1978.

"It was an act of insanity," says Franklin Murphy. "He just didn't have the cards."[61]

After thirty years of superbly proficient politicking and climbing, Lee Iacocca had lost sight of the basic rule by which he had always played the game. The Ford Motor Company simply was not a public company which worked the way the business schools say things work. Forty percent of its votes were controlled by the Ford family, and there was nothing that Iacocca, or any other non-Ford, could do about that.

"Lee had a lot of loyal chums out in the system," says Franklin Murphy, "and anybody other than Henry Ford, Lee could have castrated—absolutely, quickly. But you don't castrate the man who represents the family who owns the company. And this is something that he didn't understand."[62]

Henry Ford II went to meet his directors on the afternoon of July 12, 1978, with an ultimatum. He had listened to them last month, and then he had bowed to their will. But this was the end. They would have to choose—and the choice was a simple one.

"Henry said, 'It's me or Iacocca,'" remembers Franklin Murphy. "There was not one negative vote."[63]

And so the stage was set for the encounter that is already

a legend in the Motor City and far beyond—the O.K. Corral of recent American corporate history. On the evening of July 12, after the Ford directors had met, Lee Iacocca received a phone call from Keith Crain, the publisher of *Automotive News*.

"Say it isn't so," said Crain.[64]

Iacocca jumped to the conclusion that Crain, a friend of Edsel Ford, had got inside information from the family. But Edsel was working in Australia at the time. Crain had picked up the talk around town and he wanted to finalize his story before his magazine went to bed next day.[65] In the event, Crain had to hold the presses.

At three o'clock on the afternoon of Thursday, July 13, 1978, Lee Iacocca received the phone call summoning him to the office of Henry Ford II, and when he arrived, he was surprised to discover that Henry was not alone. He was waiting for him with his brother William Clay Ford.

In his memoirs, Lee Iacocca interprets the presence of brother Bill at the final showdown as a matter of Henry II wanting a witness.[66] But it was more complicated than that, for William Clay Ford, the company's largest single shareholder, had been one of the people to whom Iacocca had been talking in his last desperate weeks of lobbying, and Bill Ford had given Iacocca a sympathetic ear.

"I thought he was a good person for the job," says William Clay today.[67]

Over the months Bill Ford had talked quite frequently with his brother, and with Iacocca as well, acting as a sort of family go-between.

"You're a better friend of Lee's than I am," Henry said to him accusingly on one occasion—a comment that Bill recalls today with his oddly leftward-twisting smile.

"Cripes! They had offices ten feet apart! I mean, doors. I mean, great! They've been working together, I don't know for how many years, and supposedly I'm closer to him than he is! So I guess that's why I was present."[68]

Henry Ford wanted to make sure that Lee Iacocca got the message in no uncertain terms. The board was behind him, and so was the family. There was no court of appeal. When Henry had fired Bunkie Knudsen nine years earlier, he had brought Bill in to make the same thing quite clear[69] —and that was how one ordinary mortal now came to be present at this final, skull-jarring encounter between two bull males, each so potent, so talented, and so raging mad.

Bill wept at the sheer power of it. He had "tears running down his face," Lee Iacocca remembers, and William Clay Ford does not deny that today.[70] It was the dismissal by a father of his son, the final, bitter disinheritance by a king of his erstwhile crown prince—and also, quite simply, the tragic parting of the ways between two men who were so much alike they could not possibly get along.

Lee Iacocca dealt with it in his customary fashion, jabbing, weaving, attacking—a ferocious onslaught of words and insults and anger. He was good when he was calm, and when he was moved, he was very good indeed.

Henry Ford II had comparatively little to say. A better smoulderer than talker, he was most verbose when it came to the incidentals, Lee's "resignation" date and the pension details.

"There comes a time when I have to do things my way . . . ," he said. "It's personal, and I can't tell you any more. It's just one of those things."[71]

It was not really a very impressive performance. If it had been the Academy Awards, Lee Iacocca would have won the Oscar—and Bill Ford told him as much as they left, congratulating the ex-president on how well he had argued his case.

Lee Iacocca considered the compliment. "Thanks, Bill," he replied. "But I'm dead, and you and he are still alive."[72]

The warehouse was the epilogue. Under the terms of his departure, Lee Iacocca was to stay on at the Ford Motor Company for another three months, until October 15, 1978, his fifty-fourth birthday. Staying until then would entitle him to receive his full retirement benefits, a cash and stock package worth over $1.1 million,[73] so long as he did not work for a competitor.

Lee Iacocca tried very hard indeed to remove the standard Ford "no compete" clause from his severance contract, so that he could still get paid by Ford if he went to work for Chrysler. He hired Edward Bennett Williams, America's premier trial attorney—Roy Cohn not excepted—to negotiate with a Ford committee headed by Bill Ford and Carter Burgess, chairman of the Compensation Committee, and in his memoirs he describes these two men as "bastards to the bitter end."[74]

Carter Burgess regards this charge with equanimity.

"I've never said any unfortunate things about his mother," he says, "and I don't know why he says those unfortunate things about mine. Mr. Iacocca wanted me to overrule 'no compete' policy statements that he himself had signed as president, and I wasn't about to overrule his own policy decisions."[75]

Iacocca stayed in his presidential office on the twelfth floor of the Glasshouse until his birthday and "retirement" in October.[76] It had been agreed that he would, after that, have the use of another office, which he could keep until he found another job, and on October 16, 1978, he drove to this office in the Ford Parts Distribution Center, on Telegraph Road. What he found there horrified him.

"My new office," he was later to write, "was little more than a cubicle with a small desk and a telephone. My secretary . . . was already there, with tears in her eyes. Without saying a word, she pointed to the cracked linoleum floor and the two plastic coffee cups on the desk. . . . For me, this was Siberia."[77]

Lee Iacocca was to describe his exile to this "obscure warehouse on Telegraph Road" as his "final humiliation" at the hands of Henry Ford. "It was enough to make me want to kill," he said.[78] When Iacocca came to write his memoirs, he told his ghostwriter that he wanted to start with this episode, because, he said, it had been for him the great moment of truth.[79]

You might not guess from reading the dramatic opening to Lee Iacocca's autobiography that any other human being had ever occupied the miserable few feet of warehouse space to which he was consigned in October 1978. But this office had, in fact, had a previous occupant: Ernest R. Breech, chairman of the Ford Motor Company until July 1960. Driving home in that month from World Headquarters in Dearborn, where he was negotiating his own, and rather more amicable, departure from the Ford Motor Company, Ernie Breech happened to see the blue oval outside the Ford Parts Distribution Center on Telegraph Road, and he pulled in to ask if he could see the manager.

"Do you have any spare office space in here?" he inquired,[80] and the manager showed him to a very pleasant office, the best office in the building, a good twenty-one feet long by fourteen feet wide, clean and modern, well lit by windows right along one wall. It had fitted carpet, wall to wall.[81]

Breech decided that this was the retirement office he had been looking for, and he negotiated a modest commercial rent for it with Ford. He made it his headquarters for the best part of twenty-eight years—and he did not spend his time there drawing up membership lists for the country club. In March 1961, Ernest R. Breech was made a director of Trans World Airlines, and in April that year he was elected chairman of the TWA board, charged with the job of disentangling the airline from the clutches of Howard Hughes—the second time that Breech had been called on to save a major privately held company from a shambles.

Ernie Breech remained chairman of TWA for the rest of the decade, finally retiring in 1969, and throughout these years he maintained his office on Telegraph Road.

This office was the one to which Lee Iacocca was consigned in October 1978—a full 300 square feet of floor space, not counting the outer office of his secretary. There was some cracked linoleum in the secretary's office, and the occupants of the suite were expected to drink their coffee out of plastic cups from the vending machine. Ernie Breech did not, in fact, drink coffee, but for over twenty years the great postwar saviour of the Ford Motor Company was happy to take his lunch in the cafeteria whenever he was at the office, sitting unpretentiously alongside the several hundred blue- and white-collar workers in the building.

The office actually contained better furniture when Lee Iacocca went there than it did in Ernest Breech's day—a large, wide, modern teak desk, a three-cushioned sofa and chair, a stylish brass table lamp with cream shade, and a long, low occasional table. Not too uncomfortable really, as St. Helenas go.

Ernie Breech died early in July 1978, just a few days before the sacking of Lee Iacocca, and that suggested a practical solution to Lee's request for a retirement office. He could be given the premises that Ernie had rented for over twenty years on Telegraph Road. Henry Ford II, who knew about the office but had never seen it, gave orders for the arrangements to be made,[82] and one of the functionaries versed in the caste rankings of Monet reproductions, potted palms, and teak-covered filing cabinets made up the package he considered appropriate for an exiled president.

A few days later, the new furniture arrived—the sofa, the brass lamp, the wooden desk wide enough for a testing game of Ping-Pong—and it is there to this day, unused, in Lee Iacocca's Siberia. The manager of the building considers it all too grand for his own use. He makes do with a slightly smaller office, and quite a narrow, metal and formica-topped desk.[83]

# EPILOGUE

One warm May afternoon in 1979, an unusual concentration of Fords and Lincolns was to be seen drifting eastwards beneath the green shade of Lakeshore Road. All were quite new cars, all well polished, and as they reached the numerals saying 1000 Lakeshore, they all peeled off right to drive through the high, pillared gates of William Clay Ford's Grosse Pointe Shores estate. The Ford family was gathering.

The Christmas get-togethers had ended three years earlier with the death of Mrs. Eleanor. No one had kept up the tradition. But now Uncle Bill had sent out telegrams to everyone, for there was business to discuss. After thirty-three years at the helm, Henry Ford II was stepping down. The shareholders were meeting next week, and Henry II was going to tell them that he was retiring as chairman—which meant that the family would have to adjust to the company not having a Ford at its head for the first time in more than seventy-five years.

Nine months had passed since the firing of Lee Iacocca, and there was now no doubt who Ford's new chief operating officer would be. Philip Caldwell, grey and efficient, had been putting together his grey and efficient management team since the previous July. But Henry II wanted to find out how the family felt about having William Clay Ford as vice-chairman or even as a ceremonial chairman, and he wanted to explain his own future role. He was planning to stay on as a director of the company, and he would also be taking over the chairmanship of the most important of the directors' committees, the Finance Committee, from which he could keep his finger on the pulse of things.

Almost everyone was there. Charlotte and Anne had flown

764

in from New York, elegant as ever. Always beautiful, they seemed to improve with age. Edsel II and his stylish wife, Cynthia, were back from Australia, Edsel's long hair carefully trimmed to an inch more than World Headquarters' accepted length. The Ford Fords were on parade, Wally and Josephine, with their children, along with the William Clay Fords, three daughters and one son, Bill Junior, who was just finishing his studies at Princeton. Among the elders of the clan, the most obvious absentee was Benson Ford, who had died the previous summer, at the end of July 1978, just a few weeks after the firing of Lee Iacocca. Since his widow, Edie, was ill as well, that branch of the family was represented by Benson Junior and his sister, Lynn.

A stocky, square-faced young man on the threshold of his thirties, Benson Junior was just sitting down at the table with the rest of his generation when someone told him, "Your uncles want to talk to you,"[1] and going out to the library, Benson Junior found Henry II and William Clay Ford waiting for him, their faces pictures of horror and disbelief.

"Benson," said Uncle Bill. "My electronic surveillance in the house tells me that you are wearing a listening device. Is that true?"

"Yes," replied Benson—and he remembers seeing his Uncle Henry's jaw "drop open a foot."[2]

"We want to see it," said William Clay Ford.

So Benson Junior took off his jacket and shirt to reveal a Fargo radio transmitter bandaged to his chest, the device still live and broadcasting details of the conversation to a receiver and tape recorder in a car parked just outside the William Clay property. This tape was to record a sequence of colourful expletives from Uncle Bill before someone remembered to switch off the transmitter, and Benson Junior later retrieved the tape from his car after the meeting, having been readmitted, in an unwired state, to sit through the comparatively unmomentous proceedings of the family parliament.

That evening Benson Ford Junior played the tape back

to the oddly assorted bunch of allies he had assembled for the war he had been waging since his father's death upon his own family and upon Henry Ford II in particular—and among those listeners was Lee Iacocca.[3]

Benson Ford Senior cracked with relative discretion under the strain of being a Ford. He slid quietly into a decline which caused little trouble, and only the slightest embarrassment, to the rest of the family. His son, Benson Junior, exploded.

The alienation of Benson Junior went back to early in his childhood. All the Ford children came to learn, sooner or later, the ultimate price of their surname and of their trust funds, but Benson Junior was still a little boy when he started to feel like a puppet. It was nice that his parents would take him to Florida with them when they went cruising in the winter, but it meant that he was never in the same school for more than a few months at a time.[4]

"Benson was the kid who always got yanked out of class every January," remembers Billy Chapin.[5]

One voyage on his father's beloved motor yacht, the *Onika*, had been disrupted when Benson Junior had to be rushed ashore with suspected appendicitis, so as a precaution before the next voyage, his mother took him, and his sister, Lynn, to the Ford Hospital to take care of the problem. Both children embarked on the next trip appendix-less.[6]

Apparently very aggressive, but in reality desperately insecure, scared, and even rather shy, Benson Ford became a rebellious teenager. He went through a couple of schools, and chose a university as far away from home as possible both in terms of miles and lifestyle, Whittier College, Richard Nixon's alma mater in the suburbs of Los Angeles. There he delivered up his youthful existence to sun, sand, fast cars, and most of the mind-expanding substances that money could buy. Before he was thirty he was to be arrested twice on drugs charges.[7]

Benson Ford Junior and his sister, Lynn, were the richest of all Henry Ford I's great-grandchildren. Their money came to them in various trust funds set up by Henry, Clara, Edsel, and Eleanor, bypassing Henry II, his brothers, and his sister, who had their own share of the Ford fortune. The generation-jumping was for tax-avoidance purposes, and since Benson Ford had the smallest number of children, Benson Junior and his sister came into particularly generous inheritances when they reached the age of twenty-one— some $20 million apiece, largely in Ford Class B stock.[8]

It had become the custom for these inheritances to be administered by Ford Estates, the family business office whose legal adviser was Pierre Heftler, the Ford family lawyer for many years. But soon after Benson reached the age of twenty-one, he decided that he would run his fortune himself, and after an acrimonious meeting with his parents and Heftler in December 1972, he got his way. At Whittier, Benson had started having sessions with a local therapist, Lou Fuentes, who had helped a number of other students sort out their emotional problems, and it had been at Fuentes's suggestion that young Ben had made this bid for more say in his destiny.

Lou Fuentes was to play a major role in the life of the young Benson Ford for the next half-dozen years or so, and, through Ben, his impact on the entire Ford family was to be considerable. No one had ever rocked the boat before. Edsel I had established the pattern of silence and submission, the covering up of family disagreements—public unity at the price of private pain.

Lou Fuentes taught Benson Ford Junior to put it all up front. Fierce, masculine, and decisive, the dark-bearded Fuentes was outspoken on the subject of the Ford family and the damage he felt they had inflicted on the psyche of his patient.

"As human beings," he declared on one occasion, "they're like a poor pimple on some whore's ass."[9]

Fuentes pushed Benson to get control of his inheritance, and then, in a strange development of therapeutic practice, which is, at the time of writing, the subject of a lawsuit between the two men, he offered himself to his patient as a business partner. Early in the 1970s, Luben Inc. went into business manufacturing roll bars and accessories for the West Coast hot-rod market, and the Ford-Fuentes partnership branched into other fields—some of their business meetings, according to Benson Junior today, being conducted while Benson lay on the couch in his therapist's consulting room.[10]

The businesses were almost uniformly unsuccessful. They consumed money by the millions—some $10 million, says Benson Junior[11]—and the final twists of the plot, together with the fortune, would probably have played themselves out in the sad yet not unusual traditions of inherited wealth, if the death of Benson Senior had not occurred in July 1978. This came at the very climax of his brother Henry's mortal battle with Lee Iacocca, and it suddenly thrust Benson Junior and Fuentes into the heart of the drama, for Benson Senior had altered his will in order to stop his son getting his hands on any more Ford money. Trustees were named to control young Ben's access to his share of his father's estate, and since those trustees included both his uncles, William Clay and Henry Ford II, the battle which Benson Junior joined to contest his father's will in the autumn of 1978 came to be a problem for the whole family.

Its ramifications spread even further, for as he had watched his son veering off course in the early 1970s, Benson Ford Senior had turned for help to Lee Iacocca. He had asked the Ford president to cultivate young Benson's friendship, to try to steer the boy in the right direction, and the tactic had worked, to a point.

"Lee and myself, we really hit it off," remembers Benson Junior today. "Mr. Iacocca really talked to me straight. I liked that."[12]

Whenever Benson Junior came to Detroit, he got in the habit of going to see the Ford president, often taking Lou Fuentes with him. They would have drinks together, go out for a meal. Benson Junior got to know Mary Iacocca, whom he liked, and today he still considers Lee Iacocca a friend.

"I like the guy. He's a brilliant guy. I think he's got a lot of common sense."[13]

Interviewed by Kirk Cheyfitz in 1984 on the subject of his own relationship with the Ford family's most notorious rebel, Lee Iacocca remembered being pulled aside by Henry II on one occasion as he was about to enter the double doors of the Glasshouse boardroom:

Henry said, "What the hell are you always talking to Benson for?"
And I got mad, and I said, "'Cause your fuckin' brother told me to."
Then Henry said, "Look out because he hangs out with tough hombres."[14]

Both Benson Junior and Lou Fuentes were by this date in the habit of travelling with armed bodyguards, and Henry II advised his president that he should break off his relations with this curious couple who meant nothing but trouble for the house of Ford.

Lee Iacocca told Kirk Cheyfitz that he took this advice so long as he was president of Ford. But following his dismissal, he evidently felt free to assist young Benson's attempts to embarrass Henry II—and so did his friends. Sometime in the autumn of 1978, Benson Junior and Fuentes flew to New York for a meeting with Bill Fugazy.

"I remember Fugazy talked very highly of Lee Iacocca . . . ," says Benson, "and how Fugazy *lived* for Mr. Iacocca. . . . We talked with him a couple of hours."[15]

From New York, Benson and Fuentes flew down to Florida to see Iacocca, who was there at the time. "And then," Benson remembers, "Roy Cohn got in the picture somehow. I can't remember how, but I think Fugazy was the one who recommended to use Roy Cohn. . . . We wanted to pick out a guy who was tough, mean, a mean son-of-a-bitch. . . . He was kind of a thorn in Ford's side, and I thought, well, that fits right along with my programme."[16]*

* On February 22, 1986, the *New York Post* reported that two of the principal guests at Roy Cohn's fifty-ninth birthday party were Bill Fugazy and Lee Iacocca.

Benson Junior hired Roy Cohn to represent him in his suit against his father's will, and he also kept in touch with Lee Iacocca. So when he got back to his hotel on the evening of his adventure at the home of Uncle Bill in May 1979, he telephoned the ex-president of Ford.

"I told him to come over," remembers Benson, "I had something interesting for him." Iacocca, who was by now embroiled in the troubles of Chrysler, was around in no time.

"He laughed his ass off. He laughed his ass off," remembers Benson Ford. "He couldn't believe it. He said, 'That's one of the most daring things I ever heard in my life.' He thought that was neat. He really thought that was neat. . . . He listened to the tape about four times."[17]

The annual stockholder meetings of the Ford Motor Company, like those of a number of other major American corporations, are notable for the declamations, interruptions, and general confusion created by two "professional" shareholders, Mrs. Evelyn Y. Davis and Mr. Lewis D. Gilbert, both of whom hold a few dozen shares in many companies, including Ford,[18] and who spend their lives travelling from stockholder meeting to stockholder meeting, rising to make points of order and to ask awkward questions of the directors. As he sat beneath the bright lights on the podium of the Edsel and Eleanor Ford Auditorium beside the Detroit River on May 10, 1979, waiting to start his final stockholder meeting as chairman, Henry Ford II peered out into the darkened hall.

"I see Evelyn Davis out there," he said to Philip Caldwell beside him. "She's gone crazy. . . . I hear Gilbert's got a question planned: 'Why did it take so long to get rid of Iacocca?' "[19]

Both Henry II and Caldwell knew that they had a difficult few hours ahead. Benson Ford Junior had double-barrelled his attack on his uncle by filing a request for a seat on the board of directors, a request he was planning to explain today to the assembled shareholders. That would cause trouble enough—but worse, Roy Cohn was back in town.

"Let's get this goddamn thing out of the way," said Henry Ford II.

"We may look back at that," said Caldwell, referring to past affrays with Evelyn Davis and Lewis Gilbert, "and say they were the good old days."

"God, I hope not, I hope not," responded Henry II, and banged his gavel to start the meeting.[20]

Henry Ford II was looking his best for his swan song. He was wearing a broad, blue-spotted tie with a matching handkerchief, and, on his breast pocket, that odd, superfluous label he had worn at shareholder meetings for twenty-four years, saying who he was.

He started with a tribute to his brother Benson. "His death leaves a great void," he said. "May I ask all of you to stand for a moment in prayer."[21]

It was the last moment of calm in the entire meeting. Trying to forestall trouble, Henry II started with a review of the company's history under his stewardship since 1945.

"You could count the number of stockholders on the fingers of both hands," he said, recalling those days when stockholder meetings "took place inside my grandfather's head."[22]

In 1945 the company had had 160,000 employees worldwide. Now it had 518,000, with 14,000 dealers selling Fords in 200 different countries. In 1946 the company had sold 900,000 units. Last year it sold 6.5 million. Ford Aerospace had played a key role in getting men to the moon. If separated from the main company, Ford of Europe, which Henry II had started in 1967, would rank as the world's eighteenth-largest industrial corporation in its own right. Every ten days Ford sold $1 billion worth of products worldwide.[23]

"As long ago as 1975," said Henry II, "I began to devote a lot of my time to planning how the future management of this company should be organized and who should replace me as chief executive." He had discussed this with the outside directors, he said, and now he felt happy that management had been reorganized and was on a sound footing for the 1980s—which brought him to the question of "the part the Ford family plays" and should play in the running of the company.[24]

"Until recently," he said, "I had not thought there would be any worthwhile purpose in making this kind of statement. The considerations involved in the appointment of top management seemed to me to be self-evident. But clearly this is not so, at least not to everybody"—and at this point the chairman peered hard over his glasses down to his left, towards that area of the auditorium where the members of the family were sitting, Benson Ford Junior among them.

"Since this is a time for frankness," he continued, "I have decided to make it clear beyond any shadow of doubt. . . . The ownership of B stock is no passport to a top position in Ford, either on its board of directors or its management. It confers no special privilege. If any other member of my family achieves a senior position in the company, it will be through merit and by a decision of the board of directors. There are no crown princes in the Ford Motor Company."[25]

Tumultuous applause greeted these remarks, and Henry II paused to sip from a glass of water.

"My main concern in life," he said, "has been what it remains today, the future of the Ford Motor Company"—and no one could quarrel with that. "I leave the management in the best possible hands, and I believe it to be the best management the company has ever had. . . . After thirty-four years on the job, I am now ready to step aside."[26]

It was a poignant moment. The entire auditorium rose in applause, and since many of the stockholders were Ford retirees who had themselves lived and worked through the years of Henry II, the tribute was especially moving. The applause went on and on, and it did not halt until finally, diffidently, Henry II rose to his feet to lift his arm in farewell.

*

Then the nastiness started. Evelyn Davis kicked off with a question about Benson Junior. Why would his uncle not allow him on the board?

"Not qualified," snapped Henry II gruffly.

As predicted, Lewis Gilbert asked his question about Iacocca, and also wanted to know the details of the ex-president's compensation package, since Iacocca was now working for a competitor.

"I couldn't understand it myself," said Henry II frankly, referring his questioner to the proxy statement in which all the details were disclosed.

Roy Cohn went straight for the jugular. The very first charge he had brought against Henry Ford II more than a year ago related to the Ford chairman's apartment in the Carlyle, and now this year's proxy statement referred to a payment of $34,585 which Henry II had made to the company. Was there a connection?

Henry II confessed that there was. He had discovered that his wife, and various friends of his wife, had stayed in the apartment without his knowledge, and that their personal expenses had been billed to the company. So Henry II had paid the company back.

Roy Cohn sniffed blood. This proved the validity of his charges, he said. The wrong billing would never have been discovered if he had not called for an investigation, and he moved on to the Iacocca affair. He had chapter and verse for the number of managers who had left Ford to join Lee Iacocca at Chrysler.

"We've got a solid team," he complained, speaking on behalf of his Ford shareholder clients, "who have gone to a competitor." This was a heavy and reckless loss of talent from which the Ford Motor Company would suffer, and for which Henry II was personally responsible.[27]

"You put your money in Chrysler and go to their meeting," shot back Henry II. "Okay?"—a riposte greeted with applause and audible cheers.

Benson Junior rose. "I am a successful businessman," he declared in the course of a surprisingly compelling and impressive speech on behalf of his bid for a seat on the board. "I know something about cars," he said, and acknowledging that he had probably lost this round in his battle, he concluded bravely, "I do not intend to fade away."[28]

The worst was still to come. Roy Cohn's succession of attacks on Henry II had appeared to run out of steam the previous year in the months following the departure of Lee Iacocca. It was as if the campaign had been robbed of its goal. Ford lawyers had secured a court order requiring Cohn's clients to deposit a bond of $250,000 on the grounds that their complaints represented such a small proportion of the shareholding body—shares worth less than $600, only .0000115 percent of the company's common stock.[29] Lacking the money, the suit was about to founder, when an unexpected saviour had appeared. In December 1978, Lee Iacocca's old friend Alejandro de Tomaso, the Pantera maker, had stepped forward and placed his own Ford shareholding, 10,912 shares valued at nearly half a million dollars, behind Cohn's charges[30]—and Cohn was also supplied with a confidential Ford document which enabled him to present his most substantive charges yet.

The document was an embarrassing memorandum from Henry Nolte, Ford's general counsel, in which Nolte revealed an additional dimension to the old Indonesian bribe scandal. The company had been able to stop the $1 million bribe that had been the subject of Cohn's earlier allegations, but Nolte had since discovered that another bribe might possibly have been paid, some $889,000, to the original Indonesian general. Worse, junior Ford employees had deliberately falsified and back-dated documents which had been submitted by Nolte to the Department of Justice. So Ford had not only, perhaps, paid a bribe, it had effectively perjured itself, albeit unwittingly, to the U.S. government.

Cohn finally had his piece of paper. The Department of Justice was eventually to conclude that Ford's bookkeeping sleight-of-hand had been at a lower level and that the company's senior officers, including Henry II, had all acted in good faith. Most important of all, it was established that no bribe had, in fact, been paid.

But this was not clear in May 1979, and for the best part of ten minutes Roy Cohn grilled Henry II mercilessly, treating Ford's shareholders to a glimpse of the piranha-like attacks to be enjoyed by his admirers in New York's trial courts most days of the week. One question which Henry II might have shot back, but did not, was where Cohn had got his document from, since the circulation of Nolte's memorandum had been strictly confined to Ted Mecke, the vice-president in charge of P.R.; Ed Lundy, the Whiz Kid who was now Executive Vice-President, Finance; P. J. Sherry, in charge of Personnel; and the Office of the Chief Executive: Henry II, William Clay Ford, Philip Caldwell, and Lee Iacocca.[31]

Henry II confined himself to stonewalling. He had known nothing of the wrongdoing in advance, or at the time, he said. He had ordered full disclosure to the Justice Department as Nolte's memorandum had recommended, and by the end of his cross-examination the most partial observer had to feel he was telling the truth. Still, it was a sour note on which to conclude his final and longest-ever stockholder meeting—and fortunately a member of the audience now rose to round off the proceedings with a happier valedictory.

Charlotte Ford had been sitting throughout the four-hour-long meeting making notes on a yellow legal pad, and rising to speak, she said meaningfully, "on behalf of the family, especially our generation," that she wanted to praise her father and everything he had done for "the company, its stockholders, employees, the city of Detroit, and the world in the past thirty-eight years."

"You are a great human being," she said to her father. "Generous, loyal, and above all, honest. We are proud of you."[32]

In the outburst of applause which followed, Henry Ford II was visibly moved.

"Thank you very much, Charlotte," he replied, with a

catch in his voice. "I appreciate that from the bottom of my heart—and I love you."[33]

Henry Ford II formally relinquished his responsibilities as chief executive officer of the Ford Motor Company on October 1, 1979, five months after his final stockholder meeting. Early in 1980 he also wrapped up a phase in his personal life when he settled the details of his divorce from his second wife. Cristina Ford had been making free with accusations about her husband's drinking, and as the bitterness mounted, rumours and counter-rumours circulated of bizarre sexual escapades.[34]

But with several dozen witnesses subpoenaed by both sides, and many more journalists on hand, their pens poised, the couple withdrew from the brink at the very last moment. Their lawyers negotiated an out-of-court settlement believed to be in the region of $16 million, and Henry Ford, the marriage lover, was free to legalize his relationship with Kathy DuRoss, which he did within the year, in Carson City, Nevada, on Tuesday, October 14, 1980, at 10:40 A.M. —the time and date having been chosen by an astrologer. "From Bishop Sheen to Carson City," remarked the latest Mrs. Ford contentedly.

On the Thursday before the wedding, Henry II telephoned his daughters, Charlotte and Anne, to invite them out to Nevada for the ceremony the following week. The sisters said they could not come at such short notice.[35] As for Edsel II, he was on company business on the far side of Australia, which meant he could scarcely get back in time either. So Henry Ford II's third wedding was quite a solitary affair, the audience coming principally from the bride's side: a group of Kathy's ex-model girlfriends and her two daughters, Debi and Kimberly.

A few days after the wedding, the phone rang late one evening in Anne Ford's Park Avenue apartment. It was her father calling from Europe, where he had flown with his new wife on a sort of business honeymoon. (Much of Henry II's time for the two years following his retirement was consumed with journeys to various corners of the world saying goodbye to people.)

It was sometime after ten o'clock at night in New York —three or four in the morning in Europe—and Henry II had clearly been drinking. His voice was slurred, and the moment he had made sure that he was speaking to his favourite daughter, the little girl to whose bedroom he would go on the lonely, sleepless nights when his first marriage was falling apart in Grosse Pointe, he started to curse and swear, uttering the most ugly sort of obscenities. He was screaming and yelling. He called his favourite daughter every four-letter word under the sun, and more.[36]

Anne Ford put the phone down. Some time later it rang again. It was her father on the line once more. But he was not calling to apologize. He wanted to give her more of the same, and after a third call, Anne Ford took the phone off the hook. She has not spoken more than a few words to her father since that night.

When you talk about Henry Ford II today with members of his own close family, all of them, without exception, loved by him and also wounded by him, sometimes terribly—they search for the link. It seems scarcely possible that a man who has often proved capable of great warmth and sensitivity, a man dusted in some ways with a certain innocence, could also inflict such brutality and pain upon the people who are closest to him. Kind and cruel, caring and callous, Henry Ford II, now in his late sixties, is a full-grown, havoc-wreaking child.

What makes him like that? asks the family in its puzzlement. Do you think he has any real feelings?[37]

It is the same question, presumably, that Clara Ford used to ponder as she contemplated her husband's loving but lethal treatment of their only son, the conundrum that bedevilled the life of Henry Ford I—and which is now also souring the final years of Henry Ford II as well. The earnest disciple of "human engineering," who, says his P.R. man Walter Hayes, treats "housemaids and hotel maids and secretaries and drivers and the people in the plants like

Dukes and Duchesses,"[38] is ending his life isolated and estranged, cut off from his own flesh and blood as effectively as Henry I was—public achievement and private emptiness.

The Ford family today is split by a rift which goes back to the phone calls of Thursday, October 9, 1980, when Henry II invited his daughters to his third wedding, and they refused. Charlotte Ford, who has worked very hard to heal the rift, remembers the phone call vividly.

"I'd just walked into my house in the country and he said, 'Hi, how are you?' 'Fine, how are you?' Shooting the bull for a minute, then he said, 'Well, just wanted you to know that Kathy and I are getting married on Tuesday in Nevada.' It was sort of offhand. I said, 'Oh,' and probably I was wrong. I'm not going to say I was right in not going to the wedding, but you don't know these things until you make the mistake. I said: 'Oh, my God. I can't make it. I've just fired my secretary.' There were all sorts of things going on, my daughter, her school. I said, 'I've got nobody. . . .' Well, O.K., we should all have dropped everything and gone, but we didn't, and he's never forgiven us for that."[39]

Charlotte and Anne had heard about their father's marriage to Cristina on the radio. They disliked Kathy and had made their dislike very plain. They had got their father to promise that he would sit down and talk to them and try to sort out all the differences before he married again. The girls felt discarded, betrayed.

Kathy Ford has little sympathy with them. "Poor little rich girls," she says, "with all this complaining, you know, about Daddy never did this and Daddy never did that. Well, I just feel like saying, 'You were damn lucky you had a father. My kids didn't. . . .' I don't ever want to stay in their home or have to take a trip with them again. I mean, I've been subjected to just enough."[40]

The precise history of the ill-feeling that has developed between Henry Ford's daughters and the stepmother who is just one year Charlotte's senior is a tale of antipathies familiar to many families. There is justice and pettiness on both sides, and it would make up quite a banal recital if its progressions had not been acted out on luxury yachts in the Mediterranean. Having made quite an effort to get on well with Cristina, and having grown rather fond of her for a time, the Ford children felt disinclined to make the effort with a second stepmother, especially one they considered demeaning to their father. Kathy Ford, for her part, makes no secret of her feeling that they are spoiled kids who should get used to the real world, and she remains furious with them for shunning her wedding.

"If you received a phone call that your father had died," she asked Charlotte later, "would you have been able to make it to his funeral?"[41]

The mutual rancour has not been helped by the emotional inarticulateness of Henry Ford II, who is at the eye of the storm.

"The trouble with the Fords," says the former Mrs. DuRoss, "is that they bottle things up, and then it all comes out in a nasty way."[42]

No one could accuse Kathy Ford of that. She is a very direct person indeed. She says exactly what is on her mind, and she is not afraid to be quite open about interests which, in other people, might be considered eccentric. She studies the stars, consults fortune-tellers, and has deep faith in the spirit world and the power of psychic communication, believing that the spirit of old Henry Ford I himself may have played a part in bringing her together with her present husband.

"I played a violin," she says, "and the grandfather also played a violin and his favourite song was 'I'll Take You Home Again, Kathleen.' So probably my first husband and the grandfather were just bored up in heaven and just thought they'd play this little game, maybe, and work it out. You never know. Those are the mysteries."[43]

Kathy Ford believes it is the psychic dimension that makes the whole planet move.

"It's very important," she says, "for a person to become aware and open your mind to the psychic world because it's really as much a part of our lives as the air we breathe and the water we drink. It's just there."[44]

When you meet her she will, if she likes you, introduce you to her own spirit, Helta, a very proper piece of English ectoplasm with quaint expressions like "larder" and "quell" whom she talks to frequently through her Ouija board.[45]

"The Ouija board," she explains, "is an alphabet. It is a form of table-tipping. . . . You have a planchette, a triangular planchette. You just rest your hand on it, you ask a question, and the circle in the middle of it goes over the letters. . . . I must tell you, it's energy. I mean, energy is around everything, and she is like a sender and I'm a receiver. I'm the sender, she's the receiver. We pull in. . . .

"I've said, 'Well, how does this work?' because when I'm in an airplane and I look down on all these little houses, how does the spirit find that little spot? You know, where we are. And it said, 'It is just like radar.' You know, it's an antenna which we just tune in to."[46]

Kathy Ford says that her husband has been "very open-minded" towards Helta. "It gets his attention. Absolutely."

"I like to hear it," agrees Henry II. "I like to hear what the hell it says, which is interesting. But I don't consult the Ouija board on very important problems. I ask, you know, what's the problem with my boat? Is it serious? Or are we going to have a good trip to Europe?"[47]

Anne Ford can remember Helta coming into the troubled question of the wedding invitation.

"Daddy," she said, "why can't you delay it a little bit, have a proper wedding in Detroit? Then Edsel could come back from Australia."

"No," she recalls her father saying. "The Ouija board says it's got to be on a mountain near Las Vegas next week."[48]

There will probably never be another Ford at the head of the Ford Motor Company. Since Edsel Ford II graduated from college in the early 1970s, Detroit has imagined Henry

Ford II working to smooth and advance the path of his only son to the top of the company.

But Detroit is wrong. Edsel Ford II is doing very nicely at Ford, as a young Ford should. At the age of thirty-seven he currently holds the position of Marketing and Advertising Manager, Lincoln-Mercury Division. No other executive of his age is as far up the Ford hierarchy as he is, and he has been given a broad-based preparation for life at the top—some time in product planning, some time abroad.

But every bright young man on the Ford fast track gets as much. The company's personnel policy is to pick out high-fliers at an early stage and to massage their careers in the same way that Edsel II's has been. By the time he is in his middle forties, Edsel Ford will be surrounded by a pack of talented contemporaries—and he may then well find that his surname counts against him, for since the retirement of Henry II, the Ford Motor Company has discovered that it can operate rather well without a Ford at the helm. The spell has been broken. The chaos of Henry II's latter years is a bad dream when compared with the smooth management that the company has enjoyed since his departure.

So, just like his father and grandfather, Edsel Ford II would not be where he is today if he were not a Ford, and, also like his father, he is not going to get to the top unless he can disassociate himself in quite a distinct fashion from the regime of the Ford who preceded him. The problem is the same for his bright younger cousin, William Clay Ford Junior, who, at the age of twenty-nine, is also moving fast through the company, but who will not face the real challenge for another dozen years.

There is a subcompact Henry Ford III in the wings, a wistful little snow-white blond boy, now in his sixth year and just beginning to make the connection between his own surname and the name on the motorcars. But Henry Ford III does not yet know the full, awful import of his name. He does not even think of himself as a Henry, since his mother and his father—who grew up himself with the burden of an historic name—have called the boy "Sonny" from the day he was born. As names go, it is debatable which of the available alternatives, Edsel or Henry, is worse to live up to.

Henry II has not, in any case, devoted that much effort to teaching Henry III what being a Henry Ford is all about. The first Henry took his grandchildren very seriously, playing with them so much that the time they spent at Fair Lane was a source of some irritation to Edsel and Eleanor, according to Henry II.[49] But his own children have no such cause for complaint. In his own way, Henry II manages as best he can on the few occasions he sees any of his six grandchildren—"Our kids are crazy about him," says Cynthia Ford—but wrapped up in his own life and in his third marriage, he does not yet appear to see himself as a full-time grandparent.[50]

If little Henry III is lucky, he could well remain a "Sonny" for the rest of his life—and the latest Henry Ford is not even an American, since he was born during his parents' tour of duty in Australia and carries an Australian passport. His father will be quite happy if his son, when he reaches the age of eighteen, chooses to leave things that way.

"Who knows?" says Edsel. "It may not be such a good thing to be an American by then."[51]

The younger male Fords have adopted diverse strategies towards the problem of their surname. Edsel II and William Clay Junior have chosen the path to company success, which will never yield them quite what they hope for. If they succeed in making it to the very top, people will say it is because they are Fords, and if they achieve anything less than the very best, the world will, kindly, judge them failures.

Having opted for rebellion, Benson Ford Junior is, at the time of writing, back in Detroit, a chastened figure, seeking reconciliation with his family and legal damages from his former therapist and business partner as some sort of compensation for a dozen bitter, wasted years.

Walter Buhl Ford III, son of Josephine and Wally, the eldest of the Ford Fords who is known as "Buhl," has energetically devoted his inheritance to his own expensive divorce settlements—which have afforded revealing glimpses of the budgetary necessities of the super rich: $6,000 a year spent on cut flowers, $5,000 a year on private showings of first-run movies.[52]

Spiritually, the Ford who seems more at ease with himself than any other of his relatives is Buhl's younger brother, Alfie, a relaxed and amusing thirty-five-year-old who has been a member of the Hare Krishna movement for more than ten years. Taking the name Ambarish Das, after an ancient Hindu king who, according to mythology, gave up his kingdom and wealth to serve the god Krishna, Alfred Brush Ford has given more than $2 million to the Society for Krishna Consciousness. Working with a fellow devotee, Lisa Reuther, the daughter of Walter, he has helped create a temple-monastery beside the Detroit River which distributes food to the poor, and he is currently involved in several projects to bring North America towards a clearer understanding of his movement's principles—among them vegetarianism and reincarnation.

Embryo tycoons, a reformed rebel, a saffron-robed mystic —what can pass between these disparate human beings when they all assemble? The answer is nothing, for they do not. The Ford family may exist in the minds of outsiders as an integrated and coherent clan, meeting, planning, and working together for their mutual advancement. But in reality they display a notable lethargy of family spirit. There is no Hyannis Port where Fords gather to play touch football and plot the strategy of their B class votes. The modern Fords lead coincidental, rather isolated lives, less ashamed than unimpressed by what makes them special. There are today no Fords among the trustees of the Ford Foundation, which, in 1974, disposed of its last piece of Ford stock, and when, in February 1986, the Detroit Institute of Arts celebrated the centennial of Diego Rivera with an exhibition whose centrepiece was the frescoed courtyard which was Edsel Ford's finest legacy—his rare and bravest triumph— only one of his children, Josephine, bothered to attend, while the sole representative of his eleven grandchildren was

Benson's daughter, Lynn, who came with her husband, Paul Alandt.

Before Mrs. Eleanor Ford died, she called all her children together. There would, she said, be no cocktails on this occasion until after she had said what she had to say, because she wanted to make sure that they were all paying attention.[53] Distressed to see so many of Grosse Pointe's great mansions and estates being destroyed, she had decided that she wanted the home she had created with Edsel to be preserved as a memorial, and also as a centre for the ideals of culture and community service which she and her husband had tried to uphold. She left $15 million to keep the Edsel & Eleanor Ford House alive in that tradition, but her children have not proved able to replace the warm, personal focus for family unity which Mrs. Eleanor herself supplied.

One reason for this is the chill in the never-warm relations between Henry Ford II and his younger brother, Bill. Their reserves of brotherly love have been running on empty for several years now. When Henry Ford II asked the family on his retirement in 1979 whether they would like to see Uncle Bill actually sitting in the chairman's position, the general feeling was that they would. So William Clay Ford started coming into the Glasshouse more often. He spent a little less time with his football team and he generally assumed a higher profile in the company—although it was always assumed that his position as chairman would be essentially a ceremonial one.

On Thursday, March 13, 1980, William Clay Ford was in his vice-chairman's office on the twelfth floor of World Headquarters, waiting for the directors' meeting at which he confidently expected his chairmanship to be approved, when his elder brother came into the room looking embarrassed. There had been a change of plan, said Henry II. Philip Caldwell was going to have the chairmanship, and Bill would have to stay in his present position.

William Clay Ford was furious. Quite content with the vice-chairmanship, he had only prepared himself for the higher position at his brother's suggestion, and now he found himself discarded at the very last moment without even the pretence of consultation.

"You treat your staff like that," he complained, according to one of his friends. "You treat your wives like that, and your children like that—and now you treat your brother in the same way."[54]

Philip Caldwell had insisted on having the old chairman's title if he was going to do the old chairman's job, and in the clash which this created between family and company, Henry Ford II had no difficulty in choosing sides. When reflecting today occasionally upon the barren state of his family relations, he shrugs his shoulders with resignation, but with a certain defiant pride.

"I made my choice," he says. "I married the company."[55]

On February 1, 1985, Philip Caldwell, who had reached the age of sixty-five, retired from the chairmanship of the Ford Motor Company to be succeeded by Donald E. Petersen. Petersen had previously been company president, and now he was succeeded in that position by the man who had until then been number three in the hierarchy, Harold A. "Red" Poling.

Detroit could not quite believe it. For the first time in living memory a smooth transition of power had taken place in the Glasshouse. There had been no sackings, feudings, or "early retirements." There had been no unpredicted injections of outside talent, or offices of the chief executive. Everyone just moved up a place in the best General Motors tradition. The transformation aimed at forty years previously by Ernest Breech and Henry Ford II had finally been accomplished. Ford actually looked like becoming a normal company.

As Ford moves forward into the late 1980s, the capricious and confused reign of Henry Ford II, which ended only a matter of a few years ago, already seems to be remarkably distant, improbable even—an aberration. If Henry Ford II had withdrawn from the company when it went public in

1956, or even in the middle of the 1960s, his stewardship would have been looked back upon as one of almost total success, a golden era of revival. As it is, his faltering response to the admittedly severe challenges of the 1970s means he must be judged, ultimately, like his grandfather, to have been a great leader who outstayed his welcome.

The Ford machine is working smoothly at last. The company has a proper, long-term, planned product cycle with new medium-sized cars, the Taurus and Sable, which are the first Ford products since the Mustang and Falcon to give General Motors serious grounds for concern. Ford is gaining market share even faster than the revived Chrysler Corporation under Lee Iacocca—and it has come back from the dead without the help of government money. Lee Iacocca became a folk hero when he took over an ailing giant in 1979 and turned it around dramatically. But in those very same years Philip Caldwell took over a company whose costs and product line were as deplorable as Chrysler's—and whose president for the best part of the previous decade had been Lee Iacocca.

Henry Ford II can take not a little credit for this. The turn-around wrought by the uncharismatic Caldwell is a vindication of Henry II's battle to exclude Lee Iacocca from his company, for the humiliated and driven Iacocca who saved Chrysler is a different character from the complacent, arrogant man who would have taken over at Ford.

"If Iacocca had just succeeded Henry smoothly," says one of his former colleagues, "he would have been like a pig in shit. He had grown lazy, self-indulgent. He should thank Henry for driving him back to basics. Getting sacked shocked Lee. It drove him back to being the lean, tough, car man he was when he started out."[56]

In many ways, Lee Iacocca is the key to the confusion of Henry II's later years. Henry II encouraged the bright young salesman, and then found that he had got more than he had bargained for. Once Lee was up there near the top, Henry II never felt he could relax. The king never really trusted his heir apparent. If he had, he would have made Iacocca president after Arjay Miller, not brought in Bunkie Knudsen, whose arrival acted as a catalyst to the cult of personality developing around Iacocca. Reacting against this, Henry II developed a personality cult of his own, blocking Iacocca's decisions, on occasions, for no more obvious reason than that they were Iacocca's—although it is also possible, with hindsight, to appreciate Henry II's unwillingness to have Iacocca succeed him. If *you* were the grandson of Henry Ford and the son of Edsel Ford, would *you* hand their company over to Lee Iacocca? He is a great businessman, a great Chrysler-saver, a splendid fellow, in fact—but let him save someone else's company.

Lee Iacocca has got his sweetest revenge, of course, from being a better Henry Ford than Henry Ford. In the early years of the century, there was a great carmaker of humble birth, the son of immigrants, who was snubbed by the establishment, who was apparently quite defeated, at one stage, by the privileged and the mighty, but who fought back with anger, with talent, and with sheer hard work, and who provided, in the process, a lot of jobs, not to mention inspiration, for humble people.

It was only right that he should become a folk hero. His cars were not always that good, but people bought them because he told them to. You could trust him. A lot of ordinary men and women felt they could identify with his blunt, no-nonsense ways. They wrote him letters about their problems, and even offered him their advice. They thought of him by his first name. He became a national personality. Highly paid aides helped craft his columns for the newspapers, and when a ghostwriter helped the hero produce what passed for the truth about his life, mixed in with his thoughts on the state of the nation and some simplistic nostrums about how readers could duplicate his business success, it naturally produced a runaway best-seller. It was small wonder people started talking about him for the presidency.

Henry Ford II has feigned indifference to the astonishing

apotheosis of the man he fired nearly a decade ago. But in reality he is mortified.

"Are you still sucking ass around that Iacocca?" he growled recently to an acquaintance brave enough to have stayed on good terms with the former Ford president.[57]

But the meteoric career of Lee Iacocca since his departure from Ford has at least vindicated the basic reason why Henry II did not want him running his family company. Lee Iacocca today *is* Chrysler. He has made the company his own personal fiefdom. How is Chrysler going to sell its fairly ordinary cars in the future without his smiling face? It is the only way that Lee Iacocca knows how to do things. Between 1984 and 1986, he even managed to make the Statue of Liberty his property for a time.

The final twist, however, is that Iacocca learned it all at Ford. The Ford Motor Company taught him everything that he knew. It provided him with the launching pad for his great achievements elsewhere—and when he got to Chrysler, it was a team of Ford men that he assembled to help him save the day. Lee Iacocca, in fact, relied even more heavily on Ford men and Ford techniques to save Chrysler than Ernie Breech relied on General Motors men to save Ford.

It is the autumn of 1984 and Henry Ford II is in his office, sorting papers. He no longer occupies the topmost office in the Glasshouse, and he does not come in every day by any means. Since his retirement he has spent most of his time in England or Florida, where he has taken up residence, and where he sits on the boards of a hospital and a bank in order to emphasize his Florida residence for tax purposes. The tax advantage of living in Florida is the absence of any local inheritance tax, and since Henry II has publicly announced his intention not to bequeath his children any more than they have already received from him and from the family trusts, this must be presumably for the benefit of his third wife and his grandchildren.

So far as the Ford Motor Company is concerned, Henry

II is today like any other outside director flying into Dearborn on the second Wednesday of every month—with a difference. When he retired, the rules of membership of the crucial Finance Committee were altered so that an outside director could sit on this body which exercises ultimate control over company spending,[58] and this outside director was Henry Ford II. He became chairman.

So the old monarch has not finally resigned his prerogatives. Every major company programme still has to pass his scrutiny, and when it comes to top management changes at Ford, there is no move from the level of vice-president upwards which is not submitted for his personal approval.[59]

But Henry Ford II is not concerned with the current activities of his company on this autumn afternoon. The papers that he is shuffling are to do with history, the letters and reports and memoranda which make up the record of his years in the company—and most of them are going into his paper shredder.

Everyone who went to see Henry Ford II in the months that surrounded his retirement can remember it—the paper shredder chewing away in the corner, and the smile on the face of Henry II. Not content with destroying most of his own papers, he also secured and personally shredded the medical records of his parents and grandparents to preserve their secrets from posterity.[60]

"I did a good job on that," he says with satisfaction.[61]

Are there any papers at all that he is keeping?

"Absolutely nothing," he replies, "except letters that I think are interesting. . . . Letters from presidents or people of importance, and I save a few documents that are of special interest to me—otherwise everything goes."[62]

His grandfather spent the last two decades of his life rearranging history, and the results are to be seen spread across 250 acres to the southwest of Henry II's office. To the southeast lies the Rouge. Still further around are the shiny glass silos of the Renaissance Center rising above the distant skyscrapers of downtown Detroit.

But Henry Ford II is not focusing on the scenery. He has

his head down, shuffling papers, feeding the humming, voracious little beast by his side. Nearly seventy now and rather shaky, he looks quite an old man.

Is he ashamed of what he has done, in some way? Bashful? Bored with it? Why this eagerness to edit a lifetime of dynamic, brave, flawed achievement to the polite and unexceptional contents of one cardboard box?[63] The hero shrugs his shoulders, quite content with the enigma.

"What I've done in my life," says Henry Ford, "is nobody's business."[64]

# APPENDIX: THE FORD FAMILY

Henry Ford's parents were William Ford (1826–1905) and Mary Litogot (1839–1876). They married in 1861.

Their children were an unnamed infant son (d. 1862), Henry (1863–1947), John (1865–1927), Margaret (1867–1960), Jane (1869–1906), William (1871–1959), Robert (1873–1877), and a last, unnamed infant son (d. 1876).

Margaret married James Ruddiman, the brother of Henry's school friend Edsel Ruddiman, and had a daughter, Catherine (b. 1902).

Henry Ford married Clara Jane Bryant (1866–1950) in 1888. Their only child was Edsel Bryant Ford (1893–1943).

Edsel Ford married Eleanor Clay (1896–1976) in 1916. Their children are Henry II (b. 1917), Benson (1919–1978), Josephine Clay (b. 1923), and William Clay (b. 1925).

Henry Ford II has been married three times, first to Anne McDonnell (b. 1919), married in 1940, divorced in 1964; second to Maria Cristina Vettore Austin (b. 1926), married in 1965, divorced in 1980; and third to Kathleen King DuRoss (b. 1940), married in 1980. Henry Ford II is now officially resident in Florida, but retains homes in Grosse Pointe Farms and near Henley-on-Thames, England.

Henry II has had no children by his latter two wives. His children by his first wife, Anne McDonnell, are Charlotte (b. 1941), Anne (b. 1943), and Edsel Bryant Ford II (b. 1948). Henry Ford II is stepfather to the daughters of Kathleen DuRoss, Debi (b. 1956) and Kimberly (b. 1957).

Charlotte Ford's husbands have been Stavros Niarchos (b. 1910), married in 1965, divorced in 1967; and Tony

Forstmann (b. 1939), married in 1973, divorced in 1978. In 1986 she married Edward Reynolds Downe Jnr (b. 1929). They live in New York.

Charlotte's daughter by Stavros Niarchos is Elena Anne (b. 1966). Charlotte had no children by Tony Forstmann.

Anne Ford's husbands have been Giancarlo Uzielli (b. 1934), married in 1965, divorced in 1975; and Charles Scarborough (b. 1943), married in 1982. They live in New York.

Anne's children by Giancarlo Uzielli are Alessandro (b. 1966) and Allegra (b. 1972). She has had no children by Charles Scarborough.

Edsel Ford II married Cynthia Layne Neskow (b. 1951) in 1974. They live in Grosse Pointe Farms. Their children are Henry III (b. 1980), Calvin (b. 1983), and Stewart (b. 1986). Edsel has worked at Ford since 1974 and currently holds the position of Marketing Manager, Lincoln-Mercury Division.

Benson Ford (1919–1978) married Edith McNaughton (1920–1980) in 1941. Their children are Benson Junior (b. 1949) and Lynn (b. 1951).

Benson Junior married Lisa Adams (b. 1953) in 1984. They have a house in Grosse Pointe Farms.

Lynn married Paul Alandt (b. 1949) in 1975. They live in Grosse Pointe Shores. Paul Alandt is executive director of the Edsel & Eleanor Ford House in Grosse Pointe Shores.

Josephine Clay Ford married Walter Buhl Ford II (b. 1920) in 1943. They live in Grosse Pointe Farms. Walter Buhl Ford II is an interior and industrial designer. Their children are Walter Buhl III (b. 1943), Eleanor Clay (b. 1946), Josephine Clay (b. 1949), and Alfred Brush (b. 1950).

Walter Buhl Ford III married Barbara Posselius (b. 1945) in 1964 and was divorced in 1977. His 1978 marriage to Charlene Decraene (b. 1951) was dissolved in 1983. Known as Buhl, Walter Buhl III lives in Grosse Pointe Shores and works in the advertising department of Ford's Lincoln-Mercury Division.

Walter Buhl III's children by his first wife, Barbara, are Bridget (b. 1964), Lindsey (b. 1968), Wendy (b. 1971), and Barbara (b. 1973). He had no children by his second wife, Charlene.

Eleanor Clay married Frederic Bourke, Jr. (b. 1946), in 1966. They currently live in Connecticut. Their children are Avery (b. 1967), Eleanor Ford (b. 1970), and Denis (b. 1978). Frederic Bourke, Jr., is a businessman.

Josephine Clay married John Ingle, Jr. (b. 1946), in 1971. They currently live in the Finger Lakes area of New York State. Their children are Jason (b. 1974), Julie (b. 1977), John III (b. 1981), and a fourth child expected in 1986. John Ingle, Jr., is a wine grower.

Alfred Brush Ford joined the International Society for Krishna Consciousness—the Hare Krishna movement—in 1974, and took the name of Ambarish Das, the name of an ancient Hindu king who, according to mythology, gave up his kingdom and wealth to serve the god Krishna. In 1984 Alfred married Dr. Sharmilla Bhattacharya (b. 1956). They are currently resident in Florida.


William Clay Ford married Martha Firestone (b. 1925) in 1947. They live in Grosse Pointe Shores. He is vice-chairman of the Ford Motor Company, and owner of the Detroit Lions football team. Their children are Martha Parke, known as Muffy (b. 1948), Sheila Firestone (b. 1951), William Clay Junior (b. 1957), and Elizabeth Hudson (b. 1961).

Martha Parke married Peter Morse (b. 1947) in 1973. They live in Pennsylvania. Peter Morse is a businessman. Their children are Peter (b. 1977), Martha, known as Kate (b. 1979), and Lisa (b. 1983).

Sheila Firestone married Steven Hamp (b. 1948) in 1981. Their children are Michael (b. 1984) and Christopher (b. 1985). Steve Hamp is the Chairman of the Collections Department of the Ford Archives at the Edison Institute.

William Clay Ford, Jr., married Lisa Vanderzee (b. 1960) in 1983. They live in Grosse Pointe Shores. Their only child is Eleanor Clay (b. 1985). William Clay Junior works at the Ford Motor Company in the position of Planning Manager in Car Product Development.

# NOTES

*All quotations are given without altering spelling or punctuation, except where indicated. For details of the books and articles cited, see the Bibliography.*

*Abbreviations used in the Notes*

FA — Ford Archives of the Edison Institute. See MANUSCRIPT COLLECTIONS in the Bibliography.

FAE — Ford Archives of England. See MANUSCRIPT COLLECTIONS in the Bibliography.

FIA — Ford Motor Company Archives. See MANUSCRIPT COLLECTIONS in the Bibliography.

*MLW* — *My Life and Work*, Henry Ford I's autobiography. See BOOKS, CATALOGUES, AND PAMPHLETS in the Bibliography.

## The Men and the Machine

1. Henry Ford II, interview, April 17, 1986.
2. The figures for the sign are compiled by *Automotive News* for the Goodyear tyre company. They are based on the previous week's production, in all United States assembly plants, by General Motors, Ford, Chrysler, and American Motors. They also include small numbers of cars produced by the U.S. plants of Honda, Nissan, Volkswagen, and New United, the GM–Toyota joint venture producing Nova automobiles.
3. *Fortune*, August 18, 1985, p. 179.
4. Henry Ford II interview, September 11, 1984.
5. Ibid., April 17, 1986.
6. Ibid., September 11, 1984.

## 1. Farmboy

1. Tocqueville, *Journey to America*, p. 351.
2. Ibid., p. 350.

3. Ibid., p. 364.

4. Ibid., pp. 363, 364.

5. Ibid., p. 367.

6. FA, *Reminiscences*, Clyde Ford, contains an account of the early settlement of Dearborn. Clyde Ford was a cousin of Henry Ford.

7. FA, Acc. 1, Box 1. Spelling unchanged, author's punctuation.

8. FA, Acc. 1, Box 14.

9. *Illustrated Historical Atlas*, Wayne County, Michigan, 1876; cited by Bryan, "Patrick Ahern, Henry Ford and Fair Lane," p. 15.

10. This seems the most likely interpretation of the rather sketchy evidence about the early history of the Ford family. There is a theory that Henry Ford's grandfather was only briefly in Ireland before emigrating to America, having spent most of his life on a farm in Essex. But this does not seem to square with the quite complex network of brothers and cousins who all moved from Ireland to Dearborn about the same time. For details see Nevins and Hill, Olson, and the articles of Ford R. Bryan.

11. Bryan, "William Ford South."

12. For more details about Henry Ford's grandfather, see Ford R. Bryan's article "Patrick Ahern, Henry Ford and Fair Lane."

13. Interview with Edgar A. Guest, "Henry Ford Talks About His Mother," *American Magazine*; cited in Nevins and Hill, vol. 1, pp. 49–51.

14. Simonds, p. 27.

15. FA, *Reminiscences*, Ruddiman, unbound. From discussions with Margaret's daughter, Catherine Ruddiman, and with Owen Bombard, in charge of the Ford oral-history programme in the early 1950s, it would seem that there were originally three different sets of Ruddiman reminiscences: as given by Margaret Ruddiman to Bombard in an interview, as given to Frank Hill in an interview, and as written in a long article, with the help of her daughter, "Memories of My Brother, Henry Ford," in *Michigan History*, Vol. 37, No. 3, for September 1953. Of these, only the Hill interview is not easily available in the Ford Archives, although it may survive in some as-yet-uninventoried collection.

16. Olson, p. 16.

17. FA, *Reminiscences*, Ruddiman, unbound.

18. Ibid.

19. Ruddiman, "Memories," pp. 243–244.

20. FA, *Reminiscences*, Ruddiman, unbound.

21. Interview with Edgar A. Guest; cited in David E. Nye, p. 97.

22. Simonds, p. 34.

23. David E. Nye, p. 96.

24. Olson, p. 18.

25. Ibid.

26. Dahlinger, p. 75.

27. *MLW*, p. 22.

28. Ibid.

29. Ibid., pp. 22, 23.

30. Selden Case Record/*Chicago Tribune* trial; cited in Nevins and Hill, vol. 1, p. 55.

31. MLW, p. 23.

32. Ibid., p. 24.

33. Benson, pp. 28–30.

34. *MLW*, p. 24.

35. Benson, p. 33.

36. Ibid., pp. 30–34.

37. Ruddiman, "Memories," p. 249.

38. Ibid.

39. Benson, p. 34.

40. *MLW*, p. 24. The actual name of the firm was the Detroit Dry Dock Company, not the Drydock Engine Works.

41. Arnold and Faurote, p. 9.

42. FA, *Reminiscences*, Strauss, p. 2.

43. Ibid., p. 4.

44. Ibid.

45. Ruddiman, "Memories," p. 248.

46. Ibid., p. 254.

47. FA, *Reminiscences*, Strauss, p. 4.

48. Ruddiman, "Memories," p. 255.

## 2. Machine Age

1. Hatcher and Walter, p. 54.

2. Brown et al., p. 23.

3. Ibid., p. 24.

4. Ferry, p. 7.

5. Conot, p. 10.

6. Ferry, p. 11.

7. Olson, p. 113.

# NOTES

8. Conot, p. 17.

9. Hatcher and Walter, p. 212.

10. Conot, p. 94.

11. FA, *Reminiscences*, Strauss, p. 3.

12. Benson, p. 40.

13. Olson, p. 28. The Magill jewellery shop was later moved and reconstructed by Henry Ford, and stands in Greenfield Village.

14. *MLW*, p. 30.

15. Ibid., pp. 45–46.

16. *Fortune*, "Mr. Ford Doesn't Care," p. 134.

17. Olson, p. 33.

18. Ibid.

19. Ibid.

20. The original inspiration of this search appears to have been commercial, not nostalgic. Charles Knight had patented a certain sort of slide valve for his Willys Knight car, and, remembering that he had devised and fitted a similar sort of sleeve valve to 345 more than twenty years earlier, Henry instituted the search to prove his prior invention.

21. Bryan, "Revival of Old-Fashioned Harvesting."

22. Doolen, "The National Greenback Party," p. 161.

23. Ibid., p. 176.

24. Hurt, "The Ohio Grange," p. 19.

25. Chicago Tribune, July 12, 1935; cited in Wik, p. 12.

26. FA, Fair Lane Papers, Box 118; cited in Nevins and Hill, vol. 1, p. 88.

27. Breuer, "Henry Ford and the Believer," p. 124.

28. FA, "Memories," Margaret Ford Ruddiman, pp. 261, 262.

29. Breuer, "Henry Ford and the Believer," p. 124.

30. Ibid.

31. FA, "Memories," Margaret Ford Ruddiman.

32. FA, Acc. 1, Box 1.

33. Olson, p. 47.

34. Ford Bryan to author, April 12, 1986.

35. Olson, p. 45.

36. These extracts come from two letters in the Ford Archives (Acc. 1, Box 1), one dated March 3, 1891, the other "1891" and "Friday morning."

37. Ruddiman, "Memories," p. 265.

38. *MLW*, p. 30.

## 3. First Ford

1. Olson, p. 53. Henry started work for Edison at an electrical substation at the junction of Willis and Woodward avenues. The Fords' first lodgings were at 618 (today 4426) John R. Street.

2. Rae, *American Automobile Manufacturers*, p. 28.

3. Nevins and Hill, vol. 1, pp. 139, 140.

4. Douglas Dow, interview, September 19, 1984.

5. FA, *Reminiscences*, Strauss, p. 18.

6. Ford R. Bryan, letter to the author, December 13, 1985.

7. Warnock, p. 76.

8. Shapiro and Hendricks, p. 27.

9. Nevins and Hill, vol. 1, pp. 135–136.

10. Brendan Gill, "To Spare the Obedient Beast," *New Yorker*; cited in Nevins and Hill, vol. 1, p. 13.

11. *MLW*, pp. 25, 26.

12. National Automotive History Collection, Papers of Charles B. King, Box 3. Statement of Oliver E. Barthel, March 29, 1940.

13. Ibid. Correspondence between Charles B. King and George W. Cato, October 2, 1930, and February 15, 1931.

14. Olson, p. 73.

15. Nevins and Hill, vol. 1, p. 193.

16. Ibid., p. 149.

17. *Detroit Journal*, March 7, 1896.

18. Nevins and Hill, vol. 1, p. 154.

19. Ibid.

20. *MLW*, p. 14.

21. Nevins and Hill, vol. 1, p. 156.

22. FA, *Reminiscences*, Bush, p. 9.

23. FA, Margaret Ford Ruddiman, Written Memoir IV, p.1.

24. Brough, p. 48.

25. Olson, p. 98.

26. Ibid., p. 116.

27. Nevins and Hill, vol. 1, p. 175.

28. *Detroit Journal*, August 5, 1899; cited in Nevins and Hill, vol. 1, p.175.

29. Detroit Free Press, August 19, 1899.

30. Ch. 14 of Olson contains a most detailed and illuminating review of the major shareholders in the Detroit Automobile Company.

31. Nevins and Hill, vol. 1, p. 176.

32. FA, *Reminiscences*, Strauss, p. 53.

33. *Detroit News-Tribune*, February 4, 1900.

34. Ibid.

35. *MLW*, p. 36.

36. FA, *Reminiscences*, Strauss, p. 53.

37. Ibid.

38. Olson, p. 121.


# 4. Racing

1. FA, Acc. 1, Box 22.

2. Ibid.

3. See Olson for a good selection of Henry Ford's family snapshots.

4. FA, Acc. 1, Box 22.

5. Ibid.

6. Nevins and Hill, vol. 1, p. 196.

7. Olson, p. 135.

8. Ibid., p. 78. Spelling unchanged. Author's punctuation.

9. Simonds tells this story in his book *Henry Ford*, p. 69. He probably got the story about Charles Shanks preselecting the trophy from Henry Ford himself, who provided much of the material in the book. After Henry Ford had won, Clara refers to him receiving "a beautiful cut glass punch bowl" (FA, Acc. 102, Box 1).

10. See Silas Farmer, *Grosse Pointe on Lake Sainte Claire*, for a contemporary description of Grosse Pointe in 1886.

11. *Detroit Tribune*, October 11, 1901; cited in Nevins and Hill, vol. 1, p. 204.

12. FA, Acc. 102, Box 1: Clara Bryant Ford to Milton D. Bryant, December 3, 1901.

13. FA, *Reminiscences*, Barthel, p. 70.

14. Ibid., Ruddiman, p. 3.

15. London *Sunday Express*, "Henry Ford, discussing his Religion, says I Believe in a Master Mind," November 4, 1928. No author given.

16. Henry Ford described his conviction that he was a soldier in a previous life to Dr. William R. Valentiner, who recorded the conversation in his diary for October 31, 1939. Sterne, p. 267.

17. For example, in an interview with John Bradford Maine of the *Detroit Times*, on April 26, 1938. Cited in FA, *Reminiscences*, Barthel, p. 71.

18. London *Sunday Express*, November 4, 1928.

19. FA, Acc. 102, Box 1: Clara Ford to Milton Bryant, December 3, 1901; cited in Nevins and Hill, vol. 1, p. 207.

20. Ibid.: Henry Ford to Milton Bryant, January 6, 1902. Author's punctuation.

21. FA, *Reminiscences*, Barthel, p. 28.

22. Ibid., p. 74.

23. Ibid., p. 29.

24. Rae, *American Automobile Manufacturers*, p. 31.

25. FA, *Reminiscences*, Pring, p. 24.

26. London *Sunday Express*, November 4, 1928.

27. Nevins and Hill, vol. 1, p. 234.

28. Motor Vehicle Manufacturers Assn., p. 48. The precise number was 290.

29. Hyde, p. 20.

30. FA, Acc. 102, Box 1: Clara Bryant Ford to Milton Bryant, March 3, 1902.

31. *MLW*, p. 50.

32. Simonds, p. 75.

33. Ibid., p. 76.

34. FA, Acc. 102, Box 1.

## 5. Dr. Pfennig Buys a Car

1. Sterne, p. 193.

2. Ferry, *Buildings of Detroit*, p. 179.

3. Rae, *American Automobile Manufacturers*, p. 36.

4. Rae, "Why Michigan?," in Lewis, "The Automobile in American Culture," p. 437.

5. Hyde, p. 10.

6. FA, Acc. 1, Box 1.

7. Nevins and Hill, vol. 1, p. 233.

8. Ibid., p. 226.

9. Olson, p. 163.

10. Hyde, pp. 11, 13.

11. I am grateful to Martin S. Hayden for lending me the manuscript of the unpublished biography of James Couzens by his father, Jay Hayden. This was based on interviews with Couzens, and though it was not completed, it does cover Couzens's early years and work with Ford in some detail.

12. FA; these figures are taken from the letter written by John W. Anderson to his father on June 4, 1903.

13. Olson, p. 189.

14. Nevins and Hill, vol. 1, p. 246.

15. *Detroit Journal*, April 24, 1905.

16. Interview with Mrs. Myrle Miller (nee Clarkson), *Detroit News*, September 16, 1941.

17. Simonds, p. 102.

18. Harry Barnard, pp. 46, 47.

19. Dominguez, pp. 10, 11.

20. *MLW*, p. 57.

21. *Detroit Journal*, May 9, 1905.

22. Milton A. McRae, *Forty Years in Newspaperdom;* cited in Nevins and Hill, vol. 1, p. 274.

23. Nevins and Hill, vol. 1, p. 279.

24. FAE, Percival Perry memoir.

25. Nevins and Hill, vol. 1, p. 273.

26. FAE, Perry memoir.

27. FA, *Reminiscences*, Wandersee, p. 37; cited in Nevins and Hill, vol. 1, p. 271. See also Olson, p. 132.

28. Olson, p. 127.

29. FA, *Reminiscences*, Fred Rockelman, p. 25.

## 6. Model T

1. Susman, p. 136.

2. *MLW*, p. 66.

3. Ibid., spelling corrected ("Very litle vanadium" to "Very little vanadium").

4. *Detroit Journal*, March 21, 1907.

5. *Cycle and Automobile Trade Journal X*, January 1, 1906, p. 105.

6. Figures from the Secretary's Office Records, Ford Motor Company; cited in Nevins and Hill, vol. 1, p. 338. In *My Life and Work*, Henry Ford gives the sales figure for the twelve months to September 30, 1907, as 8,423 cars.

7. Charles E. Sorensen, p. 96.

8. Ibid.

9. FA, *Reminiscences*, Galamb, p. 15.

10. Ibid., p. 25.

11. Charles E. Sorensen, p. 103.

12. Ibid.

13. Ibid., pp. 99–100.

14. Ibid., p. 107.

15. Ibid., p. 108.

16. Ibid., p. 109.

17. Ibid., p. 105.

18. Both letters dated March 21, 1908, published in *Ford Times* I, April 15, 1908, pp. 14–15.

19. *Ford Times* II, October 15, 1908, p. 10.

20. Nevins and Hill, vol. 1, pp. 396–397.

21. Lewis, "Ford Country."

22. E. B. White, *Letters*; see pages 31–61 for details of the expedition.

23. E. B. White, "Farewell, My Lovely!" *The Second Tree from the Corner*, pp. 36–37. White's essay, suggested by a manuscript submitted by Richard L. Strout of the *Christian Science Monitor*, originally appeared in the *New Yorker* over the pseudonym Lee Strout White. It was published as a little book in its own right, *Farewell to Model T*, by G. P. Putnam's Sons in 1936.

24. Edsel B. Ford, *Souvenir Transcontinental Tour: Detroit to San Francisco—June 17, 1915, to June 25, 1915.* Unpublished journal in the archives of the Edsel & Eleanor Ford House, Grosse Pointe.

25. FA, Acc. 62, Box 4: Letter of Mrs. John P—, Rome, Georgia, June 3, 1918; cited in Wik, p. 1.

26. See Gertrude Stein, *Wars I Have Seen*, and Ernest Hemingway, *A Moveable Feast*, p. 29.

27. Grace Hegger Lewis, *With Love from Gracie: Sinclair Lewis 1912 —25*; cited in Wik, p. 1.

28. Nevins and Hill, vol. 1, p. 295.

29. Ibid.

30. Ibid., pp. 296, 297.

31. Ibid.

32. *Detroit Free Press*, July 28, 1903.

33. Nevins and Hill, vol. 1, p. 421.

34. Ibid., p. 423, 424.

35. Ibid.

36. *Detroit News*, October 19, 1909.

37. Nevins and Hill, vol. 1, p. 424.

38. *Detroit Journal*, February 12, 1910.

39. Ibid., February 26, 1910.

40. *Detroit Free Press*, March 1, 1910.

41. Lewis, p. 24.

42. Nevins and Hill, vol. 1, p. 644.

43. FA, *Reminiscences*, Wollering, p. 34.

44. *Detroit Journal*, October 1, 1910.

45. *American Machinist*, May 8, 1913, through September 18, 1913; cited in Jardim, p. 88.

46. See Hounshell, ch. 6, for a very detailed analysis of the introduction of movement to Ford production processes. Hounshell produces good evidence for doubting whether radiator conveyors were introduced in 1912, as claimed by Sorensen and as accepted by Nevins and Hill.

47. *MLW*, p. 83.

48. Ibid.

49. Garrett, p. 85.

50. Nevins and Hill, vol. I, pp. 644, 648.

## 7. Birds and the Spirit

This chapter is largely based on a paper, "Images of an Idealist: Henry Ford's Vision for Highland Park," delivered by the author to the Society for the History of Technology meeting at the Edison Institute, Dearborn, on October 18, 1985. I am grateful to the seminar organizer, Kathleen Anderson Kraus, to its moderator, Stephen Meyer III, and to Professor David L. Lewis and Dr. Howard Segal for their comments on the paper.

I am grateful to Barry F. Machado for first drawing my attention to the importance of the relationship between John Burroughs and Henry Ford, and for showing me his unpublished article "The Olde Ford Way: A New Perspective."

1. FA, Acc. 1, Box 1: Notebooks and jottings.

2. Barrus, vol. 2, p. 185.

3. Ibid.

4. Burroughs, *John Burroughs Talks*, p. 326.

5. *MLW*, p. 239.

6. FA, Acc. 1, Box 14.

7. I am grateful to Barry Machado for this date. He says that the earliest quoting of Emerson by Ford he can discover is in an interview in the *New York Herald* of January 1, 1915.

8. Benson, pp. 331, 332.

9. The book and dust jacket are to be found in the Ford Archives in the Edison Institute at Dearborn, Acc. 1, Box 14, along with other notebooks and jottings.

10. Emerson, *Essays*, p. 190.

11. Ibid., p. 93.

12. Ibid., p. 54.

13. Ibid., p. 215.

14. Kasson, p. 117.

15. Emerson, *Essays*, p. 47.

16. From the manuscript of Jay Hayden's unpublished biography of Couzens, p. 65.

17. Charles Sorensen claims (pp. 136–140) that Couzens was not even present at the meeting which decided on the Five Dollar Day.

18. For detailed figures, see Nevins and Hill, vol. 1, p. 525.

19. Meyer, p. 103.

20. Ford Motor Company pamphlet, *Helpful Hints and Advice to Employes*, p. 8. I am grateful to Dr. Phil Mason of the Walter Reuther Library for first showing me this pamphlet.

21. These and other citations can be found in Lewis, ch. 5, pp. 69–77, which is quite the most comprehensive account of media reaction to the Five Dollar Day.

22. Conot, p. 169.

23. Ibid.

24. Ibid., p. 170.

25. Lewis, p. 71.

26. Ibid.

27. Benson, p. 332.

28. Emerson, *Best of RWE*, p. 161.

29. Ibid.

30. Sward, p. 49.

31. Hounshell, p. 258.

32. Emerson, *Best of RWE*, pp. 161, 162.

33. Charles E. Sorensen, p. 139.

34. *Syracuse Herald*, January 11, 1914; cited in Nevins and Hill, vol. 1, p. 534.

35. *MLW*, p. 126.

36. Ibid., p. 147.

37. Marquis, pp. 152–153.

38. Ibid.

39. Ford Motor Company pamphlet, *Helpful Hints and Advice to Employes*, pp. 8–9.

40. Samuel M. Levin, "Ford Profit-Sharing, 1914–1920," *Personnel Journal*; cited in Meyer, p. 111.

41. *New York Times*, January 1914; cited in Sward, p. 61.

42. Stevenson, pp. 48–49.

43. Conot, p. 188, the best survey of social conditions in Detroit at this period.

44. All the preceding are taken from the Ford Motor Company pamphlet *Helpful Hints and Advice to Employes*.

45. Ford Motor Company pamphlet, *Profit Sharing Plan of the Ford Motor Company*, and FA, *Reminiscences*, Baxter, p. 547; cited in Nevins and Hill, vol. 1, p. 555.

46. *New York Times*, November 15, 1914; cited in Meyer, p. 77.

47. *Forum*, April 1928; cited in David E. Nye, p. 71.

48. Breuer, "Henry Ford and the Believer."

49. Ford Motor Company pamphlet (J. E. Mead), *Salvage of Men*; cited in Nevins and Hill, vol. 1, p. 562.

50. Marquis, p. 153.

51. David E. Nye, p. 71.

52. *Detroit Times*, January 12, 1914; cited in Nevins and Hill, vol. 1, p. 545.

53. FA, *Reminiscences*, McDonnell ("Life with Uncle Henry" by Orry Barrule), p. 3.

54. Madison, "My Seven Years of Automotive Servitude," pp. 445—458. Madison's account has additional interest in that he had also worked for Ford before the introduction of the moving assembly line.

55. Ibid.

56. FA, Acc. 1, Box 120: "Personnel Complaints"; cited in Hounshell, p. 259.

57. Conot, p. 175.

58. Marquis, p. 34.

59. Ibid.

60. Ibid., p. 35.

61. These figures are based on data compiled by John R. Lee and by the *Ford Times*; cited in Nevins and Hill, vol. 1, pp. 558–559.

62. FA, *Reminiscences*, McDonnell, p. 9.

63. Herndon, p. 15.

## 8. The Peace Ship

1. Schlesinger, *Age of Jackson*; cited in Kraft, p. vii.

2. FA, Acc. 1, Box 1.

3. FA, *Reminiscences*, Rockelman, p. 85.

4. Jane Addams, *Peace and Bread*; cited in Kraft, p. 5.

5. Kraft, p. 4.

6. This sounds like direct repetition of the lessons in the McGuffey Readers, but, according to Barbara Kraft (p. 50), the *New York Times* reporter told Ford that this was the opinion of the pacifist Jane Addams, and Ford agreed with it.

7. Smith, *Rise of Industrial America*, p. 745.

8. *New York Times Magazine*, April 11, 1915.

9. *Detroit News*, June 18, 1915.

10. *Detroit Journal*, November 29, 1915; cited in Kraft, p. 34, and Lewis, p. 78.

11. Kraft, p. 62.

12. Lochner; cited in Nevins and Hill, vol. 2, p. 27.

13. Nevins and Hill, vol. 1, p. 511.

14. Villard, "Unveiling of Henry Ford," *Nation*; cited in Lewis, p. 80.

15. Villard, *Fighting Years*; cited in Kraft, p. 68.

16. *New York Tribune*, November 25, 1915; cited in Kraft, p. 68.

17. *Detroit Free Press*, November 25, 1915; cited in Kraft, p. 68.

18. Barrus, vol. 2, p. 227.

19. Lochner; cited in Kraft, p. 74.

20. Clara Ford to Rosika Schwimmer, August 12, 1916, Evans Papers; cited in Kraft, p. 90.

21. Breuer, "Henry Ford and the Believer."

22. Ibid.

23. FA, *Reminiscences*, Caritte, p. 6, and Marquis, p. 19.

24. *Detroit Free Press*, December 5, 1915.

25. Good descriptions of the Peace Ship's sailing are in Kraft, ch. 6, Lewis, ch. 6, and Nevins and Hill, vol 2, ch. 2.

26. Kraft, p. 89.

27. Ibid.

28. Lewis, p. 90.

29. Kraft, p. 137.

30. Ibid.

31. Lewis, p. 90.

32. Nevins and Hill, vol. 2, p. 45.

33. Lochner; cited in Nevins and Hill, vol. 2, p. 45.

34. Marquis, p. 8.

35. Ibid.

36. Lewis, p. 91.

37. FA, Acc. 66, Box 6: "Henry Ford and His Peace Mission: A Discourse at Temple Keneseth Israel"; cited in Wik, p. 167.

38. Lewis, p. 90.

39. *Ford Times*, October 1915; cited in Lewis, p. 79.

## 9. Blood Money

1. Richards, p. 1.

2. Nevins and Hill, vol. 1, p. 649.

3. I am grateful to Jerald and Marilyn Mitchell, the current occupants of 66 Edison Avenue, for showing me around the house.

4. Breuer, "Henry Ford and the Believer."

5. Samuel S. Marquis, *Henry Ford*; cited in Greenleaf, p. 11.

6. Barfknecht, p. 111. The road was laid in order to cope with the heavy traffic around Highland Park on Woodward Avenue between Six Mile and Seven Mile roads, and cost $13,537.

7. Ford Bryan examined the origin of Fair Lane's name in his research for the article "Patrick Ahern, Henry Ford and Fair Lane," and I am grateful to him for his assistance with this and other points.

8. Ferry, *Buildings of Detroit*, p. 300. This book provides the definitive architectural history of Fair Lane and of all the other significant buildings of Detroit.

9. I am grateful to Donn Werling, the director of Fair Lane, for showing me the house and, in particular, the power station.

10. Van Tine, "The Henry Ford Estate," p. 59.

11. Catherine Ruddiman, letter and floor plan sent to Richard Folsom, November 12, 1985.

12. FA, Acc. 1, Box 27.

13. FA, *Reminiscences*, Lepine, pp. 61, 62.

14. Marquis, pp. 186–187.

15. FA, Acc. 1, Box 27.

16. Ibid.

17. I am grateful to Mrs. Alvan Macauley, Jr.; Jane, Lady Easton; Ray Smith; Donald Thurber; and other former pupils for their memories of Miss Ward-Foster's Dancing Academy.

18. Mrs. Alvan Macauley, Jr., interview.

19. *Detroit News*, November 2, 1916.

20. *Detroit Free Press*, November 2, 1916; cited in Brough, p. 7. I am grateful to Miss Esther Cutler, one of the bridesmaids, for her memories of the wedding.

21. See Lewis, p. 91, for details of Ford's peace advertising campaign.

22. Nevins and Hill, vol. 2, p. 117.

23. *New York Times*, February 10, 1917.

24. Jonathan Daniels, *The End of Innocence*; cited in Lewis, p. 503, note 2.

25. *New York Tribune*, April 3 and 7, 1917; cited in Nevins and Hill, vol. 2, p. 56.

26. Ibid.

27. *New York Herald*, February 6, 1917; cited in Nevins and Hill, vol. 2, p. 55.

28. Elliott Stevenson, *Chicago Tribune* attorney in the Mount Clemens Trial, July 7, 1919; cited in Gelderman, p. 169.

29. Nevins and Hill, vol. 2, p. 71.

30. Ibid.

31. Ferry, *Legacy of Albert Kahn*, pp. 23, 113.

32. Sward, p. 96.

33. *New York Times*, November 7, 1922; cited in Sward, p. 95.

34. Edwin G. Pipp, "Facts About Edsel Ford," *Pipp's Weekly* I, May 15, 1920; cited in Nevins and Hill, vol. 2, p. 78.

35. Nevins and Hill, vol. 2, p. 78.

36. *Omer Progress*; cited in *Detroit Saturday Night*, July 13, 1918.

37. Nevins and Hill, vol. 2, p. 115.

38. Ibid., p. 118.

39. John Burroughs, *John Burroughs Talks*; cited in Sward, p. 116.

40. Spencer Ervin, *Henry Ford Versus Truman H. Newberry*; cited in Sward, p. 119.

41. FA, *Reminiscences*, Liebold, p. 410.

42. Nevins and Hill, vol. 2, p. 122.

43. Ervin, *Henry Ford Versus Truman H. Newberry*; cited in Sward, p. 122.

44. Sward, p. 123.

45. Bushnell, p. 96.

46. Ibid., p. 7.

47. FA, Acc. 572, Box 26; also *New York Times*, April 20, 1922.

48. *New York Times*, April 20, 1922.

49. Sward, p. 99.

50. *Detroit News*, October 13, 1923.

51. *New York Times*, October 14, 1923.

52. Sward, p. 99.

53. *Detroit News*, November 8, 1917, p. 99.

54. *Detroit Saturday Night*, June 15, 1935.

55. *Detroit News*, July 30, 1938.

## 10. No Stockholders, No Parasites

1. FA, Acc. 1, Box 1.

2. Reed, "Industry's Miracle Maker," p. 66.

3. Ibid., p. 10.

4. There are several accounts of James Couzens's resignation

from Ford, all of them broadly similar. This account comes from Couzens's own recollections to Jay Hayden, recorded by Hayden in his unpublished manuscript biography of Couzens in the possession of his son Martin.

5. *Pipp's Weekly* IV, January 19, 1924; cited in Nevins and Hill, vol. 2, p. 24.

6. Nevins and Hill, vol. 1, p. 570.

7. Ibid., p. 649.

8. Ibid., vol. 2, p. 94.

9. *Detroit News*, November 14, 1916; cited in Jardim, p. 93.

10. Ibid.

11. Nevins and Hill, vol. 1, p. 646.

12. Ibid.

13. Ibid., vol. 2, p.9.

14. *Detroit Journal*, June 15 and 19, 1915; cited in Nevins and Hill, vol. 2, p. 201.

15. *Dearborn Independent*, October 8, 1915; cited in Nevins and Hill, vol. 2, p. 88.

16. On June 16, 1915, the *Detroit Journal* reported, "It is the intention of Henry Ford to bring iron ore in boats to the blast furnace and turn the ore into motor cylinder heads and other auto and tractor parts without having either ore or iron pass through the hands of middlemen." (Jardim, p. 99)

17. Dodge Suit Record II, 490–492; cited in Nevins and Hill, vol. 2, p. 90.

18. Ibid.

19. Sward, p. 72.

20. *Los Angeles Examiner*, March 5, 1919; cited in Nevins and Hill, vol. 2, p. 106.

21. Ibid.

22. Lewis, pp. 102–103.

23. Ibid.

24. FA, Acc. 62, Box 107; Liebold to Plantiff, March 19, 1919; cited in Nevins and Hill, vol. 2, p. 106.

25. Dodge versus Ford, 204 Michigan 505; cited in Sward, p. 71.

26. Ibid.

27. Nevins and Hill, vol. 1, p. 570.

28. *Los Angeles Examiner*, March 5, 1919; cited in Nevins and Hill, vol. 2, p. 106.

29. Ibid.

30. *New York Times*, March 11, 1919.

31. Ford versus Dodge brothers; cited in Nevins and Hill, vol. 2, p. 99.

32. Jardim, p. 109.

33. Ibid.

34. *Detroit Times*, February 15, 1927.

35. *New York Times*, March 11, 1919.

36. These figures have been rounded off to the nearest dollar. The precise purchase price of James Couzens's shares, for example, was $29,308,857.90. FA, Acc. 352, Box 1: "Memo of Financial Transactions re: Purchase of Stock," September 2, 1919; cited in Nevins and Hill, vol. 2, p. 110.

37. Sward, p. 73.

38. FA, Acc. 33, Box 41: Dana Mayo, Memorandum; cited in Nevins and Hill, vol. 2, p. 110.

39. Nevins and Hill, vol. 2, p. 111.

40. *New York Times*, July 12, 1919.

41. *Detroit News*, May 18, 1920.

42. Ibid.

43. Marquis, p. 165.

44. Ibid., p. 94.

45. Ibid., p. 170.

## 11. Evangeline

Most of what we know about the relationship between Henry Ford and Evangeline Dahlinger comes from John Dahlinger's book, *The Secret Life of Henry Ford*. John Dahlinger died in November 1984.

1. Dahlinger, p. 17.

2. Nevins and Hill, vol. 1, p. 644.

3. Charles E. Sorensen, p. 90.

4. FA, *Reminiscences*, Gleason, p. 22.

5. FA, Acc. 1, Box 1: "Henry Ford Health." The fact that this prescription survives in Henry Ford's papers suggests, sadly, that Henry Ford did not use it.

6. Bennett, p. 103.

7. Ibid.

8. Douglas Dow, interview, September 19, 1984.

9. Dahlinger, p. 18.

10. Ibid., p. 35.

11. FA, *Reminiscences*, Bacon, pp. 65–66.

12. Dahlinger, pp. 22–26.

13. Evangeline's flying boat can today be seen in the Henry Ford Museum at Greenfield Village.

14. Lewis, *Car Collector*, Vol. I, No. 6, p. 120.

15. David Crippen, interview, March 17, 1986.

16. FA, *Reminiscences*, Bacon, pp. 143–144.

17. I am grateful to Thomas W. Brunk for his information about Jenssen's unpaid accounts, which he came across during his research for his forthcoming book on the architect and designer Leonard C. Willeke.

18. Grace Prunk, interview, January 23, 1985.

19. Lewis, "Ford Country."

20. Bennett, p. 102.

## 12. Chronicle of the Neglected Truth

1. Interview with Upton Sinclair, "Henry Ford Tells Just How Happy His Great Fortune Made Him," *Reconstruction*; cited in Jardim, p. 140.

2. *Dearborn Independent*, January 11, 1919; cited in Nevins and Hill, vol. 2, p. 126.

3. Nevins and Hill, vol. 2, p. 124.

4. Kenneth F. McCormick, "Spokesman for Henry Ford," *Radio Guide*; cited in Sward, p. 143.

5. *Detroit Saturday Night*, January 18, 1919.

6. Nevins and Hill, vol. 2, pp. 129–130.

7. FA, *Reminiscences*, Liebold, vol. 4, p. 295.

8. Magee, p. 95. I am grateful to Donald E. Worrell, Jr., for his help acquainting me with the history of Mount Clemens, and, in particular, for permission to quote from his article "Mount Clemens's Fabulous Bath Era" in *Chronicle: The Magazine of the Historical Society of Michigan*, Summer 1978.

9. Sward, p. 101.

10. Lewis, p. 105; the best account of the media aspects of the *Chicago Tribune* trial.

11. *Pipp's Weekly* II, October 22, 1921; cited in Nevins and Hill, vol. 2, p. 137.

12. Sward, p. 104, and Nevins and Hill, vol. 2, p. 138.

13. Ibid.

14. *Nation* CIX; cited in Nevins and Hill, vol. 2, p. 140.

15. *Chicago Herald*, July 16, 1919; cited in Wik, p. 54.

16. Wik, p. 55.
17. Ibid.
18. John Burroughs, "Our Vacation Days of 1918" (private publication). I am grateful to Mrs. Alvan Macauley, Jr., for lending me her illustrated copy of Burroughs's journal.
19. Ibid.
20. Ibid.
21. Henry Ford later taught this recipe to John Dahlinger (Dahlinger, p. 142).
22. Lewis, p. 223.
23. FA, Acc. 940, Box 7: "Notes on auto-camping trip with Henry Ford, Thomas A. Edison, H. S. Firestone, and others by John Burroughs," August 8, 1919; cited in Jardim, p. 141.
24. Kraft, p. 280.
25. Liebold's voluminous *Reminiscences* make his anti-Semitic assumptions quite clear.
26. Kraft, p. 104.
27. Ibid., p. 281.
28. Emerson, *Essays*, p. 83.
29. David E. Nye, p. 108.
30. "Henry Ford at Bay," *Forum*; cited in Jardim, p. 141.
31. *Dearborn Independent*, August 6, 1921.
32. Conot, p. 210.
33. *MLW*, p. 250.
34. Ibid.
35. Henry Ford, *Ford Ideals*, p. 290.
36. FA, Acc. 62, Box 9: Liebold to Plantiff, January 26, 1921; cited in Jardim, p. 145.
37. Nevins and Hill, vol. 2, p. 316.
38. Upton Sinclair, p. 59.
39. Nevins and Hill, vol. 2, p. 302.
40. Lee, pp. 43, 44.
41. Lewis, p. 215.
42. Susman, p. 146.
43. Lewis, p. 215.
44. Lee, p. 68.
45. Wik, p. 111.
46. Ibid.
47. FA, Acc. 572, Box 9: *The Ford Interview on Muscle Shoals*.
48. Jardim, p. 147.
49. Nevins and Hill, vol. 2, p. 308.

50. FA, *Reminiscences*, Black, p. 29.

51. Ibid.

52. Nevins and Hill, vol. 2, p. 304.

53. Wik, p. 130.

54. *Dearborn Independent*, April 23, 1924; cited in Lee, p. 69.

55. Wik, p. 130.

56. *New York Times*, July 24, 1927; cited in Wik, p. 136.

57. FA, Acc. 48; cited in Wik, pp. 137, 138.

58. Lewis, p. 142.

59. Bennett, p. 56.

60. For evidence of Henry Ford's enduring anti-Jewish feeling in 1939, see Sterne, p. 267.

61. Lee, pp. 57–66.

62. Ibid., p. 59.

63. Bentley Historical Library, Gomon papers, Box 10, Draft Manuscript, "The Poor Mr. Ford."

64. Lee, p. 34.

65. Ibid.

## 13. Food For Thought

I am grateful to Ann Eisel for her help gathering material on the immigrant communities of Detroit and to Dr. Conrad Lam for sharing his unparalleled knowledge on the history of the Henry Ford Hospital. The *Reminiscences* of Ernest Liebold, who administered the hospital in its early years, are the best contemporary source material.

1. Marquis, p. 8.

2. Zunz, p. 288.

3. John Brown brought fourteen fugitives through Detroit in March 1859. Lockbiler, p. 20.

4. Conot, p. 233.

5. Ibid., p. 234.

6. Bentley Historical Library, Gomon papers, Box 10, "Racial Record."

7. Welliver, "Henry Ford, Dreamer and Worker," p. 492.

8. Nevins and Hill, vol. 2, p. 539.

9. Ibid., pp. 539, 540.

10. Bentley Historical Library, Gomon papers, Box 10, "Racial Record."

11. Nevins and Hill, vol. 2, p. 540.

12. Lasky, p. 34.

13. Ford R. Bryan, letter to the author, December 13, 1985.

14. *MLW*, p. 216.

15. Ibid., p. 215. The hospital was open prior to the First World War but without its own surgical facilities for most of this time. Patients were wheeled across West Grand Boulevard for their operations, to Providence Hospital.

16. FA, *Reminiscences*, Liebold, p. 74.

17. Nevins and Hill, vol. 2, p. 408.

18. Greenleaf, p. 31.

19. Ibid., p. 53.

20. Conrad Lam, interview, March 12, 1985.

21. Sward, pp. 138, 139.

22. Greenleaf, p. 41.

23. Lam, pp. 80–82.

24. Henry Ford II, interview, September 11, 1984.

25. Deutsch, p. 56.

26. *New York Times*, May 10, 1929; cited in Greenleaf, p. 32.

27. Deutsch, p. 71.

28. Barnard, p. 92.

29. Welliver, "Henry Ford, Dreamer and Worker," p. 488.

30. FA, Acc. 69, Box 9. I am grateful to Ford R. Bryan for drawing my attention to this company in his unpublished article "Henry Ford & Son, Tractors."

31. Bryan, "A Prized Friendship," p. 90.

32. Kahn, "The Staffs of Life," pp. 50ff.

33. Ibid., p. 64.

34. Ibid., p. 57.

35. Conot, p. 313.

36. Bryan, "A Prized Friendship," p. 10.

37. Ibid.

38. Wik, p. 151.

39. Ibid.

40. The printed proceedings of the Dearborn chemurgical conferences of 1935 and 1936 are in the library of the Ford Archives.

41. "Proceedings of the National Chemurgical Conference," Vol. II, p. 334.

42. Kahn, "The Staffs of Life," p. 68.

43. Statistics from the U.S. Department of Agriculture, Crop Reporting Board. I am grateful to David Hagel of the Michigan

Department of Agriculture for making these figures available.

44. *Detroit News*, Sunday, February 7, 1926.

45. Frank J. Sladen, Jr., interview.

46. Welliver, "Henry Ford, Dreamer and Worker," p. 481.

47. Ibid., p. 495.

## 14. Time Machine

1. Walter Karp, "Henry Ford's Village," *American Heritage*; reprinted in *A Sense of History*, American Heritage Magazine, pp. 658–669.

2. *New York World*, July 18, 1919; cited in Jardim, p. 124.

3. FA, *Reminiscences*, Liebold, p. 890.

4. Lewis, "The Flivver of Hostelries," p. 126.

5. Ibid.

6. Lewis, *Public Image of Henry Ford*, p. 255.

7. Jay Anderson, pp. 25ff. I am grateful to Donn Werling, Director of Fair Lane, for drawing my attention to this book, and for lending it to me.

8. Richards, p. 103.

9. Ibid., p. 104. I am grateful for the help of Eva O'Neal Twork, author of *Henry Ford and Benjamin B. Lovett: The Dancing Billionaire and the Dancing Master*.

10. Twork, p. 56.

11. Gelderman, p. 278.

12. *Good Morning*; cited in Sward, p. 260.

13. *Good Morning*; cited in Twork, p. 86.

14. Ibid.

15. Nevins and Hill, vol. 2, p. 240.

16. Karp (see note 1), p. 658.

17. Richards, p. 180.

18. Glick, "A Favorite Subject," p. 149.

19. Sward, p. 268.

20. Conot, p. 257.

## 15. Heir Apparent

1. These home movies are in the Ford Film Collection in the National Archives in Washington, and also in the Henry Ford Centennial Library at Dearborn. I am grateful to Rollin P. Marquis, City Librarian of Dearborn, for making these films available.

2. Nevins and Hill, vol. 2, p. 105.

3. *Ford Times* IX, October 1915; cited in Nevins and Hill, vol. 2, p. 14.

4. FA, Acc. 1, Box 27.

5. FA, Acc. 6, Restricted.

6. Ibid.

7. FA, *Reminiscences*, Bacon, p. 48.

8. Ibid., Lepine, p. 25.

9. Ibid., p. 26.

10. Ibid., p. 66.

11. Ibid., p.79.

12. I am grateful to Thomas W. Brunk, author of the forthcoming biography of Willeke, for letting me share his research material on the early homes of the Edsel Fords.

13. Mrs. Alvan Macauley, Jr. (nee Katie Shiell), interview.

14. Lewis, "Edsel Ford's Farm Environmental Center."

15. *FA, Reminiscences*, Backus, p. 11.

16. FA, Acc. 1, Box 32: Eleanor Clay Ford to Henry Ford, August 1918; cited in Nevins and Hill, vol. 2, p. 489.

17. Freda Pepper Hewlitt, interview, February 20, 1985.

18. Lynn Pierson, interview, September 18, 1984.

19. Nevins and Hill, vol. 2, p. 507.

20. Catherine Ruddiman, interview, August 26, 1985.

21. FA, Acc. 1, Box 27.

22. Ibid.

23. FA, *Reminiscences*, Bacon, p. 10.

24. Ibid., p. 7.

25. FA, Acc. 1, Box 31: Excelsior Diary, 1911.

26. Herndon, p. 142.

27. Nevins and Hill, vol. 2, p. 276.

28. Dahlinger, p. 152.

29. Montgomery, "Henry Ford & Son, Partners," p. 7.

30. Nevins and Hill, vol. 2, p. 270. Nevins and Hill give the source of this document as FA, Acc. 6, Box 108, but, as is so often the case with documents relating to Edsel Ford, it is no longer to be found where it was once catalogued.

31. Emerson, *Essays*, p. 83.

32. Dahlinger, p. 201.

33. Bennett, p. 23.

34. *MLW*, p. 265.

35. Bennett, p. 24.

36. Herndon, pp. 139–140. I am grateful to Emmet Tracy, one of the accountants who was dismissed, for confirming the details of this story. He dates it as 1921 or 1922, possibly 1923.

## 16. Hard Times, Hard Dealing

1. Nevins and Hill, vol. 2, p. 482.
2. Benson, p. 21.
3. I am grateful to Thomas W. Brunk for his help with the history of Indian Village.
4. Nevins and Hill, vol. 2, pp. 61, 62.
5. Ibid., p. 62.
6. Bryan, "Henry Ford & Son, Tractors," p. 6.
7. Rae, *American Automobile Manufacturers*, pp. 109–110.
8. Ford, Anne and Charlotte, p. 17.
9. Ibid.
10. Conot, p. 202.
11. Figures from Nevins and Hill, vol. 2, p. 152.
12. FA, *Reminiscences*, Black; cited in Nevins and Hill, vol. 2, p. 153.
13. Nevins and Hill, vol. 2, p. 193.
14. Ibid., p. 154.
15. Ibid., p. 158.
16. *MLW*, p. 174.
17. For details of the Ford clearance sale, see Nevins and Hill, vol. 2, pp. 158–159.
18. *New York Times*, February 9, 1921; cited in Nevins and Hill, vol. 2, p. 160.
19. Conot, p. 202.
20. *MLW*, p. 176.
21. Memorandum of Release and Agreement, Secretary's office file, Box 13; cited in Nevins and Hill, vol. 2, p. 146.
22. Lord Perry, interview, March 28, 1952; cited in Nevins and Hill, vol. 1, p. 362.
23. Nevins and Hill, vol. 2, p. 168.
24. Lord Perry, interview, March 28, 1952; cited in Nevins and Hill, vol. 2, p. 168.
25. Malcolm W. Bingay, *Detroit Is My Own Home Town*; cited in Beasley, p. 109.
26. Beasley, pp. 92–94.
27. *MLW*, p. 265.
28. Jardim, p. 196.

29. Marquis, pp. 164–165.

30. *MLW*, p. 263.

31. Lewis, p. 183.

32. *Detroit News*, February 5, 1922; cited in Sward, p. 166.

33. Ibid.

34. Lewis, p. 183.

35. Nevins and Hill, vol. 2, p. 177.

36. Ibid., p. 190.

37. FA, *Reminiscences*, Getsinger; cited in Nevins and Hill, Vol. 2, p.191.

38. Nevins and Hill, vol. 2, p. 184.

39. *Pipp's Weekly* II, January 21, 1922; cited in Nevins and Hill, vol. 2, p. 181.

40. Ibid.

41. *Detroit Saturday Night*, April 5, 1924; cited in Sward, p. 169.

42. These paragraphs are based on Joseph Duveen's account of his meeting with Henry Ford as related by S. N. Behrman in *Duveen* (New York: Random House, 1951).


## 17. Farewell, My Lovely

Details about the Ford family conflicts over Ernest Kanzler are hard to come by. Charles E. Sorensen and Bennett both contain some details, and I am grateful for the help of Emmet Tracy and George Reindel, business associates of Ernest Kanzler, and for the help of Kanzler's son, Robert.

1. *MLW*, p. 43.

2. Pettifer and Turner, p. 130, where the advertisement is reproduced.

3. Nevins and Hill, vol. 2, p. 400.

4. Lewis, p. 192.

5. For this and other examples of the Ford Joke, see the illuminating survey in Lewis, pp. 121–126.

6. Sales figures from Nevins and Hill, vol. 2, pp. 264, 685.

7. Pettifer and Turner, p. 131.

8. Nevins and Hill, vol. 2, p. 412.

9. FA, *Reminiscences*, Brown, pp. 110–111. See also the *Reminiscences* of Mallon, p. 117; Galamb, p. 37; Wibel, p. 5. Cited in Jardim, p. 28.

10. FA, *Reminiscences*, Hadas; cited in Nevins and Hill, vol. 2, p. 407.

11. FA, Acc. 572, Box 22: Letter from W. S. Nordburg, 489 Sunset Road, Winnetka, Illinois, May 17, 1926.

12. Ibid.: Letter from J. C. Henning, 5338 Enright Avenue, St. Louis, Missouri, August 2, 1926.

13. Ibid.

14. Ibid.: Letter from B. F. O'Brien, Caxton Block, Moline, Illinois, December 7, 1926.

15. Ibid.

16. FA, *Reminiscences*, Gehle, vol. 2, p. 184.

17. From an unedited draft manuscript of Bennett, *We Never Called Him Henry*, in the possession of David C. Smith; p. 123.

18. Charles E. Sorensen, p. 308.

19. Ibid., p. 310.

20. Emmet Tracy (June 13, 1985) and George Reindel (August 2. 1985), interviews.

21. FA, *Reminiscences*, Lepine, p. 6.

22. FA, Acc. 6, Box 447: S. A. Stellwagen, report, June 17–19, 1926; cited in Nevins and Hill, vol. 2, p. 416.

23. For George B. Carter's complaint, and other details of the "crossroads policy," see Nevins and Hill, vol. 2, pp. 421–426.

24. The quotes from Kanzler are from FA, Acc. 1, Box 116: Ford Motor Co. Engineering, 1–26–26, Kanzler Memorandum. Author's punctuation added.

25. Charles E. Sorensen, p. 308.

26. Ibid., p. 307.

27. Ibid., p. 310.

28. Bennett, p. 25.

29. Hounshell, p. 278.

30. Ibid.

31. E. B. White, *Second Tree from the Corner*, unpaged.

32. *Ford Times*, July 1953; cited Stern, p. 118.

33. *New York World*, September 11, 1927; cited in Sward, p. 201.

34. Beasley, p. 135.

35. Conot, p. 248. Also Lewis, p. 201.

36. *New York Sun*, December 2, 1927; cited in Lewis, p. 202.

37. Lewis, p. 203.

38. FA, Acc. 6, Box 274: Edsel Ford correspondence, 1928; Douglas Fairbanks to Edsel Ford, January 3, 1928, 5:24 P.M.

39. Ibid., Box 87: Couzens to Edsel Ford, December 7, 1927.

40. FA, *Reminiscences*, Sheldrick, p. 82.

41. Hounshell, p. 288.

42. Nevins and Hill, vol. 2, p. 468. The excessive use of steel forgings in early versions of the Model A was a factor in raising the cost of the car, and the substitution of malleable castings saved Ford some $30 or $40 per vehicle. But the principal factor in reducing unit cost was speeding up the line, thus spreading fixed overheads across increased output.

43. Charles E. Sorensen, p. 225.

44. Nevins and Hill, vol. 2, p. 458.

45. Rae, *American Automobile Manufacturers*, p. 157.

## 18. Depression

1. Sterne, p. 187.

2. Figures from Nevins and Hill, vol. 2, pp. 570–573.

3. Sward, p. 223.

4. "Interview, Model 1931," *Outlook and Independent*; cited in Lewis, p. 233.

5. Sward, p. 221.

6. Motor Vehicle Manufacturers Association, p. 89.

7. Nevins and Hill, vol. 2, p. 573.

8. John W. Scoville, *Behavior of the Automobile Industry in Depression*; cited in Nevins and Hill, vol. 2, p. 574 (footnote).

9. Lewis, p. 233.

10. Ibid., p. 588.

11. Harvey Burleson, interview, July 12, 1984. Nevins and Hill have further evidence of car-for-job barters (vol. 2, p. 590).

12. Garret Garrett, *The Wild Wheel*; cited in Lewis, p. 234.

13. Conot, pp. 277–279.

14. Hollander and Marple, p. 2.

15. FA, *Reminiscences*, Liebold, p. 1432; cited in Conot, p. 278.

16. Lewis, pp. 233–234.

17. Ibid., p. 233.

18. *Philadelphia Record*, May 30, 1932; cited in Lewis, p. 224.

19. Ibid., p. 234.

20. Ibid.

21. *New York Times*, May 9, 1932; cited in Lewis, p. 234.

22. FA, *Reminiscences*, Thoms, p. 59.

23. Motor Vehicle Manufacturers Association, pp. 58, 89.

24. FA, *Reminiscences*, Thoms, p. 67.

25. Ibid.

26. Ibid.

27. Charles E. Sorensen, p. 228.
28. Ibid., p. 229.
29. Ibid.
30. Ibid., pp. 227, 228.
31. Lewis, p. 207.
32. Charles E. Sorensen, p. 229.
33. Lewis, p. 207.
34. Rich, "Clyde Barrow's Last Ford," p. 635.

## 19. Patron of Art

This chapter has drawn extensively upon the works and archives of the Detroit Institute of Arts, and I am grateful to its directors, Dr. Frederick J. Cummings and Samuel Sachs II, to Linda Downs, for sharing her special expertise on Rivera and his murals, to Marilyn Ghaussi for tracking down some correspondence between Edsel Ford and William Valentiner, to Ellen Sharp, and to James A. Bridenstine, now Director of the Edsel & Eleanor Ford House in Grosse Pointe.

1. Brunk, "A Note on Charles Lang Freer," p. 17.
2. I am grateful to Ted Mecke for showing me his unpublished paper, delivered to the Witenagemote Club, on Charles Lang Freer.
3. Sterne, p. 171. In 1922 the DIA purchased Raoul Dufy's *Still Life* for $75 and Van Gogh's *Self-Portrait* for $4,200.
4. Ibid., p. 153.
5. Ibid., p. 154.
6. Ibid.
7. Ibid., p. 155.
8. Ibid., p. 162.
9. Richards, p. 200.
10. I am grateful to James Bridenstine for his help explaining the Edsel and Eleanor Ford art collection.
11. Sterne, p. 186.
12. Ibid.
13. Ibid., p. 189.
14. On December 26, 1931, Henry McBride described Rivera as "the most talked about man on this side of the Atlantic." Herrera, p. 131.
15. Wolfe, pp. 235ff.
16. Downs and Jacob, p. 47.

17. *New York Herald Tribune*, November 14, 1931; cited in Herrera, p. 128.

18. Sterne, p. 194.

19. Rivera, *My Art, My Life*; cited in Gelderman, p. 318.

20. Ibid.; cited in Herrera, p. 134.

21. Ibid., p. 135.

22. Herrera, p. 135.

23. Ibid., pp. 136–137.

24. Sheryl Freidland, interview, September 5, 1985.

25. Sterne, p. 195.

26. Ibid., p. 197.

27. Ibid., p. 201.

28. Rivera, *My Art, My Life*; cited in Gelderman, p. 317.

29. *Age of Steel*, sound track.

30. Ibid.

31. I am grateful for the help of Sheryl Freidland, who has made a special study of Detroit's reaction to the Rivera murals.

32. *Detroit Times*, March 21, 1933; cited in Greenleaf, *From These Beginnings*, p. 166.

## 20. Bank Holiday

1. Guardian Group, p. 24. I am grateful to John Lord Booth II for lending me this prospectus.

2. It is sometimes said that Henry Ford gave his Gaukler Pointe property to his son, but the reminiscences of Edsel's private secretary, A. J. Lepine, are specific: "Mr. Edsel Ford bought the property from his father." (FA, *Reminiscences*, Lepine, p. 71).

3. Emmet Tracy, interview, June 13, 1985.

4. Guardian Group, p. 24.

5. Ibid.

6. Conot, p. 302.

7. Guardian Group, pp. 28–32.

8. *Detroit News*, March 31, 1929.

9. Nevins and Hill, vol. 3, p. 12.

10. Howard R. Neville, *The Detroit Banking Collapse of 1933*; cited in Conot, pp. 302, 303.

11. *Detroit News*, March 1, 1934; cited in Sward, p. 246.

12. Conot, p. 303.

13. *Detroit News*, May 9, 1937.

14. Sward, p. 247.

15. Off-the-record interview.

16. Lewis, p. 238.

17. Conot, p. 303.

18. Nevins and Hill, vol. 3, p. 13.

19. Patricia O'Donnell McKenzie, "Banking, Economics and Politics: The Detroit Bank Crisis of 1933" (Ph.D. diss.), ch. 2; also Harry Barnard, pp. 221–227. Both cited in Lewis, p. 524.

20. Sterne, p. 211.

21. FA, *Reminiscences*, Backus, p. 11. Backus also describes how he put his own money into the Union Guardian Trust Company: "I got smart and bought what I could afford as I assumed it was at the bottom and I would be able to make a nice profit. It didn't work and I lost all my own investment." (p. 10).

22. FA, *Reminiscences*, Bacon, p. 223.

23. Sward, p. 244.

24. Federal Trade Commission, *Report on Motor Vehicle Industry*; cited in Sward, p. 243.

25. Emmet Tracy, interview, June 13, 1985.

26. Bennett, p. 161.

27. Ibid., p. 26.

28. FA, *Reminiscences*, Bacon, p. 96.

29. Nevins and Hill, vol. 3, pp. 13, 14.

30. Conot, pp. 305, 306.

31. Sward, p. 251.

32. Conrad Lam, interview, March 12, 1985.

33. Herrera, p. 135.

34. *New Republic*, September 30, 1936; cited in Sward, p. 254.

35. Nevins and Hill, vol. 3, p. 14.

36. Ibid.

37. Sward, p. 252.

38. Conot, p. 306.

## 21. Overpass

1. Reuther, pp. 198–199.

2. Ibid., p. 45.

3. Ibid.

4. Nevins and Hill, vol. 3, p. 32.

5. Death and injury statistics from Nevins and Hill, vol. 3, p. 33. This account of the Hunger March is based on the descriptions in Conot, pp. 283–286, Sward, pp. 231–242, and Harry Bennett's own account in *We Never Called Him Henry*, pp. 91–95.

6. *New York Times*, March 8, 1932; cited in Sward, p. 237.

7. *New York Herald Tribune*, March 8, 1932; cited in Sward, p. 236.

8. Conot, pp. 285–286.

9. Dos Passos, p. 56.

10. Robert L. Cruden, *The End of the Ford Myth*; cited in David E. Nye, p. 45.

11. FA, Acc. 572, Box 1: Ford Motor Company Labor Relations —Es., 104–H.2, pp. 2, 3.

12. FA, Acc. 572, Box 1: Ford Motor Company Labor Relations —Es. Report re. J–6347, Frank F. Conner, 10 Highland Avenue, Captain 32, 9–11–18.

13. Ibid., Report of Operative 15, July 23, 1919.

14. Ibid., author's punctuation. The original reads, "You invest you money in a Capitalist proposition,".

15. Ibid.

16. Céline, p. 222.

17. Ibid., p. 224.

18. Ibid., pp. 224–225.

19. Upton Sinclair, p. 88.

20. Nevins and Hill, vol. 2, p. 349.

21. Ibid., p. 351.

22. Ibid., p. 511.

23. Ibid., pp. 510–514.

24. Cuningham, p. 15.

25. Nevins and Hill, vol. 2, p. 526.

26. FA, *Reminiscences*, Klann, p. 155.

27. Fountain, *Union Guy*, pp. 44, 42.

28. Ibid.

29. Bennett, p. 109.

30. Nevins and Hill, vol. 2, p. 509.

31. Pflug, *The UAW in Pictures*, pp. 23, 24.

32. Nevins and Hill, vol. 3, p. 51.

33. Pflug, *The UAW in Pictures*, p. 31.

34. Nevins and Hill, vol. 3, p. 140.

35. Reuther, pp. 65, 66.

36. Conot, p. 353, and Reuther, p. 202. This account of the Battle of the Overpass is based on that given in Conot; in Nevins and Hill, vol. 3, pp. 139–142; and on the memories of Reuther himself as given in the book by his brother Victor, p. 201.

37. Herndon, p. 14.

## 22. Dark Angel

I am grateful to David C. Smith for allowing me to listen to the tapes of a series of interviews that he conducted with Harry Bennett towards the end of Bennett's life. These shed new light on several aspects of Bennett's career with Ford, including the commonly accepted version of how he first met the carmaker. This is related on pages 6–8 of *We Never Called Him Henry*, Bennett's autobiography ghostwritten by Paul Marcus. But in Bennett's interviews with Smith, he stated that "the man who first took me to Ford was the man from Eagle boat," and he told Smith a garbled story suggesting that he first came to work at Ford as a Navy "spotter" looking for sabotage of the Eagle submarine-chaser contract.

At the time of the interview, Bennett also gave Smith a draft copy of Marcus's manuscript, on the flyleaf of which he had scrawled, "This Book is so slanted I don't think it should be printed. Harry H."—thus appearing to cast further doubt on the story according to Marcus.

However, it was Smith's impression that Bennett's mind was wandering sometimes when he met him. The handwriting on the manuscript flyleaf was erratic and senile, of a piece with other scribbled ramblings which Bennett gave to Smith.

The handwriting with which Bennett had made quite a number of corrections on the manuscript itself was distinctly more coherent. It appeared to date from the time when the manuscript itself had been prepared around 1950—and Bennett made no alterations then to the account of how he met both Brisbane and Henry Ford as a result of the street brawl, which is the account given here.

Harry Bennett died on January 4, 1979, age eighty-seven.

1. Lens, p. 121.
2. Charles E. Sorensen, p. 260.
3. Ibid.
4. Ibid.
5. Bennett, pp. 6–8.
6. FA, *Reminiscences*, Bacon, p. 177. As Irving Bacon tells the story, Bennett was recruited from the art department by William Knudsen to join the security staff protecting the Eagle boat production, and it was Bennett's valour as a small man taking on mountainous troublemakers that first won him the attention of Henry Ford (*Reminiscences*, pp. 38ff). Knudsen always said, without taking particular pride in it, that he "got Harry Bennett

started." (Author interviews with Semon "Bunkie" Knudsen, July 30, 1985, and Robert and Tutie Vanderkloot, August 1, 1985.)

7. David L. Lewis, *Detroit Magazine* interviews with Harry Bennett, *Detroit Free Press*, January 20 and 27, 1974.

8. Bacon credits Bennett with these achievements in his *Reminiscences*, p. 177.

9. Bennett, p. 15.

10. Ibid., p. 17.

11. Ibid., p. 34.

12. Off-the-record interview.

13. "Mr. Ford and I got closer after the Sapiro trial," Bennett told David C. Smith in 1974.. "He got so he wouldn't leave me. He wouldn't let me do anything on my own." (Transcript of interview, p. 6.)

14. This unlikely sounding tale is echoed from many sources. Martin Hayden, former editor of the *Detroit News*, told me that Harry Bennett took out his pistol and shot over his visitors' heads on one occasion when Hayden was in the office. (Interview, April 27, 1984.)

15. Conot, p. 274.

16. Bennett, p. 39.

17. Off-the-record interview.

18. The figure for 1928 was 1,169,000 gallons. Conot, p. 265.

19. Ford R. Bryan, letter to author, February 8, 1986.

20. Andrew Sinclair, pp. 242, 243.

21. Conot, pp. 265, 266.

22. These photographs, from a *Detroit News* of 1929, together with other photographs of Prohibition, are reproduced in the article on Detroit rum-running by Larry Engelmann in the *Smithsonian* magazine for June 1979, Vol. 10, No. 3, pp. 113–125.

23. Rockaway, "Rise of the Jewish Gangster," p. 35.

24. Ibid., p. 36.

25. Conot, p. 267.

26. Ibid.

27. *New Yorker* quoted in Krutch, p. 249.

28. Brough, p. 118.

29. Nevins and Hill, vol. 3, p. 237.

30. Copies of the handgun licenses of the Edsel Ford staff are in Acc. 6 of the Ford Archives.

31. These security arrangements were organized by Thomas

Laughlin, who worked for the Edsel Ford family for more than fifty years, and I am grateful for the help of his daughter, Eleanor Collins, in describing this and other aspects of her father's work.

32. Bennett, p. 68. In the draft manuscript of the book (p. 122), Bennett stated, "All of Edsel's children hated Holland and Brady."

33. Ibid., p. 65.

34. Ibid.

35. Rockaway, "Rise of the Jewish Gangster," p. 36.

36. Andrew Sinclair, p. 244.

37. Bennett, p. 68.

38. Sward, p. 317.

39. Bennett, p. 80.

40. Andrew Sinclair, p. 244, and Nevins and Hill, vol. 3, pp. 238, 239.

41. I am grateful to Charles A. Bigelow for taking me to visit Harry Bennett's old office in the basement of the Administration Building.

42. Bentley Historical Library, Gomon papers.

43. Reuther, p. 203.

44. Walter Reuther Library: UAW–Ford vertical file, clippings.

45. Lindbergh, p. 285.

46. Ibid., p. 286.

47. FA, *Reminiscences*, Bacon, p. 204.

48. Herndon, p. 162.

49. Peter Pestillo, Ford Motor Company, interview, May 29, 1984.

50. Walter Reuther Library: UAW—Ford vertical file.

51. Nevins and Hill, vol. 3, p. 142.

52. 26 NLRB, 348, 351, 353–365 (Dallas beatings); cited in Nevins and Hill, vol. 3, p. 142.

53. Nevins and Hill, vol. 3, p. 145.

54. *Detroit Free Press*, December 23, 1937; cited in Nevins and Hill, vol. 3, p. 145.

55. Lewis, p. 75.

56. Ibid., p. 251.

57. *Detroit Labor News*, July 27, 1923; cited in Nevins and Hill, vol. 2, p. 353.

58. David E. Nye, p. 88.

59. U.S. Department of Justice. FBI 94-4-3815-2.

60. Ibid., 94-1-5576-144.

61. Ibid., 62–28131–16.

62. Ibid., 99–313–1.

63. Ibid., 61–7559–5127.

64. Ibid., 62–43818–79.

65. Bennett, p. 117.

66. Ford eventually lost its cases on February 10, 1941, when the Supreme Court refused the Ford Motor Company's request to review the October 1940 ruling of the Sixth U.S. Circuit Court of Appeals, which had been in favour of the union.

67. Bennett, pp. 109, 110.

68. Ibid., p. 116.

69. Nevins and Hill, vol. 3, p. 158.

70. *Louisville Courier Journal*, April 4, 1941; cited in Lewis, p. 265.

71. Bennett, p. 136.

72. Charles E. Sorensen, p. 268.

73. Ibid., p. 256.

74. Ibid., p. 271.

75. Nevins and Hill, vol. 3, p. 166.

76. Bennett, p. 5.

77. Herndon, p. 160.

78. Bennett draft manuscript, p. 43.

79. FA, 104– J–2: J. R. Davis interview, July 25, 1960.

80. Off -the-record interview.

81. Off -the-record interview.

## 23. Broken Heart

1. FA, 104– J–2: J. R. Davis interview, July 25, 1960.

2. Grace Prunk, interview, January 23, 1985.

3. Bennett draft manuscript, p. 114.

4. Dahlinger, p. 201.

5. Linda Downs, interview, June 13, 1984.

6. Nevins and Hill, vol. 2, p. 171.

7. Downs, "Diego Rivera's Portrait of Edsel Ford," p. 51.

8. Sedgwick, p. 124.

9. FA, *Reminiscences*, Bacon, p. 48.

10. Nevins and Hill, vol. 3, p. 16.

11. Ibid., p. 17.

12. Conot, p. 335.

13. I am grateful to Martin Hayden for telling me this story about his father.

14. Ford R. Bryan, interview, August 26, 1985. See also Bryan, "From Flats to Field," p. 81.

15. Nevins and Hill, vol. 3, p. 169.

16. Off-the-record interview.

17. Nevins and Hill, vol. 3, p. 172.

18. Ibid.

19. John Dykema, interview, May 1985.

20. Nevins and Hill, vol. 3, p. 174.

21. Ibid.

22. Beasley, p. 264.

23. Charles E. Sorensen, p. 275.

24. Ibid.

25. FA, *Reminiscences*, Backus, p. 18.

26. Lewis, p. 365.

27. Ibid., p. 363.

28. Bentley Historical Library, Gomon papers, Box 10, "The Poor Mr. Ford," p. 53.

29. Ibid., pp. 54, 55.

30. *Detroit Free Press*, February 1, 1942.

31. *New York World-Telegram*, February 4, 1942; cited in Lewis, p. 349.

32. Lindbergh, *Wartime Journals*; cited in Gelderman, p. 352.

33. *Manchester Leader and Evening Union*, March 9, 1943; cited in Lewis, p. 359.

34. Polls cited in Lewis, p. 363.

35. *Christian Science Monitor*, November 25, 1944; cited in Lewis, p. 361.

36. Lewis, p. 350.

37. *Detroit Free Press*, May 16, 1942.

38. FA, Ford Clipbook 124; cited in Lewis, p. 351.

39. Lewis, p. 350.

40. Ibid., p. 355.

41. *New York Times*, December 5, 1942.

42. *Flying*, p. 21, *Detroit News*, February 22, 1943; cited in Lewis, note 34, pp. 539–540.

43. FA, Ford Clipbook 126, p. 95, unidentified article; cited in Lewis, p. 356.

44. Charles E. Sorensen, p. 296.

45. Nevins and Hill, vol. 2, p. 273.

46. FA, Acc. 6: Letter of Dr. John G. Mateer to Edsel Ford, November 15, 1940.

47. Off-the-record interview. Edsel Ford's medical records, along with those of other members of the Ford family, were removed from the Ford Hospital sometime in the early 1980s at the request of Henry Ford II, who, after consultation with his brother William Clay Ford, decided they should be destroyed. In September 1984, he told this author that he put the medical records into the paper shredder in his office.

48. Lewis, p. 358.

49. Charles E. Sorensen, p. 318.

50. Ibid.

51. FA, Acc. 1, Box 27: Undated letter from Edsel Ford. The letter describes the christening of Anne, the second daughter of Henry Ford II, which took place in Chicago early in 1943.

52. Charles E. Sorensen, p. 322.

53. Ibid., p. 320.

54. Ibid.

55. Ibid., p. 321.

56. Ibid.

57. Ibid., p. 322.

58. Henry Ford II, interview, September 11, 1984.

59. FA, *Reminiscences*, Buhler, p. 17.

60. Off -the-record interview.

61. Charles E. Sorensen, p. 323.

## 24. Young Henry

This chapter presents a reinterpretation of an important, but confused episode in the history of the Ford family. It has often been stated that, after the death of Edsel, conflict developed between his widow, Eleanor, and Henry Ford, and that this climaxed in Eleanor threatening to sell her shares in the company if Henry Ford persisted in ignoring her wishes.

Henry Ford II has always downplayed this story, without denying it directly. "My mother," he told this author, "was not a threatening sort of person." His point is that he was not personally present at any such confrontation, and that neither his mother, nor his grandfather—the only people in a position to know—ever discussed the subject with him. His sister, Josephine, and his brothers, Benson and William Clay, have spoken in similar terms.

The "authorized" version of events, presented by Allan Nevins and Frank Ernest Hill in volume 3 of their official history (p. 250), appears largely based on the memory of Ernest Kanzler, whom the Nevins team interviewed. This version sets the decisive confrontation 2¼ years after Edsel's death—in September 1945, when Henry Ford reluctantly agreed to transfer the company presidency to his grandson, Henry II.

However, the entry from Charles Sorensen's diary and the deleted section of Harry Bennett's memoirs quoted in the text suggest a much earlier confrontation—and a close, lifelong friend of Edsel and Eleanor Ford recalled to this author a conversation that he had with Eleanor Ford on the subject. She told him that her great moment of confrontation with Henry Ford was immediately following Edsel's death, when Henry Ford wanted to give the Ford presidency to Harry Bennett.

1. FA, Acc. 1, Box 32: Letter from Eleanor Ford, August 11, 1943.

2. FA, Acc. 1, Box 32: Eleanor Ford, undated letter.

3. William Clay Ford, interview, May 30, 1985.

4. Off-the-record interview.

5. Richards, p. 229.

6. Off-the-record interview.

7. Charles E. Sorensen, p. 326.

8. The details of this are obscure, but early in 1951, someone representing the Ford Motor Company flew to Arizona where Harry Bennett was living in retirement. Prior to the meeting, the manuscript of Bennett's memoirs contained several graphic descriptions of ill feeling between Eleanor Ford and Henry Ford I, and also between Henry Ford I and his grandsons Henry II and Benson. None of these passages appeared in the book as published. This author read the deleted passages in the draft manuscript which Harry Bennett gave to David C. Smith in 1974.

9. Bennett draft manuscript, p. 308.

10. Ibid. Also printed in Bennett's book, p. 168.

11. Ibid.

12. *New York Times Magazine*, March 5, 1978. Galbraith describes this discussion taking place in 1941 and 1942, and in September 1943, a similar suggestion was made by the Army Material Command. Galbraith confirmed this to the author in April 1986. See also Lewis, p. 360.

13. Nevins and Hill, vol. 3, p. 259.

14. Al Esper, interview, May 14, 1985.

15. Robert Kanzler, interview, October 29, 1985, and Henry Ford II interview, April 17, 1986.

16. Off -the-record interview.

17. Off -the-record interview.

18. Herndon, p. 43. Herndon investigates this episode thoroughly.

19. Ibid., p. 42.

20. Dahlinger, p. 36.

21. Ibid.

22. Donald Thurber, interview.

23. Lasky, p. 51.

24. FA, Acc. 6, Box 360: Office of the President subject file.

25. Ibid.

26. Henry Ford II, interview, September 11, 1984.

27. Off -the-record interview.

28. Off -the-record interview.

29. Henry Ford II, interview, April 17, 1986. See also FA, Acc. 880, Box 1: Ford, Henry II. This box contains evidence relating to other motor accidents involving Henry Ford II in these years. Fuller details originally existed in Acc. 6, Box 360, but these are no longer in the Archives.

30. FA, Acc. 6, Box 211.

31. Birmingham, *Real Lace*, p. 5.

32. Off -the-record interview.

33. Bennett, p. 126.

34. Ibid.

35. *Detroit Free Press*, January 20, 1974.

36. Louise Clancy and Florence Davies's adulatory biography of Clara, *The Believer* (p. 201), hints at the rift which followed Edsel's death.

37. Considine, p. 7.

38. Bennett draft manuscript.

39. Charles E. Sorensen, pp. 314, 315.

40. Ibid., p. 320.

41. Off -the-record interview.

42. Bennett, p. 172.

43. Harry Bennett, interview with David C. Smith, Tape Sony A, no. 1.

44. Ibid.

45. FA, *Reminiscences*, Bacon, p. 256.

46. Nevins and Hill, vol. 3, p. 249.

47. Bennett draft manuscript, p. 320.

48. Nevins and Hill, vol. 3, p. 266.

49. Freedom of Information Act. FBI file 76–50997–349. Letter of Bugas to J. Edgar Hoover, December 18, 1943.

50. For some details of how Bugas was offered the job on November 19, 1943, by Harry Bennett, Henry Ford I, and Henry Ford II, see Bugas's letter to J. Edgar Hoover of December 18, 1943. FBI file 67–50997–349.

51. Nevins and Hill, vol. 3, p. 266.

52. Ibid.

53. Ibid.

54. Ibid.

55. John Weld, interview, October 13, 1985.

56. Henry Ford II interview, June 16, 1959, cited in Nevins and Hill, vol. 3, p. 265.

57. FA, Acc. 975, Box 1, 104– J-2. J. R. Davis interview, July 25/26, 1960.

58. Bennett draft manuscript, p. 324.

59. Ibid.

60. Bennett interviews with David C. Smith.

61. Nevins and Hill, vol. 3, p. 268.

62. Joe McCarthy, "The Ford Family," Part III, *Holiday*; cited in Nevins and Hill, vol. 3, p. 268.

63. Considine, p. 20.

64. Herndon, p. 67.

65. Bennett interview with David C. Smith.

66. Bennett, p. 178.

67. Lasky, p. 67.

68. Ibid.

## 25. The Whiz Kids

1. Nevins and Hill, vol. 3, p. 294.

2. Ibid., vol. 2, p. 119.

3. "U.S. New-Car Registrations by Make Since World War II," p. 26.

4. *Life*, October 1, 1945; cited in Herndon, p. 214.

5. Arjay Miller, interview, October 12, 1985.

6. Walter and Peter.

7. Halberstam, p. 221.

8. Names from Nevins and Hill, vol. 3, p. 309.

9. FA, Acc. 975, Box 1, 104–5–2: Nevins team interview with Ben Mills, November 17, 1959.

10. Ibid.

11. Herndon, p. 215.

12. Off-the-record interview.

13. Off-the-record interview.

14. Off-the-record interview.

15. *Detroit News*, April 22, 1979.

16. FA, Acc. 975, Box 1, 104 J–2: Kanzler interview, January 14, 1960.

17. Lewis, p. 425.

18. Hickerson, p. 26.

19. Ibid., pp. 113, 116.

20. Ibid., p. 119.

21. William T. Gossett, interview, May 17, 1985.

22. FA, Acc. 975, Box 1, 104– J–2: Breech interview, January 6, 1960.

23. Hickerson, p. 133.

24. Ibid.

25. Ibid.

26. Proxy statements to stockholders of the Chrysler Corporation, April 10, 1985, and of the Ford Motor Company, April 12, 1985.

27. Ford Motor Company Proxy Statement, April 24, 1956, p. 6, Stock Options. Henry Ford II does not remember offering Ernest Breech stock options during Breech's negotiations to join the company. However, he thinks it possible that Breech raised the subject with Ford lawyers. Henry Ford II, interview, April 17, 1986.

28. Off-the-record interview.

29. Herndon, p. 74.

30. Crusoe formally joined Ford at the same time as Breech, in July 1946. Youngren and Harder also signed on that summer, and William T. Gossett, who had supervised all the recruiting paperwork as an outside attorney, arrived as vice-president and general counsel in February 1947.

31. *New York Times*, March 5, 1978.

32. *Look*, Vol. XVII, June 30, 1953; cited in Nevins and Hill, vol. 3, p. 254.

33. Lewis, p. 425. Lewis gives the cash balance of the Ford Motor Company on June 30, 1945, as $697,298,372, and assets valued at $815,515,214.

34. Off-the-record interview.

35. FA, Acc. 975, Box 1, 104 J–2: Kanzler interview, January 14, 1960.

36. Ibid.

37. Henry Ford II, interview, September 11, 1984.

38. Ibid.

39. Ibid.

40. Herndon, p. 206.

41. For some examples of the new policy, see the transcripts of the Management Meetings in FIA, AR–65–71:36.

42. Ford R. Bryan, interview, September 20, 1984.

43. Hickerson, p. 130.

44. Nevins and Hill, vol. 3, p. 332.

45. Ibid.

46. Ibid.

47. The sales figures for 1949 were 1,031,086 for Ford and 1,035,272 for Chrysler. "U.S. New-Car Registrations," p. 26.

48. Abodaher, p. 290.

49. FA, Acc. 975, Box 1, 104– J–2: Jack Davis interview, July 25/26, 1960.

50. Arjay Miller, interview, March 9, 1986.

51. Ibid.

52. Ibid.

53. Lewis, p. 432.

54. Arjay Miller, interview, March 9, 1986.

55. Ross, p.91.

56. Ibid., p. 88.

57. Lewis, p. 429.

58. Ibid., p. 432.

59. Ibid.

60. *Time*, February 4, 1946, p. 74.

61. Mrs. Deane Johnson, interview, December 1, 1985.

62. *Detroit News*, January 9 or 10, 1946; cited in Lewis, p. 430.

63. Lewis, p. 433.

64. Ibid.

65. Victor Reuther, interview, October 26, 1985.

66. Douglas Fraser, interview, October 1985.

67. William Gossett, interview, May 17, 1985.

68. Joan Bugas, interview, October 30, 1985.

## 26. Candlelight

I am grateful for the help of Richard Folsom, who carried out the fullest interview with Rosa Buhler, the Fords' maid, on the events on the day of Henry Ford's death, and to Charles W. Davis, Jr., for lending me his collection of newspapers relating to Henry Ford, and to his funeral in particular.

The account of the Ford family's inheritance arrangements has necessarily omitted some of the financial complexities. Thus, although the Ford Foundation's sale of shares in January 1956 is generally—and correctly—referred to as the moment when the company went "public," only 22 percent of the company's total stock was actually put on the market then. The Ford Foundation retained some 67 percent of the equity, which it sold off in offerings in subsequent years. These subsequent offerings—and all other Ford stock splits or offerings—do not affect the 60:40 vote proportions, since this is basically a matter of the weightings assigned to the two classes, which vote separately, not to the number of shares within them at any one time.

For fuller details of the 1956 flotation, see Nevins and Hill, vol. 3, chapter 17, and the footnotes in particular. For details of the Class A, Class B voting arrangements, see the Ford Motor Company's Composite Certificate of Incorporation, as amended to 12.27.84. This shows that Class B voting power will reduce to 30 percent if the number of B shares falls below 10.1 million, and will vanish altogether if the number of B shares held by the family falls below 5.6 million.

The company's proxy statement of April 12, 1985, listed some 173 million shares of common stock and 13.8 million Class B shares, with each Class B, "Ford," share carrying 8.337 votes as compared to the single vote carried by one share of common stock.

1. Trine, p. 107.

2. FA, Acc. 1, Box 1: Henry Ford health.

3. Hawkins Ferry, interview, February 1, 1985.

4. I am grateful to John and Rosemary Dykema for their hospitality at the Huron Mountain Club.

5. Mrs. Renville Wheat, interview, July 13, 1985.

6. Bennett, p. 168.

7. Ibid., p. 165.

8. Ibid.

9. Henry Ford, "Looking Under the Human Hood," p. 10.

10. David E. Nye, p. 117.

11. FA, *Reminiscences*, Bacon, pp. 213, 214.

12. George Holley, unpublished reminiscences with photographs. I am grateful to George Holley's nephew, Danforth Holley, for showing me this manuscript.

13. Bryan, "Henry Ford's Experiment at Richmond Hill."

14. FA, *Reminiscences*, Buhler, p. 17. This interview by Richard B. Folsom is the principal source for the account given here of Henry Ford's final hours.

15. Ibid., p. 18.

16. Mrs. Deane Johnson, interview, December 1, 1985.

17. Ibid.

18. Henry Ford II, interview, April 17, 1986.

19. *Detroit Free Press*, April 10, 1947.

20. FA, *Reminiscences*, Bacon, p. 215.

21. *Detroit News*, April 10, 1947. See the photograph on page 64.

22. Lewis, p. 475.

23. Ibid.

24. Lewis, p. 475.

25. *Detroit Times*, April 11, 1947.

26. *MLW*, pp. 206, 207.

27. Nevins and Hill, vol. 3, p. 411.

28. Ibid.

29. Ibid., vol. 2, p. 113. The precise percentages were: Henry 55.212, Edsel 41.652, and Clara 3.136.

30. Ibid., vol. 3, p. 413.

31. FA, Acc. 975, Box 1, 104–J–2: J. R. Davis interview, July 25/26, 1960.

32. MacDonald, "Foundation."

33. Nevins and Hill, vol. 3, p. 420.

34. Alan Gornick, interview, October 31, 1985.

35. Nevins and Hill, vol. 3, p. 423.

36. Ibid., p. 422.

37. Ibid., p. 424.

## 27. The New Mr. Ford

1. Off-the-record interview.

2. Mrs. Deane Johnson, interview, December 1, 1985.

3. Ibid.

4. *Ten Important Paintings from the Collection of Henry Ford II.*

5. I am grateful to Donald M. D. Thurber for lending me the history of the Detroit Grand Opera Association by Frank W. Donovan, published in *The Metropolitan Opera Centennial Tour*, 1984, pp. 72–78.

6. Ford Foundation, *Annual Report for 1951*, December 31, 1951.

7. *New York Times Magazine*, March 12, 1978.

8. Dwight MacDonald, *New Yorker*, November 26, 1955, p. 83.

9. Off-the-record interview.

10. Off-the-record interview.

11. Off-the-record interview.

12. *New York Times Magazine*, December 3, 1978.

13. Ibid.

14. Herndon, p. 323.

15. *Time*, May 18, 1953, p. 102.

16. FIA, AR–65–71–10. June 19, 1952. Report of Subcommittee on Lincoln Continental: "even though not directly justifiable on a financial basis, the institutional advertising value of the Continental, we believe, warrants adoption of the program."

17. Anne Ford Scarborough, interview, November 30, 1985.

18. *Great Homes of Grosse Pointe Calendar*. Grosse Pointe: House & Apartment, Inc., 1986.

19. Charlotte Ford, interview, September 30, 1984.

20. Ibid.

21. Ibid.

22. Mrs. Deane Johnson, interview, December 1, 1985.

23. Edsel Ford II, interview, December 18, 1984. The Pope was John XXIII.

24. Anne Ford Scarborough, interview, November 30, 1985.

25. Off-the-record interview.

26. Billy Chapin, interview, November 10, 1985.

27. Anne Ford Scarborough, interview, November 30, 1985.

28. Lloyd Semple, interview, November 29, 1985.

29. "Charlotte," by Meyer Davis and Toby Tyler. Copyright 1959 by Meyer Davis. All rights reserved.

30. *Time*, January 4, 1960, p. 15.

31. Ibid.

32. William Clay Ford, interview, May 30, 1985.

33. Mrs. Deane Johnson, interview, December 1, 1985.

34. Charlotte Ford, interview, September 30, 1984.

35. William Clay Ford, interview, May 30, 1985.

36. Alfred Ford and Benson Ford, Jr., interviews.

37. Ford R. Bryan, notes to the author, December 13, 1985.

38. Grace Prunk, interview, January 23, 1985.

39. Frank Donovan, interview.

40. Lloyd A. Semple, interview, October 18, 1985.

41. Off-the-record interview.

42. Lloyd A. Semple, interview, October 18, 1985.

## 28. Graduation

1. Warnock, p. 133.
2. "U.S. New-Car Registrations by Make Since World War II," p. 86.
3. Ibid., p. 25.
4. Ibid.
5. Ibid., p. 26.
6. FIA, AR–65–71:20. See *Plan for Strengthening Ford's Position Relative to Chevrolet in the Car Market*, December 9, 1958.
7. Wilkins and Hill, pp. 393–397.
8. FA, Acc. 975, Box 1, 104– J–2. William Clay Ford interview, April 12, 1960.
9. Warnock, p. 41.
10. Ibid., pp. 56, 57.
11. FIA, Ar–65–71. "E" Car Name Evaluation Program.
12. Warnock, p. 75.
13. Ibid., p. 76.
14. Ibid., p. 62.
15. Ibid., p. 75.
16. Keats, p. 37.
17. Larry Shinoda, interview, September 12, 1985.
18. Pettifer and Turner, p. 137.
19. Eugene Bordinat, interview, November 6, 1985.
20. Robert Kanzler, interview, October 29, 1985.
21. *Life*, September 2, 1957; *Time*, September 2, 1957.
22. Off -the-record interview.
23. *Fortune*, September 1957; cited on Warnock dust jacket.
24. *Detroit Free Press*, Tuesday, August 27, 1957.
25. Warnock, p. 239.
26. Herndon, p. 86.
27. Cortz, "A New Generation of Whiz Kids."
28. Off -the-record interview.
29. Arjay Miller, interview, October 12, 1985.
30. Ibid.
31. Warnock, p. 243.
32. The cartoon, by Paul Conrad, appeared in the *Los Angeles Times* in 1963, according to Warnock, p. v.
33. Henry Ford II, interview, September 11, 1984.
34. Off -the-record interview.

35. Eugene Bordinat, interview, November 6, 1985.

36. Arjay Miller, interview, March 9, 1986.

37. FIA, AR–66–12:8. Program, 1956, Ford Motor Company Management Conference, June 14, 15, 16, The Greenbrier.

38. Alan Gornick, interview, January 14, 1985.

39. Arjay Miller, interview, March 9, 1986.

40. Hickerson, p. 132.

41. Off -the-record interview.

42. Off -the-record interview.

43. Halberstam, p. 233.

44. Ted Mecke, interview, March 9, 1986.

45. Henry Ford II, interview, April 17, 1986.

46. FIA, AR–66–12:8. Robert S. McNamara. Letters of July 7, 1950, and of 1954, no day or month given.

47. It has been said that McNamara forfeited as much as $3 million when he left Ford, but although the Ford Motor Company proxy statement of April 25, 1961, shows him holding options on shares worth approximately $2.7 million, his profit on these would only have amounted to some $1.05 million.

48. Henry Ford II, interview, April 17, 1986.

## 29. Mustang

On April 2, 1985, the author wrote to the public-relations office at Chrysler requesting an interview with Lee Iacocca in order to discuss the contents of this and subsequent chapters. The request was turned down, as were a number of other requests made directly to Mr. Iacocca and also via his representatives.

Gary Witzenburg's *Mustang!* is the most meticulous published account of the car's birth, based on interviews with Gene Bordinat, Don Frey, Lee Iacocca, Don Petersen, Hal Sperlich, and others in the original team. His book contains the dates and details for the account given here, together with photographs which illustrate the original Monza, the Bordinat-DeLaRossa Allegro, and the other prototypes that eventually became the Mustang—including an attempt by the Budd Company to create a Thunderbird-Falcon hybrid. Witzenburg also deals fully with the very first Mustang of all, the mid-engined Mustang I.

1. Iacocca, p. 5.

2. Ibid., pp. 5–7.

3. Abodaher, p. 36.

4. Ibid., 35.

5. Ibid., p. 37.

6. Cheyfitz and Wright, p. 52. I am grateful to Kirk Cheyfitz, who spent a week in Allentown in 1978, for confirming this material.

7. Iacocca, p. 25.

8. Ibid., p. 32.

9. Chevrolet sales for 1955 were 1,640,681 as compared to 1,573,882 for Ford, a gap of 66,799. In 1956 the figures were 1,565,399 for Chevrolet, against 1,375,343 for Ford, a margin of 190,056. "U.S. New-Car Registrations," p. 26.

10. Abodaher, p. 65.

11. Iacocca gives this date as December 1960 in his memoirs, but his official Ford biography has always listed November 1960 as the date when he took over the Ford Division.

12. Iacocca, p. 46.

13. Nevins and Hill, vol. 3, p. 349.

14. Ibid., p. 338.

15. Ted Mecke, interview.

16. Nevins and Hill, vol. 3, p. 379.

17. Warnock, p. 36.

18. Ibid.

19. Witzenburg, p. 11.

20. *Mustang Monthly Magazine*, May 1983, pp. 25–61.

21. Gene Bordinat, interview, November 6, 1985.

22. Iacocca, p. 69.

23. Ford Motor Company, Research and Analysis Department.

24. Charles Bosworth, interview.

## 30. Mediterranean Phase

1. Mrs. Deane Johnson, interview, December 1, 1985.

2. Robert Kanzler, interview, October 29, 1985.

3. Alfred Ford, interview, January 29, 1984.

4. George Reindel interview, August 2, 1985.

5. Lasky, p. 99.

6. Off -the-record interview.

7. Mrs. Deane Johnson, interview, December 1, 1985.

8. Anne Ford Scarborough, interview, November 30, 1985.

9. Charlotte Ford, interview, September 30, 1984.

10. Lasky, p. 107.

11. Charlotte Ford, interview, September 30, 1984.

12. William G. Curran, interview, May 4, 1984.

13. Lasky, p. 103.

14. Anne Ford Scarborough, interview, November 30, 1985.

15. Lloyd Semple, interview, November 29, 1985.

16. Off-the-record interview.

17. Off-the-record interview.

18. Charlotte Ford, interview, September 30, 1984.

19. Anne Ford Scarborough, interview, November 30, 1985.

20. Charlotte Ford, interview, September 30, 1984.

21. Ibid.

22. Lasky, p. 116.

23. Off-the-record interview.

24. FA, Acc. 6 contains accounts and diaries relating to the Edsel Fords' foreign holidays.

25. Henry II's London townhouse off Grosvenor Square went to Cristina Ford in their divorce settlement.

26. Rose, p. 20.

27. Wilkins and Hill is the definitive account of Ford's development overseas from 1903 to the early 1960s.

28. Walter Hayes, interview.

29. Seidler gives a more than adequate contemporary account of the development of the Fiesta, and should be read in conjunction with Lee Iacocca's memoirs in order to arrive at a balanced assessment of how much credit Iacocca can really claim for this car.

30. B. Bruce-Briggs, "Ford of Europe Is Under Seige," *Detroit News*, October 28, 1984.

31. Jonathan Aitken, "The Battle of Wits over Mr. Ford's Lost 63 Million Pounds," London *Evening Standard*, March 15, 1971.

## 31. Trouble on Twelfth Street

Robert Conot's *American Odyssey* contains a detailed account of the Detroit riots of 1967, together with the events leading up to them. The Ford Motor Company's black hiring programme is well described by Booton Herndon, who was in Detroit at the time. Henry Ford II's personal role in the reconstruction of Detroit is described here from interviews as listed below. I am particularly grateful for the help of Larry Doss, Max Fisher, Joe Hudson, Jr., Robert McCabe, and Ted Mecke.

1. FA, Acc. 1, Box 1: Draft article by Henry Ford on the future.

2. Conot, p. 523.

3. Ibid., p. 524.

4. Lee and Humphrey, p. 8.

5. Ibid.

6. Conot, p. 468.

7. Ibid., p. 449.

8. Ibid., p. 160.

9. Babson, p. 168.

10. Joseph L. Hudson, Jr., interview.

11. Conot, p. 456.

12. Johnson spoke at the University of Michigan. Conot, p. 489.

13. For a sketch map showing this location, see Babson, p. 242.

14. Babson, p. 167.

15. Car registrations fell in 1967 to 8.357 million from 9.008 million in 1966.

16. Ted Mecke, interview, April 5, 1984.

17. Levi Jackson, interview, summer 1984.

18. Herndon, pp. 103, 104.

19. Ibid., p. 105.

20. Ibid.

21. Max Fisher, interview, July 29, 1985.

22. Herndon, p. 342.

23. William Curran, interview, May 4, 1984.

24. Herndon, p. 331.

25. Max Fisher, interview, July 29, 1985.

26. Ibid.

27. Ibid.

28. Herndon, pp. 238, 239.

29. Joseph Hudson, Jr., interview.

30. Max Fisher, interview, December 24, 1985.

31. Conot, p. 529.

32. Herndon, p. 336.

33. Ibid., p. 335.

34. Larry Doss, interview, December 27, 1985.

35. Ibid.

36. Herndon, p. 336.

37. Max Fisher, interview, July 29, 1985.

38. Larry Doss, interview, December 27, 1985. The other founders of ICBIF were Karl Gregory, Charlie Diggs, Walt McMurtry, and the Rev. Charles Morton.

39. Ibid.

40. Ibid.
41. Ibid.
42. Henry Ford ll, interview, September 11, 1984.
43. Robert McCabe, interview, December 17, 1985.
44. Max Fisher, interview, December 24, 1985.
45. Alfred A. Taubman, interview, February 15, 1985.
46. Ford Bryan, interview, December 6, 1985.
47. Off -the-record interview.
48. Larry Doss, interview, December 27, 1985.
49. *Time*, November 26, 1984.
50. Ferry, *Buildings of Detroit*, first edition, p. xix.

## 32. Bunkie

On March 27, 1986, the author telephoned the office of William Fugazy in New York in order to discuss the contents of this and subsequent chapters. Unable to make contact, he sent a telegram that was delivered on March 28, 1986, inviting Mr. Fugazy to discuss a number of points that were set out in the telegram and to make his views known by April 14, 1986. Mr. Fugazy did not respond.

1. Off -the-record interview.
2. Arjay Miller, interview, October 12, 1985.
3. Herndon, p. 337.
4. Bunkie Knudsen, interview, July 30, 1985.
5. Lyndon Baines Johnson Library, Austin, Texas. WHCF, Name File, No. 182. "Ford, Henry II." Letter of September 18, 1964.
6. Lyndon Baines Johnson Library, Austin, Texas. Office Files of John Macy, "Ford, Henry II." Box 188.
7. Ibid.
8. Bunkie Knudsen, interview, July 30, 1985.
9. Ibid.
10. *Time*, May 23, 1959.
11. This tale, now part of the folklore of Detroit, is well told by Herndon, pp. 131–134, based on his interviews with Knudsen and Jack Davis.
12. Bunkie Knudsen, interview, July 30, 1985.
13. Ted Mecke, interview, April 5, 1984.
14. Larry Shinoda, interview, September 12, 1985.
15. Ibid.

16. See for example, the *Wall Street Journal*, May 14, 1970, and also the *New York Times Magazine*, July 18, 1971.

17. *Time* September 19, 1969.

18. *New York Times Magazine*, October 19, 1969.

19. Ibid.

20. Iacocca, pp. 83–85.

21. Bunkie Knudsen, interview, July 30, 1985.

22. Larry Shinoda, interview, September 12, 1985.

23. Ibid.

24. *Wall Street Journal*, September 17, 1969.

25. Larry Shinoda, interview, September 12, 1985.

26. Ibid.

27. *Manhattan Inc.*, September 1985, p. 136.

28. Iacocca, p. 80.

29. Ibid., pp. 80–81.

30. Bunkie Knudsen, interview, July 30, 1985.

31. Ibid.

32. Ibid.

33. Gene Bordinat, interview, November 6, 1985.

34. Off-the-record interview.

35. *New York Times Magazine*, July 18, 1971.

36. Bunkie Knudsen, interview, July 30, 1985.

37. Charlotte Ford, interview, September, 30, 1984.

38. *Wall Street Journal*, September 17, 1969.

39. Bunkie Knudsen, interview, July 30, 1985.

40. *New York Times*, September 12, 1969.

41. Ibid., July 18, 1971.

42. Ibid., September 12, 1969.

43. Henry Ford II, interview, April 17, 1986.

44. *New York Times*, July 18, 1971.

45. Gene Bordinat, interview.

46. *Wall Street Journal*, September 17, 1969. I am grateful to Henry Ford II for sending me this material.

47. *New York Times Magazine*, October 19, 1969.

48. Off-the-record interview.

49. Off-the-record interview.

## 33. Thrifting

This chapter has drawn extensively on the help and facilities of the Center for Auto Safety in Washington, and I am particularly grateful for the help of Robert Dewey there. The chapter also relies on the expertise of Byron Bloch, the Los Angeles-based automotive-safety consultant, who has testified in a number of cases involving the Pinto, and who provided much of the data for the *Mother Jones* article "Pinto Madness," by Mark Dowie, in September/October 1977. Mary Joseph of Ford Corporate News kindly provided very prompt and thorough answers to a number of questions, and Richard J. Molloy, Assistant General Counsel, compiled a most helpful folder of data which he explained. I am grateful to Larry Deitch and Matt Schlegel of Simon Deitch Tucker and Friedman for tracking down some important legal details and for talking to the attorney of Richard Grimshaw, Arthur N. Hews.

1. *Wall Street Journal*, February 8, 1978. Ford have the date of the accident recorded as May 28, 1972.

2. U.S. Government Fatal Accident Reporting System, 1975–1984.

3. Iacocca, p. 162.

4. Bunkie Knudsen, interview, July 30, 1985.

5. Ibid.

6. Ibid.

7. Byron Bloch, interview, October 14, 1985.

8. Tom Feaheny, interview, April 15, 1986.

9. Cited in Dowie, "Pinto Madness."

10. Ibid.

11. Mary Joseph, Ford Corporate News department, March 27, 1986.

12. Off-the-record interview.

13. Herndon, p. 262.

14. Ibid., p. 263.

15. "Societal Cost Components for Fatalities," NHTSA, 1972.

16. "Fatalities Associated with Crash-Induced Fuel Leakage and Fires," by E. S. Grush and C. S. Saunby. Countersigned by J. D. Hromi and R. B. Maclean. Ford Inter Office, Environmental and Safety Engineering. Copy in the files of the Center for Auto Safety, Washington.

17. Ibid, p. 7.

18. The hearing was denied on September 10, 1981. 174 California Reporter 348, 119 California Appeals 3d, p. 757 (1981). Settlement confirmed by Arthur N. Hews to Matt Schlegel, March 28, 1986.

19. *Time*, February 12, 1979.

20. Off-the-record interview.
21. Tom Feaheny, interview, January 10, 1986.
22. Byron Bloch, interview, October 14, 1985.
23. Gene Bordinat, interview, January 9, 1986.
24. Ibid.
25. Tom Feaheny, interview, January 10, 1986.
26. Ibid.
27. Ibid.
28. Department of Justice, News Release, February 13, 1973. Copy in the files of the Center for Auto Safety, Washington. These figures are confirmed by Ford Corporate News.
29. Lasky, p. 138.

## 34. Strega

1. Herndon, pp. 384, 385.
2. Off-the-record interview.
3. Kay Wise, interview.
4. Benson Ford, interview, February 18, 1986.
5. Lee Hills, interview, March 22, 1985.
6. Ibid.
7. Yale University, Associate Secretary's Office.
8. Lasky, p. 117.
9. *Look*, as quoted by Jeremy Campbell in London *Evening Standard*, September 10, 1969.
10. Lloyd Semple, interview, November 29, 1985.
11. Sergeant Milton Turner, interview, October 14, 1985.
12. Otie Hunter, interview, October 14, 1985.
13. Off-the-record interview.
14. Kathy Ford, interview, April 22, 1985.
15. Ibid.
16. Whelan, p. 55.
17. Kathy Ford, interview, April 22, 1985.
18. John Bugas, interview, October 30, 1985.
19. Ibid.
20. Off-the-record interview.
21. *Detroit News*, June 11, 1978.
22. Off-the-record interview.
23. Kathy Ford, interview, April 22, 1985.
24. Walter Hayes, interview.
25. Kay Wise, interview.
26. Ibid.

27. Off -the-record interview.
28. Off -the-record interview.

## 35. Keys to the Kingdom

On March 27, 1986, the author telephoned the offices of Alejandro de Tomaso in New Jersey and Modena in order to discuss the contents of this and subsequent chapters. Unable to make contact, he sent a telegram to Modena that was delivered on March 28, 1986, inviting Mr. de Tomaso to discuss a number of points that were set out in the telegram and to make his views known by April 14, 1986. Mr. de Tomaso did not respond.

1. Iacocca, p. 127.
2. Ibid., p. 92.
3. Dr. Franklin D. Murphy, interview, May 8, 1985.
4. Ford Motor Company Proxy Statement, April 21, 1959. As of March, 2, 1959, Henry Ford II owned 125,442 shares of Ford Motor Company Common Stock and 819,185 of Class B stock. William Clay Ford owned 966,008 shares of Ford Motor Company Class B stock.
5. Ford Motor Company Proxy Statement, April 10, 1970. Henry II had more ordinary shares, thanks to his participation in company stock-option schemes—122,676 of Ford Motor Company Common Stock, to William Clay Ford's 4,602.
6. The interview was shown on WKBD-TV, Channel 50, May 26, 1974.
7. Off -the-record interview.
8. Iacocca, p. 121.
9. Ibid., pp. 96, 97.
10. Ibid., pp. 105, 106.
11. Off -the-record interview.
12. David Metcalfe, interview, January 29, 1986.
13. FIA, AR–71–24570:3 and AR–78–24572:2.
14. Iacocca, p. 117.
15. Ibid., p. 121.
16. Ibid., p. 116.
17. Ibid.
18. Edsel Ford II, interview, December 18, 1984.
19. Burgess-Wise, p. 99.
20. Ibid., p. 102.
21. Ibid., p. 114.

22. Ibid.

23. David C. Smith, interview.

24. Burgess-Wise, p. 122.

25. National Highway Traffic Safety Administration, Office of Defects Investigations. De Tomaso of America, Inc. Documents obtained by author November 21, 1985, under the Freedom of Information Act.

26. Don Kopka interview, in Burgess-Wise, p. 126.

27. Smith, "Under the Influence," p. 40.

28. David Benson, interview, November 1985.

29. William Clay Ford, interview, May 30, 1985.

30. Lasky, pp. 85, 124–125.

31. William Clay Ford, interview, May 30, 1985.

32. Marian S. Heiskell, interview, May 1, 1985.

33. Ibid.

34. Ibid.

35. Ibid.

36. Ibid., January 21, 1986.

37. Dr. Franklin D. Murphy, interview, May 8, 1985.

38. Ibid.

39. Ibid.

40. Ibid.

41. Marian Heiskell, interview, January 21, 1986.

42. Letter of D. R. Jolliffe to J. J. Sullivan, April 2, 1986.

43. Marian Heiskell, interview, May 1, 1985.

44. Dr. Franklin D. Murphy, interview, May 8, 1985.

45. Iacocca, p. 124.

46. Dr. Franklin D. Murphy, interview, May 8, 1985.

47. Ibid.

48. Gene Bordinat, interview, November 6, 1985.

49. Off-the-record interview.

50. Marian Heiskell, interview, May 1, 1985.

51. Iacocca, p. 125.

52. Dr. Franklin D. Murphy, interview, May 8, 1985.

53. Letter from David W. Scott, Vice President, Public Affairs, Ford Motor Company, 3 November 1986.

54. Tom Feaheny, interview, July 10, 1984.

## 36. Say It Isn't So

1. Supreme Court of the State of New York, County of New York, index number 1992/78.

2. Off -the-record interview.

3. Supreme Court of the State of New York, County of New York, index number 71891/78. John F. Lang, as trustee for the benefit of T. Sean Bolan, Douglas Bolan, Mary Bolan, and Jacqueline Bolan, against Henry Ford II and others, New York, New York, April 24, 1978, p. 2.

4. Ibid., p. 4.

5. Ibid., p. 5.

6. Ibid., p. 8.

7. Ibid. First amended complaint, May, 1979, pp. 10, 11.

8. Ford Motor Company news release, May 2, 1978.

9. Auletta, "Don't Mess With Roy Cohn," p. 39.

10. Ibid., p. 41.

11. Ibid.

12. Ibid.

13. Videotape of 23rd Stockholders' Meeting, May 11, 1978.

14. Ibid.

15. See note 3. Clause 57, p. 17.

16. See note 3. Third amended complaint, p. 14.

17. Floral beachwear: off-the-record interview. Quote from joint statement for public release, Ford Motor Company and Roy M. Cohn, signed in the offices of Hughes Hubbard and Reed, One Wall Street, New York, January 11, 1980.

18. This judgement was confirmed on January 31, 1986, in the U.S. Court of Appeals for the Second Circuit.

19. See note 3. Clause 40, p. 13.

20. Iacocca, p. 113.

21. Paul Lorenz to author, April 4, 1986.

22. Dr. Franklin D. Murphy, interview, May 8, 1985.

23. Ibid.

24. *Ward's Auto World*, Vol. 14, No. 8, August 1978, p. 22.

25. Ibid., p. 25.

26. *New Republic*, July 16 and 23, 1984, p. 21.

27. Dr. Franklin D. Murphy, interview, May 8, 1985.

28. Iacocca, p. 158.

29. "Comparative Sources of Earnings Growth and Changes in Profit Composition, 1972–1977." Donaldson, Lufkin and Jenrette Securities Corporation, July 1978.

30. Ibid.

31. Dr. Franklin D. Murphy, interview, May 8, 1985.

32. *Detroit News*, February 2, 1976.

33. "Mustang Sales in U.S., 1964–1985." Ford Research and Analysis, L. Ray Windecker.

34. Marian Heiskell, interview, January 21, 1986.

35. Ibid.

36. Lasky, p. 168.

37. Walter Hayes, interview, January 29, 1986.

38. Ford total worldwide factory sales for 1978 were 6,557, 302.

39. Off-the-record interview.

40. Dr. Franklin D. Murphy, interview, May 8, 1985.

41. Ibid.

42. "Decade of Zaps," *New York Times*, April 14, 1983.

43. News conference, Dearborn, Michigan, May 2, 1978. Henry Ford's answer to Jimmy Jones.

44. *Detroit News*, February 17, 1978.

45. *Detroit News*, February 19, 1978, quoting from testimony by Cristina Ford in Wayne Circuit Court, February 18, 1978.

46. Ibid.

47. Off-the-record interview.

48. Off-the-record interview. Cristina Ford rebutted these rumours, published by Liz Smith in the *New York Post*, in a statement of May 5, 1978: "I am not about to engage Mr. Cohn, nor do I have any intention of doing so."

49. *Detroit News*, May 5, 1978.

50. *Detroit Free Press*, May 11, 1978.

51. *Esquire*, June 20, 1978.

52. Off-the-record interview.

53. Carter L. Burgess, interview, July 10, 1985.

54. Ibid.

55. Dr. Franklin D. Murphy, interview, May 8, 1985.

56. Ibid.

57. Iacocca, p. 125.

58. Dr. Franklin D. Murphy, interview, May 8, 1985.

59. Joseph Cullman III, interview, February 28, 1986.

60. Ibid.

61. Dr. Franklin D. Murphy, interview, May 8, 1985.

62. Ibid.

63. Ibid.

64. Iacocca, p. 126, and Keith Crain, interview.

65. Keith Crain, interview.

66. Iacocca, p. 127.

67. William Clay Ford, interview, May 30, 1985.

68. Ibid.

69. William Clay Ford, interview, May 30, 1985.

70. Lee Iacocca describes William Clay Ford as having "tears running down his face" as he left his brother's office (Iacocca, p. 128). In answer to the author's question about this, William Clay Ford replied: "Well, I thought the whole thing was unfortunate, let's put it that way. . . . I didn't think it had to come down to what it'd come down to. . . . Close to tears? I was upset by it, sure I was upset by it. I thought it was very unfortunate. I thought he was a very capable man, and I was really sorry to see it happen."

71. Iacocca, p. 127.

72. Ibid., p. 128.

73. Ford Motor Company Proxy Statement, April 13, 1979, p. 15.

74. Iacocca, p. 134.

75. Carter Burgess, interview, July 10, 1985.

76. Iacocca, p. xiii. "On October 15, my final day at the office, and, just incidentally my fifty-fourth birthday, my driver drove me to World Headquarters in Dearborn for the last time." In 1978, October 15 fell on a Sunday, so it was presumably on the previous Friday that Iacocca "retired."

77. Ibid., p. xiv.

78. Ibid.

79. Off-the-record interview.

80. Robert Normand, interview, September 15, 1985.

81. The author visited this office and measured it on September 15, 1985. He also interviewed Robert Normand, who was in charge of the building at the time of Lee Iacocca's brief residence, as well as in the days of Ernest R. Breech.

82. Henry Ford II, interview, April 17, 1986.

83. The author is grateful for the help of Walter Feehily, Executive Assistant to Ernie Breech, and to Jack Maison, Industrial Relations Manager of the Parts Distribution Center on Telegraph Road.

**Epilogue**

1. Benson Ford Junior, interview, February 18, 1986.

2. Ibid.

3. Ibid.

4. Ibid.

5. William R. Chapin, interview.

6. Off-the-record interview.

7. Cheyfitz and Levin, "Crashing in the Fast Lane," January 1985, p. 153.

8. Ibid.

9. Ibid., December 1984, p. 68.

10. Benson Ford Junior, interview, February 18, 1986.

11. Ibid.

12. Ibid.

13. Ibid.

14. Cheyfitz and Levin, "Crashing in the Fast Lane," January 1985, p. 56.

15. Benson Ford Junior, interview, February 18, 1986.

16. Ibid.

17. Ibid.

18. In proposals printed in the Ford Motor Company proxy statement of April 12, 1985, Mrs. Evelyn Y. Davis stated that she held 75 shares of the common stock, while Lewis D. Gilbert disclosed a shareholding of 37 shares, with an additional family interest of 187 shares.

19. Videotape of twenty-fourth Annual Meeting of Stockholders, Ford Motor Company, May 10, 1979.

20. Ibid.

21. Ibid.

22. Ibid.

23. Ibid.

24. Ibid.

25. Ibid.

26. Ibid.

27. Ibid.

28. Ibid.

29. *Detroit News*, February 11, 1979.

30. Supreme Court of the State of New York, County of New York. Index No. 71891/78. Affidavits of Alejandro de Tomaso, December 4, 1978, and of Roy M. Cohn, December 15, 1978. De Tomaso's shares were valued at $41 per share, the quoted price of Ford Motor Company stock as published in the *Wall Street Journal* at the close of trading on December 14, 1978.

31. A copy of Nolte's memorandum of April 6, 1978, together with a copy of his letter of that date to Harold Webb, Criminal

Division, U.S. Department of Justice, was attached as exhibit D to the fourth amended complaint, November 9, 1978, of Index No. 71891/78, Supreme Court of the State of New York, County of New York.

32. See note 19.

33. Ibid.

34. Kay Wise, interview, March 25, 1986. See also Lasky, p. 162.

35. Charlotte Ford, interview, September 30, 1984, and Anne Ford Scarborough, interview, November 30, 1985.

36. Anne Ford Scarborough, interview, November 30, 1985.

37. Off-the-record interview.

38. Walter Hayes, letter to the author, April 3, 1986.

39. Charlotte Ford, interview, September 30, 1984.

40. Kathy Ford, interview, April 22, 1985.

41. Ibid.

42. Ibid.

43. Ibid.

44. Ibid.

45. Ibid.

46. Ibid.

47. Henry Ford II, interview, April 17, 1986.

48. Anne Ford Scarborough, telephone conversation, April 3, 1986.

49. Lewis, "A Super Existence."

50. Cynthia Ford, telephone conversation, April 9, 1986.

51. Edsel Ford, interview, June 9, 1984.

52. *Detroit Free Press*, February 10, 1977.

53. Off-the-record interview.

54. Off-the-record interview. Confirmed by William Clay Ford, April 15, 1986.

55. Off-the-record interview. Confirmed by William Clay Ford, April 17, 1986.

56. Off-the-record interview.

57. Off-the-record interview.

58. Letter of D. R. Jolliffe to J. J. Sullivan, Stockholder Relations, April 2, 1986. "Outside Directors' Fees."

59. Off-the-record interview.

60. Henry Ford II, interview, September 12, 1984.

61. Ibid.

62. Ibid.

63. "I've only got one box, that big, from '45 to '68," Henry Ford II told this author on September 12, 1984, "and it's not full. . . . I can't remember how much I've saved, but it's maybe one of those cardboard boxes, about like this, maybe three quarters full, and that's twenty-three years."

64. Ibid.

# PHOTO CREDITS

Frontispiece photograph is from the Henry Ford Museum, The Edison Institute, Dearborn, Michigan.

All photographs in the first inset are from the Henry Ford Museum, The Edison Institute, Dearborn, Michigan, with the exception of the top photograph on page 11, which is from Ford of Britain.

Photographs in the second inset are from the Henry Ford Museum, The Edison Institute, Dearborn, Michigan, with the exception of the following: page 2, bottom, *Detroit News*; page 3, bottom, Ford Motor Company Archives; page 5, top left and right, Catherine Ruddiman; page 9, bottom, *Detroit News*; page 12, top, Founders Society Purchase, Edsel B. Ford Fund and Gift of Edsel B. Ford; bottom, Detroit Institute of Arts; page 13, bottom, Founders Society Purchase, Edsel B. Ford Fund and Gift of Edsel B. Ford; pages 14 and 15, Archives of Labor and Urban Affairs, Wayne State University; page 16, top, The Bettmann Archive, Inc.

The photographs in the third inset are from the following sources: page 1, Henry Ford Museum, The Edison Institute, Dearborn, Michigan. Page 2, top, *Detroit News*; bottom, Paul Popper Ltd. Page 3, Paul Popper Ltd. Page 4, top, Ford News Department; bottom, Henry Ford Museum, The Edison Institute, Dearborn, Michigan. Page 5, Henry Ford Museum, The Edison Institute, Dearborn, Michigan. Page 6, top left, *Detroit News*; top right, Henry Ford Museum, The Edison Institute, Dearborn, Michigan; bottom, Ford Motor Company. Page 7, top, Henry Ford Museum, The Edison Institute, Dearborn, Michigan; bottom, Associated Press Ltd. Page 8, Popperfoto. Page 9, top, Ford Motor Company; bottom, AP/Wide World Photos. Page 10, Popperfoto. Page 11, top, Popperfoto; bottom, *Detroit Free Press*. Page 12, top, *Detroit Free Press*; bottom, Detroit Lions. Page 13, top, Linda Solomon; bottom, *Detroit News*. Page 14, top left, Ford Motor Company;

# BIBLIOGRAPHY

*The bibliography is arranged as follows:*
INTERVIEWS CONDUCTED BY THE AUTHOR
MANUSCRIPT COLLECTIONS
DOCUMENTS OBTAINED UNDER THE FREEDOM OF INFORMATION ACT
UNPUBLISHED DOCUMENTS
VIDEO RECORDINGS AND TRANSCRIPTS
ARTICLES
BOOKS, CATALOGUES, AND PAMPHLETS

## Interviews

Research for this book started in November 1983, and since then the author has undertaken over 200 interviews. A number were off the record and are not listed here. The following were on the record. Where no date is given, this indicates frequent meetings or conversations.

Alandt, Lynn: Grosse Pointe, Michigan, June 17, 1985.

Alandt, Paul: Grosse Pointe, May 14, 1984.

Anderson, Kim: Grosse Pointe, February 2, 1985, and other conversations.

Bachrach, Chuck: St. Clair Shores, Michigan, telephone interview, November 26, 1985.

Benson, David: interviewed by Victoria Mather, London, November 1985.

Bigelow, Chuck: Grosse Pointe.

Biggar, Gladys: Fort Myers, Florida, March 28, 1985.

Bloch, Byron: Los Angeles, October 14, 1985; telephone interview, January 8, 1986; and other conversations.

Bombard, Owen: New York, two telephone interviews.

Booth, John Lord II: Grosse Pointe.

Bordinat, Eugene: Clarkston, Michigan, November 6, 1985; telephone interview, January 9, 1986; and other conversations.

# BIBLIOGRAPHY

Boyer, Robert A.: Florida, telephone interview, March 30, 1985.

Bridenstine, James A.: Grosse Pointe.

Brokaw, Tom: New York, September 27, 1984.

Brunk, Thomas W.: Indian Village, Detroit, August 20, 1984, and other conversations.

Bryan, Ford R.: Dearborn.

Bugas, Joan: Southfield, Michigan, October 30, 1985, and telephone conversation, January 10, 1986.

Burgess, Carter: Dearborn, July 10, 1985.

Burleson, Harvey: Northville, Michigan, July 12, 1984, and other conversations.

Chapin, William R.: Grosse Pointe Farms, November 10, 1985, and other conversations.

Chapin, Roy, Jr.: Grosse Pointe, May 23, 1985.

Cheyfitz, Kirk: Detroit, May 25, 1984, and other conversations.

Collins, Eleanor: Grosse Pointe, December 6, 1984.

Crain, Keith: Grosse Pointe.

Crippen, David: Dearborn and Ann Arbor, Michigan.

Cullman, Joseph III: New York, telephone interview, February 28, 1986.

Cummings, Dr. Frederick: Detroit, June 4, 1984.

Curran, William: Grosse Pointe, May 4, 1984, and other conversations.

Curran, Mrs. William: Grosse Pointe, March 14, 1984.

Cutler, Esther: New York, September 29, 1984.

Davis, Charles W., Jr.: Grosse Pointe.

Davis, David E.: Ann Arbor, April 9, 1984, and other conversations.

DeRosen, Donald: Henry Ford Hospital, Detroit, July 15, 1985.

Dewey, Robert: Center for Auto Safety, Washington, D.C., October 4, 1985, and other conversations.

Donovan, Frank: Grosse Pointe.

Doran, Maureen Keane: Dearborn, June 18, 1985.

Doss, Larry: telephone interview, December 27, 1985.

Dow, Douglas: Indian Village, Detroit, September 19, 1984.

Downs, Linda: Detroit Institute of Arts, Detroit, June 13, 1984, and other conversations.

Dykema, John: Detroit, March 5, 1985; May 1985; and Huron Mountain Club, Big Bay, Michigan, July 12–16, 1985.

Esper, Al: Dearborn, May 14, 1985.

Feaheny, Tom: Bloomfield Hills, Michigan, July 10, 1984; Dearborn, November 18, 1985; telephone interview, January 10, 1986; and other conversations.

Feehily, Walter: Arizona, telephone interview, April 22, 1986.

Ferry, Hawkins: Grosse Pointe.

Fisher, Max: Detroit, July 29, 1985; telephone interview, December 24, 1985; and other conversations.

Ford, Alfred Brush: Indian Village, Detroit, January 29, 1984, and the Hare Krishna Temple, Detroit, May 13, 1985.

Ford, Benson: Grosse Pointe, February 18, 1986.

Ford, Charlotte: New York, September 30, 1984; Grosse Pointe, December 12, 1984; and other conversations.

Ford, Edsel II: Grosse Pointe Farms, June 9, 1984; Renaissance Center, Detroit, December 18, 1984; and other conversations.

Ford, Henry II: Renaissance Center, Detroit, September 11, 1984, and Dearborn, April 17, 1986.

Ford, Josephine: Grosse Pointe, October 22, 1985.

Ford, Kathy: Grosse Pointe, April 22, 1985, and telephone conversation, January 24, 1986.

Ford, Walter Buhl II: Warren, Michigan, October 31, 1985.

Ford, William Clay: Dearborn, May 30, 1985, and telephone conversation, April 15, 1986.

Ford, William Clay, Jr.: Grosse Pointe Shores, January 22, 1985, and other conversations.

Fraser, Douglas: telephone interview, October 1985.

Freidland, Sheryl: Grosse Pointe, September 5, 1985.

Galbraith, J. K.: New York, April 17, 1986.

Gornick, Alan: Bloomfield Hills, January 14, 1985, and telephone conversation, October 31, 1985.

Gossett, William T.: Bloomfield Hills, May 17, 1985.

Hayden, Martin: Grosse Pointe, April 27, 1984.

Hayes, Walter: Dearborn and London.

Heiskell, Marian S.: New York, telephone interviews, May 1, 1985, and January 21, 1986.

Herndon, Booton: Charlottesville, Virginia, telephone conversation, September 1984.

Hewlitt, Mrs. Freda Pepper: Birmingham, Michigan, February 20, 1985.

Higbie, Carlton M., Jr.: Detroit, July 29, 1985.

Hills, Lee: Miami, Florida, March 22, 1985.

Holley, Danforth: Grosse Pointe.

Humberstone, Jordon: Greenfield Village, Michigan, July 17, 1984.

Hudson, Joseph L., Jr.: Grosse Pointe, January 28, 1986, and other conversations.

Hunter, Otie: Santa Barbara, California, October 14, 1985.

Jackson, Levi: Dearborn, July 17, 1984.

Johnson, Mrs. Deane: New York, December 1, 1985, and telephone conversations, October 7, 1985, and March 9, 1986.

Kanzler, Robert: Detroit, October 29, 1985.

Knudsen, Semon E., "Bunkie": Bloomfield Hills, July 30, 1985.

Lam, Dr. Conrad: Henry Ford Hospital, Detroit, March 12, 1985.

Lapteff, Alexis V.: New York, letter of October 24, 1984.

Lepard, Mrs. Robin: Grosse Pointe.

Lewis, Dr. David L.: Ann Arbor, April 8, 1984, and other conversations.

Litogot, Art: Bloomfield Hills, November 22, 1985.

Lorenz, Paul: Bloomfield Hills, June 10, 1985, and other conversations.

Macauley, Mrs. Alvan: Grosse Pointe.

McCabe, Robert: Renaissance Center, Detroit, April 24, 1984, and telephone interview, December 17, 1985.

McClure, Doug: Dearborn, July 1, 1985.

Mecke, Ted: Grosse Pointe, April 5, 1984, and other conversations.

Merry, Maggie: Grosse Pointe.

Metcalfe, David: interviewed by Victoria Mather, London, January 29, 1986.

Miller, Arjay: Woodside, California, October 12, 1985, and telephone interview, March 9, 1986.

Morris, George: Monroe, Michigan, November 21, 1985.

Morrow, Thirza: Grosse Pointe, January 15, 1985.

Murphy, Dr. Franklin D.: Dearborn, May 8, 1985.

Normand, Robert: Livonia, Michigan, September 15, 1985.

Pestillo, Peter: Dearborn, May 29, 1984.

Pierson, Lynn: Grosse Pointe, September 18, 1984.

Prunk, Grace: Grosse Pointe, January 23, 1985.

Reindel, George: Detroit, August 2, 1985.

Reuther, Lisa: Hare Krishna Temple, Detroit, November 19, 1985.

Reuther, Victor: Detroit, October 26, 1985.

Robine, Paul: Dearborn, August 29, 1985.

Ruddiman, Catherine: Boca Raton, Florida, March 26, 1985.

Scarborough, Mrs. Anne Ford: New York, November 30, 1985.

Secrest, Frederick: Dearborn, August 3, 1984.

Semple, Lloyd: Grosse Pointe, November 29, 1985.

Sharp, Ellen: Detroit Institute of Arts, Detroit, April 19, 1984.

Shinoda, Lawrence: Farmington Hills, Michigan, September 12, 1985, and telephone interview, November 22, 1985.

Sladen, Frank J., Jr.: Grosse Pointe.

Sloan, Jerry: Southfield, April 10, 1985, and telephone interview January 27, 1986.

Smith, David C.: Detroit, 1984.

Smith, Raymond: Grosse Pointe, June 18, 1984.

Smith, Robert: Detroit, September 26, 1985.

Taubman, A. Alfred: Troy, Michigan, February 15, 1985.

Taubman, Robert: Bloomfield Hills.

Tassinare, Bruce: Hare Krishna Temple, Detroit.

Thurber, Donald: Grosse Pointe, February 7, 1985, and other conversations.

Townsend, LaBonnie: Dearborn, July 17, 1984, and other conversations.

Tracy, Emmet: Grosse Pointe, June 13, 1985.

Tracy, Mrs. Emmet: Grosse Pointe, January 29, 1985.

Turner, Sgt. Milton: Los Angeles, telephone interview, October 14, 1985.

Vanderkloot, Mr. and Mrs. Robert: Bloomfield Hills, August 1, 1985.

Welcenbach, Kay: Grosse Pointe, May 30, 1984.

Weld, John: Laguna Niguel, California, October 13, 1985.

Wheat, Mrs. Renville: Huron Mountain Club, Big Bay, Michigan, July 13, 1985.

White, Gary: Dearborn, July 17, 1984.

Wise, Kay: Grosse Pointe and Palm Beach, Florida.

## Manuscript collections

*Edison Institute (Ford Archives)*

The personal papers of Henry Ford I, together with the archives of the Ford Motor Company for most of his lifetime, were gathered together after his death and are now in the Ford Archives of the Edison Institute, which is the collective name for Greenfield Village, the Henry Ford Museum, and the various research and educational facilities connected with them in Dearborn, Michigan.

In addition to the original documentary material, the Ford Archives contain a major and comprehensive collection of oral histories. These consist of interviews conducted in the early 1950s under the supervision of Owen W. Bombard. More than 300 people who knew or had contacts with Henry Ford were interviewed. Their interviews were edited, transcribed, and bound, and are filed in the archives by name, alphabetically, under the general title of *Reminiscences*.

One significant gap in the archives is of personal papers relating to Edsel Ford, the son of Henry Ford I. These were originally accessioned and filed in the archives when they were established in the early 1950s. But late in 1964, shortly before the archives were transferred from the Ford Motor Company to the Edison Institute—which is an independent body—many of Edsel Ford's personal papers were removed from their boxes and taken away on the instructions of the Ford Motor Company. When questioned by this author as to the current whereabouts of these papers, Henry Ford II said he did not know where they were—and that, indeed, he had no recollection of their removal.

Also in 1964, a Ford Motor Company official wrote a memorandum suggesting that "controversial" documents in the personal and corporate papers of Henry Ford I should also be destroyed. Fortunately this was not acted upon—and it is possible slightly to reconstruct Edsel's personal papers by reference to the original catalogue and to descriptions of them in other accessions which the company did not censor. The corporate papers of Edsel Ford are filed in Accession 6.

References to Ford Archives material in this book are indicated by the abbreviation FA, followed by an accession and box number, or by FA, *Reminiscences*, followed by a name.

In addition to documents, the Ford Archives also contain a rich supply of photographic material. Photographs from this collection that appear in this book are credited to the Edison Institute.

The extensive film material relating to Henry Ford, some 1.5 million feet, has been transferred to the National Archives in Washington, where it can be consulted in the Ford Film Collection.

*Ford Motor Company Industrial Archives*

These archives, which can be consulted by application to the Archivist, Ford Industrial Archives, 26305 Glendale, Redford, Michigan 48239, contain confidential material relating to the early years of the company, as well as a wide variety of executive files and other materials relating to the company since the Second World War, including the files of Lee Iacocca. Admission to the archives is at the discretion of the Ford Motor Company.

If admitted to the archives, researchers may request photocopies of documents, but may not take notes. These photocopies are then submitted for review and approval by various offices inside the Ford Motor Company, who decide which documents, if any, may be released.

The following collections were consulted in the preparation of this book, and are referred to in the source notes by the abbreviation FIA, followed by the accession number:

| Acc. No. | Subject |
|---|---|
| AR–65–71 | Executive files: E. R. Breech, 1946–1960. |
| AR–65–87 | Executive files: Henry Ford II, 1945–1955. |
| AR–65–110 | Personal papers of Mr. E. R. Breech, 1946–1960. |
| AR–66–12 | Executive files of Robert S. McNamara, 1956–1960. |
| AR–68–1 | Exec. files: L. A. Iacocca, Exec. V.P., NAAO, 1965. |
| AR–69–1 | L. A. Iacocca correspondence files from Ford Div.,1961–1962. |
| AR–69–3 | Exec. files: L. A. Iacocca, Exec. V.P., NAAO, 1966, and C. H. Patterson, Chron. files, 1963–67. |
| AR–70–4 | Prince of Wales visit to Detroit, Oct. 14, 1924: Mr. Ford's gift to him of a Model T. |
| AR–70–5 | Flying saucers: sighting by Henry Ford II and other execs. on Company plane. |
| AR–70–18 | Exec. files: L. A. Iacocca, Pres. NAAO, 1967. |
| AR–71–8 | Exec. files: L. A. Iacocca, President, 1968. |
| AR–71–20 | Exec. speeches, 1944–1955. |
| AR–72–00675 | Exec. files of L. A. Iacocca, Pres., 1968–1969. |
| AR–73–15824 | Exec. files: L. A. Iacocca, President, 1970. |
| AR–73–18038 | Office of Henry Ford II: estate of Edsel B. Ford; Benson and William C. regarding Eleanor Clay Ford; Benson and William Clay Ford regarding Eleanor Clay Ford and trust accounts; Henry |

Ford II and family records from offices of Benson and William Clay Ford; William C. Ford and Benson Ford office records regarding Henry Ford II, Benson Ford and family, Josephine C. Ford and family, William Clay Ford and family, Eleanor Clay Ford and family; stock and bond certificates.

AR–74–19368   Exec. Communications (Blue Letters)—Master File: 1946 to date.

AR–75–11394   Exec. files: L. A. Iacocca, President 1965–1973.

AR–77–24570   Exec. files: L. A. Iacocca, 1973–1974.

AR–77–24571   Exec. files: L. A. Iacocca for 1970–1971, 1973 and 1975.

AR–77–28750   Executive files, B. E. Bidwell, V. P. Ford div., 1973.

AR–78–24572   Exec. files: L. A. Iacocca, 1966–1978.

AR–78–24573   Exec. files: L. A. Iacocca, 1975–1977.

AR–78–24574   Exec. files: L. A. Iacocca, 1969–1978.

AR–83–56–1699   Purchase by Ford in 1953 of assets of Dearborn Motors Corp. and Wood Brothers, Inc.

AR–85–26232   Misc. items from Secretary's Office.

AR–85–57036   Misc. drawings related to a variety of Ford activities, buildings, projects, 1918—1949.

AR–85–57038   Journal vouchers, 1907–1946, etc.

AR–85–57043   Misc. items dated 1954–1973.

## The Ford Archives of England

These archives, at Eagle Way, Brentwood, Essex, consist of documentary material accumulated over the years, but still awaiting classification, organization, and formal storage, hopefully in a future Ford museum at Dagenham. Access is at the discretion of the Ford Motor Company, by application to the Archivist.

Interesting material includes a draft history of Ford of England, written around 1952 by Norman St. John Stevas but never published, some papers of Sir Percival Perry, and records of Ford's early dealings with the British royal family.

The Ford photographic department at Arisdale Avenue, South Ockenden, Essex, contains a well-indexed collection of photographs. Access is at the discretion of the company, by application to the Manager.

### Henry Ford and Anti-Semitism

The Ford Archives contain useful material on this subject. Another important resource is the papers of the Rabbi Leo Franklin, kept in the Burton Historical Collection (see below) and also at Temple Beth El, Birmingham, Michigan. Despite repeated attempts, however, the author was unable to secure access to these papers, or even to ascertain who really controls access.

The following libraries did supply useful material: in London, the Wiener Library, London W.1.; in New York, the Anti-Defamation League of the B'nai B'rith, the Leon Baeck Institute, and the YIVO Institute for Jewish Research.

### Bentley Historical Library

This library, part of the University of Michigan, at 1150 Beal Avenue, Ann Arbor, Michigan 48109, contains a number of valuable collections relating to Michigan history. Of particular interest are the papers of Josephine Gomon, who worked for Henry Ford and Harry Bennett in the 1940s, and the papers of Joseph L. Hudson, Jr., documenting his work as chairman of New Detroit in the aftermath of the 1967 Detroit riots. The Bentley Library also contains papers relating to John Harvey Kellogg and his work at Battle Creek, and records of the Gordy family, with special reference to Berry Gordy, founder of Tamla Motown.

### Burton Historical Collection

This is a rich and well-catalogued collection of documents, photographs, and newspaper clippings on the history of Detroit. It can be consulted during library hours at the Detroit Public Library, 5201 Woodward Avenue, Detroit, Michigan 48202.

### Detroit Institute of Arts, Museum Archives

These archives contain documents relating to the history of the museum, including material with special relevance to Edsel Ford and to the commissioning of the Rivera murals (classified under the heading of the William R. Valentiner Records). Access is by application to the Archivist, Detroit Institute of Arts, 5200 Woodward Avenue, Detroit, Michigan 48202.

### Henry Ford Hospital Archives

This is a collection of printed and documentary material relating to the foundation and history of the Henry Ford Hospital, gathered by Dr. Conrad Lam and located at the hospital on West Grand

Boulevard, Detroit, as part of the library department. Access is by application to the Librarian.

## National Automotive History Collection

This is a collection of printed material and documents located, like the Burton Historical Collection, in the main branch of the Detroit Public Library on Woodward Avenue. Of particular interest are the papers of Charles B. King, documents relating to the Ford Tax Case, the papers of Henry and Wilfred Leland, and the papers of Charles E. Sorensen.

## Presidential Libraries

The Franklin D. Roosevelt Library at Hyde Park, New York, contains valuable material relating to Roosevelt's relations with both Henry Ford and Edsel Ford.

The Lyndon Baines Johnson Library at Austin, Texas, contains material relating to Henry Ford II.

## Walter P. Reuther Library

This collection of labour documents is gathered on the campus of Wayne State University, Detroit, Michigan 48202, and is officially titled the Archives of Labor History and Urban Affairs. It contains the personal papers of many union activists, including those of Walter P. Reuther and his brother Victor. It also contains documents relating to the history of the United Auto Workers and other unions, together with a section of oral histories on the unionization of the car industry and on the history of blacks and the labour movement. For full details consult Warner W. Pflug, *A Guide to the Archives of Labor History and Urban Affairs* (Detroit: Wayne State University Press, 1974).

Photographs appearing in this book from the Walter P. Reuther Library are credited to the Archives of Labor and Urban Affairs, Wayne State University.

## Other Libraries Consulted

In London: the British Library, W.C.1; the Hans Tasiemka Archives, N.W.11; the London Library, S.W.1; the U.S. Embassy Library, W.1.

In the United States: the Detroit Public Library; the Grosse Pointe Public Library; the Mount Clemens Public Library; the New York Public Library.

## Freedom of Information Act

Several collections of documents were secured by applications under the Freedom of Information Act. The following are the serial numbers of documents supplied by the Federal Bureau of Investigation, Washington, D.C., relating to Harry Bennett, the Ford Motor Company, Henry Ford I, Edsel Bryant Ford, and John Bugas:

| | | |
|---|---|---|
| 62–99197–15 | 62–6540 | 94–1–29436–6X2 |
| 92–6063 | 62–66816–49 | 61–10497–43 |
| 62–26664–9 | 62–53409–133 | 44–2925–956 |
| 62–53567–8X | 44–2925–840 | 26–176857–32 |
| 62–75147–15 | 87–2068–226 | 94–1–5576–144 |
| 44–2925–468 | 62–4381–90 | 62–28131–16 |
| 71–1788–76 | 67–50997–349 | 99–313–1 |
| 62–7514715–4 | 62–98006–2 | 61–7559–5127 |
| 163–143–1 | 116–421930–302 | 62–43818–79 |
| 62–302–15–8 | 62–31777–1 | |

The following document was supplied by the National Highway Traffic Safety Administration, Office of Defects Investigations, Vehicle Safety Defect Recall Campaigns:

De Tomaso of America, Inc. Service bulletin report. Thirty pages of printout, reference numbers 02170000 to 92000000.

## Unpublished documents

Bennett, Harry. *We Never Called Him Henry*. Draft manuscript in the possession of David C. Smith, Detroit.

Dow, Alex. "About Certain Celebrities," *Autobiographical Notes*, in the possession of his son, Douglas, dated September 24, 1940.

Ford, William Clay, Jr., *The Detroit Lions: Gaining a Competitive Edge*, a paper prepared in the Alfred P. Sloan School of Management, M.I.T., June 1984.

Hayden, Jay. *James Couzens*, an uncompleted biography in the possession of Hayden's son Martin.

Holley, George. *Forty Years in Transportation*, memoirs in the possession of his nephew Danforth Holley.

Mecke, Theodore H., Jr. Paper on Charles Lang Freer, Gari Melchers, and one other, delivered to the Witenagemote Club, Detroit, October 24, 1984.

Smith, Dr. Richard W. "Opening Address" to the Frank Sladen Memorial Society, an unpublished paper in the possession of Frank Sladen, Jr., Detroit, 1982.

## Video recordings and transcripts

"Age of Steel," 1978. Film produced for the exhibition "The Rouge: The Image of Industry in the Art of Charles Sheeler and Diego Rivera" at the Detroit Institute of Arts, funded by the Ford Motor Company. (Film is now owned by the Walter P. Reuther Archives.)

"American Road." A film history of the Ford Motor Company and its founder, narrated by Raymond Massey. Ford World Headquarters, Dearborn.

"The Ballad of Henry Ford II." Written and produced by Dick Gilling, for the BBC, London.

Ford family home movies, shot at Fair Lane and elsewhere. Assembled and edited by Michael Skinner.

Edsel Ford II. Interviewed by J. P. McCarthy. WJBK–TV, Detroit, May 3, 1983.

"Henry Ford's America." A BBC film by Donald Brittain. Recorded from CBET–TV, Windsor, Ontario, Canada, November 28, 1976.

Henry Ford II. Interviews with Barbara Walters. ABC–TV, April 30, 1980, and May 2, 1980.

Henry Ford II. Interview with Dennis Wholly, *Late Night America*. PBS–TV, November 1, 1983.

Henry Ford II. Interview with Max Fisher. Undated video recording. Ford World Headquarters.

Henry Ford II. *Meet the Press*. April 29, 1973.

Henry Ford II. Interview with Lou Gordon. WKBD–TV, May 26, 1974.

Henry Ford II. Resignation as Chief Executive Officer. Various news reports, local and network, October 1, 1979.

Henry Ford II. Resignation as Chairman of the Board of Directors. Various news reports, local and network, March 13, 1980.

Ford Motor Company Stockholders' Meeting. Untitled video recording, Ford World Headquarters, Dearborn, May 1978.

Ford Motor Company Stockholders' Meeting. Untitled video recording, Ford World Headquarters, Dearborn, May 1979.

*Modern Times*. Charlie Chaplin and Paulette Goddard, R.B.C. Films, Playhouse Video.

"People and Technology." Ford World Headquarters, Dearborn.

"The People Factor." Employee-involvement training film. Ford World Headquarters, Dearborn.

"Probe IV and Concept 100." Ford World Headquarters, Dearborn.

"The Road to Happiness." Written and produced by Francis Gladstone and Patrick Griffin. *Nova*. PBS–TV.

"Rouge Steel." A film history of the company. Ford World Headquarters, Dearborn.

"Taking Care of Miss Liberty." *20/20*. ABC–TV, December 12, 1985.

"A World Car Is Born." A film history of the development of the Ford Escort. Ford World Headquarters, Dearborn.

"The World of Ford." A film history of the Ford Motor Company on its 75th anniversary. Ford World Headquarters, Dearborn.

## Articles

Auletta, Ken. "Don't Mess with Roy Cohn." *Esquire*, Vol. 90, No. 12, December 5, 1978.

Breuer, Elizabeth. "Henry Ford and the Believer." *Ladies' Home Journal*, September 1923.

Brunk, Thomas W. "A Note on Charles Lang Freer." *Bulletin of the Detroit Institute of Arts*, Vol. 59, No. 1 (1981), p. 17.

———. "The House That Freer Built." *Dichotomy: A Semi-annual Review of Art and Architecture* (University of Detroit School of Architecture), Vol. 3, No. 4 (Spring 1981), p. 5.

Bryan, Ford R. "Henry Ford's Experiment at Richmond Hill." *Dearborn Historian*, Vol. 24, No. 4 (Autumn 1984).

———. "Henry Ford & Son, Tractors." Unpublished.

———. "Patrick Ahern, Henry Ford and Fair Lane." *Dearborn Historian*, Vol. 22, No. 1 (Winter 1982).

———. "A Prized Friendship: Henry Ford and George Washington Carver." *Greenfield Village Herald*, Vol. 12, No. 2 (1983).

———. "Revival of Old-Fashioned Harvesting." Unpublished.

———. "William Ford South." Unpublished.

Cheyfitz, Kirk, and Wright, J. Patrick. "The Rise and Fall and Rise of Lee Iacocca." *Monthly Detroit*, February 1979.

Cortz, Dan. "A New Generation of Whiz Kids." *Fortune*, January 1967.

Cummings, Frederick J. "Preface." *Bulletin of the Detroit Institute of Arts*, Founders' Society, Detroit Institute of Arts, Detroit, Michigan, Vol. 57, No. 1, on bequest of Mrs. Edsel Ford (1979).

*Cycle and Automobile Trade Journal*, X, January 1, 1906.

Dearborn Press. "A Tribute to Henry Ford on His Eightieth Birthday." *Dearborn Press*, Dearborn, Michigan (1943).

Doolen, Richard M. "The National Greenback Party in Michigan Politics, 1876–88." *Michigan History*, Vol. 47, No. 2 (June 1963).

Dowie, Mark. "Pinto Madness." *Mother Jones*, September/October 1977.

Downs, Linda. "The 'Detroit Industry' Frescoes by Diego Rivera." *Detroit Institute of Arts Gallery Sheet*, undated.

———. "Diego Rivera's Portrait of Edsel Ford." *Bulletin of the Detroit Institute of Arts*, Vol. 57, No. 1 (1979).

Ford, Henry, as told to William L. Stidger. "Looking Under the Human Hood." *The Rotarian*, January 1947.

*Fortune* staff writers. "Mr. Ford Doesn't Care." *Fortune*, Vol. VIII, December 1933.

Gates, Dick. "Behind That Edsel Ford Gatehouse." *Sunday News Magazine* (September 4, 1977).

Glick, David T. "A Favorite Subject: Henry Ford as Viewed by Cartoonists." *Greenfield Village Herald*, Vol. 12, No. 2 (1984).

Gnau, Tara. "From Flats to Field." *Dearborn Historian*, Vol. 25, No. 3.

Hurt, Douglas R. "The Ohio Grange, 1870–1900." *Northwest Ohio Quarterly*, Vol. LIII, No. 1 (Winter 1981).

Kahn, E. J., Jr. "The Staffs of Life V—The Future of the Planet." *New Yorker*, March 11, 1985.

Lam, Conrad R. "He Got Up and Lived: The Story of an Unusual Hernia Operation on an Unusual Man." *Surgical Rounds*, September 1982.

Lewis, David L., editor. "The Automobile in American Culture." *Michigan Quarterly Review*, Vol. 19, No. 4 (Fall 1980), and Vol. 20, No. 1 (Winter 1981), Ann Arbor, University of Michigan Press.

Lewis, David L. "Edsel Ford's Farm Environmental Center." *Cars and Parts*, February 1975.

———. "The Flivver of Hostelries: Ford's Wayside Inn." *Cars and Parts*, April 1974.

———. "A Super Existence: The Boyhood of Henry Ford II." *Michigan Quarterly Review*, Vol. 25, No. 2 (Spring 1986).

McCann, Hugh, and Smith, Dave. "Mustang." *Detroit Free Press* (October 11, 1970).

MacDonald, Dwight. "Foundation." *New Yorker* XXXI, November 26, 1955. Also December 3, 10, and 17, 1955, and February 11, 1956.

Madison, Charles. "My Seven Years of Automotive Servitude." *Michigan Quarterly Review*, Vol. XIX, No. 4, and Vol. XX, No. 1 (double issue, Fall 1980/Winter 1981).

Montgomery, James. "Henry Ford & Son, Partners. Edsel's Influence Grows, but the Father Is Still Ruler of Their Vast Business." *Personality Magazine*, December 1927.

Reed, John. "Industry's Miracle Maker." *Metropolitan Magazine*, October 1916.

Rich, Carroll Y. "Clyde Barrow's Last Ford." *Journal of Popular Culture*, Vol. VI, No. 4 (Spring 1973).

Rockaway, Robert A. "The Rise of the Jewish Gangster in America." *Journal of Ethnic Studies*, Vol. 8, No. 2.

Ruddiman, Margaret Ford. "Memories of My Brother, Henry Ford." *Michigan History*, Vol. 37, No. 3 (September 1953).

Smith, David C. "Under the Influence: U.S. Styling Takes on Foreign Flavor." *Ward's Auto World*, Vol. 8, No. 4, April 1972.

"U.S. New-Car Registrations by Make Since World War II." *Automotive News*, 1985 Market Data Book Issue (source: R. L. Polk and Co.).

Van Tine, W. H., Architect. "The Henry Ford Estate, Dearborn, Mich." *Architecture*, March 1915.

Walter, Connecticut, and Peter, Viviane. "The 'Whiz Kids' and How They Grew." *Parade*, November 15, 1970.

Welliver, Judson C. "Henry Ford, Dreamer and Worker." *The American Review of Reviews*, November 3, 1921.

Whelan, Edward P. "The Real Kathy Ford." *Monthly Detroit*, July 1981.

## Books, catalogues, and pamphlets

The following books, catalogues, and pamphlets have been consulted. The chapter reference notes make clear where particular reliance has been placed upon certain sources. I am grateful to those publishers and authors who have granted permission to quote brief extracts.

## BIBLIOGRAPHY

Abodaher, David. *Iacocca: America's Most Dynamic Businessman*. New York: Zebra, 1985.

Allsop, Kenneth. *The Bootleggers*. London: Hutchinson, 1961.

American Heritage Magazine, compiler. *A Sense of History: The Best Writing from American Heritage*. New York: American Heritage, 1985.

Amory, Cleveland. *Who Killed Society?* New York: Harper & Brothers, 1960.

Anderson, Jay. *Time Machines: The World of Living History*. Nashville: American Association for State and Local History, 1984.

Anderson, Rudolph E. *The Story of the American Automobile: Highlights and Sidelights*. Washington, D.C.: Public Affairs Press, 1950.

Arnold, Horace Lucien, and Faurote, Fay Leone. *Ford Methods and the Ford Shops*. New York: The Engineering Magazine Co., 1915.

Babson, Steve; Alpern, Ron; Elsila, Dave; and Revitte, John. *Working Detroit: The Making of a Union Town*. New York: Adama Books, 1984.

Barfknecht, Gary W. *Michillaneous*. Davison, Mich.: Frieda Publications, 1982.

Barnard, Harry. *Independent Man: The Life of Senator James Couzens*. New York: Charles Scribner's Sons, 1958.

Barnard, John. *Walter Reuther and the Rise of the Auto Worker*. Boston: Little, Brown, 1983.

Barrus, Clara. *The Life and Letters of John Burroughs*. 2 volumes. Boston: Houghton Mifflin, 1925.

Beasley, Norman. *Knudsen: A Biography*. Introduction by William S. Knudsen. New York: Whittlesey House, 1947.

Bedford, Sybille. *Aldous Huxley: A Biography*. Volume 1, 1894–1939. London: Chatto & Windus; Collins, 1973.

Belasco, Warren James. *Americans on the Road: From Autocamp to Motel, 1910–1945*. Cambridge: M.I.T. Press, 1979.

Belloc, Hilaire. *Selected Cautionary Verses*. Harmondsworth, Middlesex: Puffin Books, 1983.

Bennett, Harry, as told to Marcus, Paul. *We Never Called Him Henry*. New York: Fawcett, 1951.

Benson, Allan L. *The New Henry Ford*. New York: Funk & Wagnalls, 1923.

Berger, Michael. *The Devil Wagon in God's Country: The Automobile and Social Change in Rural America, 1892–1929*. Hamden, Conn.: Archon Books, 1979.

Betjeman, John. *The Best of Betjeman*. Edited by John Guest. London: John Murray, 1978.

Beynon, Huw. *Working for Ford*. Second edition. Harmondsworth, Middlesex: Pelican Books, 1984.

Bingay, Malcolm W. *Detroit Is My Own Home Town*. Indianapolis: Bobbs-Merrill, 1946.

Birmingham, Stephen. *Real Lace: America's Irish Rich*. London: Hamish Hamilton, 1973.

———. *The Right People*. Boston: Little, Brown, 1958.

Blunsden, John. *The Power to Win*. London: Motor Racing Pub., 1983.

Bonosky, Phillip. *Brother Bill McKie: Building the Union at Ford*. New York: International Publishers, 1953.

Bowdidge, Elizabeth. *The Soya Bean: Its History, Cultivation (in England) and Uses*. London: Oxford University Press, 1935.

Bray, Mayfield. *Guide to the Ford Film Collection in the National Archives*. Publication No. 70–6. Washington, D.C.: National Archives, 1970.

Brough James. *The Ford Dynasty*. London: W. H. Allen, 1978.

Brown, Henry D.; Négrié, Henri; Place, Frank R.; Toujas, René; Simons,Leonard N.; Weeks, Solan; and others. *Cadillac and the Founding of Detroit*. Detroit: Wayne State University Press, 1979.

Burgess-Wise, David. *Ghia, Ford's Carrozzeria*. London: Osprey Publishing, 1985.

Burroughs, John. *John Burroughs Talks*. Boston: Houghton Mifflin, 1922.

———. *Our Vacation Days of 1918*. Photo album and text. Private publication, circa 1920.

Bushnell, Sarah T. *The Truth About Henry Ford*. Chicago: Reilly & Lee, 1922.

Cameron, William J. *You and the Ten Commandments*. Indianapolis: Bobbs-Merrill, 1941.

Carson, Gerald. *Cornflake Crusade*. London: Victor Gollancz, 1959.

Céline (Destouches, Louis Ferdinand). *Death on the Installment Plan*.New York: Duenewald Printing Corp., 1938.

———. *Journey to the End of Night*. Boston: Little, Brown, 1934.

Chandler, Alfred D. *Strategy and Structure: Chapters in the History of the Industrial Enterprise*. Cambridge: M.I.T. Press, 1962.

Clancy, Louise B., and Davies, Florence. *The Believer: The Life Story of Mrs. Henry Ford*. New York: Coward-McCann, 1960.

Cohn, Norman. *Warrant for Genocide*. London: Eyre & Spottiswoode, 1967.

Conot, Robert. *American Odyssey: A Unique History of America Told Through the Life of a Great City*. New York: William Morrow, 1974.

Considine, Bob. *The Fabulous Henry Ford II*. A series of articles reprinted from the Hearst Newspapers. New York: The Hearst Corp., 1964.

Cuningham, W. M. *"J8": A Chronicle of the Neglected Truth about Henry Ford and the Ford Motor Company*. Private publication, undated.

Curtis, Creswell. *Survival of the Slickest*. London: Jonathan Cape, 1939.

Dahlinger, John Côté, and Leighton, Frances Spatz. *The Secret Life of Henry Ford*. Indianapolis: Bobbs-Merrill, 1978.

Davidson, Eugene. *The Trial of the Germans*. New York: Macmillan, 1966.

Detroit Institute of Arts. *Selected Works, 1979*. Detroit: Detroit Institute of Arts, 1979.

————. *Treasures*. Detroit: Detroit Institute of Arts, 1960.

Detroit Public Library. *Detroit in Its World Setting: A 250-Year Chronology, 1701–1951*. Detroit: Detroit Public Library, 1953.

Deutsch, Ronald M. *The Nuts Among the Berries: An Exposé of America's Food Fads*. Foreword by Frederick J. Stare, M.D. New York: Ballantine Books, 1967.

Dickens, Charles. *American Notes*. London: Oxford University Press, 1957.

Dominguez, Henry L. *The Ford Agency: A Pictorial History*. Osceola, Wis.: Motorbooks International Publishers & Wholesalers, 1981.

Dos Passos, John. *The Big Money*. New York: Harcourt Brace, 1933.

Downs, Linda, and Jacob, Mary Jane. *The Rouge: The Image of Industry in the Art of Charles Sheeler and Diego Rivera*. Foreword by Frederick J. Cummings. Detroit: Detroit Institute of Arts, 1978.

Dreiser, Theodore. *Tragic America*. London: Constable, 1932.

Dreyfus, René, with Kines, Ray. *My Two Lives: Race Driver to Restaurateur*. Foreword by Walter Cronkite. Tucson, Ariz.: Aztex, 1983.

Drucker, Peter F. *The Future of Industrial Man*. London: Heinemann, 1943.

DuBois, Josiah E. *Generals in Grey Suits*. London: Bodley Head, 1933.

Emerson, Ralph Waldo. *The Best of Ralph Waldo Emerson: Essays, Poems, Addresses*. New York: Walter J. Black, 1941.

———. *Essays*. "The World's Classics." New York: Oxford University Press, 1936.

Fallon, Ivan, and Srodes, James. *De Lorean*. London: Hodder and Stoughton, 1984. (Published in the U.S. as *Dream Maker: The Rise and Fall of John Z. De Lorean*. New York: Putnam, 1983.)

Ferry, W. Hawkins. *The Buildings of Detroit: A History*. Revised edition. Detroit: Wayne State University Press, 1980.

———. *The Legacy of Albert Kahn*. Detroit: Detroit Institute of Arts, 1970.

Fine, Sidney. *The Automobile Under the Blue Eagle*. Ann Arbor: University of Michigan Press, 1963.

Ford, Anne and Charlotte. *How to Love the Car in Your Life*. Chicago: Mobium Press, 1980.

Ford, Charlotte. *Charlotte Ford's Book of Modern Manners*. New York: Simon & Schuster, 1980.

Ford, Henry. *Ford Ideals: Being a Selection from "Mr. Ford's Page" in the Dearborn Independent*. Dearborn, Mich.: Dearborn Publishing Co., 1926.

———. *My Philosophy of Industry*. New York: Coward-McCann, 1929.

———. *Things I've Been Thinking About*. New York: Fleming H. Revell, 1936.

Ford, Henry, with Crowther, Samuel. *My Life and Work*. Garden City, N.Y.: Doubleday, 1923.

———. *Today and Tomorrow (Being a Continuation of "My Life and Work")*. Garden City, N.Y.: Garden City Pub. Co., 1926.

Ford, Henry & Son Ltd. *Ford in Ireland: The First 60 Years: 1917–1977*. Cork, Ireland: Henry Ford & Son Ltd., 1977.

Ford Motor Company Pamphlets:
*Profit-Sharing of the Ford Motor Company.*
*Helpful Hints and Advice to Employees—To Help Them Grasp The Opportunities Which Are Presented To Them By The Ford Profit-sharing Plan.* 1915.
*Salvage of Men.* J. E. Mead. 1919.

Ford Trade School. *Shop Theory*. Dearborn, Mich.: Henry Ford Trade School, 1941.

Fountain, Clayton W. *Union Guy*. New York: Viking, 1949.

# BIBLIOGRAPHY

Galbraith, J. K. *The Liberal Hour*. London: Hamish Hamilton, 1960.

Garrett, Garet. *The Wild Wheel: The World of Henry Ford*. London: Cresset Press, 1952.

Gelderman, Carol. *Henry Ford: The Wayward Capitalist*. New York: Dial Press, 1981.

Glad, Paul W. *Trumpet Soundeth: William Jennings Bryan and his Democracy, 1896–1912*. Lincoln, Neb.: University of Nebraska Press, 1960.

Graves, Ralph H. *The Triumph of an Idea: The Story of Henry Ford*. Garden City, N.Y.: Doubleday, Doran, 1935.

Greenleaf, William. *From These Beginnings: The Early Philanthropies of Henry and Edsel Ford, 1911–1936*. Detroit: Wayne State University Press, 1964.

———. *Monopoly on Wheels: Henry Ford and the Selden Automobile Patent*. Detroit: Wayne State University Press, 1967.

Guardian Group. *The Straits of High Adventure. "Le Detroit des Grandes Adventures."* Detroit: The Guardian Group, 1928.

Hailey, Arthur. *Wheels*. London: Pan Books, 1983.

Halberstam, David. *The Best and the Brightest*. New York: Random House, 1972.

Hale, William J. *Farmward March: Chemurgy Takes Command*. New York: Coward-McCann, 1939.

———. *The Farm Chemurgic*. Boston: The Stratford Company, 1934.

Hall, Theodore Parsons. *Grosse Pointe on Lake Sainte Claire*. Reprint of 1886 edition published by Silas Farmer & Co. Detroit: Gale Research Company, 1974.

Hapgood, Norman. *The Inside Story of Henry Ford's Jew Mania*. New York: Hearst International, 1922.

Hatcher, Harlan. *The Great Lakes*. New York: Oxford University Press, 1944.

Hatcher, Harlan, and Walter, Erich A. *A Pictorial History of the Great Lakes*. New York: Bonanza/Crown, 1963.

Hemingway, Ernest. *A Moveable Feast*. New York: Bantam, 1965.

Herman, Victor. *Coming Out of the Ice: An Unexpected Life*. Oklahoma City: Freedom Press Ltd., 1979.

Herndon, Booton. *Ford: An Unconventional Biography of the Men and Their Times*. New York: Weybright and Talley, 1969.

Herrera, Hayden. *Frida: A Biography of Frida Kahlo*. New York: Harper & Row, 1983.

Hickerson, J. Mel. *Ernie Breech: The Story of His Remarkable Career at General Motors, Ford, and TWA.* Foreword by Henry Ford II. New York: Meredith Press, 1968.

Hicks, John D. *The Populist Revolt: A History of the Farmers' Alliance and the People's Party.* Lincoln, Neb.: University of Nebraska Press, 1961.

Higham, Charles. *Trading with the Enemy: An Exposé of the Nazi-American Money Plot.* New York: Delacorte, 1983.

Higham, John. *Strangers in the Land: Patterns of American Nativism.* New Brunswick, N. J.: Rutgers University Press, 1955.

Hobbs, Susan. *The Whistler Peacock Room.* Washington, D.C.: Freer Gallery of Art, Smithsonian Institution, 1980.

Hofstadter, Richard. *The Age of Reform.* London: Jonathan Cape, 1962.

Hollander, S. C., and Marple, G. A. *Henry Ford: Inventor of the Supermarket?* East Lansing, Mich.: Department of Marketing and Transportation Administration, Michigan State University, 1960.

Hounshell, David A. *From the American System to Mass Production, 1800–1932.* Baltimore: Johns Hopkins University Press, 1984.

Hughes, Jonathan. *The Vital Few.* Boston: Houghton Mifflin, 1966.

Huxley, Aldous. *Brave New World.* London: Chatto & Windus, 1932.

———. *Brave New World Revisited.* London: Chatto & Windus, 1959.

Huxley, Julian. *Memories.* London: Allen & Unwin, 1970.

Hyde, Charles K. *Detroit: An Industrial History Guide.* Detroit: Detroit Historical Society, 1980.

Iacocca, Lee, with Novak, William. *Iacocca: An Autobiography.* New York: Bantam Books, 1984.

International Society for Krishna Consciousness. *Chant and Be Happy: The Power of Mantra Meditation.* Los Angeles: The Bhaktivedanta Book Trust, 1983.

———. *Coming Back: The Science of Reincarnation.* Los Angeles: The Bhaktivedanta Book Trust, 1984.

Jackson, Stanley. *J. P. Morgan: The Rise and Fall of a Banker.* London: Heinemann, 1984.

Jacobs, Jane. *The Death and Life of Great American Cities.* London: Jonathan Cape, 1962.

Jardim, Anne. *The First Henry Ford: A Study in Personality and Business Leadership.* Cambridge: M.I.T. Press, 1970.

Jones, Howard Mumford. *Ideas in America.* Cambridge: Harvard University Press, 1944.

————. *O Strange New World: American Culture, the Formative Years*. London: Chatto & Windus, 1965.

Kasson, John F. *Civilizing the Machine: Technology and Republican Values in America, 1776–1900*. New York: Penguin, 1977.

Keats, John. *The Insolent Chariots*. Philadelphia: J. B. Lippincott, 1958.

Kelly, Brian, and London, Mark. *Amazon*. London: Robert Hale, 1984.

Kimes, Beverly Rae. *The Cars That Henry Ford Built*. Princeton: Princeton Publishing, 1978.

Kirkland, Edward C. *Industry Comes of Age: Business, Labor, and Public Policy, 1860–1897*. New York: Holt, Rinehart & Winston, 1961.

Kraft, Barbara S. *The Peace Ship: Henry Ford's Pacifist Adventure in the First World War*. New York: Macmillan, 1978.

Krutch, J. *Our Modern Temper*. New York: Harcourt Brace, 1929.

Lane, Rose Wilder. *Henry Ford's Own Story*. Forest Hills, N.Y.: Ellis O. Jones, 1917.

Lasky, Victor. *Never Complain, Never Explain: The Story of Henry Ford II*. New York: Richard Marek, 1981.

Lee, Albert. *Henry Ford and the Jews*. New York: Stein and Day, 1980.

Lee, Alfred M., and Humphrey, Norman D. *Race Riot Detroit, 1943*. New York: Octagon, 1967.

Lens, Sidney. *Strikemakers and Strikebreakers*. New York: Lodestar/ E. P. Dutton, 1985.

Leonard, Elmore. *City Primeval: High Noon in Detroit*. New York: Avon, 1982.

Leonard, Jonathan Norton. *The Tragedy of Henry Ford*. New York: G. P. Putnam's Sons, 1932.

Lewis, David L. *The Public Image of Henry Ford: An American Folk Hero and His Company*. Detroit: Wayne State University Press, 1976.

Lindbergh, Anne Morrow. *War Within and Without: Diaries and Letters, 1939–1944*. New York: Harcourt Brace Jovanovich, 1980.

Lochbiler, Don. *Detroit's Coming of Age, 1873 to 1973*. Detroit: Wayne State University Press, 1982.

Lochner, Louis P. *Henry Ford: America's Don Quixote*. New York: International, 1925.

Ludecke, Kurt G. W. *I Knew Hitler: The Story of a Nazi Who Escaped the Blood Purge*. London: Jarrolds, 1938.

McAleer, John. *Ralph Waldo Emerson: Days of Encounter*. Boston: Little, Brown, 1984.

McCarthy, Joe. *Ford at Fifty, 1903–1953*. New York: Simon & Schuster, 1953.

MacDonald, Donald. *Detroit 1985*. Foreword by the Hon. George Romney. Garden City, N.Y.: Doubleday, 1980.

McGuffey, William H. *McGuffey's First Eclectic Reader*. New York: American Book Co., 1920.

———. *McGuffey's Third Eclectic Reader*. New York: American Book Co., 1920.

McNairn, William and Marjorie, compilers. *Quotations from the Unusual Henry Ford*. Redondo Beach, Calif.: Quotamus Press, 1978.

Magee, Dorothy M., editor. *Centennial History of Mount Clemens, Michigan, 1878–1979*. Mount Clemens, Mich.: Mount Clemens Public Library, 1980.

Marquis, Samuel S. *Henry Ford: An Interpretation*. Boston: Little, Brown, 1923.

May, George, and Banks, Herbert, editors. *A Michigan Reader: 11,000 B.C. to A.D. 1865*. Grand Rapids, Mich.: William B. Ferdmans, 1974.

Meier, August, and Rudwick, Elliott. *Black Detroit and the Rise of the UAW*. New York: Oxford University Press, 1979.

Meyer, Stephen III. *The Five Dollar Day: Labor Management and Social Control in the Ford Motor Company, 1908–1921*. Albany, N.Y.: State University of New York Press, 1981.

Motor Vehicle Manufacturers Association of the United States. *Automobiles of America*. Detroit: Wayne State University Press, 1974.

Nader, Ralph. *Unsafe at Any Speed: The Designed-in Dangers of the American Automobile*. New York: Grossman, 1965.

National Farm Chemurgic Council. *Proceedings: First Dearborn Conference*. New York: The Chemical Foundation Inc., 1935.

———. *Proceedings: Second Dearborn Conference*. New York: The Chemical Foundation Inc., 1936.

Nevins, Allan. *The Emergence of Modern America: 1865–1878*. New York: Macmillan, 1927.

Nevins, Allan, and Hill, Frank Ernest. *Ford: The Times, the Man, the Company*. Volume 1. New York: Charles Scribner's Sons, 1954.

———. *Ford: Expansion and Challenge, 1915–1933*. Volume 2. New York: Charles Scribner's Sons, 1957.

————. *Ford: Decline and Rebirth, 1933–1962.* Volume 3. New York: Charles Scribner's Sons, 1963.

Nye, David E. *Henry Ford, "Ignorant Idealist."* Port Washington, N.Y.: Kennikat Press, 1979.

Nye, Russell B. *Midwestern Progressive Politics.* Lansing, Mich.: Michigan State University Press, 1959.

Olson, Sidney. *Young Henry Ford: A Picture History of the First Forty Years.* Detroit: Wayne State University Press, 1963.

Parkman, Francis. *The Jesuits in North America in the Seventeenth Century.* 2 volumes. Boston: Little, Brown, 1905.

Pettifer, Julian, and Turner, Nigel. *Automania.* London: William Collins Sons, 1984.

Pflug, Warner W. *A Guide to the Archives of Labor History and Urban Affairs.* Detroit: Wayne State University Press, 1974.

————. *The UAW in Pictures.* Detroit: Wayne State University Press, 1971.

Pitkin, Thomas M., and Cordasco, Francesco. *The Black Hand: A Chapter in Ethnic Crime.* Jotowa, N. J.: Littlefield, Adams, no date.

Pitrone, Jean Maddern, and Elwart, Joan Potter. *The Dodges: The Auto Family Fortune and Misfortune.* South Bend, Ind.: Icarus Press, 1981.

Pool, James and Suzanne. *Who Financed Hitler?* New York: Dial Press, 1978.

Rae, John B. *American Automobile Manufacturers: The First Forty Years.* Philadelphia: Chilton, 1959.

————. *The Road and the Car in American Life.* Cambridge: M.I.T. Press, 1971.

Reuther, Victor G. *The Brothers Reuther and the Story of the UAW.* Boston: Houghton Mifflin, 1976.

Richards, William C. *The Last Billionaire: Henry Ford.* New York: Charles Scribner's Sons, 1948.

Robbins, Harold. *The Betsy.* London: New English Library/Times Mirror, 1981.

Rose, Kenneth. *King George V.* London: Weidenfeld and Nicolson, 1983.

Ross, Irwin. *The Image Merchants: The Fabulous World of Public Relations.* Garden City, N.Y.: Doubleday, 1959.

Schlesinger, Arthur M. *The Rise of the City.* New York: Macmillan, 1933.

Sedgwick, Michael. *Cars of the Thirties and Forties.* Gothenburg, Sweden: Nordbok, 1979.

Seidler, Edouard. *Let's Call It Fiesta: The Auto-biography of Ford's Project Bobcat.* Switzerland: Edita, 1976.

Serrin, William. *The Company and the Union.* New York: Knopf, 1973.

Shapiro, Max S., and Hendricks, Rhoda A. *A Dictionary of Mythologies.* London: Granada (A Paladin Book).

Shelby, Carroll, with Bentley, John. *The Cobra Story.* New York: Trident Press, 1965.

Simonds, William A. *Henry Ford: His Life, His Work, His Genius.* Indianapolis: Bobbs-Merrill, 1943.

Sinclair, Andrew. *Prohibition, The Era of Excess.* London: Faber & Faber, 1962.

Sinclair, Upton. *The Flivver King: A Story of Ford-America.* Pasadena, Calif.: Published by Author, Station A, 1937.

Sladen, Frank J., and staff of the Henry Ford Hospital, Detroit. *Collected Papers, 1915–1925.* New York: Paul B. Hoeber, 1926.

Sloan, Alfred P. *My Years with General Motors.* Edited by John McDonald with Catharine Stevens. Garden City, N.Y.: Doubleday, 1964.

Smith, Page. *America Enters the World: A People's History of the Progressive Era and World War I.* Volume 7. New York: McGraw-Hill, 1985.

―――. *The Rise of Industrial America: A People's History of the Post-Reconstruction Era.* Volume 6. New York: McGraw-Hill, 1984.

Smithsonian Institution. *The Freer Gallery of Art.* Washington, D.C.: Smithsonian Institution, undated.

Sorensen, Charles E., with Williamson, Samuel T. *My Forty Years with Ford.* New York: W. W. Norton, 1956.

Sorensen, Lorin. *The Ford Road: 75th Anniversary: Ford Motor Co., 1903–1978.* St. Helena, Calif.: Silverado, 1978.

Stein, Gertrude. *Wars I Have Seen.* New York: Random House, 1945.

Steinbeck, John. *Cannery Row.* London: Heinemann, 1945.

―――. *The Grapes of Wrath.* London: Heinemann, 1939.

Stern, Philip Van Doren. *Tin Lizzie: The Story of the Fabulous Model T Ford.* New York: Simon & Schuster, 1955.

Sterne, Margaret. *The Passionate Eye: The Life of William R. Valentiner.* Detroit: Wayne State University Press, 1980.

Stevenson, Robert Louis. *Across the Plains.* London: Chatto and Windus, 1892.

Stidger, William L. *Henry Ford: The Man and His Motives*. New York: George H. Doran Co., 1923.

Susman, Warren I. *Culture as History: The Transformation of American Society in the Twentieth Century*. New York: Pantheon Books, 1985.

Sward, Keith. *The Legend of Henry Ford*. New York: Russell & Russell, 1948.

*Ten Important Paintings from the Collection of Henry Ford II*. New York: Christie, Manson and Woods International, 1980.

Tennyson, Alfred, Lord. *Selected Poems*. London: Macmillan, 1947.

Tingley, Katherine. *Theosophy: The Path of the Mystic*. Pasadena, Calif.:Theosophical University Press, 1977.

Tocqueville, Alexis de. *Democracy in America*. Edited by Richard D. Heffner. New York: New American Library, 1956.

———. *Journey to America*. Garden City, N.Y.: Doubleday, 1971.

Trachtenberg, Alan. *The Incorporation of America*. New York: Hill &Wang, 1982.

Trine, Ralph Waldo. *The Power That Wins: Henry Ford and Ralph Waldo Trine in an Intimate Talk on Life—The Inner Things—The Things of the Mind and Spirit—and the Inner Powers and Forces That Make for Achievement*. Indianapolis: Bobbs-Merrill, 1928.

Twork, Eva O'Neal. *Henry Ford and Benjamin B. Lovett: The Dancing Billionaire and the Dancing Master*. Detroit: Harlo Press, 1982.

Veblen, Thorstein. *The Theory of the Leisure Class*. New York: Macmillan, 1899.

Warner, Robert, and Vanderbilt, C. Warren. *A Michigan Reader: 1865 to the Present*. Grand Rapids, Mich.: William Ferdmans, 1974.

Warnock, C. Gayle. *The Edsel Affair*. Paradise Valley, Ariz.: Pro West, 1980.

Webster, E. Lucille. *An Autobiography of a One-Room School Teacher: Scotch Settlement School of Henry Ford's Greenfield Village*. Dearborn, Mich.: E. Lucille Webster, 1978.

White, E. B. *Letters of E. B. White*. Collected and edited by Dorothy Lobrano Guth. New York: Harper and Row, 1976.

———. *The Second Tree from the Corner: Time Past, Time Future*. New York: Harper & Brothers, 1954.

White, Lawrence J. *The Automobile Industry Since 1945*. Cambridge: Harvard University Press, 1973.

Whiteside, Thomas. *The Investigation of Ralph Nader: General Motors vs. One Determined Man*. New York: Arbor House, 1972.

Wik, Reynold M. *Henry Ford and Grass-roots America*. Ann Arbor, Mich.: University of Michigan Press, 1973.

Wilkins, Mira, and Hill, Frank Ernest. *American Business Abroad: Ford on Six Continents*. Introduction by Allan Nevins. Detroit: Wayne State University Press, 1964.

Wilson, Paul C. *Chrome Dreams: Automobile Styling Since 1893*. Radnor, Penn.: Chilton, 1976.

Witzenburg, Gary L. *Mustang! The Complete History of America's Ponycar*. Princeton, N. J.: Princeton Publishing, 1979.

Wolfe, Bertram D. *Diego Rivera—His Life and Times*. New York: Knopf, 1939.

Woodford, Frank B., and Woodford, Arthur M. *All Our Yesterdays: A Brief History of Detroit*. Detroit: Wayne State University Press, 1969.

Woodham-Smith, Cecil. *The Great Hunger*. London: Hamish Hamilton, 1962.

Wright, J. Patrick. *On A Clear Day You Can See General Motors: John Z. De Lorean's Look Inside the Automotive Giant*. Grosse Pointe, Mich.: Wright Enterprises, 1979.

Zunz, Oliver. *The Changing Face of Inequality*. Chicago: University of Chicago Press, 1982.

# ACKNOWLEDGEMENTS

This book would have been much harder to write without the quite remarkable honesty and bluntness of the Ford family. I am grateful to Henry Ford II for the many doors he opened, and to his wife, Kathy, for her frankness in every respect. The interviews listed in the Bibliography show which members of the family were kind enough to talk to me at length. I am especially grateful for the warmth, friendship, and support extended by Edsel and Cynthia Ford to myself and to my family during the two and a quarter years we have spent away from home.

The Ford Motor Company has an honorable tradition of openness to outside inquiry. No other great industrial corporation has gone to such trouble to preserve its own records and to have them organized for the benefit of historians and researchers, and this yields rich treasure for a writer. Coming to live in the Detroit area has been made especially worthwhile by the vast mass of documentation to be studied in the Ford Archives of the Edison Institute and in the Ford Industrial Archives, whose collections are both described in more detail in the Bibliography. David Crippen at the Ford Archives—which are now independent of the Ford Motor Company—has been particularly generous and knowledgeable in pointing me towards new and interesting material. At the Ford Archives I would also like to thank Steve Hamp, Betty Jordan, and Cynthia Read-Miller. At the Ford Industrial Archives, Darleen Flaherty, the only tarantula-keeping archivist I have ever met, made her warehouse a very hospitable place.

At the Ford Motor Company, Walter Hayes was my initial and closest contact, unstinting with his help and patience, even when it became obvious that my writing was not going in the direction that he might have wished. We part, I hope, more in sorrow than in anger. David Scott and his wife, Ginger, have proved good friends, and inside the company for their many and varied kindnesses, I should like to thank Carol Bonamichi, Gerry Boston, the late Stan Cousineau, Allan Dreyfuss, Les Langlois, J. W. Martin, Jr., Jack Maison, Bernie Miller, Bob Normand, Roy Pask, Jerry Sullivan, Robert Taub, and LaBonnie Townsend.

In May 1985, I spent a few days tasting the life of an assembly-line worker, and I am grateful to Peter Pestillo for making this possible. I should also like to thank Tony Ruggiero and Terry Smith of Ford's Industrial Relations Department, as well as the tolerant and welcoming staff of the Wixom Assembly Plant alongside whom I briefly worked.

Detroit's writing fraternity has been more than gracious to an outsider coming in to poach upon their preserve. It is good to know one is not alone, and I thank, for their professional fellowship, Eleanor Breitmeyer, Kirk Cheyfitz, Keith and Mary Kay Crain, David E. and Jeannie Davis, Hillel Levin, Bill Mitchell, Isabel and David C. Smith, Bob Talbert, Paul Witteman, and J. Patrick Wright. In the very special field of Fordiana, I am particularly grateful for the advice and generosity of Ford R. Bryan and Professor David L. Lewis.

The logistics of transporting two grown-up children, a newborn baby, two cats, and twenty-four suitcases to and fro across the Atlantic involves not a little expertise and resourcefulness, and for help with many practical details we are grateful to Ed Gudeon, visa king, to Transpet Limited of Chingford, Essex, to Mary Wilson of British Airways, and to Jeffrey Slatkin and Richard Maziarz of Royal International Travel. Thanks to Winifred Weyhing for finding our first rented house, and to Bill and Marion Touscany for providing our second one.

Our first friends in Michigan were Larry and Penny Deitch. They head a roll of warm and generous new acquaintances who advanced the progress of the book in many ways, and whose friendship has been the most valuable legacy we will take home with us: Kim and Mary Anderson; Chuck and Judy Bigelow; Dr. Robert Birk; John and Becky Booth; Ralph and Dede Booth; James A. Bridenstine; Joy and Micky Briggs; Mike and Marcie Brogan; Harvey and Jan Burleson.

Billy Chapin; Myra and Marty Citrin; Paul Dorman; Ray and Gilly von Drehle; Charlie and Peggy Davis; Linda Downs; Frank and Ana Maria Donovan; John and Rosemary Dykema; Sir James Easton and Jane, Lady Easton; Joy and Jack Emory.

Hawkins Ferry; Max and Marjorie Fisher; Rodger and Henrietta Fridholm; Pat and Jane Gage; Connie and Dick Goodyear; Glenda

Greenwald; Danforth and Jane Holley; Jean and Joe Hudson; Dr.
Tom Kelly; Kenneth E. King; Mary and Ron Lamparter; Mary
and Jim Lark; John and Gill Lazar; Robin Lepard.

Katie Macauley; Bob and Beatrice McCabe; Dr. Douglas Mac-
Donald; Ted and Eleanor Mecke; Lou Miller; Bob Mounsey; Jim
and Anne Nicholson; Ann Petrovich; Max and Lainie Pincus;
Sophia Rivard; Sam Sachs and Beth Gordon; Harry and Mary
Satchwell; Dr. Kenneth Schoof; Jutta and Charlie Schridde; Fred
and Janet Schroeder; Ray E. Scott, Jr.; Betty and Frank Sladen,
Jr.; the Hon. Peter and Anne Spivak; Peter and Nicole Stroh.

Jack Tarpley; Bruce and Miriam Tassinare; Bobby and Linda
Taubman; Donald E. Worrell, Jr.; Saad and Josephine Zara.

Based away from home, I have not been able to work as closely
as usual with my British publisher, Brian Perman, nor with my
London agent, Michael Shaw, but they have proved as cheering
and supportive as ever.

My research assistant, working in London, has been Victoria
Mather, who has supplied the entire Lacey family with transatlantic amusement and encouragement for more than two years, while
also unearthing and checking all manner of factual information
from cylinder capacities to secrets of the Freedom of Information
Act. I should like to thank her, and she would like to thank for
their help: Miss Dina Abramowitz at the YIVO Institute for Jewish
Research, New York; David Benson, motoring editor of the *Daily
Express*; the British Heart Foundation; Colonel Maurice Buckmas-
ter; the Hon. Isabel Catto; Terence Charman at the Imperial War
Museum, London; Jill Frisch at the *New Yorker*; Joan Gartland at
the Burton Historical Collection, Detroit; Oliver Gillie, medical
correspondent of the *Sunday Times*; Anna Girvan and her colleagues
at the Reference Library, U.S. Embassy, London; Dr. Michael
Harding; Philip Jordan at the *Mail on Sunday*; Colin and Virginia
Keith; Mark Law at the *Times*; Philip Ling; David Metcalfe; the
New York Public Library; Alan Ogden at Charles Barker City
Ltd.; Andrew Pfeiffer; Michael Rif at the Leon Baeck Institute,
New York; Anita Ross; Martin Smith; John Southgate; Edda
Tasiemka at the Hans Tasiemka Archives, London; John Taylor
at the National Archives, Washington; Raymond Teichman and
his staff at the Franklin D. Roosevelt Library, Hyde Park, New
York; James Whittaker of the *Daily Mirror*; the Wiener Library,
London; Jacqueline Williams; and especially David Burgess-Wise,
archivist at Ford of Britain, for his unfailing good humour and

patience with a multitude of arcane queries, and John Raymond for his support and invaluable help.

The excellent selection of pictures was researched by Maureen Monroe. Interviews were faithfully transcribed down to the last "Um" by Connie Bonner. Lois Folsom cheerfully blackened her fingers to check newspaper references. Her son, Dick, compiled and checked the family tree and genealogical appendix. Michael Skinner unsparingly offered his knowledge of Ford home movies and just about everything else Ford. Tom Schlintz at John K. King Books laid hands for me on several dozen invaluable out-of-print books—may it be many years before he lays hands on this one. Eleanor Poteracki raised the art of photocopying to new heights. Douglas Rossdale advised on Alzheimer's Disease and aphrodisiacs. William Brock helped with populism. Scott Bowles investigated the Goodyear car counter. Donna Estry and Sheila Mahoney let me use their microfilm reader. Randy Mason shared his knowledge of the Model T. Gerald Grant found out about Edsel. Charles Wright lent me his beloved E. B. White. Micky Ross showed me around Highland Park. My thanks to all these, and to the other helpers named specifically in the Notes.

This book has been written on an IBM PC-XT personal computer using SSI Wordperfect 4.0, on a desk kindly loaned to the author by Ted Mecke. It would not have got started when it did if my former secretary, Frances Ullman, had not been willing to disrupt her personal life and brave two months of a Michigan winter to push me into the early chapters. My debt is still greater to her successor, Marge Lamkin, who has submitted to endless hours in front of the green screen in order to get the manuscript finished, and who has been an unfailing source of humour, encouragement—and even the odd word or two.

My elder children, Sasha and Scarlett, have become resigned to being dragged around the world in pursuit of my writing projects.

My younger son, Bruno, knows nothing else, having spent most of his life to date in the Motor City, though he would probably be just as fond of cars anyway. Thank you all for your good humour and adaptability, and thank you too to Audrey Newton and to Grace Harkins who helped look after you.

My greatest debt is to my wife, Sandi. Detroit was not the obvious resort after a stint in Saudi Arabia, but she tackled it with love and strength. She made friends for us. She was my best friend. In the last two and a half years there have been challenges to

## ACKNOWLEDGEMENTS

face whose power no one else knows, and the victory has been hers.

I was first moved to write this book by my editor, Bill Phillips, who suggested the idea, edited me as I have never been edited before, and then inspired his colleagues at Little, Brown to advance publication to an impossibly early date. If this book looks good, makes sense, and is being delivered to the shops within six weeks of the final chapter being written, it is to his credit. If its spelling and punctuation are correct, that is thanks to Peggy Freudenthal, and if it avoids lawsuits, that is to the credit of Ike Williams at Palmer and Dodge. My thanks to Ruth C. Cross for the index.

When I first met John Cushman, my friend and agent, in New York in the winter of 1968, he urged me to write a book with a major American theme. It nearly happened at least once, but it was not until the autumn of 1983 that I finally, sensibly, took his advice. It felt very good to be on his side of the Atlantic. The phone bills were cheaper. The warmth and wisdom, somehow, that much more tangible. And then suddenly, within a few months of our arrival, he was dead. It has not really been the same since, and this book is dedicated to him.

# INDEX

*Index compiled by Peva Keane*

Peter Collier
and David Horowitz
**The Kennedys** £3.95

An American Drama

Years in the making, based on hundreds of interviews with family
members and associates, extensive research into archives, and
sources unused until now, this is the nationwide bestseller whose
very publication caused an uproar in the press ... the first and only
book to penetrate fully the Kennedy inner sanctum and reveal the
true, all too human saga behind America's most famous family.

edited by Elaine Steinbeck
and Robert Wallsten
**Steinbeck: A Life in Letters** £3.95

'The letters of John Steinbeck provide an insight into the mind and
life of a writer: the compulsion to write, perpetual planning of new
books, the build-up of work, the danger of the crack-up ... The
Nobel Prize was well awarded, for Steinbeck must be listed among
those writers who effectively convey their understanding of life, and
their emotional, exuberant delight in its complexities. He had, in sixty
years, left a lot of tracks: and we can retrace them through the
outspoken letters he wrote' YORKSHIRE POST

'His friend and his widow have raised a fitting memorial, carved from
his own words, to both his life and his art' OBSERVER

Betty Tootell
**All Four Engines Have Failed** £2.50

The True and Triumphant Story of Flight BA 009
and the 'Jakarta Incident'

It was the nightmare that haunts every airline passenger. Flying at
37,000 feet over Java, on a dark night in June 1982, a British
Airways Jumbo jet ran into serious trouble. First one, then another,
and finally all four engines flamed, surged, shuddered and died.
Betty Tootell was a passenger on Flight 009. She recounts in detail
what happened during the tense minutes that followed the engine
failure, how the passengers and crew reacted and how the ordeal
changed the course of many of their lives. A gripping story of
survival and the heroism of ordinary people.

Michael Thornton
**Royal Feud** £3.95

**The Queen Mother and the Duchess of Windsor**

For more than three decades the acrimony between the Queen Mother and the woman branded as the temptress who distracted King Edward VIII from the paths of decency and duty, the Duchess of Windsor, haunted the corridors of power. British prime ministers, American presidents, cabinet ministers, ambassadors and even foreign dictators found themselves caught up in it.

Now for the first time, Michael Thornton traces the course of this astonishing feud and explains its origins, drawing upon much hitherto unpublished material from sources close to the Royal Family and to the Windsors. In an account that is both devastatingly frank and hugely entertaining, he examines their characters, their relationships with their husbands and with each other, and their contrasting histories as wives of kings of England.

'I devoured it, loved it. It is fascinating, objective, yet compassionate at the same time' ARTHUR HAILEY

'An engrossing double biography that examines every nuance of their bitter mutual dislike' SUNDAY EXPRESS